ALL IN ONE

CompTIA Network+™ Certification

NINTH EDITION

(Exam N10-009)

Jonathan S. Weissman
Mike Meyers, Series Editor

TOTAL SEMINARS
HOUSTON

CompTIA Network+™ Certification All-in-One Exam Guide, Ninth Edition (Exam N10-009)

1 2 3 4 5 6 7 8 9 QVS 31 30 29 28 27 26

Printed in the United States of America on certified mill sourced paper.

ISBN 978-0-816217-3-9

Sponsoring Editor & Editorial Supervisor
Tim Green

Project Editor
Rachel Monaghan

Technical Editor
Ed Tetz

Copyeditor
Rachel Monaghan

Proofreader
James M. Fraleigh

Indexer
Rachel Kuhn

Composition
Maureen Forys,
Happenstance Type-O-Rama

Art Director, Cover
Jeff Weeks

A catalog record of this book is available from the Library of Congress. The Library of Congress issued the following Cataloging-in-Publication data for the previous edition:
Names: Meyers, Mike, 1961- author. | Jernigan, Scott, author. | Jernigan, Scott. CompTIA Network+ all-in-one exam guide (exam N10-008)
Title: CompTIA Network+ Certification all-in-one exam guide, Eighth (Exam N10-008) / Mike Meyers, Scott Jernigan
Description: Eighth edition. | New York : McGraw-Hill Education, [2021] |
Other titles: CompTIA Network+ all-in-one exam guide, Seventh Edition (exam N10-007)
Description: Seventh edition. | New York : McGraw-Hill Education, [2018] |
Based on: CompTIA Network+ all-in-one exam guide (exam N10-007) / Scott Jernigan, Mike Meyers. 2018. | Includes index.
Identifiers: LCCN 2018054260| ISBN 9781260441871 (soft cover : alk. paper) | ISBN 1260441873 (soft cover : alk. paper)
Subjects: LCSH: Computer science—Examinations—Study guides. | Information technology—Examinations—Study guides. | Computer technicians—Certification—Study guides.
Classification: LCC QA76.28 .M49 2019 | DDC 004.076—dc23 LC record available at https://lccn.loc.gov/2018054260.

Total Seminars books are available at special quantity discounts to use as premiums and sales promotions, or for use in corporate training programs. To contact a representative, please visit the Contact Us pages at *https://www.totalsem.com/*. Information has been obtained by Total Seminars from sources believed to be reliable. However, because of the possibility of human or mechanical error by our sources, Total Seminars, or others, Total Seminars does not guarantee the accuracy, adequacy, or completeness of any information and is not responsible for any errors or omissions or the results obtained from the use of such information.

To my beautiful wife, Eva Ann,
and our amazing sons, Noah Harrison and Jacob Meir.
Thank you for being my constant source of love, inspiration, and joy.
I love you all so much.

ABOUT THE AUTHOR

Jonathan S. Weissman, MA, CompTIA A+, CompTIA Network+, CompTIA Security+, CompTIA Server+, CompTIA Linux+, CCNP, CCNA, CEH, CHFI, is a principal lecturer, the highest teaching-rank appointment in the Department of Cybersecurity at Rochester Institute of Technology (RIT), and concurrently a tenured full professor at Finger Lakes Community College (FLCC). His teaching focuses on demystifying complex technical concepts, making elite-level networking and cybersecurity education accessible to every learner.

Professor Weissman was awarded the RIT Outstanding Teaching Award in 2014, the RIT B. Thomas Golisano College of Computing and Information Sciences (GCCIS) Outstanding Educator Award in 2018, and RIT Distinguished Teacher Recognition Program Honors in 2019. Weissman developed and teaches three courses for the edX RITx Cybersecurity MicroMasters program, which together have reached more than 300,000 learners worldwide. He also developed and teaches two courses for RIT Certified, the professional and workforce training division of RIT.

For his work at FLCC, Professor Weissman was awarded the State University of New York (SUNY) Chancellor's Award for Excellence in Teaching in 2021. Overall, across institutions past and present, Weissman has received 12 institutionally recognized teaching honors and awards.

In addition to his two full-time academic positions, Weissman teaches part-time at Syracuse University in the Department of Electrical Engineering and Computer Science and the Monroe Community College (MCC) Economic & Workforce Development Center.

Since beginning his teaching career in 2001, Weissman has taught more than 50 graduate- and undergraduate-level courses in networking, cybersecurity, routing and switching, systems administration, cryptography, cryptocurrency, ethical hacking/pentesting, digital forensics, malware reverse engineering, programming, scripting, web design, database design, computer organization and architecture, and operating system design.

Weissman is the author of four books, including three on Network+ certification and one on Security+ certification. He also serves as a technical editor for many industry textbooks.

Weissman is widely recognized for his expertise in networking and cybersecurity. He regularly appears on TV news and talk radio, as well as in print and online articles, as a subject-matter expert. He also consults for local businesses and individuals; presents at conferences, workshops, and webinars; and appears on podcasts.

Weissman has a master's degree in computer science from Brooklyn College and holds 47 earned industry certifications, including but not limited to CCNP Enterprise, Cisco Certified Specialist (Enterprise Core, Enterprise Advanced Infrastructure Implementation, Security

Core), CCNA Security, CCNA, CompTIA Security+, CompTIA Network+, CompTIA A+, CompTIA Linux+, CompTIA Server+, EC-Council Certified Ethical Hacker, EC-Council Computer Hacking Forensic Investigator, and IPv6 Forum Certified Network Engineer (Gold). He was inducted into the IPv6 Forum's New Internet IPv6 Hall of Fame as an IPv6 Evangelist in 2021.

For more, see the following:

- **LinkedIn:** *linkedin.com/in/jonathan-s-weissman*
- **X and Instagram:** *@CSCPROF*
- **YouTube:** *youtube.com/Weissman52*
- **Amazon author page:** *amazon.com/author/jonathansweissman*
- **More links:** *linktr.ee/CSCPROF*

About the Technical Editor

Ed Tetz graduated in 1990 from Saint Lawrence College in Cornwall, Ontario, with a degree in business administration. Since that time, he has spent his career delivering certified technical training for a Microsoft Training Center and working as a service delivery professional in both Halifax, Nova Scotia, and Ottawa, Ontario. Over his career, Ed has supported Apple Macintosh, IBM OS/2, Linux, Novell Netware, and all Microsoft operating systems from MS-DOS to the current Windows Server OS, as well as hardware from most of the major manufacturers. Over his career, he had held certifications from Microsoft, Cisco, CompTIA, VMware, and others. Ed currently works for Microsoft in Enterprise Service Delivery in Ottawa, Ontario, supporting enterprise and government customers.

When not working with technology, Ed spends time with his wife, Sharon, and ever-growing family.

ABOUT THE SERIES EDITOR

Mike Meyers is the industry's leading authority on CompTIA A+ and CompTIA Network+ certification. He is the founder of Total Seminars, LLC. Mike is the author of many books, including *Mike Meyers' Network+ Guide to Managing and Troubleshooting Networks.*

Email: *michaelm@totalsem.com*

BECOMING A COMPTIA CERTIFIED IT PROFESSIONAL IS EASY

Becoming certified is not only easy, it's the best way to reach greater professional opportunities and rewards.

Why Get CompTIA Certified?

In fact, there are many benefits.

GROWING DEMAND

According to CompTIA, tech jobs are projected to be among the fastest-growing occupations from 2023 to 2033 (source: US Bureau of Labor Statistics). CompTIA has also reported that "employers listed 8.95 million job postings in the US seeking candidates with digital and tech fundamental skills during 2023" (Lightcast US active job postings Jan. 2023–Dec. 2023).

HIGHER SALARIES

IT professionals with certifications on their résumés command better jobs, earn higher salaries, and have more doors open to new multi-industry opportunities.

VERIFIED STRENGTHS

Ninety-one percent of hiring managers indicate that CompTIA certifications are valuable in validating IT expertise, making certification the best way to demonstrate your competency and knowledge to employers (according to CompTIA's "Employer Perceptions of IT Training and Certification" report).

UNIVERSAL SKILLS

CompTIA certifications are vendor neutral, which means certified professionals can proficiently work with an extensive variety of hardware and software found in most organizations.

You can learn more about the Network+ certification on the CompTIA website, *comptia.org*.

CONTENTS AT A GLANCE

Acknowledgments xxxi

Introduction xxxiii

Part I **Networking Concepts and Protocols**

CHAPTER 1 OSI Model and Numeral Systems 3

CHAPTER 2 Local Communication vs. Remote Communication 41

CHAPTER 3 IPv4 59

CHAPTER 4 Ports, Protocols, and Services 83

Part II **Network Infrastructure and Connectivity**

CHAPTER 5 Routing 109

CHAPTER 6 Switching 147

CHAPTER 7 DNS and DHCP 171

CHAPTER 8 IPv6 203

CHAPTER 9 Cabling 225

CHAPTER 10 Ethernet 245

CHAPTER 11 Installing a Physical Network 279

CHAPTER 12 Wireless Networking 343

Part III **Modern Operations and Cloud Architectures**

CHAPTER 13 Virtualization and Cloud Computing 415

CHAPTER 14 Data Centers 455

CHAPTER 15 Devices, Access, Management, and Monitoring 485

CHAPTER 16 Processes and Procedures 525

Part IV Network Security and Troubleshooting

CHAPTER 17 Network Security 541

CHAPTER 18 The Troubleshooting Methodology 607

Part V Appendixes

APPENDIX A Exam Objective Reference 621

APPENDIX B About the Online Content 639

Index 643

CONTENTS

Acknowledgments xxxi

Introduction xxxiii

What Is CompTIA? xxxiii
    CompTIA Certifications. xxxiv
    CompTIA Network+. xxxiv
About the Book xxxv
Getting the CompTIA Tech+ Certification. xxxvi
    Studying for the Exam xxxvi

Part I Networking Concepts and Protocols

CHAPTER 1 OSI Model and Numeral Systems 3

Working with Models 4
    The Purpose of a Model 4
    Network Models. 5
The OSI Model on a Simple Network. 6
    Welcome to CSCPROF! 7
    Layer 7, the Application Layer. 8
    Layer 6, the Presentation Layer 9
    Layer 5, the Session Layer 9
    Layer 4, the Transport Layer. 11
    Layer 3, the Network Layer 12
    Layer 2, the Data Link Layer 14
        The NIC 14
        MAC Addresses 15
        Frames 17
        Switches 19
        The Complete Frame Movement 20
        The Two Sublayers of Layer 2. 22
    Layer 1, the Physical Layer 23
The OSI Model as a Diagnostic and Collaboration Tool 25
Numeral Systems 26
    The Decimal Numeral System. 26
    The Binary Numeral System 27

Binary-to-Decimal Conversion 28
Decimal-to-Binary Conversion 28
The Hexadecimal Numeral System 32
Hexadecimal-to-Binary Conversion 34
Hexadecimal-to-Decimal Conversion 35
Decimal-to-Hexadecimal Conversion 37
Chapter Review 38
Questions 38
Answers 40

CHAPTER 2 Local Communication vs. Remote Communication 41

Addressing and Communication 42
MAC Addresses and IP Addresses 42
Local Communication 44
Remote Communication 47
Why Both a MAC Address and an IP Address Are Needed 52
Finding Your MAC Address and IP Address 54
Chapter Review 56
Questions 56
Answers 58

CHAPTER 3 IPv4 59

IP Addresses 60
IPv4 Address Classes 62
Class A 63
Class B 64
Class C 65
Classes D and E 66
Limitations of Classful Addressing 66
Subnetting 66
Designing a Network Layout 68
Calculating the Number of Hosts 70
Creating Subnets 71
Calculating Subnets 72
CIDR 76
IP Address Configuration and Special Addresses 77
Chapter Review 79
Questions 79
Answers 81

CHAPTER 4 Ports, Protocols, and Services 83
How Ports Work 84
Types of Ports 85
Well-Known Ports 85
Registered Ports. 85
Dynamic Ports 86
Port States 86
Layer 4 Protocols and Utilities 90
TCP 90
UDP 94
netstat 96
Layer 3 Protocols and Utilities 97
IP 97
ICMP 98
ping. 99
traceroute/tracert 100
Chapter Review 103
Questions 103
Answers 104

Part II **Network Infrastructure and Connectivity**

CHAPTER 5 Routing 109
Introduction to Routers 110
Static Routing 113
Dynamic Routing. 113
IGP. 117
OSPF 117
EIGRP 120
EGP 121
BGP. 121
Working with Routers 125
Routing Tables 125
Reading and Interpreting Routing Table Entries. 126
Examining Routing Tables in Other Devices 128
Troubleshooting Routing Table Issues 132
Router Technologies Beyond Ethernet 133
Router Connections. 134
Cisco IOS 135

Web Access and Other Connection Methods 138
Router Redundancy. 139
Network Address Translation 140
The Setup 140
Port Address Translation. 141
Large-Scale NAT and Carrier-Grade NAT 143
Port Forwarding. 143
Chapter Review. 144
Questions 144
Answers 146

CHAPTER 6 Switching 147

Introduction to Switches 147
How a Switch Learns and Makes Decisions 148
VLANs. 151
Trunking 153
Layer 3/Multilayer Switch 154
VLAN Database 156
Link Aggregation. 157
Duplex 157
Speed 157
Jumbo Frames. 158
Spanning Tree Protocol 158
STP Port States 159
Root Bridge Selection. 161
Root Port Selection 163
Designated Port Selection 164
Topology Changes. 166
Interface Issues 166
Cyclic Redundancy Checks 167
Runts. 167
Giants 167
Drops 167
ACLs 168
Chapter Review. 168
Questions 168
Answers 170

CHAPTER 7 DNS and DHCP. 171

The DNS Structure and Query Resolution Process. 174
Zone Transfers 175

Global Hierarchy 176
Root DNS Servers 176
Authoritative TLD DNS Servers 177
DNS Caching and TTL 179
DNS Resource Record Types 180
A 180
AAAA. 181
CNAME 181
MX. 183
SOA 184
PTR 185
TXT 186
SRV. 187
NS 187
Authoritative vs. Non-Authoritative Responses. 188
Internal vs. External DNS. 189
DHCP Operations and Configuration 190
THE DORA Process 190
Discover 190
Offer 191
Request 192
Acknowledge 193
DHCP Commands 193
Options 193
Lease 194
Dynamic vs. Static Assignment 195
Exclusion Ranges 196
Reservation 196
DHCP Message Types 196
DHCP Relay and IP Helper/UDP Forwarding 197
Common DHCP Issues 198
Address Pool Exhaustion. 198
Incorrect Default Gateway. 199
Incorrect IP Address 199
Duplicate IP Address 199
Incorrect Subnet Mask 199
Incorrect DNS 199
Chapter Review 199
Questions 199
Answers 201

CHAPTER 8 IPv6 203

IPv6 Addressing. 205
IPv6 Address Allocation 205
IPv6 Address Notation 206
Link-Local Address 208
Global Unicast Address 209
Multicast Addresses 210
Anycast Address 211
Neighbor Discovery Protocol. 212
Solicited-Node Multicast Address 212
Neighbor Solicitation 214
Neighbor Advertisement 214
Router Solicitation 215
Router Advertisement 215
Redirect 216
IPv6 Deployment 216
SLAAC 216
DHCPv6 217
IPv6 and DNS 218
Subnetting 218
Connecting IPv4 and IPv6 Infrastructures:
Compatibility Requirements 219
Dual Stack 219
Transition Mechanisms 219
Tunnel Brokers. 220
Overlay Tunnels 220
NAT64 220
Chapter Review 221
Questions 221
Answers 223

CHAPTER 9 Cabling 225

Copper Cables and Connectors 226
Coaxial Cables 226
Twinaxial Cables 230
Twisted-Pair Cables 231
Fiber-Optic Cables and Connectors. 235
Fire Ratings 238
IEEE Networking Industry Standards 239

Chapter Review . . . 241
Questions . . . 241
Answers . . . 243
CHAPTER 10 Ethernet . . . 245
Ethernet Origins . . . 246
802.3 Standards . . . 246
Ethernet Frames . . . 247
Early Ethernet Standards . . . 250
Bus Ethernet . . . 250
10BASE-T . . . 250
UTP . . . 251
10BASE-T Limits and Specifications . . . 255
10BASE-FL . . . 255
CSMA/CD . . . 257
Enhancing and Extending Ethernet Networks . . . 259
The Trouble with Hubs . . . 259
Switches to the Rescue . . . 260
Problems with Switches . . . 261
100-Megabit Ethernet . . . 261
100BASE-T . . . 261
100BASE-FX . . . 263
100BASE-SX . . . 264
Full-Duplex Ethernet . . . 264
Gigabit Ethernet . . . 265
1000BASE-SX . . . 266
1000BASE-LX . . . 266
SFF Fiber Connectors . . . 266
Mechanical Connection Variations . . . 268
Gigabit Ethernet Implementation . . . 268
Ethernet Evolutions . . . 269
10-Gigabit Ethernet . . . 269
Fiber-Based 10 GbE . . . 269
The Other 10 GbE Fiber Standards . . . 271
Copper-Based 10 GbE . . . 272
10 GbE Physical Connections . . . 272
Characteristics of Fiber Transceivers . . . 273
Backbones . . . 274
40GbE, 100GbE, and Terabit Ethernet . . . 275

Chapter Review 276
Questions 276
Answers 278

CHAPTER 11 Installing a Physical Network 279

Understanding Structured Cabling 280
Structured Cabling Basics: A Star Is Born 281
Structured Cabling: Network Components 282
Horizontal Cabling 284
The Telecommunications Room 286
The Work Area 297
Structured Cabling: Beyond the Star 299
Demarc 299
Connections Inside the Demarc 302
Installing Structured Cabling 303
Getting a Floor Plan 303
Mapping the Runs 304
Determining the Location of the Telecommunications Room . . . 305
Pulling Cable 307
Making Connections 310
Connecting the Work Areas 310
Rolling Your Own Patch Cables 311
Connecting the Patch Panels 314
Testing the Cable Runs 316
Addressing Copper Challenges 317
Addressing Fiber Challenges 323
NICs 327
Buying NICs 328
Physical Connections 328
Drivers 330
Understanding Link Lights 330
Diagnosing and Repairing Physical Cabling Issues 332
Check Your Lights 332
Check the NIC 333
Test Your Cables 334
Problems in the Telecommunications Room 335
Toners 337
Taps 338
Chapter Review 339
Questions 339
Answers 341

CHAPTER 12 Wireless Networking 343
Wi-Fi Standards. 344
802.11 345
Hardware 345
Software 347
Network Types 349
Range. 351
BSSID, SSID, and ESSID. 351
Transmission Frequency 352
Transmission Methods 352
Channels. 353
CSMA/CA 354
802.11b 356
802.11a 356
802.11g 357
802.11n 358
802.11ac. 359
802.11ax. 360
802.11be. 360
802.11bn. 361
WPS 361
Wi-Fi Security. 361
Data Encryption. 362
WEP 362
WPA 362
WPA2 367
WPA3 368
Additional Security Measures. 368
SSID Broadcast Disabling 369
MAC Address Filtering. 369
Network Isolation 370
Captive Portals 370
Geofencing 371
Enterprise Wireless. 371
Robust Device Construction 371
Enterprise Wireless Administration 372
VLAN Pooling. 374
Power over Ethernet. 374
Implementing Wi-Fi 376

Performing a Site Survey . . . 376
Existing Wireless Networks . . . 376
Congestion/Contention . . . 378
Interference Sources . . . 378
Installing the Client. . . . 379
Setting Up an Ad Hoc Network . . . 380
Setting Up an Infrastructure Network . . . 381
Placing the Access Points/Antennas . . . 381
Configuring a Consumer Access Point. . . . 386
Configuring the Client . . . 392
Extending the Network . . . 392
Adding a WAP . . . 393
Adding Wireless Bridges . . . 393
Verifying the Installation . . . 394
Troubleshooting Wi-Fi . . . 394
No Connection . . . 395
Channel Problems . . . 395
Security Type Mismatches . . . 395
Signal/Power Levels . . . 396
Slow Connections . . . 398
Overworked WAPs . . . 399
Physical Issues. . . . 400
Interference . . . 400
Weird Connections . . . 402
Open Networks. . . . 402
Wrong SSID. . . . 402
Untested Updates/Incompatibilities . . . 403
Rogue Access Points . . . 403
Client Disassociation Issues . . . 404
Roaming Misconfiguration. . . . 404
Satellite . . . 405
Cellular WAN. . . . 405
GSM and EDGE. . . . 407
CDMA . . . 408
HSPA+ . . . 408
LTE . . . 408
5G . . . 409
Chapter Review . . . 410
Questions . . . 410
Answers . . . 412

Part III Modern Operations and Cloud Architectures

CHAPTER 13 Virtualization and Cloud Computing 415

Virtualization 416
The Hypervisor 417
Abstraction 421
Flexibility 423
Reroute an Input or Output 423
Relocate Components 423
Divide and Combine Resources 424
Scaling 424
Virtual Networking 425
Virtual Networking Inside the VM Host 425
Virtual Network Interface Cards 425
Virtual Switches 426
Distributed Switches 426
Virtual Routers 427
Virtual Firewalls 427
Virtual Networking Outside the VM Host 428
Network Function Virtualization 429
NFV Architecture 429
NFV vs. Software-Defined Networking 430
Cloud Computing 431
The Service-Layer Cake 432
Infrastructure as a Service 433
Platform as a Service 433
Software as a Service 436
Cloud Deployment Models 437
Public Cloud 437
Private Cloud 438
Hybrid Cloud 438
Virtual Private Cloud 439
Virtualization's Role in Cloud Computing 439
Infrastructure as Code 440
Automation 440
Source Control 441
Orchestration 442
Putting Network Virtualization and Cloud Computing to Work 442
Cloud Resource Management 443

Scalability 443
Elasticity 444
Security Implications 444
Desktop Virtualization 446
Interconnecting Local and Cloud Resources 448
Virtual Private Networks 450
Direct Connect 451
Chapter Review 451
Questions 451
Answers 453
CHAPTER 14 Data Centers 455
Classic Data Center Architecture and Design 456
Three-Tiered Architecture 457
Access Layer 458
Distribution Layer 459
Core Layer 460
Collapsed Core Architecture 460
Spine-and-Leaf Architecture 461
Traffic Flows 462
North-South 462
East-West 462
Data Storage 463
Data Center Location 464
The Modern Data Center 466
Virtualization 466
SDN and SD-WAN 466
Application Awareness 467
Zero-Touch Provisioning 467
Transport Agnosticism 467
Central Policy Management 467
Virtual Extensible Local Area Networks 467
Zero Trust Architecture 468
Policy-Based Authentication 468
Authorization 469
Least Privilege Access 469
SASE and SSE 469
High Availability in the Data Center 470
HA Approaches 470
Load Balancing 470

Redundancy 471
Facilities and Infrastructure Support 472
Power 472
Environment 473
Emergency Procedures. 473
Documenting the Data Center. 474
Network Diagrams 474
Physical Network Diagrams 474
Logical Network Diagrams. 478
Rack Diagrams 478
Cable Maps and Diagrams 479
Asset Inventory 480
Baseline Configurations 480
Assessments. 481
Site Surveys 481
Chapter Review 482
Questions 482
Answers 484
CHAPTER 15 Devices, Access, Management, and Monitoring 485
Devices 485
Load Balancers 486
Proxies 486
Firewalls. 489
Stateless vs. Stateful Packet Filtering 490
ALG 491
DPI 491
DCI 491
UTM Appliance vs. NGFW/Layer 7 Firewall 492
IDSs and IPSs 492
Access and Management. 496
QoS Policies 496
VPNs. 496
Client-to-Site VPNs 497
Clientless VPNs 501
Split-Tunnel vs. Full-Tunnel VPNs 501
Site-to-Site VPNs. 502
IPsec Tunneling Protocols 503
AH/ESP 503
IKE 503

GRE 504
Past vs. Present Protocols 504
NTP 505
PTP 505
NTS 505
Port Scanners 505
SSH 506
RDC 507
Remote Desktop Gateway 508
Jump Box/Host 508
In-Band vs. Out-of-Band Management 509
Monitoring 511
SNMP 511
Authentication and Encryption 511
Architecture 512
Packet Capture 514
Flow Data 516
Performance Monitoring 517
Baseline Metrics 517
Logs 518
Log Aggregation 518
API Integration 520
Network Discovery 520
Ad Hoc 520
Scheduled 520
Availability Monitoring 520
Configuration Monitoring 521
Chapter Review 522
Questions 522
Answers 524

CHAPTER 16 Processes and Procedures 525

Documentation 525
Asset Inventories 525
Hardware 526
Software 526
Licensing 526
Warranty Support 526
IP Address Management 526
Service-Level Agreements 527

Life-Cycle Management . . . 527
Software Management . . . 527
Patches and Bug Fixes . . . 528
Firmware Updates . . . 528
Operating System Updates . . . 529
End of Life . . . 529
End of Support . . . 529
Decommissioning . . . 530
Change Management . . . 530
Service Requests . . . 530
Request Process Tracking . . . 531
Configuration Management . . . 531
Production Configuration . . . 532
Backup Configuration . . . 532
Baseline/Golden Configuration . . . 532
Disaster Recovery . . . 532
DR Metrics . . . 533
Recovery Point Objective . . . 533
Recovery Time Objective . . . 533
Mean Time to Repair . . . 534
Mean Time Between Failures . . . 534
DR Sites . . . 534
Testing . . . 535
Tabletop Exercises . . . 535
Validation Tests . . . 535
Chapter Review . . . 536
Questions . . . 536
Answers . . . 538

Part IV Network Security and Troubleshooting

CHAPTER 17 Network Security . . . 541

Foundational Network Security Concepts . . . 542
Vulnerabilities . . . 542
Exploits . . . 543
Threats . . . 544
Internal . . . 544
External . . . 545
Threat Agents . . . 545

Risk 545
Confidentiality, Integrity, and Availability 549
Cryptography 550
Encryption 550
XOR and Encryption 551
Data in Transit 554
Data at Rest 554
Symmetric Encryption 554
Asymmetric Cryptography 555
Certificates 558
Public Key Infrastructure 558
Self-Signed Certificates 559
The Issuance Process 560
Hashing 560
Integrity of Files 561
Integrity of Messages 562
Integrity of Certificates 562
Integrity of Software Updates 562
Secure Password Storage 562
Identity and Access Management 563
Authentication 564
Multifactor Authentication 564
Single Sign-On 565
Terminal Access Controller Access-Control System Plus . . 565
Remote Authentication Dial-in User Service 565
Lightweight Directory Access Protocol 566
Security Assertion Markup Language 566
Time-Based Authentication 566
Kerberos 567
Geofencing 568
Authorization 568
Least Privilege 568
Role-Based Access Control 568
Physical Security 569
Cameras 569
Locks 569
Deception Technologies 570
Honeypots 570
Honeynets 570

Audits and Regulatory Compliance 570
Data Locality Laws 571
PCI DSS 571
GDPR 571
ISO/IEC 27001 571
ISO/IEC 27002 571
HIPAA 571
Network Segmentation Enforcement 572
Internet of Things 572
Industrial Internet of Things 573
Operation Technology 574
Industrial Control Systems 574
Distributed Control Systems 576
Supervisory Control and Data Acquisition 577
Programmable Logic Controllers 578
Guest Network 579
Bring Your Own Device 579
Types of Attacks and Their Network Impact 580
Denial-of-Service and Distributed Denial-of-Service 580
VLAN Hopping 580
MAC Flooding 581
On-Path Attacks 582
ARP Poisoning/Spoofing 582
DNS Poisoning 585
DNS Spoofing 585
DNS Snooping 586
DNS Attack Mitigations 586
Domain Name System Security Extensions 586
DNS over TLS and DNS over HTTPS 587
Rogue Devices and Services 587
Rogue DHCP Servers 587
Rogue APs 588
Evil Twin 588
Social Engineering 588
Phishing 590
Dumpster Diving 592
Shoulder Surfing 592
Tailgating and Piggybacking 592
Malware 593

Viruses and Worms 593
Macro Viruses. 594
Logic Bombs. 594
Trojan Horses 594
RATs 595
Rootkits 595
Adware and Spyware. 595
Network Security Features, Defense Techniques, and Solutions. 596
Device Hardening 596
Disable Unused Ports and Services 596
Change Default Passwords 597
Increase Password Length 597
Network Access Control 597
Port Security 597
Key Management 599
Security Rules 599
Access Control Lists 600
URL Filtering. 600
Content Filtering. 601
Zones 601
Screened Subnet 601
Trusted vs. Untrusted Networks 602
Chapter Review 603
Questions 603
Answers 604

CHAPTER 18 The Troubleshooting Methodology 607

Identify the Problem 608
Gather Information 608
Question Users 608
Identify Symptoms 608
Determine Whether Anything Has Changed 609
Try to Duplicate the Problem 609
Approach Multiple Problems Individually 610
Establish a Theory of Probable Cause 610
Question the Obvious 610
Consider Multiple Approaches 610
Top-to-Bottom/Bottom-to-Top OSI Model 610
Divide and Conquer 611
Test the Theory to Determine the Cause 612

If Theory Is Confirmed, Determine the Next Steps to Resolve Problem . . . 612
If Theory Is Not Confirmed, Establish a New Theory or Escalate . . . 612
Establish a Plan of Action . . . 613
Implement the Solution or Escalate . . . 613
Verify Full System Functionality and Implement Preventive Measures 614
Document Findings, Actions, Outcomes, and Lessons Learned . . . 614
Chapter Review . . . 615
Questions . . . 615
Answers . . . 617

Part V Appendixes

APPENDIX A Exam Objective Reference . . . 621
CompTIA Network+ Certification Exam . . . 621

APPENDIX B About the Online Content . . . 639
System Requirements . . . 639
Your Total Seminars Training Hub Account . . . 639
Privacy Notice . . . 639
Single-User License Terms and Conditions . . . 640
TotalTester Online . . . 641
Other Book Resources . . . 641
CompTIA Network+ Video Training Sample . . . 642
Playing the CompTIA Network+ Introduction Video . . . 642
TotalSims sample for CompTIA Network+ . . . 642
Mike's Cool Tools . . . 642
Technical Support . . . 642

Index . . . 643

ACKNOWLEDGMENTS

Tim Green, director of Publication Development, used his powerhouse publishing expertise to shape this book into what you see today. He was involved in both the big picture and the details, from lining up an all-star project team to personally editing each chapter and making helpful suggestions. Ed Tetz caught every little technical error and kept us honest. His knowledge and attention to detail were invaluable, as was his commitment to making sure every exam objective was thoroughly covered.

To the project editor and copyeditor, Rachel Monaghan; proofreader, James Fraleigh; indexer, Rachel Kuhn; and Maureen Forys at Happenstance Type-O-Rama, who laid out the book—superb work in every facet. Thank you for being the best.

INTRODUCTION

Congratulations—you've just taken the first step toward mastering networking! But here's the truth: networking is huge. Vast. Complex. Too big for any single book, course, or certification to cover in its entirety.

So, what do *you* want to do with it? Configure routers and switches? Manage a massive network with Windows and Linux devices? Build wide area connections? Set up web servers? Defend networks from attacks?

If you're here for CompTIA Network+, you might not have all the answers yet—and that's exactly why this certification is perfect for you. Network+ gives you a **big-picture view of networking**, helping you explore the parts of the field that excite you most.

Network+ is a game-changer that will:

- **Map out the landscape:** It teaches you about local and wide area networks (LANs and WANs), the internet, security, cabling, and applications—all in one certification.
- **Open doors:** You can use it as a launchpad to more advanced certifications.
- **Make learning enjoyable:** Every concept you master brings a satisfying "a-ha!" moment.
- **Boost your career:** Networks run the world, and skilled tech professionals are in high demand.

Network+ doesn't just teach you networking, it gives you **the foundation, confidence, and curiosity** to thrive in the tech world. By the time you're done, you'll know how networks work, why they matter, and where you want to go next.

Ready to dive in, earn a respected certification, and have fun doing it? Let's get started—welcome to CompTIA Network+!

What Is CompTIA?

In many fields, people demonstrate knowledge of subjects by passing tests, passing classes, and earning degrees. In computing, people get certificates (or, more commonly, *certifications*) to prove their skills. The most important general certifying body for computing is the Computer Technology Industry Association (CompTIA).

CompTIA is a nonprofit industry trade association based in Oakbrook Terrace, Illinois. It consists of more than 20,000 members in 102 countries. You'll find CompTIA offices in such diverse locales as Amsterdam, Dubai, Johannesburg, Tokyo, and São Paulo.

Virtually every company of consequence in the IT industry is a member of CompTIA. Here are a few of the biggies:

Adobe Systems	Cisco Systems	Intel	Symantec
AMD	Facebook	Kyocera	Toshiba
Best Buy	Fujitsu	McAfee	Total Seminars, LLC (that's our company!)
Brother International	Hewlett-Packard	Microsoft	Xerox
Canon	IBM	NCR	*Plus many thousands more*

CompTIA provides a forum for people in these industries to network (as in meeting people), represents the interests of its members to the government, and provides certifications for many aspects of the computer industry. CompTIA watches the IT industry closely and provides new and updated certifications to meet the ongoing demand from its membership.

CompTIA Certifications

CompTIA certifications enable techs to offer proof of competency in a variety of technology fields. Attaining the CompTIA A+ certification, for example, proves that you're a PC technician of some skill. You know how to build and fix PCs, and you know the basics of networking because modern PCs almost always connect to some network. The CompTIA Network+ certification, in contrast, dives deep into networking. It's designed for network technicians.

Earning a CompTIA A+ or CompTIA Network+ certification takes time and commitment. Most commonly, the successful candidate is a working tech already and wants to prove their merit to an employer. But what about people who might want to become a tech but aren't there yet?

CompTIA Network+

The CompTIA Network+ certification covers foundational networking subjects and demonstrates a broad, practical understanding of modern networks. The successful candidate can explain the principles of network design and management, configure and troubleshoot network devices, and understand protocols that drive network communication. The candidate can secure networks, implement basic wireless and wired connections, and identify common network issues. In short, a successful CompTIA Network+ certification recipient can handle a variety of networking tasks competently.

People pursue the CompTIA Network+ certification for a couple of reasons. First, Network+ establishes a baseline core of networking knowledge. The certification explores networks of all types—LANs, WANs, the internet, wireless, and more—helping the student learn what is possible in networking.

CompTIA Network+ also creates an entry point for people who are interested in pursuing a career in IT or networking. To take the exam successfully, you'll need to understand the concepts and terminology of networking, protocols, cabling, security, and troubleshooting. You'll need a working knowledge of routers, switches, wireless access points, and network monitoring tools. This is an essential starting point for network professionals.

The CompTIA Network+ certification, therefore, applies to two groups of people:

- Those who want to understand networks and operate effectively in a networked world
- Those who aspire to become network technicians or IT professionals

About the Book

I designed the *CompTIA Network+ Certification All-in-One Exam Guide* to address the needs of the two groups just mentioned: those who want to understand networks and those who aspire to become network technicians or IT professionals. The book approaches topics in plain language, gradually introducing you to networking terminology, technologies, and best practices.

PART I: NETWORKING CONCEPTS AND PROTOCOLS Chapters 1–4 establish the essential building blocks of networking. You will master the "language" of data by breaking down the Open Systems Interconnection (OSI) model, number systems, and the fundamentals of local versus remote communication. This section provides a deep dive into MAC addresses, IPv4 addresses, and ports, alongside the protocols that facilitate network communication, such as ARP, ICMP, TCP, and UDP. This conceptual bedrock is designed to give you a packet-level understanding before you ever touch a piece of hardware.

PART II: NETWORK INFRASTRUCTURE AND CONNECTIVITY Chapters 5–12 transition from theory to the physical and logical components that power modern networks. You will explore the meat of the exam: the mechanics of routing and switching, and the essential network services of DNS and DHCP. This section also introduces IPv6 and emphasizes practical implementation, including cabling, Ethernet standards, physical network installation, and wireless networking. By the end of this part, you will understand how to design and build a functional, scalable physical network environment.

PART III: MODERN OPERATIONS AND CLOUD ARCHITECTURES Chapters 13–16 cover the day-to-day responsibilities of a network professional in a modern, software-defined environment. You'll explore data center architecture and the specialized devices used for load balancing and high availability. A major focus is placed on the shift to virtualization and cloud computing—transitioning from physical hardware to virtualized environments. You'll also learn operational best practices for access control, network management, and monitoring, along with the policies and procedures that support them.

PART IV: NETWORK SECURITY AND TROUBLESHOOTING Chapters 17 and 18 cover two high-stakes domains of both the Network+ exam and the real world: security and troubleshooting. You'll explore network security fundamentals, from hardening devices to mitigating common risks and threats. The book concludes with an expanded focus on systematic troubleshooting, where you'll apply the CompTIA troubleshooting methodology to real-world scenarios. This part will give you the tactical skills needed to identify points of failure and resolve complex connectivity issues, ensuring maximum uptime.

Getting the CompTIA Network+ Certification

To become CompTIA Network+ certified, you simply pass one computer-based exam. There are no prerequisites for taking the CompTIA Network+ exam, and no networking experience is needed. You're not required to take a training course or buy any training materials. The only requirements are that you pay a testing fee to an authorized testing facility and then sit for the exam. Upon completion of the exam, you will immediately know whether you passed or failed.

Once you pass, you become CompTIA Network+ certified for three years. After three years, you'll need to renew your certification by taking the current exam or completing approved Continuing Education activities. By completing these activities, you earn credits that (along with an annual fee) allow you to keep your CompTIA Network+ certification. For a full list of approved activities, check out CompTIA's website (*comptia.org*) and search for CompTIA Continuing Education Program.

Studying for the Exam

To get the most out of your study time, I recommend reading this book twice:

- **Pass 1: The big picture.** Dive in like it's a story. Enjoy the illustrations, explore the new terms, and get comfortable with the concepts. Don't stress about memorizing details yet—just absorb the ideas and have fun building your foundation.
- **Pass 2: Game time.** This is your deep dive. Keep a copy of the official CompTIA Network+ objectives nearby. Read carefully, check off each topic as you master it, and ensure you understand how it all fits together.

By the end of this second pass, you'll be confident, prepared, and ready to tackle the exam with authority.

NOTE Appendix A lists where I cover each objective in the book.

As I tell my students, if you have questions or comments, please feel free to contact me through any of the platforms listed at *linktr.ee/CSCPROF*.

Good luck with your studies and with the CompTIA Network+ exam!

PART I

Networking Concepts and Protocols

IN THIS PART:

- CHAPTER 1: OSI Model and Numeral Systems
- CHAPTER 2: Local Communication vs. Remote Communication
- CHAPTER 3: IPv4
- CHAPTER 4: Ports, Protocols, and Services

OSI Model and Numeral Systems

IN THIS CHAPTER YOU WILL LEARN HOW TO

- Use the Open Systems Interconnection (OSI) reference model as a tool to learn about and troubleshoot networks
- Convert between different number systems used in networking

Networks enable connected hosts—computers and other digital devices—to share and access resources. The sharing host (a server) runs special software to enable the accessing host (a client, also running special software) to get the desired resource. That resource can be any number of things, from a web page on the internet to files on a server in your office. Networking protocols like Hypertext Transfer Protocol (HTTP), File Transfer Protocol (FTP), Secure Shell (SSH), Domain Name System (DNS), Dynamic Host Configuration Protocol (DHCP), and many more operate with this client-server paradigm. Networking professionals need to know how all these connections happen and understand all the hardware and software that enables this exchange of resources.

Although we call the machines "clients" and "servers," the hardware is just the platform. The true clients and servers are the software services; for example, both a DHCP client service and the DHCP server service it communicates with are software.

The CompTIA Network+ exam challenges you to understand this and virtually every other aspect of networking—not a small task. Networking professionals use models to conceptualize the many parts of a network, relying primarily on the *Open Systems Interconnection (OSI) model.*

The OSI model provides two tools that make it essential for networking techs. First, it provides a powerful mental tool for diagnosing problems. Understanding OSI enables a tech to determine quickly at what layer a problem can occur and helps the tech zero in on a solution without wasting a lot of time on false leads. Second, the OSI model provides a common language that techs use to describe specific network functions. Figure 1-1 shows product information for a Cisco-branded advanced networking device. Note the use of the terms *L3* and *layer 7.*

Both terms directly reference the OSI model, which has seven layers. Techs who understand the OSI model know what those numbers mean, allowing them to quickly grasp what the device provides to a network.

In this chapter, we'll look first at models in general and how they help conceptualize and troubleshoot networks. We'll then explore the OSI model to see how it helps clarify network architecture for techs. The chapter concludes with a deep dive into numeral systems, which are fundamental to many networking concepts ahead.

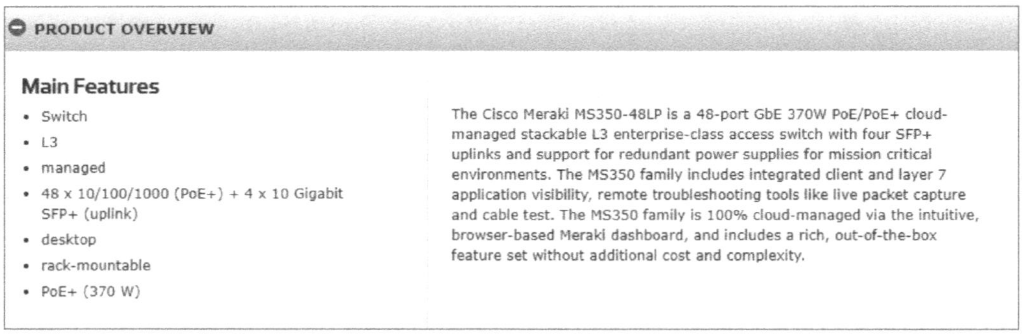

FIGURE 1-1 Using OSI terminology in device documentation

Historical/Conceptual

Working with Models

Networking is really a lot of fun! It takes a lot of pieces, both hardware and software, all working incredibly quickly and in perfect harmony, to get anything done. Whenever we encounter highly complex technologies, we need to simplify the overall process by breaking it into discrete, simple, individual processes. We do this using a network *model*.

The Purpose of a Model

What does the word *model* mean to you? Does it make you think of someone walking the catwalk at a fashion show in some outrageous costume or showing off the latest style of blue jeans on a huge billboard? Maybe it makes you think of a plastic model airplane or a diecast train. What about those computer models that try to predict weather? We use the term *model* in several ways, all of which share certain themes.

All models are a simplified representation of the real thing. The human model ignores the many different types of body shapes, using only a single "optimal" figure. The model airplane lacks functional engines or the internal framework of a real plane. The computerized weather model might disregard subtle differences in wind temperatures or geology (Figure 1-2).

FIGURE 1-2 Types of models

Additionally, a model must have at least all the major functions of the real item, but what constitutes a major rather than a minor function is open to opinion. Figure 1-3 shows a different level of detail for a model airplane.

FIGURE 1-3
Simple model airplane

Does it contain all the major components of a real airplane? You could argue that the model should have landing gear to go along with the propeller, wings, and tail.

Network Models

Network models face similar challenges. What functions define all networks? What details can you omit without rendering the model inaccurate? Does the model retain its usefulness when describing a network that does not employ all the layers?

In the early days of networking, different manufacturers made unique types of networks that functioned well. Part of the reason the networks worked was that back then, each manufacturer provided everything customers would need when they purchased a network solution. All the hardware and all the software came in one complete and expensive package. Although these networks worked fine on a standalone basis, the proprietary nature of the hardware and software made it difficult—to put it mildly—to connect the networks of multiple manufacturers. To interconnect networks and therefore improve the networking industry, someone needed to create a guide, a model, that described the functions of a network. Using this model, the people who made hardware and software could collaborate to make networks that worked together well.

NOTE The International Organization for Standardization (ISO) created the OSI model. ISO may look like a misspelled acronym, but it's actually a word derived from the Greek word *isos*, which means "equal." The organization sets standards that promote *equality* among network designers and manufacturers, thus "ISO."

The best way to learn the OSI model is to see it in action. Next, I'll introduce you to a small, simplified network in which a user needs to copy a file from one computer to another. This example goes through each of the OSI layers needed to copy that file, and I'll explain each step and why it is necessary. By the end of the chapter, you should have a definite handle on using the OSI model as a tool to conceptualize networks. You'll continue to build on this knowledge throughout the book and turn your OSI model knowledge into a powerful troubleshooting tool.

The OSI Model on a Simple Network

Each layer in the OSI model defines an important function in computer networking, and the protocols that operate at each layer offer solutions for those functions. *Protocols* are sets of clearly defined rules, regulations, standards, and procedures that enable hardware and software developers to make devices and applications that work properly at a particular layer. The OSI model encourages modular design in networking, meaning that each layer has as little to do with the operation of other layers as possible. Think of it as an automobile assembly line. The person painting the car doesn't care about the person putting doors on it—he expects the assembly line process to make sure all the cars he paints have doors. Each layer on the model trusts that the other layers are doing their jobs.

The seven layers of the OSI model are

- **LAYER 7,** Application
- **LAYER 6,** Presentation
- **LAYER 5,** Session
- **LAYER 4,** Transport
- **LAYER 3,** Network
- **LAYER 2,** Data Link
- **LAYER 1,** Physical

The OSI model's seven layers are not laws of physics. Although many protocols fit neatly into one of the seven layers, others do not.

EXAM TIP Be sure to memorize both the name and the number of each OSI layer. Network techs use OSI model terms such as *Layer 4* and *Transport layer* synonymously. Students have long used mnemonics for memorizing such lists. The one I use when teaching is "All People Seem To Need Data Processing."

Now that you know the names of the layers, let's look at what each layer does. We'll see them at work at the fictional company CSCPROF. (You can find me on X and Instagram with my handle *@CSCPROF*.)

NOTE This section is a conceptual overview of the hardware and software functions of a network. Your network may have different hardware or software, but it will share the same functions.

Welcome to CSCPROF!

CSCPROF has a small network of PCs (desktops and laptops) running Windows as well as machines running various Linux distributions and macOS. Any operating system comes with all the network software it needs to connect to a network. Some computers in the CSCPROF network are connected by network cabling, while others are connected wirelessly.

As in most offices, everyone at CSCPROF has their own PC, including Noah and Jacob, who handle all the networking and cybersecurity functions at CSCPROF. Because of the kinds of work they do, these two often need to exchange data between their two PCs. Noah has just completed a new cybersecurity training document in Microsoft Word that is part of CSCPROF's cybersecurity education for its employees, and he wants Jacob to check it out. Noah could transfer a copy of the file to Jacob's computer by the tried-and-true Sneakernet method—saving the file on a flash drive and walking it over to him—but thanks to the wonders of computer networking, Noah doesn't even have to get up from his chair.

Long before Noah ever saved the Word document on his system, the person who first installed the CSCPROF systems configured them to be part of a common network. All this setup activity resulted in multiple layers of hardware and software that can work together behind the scenes to get a copy of the Word document from Noah's system to Jacob's system. Let's examine the different pieces of the network and how they relate to the OSI model.

Test Specific

Layer 7, the Application Layer

Think of the last time you were at an airport, waiting to board a flight. After some time, you finally hear over the airport speakers, "Flight 260, now boarding." You gather your boarding pass and carry-on luggage and get in line. You're not flying. You're getting ready to fly. That's the Application layer (Layer 7), which is all about preparing your network for traffic.

This layer represents the network-related program code and functions running on a computer system that either initiate the request on the sending system or service the request on the receiving system. At the Application layer are *Application Programming Interfaces* (APIs), which are tools and protocols that allow programs on one machine to communicate with other programs on the same machine, the operating system, and even programs on other machines. An API, in general, provides a standard way for programmers to enhance or extend an application's capabilities by communicating with classes and functions in library files. The key is that APIs are reusable within the same program or by different programs. As an example, consider a weather app on a phone that uses APIs to communicate with the weather bureau's software and database.

The word *Application* here doesn't refer to actual applications like Zoom or Microsoft Word. Instead, it refers to protocols like DNS and DHCP, or APIs on which programs rely. For example, Internet Message Access Protocol (IMAP) and Simple Mail Transfer Protocol (SMTP) are important Application layer protocols for email, but many different end-user applications use those protocols, such as Microsoft Outlook and Mozilla Thunderbird.

Other protocols at Layer 7 include FTP, HTTP, Lightweight Directory Access Protocol (LDAP), and Simple Network Management Protocol (SNMP).

When you start the networking process, the system makes API calls. You're not sending traffic across networks yet, but you're preparing to. That's just like boarding the flight: you're not yet flying, but you're getting ready to.

The first and last parts of any network communication are the software applications that use it. They are also the most visible. If you want to copy a file residing on another system in your network, you need an applet like Network in Windows that enables you to access files on remote systems. If you want to view web pages, you need a web browser like Google Chrome or Mozilla Firefox. You experience a network through an application. A user who knows nothing about all the other parts of a network still knows how to open an email application to retrieve mail.

Applications may include additional functions, such as encryption, user authentication, and tools to control the look of the data, but these functions are specific to the given applications. In other words, if you want to put a password on your Word document, you must use the password functions in Word to do so, just like you'd use Word's formatting menu.

In our story, Jacob uses the Network applet to access a shared folder on Noah's computer to download a copy of the cybersecurity training document. The Network applet hooks into the operating system and gets the networking ball rolling through the Server Message Block (SMB) protocol at Layer 7.

The application data, or *payload*—which is the SMB file request that has just been formed at the Application layer—is now passed to the layer below, the Presentation layer.

Layer 6, the Presentation Layer

Think of the last time you prepared for a job interview. You steamed your clothes, brushed your hair, and maybe even put on cologne or perfume. That's what the Presentation layer (Layer 6) was designed to do for data.

Compression and decompression used to be done at this layer, as did encryption, decryption, and formatting. Just about all the old functions at this layer have been offloaded to other parts of the network, but this layer remains for backward compatibility.

Thus, there are no modern protocols that operate at this layer (although there are some obsolete Layer 6 protocols), as there isn't really a functional distinction between Layer 7 and Layer 6 for applications and protocols. Consider HTTP, which is a Layer 7 protocol but handles traditional Layer 6 operations such as identifying character encoding for conversion. The actual conversion, though, happens at Layer 7.

In the traditional OSI model, the Presentation layer would turn the data in Noah's document into a generic format—that is, one that's not specific to any application. This allows the system to send the data independent of syntax or any other properties unique to Word. This layer would also compress the data to cut down on its size before sending it.

The data generated at this layer is added to what came from the layer above, the Application layer, and then sent to the layer below, the Session layer.

Layer 5, the Session Layer

Back when I used dial-up internet, many years ago, downloading a file often took a long time. Occasionally, someone in the house would pick up the phone as my file was downloading, which immediately stopped the download. In those days, it was common to use one phone line for making calls and using the internet, but you couldn't do both at the same time. So, if you were connected to your dial-up ISP and someone picked up the phone, the internet connection was terminated. I would yell "You ruined my download!" to the offending party, but in reality, this was a result of the Session layer (Layer 5), which establishes, maintains, and terminates connections between programs on different machines.

On any network, any one system may be talking to many other systems at any given moment. For example, as Jacob accesses the Word document on Noah's system, other systems could be accessing other files on Noah's system. Noah's system must direct incoming requests to the corresponding services and directories. Additionally, the operating system must enable a program on one system to connect to a program on another system to verify that the other system can handle whatever operation the initiating system wants to perform. In other words, if Eva's system wants to send a file to Noah's system, it first contacts Noah's system to ensure that it is ready to handle that file. The *session software* manages this part of networking, connecting applications to applications.

A *socket*, which represents an endpoint of an active communication session between two systems, consists of three parts:

- **IP ADDRESS** A Layer 3 unique numeric identifier for each device on a network—for example, 192.168.1.99. Internet Protocol (IP) addresses are covered in great detail in Chapters 2 and 3.
- **PORT** A Layer 4 number that identifies a program or service. For example, a web server that uses encryption will send and receive traffic on port 443, but on that same machine, an FTP server will send and receive on port 21. Think of port numbers as the way traffic enters and exits programs or services. Chapter 4 covers ports in depth.
- **LAYER 4 PROTOCOL** Either Transmission Control Protocol (TCP) or User Datagram Protocol (UDP), covered later in this chapter and in Chapter 4.

IP addresses exist at Layer 3, and ports, TCP, and UDP all exist at Layer 4. However, at Layer 5, all of those items are aggregated to connect programs on one machine to programs on another machine.

SEE YOUR SESSIONS

You can see how many sessions your system is running at one time by running the `netstat` utility from a command prompt.

On a Windows or Mac system, in the command line interface, type the following and then press ENTER:

```
netstat -an
```

On a Linux system, run the following:

```
ss -an
```

Don't worry about trying to interpret the output; we'll cover `netstat` in great detail in Chapter 4. The takeaway for now is simply that each line `netstat` outputs is a session.

In our story, Noah's PC has programs and services that are connected to many other systems at the same time, all handled by the Session layer.

The data generated at this layer is added to what came from the two layers above and is then sent to the layer below, the Transport layer.

Layer 4, the Transport Layer

At this point, the data faces a pivotal moment. It will be *encapsulated* (put inside of, like Russian nesting dolls) in a TCP segment or a UDP datagram at the Transport layer (Layer 4). Applications that require accuracy and integrity will use TCP. Applications that require speed will use UDP.

With TCP, the data, which could be quite large at this point, is chopped up into different parts (a process called *segmentation*) and placed inside multiple segments. You can think of it like multiple packages in one UPS shipment. To make sure you get all of the boxes in that shipment, UPS uses a numbering system for each box's label. Likewise, when a computer sends data over a network with TCP, a sequence number is embedded within each segment. By reading the sequence numbers, the receiving system knows both the total number of segments and how to put them back together.

With UDP, the data won't be segmented, but if necessary it might be chopped up at the Network layer (Layer 3) in a process known as *fragmentation*.

TCP segments and UDP datagrams vary greatly but have one addressing component in common: port numbers. Both include a source port and destination port number that are used at Layer 4 to correspond with a program or service on a machine that's sending or receiving traffic.

For example, when traffic comes into a machine running both a web server and an FTP server, the operating system sends traffic for the web server to port 80 (unencrypted) or 443 (encrypted), while traffic for the FTP server is sent to port 21. This is because those numbers are used as destination ports for requests from clients. When a server service responds to a client, the source port and destination port will be flipped; that is, in traffic from the server to the client, the source port will be the port that was used as a destination port in traffic from the client (in the previous examples, 80, 443, or 21). Also, the destination port will be the port that the client used as a source port in the request.

NOTE Chapter 6 covers ports, TCP, and UDP in detail.

Some protocols—like SMTP, which is used for sending email messages—require that the email client and server verify that they have a connection before a message is sent. This makes sense because you don't want your email message to be a corrupted mess when it arrives. Thus, SMTP will always use TCP as its Layer 4 protocol.

Alternatively, several protocols simply send data without waiting to verify that the receiving system is ready. This is analogous to how, when I'm teaching, I want my students to just raise their hands and ask me questions instead of introducing themselves and confirming that I heard everything they said. A DNS client, for example, sends DNS queries without first verifying that the DNS server is there. You'd want a client service to query the server service without the overhead (for integrity and accuracy) that TCP uses. This is why DNS uses UDP as its Layer 4 protocol for queries and responses.

NOTE DNS uses TCP for responses greater than 512 bytes (which are rare) and zone transfers (covered in Chapter 7).

In our story, the Word document on Noah's PC needs to have guaranteed, acknowledged, connection-oriented transmission. It needs to be broken up into multiple parts that can be reassembled at the destination, and it needs to be associated with the applications on both the source and the destination with port numbers. What handles that? The Transport layer.

Remember from Layer 7 that the server uses the SMB protocol in this case. SMB servers send and receive over port 445, and SMB messages are encapsulated in a TCP segment at Layer 4.

The TCP segment and UDP datagram start with a *header*—complementary information placed in front of the data passed from the layers above—that contains *metadata* (data about data). The source and destination port values are examples of information the TCP and UDP headers contain. The header and data combination is sent to the layer below, the Network layer.

Layer 3, the Network Layer

The Network layer involves a "container" similar to the TCP segments and UDP datagrams just described. At this layer, these header/data combinations are called *packets*.

Layer 3 packets are created and addressed so that they can go from one network to another. The logical addressing protocol in the TCP/IP suite is IP. Each device on the network gets an IP address to make sure that a piece of data gets to where it needs to go. An IP address is a *logical address*, assigned by software, as opposed to a physical address like the MAC address in Layer 2 (which we'll discuss shortly).

IP uses a rather unique dotted decimal notation based on four 8-bit numbers. Each 8-bit number ranges from 0 to 255, and the four numbers are separated by three periods. A typical IP address might look like this:

192.168.19.75

No two systems on the same network can share the same IP address. Two machines accidentally configured with the same address will produce unintended side effects. These IP addresses don't just magically appear; they must be configured by the network administrator.

THE ORIGINS OF TCP/IP

TCP/IP is ubiquitous in networking today, and although you might imagine that it had humble beginnings in someone's garage lab, that's not the case.

In the early 1970s, two researchers at the US Defense Advanced Research Projects Agency (DARPA), Robert E. Kahn and Vinton Cerf, worked out the basic parameters of what would become TCP/IP. TCP/IP offered amazing robustness in its design and eventual implementation, demonstrating government research at its most profound and world shaping!

To be accurate, TCP/IP is really several network protocols designed to work together—better known as a *protocol suite*—but TCP and IP do so much work that the suite bears their name.

I had the great honor of meeting Vint Cerf when he visited Rochester Institute of Technology many years ago, as shown here.

What makes IP addresses, and logical addressing in general, so powerful is a device called a *router* that connects networks to other networks. Routers use the destination IP address to forward data.

NOTE Try to avoid using redundant expressions like "IP protocol." It wouldn't be right to say "Internet Protocol protocol" in English, and it doesn't work in network speak either. Also, don't say "NIC card" (coming up in the next section) for the same reason!

The IP header (which contains metadata) generated at this layer encapsulates the data that came from the four layers above (including the TCP or UDP header) and is sent to the layer below, the Data Link layer.

Layer 2, the Data Link Layer

The Data Link layer (Layer 2) involves many tools and technologies, including a NIC, MAC address, frame, and switch. As you'll soon see, it's also the only layer in the OSI model that contains sublayers. Because it's more complex than the previous layers, let's break it down into the major components and examine how they work together.

THE NIC

The real magic of a network starts with the *network interface card*, or *NIC* (pronounced "nick"), which serves as the interface between the PC and the network. While NICs come in a wide array of shapes and sizes, the ones at CSCPROF look like Figure 1-4.

FIGURE 1-4
A NIC

On older systems, a NIC was literally a separate card that snapped into a handy expansion slot, hence the name. Even though NICs are now built into the motherboard, the name remains. We should really expand that acronym differently to network interface *chip*!

Figure 1-5 shows a typical laptop with a dongle providing an Ethernet (wired networking technology) port. Note how the cable runs from the NIC into the wall, and inside that wall is another cable running all the way back to a switch.

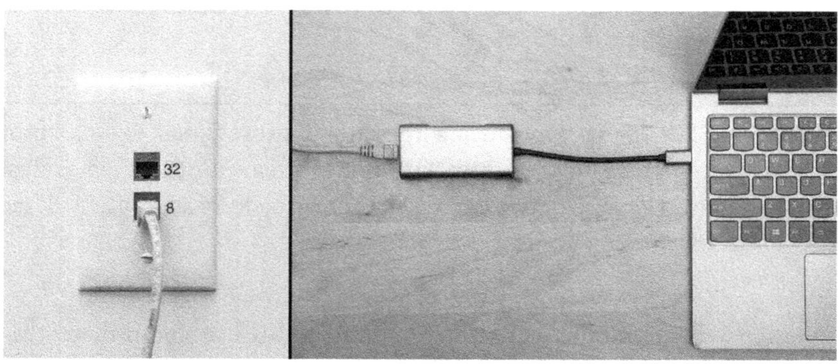

FIGURE 1-5 A dongle NIC with a cable connecting the laptop to the wall jack

To understand networks, you must understand how NICs work. The network must include a mechanism to give each system a unique identifier—like a telephone number—so that data is delivered to the right system. That's one of the NIC's most important jobs. Inside every NIC, burned onto a type of Read-Only Memory (ROM) chip, is special firmware containing a unique identifier with a 48-bit value called the *media access control (MAC) address*.

MAC ADDRESSES

Earlier you learned that port numbers uniquely identify the program or service sending and receiving traffic, and that IP addresses are logical addresses assigned by software. When I use my laptop at home, it will be assigned an IP address by a server on my home network. When I take my laptop to Rochester Institute of Technology and use it, the IP address will be assigned by an RIT server. When I take my laptop to Finger Lakes Community College and use it, the IP address will be assigned by an FLCC server. The IP address changes and is proportional to each network a device is connected to. The MAC address for my laptop, though, never changes. It's the same whether I'm at home, RIT, FLCC, or some other network location.

Any company that makes NICs must contact the Institute of Electrical and Electronics Engineers (IEEE) and request a block of MAC addresses, which the company then burns into the ROM on its NICs. Many NIC manufacturers also print the MAC address on the surface of each NIC, as shown in Figure 1-6. Note that the NIC shown here displays the MAC address in hexadecimal notation. Count the number of hex digits. Each hex digit represents 4 bits, so it takes 12 hex characters to represent 48 bits. MAC addresses are always written in hex.

TECH TIP A hexadecimal numbering system uses base 16 to represent numbers; that would be 0–15 (in base-10 values). Contrast this with the more common decimal numbering system, numbered 0–9. Just as with decimal, people who work with hexadecimal need a single character to represent each number for the 16 values. Using 0–9 makes sense, but then hex is represented in letter form for the values 10–15 (A, B, C, D, E, F).

Hexadecimal works great with binary. Four bits provide the values of 0–15. For example, 0001 is the value 1; 1000 in binary is 8; 1111 is 15. When we work with MAC addresses, it's far easier to break each 4-bit section of the 48-bit address and translate that into hex. Humans work better that way! You'll see much more on this topic in the "Numeral Systems" section later in the chapter.

FIGURE 1-6
MAC address on a NIC

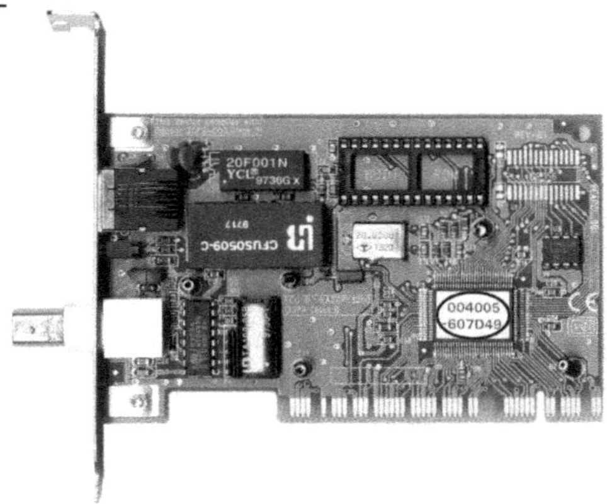

The MAC address in Figure 1-6 is 004005-607D49, although in print MAC addresses appear in the format 00–40–05–60–7D–49. The first six digits, in this example 00–40–05, represent the *organizationally unique identifier* (OUI) of the NIC manufacturer. Every NIC vendor, manufacturer, and organization purchases an OUI (also known as a *block ID*) from the IEEE, which won't issue that OUI to any other vendor, manufacturer, or organization.

The last six digits of the MAC address, in this example 60–7D–49, are the manufacturer's unique serial number for that NIC, often referred to as the *device ID*. A NIC vendor, manufacturer, or organization can assign the same device ID to multiple NICs but will ship them to different geographic areas to ensure that two NICs with the same MAC address don't wind up on the same network.

A NIC can also be configured with a locally administered address by an administrator or user. From the other side, MAC addresses can be spoofed by an attacker.

NOTE Windows uses a dash as the delimiter for the MAC address. Linux and macOS use a colon. Cisco uses dotted triplet notation, which has three groupings of 4 hex characters separated by dots.

To see the MAC address for your NIC, follow the directions for your operating system:

- For Windows, type **`ipconfig /all`** and hit ENTER from a command prompt. Note that in the output for `ipconfig`, the MAC address follows the label `Physical Address`—remember, a physical address is distinct from the *logical* IP address.
- For macOS, type **`ifconfig`** and hit ENTER from a terminal and look for the MAC address after the label `HWaddr`.
- For Linux, type **`ip a`** and hit ENTER from a terminal and look for the MAC address after the label `link/ether`.

To see the organization that made your NIC, visit *wireshark.org/tools/oui-lookup.html*, enter the MAC address of your NIC, and click **Find**.

FRAMES

Remember that the Network layer involves packets that have IP addresses to ensure that each packet gets to its intended destination. But IP packets don't leave their source device without any clothes on! Each IP packet is handed to the NIC, which encloses the IP packet in a *frame*, the "container" type used at Layer 2. The IP packet and all its data (which can include a TCP segment or UDP datagram from Layers 7 through 5) become the payload of a frame at Layer 2. Again, think of those Russian nesting dolls.

I like to visualize the packet as an envelope and the frame as a pneumatic canister containing it, as depicted in Figure 1-7.

FIGURE 1-7 An IP packet (envelope) containing data will be enclosed in a frame (canister).

Figure 1-8 shows a more conventional drawing.

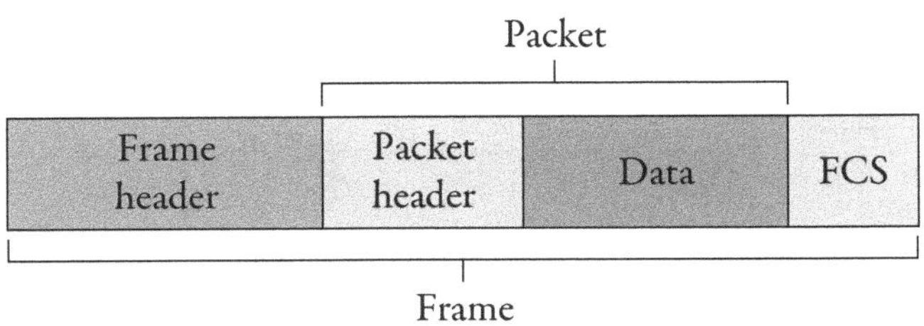

FIGURE 1-8 IP packet in a frame

Figure 1-9 illustrates a generic Ethernet frame.

Destination MAC address	Source MAC address	Type	Data	FCS

FIGURE 1-9 Generic frame

Note that the frame begins with the MAC address of the NIC to which the data is to be sent, followed by the MAC address of the sending NIC. Next comes the *Type* field, which indicates what's encapsulated in the frame. Then comes the *Data* field that contains what's encapsulated (the payload). Unlike TCP segments, UDP datagrams, and IP packets, a frame has a section that follows the payload called a *trailer*. In the frame trailer is a special piece of error checking information called the *frame check sequence* (FCS). The FCS uses a type of binary math called a *cyclic redundancy check* (CRC) that the receiving NIC uses to verify that the data arrived intact.

To summarize, think of a frame as having three sections:

- The header (source MAC address, destination MAC address, and type)
- The payload (the data encapsulated in the frame)
- The trailer (the FCS)

NICs aren't concerned with content; they don't know or care what's inside the payload. That data may be a part of a file, print job, or web page. The NIC simply takes whatever data is passed to it via its device driver and addresses it for the correct system. Special software will take care of what data gets sent and what happens to that data when it arrives. This is the beauty of imagining frames as little pneumatic canisters (Figure 1-10). A canister can carry anything from dirt to diamonds; the NIC doesn't care one bit (pardon the pun).

Like a canister, a frame can hold only a certain amount of data. Different types of networks use different sizes of frames, but the frames used in Ethernet networks hold at most 1,500 bytes of data (this doesn't count the header or trailer, just the payload). This raises a new question: What happens when the data to be sent is larger than the frame size? In that case,

FIGURE 1-10 An IP packet in a frame

packets are fragmented (broken up) at Layer 3 to adhere to the 1,500 byte limit and then sent down to Layer 2.

FCS IN DEPTH

All FCSs are only 4 bytes long, yet the Ethernet frame can carry up to 1,500 bytes of data. How can 4 bytes tell you if all 1,500 bytes in the data are correct? That's the magic of the math of the CRC. Without going into the grinding details, think of the CRC as just the remainder of a division problem. The NIC sending the frame does a little math to make the CRC. The receiving NIC applies the same math. If the receiving NIC's answer is the same as the CRC, the frame has integrity and is accepted. If not, the frame is dropped on the spot.

SWITCHES

When a system sends a frame from the NIC out onto the network, the frame goes into a network *switch*, another key piece of hardware the network uses that handles the flow of data from each device to every other device (Figure 1-11). The switch is often tucked away in a closet or an equipment room. Each non-wireless system on the network has its own cable that runs to a switch, which usually will be interconnected with other network switches. Wireless devices communicate with an access point (AP), covered in Chapter 12. Cables and wireless technologies are part of Layer 1, covered shortly.

Now that you've seen all the pieces used to send and receive frames, let's put them together and review the entire process of a frame traveling from one system to another.

FIGURE 1-11 A switch

THE COMPLETE FRAME MOVEMENT

The basic send/receive process is as follows:

1. The sending system's operating system hands what came down the OSI model from Layers 7 through 3 to its NIC. The NIC builds a frame to transport that data to the receiving NIC.
2. After the NIC creates the frame, it adds the FCS, then dumps it and the data into the frame.
3. The NIC puts both the destination MAC address and its own MAC address in the frame header. It then sends the frame through the cable to the network.

NOTE Any frame addressed specifically to another device's MAC address is called a *unicast frame*. The one-to-one addressing scheme is called *unicast addressing*. This concept also applies to IP addresses at Layer 3.

4. The frame propagates down the wire into the switch. The switch sends unicast frames to the port associated with the destination MAC address (more on this and how switches work coming up in Chapter 6) and sends broadcast frames—those destined for all devices on the network—out of all ports except the port on which the message originated.
5. The NIC on the destination checks to see that the frame has integrity by verifying the CRC in the trailer. If the CRC the NIC computes doesn't match the CRC in the frame's trailer, the NIC drops the frame on the spot.
6. The NIC checks whether the frame's destination MAC address is a broadcast, a multicast (traffic destined for multiple, but not all, devices on the network), or the unicast address of the NIC itself. If none of the above are true, the NIC drops the frame on the spot. If all is well, it strips off the frame (header and trailer) and sends the packet up to Layer 3. The networking software built into the operating system handles all the rest of the work. The NIC's driver software is the interconnection between the hardware and the software. The NIC driver knows how to communicate with the NIC to send and receive frames, but it can't do anything with the packet. Instead, it hands the packet off to other services that know how to deal with all the separate packets, send them up the OSI model layers, and turn them into web pages, email messages, files, and so forth.
7. Networking protocols and the OS's networking stack check the destination IP address in the IP header. If it's not the IP address of the destination machine, the traffic at that

point is simply dropped. If all is well, the packet is stripped off, and the TCP segment or UDP datagram is sent up to Layer 4.

8. The OS checks the destination port in the TCP or UDP header and uses that number to send the data to the correct program or service on the destination machine. If all is well, the OS strips off the TCP or UDP header and sends the data up to Layer 5, then Layer 6, and finally Layer 7.

When you send data from one computer to a device on a different network in the same organization or over the internet, that data can go through many routers before it reaches its destination. Each router strips off the incoming frame, determines which router to send the network traffic to next (as discussed in Chapter 5) according to the destination IP address in the packet, creates a new frame, and then sends the packet within a new frame on its merry way. The new frame type will be the appropriate technology for whatever connection technology connects to the next router. That could be a cable, DSL, or fiber network connection (Figure 1-12). The IP packet, on the other hand, always remains as is, unchanged.

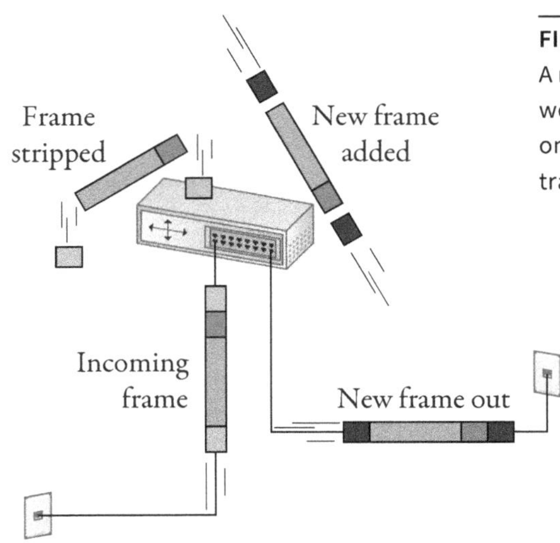

FIGURE 1-12 A router removing a network frame and adding one for the outgoing transmission

Once the packet reaches the destination network's router, that final router performs one last frame replacement. It strips off the incoming frame, looks at the destination IP address, and then adds a frame with the appropriate source MAC address (its own) and the destination MAC address corresponding to the destination IP address, which—like everything in the packet—has remained unchanged through the entire journey.

During this process on the destination, packets that were fragmented on the source are reassembled at Layer 3, segments that were broken up on the source are put together at Layer 4,

SMB at Layer 7 turns the data back into application-specific data, and finally, the destination program or service gets the data!

THE TWO SUBLAYERS OF LAYER 2

Consider how data moves in and out of a NIC. On one end, frames move into and out of the NIC's network cable connection. On the other end, data moves back and forth between the NIC and the network operating system software. The many steps a NIC performs to keep this data moving—sending and receiving frames over the wire, creating outgoing frames, reading incoming frames, and attaching MAC addresses—are classically broken down into two distinct jobs.

NOTE Sending NICs break frames down into 1s and 0s for transmission; receiving NICs rebuild the frame upon receipt.

The first job, called the *Logical Link Control* (LLC), is the aspect of the NIC that talks to the system's operating system (usually via device drivers). The LLC handles multiple network protocols and provides flow control.

The second job, the *Media Access Control* (MAC), creates and addresses the frame. It adds the NIC's own MAC address as well as the destination MAC address to the frame. Recall that each frame the NIC creates must include both the source and destination MAC addresses. The MAC sublayer adds or checks the FCS. The MAC also ensures that the frames, now complete with their MAC addresses, are then sent along the network cabling.

EXAM TIP The CompTIA Network+ exam tests you on the details of the OSI model, so remember that the Data Link layer is the only layer that has sublayers.

Most networking materials that describe the OSI model put NICs squarely into the Data Link layer of the model. It's at the MAC sublayer, after all, that data gets encapsulated into a frame, source and destination MAC addresses get added to that frame, and error checking occurs. What bothers most students about placing NICs solely in the Data Link layer is their obvious other duty: putting the 1s and 0s on the network cable for wired networks and in the air for wireless networks. How much more physical can you get?

Many people will finesse this issue by defining the Physical layer in its logical sense—that it defines the rules for the 1s and 0s—and ignoring the fact that the data sent on the cable has to come from something. The first question to ask when you hear that argument is, "What component does the sending?" It's the NIC, of course—the only device capable of sending and receiving the physical signal.

NICs, therefore, operate at both Layer 2 and Layer 1 of the OSI model.

ENCAPSULATION AND DECAPSULATION

The term *encapsulation* encompasses the entire process of preparing data to go onto a network. This includes all the steps from the Application, Presentation, Session, Transport, Network, and Data Link layers. Each layer adds more information so that the data gets to the correct recipient and the recipient knows what to do with it.

The receiving computer reverses the process, stripping all the extra header information out as the data goes up the stack. This reverse process is called *decapsulation*.

The Transport layer creates a segment or datagram and hands it down to the Network layer. That layer adds IP information, encapsulating the segment or datagram. The Data Link layer wraps up all that goodness, encapsulating the packet in a frame for delivery over the network. The NIC turns the frame into 1s and 0s for transmission over the network medium.

Layer 1, the Physical Layer

The Physical layer (Layer 1) of the OSI model defines the method of moving data between computers, so it includes anything that moves data from one system to another, such as copper cabling, fiber cables, and even radio frequency (RF) waves. Layer 1 doesn't care what data goes through; it just moves the data from one system to another system.

Now think back to the frames at Layer 2. How do they actually travel from one device to another? To answer that, we need to look at how computers transmit data at the most fundamental level: as electrical signals moving across wires.

Computer data is *binary*, which means it's made up of streams of 1s and 0s. NICs send and receive this binary data as pulses of electricity, light, or radio waves. The specific process by which a NIC uses electricity to send and receive data is exceedingly complicated but, luckily for you, not necessary to understand. Instead, just think of a charge on the wire as a 1 and no charge as a 0. A chunk of data moving in pulses across a wire might look something like Figure 1-13.

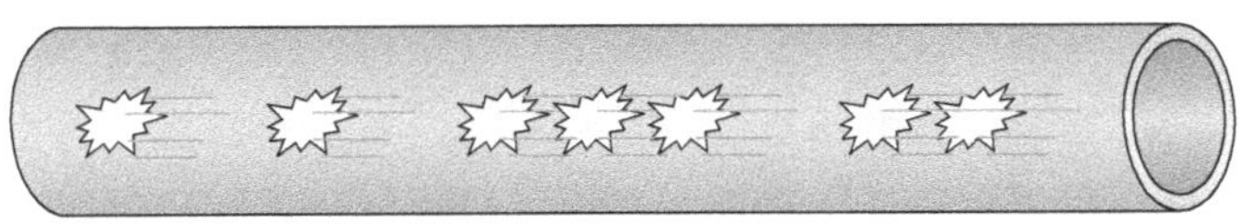

FIGURE 1-13 Data moving along a wire

If you put an oscilloscope—a powerful tool that visualizes electrical pulses—on the wire to measure voltage, you'd see something like Figure 1-14.

FIGURE 1-14
Oscilloscope of data

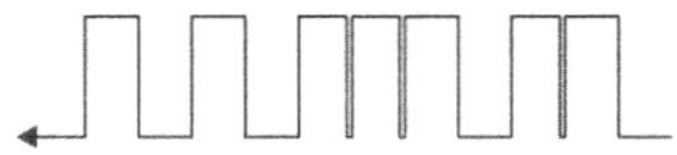

Now, keeping in mind that the pulses represent binary data, visualize instead a string of 1s and 0s moving across the wire (Figure 1-15).

FIGURE 1-15
Data as 1s and 0s

NOTE The unit of data specified by a protocol at each layer of the OSI model is called a *protocol data unit (PDU)*. A bit is the PDU of Layer 1. A frame is the PDU of Layer 2. A packet is the PDU of Layer 3. A segment (TCP) and datagram (UDP) are the PDUs of Layer 4. The PDU for Layers 5–7 is simply known as data.

Wired devices use a cable like the one shown in Figure 1-16 to move bits of data between systems. This cable, known in the networking industry as *Ethernet unshielded twisted pair* (UTP), contains four pairs of wires that can transmit and receive data.

FIGURE 1-16
UTP cabling

Note that each system has the full range of layers, so data from Noah's computer can flow to Jacob's computer.

Cabling and wireless transmission define the Physical layer of the network, and NICs provide the interface to the PC.

Computers using Wi-Fi connect to networks wirelessly; they are not plugged into an Ethernet port, and there are no local wires. So do OSI layers even apply to them? If you answered, "Of course," then you win a prize because they most definitely do.

The wireless radio waves that connect a laptop to an AP operate at Layer 1.

A wireless NIC has a MAC address and sends Wi-Fi frames to the AP. The AP strips the Wi-Fi frame header and replaces it with an Ethernet frame, then sends the traffic to the local switch, acting as a bridge between the wireless and wired networks. That's all clearly Layer 2 happiness. The difference is the frames. Wi-Fi (wireless) frames follow the 802.11 standard, while Ethernet (wired) frames follow the 802.3 standard. Each frame format varies in fields and values, but they both have Source MAC Address, Destination MAC Address, Type, and FCS in common.

NOTE The IEEE came up with local area network (LAN) standards that start with 802 (as do the names of the corresponding committees). According to this IEEE document, *ieee802.org/IEEE-802-LMSC-OverviewGuide-06-Oct-2016-v2.pdf,* 802 was just the next sequential number issued at that time. However, many people seem to believe that since this all started in February 1980 (2/80), the IEEE reversed the month and year to get 802.

The OSI Model as a Diagnostic and Collaboration Tool

Many people work remotely these days, connecting wirelessly to the internet with their laptop or desktop computers. To coordinate and collaborate with colleagues, they often also use a number of different online services, such as Microsoft 365, Dropbox, GitHub, and so forth. The OSI model provides us with a way to conceptualize a network to determine what could be causing a specific problem when one inevitably occurs. Good techs always use a model to troubleshoot their networks. The OSI model can apply to a simple network or a more advanced network.

If a remote employee can't print to a networked printer, for example, a model can help solve the problem. If their NIC shows activity, then you can use the OSI model to rule out both the Physical layer (Layer 1) and Data Link layer (Layer 2), moving up the layer ladder to the Network layer (Layer 3). If their computer has a proper IP address, then you can rule out that layer too, and move on to Layer 4 and beyond to solve the problem.

The bottom line is that understanding the OSI model is important. It is the primary diagnostic tool for troubleshooting networks as well as for communicating with your fellow techs.

Numeral Systems

The first part of this chapter, through the lens of the OSI model, provided an overview of many concepts coming up in the book in greater depth. It gave you a strong foundation to build on. This second part of the chapter does the same thing, but for a different aspect of networking.

In the world of networking, there are multiple numeral systems that you need to be well versed in to fully understand MAC addresses, IP addresses, network traffic, and more.

The numeral system we use every day is base 10 (decimal). Two others that you need to master are base 2 (binary) and base 16 (hexadecimal). Hexadecimal was briefly covered earlier in this chapter, but for consistency purposes, I'll revisit it here.

All numeral systems start with the digit and value 0, but then they start to diverge.

The number after the word *base* represents two concepts. First, that number represents the number of unique digits in the numeral system.

- Base 2 has 2 digits: 0 and 1.
- Base 10 has 10 digits: 0, 1, 2, 3, 4, 5, 6, 7, 8, 9.
- Base 16 has 16 characters: 0, 1, 2, 3, 4, 5, 6, 7, 8, 9—and since we're now out of numeric characters—A, B, C, D, E, F.

In hexadecimal, often referred to just as *hex*, A has a base-10 value of 10, B is 11, C is 12, D is 13, E is 14, and F is 15. These characters are not case sensitive.

Second, the value of the last digit is always one less than the base itself. Base 2's highest value is 1. Base 10's highest value is 9. Base 16's highest value is 15 (represented by F). The reason for this is that all numeral systems start with 0, which counts as a valid digit.

Each numeral system's numbers are represented by one or more characters, organized in columnar format. As you move from the far right (least significant digit) to the far left (most significant digit), each column's value increases. Every numeral system's rightmost column is always the ones (1s) column. As you move to the left, each column is the base times the previous column.

The Decimal Numeral System

Let's start with base 10:

1 (one)
1 × 10 = 10 (ten)
10 × 10 = 100 (one hundred)
100 × 10 = 1,000 (one thousand)
1,000 × 10 = 10,000 (ten thousand)
10,000 × 10 = 100,000 (one hundred thousand)
100,000 × 10 = 1,000,000 (one million)
1,000,000 × 10 = 10,000,000 (ten million)
10,000,000 × 10 = 100,000,000 (one hundred million)
100,000,000 × 10 = 1,000,000,000 (one billion)

In base 10, the columns (from left to right) look as follows:

BILLIONS	HUNDRED MILLIONS	TEN MILLIONS	MILLIONS	HUNDRED THOUSANDS	TEN THOUSANDS	THOUSANDS	HUNDREDS	TENS	ONES
1,000,000,000	100,000,000	10,000,000	1,000,000	100,000	10,000	1,000	100	10	1

The Binary Numeral System

In base 2, with the ones column at the far right, when you multiply each previous column with the base, you get:

$$1$$
$$1 \times 2 = 2$$
$$2 \times 2 = 4$$
$$4 \times 2 = 8$$
$$8 \times 2 = 16$$
$$16 \times 2 = 32$$
$$32 \times 2 = 64$$
$$64 \times 2 = 128$$

Putting the columns in order, you get:

128	64	32	16	8	4	2	1

Each digit (0 or 1) is known as a *bit*, short for "binary digit."

When working with large binary values, you can get confused about how many bits there are in the number. For example, take the binary numbers 1111111111111111 and 111111111111. It is difficult to see how many bits there are. That's where a *byte* comes in handy.

A byte is 8 bits. Breaking a binary number up into bytes helps you read a binary number faster and more accurately. For example, breaking up the large binary number just shown, 1111111111111111, into bytes (groups of 8 bits) gives you 11111111 11111111, which is much easier to read. Now you can easily see that you have 2 bytes, and each bit in each byte is a 1. The second example binary number, 111111111111, is also easier to read when broken up into bytes: 00001111 11111111. You have to add four leading 0s to the first group because each byte must contain exactly 8 bits.

Since a byte is 8 bits, the largest number that one byte can represent is 11111111 in binary, which is 255 (128 + 64 + 32 + 16 + 8 + 4 + 2 + 1) in decimal. Therefore, a byte can represent a decimal number between 0 and 255, for a total of 256 different numbers.

Memory and storage space are measured in bytes. When you buy a new computer, you often look at how many bytes of RAM (memory) it has and how many bytes the hard drive can store.

BINARY-TO-DECIMAL CONVERSION

The best way to convert from decimal to binary and back is to use a calculator. It's easy, fast, and accurate. There's always a chance, however, that you may find yourself in a situation where you need to convert without a calculator. Fortunately, manual conversion is also easy. Let's go back to our columnar format:

128	64	32	16	8	4	2	1

Each of these eight numbers corresponds to a column position of one of the eight binary digits. To convert an 8-bit binary value to decimal, align each binary digit under its corresponding number. For example, to convert the binary value 10010110 into decimal, you'd write:

128	64	32	16	8	4	2	1
1	0	0	1	0	1	1	0

Then, wherever there's a 1, you add those values together:

$$128 + 16 + 4 + 2 = 150$$

The decimal equivalent of 10010110 is 150.

DECIMAL-TO-BINARY CONVERSION

Converting from decimal to binary is just as easy. You start with the same column values, but this time, you place the decimal value that you're converting *above* the column values, starting from the left with 128. If the number you're trying to convert is greater than or equal to 128, you subtract 128 from it and place a 1 at the bottom of the column. If it's less than 128, you place a 0 at the bottom. Then, you move the difference to the next column above the 64, and proceed this way throughout the rest of the byte.

Let's convert 221 to binary. Begin by placing 221 over the 128:

221							
128	64	32	16	8	4	2	1

Since 221 is greater than 128, you subtract 128 from it and put the difference, 93, under the 128 and then a 1 under the 93. Then place 93 over the 64 in the second column:

221	93						
128	**64**	32	16	8	4	2	1
93							
1							

Subtracting 64 from 93 gives you 29, so you put a 29 under the 64 and then a 1 under the 29. Then place the 29 over the 32 in the third column:

	93	29					
128	64	**32**	16	8	4	2	1
	29						
1	1						

Since 29 is less than 32, you put a 0 at the bottom of the column and move the 29 over the 16 in the fourth column:

			29				
128	64	32	**16**	8	4	2	1
1	1	0					

Subtracting 16 from 29 gives you 13. Put a 13 under the 16 and a 1 under the 13. Then place the 13 over the 8 in the fifth column:

			29	13			
128	64	32	16	**8**	4	2	1
			13				
1	1	0	1				

Subtract 8 from 13 and put the remainder, 5, under the 8 and a 1 under the 5. Then place the 5 over the 4 in the sixth column:

				13	5		
128	64	32	16	8	**4**	2	1
				5			
1	1	0	1	1			

Subtract 4 from 5 to get 1, which you put under the 4, and add a 1 at the bottom of the column. Then place the 1 over the 2 in the seventh column:

					5	1	
128	64	32	16	8	4	**2**	1
					1		
1	1	0	1	1	1		

Because 1 is less than 2, put a 0 at the bottom of that column and then move the 1 over the 1 in the eighth column:

							1
128	64	32	16	8	4	2	**1**
1	1	0	1	1	1	0	

Finally, 1 is equal to 1, so put a 1 at the bottom of the column, and you're done.

128	64	32	16	8	4	2	1
1	**1**	**0**	**1**	**1**	**1**	**0**	**1**

As you can see, the number 221 in decimal is equal to 11011101 in binary.

Counting in binary revolves around a few basic binary addition problems:

$$0 + 0 = 0$$

$$0 + 1 = 1$$

$$1 + 0 = 1$$

$$1 + 1 = 10$$

Why is 1 + 1 = 10? Let's look at it vertically:

$$\begin{array}{r} 1 \\ +\,1 \\ \hline 10 \end{array}$$

Since 0 and 1 are the only digits in binary, you can't put a 2 in the 1s column, so you set the value to its lowest possible value (0), and carry the 1 to the column to the left (the 2s column). That's how you get 10, which is 2 in binary.

Now you might understand this meme a little bit (pun intended) better: *There are 10 types of people in this world—those that understand binary, and those that don't.*

Continuing on:

$$\begin{array}{r} 10 \\ +\,1 \\ \hline 11 \end{array}$$

2 (10) + 1 (1) is 3 (11).

It's just like a car odometer. When you're at 37 miles, another mile puts you at 38, and then another mile puts you at 39. The highest digit in base 10 is 9, so you set the 1s column to its lowest possible value (0) and carry a 1 to the column to the left (tens) to get 40.

In binary, the odometer would be doing the same thing:

$$\begin{array}{r} 11 \\ +\,1 \\ \hline 100 \end{array}$$

3 (11) + 1 (1) is 4 (100).

Adding 1 + 1 requires you to put the lowest possible value in the 1s column (0) and to carry the 1 to the column to the left. Now 1 + 1 gives you 10, so you put a 0 in the 2s column and carry the 1 over to the 4s column, where it comes down as is.

The Hexadecimal Numeral System

In base 16, or hexadecimal, the columns are computed as follows (I'll show just four):

$$1$$
$$1 \times 16 = 16$$
$$16 \times 16 = 256$$
$$256 \times 16 = 4{,}096$$

Putting the columns in order, you get:

4,096	256	16	1

You can express any base using *n* for the base number, with exponents starting from 0 on the far right, as shown in Table 1-1.

TABLE 1-1 Base 2, base 10, and base 16 compared with exponents

BASE *N* NUMERAL SYSTEM	N^3	N^2	N^1	N^0
Base 2 (binary)	8	4	2	1
Base 10 (decimal)	1,000	100	10	1
Base 16 (hexadecimal)	4,096	256	16	1

Table 1-2 shows the relationship between base 10, base 2, and base 16.

TABLE 1-2 The relationship between base 10, base 2, and base 16

BASE 10 (DECIMAL)	BASE 2 (BINARY)	BASE 16 (HEXADECIMAL)
0	0000	0
1	0001	1
2	0010	2
3	0011	3

BASE 10 (DECIMAL)	BASE 2 (BINARY)	BASE 16 (HEXADECIMAL)
4	0100	4
5	0101	5
6	0110	6
7	0111	7
8	1000	8
9	1001	9
10	1010	A
11	1011	B
12	1100	C
13	1101	D
14	1110	E
15	1111	F

Notice that each hex digit represents 4 bits. Since 8 bits make a byte, 4 bits is half a byte, and as such, is referred to as a *nibble* (because it's not that big of a "byte").

As noted earlier, using bytes to group bits together makes it easier to read a binary number. However, a large binary number, such as 00001111 11111111, is still cumbersome to read, write, and share with others. For example, if I wanted to share the information 01000001 01000010 01000011 with you, it would take some time to tell you all the bits, and it could get confusing. If I gave you the hexadecimal equivalent, though—41 42 43—it's much easier to share and to understand.

To count in hexadecimal, start counting just like you do in our everyday decimal system: 0, 1, 2, 3, 4, 5, 6, 7, 8, 9. But, remember, the hexadecimal numbering system has 16 characters, so after 9 come the remaining six characters: A, B, C, D, E, F.

After the largest value, F, you start over but add 1 to the position to the left and repeat the sequence: 10, 11, 12, 13, 14, 15, 16, 17, 18, 19, 1A, 1B, 1C, 1D, 1E, 1F.

Again, after the largest value, 1F, is reached, you increment the position to the left by 1 and repeat the sequence: 20, 21, 22, and so on. You can apply the car odometer analogy again here: just like a decimal odometer goes from 19 to 20, a hexadecimal counter goes from 1F to 20.

Hex is used for MAC addresses, RAM addresses, HTML color codes, IPv6 addresses, and more.

HEXADECIMAL-TO-BINARY CONVERSION

It's very easy to convert from hexadecimal to binary thanks to the magic of 4 bits. That is, each hexadecimal digit represents one of the 16 possible patterns of 4 bits. See Table 1-3.

TABLE 1-3 Each hexadecimal number represents a 4-bit pattern

BINARY	EQUIVALENT HEXADECIMAL NUMBER
0000	0
0001	1
0010	2
0011	3
0100	4
0101	5
0110	6
0111	7
1000	8
1001	9
1010	A
1011	B
1100	C
1101	D
1110	E
1111	F

Each value in the hexadecimal matches up with a 4-bit sequence in binary. Table 1-4 shows several examples.

TABLE 1-4 Converting from hexadecimal to binary

HEXADECIMAL NUMBER	EQUIVALENT BINARY NUMBER
A	1010
A2	1010 0010
FA2	1111 1010 0010
13	0001 0011

The reverse is also true: it's very easy to convert from binary to hexadecimal. Just break the binary number into groups of 4 bits starting from the right. If the last leftmost group has fewer than 4 bits, pad it with 0s on the left to form a 4-bit group. Replace each 4-bit group with the corresponding hex digit. That's it! Table 1-5 shows some examples.

TABLE 1-5 Converting from binary to hexadecimal

BINARY NUMBER	BINARY NUMBER BROKEN UP INTO GROUPS OF 4 BITS	EQUIVALENT HEXADECIMAL NUMBER
101111	0010 1111	2F
1111111111111111	1111 1111 1111 1111	FFFF
10100000010	0101 0000 0010	502
110010100000	1100 1010 0000	CA0
10110	0001 0110	16
11	0011	3
1000000000000000	1000 0000 0000 0000	8000
11110110	1111 0110	F6
10111101110	0101 1110 1110	5EE
110011001100	1100 1100 1100	CCC

HEXADECIMAL-TO-DECIMAL CONVERSION

You convert from hexadecimal to decimal a little bit differently. If we look at it the same way as the previous conversions, the first four columns (from the right) of a hexadecimal number would be 1, 16 (16 × 1), 256 (16 × 16), and 4,096 (256 ×16). If there were hex digits in the corresponding columns, you'd have to calculate the following to get the decimal equivalent:

$$(4{,}096 \times 14) + (256 \times 7) + (16 \times 11) + (1 \times 3) = 57{,}344 + 1{,}792 + 176 + 3 = 59{,}315$$

4,096	256	16	1
E	7	B	3

It helps to remember that each two hex digits represents 8 bits or 1 byte. Instead of working with large place values like 4,096 and 256, you can break the hex number into byte-sized pairs and work with smaller values so that you no longer have any column with a value greater than 16. However, if you do that, E won't be multiplied by 4,096, but rather by 16, and 7 won't be multiplied by 256, but rather by 1. We'll fix that shortly.

16	1
E	7

There won't be any changes to the last two columns.

16	1
B	3

Let's start with the B3. The B is 1011 in binary, and the 3 is 0011 in binary. Pushing those 4-bit patterns together gives you 10110011.

Now, we can return to our binary columns and compute the decimal value:

128	64	32	16	8	4	2	1
1	0	1	1	0	0	1	1

Adding together all the columns with 1s gives you (128 × 1) + (32 × 1) + (16 × 1) + (2 × 1) + (1 × 1) = 179. Notice that you can get the same value by multiplying (16 × 11) + (1 × 3).

Now, do the same with the E7. The E is 1110 in binary, and the 7 is 0111 in binary.

Since E7 is to the left of B3, keep doubling the column values from 128, and place the 1110 and 0111 4-bit patterns in the corresponding columns like so:

32,768	16,384	8,192	4,096	2,048	1,024	512	256
1	1	1	0	0	1	1	1

Adding the columns that have 1s in them gives you 32,768 + 16,384 + 8,192 + 1,024 + 512 + 256 = 59,136.

Now, add 59,136 to the 179 that you got earlier for B3, and you get 59,315: the decimal value of E7B3.

In most cases, though, you'll only need to worry about two hexadecimal digits (1 byte) at a time, so let's try an example like that. Say you want to turn the hexadecimal number 6C into its binary equivalent. First, represent each digit in binary.

Here's 6:

8	4	2	1
0	1	1	0

Here's C:

8	4	2	1
1	1	0	0

Since, in this case, the 6 comes to the left of the C, you'll put the binary representation of 6 to the left of the binary representation of the C:

8	4	2	1	8	4	2	1
0	1	1	0	1	1	0	0

In reality, when the 4 bits of 6 are placed to the left of the 4 bits of C, the columns can't be 1, 2, 4, and 8 anymore. Let's change those column values to what they are if they're to the left of the 8s column of the C.

~~8~~ 128	~~4~~ 64	~~2~~ 32	~~1~~ 16	8	4	2	1
0	1	1	0	1	1	0	0

Now, add the columns that have 1s in them: 64 + 32 + 8 + 4 = 108, which is 6C in decimal!

It's much easier, as you've seen, to use binary as a bridge when converting hexadecimal to binary, especially when you only have two hexadecimal digits (1 byte) to convert.

DECIMAL-TO-HEXADECIMAL CONVERSION

Converting from decimal to hexadecimal is just as easy. You'll use binary as the "bridge" in reverse!

Say you have a decimal number of 185. Turning 185 into binary looks like this, since 128 + 32 + 16 + 8 + 1 = 185:

128	64	32	16	8	4	2	1
1	0	1	1	1	0	0	1

If you treat each group of 4 bits separately, you can think of the left 4 bits as being in the 1, 2, 4, and 8 columns, like the 4 bits on the right:

~~128~~ 8	~~64~~ 4	~~32~~ 2	~~16~~ 1	8	4	2	1
1	0	1	1	1	0	0	1

Adding 8 + 2 + 1 (the columns of the left 4 bits that have 1s in them), you get 11, or B in hexadecimal.

If you add 8 + 1 (the columns of the right 4 bits that have 1s in them), you get 9, which is also 9 in hexadecimal.

When you put the B and the 9 together, B9 is the hexadecimal representation of the decimal number 185! If you have fewer than 8 bits, pad the left with 0s to reach 8 bits.

Chapter Review

Questions

1. What Windows command do you use to find the MAC address for a system?
   A. `ipconfig /all`
   B. `netstat`
   C. `ping`
   D. `mac /show`

2. Which of the following is not associated with Layer 4?
   A. TCP
   B. UDP
   C. Frames
   D. Port numbers

3. Which of these devices operates at Layer 3?
   A. Switch
   B. Router
   C. Server
   D. PC

4. Which of the following layers contain data created and read by applications?
   A. 5 through 7
   B. 1 and 2
   C. 4 through 6
   D. 3 through 5
5. Which of the following is true?
   A. Routers connect devices of the same network together.
   B. Switches connect different networks together.
   C. Routers connect clients of the same network together.
   D. Switches connect devices of the same network together.
6. Which of the following differ between wired and wireless devices?
   A. Frames
   B. Packets
   C. Segments
   D. Datagrams
7. Which of the following always uses TCP at Layer 4?
   A. DNS
   B. DHCP
   C. Email
   D. VoIP
8. If you're having an issue due to something at Layer 2, which of the following won't be related to it?
   A. IP address
   B. NIC
   C. Switch
   D. MAC address
9. Which of these represents a valid MAC address and a valid IP address?
   A. MAC address F8-B5-4D-61-AA-B2; IP address 192.168.1.246
   B. MAC address F8-B5-4D; IP address 192.168.1
   C. MAC address F8-B5-4D-61-R2-D2; IP address 192.168.1.490
   D. MAC address F8-B5-4D-61-BB-C2-11; IP address 1.2.3.4.5

10. Which of the following represents the base 2 and base 16 representation of the base-10 number 158?
    - **A.** Base 2: 10011110; base 16: E9
    - **B.** Base 2: 10111110; base 16: E9
    - **C.** Base 2: 10011100; base 16: 9E
    - **D.** Base 2: 10011110; base 16: 9E

Answers

1. **A.** It's listed with the heading `Physical Address`.
2. **C.** Frames are Layer 2.
3. **B.** Routers are Layer 3 devices.
4. **A.** All layers below 5 add metadata to the actual data generated at Layers 7 through 5.
5. **D.** Switches connect devices of the same network, while routers connect networks.
6. **A.** Wireless (802.11/Wi-Fi) devices send and receive 802.11 frames, while wired (802.3/Ethernet) devices send and receive Ethernet frames.
7. **D.** Email requires TCP for accuracy and integrity.
8. **A.** IP addresses are found at Layer 3, while the others are all found at Layer 2.
9. **A.** MAC addresses are 12 hex characters (0–9 and A–F), while IP addresses are 4 decimal numbers from 0 to 255.
10. **D.** 128 + 16 + 8 + 4 + 2 = 158 (adding each column that has a 1 in it), and 9E is 10011110 in binary.

Local Communication vs. Remote Communication

IN THIS CHAPTER, YOU WILL LEARN HOW TO

- Differentiate between local and remote communication
- Follow the traffic related to local and remote communication
- Identify the role routers and switches play in networks
- Troubleshoot with ARP
- Explain why both MAC addresses and IP addresses are needed

Recently, a new family, the Smiths, moved into a house on our street. My wife, Eva, made them a welcome package with assorted goodies and asked me to deliver it to them. A few new houses on the block were sold recently, and I wasn't sure exactly which house the Smiths had moved into. Late one night, from my front porch, I shouted, "Hey, Bob Smith, which house did you guys move into?" In the process, I woke up the whole neighborhood, including our two kids, Noah and Jacob. However, I did get Bob's attention, and he very discreetly walked over to my front porch and said, "Hey Jonathan, it's 123 Main Street." Then, he walked home. Later that night, I brought the package over to the Smiths.

Also recently, our kids made art projects at school for their grandparents—my parents, who live in Staten Island, New York, and my in-laws, who live in Huntingdon Valley, Pennsylvania. I didn't want to drive around six hours to either of those locations from Rochester, New York, just to deliver the works of art, so I Googled for the nearest UPS Store. I took the packages of art there, paid for them, and went home.

The magical world of networking uses the same logic. Computing devices on the same network communicate directly with one another through switches, which connect devices on one network together (like the local streets that connect houses and buildings of the same city). However, computing devices on different networks indirectly communicate with one another using routers (although switches are still used to send traffic from the devices to their routers), which connect different networks together (like highway interchanges or the routing of packages by UPS). We'll go over exactly how routing and switching work in future chapters, but this distinction is all you need to know for now.

A source device (host) knows its own MAC address and IP address, but before it can send any traffic, it needs to know the destination device's MAC address and IP address. In some cases, the host will know the destination IP address, but in the vast majority of cases, the source will get the destination IP address through Domain Name System (DNS), which we'll cover in Chapter 7. Getting the destination MAC address, though, requires a protocol called Address Resolution Protocol (ARP), which works somewhat like me shouting to locate Bob's house. This process differs for local communication (meant for a device on the same network, like another house in my neighborhood) and remote communication (meant for a device on a different network, like the grandparents' homes in distant cities).

Addressing and Communication

This section will explore the mechanics of ARP and Internet Control Message Protocol (ICMP) and dissect network traffic to help you fully understand the differences between local communication and remote communication, as well as the relationship between IP addresses and MAC addresses.

MAC Addresses and IP Addresses

Let's contrast a MAC address, which was introduced in Chapter 1, with an IP address (IPv4 now, and IPv6 in Chapter 8):

- A MAC address is physical, as it is burned into the NIC (which is why it's also known as a *burned-in address*, or BIA). An IP address is logical, assigned through software.
- A MAC address is 48 bits long, represented with 12 hexadecimal characters. An IPv4 address is 32 bits long, represented with 4 decimal numbers.
- As Chapter 1 explained, a MAC address consists of two parts: the *block ID*, also known as the *organizationally unique identifier* (OUI), which identifies the manufacturer, and the *device ID*, which is like a serial number. The IP address also consists of two parts: the *network ID*, which is the first set of bits and is shared by all devices on that network (like a zip code or area code), and the *host ID*, which is the second set of bits and is unique to each device on the network (like a street address within the zip code or a phone number in that area code).
- The two parts of a MAC address are always the same length. The block ID always consists of the first 6 hex digits, and the device ID always consists of the last 6 hex digits. In other words, the MAC address is split down the middle to form each part. This differs from IP addresses, where another 32-bit value known as a *subnet mask* (which we'll cover in a moment) identifies the break between the network ID and host ID. The

subnet mask always has a string of 1s followed by a string of 0s. When it's configured or checked, though, it appears in base-10 dotted decimal format, like an IP address, as you can see in my Subnet Mask mask from the height of the COVID-19 pandemic, shown in Figure 2-1.

- MAC addresses use a flat address space. If you buy a NIC from a website, and someone in another state or country buys one from the same website, your NICs could have sequential MAC addresses. IP addresses are geographical and hierarchical. In most cases, the network ID portion of an IPv4 address can identify country, state, city, and Internet Service Provider (ISP).

FIGURE 2-1 Professor Weissman's Subnet Mask mask

Next, let's look at a couple of stories to explore how subnet masks are used, as well as why both physical MAC addresses and logical IP addresses are always needed for communication.

NOTE The following explanation simplifies how computers determine where to send traffic to, focusing only on how subnet masks help identify the network ID to differentiate between local communication and remote communication. We'll cover more complex aspects of this process—such as computer routing tables and how they handle multicast, broadcast, and loopback traffic—in Chapter 5.

Local Communication

In Story 1, Host A with IP address 10.10.1.1 wants to communicate with Host B with IP address 10.10.1.2. Host A's subnet mask is 255.255.255.0 in decimal. In binary, it looks like 24 ones followed by 8 zeroes:

	BINARY	DECIMAL
Host A IP address	00001010.00001010.00000001.00000001	10.10.1.1
Host A subnet mask	11111111.11111111.11111111.00000000	255.255.255.0

As mentioned earlier, the subnet mask consists of a string of 1s followed by a string of 0s. The 1s indicate which bit positions in an IP address are network bits, and the 0s indicate which are host bits. In other words, when you line up an IP address with its subnet mask in binary, if there's a 1 in the subnet mask row, the corresponding bit in the same column of the IP address row is a network bit, shared by all hosts on the same network. Wherever there's a 0 for a subnet mask bit, the corresponding bit in the same column of the IP address row is a host bit.

In this case, the first 24 of the 32 bits of this IP address are network bits and thus shared by every device on this network. The last 8 bits are host bits and are unique to each host on this network. Each of the four numbers in the decimal format is known as an *octet* because it's represented by 8 bits in binary.

No matter how many host bits an IP address contains, there are two patterns for host bits that are reserved and unavailable to devices. If the host bits are all 0s, that IP address represents a network ID and cannot be assigned to a host. In this example, setting all 8 host bits to 0 would give you a network ID of 10.10.1.0. Host bits can't be all 1s either, because that IP address represents a network broadcast address, which also cannot be assigned to hosts. This network's broadcast address would be 10.10.1.255. Any host bit pattern besides all 0s or all 1s is legal and can be assigned to devices on the network.

To determine its network ID, Host A lines up all 32 bits of its IP address with the 32 bits of its subnet mask to perform a *logical AND*, a binary operation that compares two bits and returns 1 only when both bits are 1 (otherwise, it returns 0). The result of the logical AND is the network ID, which in this case is 10.10.1.0:

	BINARY	DECIMAL
Host A IP address	00001010.00001010.00000001.00000001	10.10.1.1
Host A subnet mask	11111111.11111111.11111111.00000000	255.255.255.0
Logical AND operation	————————————————————	
Host A network ID	00001010.00001010.00000001.00000000	10.10.1.0

To determine if Host B is on the same network or a different one, Host A performs a second logical AND operation using Host B's IP address (10.10.1.2) and its own subnet mask (255.255.255.0).

NOTE Host B's subnet mask is unknown and never transmitted. Its IP address, however, is either already known to Host A or resolved from its name via DNS (which we'll explore in Chapter 7). Host A doesn't even need Host B's subnet mask, because if they're on the same network, their subnet masks will be the same anyway.

	BINARY	**DECIMAL**
Host B IP address	00001010.00001010.00000010.00000001	10.10.1.2
Host A subnet mask	11111111.11111111.11111111.00000000	255.255.255.0
Logical AND operation		
Host B network ID (matches the network ID of Host A)	00001010.00001010.00000010.00000000	10.10.1.0

The network ID resulting from the logical AND matches Host A's network ID, so Host A knows that Host B is on the same network and thus it can deliver traffic to Host B directly.

Next, Host A needs Host B's MAC address. Host A puts the actual traffic on hold and sends out a broadcast message using ARP (remember me shouting from my front porch?), a protocol that resolves a known IP address to its corresponding MAC address. The message in the ARP request explains that Host A, 10.10.1.1, is looking for the MAC address of Host B, 10.10.1.2. All devices on the network not only see this ARP request but read it as well. Every device but the actual destination says, "That's not for me," and discards it (see Figure 2-2). Host B sends an ARP reply to Host A. The ARP reply is *unicast*, which means it only goes to 10.10.1.1 and isn't broadcasted to everyone on the network (like the ARP request was).

Subnet masks can span multiple octets and needn't be contained to a multiple of 8 bits. For example, instead of 255.255.255.0, the mask could have been 255.255.255.192, where the first 26 bits are network bits, and the last 6 bits are host bits:

	BINARY	**DECIMAL**
Example subnet mask	11111111.11111111.11111111.11000000	255.255.255.192

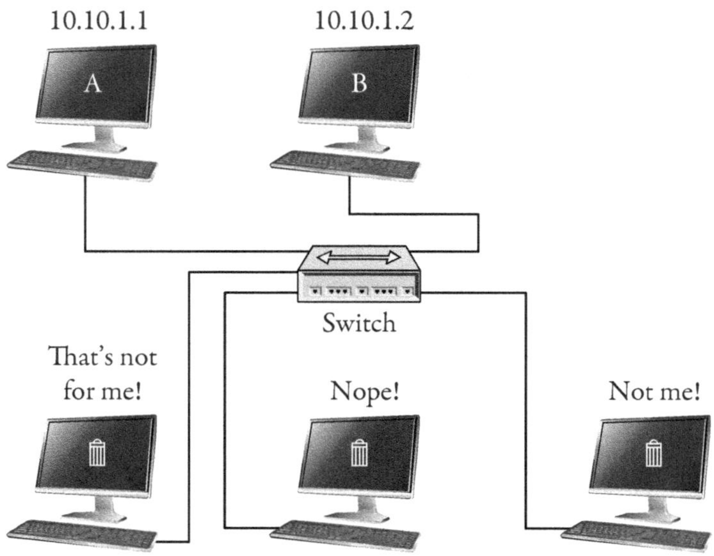

FIGURE 2-2 ARP request for local communication

NOTE After the ARP process completes, the source and destination devices both cache what they learned. Host A (which sent the ARP request) learns Host B's MAC address from the ARP reply, while Host B learns Host A's MAC address from the original ARP request. To see your machine's ARP cache, run **arp -a** from a command prompt. While ARP requests are typically broadcast messages, they can sometimes be sent as unicast to verify existing ARP cache entries, though this is less common.

Since Host A listed its MAC address in the ARP request, Host B didn't need to broadcast to find out that information. Broadcasts on networks are not a good thing. Hosts must interrupt what they're doing to parse the broadcast, only to realize in most cases that it's not even meant for them. It's like a professor emailing a 500-page PDF to the class with the subject line "Read this," but the name of the single student it was meant for is on page 500. Unfortunately, in the world of IPv4, there is no other way to get the destination's MAC address. In IPv6 (discussed in Chapter 8), though, there's a better way.

After the ARP reply comes back with Host B's MAC address, Host A can fill in that address and send the traffic. The source and destination MAC addresses are two of the fields found in the Layer 2 frame, while the source and destination IP addresses are a couple of the fields in the Layer 3 IP packet.

Remote Communication

In Story 2, Host A, the source, once again performs the Logical AND operation to determine that its network ID is 10.10.1.0.

	BINARY	DECIMAL
Host A IP address	00001010.00001010.00000001.00000001	10.10.1.1
Host A subnet mask	11111111.11111111.11111111.00000000	255.255.255.0
Logical AND operation	————————————	
Host A network ID	00001010.00001010.00000001.00000000	10.10.1.0

This time, the destination is Host X, with IP address 10.10.4.1. Using Host A's subnet mask of 255.255.255.0, the second Logical AND operation results in a Host X network ID of 10.10.4.0. The two network IDs are not the same, and Host A realizes it can't send traffic directly to Host X since they're not on the same network.

	BINARY	DECIMAL
Host X IP address	00001010.00001010.00000100.00000001	10.10.4.1
Host A subnet mask	11111111.11111111.11111111.00000000	255.255.255.0
Logical AND operation	————————————	
Host X network ID (does not match the network ID of Host A)	00001010.00001010.00000100.00000000	10.10.4.0

One of the golden rules of networking is that direct communication is only possible between devices on the same network. For communication between different networks—that is, remote communication—devices must use routers to send traffic to devices on other networks. Host A needs to get the traffic now to its *default gateway*, a router interface connected to its local network. Every device on that network is configured with the IP address of this default gateway, which takes traffic destined for other networks and forwards it appropriately, while also bringing traffic from other networks back to the local network. We'll cover more about how routers work and make decisions in Chapter 5.

Even though Host A, the source, determines that the traffic is remote, it will once again send an ARP request, which is broadcasted to all devices on its network (see Figure 2-3). This time, though, the ARP request is looking for the MAC address of Host A's default gateway. Let's say the gateway's IP address is 10.10.1.99. The gateway will send its MAC address in a unicast ARP reply back to Host A. Host A now sends the traffic with the destination MAC address of the router interface and the destination IP address of Host X, which could be 2, 5, 10, or more routers/networks away.

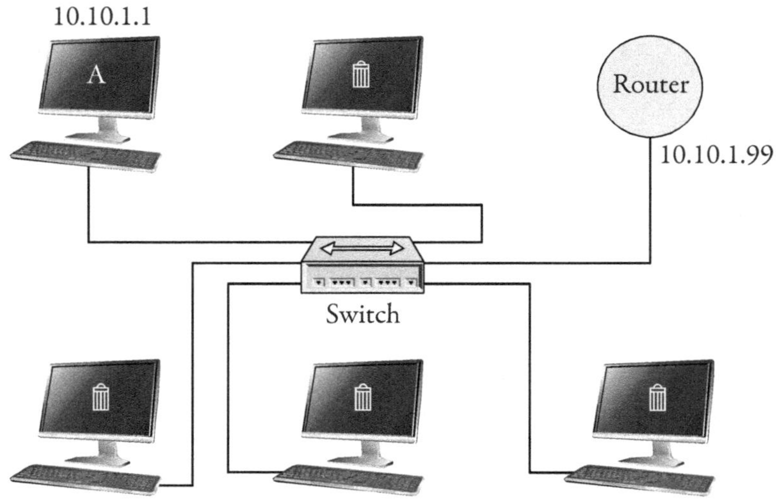

FIGURE 2-3 ARP request for remote communication

NOTE Incidentally, router interfaces will hear broadcasts on the networks they're connected to but will never forward broadcast traffic to other networks. If they did that, a simple broadcast could go around the world and back. However, a field in the IP header, TTL (time to live; discussed in Chapter 3) prevents the packet from looping forever.

Each interconnection between router interfaces, including the router interfaces themselves, is considered a separate network (see Figure 2-4). That means every device between Router 1's right interface and Router 2's left interface, including those interfaces themselves, is on that shared network. The network ID would be 10.10.2.0 if the subnet mask was 255.255.255.0. All devices on that network would need an IP address starting with 10.10.2. The last octet would be the host octet.

NOTE Router and switch interfaces are identified with names like Fast Ethernet 0/1 or Gigabit Ethernet 0/0/1, but to keep things simple, this story just identifies the interfaces with "left" and "right."

Following the IP addressing rules we've discussed, every device on a shared network starts off with the same network ID. To make it easy for this story, let's say the subnet mask for all devices and networks is 255.255.255.0, which means all hosts on each network will share the same first octets in their IP addresses. The last octet will be a host identifier for all networks. Everything between Router 2's right interface and Router 3's left interface is on that shared network. That network ID is 10.10.3.0. The last network in this topology is everything to the right of Router 3's right interface, the 10.10.4.0 network.

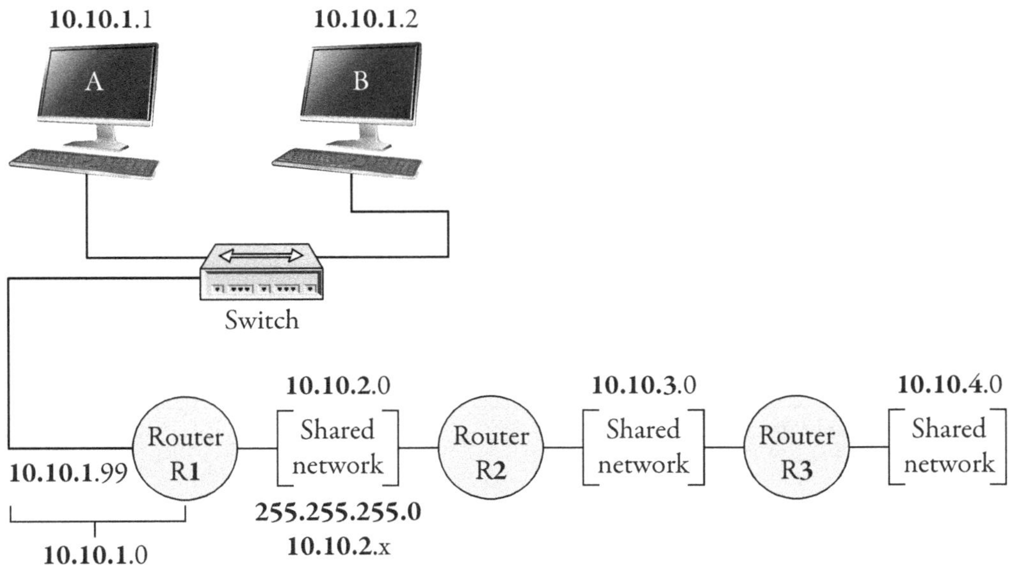

FIGURE 2-4 The topology

Now, Host A's default gateway has the actual traffic meant for Host X. Routers maintain *routing tables* to determine where to send the traffic next. The routing table tells the router which direction to forward packets based on their destination network. If the routing table doesn't know how to reach the destination network, it can use a default route—that is, a specific router interface on a different router that will have a better idea of how to get to the destination. If there's no default route, the router will drop a packet and send an error message back to the source through Internet Control Message Protocol (ICMP). In Figure 2-5, Host A's default gateway looks in its routing table and sees that the packet should go to R2's left interface next.

If the routers are connected by Ethernet infrastructure, the sending router (R1) needs the MAC address for the receiving router (R2), so it uses the same ARP process you saw earlier when Host A needed to find its default gateway's MAC address.

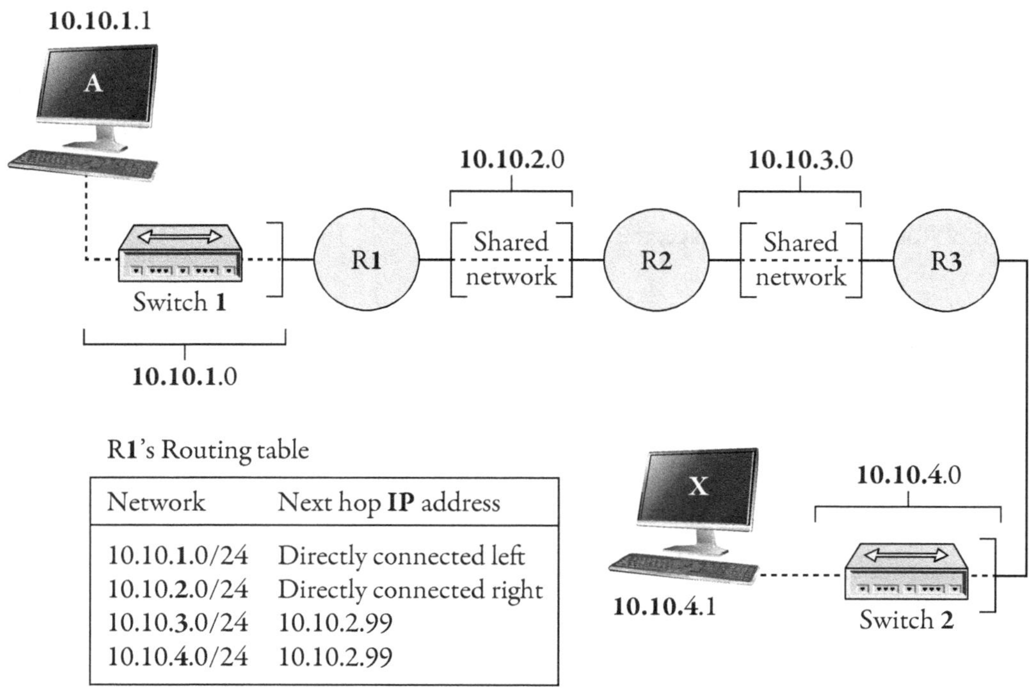

Network	Next hop **IP** address
10.10.**1**.0/24	Directly connected left
10.10.**2**.0/24	Directly connected right
10.10.**3**.0/24	10.10.2.99
10.10.**4**.0/24	10.10.2.99

FIGURE 2-5 R1's routing table

If the routers aren't connected by Ethernet, the router interfaces use a different frame type. For example, wireless NICs use 802.11 frames instead of Ethernet frames; it's the same IP packet encapsulated, just with a different frame. Point-to-point directly connected serial interfaces using protocols like Point-to-Point Protocol (PPP) or High-level Data Link Control (HDLC) don't even need to deal with MAC addresses and frames that encapsulate IP packets since their connection is just like a tunnel: only one way in and only one way out.

For this story, we'll just say all interfaces are Ethernet. There may be switches and PCs between these two router interfaces, but with or without them, the communication between routers is the same. R1 sends an ARP request, a broadcast heard and read by every device on the network, saying, "If your IP address is 10.10.2.99, I need your MAC address." The left interface of R2 sends a unicast ARP reply to R1 with its MAC address. See Figure 2-6.

FIGURE 2-6
R1 to R2 communication

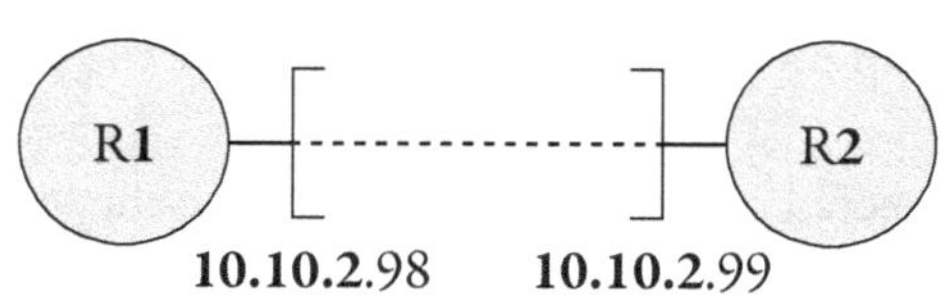

R1 then re-encapsulates the original packet sent from Host A to Host X with a new frame (see Figure 2-7). The new source MAC address represents the right interface of R1, and the new destination MAC address represents the left interface of R2.

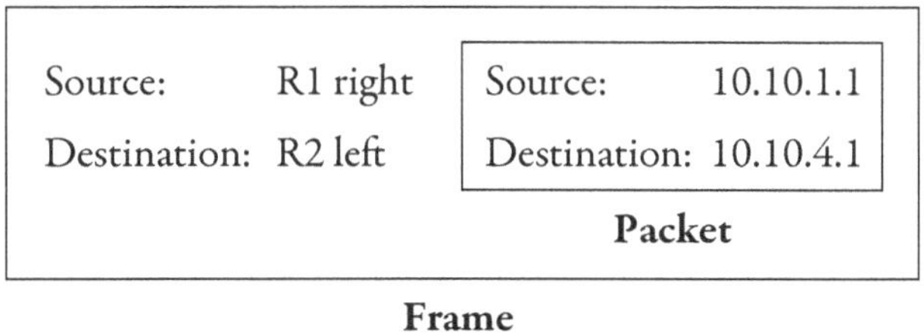

FIGURE 2-7 Re-encapsulation from R1

Next, R2 accepts the frame on its left interface and sees that the destination MAC address in the frame is its own MAC address. R2 inspects the destination IP address in the packet. That IP address is not R2's IP address nor an IP address on one of its connected networks. Therefore, R2 realizes that it must send the packet to R3. (See Figure 2-8.)

R2's right interface then sends an ARP request, looking for the MAC address of R3's left interface. After the ARP reply comes back, the new source MAC address of the frame is the right interface of R2, and the new destination MAC is the left interface of R3.

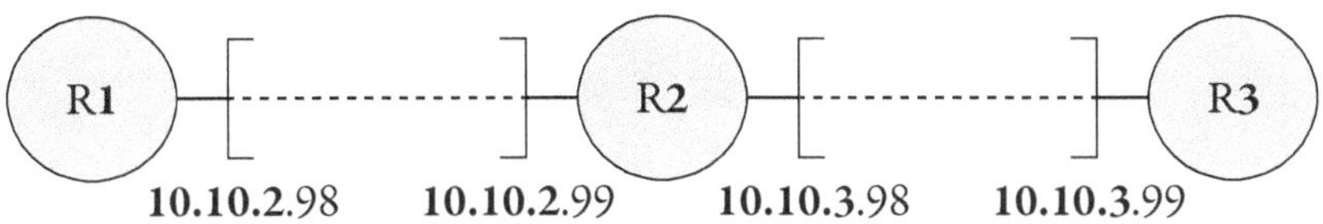

R2's Routing table

Network	Next hop IP address
10.10.1.0/24	10.10.2.98
10.10.2.0/24	Directly connected left
10.10.3.0/24	Directly connected right
10.10.4.0/24	10.10.3.99

FIGURE 2-8 R2's routing table

Then, R3's right interface finishes it off by ARPing for the destination since the right interface of R3 is on the destination's network (see Figure 2-9).

FIGURE 2-9 R3's routing table

R3's Routing table

Network	Next hop **IP** address
10.10.**1**.0/24	10.10.3.98
10.10.**2**.0/24	10.10.3.98
10.10.**3**.0/24	Directly connected left
10.10.**4**.0/24	Directly connected right

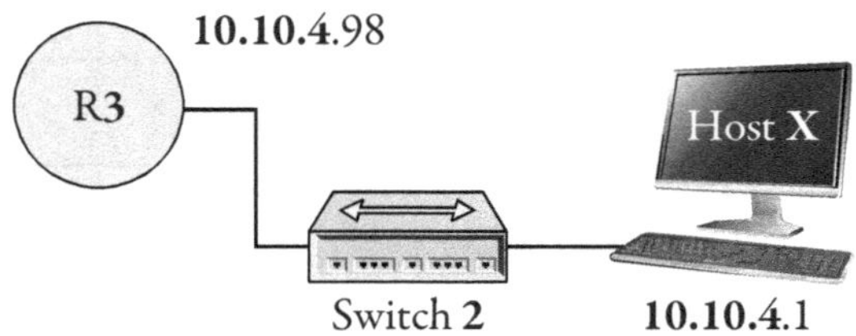

The final frame has a source MAC address of the right interface of R3 and a destination MAC address of the actual destination, Host X (see Figure 2-10). Host X gets the frame, sees its MAC address, and opens it up, saying, "Yes, that's my IP address too." Host X now strips off the IP header and sends the higher layer data up its networking stack for processing.

Frame		Packet	
Source:	R3 right	Source:	10.10.1.1
Destination:	**Host X**	Destination:	10.10.4.1

FIGURE 2-10 Final re-encapsulation from R3

Why Both a MAC Address and an IP Address Are Needed

As illustrated, MAC addresses are only locally significant and, in addition to IP addresses, they are necessary to specify the next hop to receive the packet en route to its final destination. Every time a packet passes through a router interface, the router strips off and discards the frame. After the next router figures out what the next hop IP address is, it encapsulates the packet in a new outer frame. IP addresses are logical and, for the most part, geographical and hierarchical like zip codes.

If I send a UPS package from Rochester to Staten Island, the first UPS distribution center sends it to the next one. Then, the second distribution center sends it to the third. Thanks to UPS routing stickers, the packages can be tracked as they travel between facilities. Think of those stickers as the MAC addresses. As a package leaves a UPS distribution center, the sticker indicates which distribution center it's leaving and which one it's destined for. When the package gets to the next distribution center, those stickers are removed. That's just like the Ethernet frames in our networking story, which are removed and added back with each router the packet passes through. However, each UPS package also has To and From addresses that identify the locations of the specific person sending the package and the specific person who will receive it. Those are of course analogous to the source and destination IP addresses in our story. The IP addresses, just like the To and From addresses, are geographical and never change along the packet's path to its final destination.

You can see why MAC addresses alone wouldn't be enough for network communications. They're flat addresses rather than hierarchical. You can buy a NIC on the web right after someone in another country buys one from the same website. Even with the NICs being ordered from different countries, their MAC addresses could very well be sequential. IP addresses alone wouldn't be enough for network communications, either. These logical addresses are leased to client devices temporarily, so we need a way to tie those geographical, logical addresses to the devices they're assigned to. That's why the NICs and their MAC addresses are so very important. The logical IP addresses can now be bound to and associated with a device's MAC address for some length of time, allowing us to track which device is temporarily using a network IP address at any point.

NOTE Enter the MAC address of your NIC into the Wireshark OUI Lookup tool at *wireshark.org/tools/oui-lookup.html* to identify the organization that made your NIC.

Let's consider another analogy: a restaurant. At one point on a given day, a couple might be sitting at table number 5. Later, a group of friends will be sitting there. Table number 5 will be associated with a different reservation at different points in time. Think of the table number as the host ID of the IP address. The restaurant's street address is like the network ID portion of the IP address. All tables in the restaurant, after all, are found at that location. Table number 6 would have a different host ID but the same street address as table number 5. How do we know who is using that table at any given point? The reservation name. How do we know which device is using a given IP address at any given point? The MAC address. An IP address and a MAC address: you simply can't have one without the other.

Now, think back to the beginning of this chapter when I told you a couple of stories. I had to get Bob Smith's attention so I could get his house number. I did so by shouting in the middle of the night, disturbing everyone on the block. That's what Host A did in Story 1 to get the MAC address of Host B. In Story 2, I realized that neither Staten Island nor Huntingdon Valley was local to me here in Rochester. So, I had to get the traffic to my default gateway: my local UPS store. That's what Host A did when it realized that Host X was on a different network.

Finding Your MAC Address and IP Address

Every operating system has a command-line interface (CLI) utility to display a system's IP address and MAC address in addition to other information.

> **NOTE** Every operating system also has a graphical user interface (GUI) utility to display configuration information.

In Windows, run **`ipconfig /all`** to display the IP address (as well as the subnet mask) and MAC address, as shown in Figure 2-11.

The `ipconfig` command by itself, without the `/all` switch, shows a subset of the information shown with `ipconfig /all`. One of the items omitted is the MAC address.

FIGURE 2-11 Result of running `ipconfig /all` in Windows

```
Command Prompt
Microsoft Windows [Version 10.0.19045.4651]
(c) Microsoft Corporation. All rights reserved.

C:\Users\cscprof>ipconfig /all

Windows IP Configuration

   Host Name . . . . . . . . . . . . : GCCIS-JSWICS-W1
   Primary Dns Suffix  . . . . . . . : main.ad.rit.edu
   Node Type . . . . . . . . . . . . : Peer-Peer
   IP Routing Enabled. . . . . . . . : No
   WINS Proxy Enabled. . . . . . . . : No
   DNS Suffix Search List. . . . . . : main.ad.rit.edu
                                       ad.rit.edu

Ethernet adapter Ethernet:

   Media State . . . . . . . . . . . : Media disconnected
   Connection-specific DNS Suffix  . :
   Description . . . . . . . . . . . : Intel(R) Ethernet Connection (16) I219-V
   Physical Address. . . . . . . . . : D4-93-90-15-55-A1
   DHCP Enabled. . . . . . . . . . . : Yes
   Autoconfiguration Enabled . . . . : Yes

Wireless LAN adapter Wi-Fi:

   Connection-specific DNS Suffix  . :
   Description . . . . . . . . . . . : Intel(R) Wi-Fi 6 AX201 160MHz
   Physical Address. . . . . . . . . : F8-B5-4D-61-AA-B2
   DHCP Enabled. . . . . . . . . . . : Yes
   Autoconfiguration Enabled . . . . : Yes
   IPv6 Address. . . . . . . . . . . : 2605:9480:25e:31c0::1000(Preferred)
   Lease Obtained. . . . . . . . . . : Friday, August 2, 2024 12:41:22 PM
   Lease Expires . . . . . . . . . . : Saturday, August 3, 2024 12:41:22 PM
   IPv6 Address. . . . . . . . . . . : fd7c:1a7:6666:99a0::2(Preferred)
   Link-local IPv6 Address . . . . . : fe80::191f:e724:ed11:752e%4(Preferred)
   IPv4 Address. . . . . . . . . . . : 192.168.68.158(Preferred)
   Subnet Mask . . . . . . . . . . . : 255.255.252.0
   Lease Obtained. . . . . . . . . . : Friday, August 2, 2024 12:06:41 PM
   Lease Expires . . . . . . . . . . : Friday, August 2, 2024 2:41:19 PM
   Default Gateway . . . . . . . . . : fe80::3660:f9ff:fe08:86c0%4
                                       192.168.68.1
   DHCP Server . . . . . . . . . . . : 192.168.68.1
   DHCPv6 IAID . . . . . . . . . . . : 234403149
   DHCPv6 Client DUID. . . . . . . . : 00-01-00-01-2A-E9-AA-C5-D4-93-90-15-55-A1
   DNS Servers . . . . . . . . . . . : 2001:4860:4860::8888
                                       2001:428::1
                                       8.8.8.8
                                       209.244.0.3
   NetBIOS over Tcpip. . . . . . . . : Disabled

C:\Users\cscprof>
```

In macOS, run **`ifconfig`**, as shown in Figure 2-12.

FIGURE 2-12 Result of running `ifconfig` in macOS

jonathansweissman — -zsh — 80×56

```
Last login: Fri Aug  2 12:53:08 on ttys000
jonathansweissman@jonathans-macbook-air ~ % ifconfig
lo0: flags=8049<UP,LOOPBACK,RUNNING,MULTICAST> mtu 16384
        options=1203<RXCSUM,TXCSUM,TXSTATUS,SW_TIMESTAMP>
        inet 127.0.0.1 netmask 0xff000000
        inet6 ::1 prefixlen 128
        inet6 fe80::1%lo0 prefixlen 64 scopeid 0x1
        nd6 options=201<PERFORMNUD,DAD>
gif0: flags=8010<POINTOPOINT,MULTICAST> mtu 1280
stf0: flags=0<> mtu 1280
en0: flags=8863<UP,BROADCAST,SMART,RUNNING,SIMPLEX,MULTICAST> mtu 1500
        options=400<CHANNEL_IO>
        ether 98:fe:94:42:5e:1c
        inet6 fe80::8f:2611:7504:136b%en0 prefixlen 64 secured scopeid 0x4
        inet6 2605:9480:25e:31c0::1007 prefixlen 128 dynamic
        inet 192.168.68.54 netmask 0xfffffc00 broadcast 192.168.71.255
        nd6 options=201<PERFORMNUD,DAD>
        media: autoselect
        status: active
en2: flags=8963<UP,BROADCAST,SMART,RUNNING,PROMISC,SIMPLEX,MULTICAST> mtu 1500
        options=460<TSO4,TSO6,CHANNEL_IO>
        ether 82:0d:69:71:3d:80
        media: autoselect <full-duplex>
        status: inactive
bridge0: flags=8863<UP,BROADCAST,SMART,RUNNING,SIMPLEX,MULTICAST> mtu 1500
        options=63<RXCSUM,TXCSUM,TSO4,TSO6>
        ether 82:0d:69:71:3d:80
        Configuration:
                id 0:0:0:0:0:0 priority 0 hellotime 0 fwddelay 0
                maxage 0 holdcnt 0 proto stp maxaddr 100 timeout 1200
                root id 0:0:0:0:0:0 priority 0 ifcost 0 port 0
                ipfilter disabled flags 0x0
        member: en2 flags=3<LEARNING,DISCOVER>
                ifmaxaddr 0 port 5 priority 0 path cost 0
        nd6 options=201<PERFORMNUD,DAD>
        media: <unknown type>
        status: inactive
p2p0: flags=8843<UP,BROADCAST,RUNNING,SIMPLEX,MULTICAST> mtu 2304
        options=400<CHANNEL_IO>
        ether 0a:fe:94:42:5e:1c
        media: autoselect
        status: inactive
awdl0: flags=8943<UP,BROADCAST,RUNNING,PROMISC,SIMPLEX,MULTICAST> mtu 1484
        options=400<CHANNEL_IO>
        ether a6:05:0b:97:37:54
        inet6 fe80::a405:bff:fe97:3754%awdl0 prefixlen 64 scopeid 0x8
        nd6 options=201<PERFORMNUD,DAD>
        media: autoselect
        status: active
utun0: flags=8051<UP,POINTOPOINT,RUNNING,MULTICAST> mtu 1380
        inet6 fe80::e064:1d58:e273:6c3f%utun0 prefixlen 64 scopeid 0x9
        nd6 options=201<PERFORMNUD,DAD>
utun1: flags=8051<UP,POINTOPOINT,RUNNING,MULTICAST> mtu 2000
        inet6 fe80::e28c:aeee:cd53:88eb%utun1 prefixlen 64 scopeid 0xa
        nd6 options=201<PERFORMNUD,DAD>
jonathansweissman@jonathans-macbook-air ~ %
```

On Linux systems, run **`ip a`**, as shown in Figure 2-13. This is a shortened version of the full command, `ip address`, or you could use `ip addr` (all three options work the same way).

jsw@weissman-ubuntu: ~

```
[jsw@weissman-ubuntu ~]$  ip a
1: lo: <LOOPBACK,UP,LOWER_UP> mtu 65536 qdisc noqueue state UNKNOWN group default qlen 1000
    link/loopback 00:00:00:00:00:00 brd 00:00:00:00:00:00
    inet 127.0.0.1/8 scope host lo
       valid_lft forever preferred_lft forever
    inet6 ::1/128 scope host
       valid_lft forever preferred_lft forever
2: ens33: <BROADCAST,MULTICAST,UP,LOWER_UP> mtu 1500 qdisc fq_codel state UP group default qlen 1000
    link/ether 00:0c:29:1d:02:4e brd ff:ff:ff:ff:ff:ff
    altname enp2s1
    inet 192.168.68.74/22 brd 192.168.71.255 scope global dynamic noprefixroute ens33
       valid_lft 6557sec preferred_lft 6557sec
    inet6 2605:9480:25e:31c0::1006/128 scope global dynamic noprefixroute
       valid_lft 85760sec preferred_lft 85760sec
    inet6 fe80::9142:6290:553b:9fd6/64 scope link noprefixroute
       valid_lft forever preferred_lft forever
[jsw@weissman-ubuntu ~]$
```

FIGURE 2-13 Result of running `ip a` in Ubuntu

Chapter Review

Questions

1. What's the purpose of a subnet mask?
   A. To identify the routers on a network
   B. To identify the servers on a network
   C. To identify the network ID in an IP address
   D. To identify the device ID in a MAC address
2. Which of the following describes the format of a subnet mask in binary?
   A. A string of 0s followed by a string of 1s
   B. A string of 1s followed by a string of 0s
   C. Intermixing of 1s and 0s
   D. All 1s
3. In local communication, what device's MAC address is the source looking for?
   A. The switch
   B. The default gateway
   C. The DNS server
   D. The actual destination
4. In remote communication, who is the ARP request sent to?
   A. The switch
   B. The default gateway
   C. All devices
   D. The actual destination
5. Which addresses change with each hop?
   A. Source MAC and destination MAC
   B. Source IP and destination IP
   C. Source IP and source MAC
   D. Destination IP and destination MAC

6. Which of the following is valid?
   A. An IP address assigned to a device with a host ID of all 0s
   B. An IP address assigned to a device with a host ID of all 1s
   C. An IP address of a host on a different network from its default gateway
   D. An IP address of a host on the same network as its default gateway
7. Does a device on a different network see the source's MAC address?
   A. Never
   B. Sometimes
   C. Always
   D. Not enough information given
8. What Windows command do you use to find the IP address for a system?
   A. `ifconfig`
   B. `ipconfig`
   C. `ip a`
   D. `ip /show`
9. Which of the following is true, if I used my laptop at Rochester Institute of Technology, at Finger Lakes Community College, and at the Weissman home on the same day (which I actually do Monday through Friday)?
   A. My laptop would have used three MAC addresses and one IP address.
   B. My laptop would have used three IP addresses and one MAC address.
   C. My laptop would have used three MAC addresses and three IP addresses.
   D. My laptop would have used one MAC addresses and one IP address.
10. Which of the following is true?
   A. Routers never forward broadcasts.
   B. Routers always forward broadcasts.
   C. Switches never forward broadcasts.
   D. An ARP request from a network can be seen on another network.

Answers

1. **C.** When an IP address and a subnet mask are logically ANDed together, the result is the network ID.

2. **B.** The 1s mean the corresponding bits in the IP address are network bits and the 0s mean the corresponding bits in the IP address are host bits.

3. **D.** In local communication, the source communicates directly (via switches) with the destination. No router is involved for local communication.

4. **C.** The question asked who the ARP request is sent to. ARP requests are always broadcasts, regardless of if it's for local or remote communication. In the ARP for remote communication, though, the source is looking for the MAC address of its default gateway, not the actual destination.

5. **A.** The frame is removed and replaced for each hop. The addresses found in a frame are source MAC address and destination MAC address.

6. **D.** In order to forward traffic from a network and receive traffic from other networks, a host needs a default gateway, which of course has to be on the same network as the host.

7. **A.** Since the frame is removed and replaced for each hop and the source MAC address is in that header, with remote communication, no device will ever see the MAC address of a device on a different network. The MAC address of the destination's default gateway will be seen as the source MAC address in the frame received by the destination.

8. **B.** `ipconfig` shows some information, including the device's IP address, while `ipconfig /all` shows even more information.

9. **B.** The MAC address is burned into the NIC and doesn't change when you move from network to network, but the IP address is assigned by a DHCP server of the network you're on. Since I was on three networks, my laptop will have used three IP addresses.

10. **A.** Routers never forward broadcasts, and ARP requests are always broadcasts.

IPv4

IN THIS CHAPTER, YOU WILL LEARN HOW TO

- Differentiate between classful and classless addressing
- Configure subnets and use appropriate IP addressing schemes for a given scenario
- Explain subnetting and CIDR
- Describe the functions of static and dynamic IP addressing
- Understand the role of special-purpose IP addresses

The CSCPROF network example in Chapter 1 provided an overview of how networks work. The foundation of every physical network is hardware: wires, network interface cards (NICs), and other stand-alone network devices that move data from one computer to another. This hardware corresponds to Layers 1 and 2—the Physical and Data Link layers of the OSI model, respectively—though some devices may also perform higher-layer functions (switches at Layer 2 and routers at Layer 3). The higher layers of the model—from Network (Layer 3) up to Application (Layer 7)—work with this hardware to make network magic.

Chapter 2 provided more details on the hardware at the Physical and Data Link layers of the OSI model. You learned how local communication differs from remote communication, as well as how MAC addresses and IP addresses work and why both are needed. You also saw how data sent by one NIC can be read correctly by another NIC.

This chapter takes you on a fun journey deep into *Internet Protocol* (IP) addressing. You'll learn all about IPv4, the IP addressing scheme that enables computers on one network to communicate with one another and with computers on other networks. You'll get the full story of how TCP/IP networks divide into smaller units, known as *subnets*, to make it easier to manage a large TCP/IP internetwork. You won't just get it from a conceptual standpoint; you'll get the practical details you've undoubtedly been craving by learning how to set up a network properly. You'll also get acquainted with different types of IP addresses and how they are classified and assigned.

Historical/Conceptual

The early days of networking, roughly the 1980s, exposed a problem in the way software developers created the programs that powered networks at the time. Unlike the hardware organizations, which worked together to make solid standards, the different organizations developing network software worked separately, secretly, and competitively. The four major players—Microsoft, Apple, Novell, and UNIX developers such as AT&T—created network software solutions that were mostly incompatible and had very different answers to the question "What do we share on a network?"

Microsoft, Apple, and Novell created networking software that for the most part did nothing more than share different computers' folders and printers (and they all did this sharing differently). AT&T and the universities developing the UNIX operating system saw networks as a way to share terminals, send email messages, and transfer files. As a result, everyone's software had its own set of Rules of What a Network Should Do and How to Do It. These sets of rules—and the software written to follow them—were broken down into individual rules or languages called *protocols*. No single protocol could do everything a network needed to do, so companies lumped together all their necessary protocols under the term *protocol suite*. Novell called its protocol suite IPX/SPX; Digital Equipment Corporation had DECnet; Microsoft's was called NetBIOS/NetBEUI; Apple called its protocol suite AppleTalk; and the UNIX folks used a protocol suite called TCP/IP. Each of those protocol suites had its own form of logical addressing. Novell's IPX/SPX, for example, used IPX addresses that looked like 1001.00e0-fc01-0001.

It took about 20 very confusing years, but eventually TCP/IP replaced every other protocol suite in all but the most rare and unique situations. To get ahead today, to get on the internet, and to pass the CompTIA Network+ exam, you only need to worry about TCP/IP. Microsoft, Apple, and Linux developers no longer actively support anything but TCP/IP. You live in a one-protocol-suite world, as the old stuff is long gone and forgotten.

Test Specific

IP Addresses

If you recall from Chapter 1, the first two layers of the OSI model, Physical and Data Link, deal with physical connectivity—wired and wireless—and protocols that interact with the physical. The TCP/IP protocol suite operates at Layers 2 through 7 of the OSI model. This chapter explores IPv4, which is found at Layer 3, the Network layer.

IP takes segments (if TCP is used) or datagrams (if UDP is used) from Layer 4, the Transport layer, and they become the IP packet's *payload*. IP then adds IP addressing and hands the final IP packet to the Data Link layer for encapsulation into a frame, where the MAC addresses are added.

Let's look at the addressing process in more depth. Here's the IPv4 address of the rit.edu web server:

129.21.1.40

This type of address—four base-10 (decimal) values ranging from 0 to 255, separated by three dots (hence the name *dotted decimal*)—is known officially as an *Internet Protocol version 4 (IPv4) address*. IPv4 is the current standard for internet addressing, but the world is in a slow transition to a newer, longer type of IP address called IPv6 (covered in Chapter 8). Here's the IPv6 address of the rit.edu web server:

2620:8d:8000:0:aba:ca:daba:217

IPv4 and IPv6 aren't the only TCP/IP protocols that work at the Network layer. *Internet Control Message Protocol* (ICMP), for example, plays a role in IP information and error reporting. TCP/IP users rarely interact directly with programs that use ICMP (or its IPv6 counterpart, ICMPv6), however. For the most part, software automatically uses ICMP as needed without direct user action. Yet there are exceptions to every rule: the ping utility, a popular network diagnostic tool, directly uses ICMP. You can use ping to answer a question like, "Can my computer communicate with the device at the IP address 192.168.1.52?"

NOTE Check out my IPv6 blog posts at *arin.net/blog/author/jonathan-s-weissman/*.

When thinking about the Network layer, remember the following protocols (there are others, but we'll focus on these three for now):

- IPv4 (normally referred to as simply "IP")
- IPv6
- ICMP

The IPv4 packet header has 13 fields:

VERSION Defines the IP address type: 4, for IPv4.

HEADER LENGTH Contains the size of the IPv4 header in bytes. While theoretically the header size can range from 20 to 60 bytes depending on the Options set (see "Options" at the end of this list), in practice it's almost never greater than 20 bytes due to security concerns related to those options.

DIFFERENTIATED SERVICES Classifies and manages network traffic by providing quality of service (QoS), which prioritizes certain types of traffic over others. For example, real-time traffic should have a higher priority than an email.

TOTAL LENGTH Contains the total size of the IP packet in octets. This includes the IP header and its payload. This field is 16 bits, which limits the packet size to 65,535 bytes.

IDENTIFICATION Groups fragments of the same packet together when it has been broken into smaller pieces for transmission. Each fragment of the packet contains the same identification value.

FLAGS Manages packet fragmentation through three 1-bit fields: Reserved (unused), Don't Fragment (DF), and More Fragments (MF).

FRAGMENT OFFSET Puts packet fragments back in order on the destination device.

TIME TO LIVE (TTL) Prevents an IP packet from indefinitely spinning through the internet (due to faulty router configuration) by decrementing a counter by one every time a packet goes through a router. When the counter reaches zero, the packet is discarded. As an 8-bit field, this number can't start higher than 255. Windows systems start this value at 128, whereas Linux and Mac systems start it at either 60 or 64.

PROTOCOL Identifies what's encapsulated inside the packet. In most cases, the protocol value is either 6 for TCP, 17 for UDP, or 1 for ICMP.

HEADER CHECKSUM Performs error checking on the header.

SOURCE IP ADDRESS Contains the IP address of the sending device.

DESTINATION IP ADDRESS Contains the IP address of the device the packet en route is meant for.

OPTIONS Allows for additional packet handling instructions, but this field hasn't been used for a long time due to security concerns.

IPv4 Address Classes

The internet is by far the biggest and the most complex TCP/IP internetwork. One challenge for the internet is to make sure no two devices share the same public IP address. To track and allocate IP addresses, computer scientists Jon Postel and Joyce K. Reynolds established the *Internet Assigned Numbers Authority* (IANA). Managed single-handedly by Postel until his death in 1998, IANA has grown dramatically and now oversees five Regional Internet

Registries (RIRs) that parcel out IP addresses to internet service providers (ISPs) and corporations that acquire their own IP address space independent of an ISP. The RIR for the United States, Canada, and many Caribbean and North Atlantic islands is the *American Registry for Internet Numbers* (ARIN).

NOTE The Internet Corporation for Assigned Names and Numbers (ICANN) indirectly manages IANA through an affiliate organization, Public Technical Identifiers (PTI). PTI was formed to perform IANA's technical work; ICANN is more focused on policy.

All end users get their IP addresses from their respective ISPs. IANA manages contiguous chunks called *network blocks* (or just *blocks*). Once upon a time, there was a "class" system for organizing and defining these blocks, which is outlined in Table 3-1 and will be explained throughout this section.

TABLE 3-1 Classful addressing

CLASS	FIRST BITS	FIRST NUMBER	DEFAULT SUBNET MASK	NETWORK ID BITS	HOST ID BITS	ADDRESSES	NUMBER OF NETWORKS	HOSTS PER NETWORK ID
A	0	1–126	255.0.0.0	8	24	1.0.0.0–126.255.255.255	126 (2^{8-1})	16,777,214 ($2^{24}-2$)
B	10	128–191	255.255.0.0	16	16	128.0.0.0–191.255.255.255	16,384 (2^{16-2})	65,534 ($2^{16}-2$)
C	110	192–223	255.255.255.0	24	8	192.0.0.0–223.255.255.255	2,097,152 (2^{24-3})	254 ($2^{8}-2$)
D	1110	224–239	N/A	N/A	N/A	224.0.0.0–239.255.255.255	N/A	Multicast
E	1111	240–255	N/A	N/A	N/A	240.0.0.0–255.255.255.255	N/A	Experimental

This class system existed only from 1981 to 1993, but techs still refer to these classes as shorthand for some private address ranges that organizations and households use for their internal networks. We'll take a closer look at these private address ranges in the "Special-Purpose IP Addresses" section at the end of the chapter.

CLASS A

In a Class A network, the first of the 32 bits in its IP address was a 0. For the first octet, the 0 in the 128s column meant that the range of base-10 values was technically 0 through 127, as shown in Table 3-2.

TABLE 3-2 Class A first octet before modification

128	64	32	16	8	4	2	1	BASE-10 VALUE
0	0	0	0	0	0	0	0	0 (with the other columns all 0s)
0	1	1	1	1	1	1	1	127 (with the other columns all 1s)

However, two first octet values are reserved and can't be used for actual networks: 0 (reserved for the local network) and 127 (reserved for the machine itself). Thus, the available range for the first number in a Class A IP address was actually 1 through 126, as shown in Table 3-3.

TABLE 3-3 Class A first octet after modification

128	64	32	16	8	4	2	1	BASE 10 VALUE
0	0	0	0	0	0	0	1	1 (lowest value for the first octet)
0	1	1	1	1	1	1	0	126 (highest value for the first octet)

With a default subnet mask of 255.0.0.0, hosts on a Class A network had only the first octet (8 bits) in common as the network ID, with the other three octets (24 bits) as host octets. Out of the 8 network bits, the first was fixed (the 0 in the 128s column, as just mentioned), while the other 7 network bits could vary. Here's how it looked (the *N*s represent network bits, and the *H*s host bits):

0NNNNNNN.HHHHHHHH.HHHHHHHH.HHHHHHHH

Thus, with 8 network bits minus 1 fixed bit, you had $2^{8-1} = 2^7 = 128$ Class A networks. Since 0 and 127 were reserved, the number of Class A networks was 126. With 24 host bits, $2^{24} - 2$ allowed for 16,777,214 possible hosts on a Class A network—not that you'd dream of putting (or even having) that many hosts on a network!

When computing hosts per network, you always raise 2 to the power of *n*, the number of host bits, and then subtract 2 from that result. The host bits in an IP address can't all be 0s, as that represents the network ID itself (so that's one excluded possibility), and they can't all be 1s, as that represents the broadcast address for that subnet (the second excluded possibility).

CLASS B

A Class B network had an IP address where the first 2 of its 32 bits were 1 and 0. For the first octet, the 1 in the 128s column meant the range of base-10 values was a minimum of 128 (if the other 7 bits were 0s). The 0 in the 64s column meant the range of base-10 values was a maximum of 191 (if the other 7 bits were 1s, since 255 – 64 = 191). Thus, the first number of a Class B IP address was between 128 and 191, as shown in Table 3-4.

TABLE 3-4 Class B first octet

128	64	32	16	8	4	2	1	BASE-10 VALUE
1	**0**	0	0	0	0	0	0	128 (with the other columns all 0s)
1	**0**	1	1	1	1	1	1	191 (with the other columns all 1s)

With a default subnet mask of 255.255.0.0, hosts on a Class B network had the first two octets (16 bits) in common as the network ID, with the other two octets (16 bits) as host octets. Out of the 16 network bits, 2 were fixed (the 1 in the 128s column and the 0 in the 64s column, as just mentioned), while 14 could vary. It looked as follows:

10NNNNNN.NNNNNNNN.HHHHHHHH.HHHHHHHH

Thus, with 16 network bits minus 2 fixed bits, you had $2^{16-2} = 2^{14} = 16{,}384$ Class B networks. With 16 host bits, $2^{16} - 2$ allowed for 65,534 possible hosts on a Class B network!

CLASS C

A Class C network had an IP address where the first three of its 32 bits were 1, 1, and 0. For the first octet, the 1 in the 128s column and the 1 in the 64s column meant the range of base-10 values was a minimum of 192 (if the other 6 bits were 0s). The 0 in the 32s column meant the range of base-10 values was a maximum of 223 (if the last 5 bits were 1s, since 255 – 32 = 223). Thus, the first number of a Class C IP address was between 192 and 223, as shown in Table 3-5.

TABLE 3-5 Class C first octet

128	64	32	16	8	4	2	1	BASE-10 VALUE
1	**1**	**0**	0	0	0	0	0	192 (with the other columns all 0s)
1	**1**	**0**	1	1	1	1	1	223 (with the other columns all 1s)

With a default subnet mask of 255.255.255.0, hosts on a Class C network had the first three octets (24 bits) in common as the network ID, with the other octet (8 bits) as a host octet. Out of the 24 network bits, 3 were fixed (the 1 in the 128s column, the 1 in the 64s column, and the 0 in the 32s column, as just mentioned), while 21 could vary. It looked like this:

110NNNNN.NNNNNNNN.NNNNNNNN.HHHHHHHH

Thus, with 24 network bits minus 3 fixed bits, you had $2^{24-3} = 2^{21} = 2{,}097{,}152$ Class C networks. With 8 host bits in a Class C network, $2^{8} - 2$ allowed for 254 possible hosts on a

Class C network, which is still a large (but paltry compared to Classes A and B) number of hosts for a single network.

CLASSES D AND E

Class D addresses were and still are used for *multicasting*, sending traffic to more than one device on a network, such as in streaming videoconferencing, but not to every device (which would be broadcasting).

Class E addresses have always been experimental (although that's not what the *E* stands for). As a result, Class D and Class E addresses—unlike Class A, Class B, and Class C addresses—were never assigned to hosts.

LIMITATIONS OF CLASSFUL ADDRESSING

IP class blocks worked well for the first few years of the internet but quickly ran into trouble, because IANA issued IP network blocks too generously. Over time, unallocated IP addresses became scarce for two main reasons.

First, the IP classful concept didn't scale well. If an organization needed 2,000 IP addresses, for example, it had to take either a single Class B network block or eight Class C blocks. Since a Class B block provided for 65,534 addresses, an organization that needed just 2,000 would be wasting over 63,000 addresses. On the other hand, using eight Class C blocks would be very cumbersome and require the internet backbone routers to learn the route to each network. (A backbone router is a high-capacity router in the core of a network that handles traffic between major network segments.) Think of it like everyone in your household having their own separate mailing address and the postal system having to send mail to each of those addresses at the same house. In fact, that created the second issue with classful addressing: the internet routing tables were starting to grow out of control due to each organization's use of multiple addressing blocks.

The "three-sizes-fit-all" model works at 7-Eleven for Slurpees (small, medium, and large), but for organizations, it simply didn't scale well. But in 1984, RFC 791 proposed a fix for these classful addressing issues: subnetting.

Subnetting

The idea behind *subnetting*—dividing a network into smaller subnetworks by dedicating some host bits to additional network identification—was to add a new dimension to the IP address between the network ID and the host ID. The internet backbone routers would still use the network ID to get traffic to the destination organization, but now that organization's router would use the subnet information to route the traffic within its own network infrastructure. That way, the internet backbone routers' routing tables wouldn't get clogged up with multiple networks for a single organization. Furthermore, an organization could make changes to its internal IP addressing schemes without affecting external routing, since its subnets were invisible to the internet anyway.

Thanks to subnetting, the organization that needed 2,000 hosts has some options for breaking up a Class B address into multiple subnets, such as:

- 16 networks with 4,094 hosts on each
- 32 networks with 2,046 hosts on each
- 64 networks with 1,022 hosts on each
- 128 networks with 510 hosts on each

Although you wouldn't really put this many hosts on a single network, you see the benefit: the organization wouldn't have to waste thousands of addresses in a Class B network, nor would it have to manage multiple Class C networks.

This flexibility allows organizations to tailor the number of subnets and hosts per subnet to its needs. Think of it as being able to go into 7-Eleven and order a Slurpee in any size you want!

Subnetting shrinks the *broadcast domain* (devices that can hear a broadcast, like an ARP request, from another network device) for each network. Routers never forward broadcasts. Think of it as the reason why college courses are taught individually in their own rooms rather than simultaneously in a single lecture hall. I don't want my students to hear the "broadcast traffic" from other professors while I teach—just mine!

In addition, subnetting allows routers (Layer 3 devices) to use stateless packet filters called *access control lists* (ACLs) to inspect packets going in and out of the network. Maybe you have some hosts on a particular subnet that should have access to other subnets in your autonomous system, except for a specific subnet where servers are storing sensitive data. Or perhaps one host from a subnet should be allowed to access a specific service on a certain machine, but not others. Even government privacy regulations might require you to prevent or allow packets from reaching certain servers. With subnetting, instead of one flat network, you can have multiple networks separated by routers that implement ACLs.

Administration is easier with subnetting as well. Searching for a specific device on a massive network can feel like looking for a needle in a haystack, but subnets allow you to more easily locate and troubleshoot any problems. Subnetting also cuts down on network congestion by limiting traffic to smaller network segments rather than jamming up a single larger network.

EXAM TIP To pass the CompTIA Network+ exam, you need to know how to subnet.

The cornerstone of subnetting is the subnet mask, introduced in Chapter 2. Later in this chapter, you'll see how classful addressing changed to classless addressing. For now, though, just know that this transformation allowed for a new way of representing subnet masks called *Classless Inter-Domain Routing* (CIDR) notation. Instead of representing the subnet mask in dotted decimal form, like an IP address, CIDR notation uses a slash (/) followed by the number of ones in the subnet mask. For example, 255.0.0.0 is 11111111.00000000.00000000.00000000 in binary. There are 8 ones in that subnet mask, so the CIDR notation of 255.0.0.0 is simply /8. The slash and number are found after an IP address, such as 10.1.2.3/8.

The default subnet mask for a Class B network, 255.255.0.0, is /16 in CIDR notation since there are 16 ones in that subnet mask.

The default subnet mask for a Class C network, 255.255.255.0, is /24 in CIDR notation since there are 24 ones in that subnet mask.

EXAM TIP CompTIA and many techs refer to a CIDR address as a *classless* address, meaning the subnet used does not conform to the big three on the classful side: A, B, or C. When you see that term on the exam, you'll know you should look for subnetting.

Now let's put CIDR notation to work in a practical subnetting scenario.

DESIGNING A NETWORK LAYOUT

With subnetting, you take an existing /8, /16, or /24 network and extend the subnet mask by replacing 0s with 1s. For example, let's say you have a café with public Wi-Fi and two internal computers in the back office for accounting and monitoring the shop's security cameras (Figure 3-1). Your network ID is 192.168.4.0/24. For security purposes, you want to set up three subnets: one for the Wi-Fi clients, one for the private internal machines, and one for the security cameras.

You need to keep two things in mind about subnetting. First, start with the given subnet mask and move it to the right until you have the number of subnets you need. Second, forget the dots. They no longer define the subnets.

Never try to subnet without first converting to binary. Too many techs are what I call "victims of the dots." They're so used to working only with class blocks that they forget there's more to subnets than just /8, /16, and /24 networks. There's no reason that network IDs must end on the dots. Computers think it's perfectly fine to have subnets that end at locations between the dots, such as /26, /27, or even /22. The trick here is to stop thinking about network IDs and subnet masks just in their dotted decimal format and instead return to thinking of them as binary numbers.

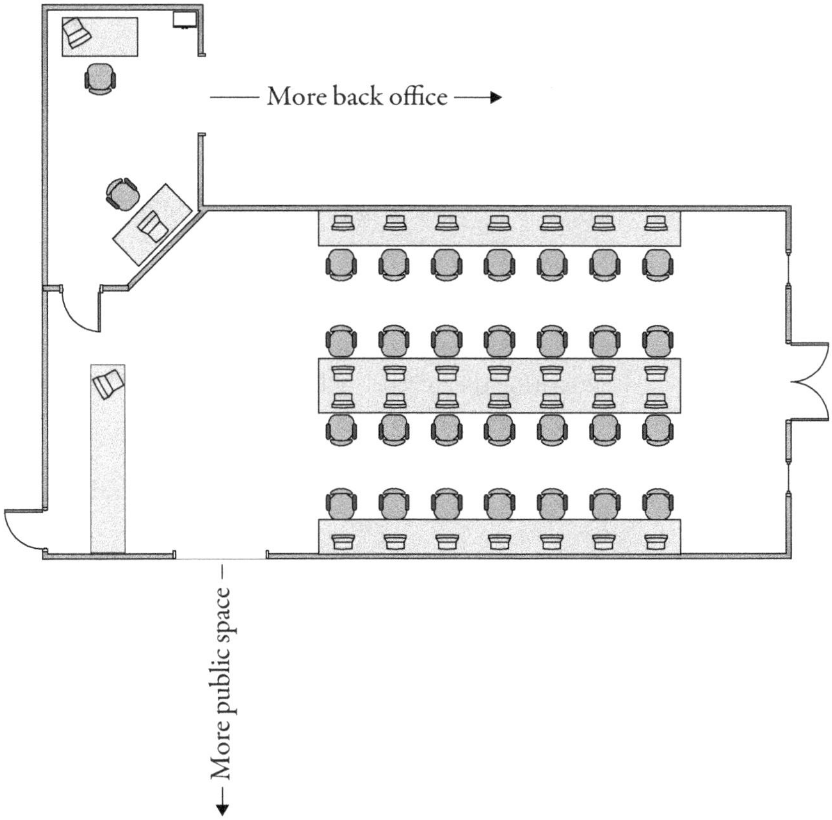

FIGURE 3-1 Layout of the network

NOTE Classful subnets were always /8, /16, or /24.

Let's begin subnetting the café's network of 192.168.4.0/24. You'll start by changing a 0 to a 1 in the subnet mask, so the /24 becomes a /25 subnet:

```
11111111.11111111.11111111.10000000
```

CALCULATING THE NUMBER OF HOSTS

Before going even one step further, you need to answer this question: On a /24 network, how many hosts can you have? If you used dotted decimal notation, you might answer as follows:

192.168.4.1 to 192.168.4.254 = 254 hosts

But do this from binary instead. In a /24 network, you have 8 zeroes that can be the host ID:

00000001 to 11111110 = 254

There's a simple piece of math here: $2^x - 2$, where x represents the number of 0s in the subnet mask. Subtract 2 for the network ID (all host bits can't be 0) and broadcast address (all host bits can't be 1), just as when calculating the number of hosts in classful addressing:

$$2^8 - 2 = 254$$

If you remember this simple formula, you can always determine the number of hosts for a given subnet.

EXAM TIP Use this formula to precisely determine the number of hosts for a given subnet: $2^x - 2$, where x = the number of 0s in the subnet mask.

If you have a /16 subnet mask on your network, what is the maximum number of hosts you can have on that network?

- Because a subnet mask always has 32 bits, a /16 subnet means you have 16 zeroes left after the 16 ones.
- $2^{16} - 2 = 65{,}534$ total hosts.

If you have a /26 subnet mask on your network, what is the maximum number of hosts you can have on that network?

- Because a subnet mask always has 32 bits, a /26 subnet means you have 6 zeroes left after the 26 ones.
- $2^6 - 2 = 62$ total hosts.

Knowing how to determine the number of hosts for a subnet mask will help you tremendously, as you'll see in a moment.

CREATING SUBNETS

All subnetting begins with a single network ID. In this scenario, you need to convert the 192.168.4.0/24 network ID for the café into three network IDs.

NOTE You can't subnet without using binary.

The primary tool for subnetting is the existing subnet mask. Write it out in binary. Place a line at the end of the 1s, as shown in Figure 3-2.

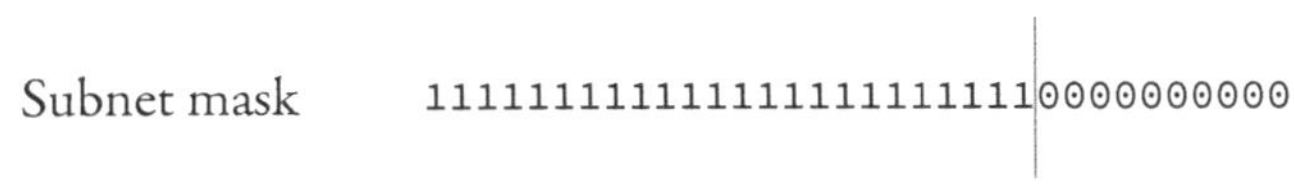

FIGURE 3-2 The subnet mask in binary

Now draw a second line one digit to the right, as shown in Figure 3-3.

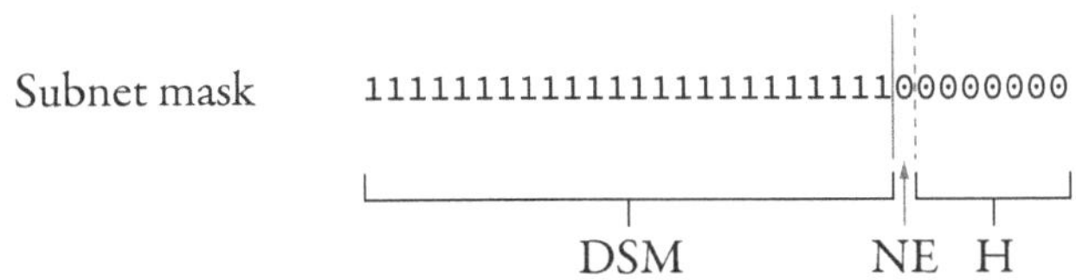

FIGURE 3-3 Organizing the subnet mask

The subnet mask is now separated into three areas that I call (from left to right) the default subnet mask (DSM), the network ID extension (NE), and the hosts (H). These aren't industry terms, so you won't see them on the CompTIA Network+ exam, but they're a handy way to make the process of subnetting more intuitive.

Now, turn that 0 in the second area into a 1, which changes it from a host bit to a network bit. This process is known as "borrowing," but I call it "stealing," since you're never going to give it back! You now have a /25 subnet mask.

At this point, most people first learning how to subnet start to freak out. They're challenged by the idea that a subnet mask of /25 isn't going to fit into one of the three pretty subnet masks of 255.0.0.0, 255.255.0.0, or 255.255.255.0. They think, *That can't be right! Subnet masks are made of only 255s and 0s.* That's not correct. A subnet mask is a string of 1s followed by a string of 0s. People only convert the masks into dotted decimal to enter them into computers. So, convert /25 into dotted decimal as follows:

1. Write out 25 ones, followed by 7 zeroes (remember, subnet masks are *always* 32 bits long):

   11111111111111111111111110000000

2. Insert the dots between every eight digits:

   11111111.11111111.11111111.10000000

3. Then convert the binary subnet mask to dotted decimal:

   255.255.255.128

Get used to the idea of subnet masks that use more than 255s and 0s. The following examples are perfectly legitimate subnet masks; try converting them to binary to see for yourself:

255.255.255.224

255.255.128.0

255.248.0.0

CALCULATING SUBNETS

When you subnet a network ID, you need to follow the rules and conventions to ensure that your new subnets can interact properly with one another and with larger networks. All you need to remember for subnetting is this: Start with a beginning subnet mask and extend it until you have the number of subnets you need. The formula for determining how many subnets to create is 2^y, where y is the number of bits you add to the subnet mask.

Let's practice this a few times. Figure 3-4 shows a starting subnet of 255.255.255.0. If you move the network ID extension over one bit position, you've just "borrowed" a single bit, 2^1.

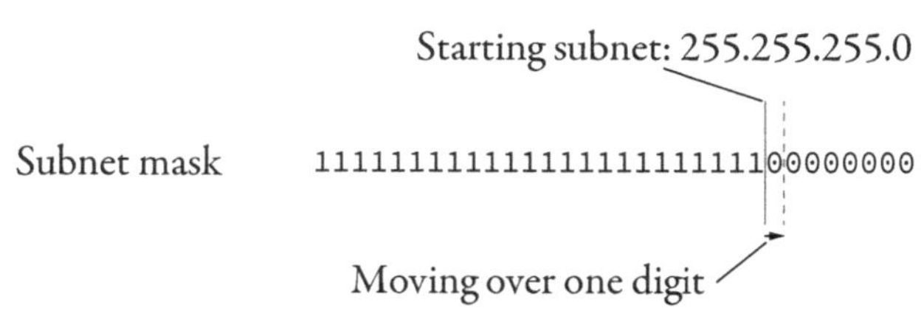

FIGURE 3-4 Moving the network extension

That bit can be a 0 or a 1, which gives you two subnets. You have only one problem—the café needs three subnets! So, take /24 and subnet it down to /26. Extending the network ID by two bits creates four new network IDs, $2^2 = 4$. To see each of these network IDs, first convert the original network ID—192.168.4.0—into binary. Then add the four different network ID extensions to the end, as shown in Figure 3-5.

Original network ID: 192.168.4.0 /24
Translates to this in binary:

```
11000000101010000000010000000000

110000001010100000000100|00|000000
110000001010100000000100|01|000001
110000001010100000000100|10|000000
110000001010100000000100|01|100010
```

FIGURE 3-5 Creating the new network IDs

Figure 3-6 shows the first four host IP addresses for each of the four new network IDs.

```
110000001010100000000100|00|000001
110000001010100000000100|00|000010
110000001010100000000100|00|000011
110000001010100000000100|00|000100

110000001010100000000100|01|000001
110000001010100000000100|01|000010
110000001010100000000100|01|000011
110000001010100000000100|01|000100

110000001010100000000100|10|000001
110000001010100000000100|10|000010
110000001010100000000100|10|000011
110000001010100000000100|10|000100

110000001010100000000100|11|000001
110000001010100000000100|11|000010
110000001010100000000100|11|000011
110000001010100000000100|11|000100
```

FIGURE 3-6 The first four host IP addresses for each of the four new networks

Table 3-6 shows the resulting network IDs, host ranges, and broadcast addresses.

TABLE 3-6 Four subnets with a /26 subnet mask

NETWORK ID	HOST RANGE	BROADCAST ADDRESS
192.168.4.0/26	192.168.4.1–192.168.4.62	192.168.4.63
192.168.4.64/26	192.168.4.65–192.168.4.126	192.168.4.127
192.168.4.128/26	192.168.4.129–192.168.4.190	192.168.4.191
192.168.4.192/26	192.168.4.193–192.168.4.254	192.168.4.255

In fact, you could have done this part of subnetting (filling in the table after working in binary with the custom subnet mask) in base 10 as well. If you start with the network ID of 192.168.4.0 and you know by $2^2 = 4$ that you're going to have four subnets, you can figure out the rest of the table:

1. Find the position of the rightmost 1 bit in the subnet mask. In this case, it's in the 64s column of the fourth octet (11111111.11111111.11111111.1**1**000000). That column value is called one of three things: multiplier, spacing, or magic number.
2. In the octet where the borrowing broke off (the fourth), increment the network ID by that number. (Alternatively, raising 2 to the number of host bits gets you that same number: in this case, $2^6 = 64$.) Therefore, the next subnet ID, after 192.168.4.0, is 192.168.4.64.
3. Again add 64 to the last octet to get the next subnet's ID: 192.168.4.128.
4. Once again add 64 to the last octet to get the fourth and final subnet ID: 192.168.4.192.

Incidentally, no matter what the custom subnet mask is and regardless of how many subnets you have, if you always add one more multiple of the multiplier, you'll always get 256, which of course is a number you can't make with 8 bits (255 is the largest number you can make with 8 bits).

The broadcast address for a subnet is the IP address that numerically comes before the next subnet's network ID. Since the second subnet's network ID is 192.168.4.64, the previous subnet's broadcast address is 192.168.4.63. In the same fashion, before .128 is .127, and before .192 is .191. You'll notice from the table that the first subnet's network ID is always the same as the network ID before subnetting, and the last subnet's broadcast address is the same as the broadcast address of the network before subnetting.

Once you've defined your network IDs and broadcast addresses, the host range for each subnet starts at the IP address that numerically follows the network ID (for example, one after 192.168.4.0 is 192.168.4.1) and ends at the IP address that numerically comes before the broadcast address (for example, one before 192.168.4.63 is 192.168.4.62).

Congratulations! You've just taken a single network ID, 192.168.4.0/24, and subnetted it into four new network IDs! Figure 3-7 shows how you can use these new network IDs in a network.

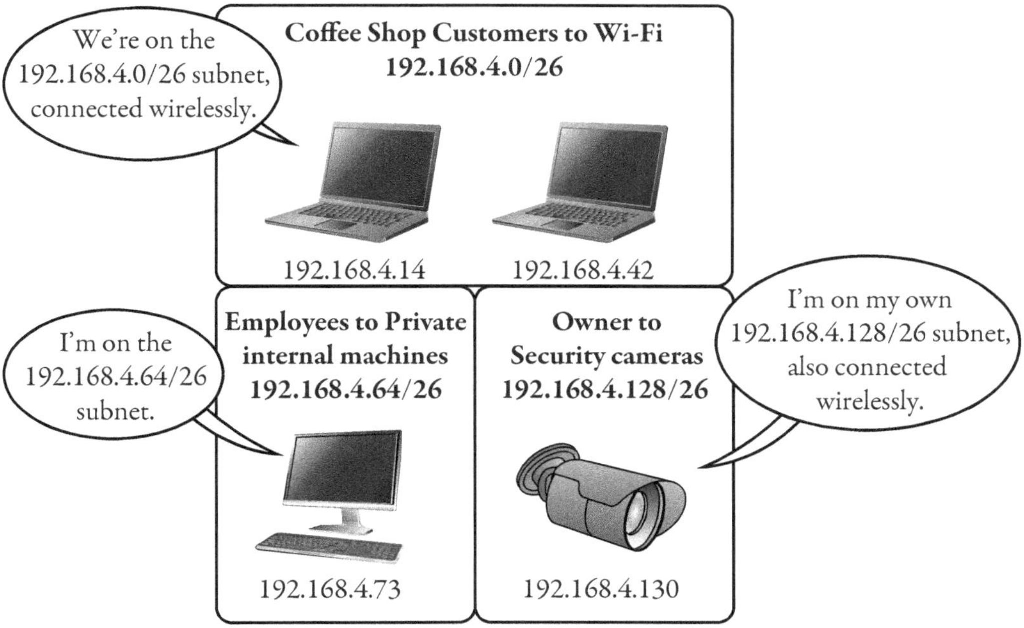

FIGURE 3-7 Three networks using the new network IDs

The café only needs three subnets, but you've created four, so you might think you're "wasting" one. Because subnets are created by powers of two, you'll often create more subnets than you need—welcome to subnetting. However, in many cases, having "spare" subnets comes in handy at the point when your infrastructure needs to grow. This gives you great scalability!

For a little more subnetting practice, let's create eight subnets on a /27 network. First, move the NE over three bits (Figure 3-8).

Note that in this case you only get $2^5 - 2 = 30$ hosts per network ID! These better be small networks!

Subnet mask	111111111111111111111111	00000000
192.168.4.0	110000001010100000000100	00000000
Add 000	110000001010100000000100	00000000
Add 001	110000001010100000000100	00100000
Add 010	110000001010100000000100	01000000
Add 011	110000001010100000000100	01100000
Add 100	110000001010100000000100	10000000
Add 101	110000001010100000000100	10100000
Add 110	110000001010100000000100	11000000
Add 111	110000001010100000000100	11100000

FIGURE 3-8 Moving the network extension three bits

Using what you learned earlier, see if you can construct a table for this /27 subnetting problem (refer to Table 3-6 for help). Hopefully, you'll get what's shown in Table 3-7.

TABLE 3-7 Eight subnets with a /27 subnet mask

NETWORK ID	HOST RANGE	BROADCAST ADDRESS
192.168.4.0/27	192.168.4.1–192.168.4.30	192.168.4.31
192.168.4.32/27	192.168.4.33–192.168.4.62	192.168.4.63
192.168.4.64/27	192.168.4.65–192.168.4.94	192.168.4.95
192.168.4.96/27	192.168.4.97–192.168.4.126	192.168.4.127
192.168.4.128/27	192.168.4.129–192.168.4.158	192.168.4.159
192.168.4.160/27	192.168.4.161–192.168.4.190	192.168.4.191
192.168.4.192/27	192.168.4.193–192.168.4.222	192.168.4.223
192.168.4.224/27	192.168.4.225–192.168.4.254	192.168.4.255

These two examples began with a Class C address. However, you can begin with any starting network ID. Nothing changes about the process you just learned.

NOTE When you work with clients, you need to be able to explain why their subnet mask is 255.255.252.0 or 255.255.255.192, when all the books they read tell them it should be 255.255.255.0!

CIDR

Classless Inter-Domain Routing was introduced in 1993 to solve the following three problems, as listed in RFC 1338 and RFC 1519:

> As the Internet has evolved and grown over in recent years, it has become evident that it is soon to face several serious scaling problems. These include:
>
> 1. Exhaustion of the class B network address space. One fundamental cause of this problem is the lack of a network class of a size which is appropriate for mid-sized organization; class C, with a maximum of 254 host addresses, is too small, while class B, which allows up to 65534 addresses, is too large for most organizations.
> 2. Growth of routing tables in Internet routers beyond the ability of current software, hardware, and people to effectively manage.
> 3. Eventual exhaustion of the 32-bit IP address space.

The first problem was solved by subnetting at the RIR and ISP level, using a *variable-length subnet mask* (VLSM), a component of CIDR that allows arbitrary-length prefixes instead of the fixed-length ones of classful addressing. Since these prefixes don't fit nicely into the classful addressing scheme, they are called *classless*. This made it possible to create subnets with different host sizes and not use the wasteful Class A, Class B, and Class C fixed host lengths.

Under the hood, VLSM is the process of subnetting a subnet. For example, instead of one organization getting a single Class B network, consisting of a possible 65,534 hosts (which would be subnetted, of course), an RIR could subnet that Class B network and then subnet the subnets differently, creating networks of many different sizes. Now, networks of appropriate sizes can be assigned to organizations, proportional to their sizes and actual host requirements.

The second problem was solved with *supernetting*, or summarizing multiple network IDs in routing tables when possible to cut down on the number of entries. For example, if all North American IP addresses start with 198.0.0.0 (using the subnet mask of 255.0.0.0), all routers from South America could have one entry pointing to routers in North America for all addresses that start with 198.0.0.0 (regardless of the values of other octets). Then, all North American routers will have more specific routes for each ISP. One ISP could control all 198.133.0.0 addresses (using the subnet mask of 255.255.0.0), and another ISP could control all 198.134.0.0 addresses (using the subnet mask of 255.255.0.0). Then, each ISP would have more specific routes for its customer companies. For example, the first ISP could have customers with IP addresses starting with 198.133.1.0, 198.133.2.0, and so on, all using the subnet mask of 255.255.255.0.

Furthermore, an organization can implement VLSM internally based on its needs. Classful addressing and traditional subnetting created subnets of the same size for the entire organization. If one network segment needed 62 devices, then all subnets in that organization had to use the same subnet mask (255.255.255.192 with 6 host bits, in this case).

With VLSM, a company can further subnet existing subnets to accommodate specific needs. It might create a subnet with just two hosts for direct router-to-router connections (there's no need for more than two host IP addresses on networks consisting of only two router interfaces), for example, or subnets sized for 14, 30, or 126 hosts.

The foundation of CIDR is, of course, subnetting. Once upon a time, subnetting was just a way that organizations broke up and organized their networks. CIDR extends this approach to the internet as a whole. RIRs and ISPs take blocks of IP addresses, break them up into multiple subnets, and assign those subnets to smaller organizations. Subnetting and CIDR have been around for quite a long time now and are a critical part of all but the smallest TCP/IP networks.

IP Address Configuration and Special Addresses

There are two ways to configure a host's IP settings (for our purposes here, those settings are its IP address, subnet mask, default gateway, and DNS servers): either by manually typing in all the information (called *static addressing*) or by having a server service automatically provide it as systems boot up on or connect to a network (called *dynamic addressing*). The dynamic addressing service, Dynamic Host Configuration Protocol (DHCP), will be covered in Chapter 7.

EXAM TIP The CompTIA Network+ exam objectives use the terms *static assignment* and *dynamic assignment* to describe these IP addressing methods.

There are several special IP addresses you need to know about. The first is 127.0.0.1, which is known as the *loopback address or localhost*. When you tell a device to send data to 127.0.0.1, you're telling it to send the packets to itself.

Although it's a common misconception that the loopback address is used to test hardware, it has absolutely nothing to do with testing a NIC (disable all NICs, ping 127.0.0.1, and it will still work!). Rather, it tests if TCP/IP is working correctly on the local machine.

The loopback address has uses beyond testing the TCP/IP stack, however. You can browse to 127.0.0.1 to test a web server running locally. In fact, you can access any server service on your local system with a destination IP address of 127.0.0.1.

EXAM TIP Even though 127.0.0.1 is used as the loopback address by convention, the entire 127.0.0.0/8 subnet is reserved for loopback addresses. This means that you could use any address on that subnet as a loopback address.

Special-purpose IP addresses also include *private addresses*, specific ranges set out by the Internet Engineering Task Force (IETF) in *RFC 1918* to slow the depletion of IPv4 addresses:

- 10.0.0.0 through 10.255.255.255 (1 Class A network block; anything that starts with 10)
- 172.16.0.0 through 172.31.255.255 (16 Class B network blocks; anything that starts with 172.16 through 172.31)
- 192.168.0.0 through 192.168.255.255 (256 Class C network blocks; anything that starts with 192.168.*x*, where *x* is a part of the network ID and can have any value from 0 to 255)

All internet backbone routers block private IP addresses.

NOTE It's a myth that private addresses are for "hiding" systems and networks. If that were the case, you wouldn't hear constant news reports of hacks, attacks, and cybercrime targeting homes and organizations. "Security through obscurity" doesn't make you more secure at all and is discouraged by standards bodies. As the National Institute of Standards and Technology (NIST) put it: "System security should not depend on the secrecy of the implementation or its components."

Anyone can use private IP addresses, but when systems with these addresses need to access the internet, they must use Network Address Translation (NAT), which will be covered in Chapter 5. NAT is often mistakenly referenced as a security protocol, but it exists only to allow devices using private IP addresses to send and receive traffic over the internet.

To learn about other special-purpose IP addresses, see *iana.org/assignments/iana-ipv4-special-registry/iana-ipv4-special-registry.xhtml.*

EXAM TIP Make sure you can quickly tell the difference between a public IP address and a private IP address for the CompTIA Network+ exam.

Chapter Review

Questions

1. Which of the following protocols does not exist at the Network layer?
   - **A.** IPv4
   - **B.** IPv6
   - **C.** TCP
   - **D.** ICMP
2. Which of these is not a field in the IP header?
   - **A.** Version
   - **B.** Header Length
   - **C.** Source IP address
   - **D.** Destination MAC address

3. Which of the following is a valid Class C IP address?
   A. 50.50.50.50
   B. 100.100.100.100
   C. 192.168.0.254
   D. 250.250.250.250
4. Which of the following masks allows for the greatest number of hosts on a network?
   A. 255.0.0.0
   B. 255.255.0.0
   C. 255.255.255.0
   D. 255.255.255.128
5. What processes are used to take a single class of IP addresses and chop it up into multiple smaller networks? (Select two.)
   A. CIDR
   B. ping
   C. Subnetting
   D. Supernetting
6. Which statements about subnet masks are true? (Select two.)
   A. Every network client has a unique subnet mask.
   B. Every client on a network shares the same subnet mask.
   C. A subnet mask consists of a string of 0s followed by a string of 1s.
   D. A subnet mask consists of a string of 1s followed by a string of 0s.
7. Which of the following represents the smallest size network?
   A. /8
   B. /12
   C. /16
   D. /26
8. How many bits do you need to borrow to make 52 subnets?
   A. 5
   B. 6
   C. 26
   D. 52

9. How many hosts are on a /22 network?
   A. 22
   B. 24
   C. 1022
   D. 1024

10. Which one of these is a private IP address?
   A. 129.21.1.40
   B. 192.156.234.2
   C. 10.11.12.13
   D. 172.32.0.1

Answers

1. **C.** TCP exists at the Transport layer.
2. **D.** MAC addresses are found in frames at the Data Link layer.
3. **C.** The address 192.168.0.254 falls within the range of Class C addresses because it starts with an octet from 192 through 223.
4. **A.** The greater number of 0s in the subnet mask, the greater the number of hosts. 255.0.0.0 has 24 bits of 0s.
5. **A** and **C.** CIDR and subnetting enable you to take a single class of IP addresses and chop it up into multiple smaller networks called subnets.
6. **B** and **D.** Every client on a network shares the same subnet mask. Subnet masks consist of a string of 1s followed by a string of 0s.
7. **D.** The more 1s in the subnet mask (the greater the number after the forward slash in CIDR notation), the fewer host bits, and thus the fewer hosts per network.
8. **B.** Using the formula 2^y = the number of subnets, $2^5 = 32$ (not enough), but $2^6 = 64$ (which gives you 52 and 12 extra).
9. **C.** Using the formula $2^x - 2$ = the number of host on each subnet, /22 leaves you with 10 host bits: $2^{10} - 2 = 1{,}022$.
10. **C.** Anything that starts with a 10 in the first octet is a private IP address. Option A is the IP address of the rit.edu web server. Option B is the IP address of the FLCC web server. Notice that the 192 in the first octet doesn't make the address private. Anything that starts with 192.168, though, is private. Option D is public, because the second octet, after 172, is not between 16 and 31.

Ports, Protocols, and Services

IN THIS CHAPTER, YOU WILL LEARN HOW TO

- Outline what role ports play in networking
- Explain the different ports and services that are used today
- Differentiate between TCP and UDP
- Describe how ICMP works in networking
- Use netstat, ping, and traceroute/tracert to troubleshoot networks

The way network communication physically enters and exits a machine is through the network interface card (NIC), which exists at both Layers 1 and 2 (the Physical and Data Link layers, respectively) of the OSI model. The NIC is the connection from your machine to the rest of the world. The way network communication *logically* enters and exits a machine, however, is through a program or service.

Historical/Conceptual

In Windows, a *service* is a program that runs in the background, independent of a sign-in. Linux and macOS use the term *daemon* to describe the same thing. As an example, Windows client machines run a workstation service in the background that uses the Server Message Block (SMB) protocol to connect to server services in order to access remote files and printers. When you start a web server, you're starting a server service that isn't tied to a specific account. This way, when the server reboots, the service automatically starts without requiring you to sign in, allowing for the constant availability of system and network components. Another advantage is that when services run from a system account or dedicated service account, permissions can be controlled, enforcing security. Technically speaking, a server is a service (software) that responds to client service requests. The term *server*, though, is often used for the machines (hardware) on which those services run.

NOTE A *process* is an instantiation of a program or service and can be broken down into multiple threads. A *thread* is a sequence of instructions executing within a process. A process will have multiple threads that run in parallel, performing different tasks. For example, a process for a web browser might have one thread that renders the page, one that deals with network requests, and one that deals with user interface events.

So, how does network communication go in and out of a program or service? Let's say a single machine is running both a File Transfer Protocol (FTP) server and a web server. If they're both accessible by the same IP address, how does the traffic for the FTP server get to the FTP server and the traffic for the web server get to the web server? The answer lies in understanding how the operating system identifies which specific service should receive the incoming data, through ports.

Test Specific

How Ports Work

Think about an apartment building with a mailbox grid in the lobby. The man in apartment 21, Frank Thomas Peterson, checks mailbox 21, and the woman in apartment 80, Helen Theresa Thomasina Parker, checks mailbox 80. The mailman brings their mail to the same building. They both live in the same building with the same street address. This is like two different servers that are accessible through the same IP address. However, when traffic is destined for the man in apartment 21, it is noted on the front of the envelope. The same goes for mail addressed to the woman in apartment 80. Similarly, the way into and out of a program or service is indicated by a *port*, a logical endpoint of communication that identifies a program or service, represented by a number.

NOTE The term *port* is used instead of *port number*. For example, you'd see or hear "port 21" instead of "port number 21."

So, in addition to source and destination MAC addresses and source and destination IP addresses, there are source and destination ports.

To summarize, in the OSI model:

- MAC addresses are found in frame headers at Layer 2 (Data Link layer).
- IP addresses are found in IP packet headers at Layer 3 (Network layer).
- Port numbers are found in either Transmission Control Protocol (TCP) segment headers or User Datagram Protocol (UDP) datagram headers at Layer 4 (Transport layer).

Based on the destination port, the operating system on the destination machine knows which program or service to send the data to, in the same way that the mail carrier knows to put the mail for apartment 21 in mailbox 21, and the mail for apartment 80 in mailbox 80.

Types of Ports

Ports are organized into three categories, summarized in Table 4-1.

TABLE 4-1 Port types

NUMBER RANGE	TYPE
0–1023	Well-known ports (aka system ports)
1024–49151	Registered ports (aka user ports)
49152–65535	Dynamic ports (aka private ports or ephemeral ports)

WELL-KNOWN PORTS

Well-known ports, also known as *system ports*, range from 0 through 1023 (0 is used by programming APIs as a wildcard to find an available port, but not directly by hosts) and are reserved for major protocols and services. FTP servers send and receive control traffic on port 21 (which is why I named the man in apartment 21 Frank Thomas Peterson). Web servers running Hypertext Transfer Protocol (HTTP) send and receive unencrypted traffic on port 80 (which is why I named the woman in apartment 80 Helen Theresa Thomasina Parker). Web servers send and receive encrypted traffic on port 443, with Transport Layer Security (TLS). This is often referred to as HTTPS (HTTP over TLS). Incidentally, there are a few client services that will use a fixed port in this range; most notably, Dynamic Host Configuration Protocol (DHCP) clients use port 68.

NOTE An IP address gets data to the intended device. A port number gets the data to the intended program/service on that device.

REGISTERED PORTS

Registered ports, also known as *user ports*, range from 1024 through 49151 and are assigned by the Internet Assigned Numbers Authority (IANA) to organizations that want to use a standard port for their programs or protocols. However, if not actively in use, these port numbers can be used by any program or service. Unlike registered IP addresses, which have global scope, registered port numbers are locally significant to a system. Common registered ports include 3306 (MySQL, a relational database management system, or RDBMS, registered by Oracle Corporation) and 3389 (Remote Desktop Protocol, or RDP, used for remote access into a Windows machine and registered by Microsoft).

NOTE IANA's official list of ports can be found at *iana.org/assignments/service-names-port-numbers/service-names-port-numbers.xhtml.*

DYNAMIC PORTS

Dynamic ports, also known as *private* or *ephemeral ports,* range from 49152 through 65535 and are used by client applications on an as-needed basis. For example, a browser might open port 60000 to send a request to a web server that will be listening for requests either on port 80 or 443 (as mentioned earlier). The web server's response is sourced from port 80 or 443 and is destined for the port that the browser opened. After the communication between the browser and the web server is complete, the browser will close the port it opened, but the web server's port will remain open for new incoming connections. The browser, or any other program or service running on the machine, will subsequently open a different port in that dynamic range for its next request. In most cases, the operating system will pick the next sequential number in that range for the next client program.

Port States

A port can be in one of three states: open, closed, or filtered. There's really just one difference between an open port and a closed port. Open ports have programs or services listening on them, whereas closed ports don't. For example, if you start a FileZilla FTP server, port 21 is open. Stop the FileZilla FTP server, and port 21 is closed. If you start an Apache web server, port 80 is now open. Stop the Apache web server, and port 80 is now closed.

A filtered port is either open or closed, but its state can't be determined because packet filtering keeps the traffic from getting to the port (*filter* in this context means to block or drop the traffic). The filtering could come from a dedicated firewall device, router rules, or a host-based firewall. Sometimes an Internet Control Message Protocol (ICMP) error message will be sent in response to a filtered port. However, firewalls often just drop the traffic without sending a response.

Firewalls don't open or close ports—they filter ports. If a network-based firewall is set to deny some or all traffic to a Secure Shell (SSH) server on port 22, the SSH server is still running on the machine and port 22 remains open (which you could confirm by running `netstat` as discussed later in this chapter). Any hosts inside the network, therefore, can still access the SSH server since the network-based firewall doesn't affect them. Likewise, when a host-based firewall on the machine running the SSH server is filtering incoming traffic on port 22, the port remains open as long as the service is running.

Let's say I'm teaching a class in the Finger Lakes Community College Victor Campus Center. Think of the class in the Networking and Cybersecurity Lab as a program or service that's running. Think of the room number (VC206) as the port number that lets students know where to enter. While class is in session, the port is open. After class, we all leave. The lights go off and the door is locked. The port is closed. Picture yourself trying to enter FLCC's Victor Campus Center, but the security guard at the front door won't let you in. That guard is the firewall. You can't get to my classroom door to even determine whether class is in session (open port) or not (closed port) because you're being filtered by the guard (filtered port).

NOTE Don't confuse these logical ports with physical ports into which connectors are plugged.

Table 4-2 lists application protocols with their corresponding port(s), corresponding Layer 4 protocol (coming up next), and purpose, as identified in the CompTIA Network+ exam objectives.

TABLE 4-2 Protocols and their associated ports

PROTOCOL	PORT(S)	LAYER 4 PROTOCOL	PURPOSE
File Transfer Protocol (FTP)	20, 21	TCP	Transfers files between clients and servers. In active mode (mostly deprecated today), the server uses port 20 for data transfer and port 21 for control information. In passive mode, the server uses a dynamic port instead of 20 but still uses port 21 for control information.
Secure File Transfer Protocol (SFTP), an extension to SSH	22	TCP	Provides secure file transfer and file system access.
Secure Shell (SSH)	22	TCP	Enables remote shell login and command execution with encryption. Replaced Telnet, which sent communications (including usernames and passwords) in plaintext.

TABLE 4-2 Protocols and their associated ports ***(continued)***

PROTOCOL	PORT(S)	LAYER 4 PROTOCOL	PURPOSE
Telnet (backronymed as Teletype Network), obsolete, replaced by SSH	23	TCP	Enabled remote shell login and command execution, sending communications (including usernames and passwords) in plaintext.
Simple Mail Transfer Protocol (SMTP)	25	TCP	Sends email off a domain, first from a mail client to a mail server, then from the sending domain's outgoing mail server to the receiving domain's incoming mail server. Clients access email from their mail server using Internet Message Access Protocol (IMAP), which uses port 143.
Domain Name System (DNS)	53	UDP (for queries and responses) TCP (in two cases: zone transfers and responses that exceed 512 bytes)	Resolves fully qualified domain names (FQDNs) into their corresponding IP addresses and performs other types of resolution, such as finding a domain's DNS and mail servers and performing reverse lookups to match IP addresses to FQDNs.
Dynamic Host Configuration Protocol (DHCP)	67, 68	UDP	Provides clients with configuration information, including IP address, subnet mask, default gateway, and IP addresses of DNS and DHCP servers. DHCP servers use port 67, and—in a very rare and unique client assignment in the well-known ports category—DHCP clients use port 68.
Trivial File Transfer Protocol (TFTP), a simplified version of FTP	69	UDP	Boots from a LAN with Preboot eXecution Environment (PXE) and uploads and downloads router and switch images and configurations.
Hypertext Transfer Protocol (HTTP)	80	TCP	Defines the formatting, transmission, and actions of web servers and clients. Passes everything in plaintext.
Network Time Protocol (NTP)	123	UDP	Synchronizes clocks between networked devices.

PROTOCOL	PORT(S)	LAYER 4 PROTOCOL	PURPOSE
Simple Network Management Protocol (SNMP)	161, 162	UDP (default) and TCP (for security)	Collects information from networking devices for management and monitoring purposes.
Lightweight Directory Access Protocol (LDAP)	389	TCP and UDP	Accesses and maintains distributed directory information services related to users, groups, computers, printers, and more. Implemented on Microsoft Windows servers through Active Directory.
Hypertext Transfer Protocol Secure (HTTPS)	443	TCP	Provides authentication, confidentiality, and integrity to exchanges between web servers and clients. Uses HTTP over Transport Layer Security (TLS) to prevent on-path (aka man-in-the-middle) attacks; secure accounts; and keep communications, identities, and browsing private.
Server Message Block (SMB)	445	TCP	Provides shared access to files, printers, and more.
Syslog (message logging standard)	514	TCP and UDP	Separates the software generating the messages, the system storing the messages, and the software reporting and analyzing the messages.
Simple Mail Transfer Protocol Secure (SMTPS), a more secure version of SMTP	587	TCP	Uses TLS encryption as well as authentication for email. Digital signatures also provide integrity to email.
Lightweight Directory Access Protocol over SSL (LDAPS), a more secure version of LDAP	636	TCP	Uses TLS encryption between the client and server.
Structured Query Language (SQL) Server	1433	TCP and UDP	Provides database connectivity to Microsoft's SQL Server via port 1433/TCP. (Port 1434/UDP, incidentally, allows for automatic discovery of SQL Server by clients.)
Remote Desktop Protocol (RDP), a Microsoft protocol	3389	TCP	Allows for connecting to another computer through a graphical user interface (GUI).

TABLE 4-2 Protocols and their associated ports ***(continued)***

PROTOCOL	PORT(S)	LAYER 4 PROTOCOL	PURPOSE
Session Initiation Protocol (SIP)	5060, 5061	TCP and UDP	Establishes, modifies, and terminates VoIP (Voice over IP) calls. Port 5060 is used for nonencrypted signaling traffic, while port 5061 is used for TLS encrypted traffic.

EXAM TIP Memorize the protocols, their purpose, and their corresponding port numbers listed in Table 4-2.

Layer 4 Protocols and Utilities

Each of the protocols listed in Table 4-2 is encapsulated within either a TCP segment or a UDP datagram at Layer 4. The segments and datagrams are then placed inside IP packets, with the Protocol field in the IP header indicating what's inside (6 for TCP and 17 for UDP). The TCP and UDP protocols take fundamentally different approaches to data transmission, each optimized for different types of communication needs. We'll compare how these two protocols work and then examine netstat, a network utility that allows you to monitor active TCP and UDP connections on your system.

TCP

TCP establishes a connection between the source and destination devices for reliable data transfer and flow control, sending data at a rate that is acceptable to both devices. TCP guarantees that every single byte sent will be received with integrity, processed in the correct order, and acknowledged by the destination. So, actually, there are three things guaranteed in life: death, taxes, and TCP.

Because TCP segments are acknowledged, the sender knows the destination got the traffic. If an acknowledgment specifically referencing byte numbers for the sent data doesn't come back, TCP resends the unacknowledged bytes. All bytes sent with TCP are ordered and sequenced. Because of this overhead, TCP is deliberately slower than UDP, striving for accuracy and integrity. The TCP header, which we'll discuss shortly, contains many fields that have functions that add latency.

TCP is used in applications where accuracy is a priority, such as file transfers (FTP), email (SMTP, IMAP), and web browsing (HTTP, HTTPS). If bytes are lost or corrupted, the whole message could be compromised.

The way TCP establishes a connection is through the *TCP three-way handshake*. In non-technical terms, it looks like this:

Source: "Hey, I want to talk to you."

Destination: "Roger that! You can talk to me. Can I talk to you too?"

Source: "Sure, let's rock!"

Take a look at Figure 4-1, as I'll focus on certain fields of the TCP header to describe the three-way handshake.

<table>
<caption>TCP Header</caption>
<tr><td>Offsets</td><td>Octet</td><td colspan="8">0</td><td colspan="8">1</td><td colspan="8">2</td><td colspan="8">3</td></tr>
<tr><td>Octet</td><td>Bit</td><td>0</td><td>1</td><td>2</td><td>3</td><td>4</td><td>5</td><td>6</td><td>7</td><td>8</td><td>9</td><td>10</td><td>11</td><td>12</td><td>13</td><td>14</td><td>15</td><td>16</td><td>17</td><td>18</td><td>19</td><td>20</td><td>21</td><td>22</td><td>23</td><td>24</td><td>25</td><td>26</td><td>27</td><td>28</td><td>29</td><td>30</td><td>31</td></tr>
<tr><td>0</td><td>0</td><td colspan="16">Source Port</td><td colspan="16">Destination Port</td></tr>
<tr><td>4</td><td>32</td><td colspan="32">Sequence Number</td></tr>
<tr><td>8</td><td>64</td><td colspan="32">Acknowledgment Number</td></tr>
<tr><td>12</td><td>96</td><td colspan="4">Data Offset</td><td colspan="3">Reserved 000</td><td>NS</td><td>CWR</td><td>ECE</td><td>URG</td><td>ACK</td><td>PSH</td><td>RST</td><td>SYN</td><td>FIN</td><td colspan="16">Window Size</td></tr>
<tr><td>16</td><td>128</td><td colspan="16">Checksum</td><td colspan="16">Urgent Pointer</td></tr>
<tr><td>20
...</td><td>160
...</td><td colspan="32">Options
...</td></tr>
</table>

FIGURE 4-1 A TCP header

The first two fields of the TCP header contain the source and destination ports, indicating which program or service is sending the message (on the source) and which should receive it (on the destination). Next are two important fields, Sequence Number and Acknowledgement Number. To understand how these fields are used, we need to look at the flags section that follows the Data Offset field (which indicates where the data begins after the TCP header) and the Reserved field (which contains three 0 bits).

Flags in the TCP header represent specific control information conveyed to and from the communicating machines. Like the red flags on a mailbox, they can be raised or lowered. TCP flags are represented by individual bits in the TCP header. Setting a flag (turning it on, or "raising" it) means assigning that bit a value of 1. Clearing a flag (turning it off, or "lowering" it) means assigning that bit a value of 0. There are nine flags (six standard ones and three specialty ones) in the TCP header. We'll focus on two of the standard ones—Synchronize (SYN) and Acknowledge (ACK)—in the three-way handshake, which follows this process:

1. (SYN) The source (client) turns on the SYN flag by placing a 1 in that bit position and generates a pseudorandom sequence number that it places in the Sequence Number field. Let's say it's 52 for this example. This is the source saying "Hey, I want to talk to

you." The source places the TCP header in an IP packet, places the packet in a frame, and, assuming remote communication, sends the frame to the default gateway.

Since the SYN flag is raised, this step is known as SYN.

2. (SYN/ACK) When the TCP segment arrives at the destination, the destination (server) responds by sending its own TCP header. The destination turns on the ACK flag, increments the sequence number that the source sent (52, in this example) by one, and puts the result (53) in the Acknowledgment Number field. This is the destination saying, "Roger that! You can talk to me." In reality, both the sequence number and acknowledgment number are 4-byte values.

   In the same TCP header, the destination also raises the SYN flag and comes up with its own pseudorandom generated sequence number, let's say 1975, which it places in the Sequence Number field. This is the destination saying, "Can I talk to you too?" It then sends this TCP segment to the source via its default gateway.

   Since the SYN and ACK flags are raised, this step is known as SYN/ACK.

3. (ACK) The source responds by sending another TCP segment with the ACK flag on, incrementing the sequence number that the destination sent by one, and putting the result in the Acknowledgement Number field (1975 + 1 = 1976). This is the source saying "Sure, let's rock!"

   Since the ACK flag is raised, this step is known as ACK.

The TCP three-way handshake, thus, is described as SYN, SYN/ACK, ACK. Figure 4-2 illustrates these three steps.

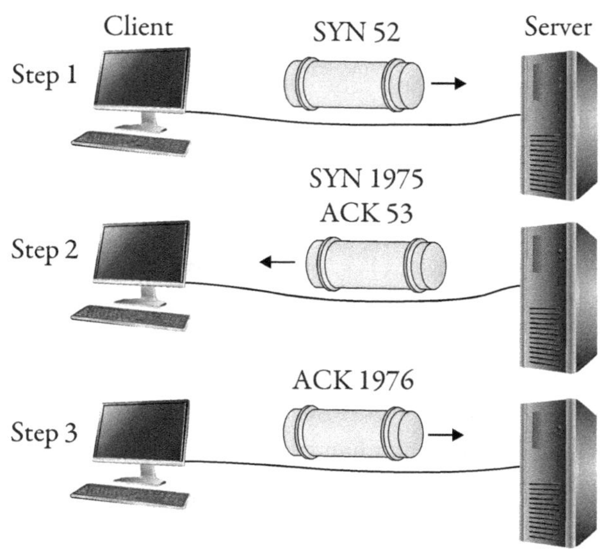

FIGURE 4-2 The TCP three-way handshake

At this point, the two systems are connected. The TCP segments in the three steps didn't have any data; the TCP header contained only control information. Now when actual data is transmitted by either station—whether by HTTP (TLS), SSH, FTP, or something else—it's encapsulated inside a TCP header. In fact, the sequence numbers now increase by the size of the data sent, and the acknowledgments increment the number of the last byte sent by one. Every byte sent is acknowledged. If not, it's resent. That's how TCP follows through on its guaranteed data delivery claim!

Tables 4-3 and 4-4 summarize other TCP fields and flags you should be aware of.

TABLE 4-3 Other TCP fields

Data Offset (Header Length)	Indicates where the data (after the TCP header) begins.
Reserved	Remains unused and is set to three 0 bits.
Window Size	Specifies the maximum number of bytes the receiving side will accept before sending an acknowledgment back to the sender.
Checksum	Handles error checking.
Urgent Pointer	Used in the past with the URG flag to prioritize data (for example, CTRL+C to kill a process over a Telnet session) that needed to be handled immediately.
Options	Comprises 35 additional TCP fields that extend the functionality of TCP from its original design, including Maximum Segment Size, Window Scale, Selective Acknowledgment permitted, Selective ACKnowledgement (SACK), Timestamps, and No-Operation (NOP).

TABLE 4-4 Other TCP flags

URG	Tells a destination system to prioritize data in a segment at a location specified by the Urgent Pointer field in the TCP header. This flag is a relic and not used by modern protocols.
PSH	Tells both the sending system to push the data down and out immediately and the receiving system to push the received data up to the receiving application without waiting for a buffer to accumulate (which would normally happen to ensure efficient data transfer for many TCP segments). The PSH flag is commonly used at the end of an HTTP or TLS session when there's no more data to be sent or received, as well as during an SSH session where the keystrokes need to be sent immediately to a remote system. Without the PSH flag there could be significant latency, making the communication unbearably slow.

TABLE 4-4 Other TCP flags *(continued)*

FIN	Tears down an established TCP connection similar to how the SYN flag establishes the connection. Unlike the TCP three-way handshake, the teardown process uses four steps (two separate two-way handshakes): 1. Side A, the side that starts the TCP connection termination (also known as the *TCP teardown*), sends a TCP segment with the FIN flag set. 2. The other side, Side B, sends a TCP segment with the ACK flag set. 3. Side B sends another segment, this time with the FIN flag set. 4. Side A sends a segment with the ACK flag set. Sequence and acknowledgment numbers are used here as well. The sequence numbers pick up from where they were at the end of the data exchange process, and the acknowledgment numbers increment the sequence numbers sent with the FINs by one.
RST	Terminates a TCP connection abruptly (in contrast to the graceful termination process with the FIN flag just described). Reasons for using RST include receiving an invalid header, not having enough resources available to support the connection, not receiving any response from the other side, and even optimizing (that is, getting rid of the other side as quickly as possible instead of initiating a graceful close with FINs, which takes more time and resources).

NOTE You can remember the six standard TCP flags (URG, ACK, PSH, RST, SYN, FIN) with the phrase Unskilled Attackers Pester Real Security Folks.

UDP

Unlike TCP, UDP is connectionless, has no flow control, and offers no guarantees about delivery, ordering, or integrity. As a result, UDP is much quicker than TCP, striving for efficiency over precision. The UDP header, shown in Figure 4-3, contains only a few fields—Source Port,

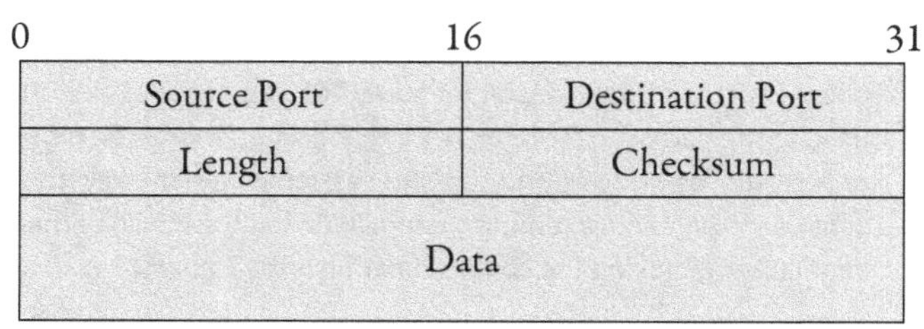

FIGURE 4-3 A UDP header

Destination Port, Length (to indicate where the actual data begins), and Checksum (for error checking)—with no additional overhead.

With UDP, if bytes are lost, we don't care and might not even notice. If we do perceive a slight degradation in image quality or sound quality, we just accept it instead of getting frustrated like we would if TCP's additional overhead were slowing down the entire communication.

UDP is used in applications where speed is a priority, such as real-time communications, conferencing, and streaming. Let's consider a scenario that illustrates why UDP is better suited than TCP for real-time communication. If every byte sent on a VoIP call over the web needed to be acknowledged, there could be problems with lost messages or even lost acknowledgments. Say a source sends the initial message, the spoken word "Hello," to the destination, but the destination's acknowledgment gets lost. TCP, on the source, would think the destination didn't get the message and would resend it. Meanwhile, as the conversation continues, the destination would hear the source's subsequent words from the voice call, "How are you doing today?" but then would receive the source's "Hello" again. In other words, you'd have past messages interrupting the current conversation—making for a very frustrating phone call!

All audio and video that is delivered in real time and streaming over the internet in UDP datagrams must still be ordered properly to ensure that it is processed correctly. Real-Time Streaming Protocol (RTSP), which exists at Layer 7, does the ordering for UDP. Using RTSP just to order UDP datagrams involves significantly less overhead than TCP would require. TCP would involve establishing and maintaining a connection, adding flow control, and sending acknowledgments—all factors that would slow down the communication between devices.

Furthermore, two major network protocols, DNS and DHCP, use UDP. When querying your DNS server to resolve a name to an IP address or querying your DHCP server to get or renew a lease for an IP address, if no reply comes back to your client, your client will simply ask again. There's no need for additional overhead.

NOTE Although not covered in the CompTIA Network+ objectives, Quick UDP Internet Connections (QUIC), a transport protocol (HTTP/3 under the hood) developed by Google, is replacing TCP on many major websites by combining TCP's reliability, TLS's encryption, and HTTP/2's multiplexing into a single, smarter protocol that deals with both efficiency and security. If TCP is like sending a giant treasure chest with locks across a shaky bridge (the internet in this case), stopping each time a bolt falls off the bridge, QUIC is like sending many small, independent, locked treasure boxes on ziplines, where the failure of a single zipline doesn't affect the others.

netstat

The netstat tool enables you to explore the sessions (think Layer 5, the Session layer, of the OSI model) between communicating systems. Check out the netstat output in Figure 4-4.

```
Command Prompt

C:\Users\jswics>netstat -a

Active Connections

  Proto  Local Address          Foreign Address        State
  TCP    0.0.0.0:21             jweissman:0            LISTENING
  TCP    0.0.0.0:135            jweissman:0            LISTENING
  TCP    0.0.0.0:445            jweissman:0            LISTENING
  TCP    0.0.0.0:5357           jweissman:0            LISTENING
  TCP    0.0.0.0:5985           jweissman:0            LISTENING
  TCP    0.0.0.0:47001          jweissman:0            LISTENING
  TCP    0.0.0.0:49664          jweissman:0            LISTENING
  TCP    0.0.0.0:49665          jweissman:0            LISTENING
  TCP    0.0.0.0:49666          jweissman:0            LISTENING
  TCP    0.0.0.0:49667          jweissman:0            LISTENING
  TCP    0.0.0.0:49673          jweissman:0            LISTENING
  TCP    0.0.0.0:49677          jweissman:0            LISTENING
  TCP    10.80.100.3:5040       jweissman:0            LISTENING
  TCP    10.80.100.3:49670      13.89.185.175:https    ESTABLISHED
  TCP    10.80.100.3:49712      13.89.188.5:https      ESTABLISHED
  TCP    10.80.100.3:49718      65.55.44.109:https     TIME_WAIT
  TCP    127.0.0.1:14147        jweissman:0            LISTENING
  TCP    127.0.0.1:49682        jweissman:4243         SYN_SENT
  TCP    127.0.0.1:49693        jweissman:62522        ESTABLISHED
  TCP    127.0.0.1:62522        jweissman:0            LISTENING
  TCP    127.0.0.1:62522        jweissman:49693        ESTABLISHED
  TCP    [::]:21                jweissman:0            LISTENING
  TCP    [::]:135               jweissman:0            LISTENING
  TCP    [::]:445               jweissman:0            LISTENING
  TCP    [::]:5357              jweissman:0            LISTENING
  TCP    [::]:5985              jweissman:0            LISTENING
  TCP    [::]:47001             jweissman:0            LISTENING
  TCP    [::]:49664             jweissman:0            LISTENING
  TCP    [::]:49665             jweissman:0            LISTENING
  TCP    [::]:49666             jweissman:0            LISTENING
  TCP    [::]:49667             jweissman:0            LISTENING
  TCP    [::]:49673             jweissman:0            LISTENING
  TCP    [::]:49677             jweissman:0            LISTENING
  TCP    [::1]:14147            jweissman:0            LISTENING
  UDP    0.0.0.0:500            *:*
  UDP    0.0.0.0:3702           *:*
  UDP    0.0.0.0:3702           *:*
  UDP    0.0.0.0:4500           *:*
  UDP    0.0.0.0:5050           *:*
  UDP    0.0.0.0:5353           *:*
  UDP    0.0.0.0:5355           *:*
  UDP    0.0.0.0:60633          *:*
```

FIGURE 4-4 The output of a netstat command

Notice that each connection is represented by a Local Address and Foreign Address. Sockets are endpoints of active communication links between two programs on separate machines, represented by a combination of IP address and port number, as well as the Layer 4 protocol (TCP or UDP) for both the source and destination. TCP sockets are actual connections between source and destination, whereas UDP sockets are connectionless. The Local Address is on the machine you're using, while the Foreign Address is on the machine you're connected to and communicating with.

The `netstat -a` command outputs all (which is what the `-a` stands for) connections and listening ports, including listening ports that are not currently in active communication. If you add the `-n` (numeric) option, the command outputs numeric IP addresses and port numbers in the Foreign Address column; without `-n`, as shown in the figure, it outputs computer names and FQDNs for IP addresses (jweissman instead of 127.0.0.1, for example) and protocol names for their corresponding port numbers (https instead of 443) when possible.

Experiment with netstat. Execute **`netstat /?`** to see other options. Along with `-a` and `-n`, some of my favorites are `-b` and `-o`. When you want to run multiple options at a time, you don't need to specify a new `-` for each one. For example, you could write `netstat -b -a -n -o` as `netstat -bano` (with the letters appearing in any order). The `-b` option requires administrator privileges: type **`cmd`** in the Windows search box, right-click **Command Prompt**, select **Run As Administrator**, and click **Yes**.

NOTE Windows still comes with the netstat tool, but in the Linux world the net-tools package that included netstat has been replaced by the iproute2 package and its ss tool. The ss tool is faster and more powerful than netstat, but it is not covered on the CompTIA Network+ exam.

Layer 3 Protocols and Utilities

IP is a connectionless protocol, as it sends packets independently, without establishing a dedicated path or confirming delivery. IP is focused solely on addressing and routing, with no guarantee for packet delivery, order, or error correction. ICMP helps to fill in those gaps by sending error and informational messages when problems occur. Since IP handles packet delivery blindly, a protocol like ICMP is needed to give the network a way to speak up when things go wrong.

IP

As you learned in Chapter 1, IP encapsulates all messages at Layer 3 in a packet. It delivers packets from source to destination based on the IP addresses in the IP header portion of the packet. The data portion contains the upper-layer headers and data. As shown in Figure 4-5, the IP header contains many fields.

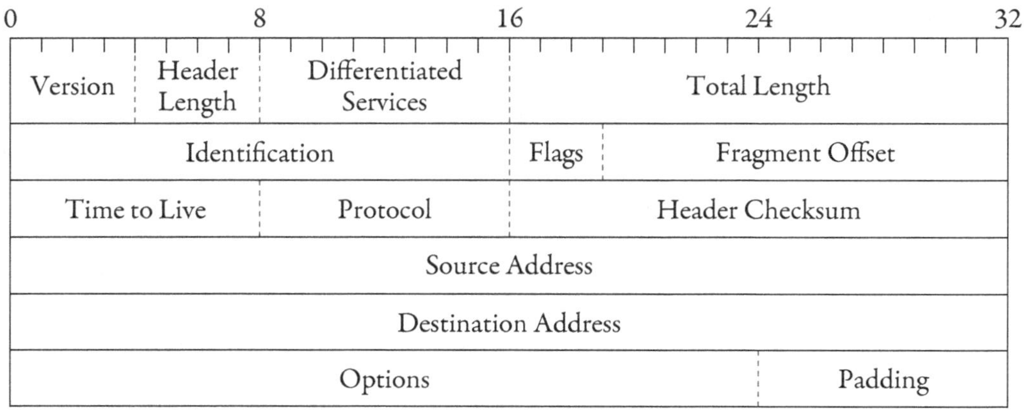

FIGURE 4-5 An IP header

For a reminder of what these fields do, see the previous chapter.

ICMP

ICMP is encapsulated directly inside of IP (a Layer 3 protocol encapsulated inside of another Layer 3 protocol). There are two types of ICMP messages: informational messages, such as the ICMP Echo request/reply messages, and error messages, such as "destination unreachable" messages, which are generated for many reasons (for example, when the router doesn't have a route for the destination network).

Every ICMP header starts off with the same three fields—Type, Code, and Checksum—and then varies based on the situation (see Figure 4-6).

Network diagnostic utilities like ping and tracert (Windows) and traceroute (non-Windows) use ICMP to provide control information to IP.

Whereas ping uses ICMP to determine if a destination is reachable ("Can you hear me?"), traceroute/tracert uses it to trace the path packets take through different networks to the eventual destination ("What are the step-by-step driving directions to your house?"), identifying each hop and where delays or failures happen.

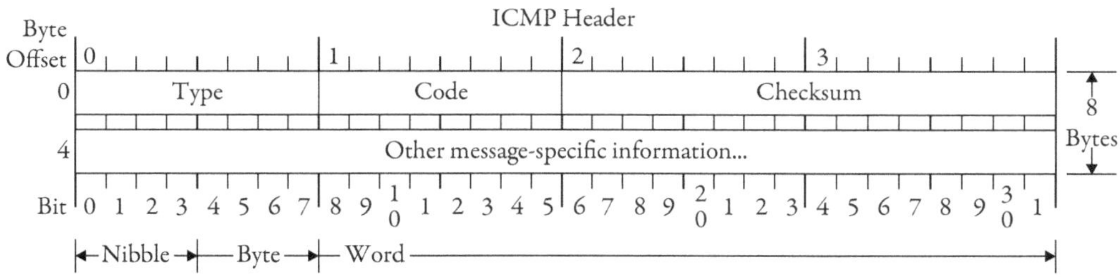

ICMP Message Types

Type code/Name
0 Echo Reply
3 Destination Unreachable
  0 Net Unreachable
  1 Host Unreachable
  2 Protocol Unreachable
  3 Port Unreachable
  4 Fragmentation required, and DF set
  5 Source Route Failed
  6 Destination Network Unknown
  7 Destination Host Unknown
  8 Source Host Isolated
  9 Network Administratively Prohibited
  10 Host Administratively Prohibited
  11 Network Unreachable for TOS

Type code/Name
3 Destination Unreachable (continued)
  12 Host Unreachable for TOS
  13 Communication Administratively Prohibited
4 Source Quench
5 Redirect
  0 Redirect Datagram for the Network
  1 Redirect Datagram for the Host
  2 Redirect Datagram for the TOS & Network
  3 Redirect Datagram for the TOS & Host
8 Echo
9 Router Advertisement
10 Router Selection

Type code/Name
11 Time Exceeded
  0 TTL Exceeded
  1 Fragment Reassembly Time Exceeded
12 Parameter Problem
  0 Pointer Problem
  1 Missing a Required Operand
  2 Bad Length
13 Timestamp
14 Timestamp Reply
15 Information Request
16 Information Reply
17 Address Mask Request
18 Address Mask Reply
30 Traceroute

Checksum

Checksum of ICMP header

RFC 792

Please refer to RFC 792 for the Internet Control Message Protocol (ICMP) specification.

FIGURE 4-6 An ICMP header

ping

You can use ping to test whether your device can communicate with another device. The ping tool sends ICMP Echo requests, hoping to elicit ICMP Echo replies. By default, Windows sends four ICMP Echo requests, so the output should show four replies, as shown in Figure 4-7.

The `ping` command can be followed by either an IP address (IPv4 or IPv6) or an FQDN. As Figure 4-7 also shows, if your system is IPv6 enabled, when pinging an FQDN, its corresponding IPv6 address will take precedence over IPv4, but you can force IPv4 with the `-4` option.

The ping tool isn't perfect. Sometimes ICMP will be filtered by a router or firewall en route to the destination or by the destination machine itself. If you get a "Request Timed Out" message instead of ICMP Echo replies, it doesn't necessarily mean you can't communicate with the destination machine. It could be that these ICMP probes are being blocked for security (a weak form of hindering an attacker's ability to quickly and easily discover devices) or efficiency (taking devices away from what they're normally doing just to say, "Yes, I'm here").

Experiment with ping. Execute **`ping /?`** to see other options.

```
Administrator: Command Prompt
Microsoft Windows [Version 10.0.19042.1110]
(c) Microsoft Corporation. All rights reserved.

C:\WINDOWS\system32>ping www.google.com

Pinging www.google.com [2607:f8b0:4006:81c::2004] with 32 bytes of data:
Reply from 2607:f8b0:4006:81c::2004: time=24ms
Reply from 2607:f8b0:4006:81c::2004: time=23ms
Reply from 2607:f8b0:4006:81c::2004: time=23ms
Reply from 2607:f8b0:4006:81c::2004: time=26ms

Ping statistics for 2607:f8b0:4006:81c::2004:
    Packets: Sent = 4, Received = 4, Lost = 0 (0% loss),
Approximate round trip times in milli-seconds:
    Minimum = 23ms, Maximum = 26ms, Average = 24ms

C:\WINDOWS\system32>ping -4 www.google.com

Pinging www.google.com [142.250.80.36] with 32 bytes of data:
Reply from 142.250.80.36: bytes=32 time=14ms TTL=116
Reply from 142.250.80.36: bytes=32 time=12ms TTL=116
Reply from 142.250.80.36: bytes=32 time=13ms TTL=116
Reply from 142.250.80.36: bytes=32 time=13ms TTL=116

Ping statistics for 142.250.80.36:
    Packets: Sent = 4, Received = 4, Lost = 0 (0% loss),
Approximate round trip times in milli-seconds:
    Minimum = 12ms, Maximum = 14ms, Average = 13ms

C:\WINDOWS\system32>
```

FIGURE 4-7 The output of two ping commands

traceroute/tracert

The ping utility is a Boolean tool: you either get a response or you don't. If a ping fails, you can use traceroute/tracert (tracert on Windows, traceroute on everything else) to identify where it failed. The traceroute/tracert tool will produce a list of all routers between you and a destination, finishing with an entry for the actual destination itself.

Check out Figure 4-8 for a tracert from my home in Rochester, New York, to *www.google.com*.

```
Administrator: Command Prompt
Microsoft Windows [Version 10.0.19042.1110]
(c) Microsoft Corporation. All rights reserved.

C:\WINDOWS\system32>tracert -4 www.google.com

Tracing route to www.google.com [172.217.6.196]
over a maximum of 30 hops:

  1     1 ms     1 ms     1 ms  192.168.0.1
  2     3 ms     5 ms     5 ms  100.65.88.1
  3     4 ms     4 ms     1 ms  172.16.0.3
  4    18 ms     5 ms     5 ms  172.16.0.9
  5    11 ms    15 ms    13 ms  lag-104.ear1.NewYork6.Level3.net [4.30.178.177]
  6     *        *        *     Request timed out.
  7    13 ms    12 ms    14 ms  Google-level3-100G.NewYork6.Level3.net [4.68.75.170]
  8    16 ms    14 ms    16 ms  108.170.225.2
  9    11 ms    13 ms    13 ms  108.170.237.205
 10    12 ms    14 ms    13 ms  lga25s54-in-f4.1e100.net [172.217.6.196]

Trace complete.

C:\WINDOWS\system32>
```

FIGURE 4-8 The output of a traceroute command

The first column in the output lists the hop number. A *hop* is a router or network that your packets pass through. The second, third, and fourth columns represent the time in milliseconds it took to hear back from a router at that particular hop—one time for each of the three attempts sent to each hop.

The fifth column shows either an IP address or FQDN and IP address (in square brackets) for each hop. The first hop in the list will always be your default gateway. The last "hop" in the list is the actual destination, so it isn't really a hop, even though the output makes it appear to be one. You can usually reach any destination machine in the world in 15 hops or fewer.

Some output from tracert might include asterisks (*) for one or more hop attempts. If one or two attempts have asterisks, either packets got lost or the ICMP Time-to-Live Exceeded messages took too long to arrive back on your system. If all three attempts for a hop have asterisks (as shown for the sixth hop in Figure 4-8), it's more likely that the router in question is filtering ICMP (all or just certain types of ICMP messages, like ICMP Echo requests) and is not sending ICMP Time-to-Live Exceeded messages. Alternatively, the router could be overworked and might not be capable of responding at that time. However, those routers will still forward the traffic (including ICMP Time-to-Live Exceeded messages) from routers closer to the destination, which is why after some asterisks, you'll see the output return to normal. If you see asterisks from a certain hop all the way down in the output, ICMP is being filtered from that point onward.

TRACERT FUN!

In a Windows Command Prompt, execute the following:

```
tracert -h 50 bad.horse
```

By default, tracert uses a maximum number of 30 hops (as shown at the top of all tracert output). The `-h` option is followed by a number to specify a new maximum number of hops—50 in this case—to allow the tracert to `bad.horse` to complete. Read about the `bad.horse` story at *a2wd.com/traceroute-bad-horse/*.

There used to be a similar one for Star Wars, but it is no longer active. Read about it in fpp's Y Combinator post at *news.ycombinator.com/item?id=5192656* and Ryan Werber's Beagle Networks post on the Internet Archive at *bit.ly/40mmYWX*.

Whenever I teach tracert in a course, I conclude the lesson with "Actually, guys, I'm sorry. Everything I just taught you is wrong. Sorry about that! Let's just watch this video that explains tracert better than anyone can." Now it's your turn to watch the legendary 2008 video by NextGenHacker101, which has close to 2 million views and still gets comments today: *youtu.be/SXmv8quf_xM*.

Windows tracert sends ICMP packets, while UNIX/Linux/macOS/Cisco traceroute sends UDP datagrams by default. Sometimes ICMP from a Windows tracert will be filtered, making a non-Windows traceroute more useful. Other times, the port numbers used in traceroute will be filtered, making a Windows tracert more useful.

Experiment with tracert. Execute **`tracert /?`** to see other options.

NOTE The Verizon Fios network handles ICMP packets differently, so if you use Windows tracert on Fios, you'll see everything as two hops, where the first hop is your default gateway and the second hop isn't really a hop but the actual destination. Some customers on the Verizon Fios Community forums suspect that this has something to do with Verizon's IPv6 deployment. By the time you're reading this, it could be fixed.

Chapter Review

Questions

1. If an FTP server and a web server are running on the same machine, how does network communication get to each of those services?
   A. They have different MAC addresses.
   B. They have different IP addresses.
   C. They have different ports.
   D. They have different logons.
2. DHCP and FTP servers listen for and send network traffic on:
   A. Well-known ports
   B. Registered ports
   C. Dynamic ports
   D. IP ports
3. Which of these does not use TCP?
   A. HTTP
   B. FTP
   C. DNS queries
   D. Email
4. Which of these does not use UDP?
   A. VoIP
   B. HTTPS (TLS)
   C. Live video stream
   D. DHCP
5. Which protocol is used for informational and error reporting?
   A. TCP
   B. UDP
   C. ICMP
   D. DNS

6. Which one of these ports isn't a secure port?
   A. 22
   B. 23
   C. 443
   D. 636
7. Which one of these ports would be used by a web browser?
   A. 80
   B. 443
   C. 587
   D. 52718
8. How do you open a port?
   A. Reboot your machine.
   B. Edit your firewall rules.
   C. Disable your firewall.
   D. Start a service that listens on that port.
9. Which of the following is true?
   A. TCP and UDP are both Layer 4 protocols.
   B. TCP is a Layer 4 protocol and UDP is a Layer 3 protocol.
   C. UDP is a Layer 4 protocol and TCP is a Layer 3 protocol.
   D. ICMP is a Layer 4 protocol and TCP is a Layer 3 protocol.
10. What tool allows you to see information about sockets, sessions, and connections on a Windows machine?
    A. ping
    B. netstat
    C. traceroute
    D. tracert

Answers

1. **C.** The operating system will differentiate server services running on the same machine by ports. On the same machine, all services are accessible through the same MAC address and IP address. Logons have nothing to do with the question.
2. **A.** These server services always send and receive on the same expected ports.

3. **C.** DNS uses UDP for standard queries and responses.
4. **B.** HTTPS (TLS) requires TCP.
5. **C.** ICMP is used for informational and error reporting.
6. **B.** Telnet servers send and receive over port 23 without cryptographically securing the data, so this port and Telnet should never be used today. Ports 22 (SSH), 443 (TLS), and 636 (LDAPS) all use cryptography to secure the data.
7. **D.** Web browsers use dynamic ports, which fall into the range 49152 through 65535, like other client services. Web servers use ports 80 and 443. SMTPS uses port 587.
8. **D.** Starting a service opens up the port that it sends and receives on. Firewalls don't open or close ports—they filter ports.
9. **A.** TCP and UDP are both Layer 4 protocols, and ICMP is a Layer 3 protocol.
10. **B.** The netstat tool shows sockets, sessions, and connections.

PART II

Network Infrastructure and Connectivity

IN THIS PART:

- CHAPTER 5: Routing
- CHAPTER 6: Switching
- CHAPTER 7: DNS and DHCP
- CHAPTER 8: IPv6
- CHAPTER 9: Cabling
- CHAPTER 10: Ethernet
- CHAPTER 11: Installing a Physical Network
- CHAPTER 12: Wireless Networking

Routing

IN THIS CHAPTER, YOU WILL LEARN HOW TO

- Describe how routers work, learn, and make decisions
- Explain the uses for static routing and dynamic routing
- Differentiate between an IGP and an EGP
- Distinguish between routing protocols, including OSPF, EIGRP, and BGP
- Establish router redundancy
- Parse and troubleshoot routing tables
- Connect, configure, and manage routers
- Troubleshoot routers and networks with utilities
- Explain how and why NAT is used

The true beauty and amazing power of networking lies in two words: *routing* and *switching*. Routing enables you to interconnect individual local area networks (LANs) to form wide area networks (WANs). Routers, the magic boxes that act as the interconnection points, have all the built-in smarts to inspect incoming packets and send them (with new frames encapsulating the packets) toward their eventual LAN destination. Routers are, for the most part, automatic. Once their initial configuration is complete, they require very little maintenance, because they can talk to each other to determine the best direction to send the packets.

Routers connect networks to other networks, while switches connect devices within a single network together. Switches, too, are magic boxes. They inspect incoming frames and forward them, as is, to one or more destination ports. For basic functionality, switches can be considered plug-and-play, as they start learning on their own, without any configuration necessary. Adding in configuration related to security and more, of course, is always a good thing.

Routers and switches, therefore, each have their own unique roles in the world of networking. Switching, and how switches work, will be covered in the next chapter. This chapter discusses many different aspects involving routers and routing, including router decision making, dynamic routing, redundancy, routing tables, working with routers, troubleshooting, and Network Address Translation (NAT).

Historical/Conceptual

Introduction to Routers

A router forwards packets based on their destination IP address, meaning it works at Layer 3 (Network layer) of the OSI model.

Unlike switches, routers don't connect devices together; instead, they connect networks together. Routers also connect to other routers that are connected to other routers that are connected to other routers, and so forth. This allows traffic from one network to travel to any interconnected network via any number of routers and allows the return traffic to make its way back to the device that initiated the traffic on the originating network. Think of routers as the highway exchanges that connect different cities and states together. Just like highways allow you to go from Rochester to Staten Island, routers allow your network traffic to reach devices on other networks in the same building, another building, another city, another state, another country, or even another continent.

Classically, routers are dedicated boxes that contain at least two ports, or connections, although they often contain many more. The Ubiquiti EdgeRouter Pro shown in Figure 5-1 has eight ports (plus the Console port, which is used for maintenance and configuration). The two "working" ports—labeled WAN (or sometimes Internet) and LAN—provide connection points between the line that goes to the internet service provider (in this case through a cable modem) and the local network. The port marked LTE is a failover to a cellular modem connection in case the cable service goes down.

FIGURE 5-1 The Ubiquiti EdgeRouter Pro router

Most techs today first encounter routers with the ubiquitous small office/home office (SOHO) wireless units (Figure 5-2) that enable PCs to connect to a cable modem, DSL modem, or, for fiber ISPs, an optical network terminal (ONT). The typical SOHO router, however, serves multiple functions, often combining a router, a switch, an access point (AP), and other features like a firewall, a DHCP server, a DNS server, a NAT gateway, and much more into the box we call "router."

FIGURE 5-2 A SOHO router

Figure 5-3 shows the logical diagram for a two-port router, whereas Figure 5-4 shows the diagram for a SOHO router.

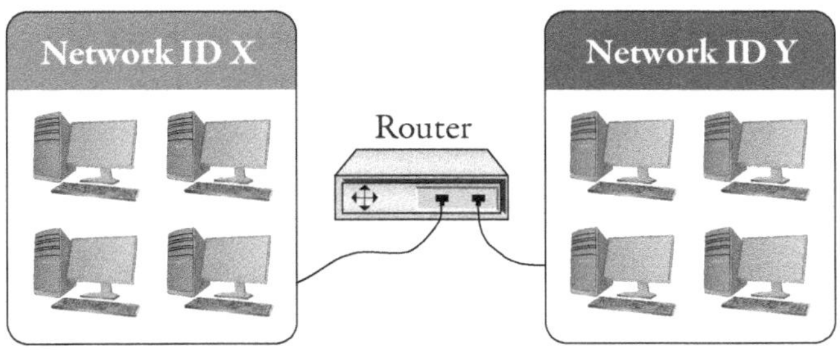

FIGURE 5-3 A router connecting two networks

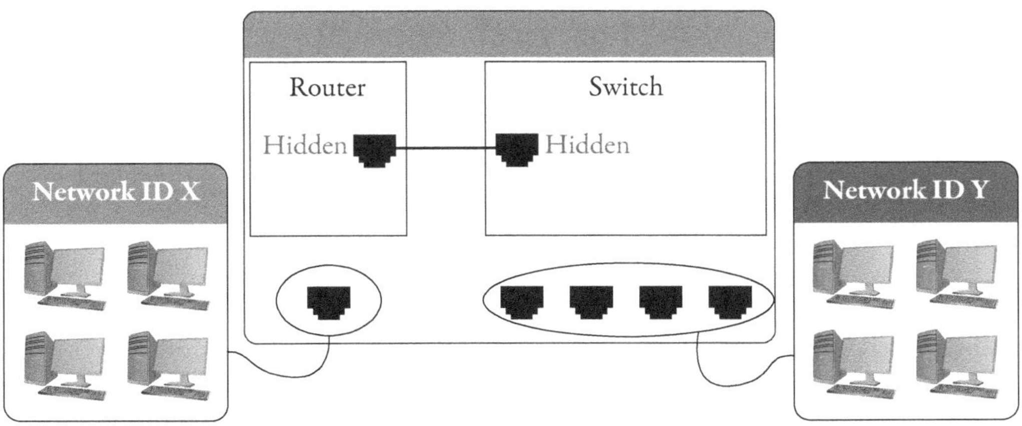

FIGURE 5-4 A SOHO router connecting two networks

Note that both boxes connect two networks. They differ in that one side of the SOHO router connects directly to a built-in switch. That's convenient—you don't have to buy a separate switch to connect multiple computers to the home router. It's like a mini switch and mini router are in the box, but they're implemented through circuitry and chips.

Test Specific

When a router receives a packet destined for an IP address, the router consults its routing table to look for a matching route. If it finds one, it then determines which router should receive the packet next. If the router finds no matching route for the destination network but has a default route configured for unknown destinations, it will use the default route to forward the packet. Without either a matching route or a default route, the router will drop the packet and send an Internet Control Message Protocol (ICMP) error message back to the source.

Internet backbone routers now contain over one million (IPv4 and IPv6) routes in their routing tables. On internal autonomous systems, there are far fewer. An *autonomous system* (AS) represents a collection of networks that share a single routing policy and are under one administrative authority, like an ISP or major entity like Rochester Institute of Technology. Why would RIT prefer a collection of internal networks to a single network? Well, for one, think back to the ARP stories in Chapter 2. ARP requests and all other broadcast traffic will always reach and be processed by every single device on a network. So, one reason why we might want multiple networks interconnected by routers instead of one big flat network is to reduce the size of the broadcast domain (devices that can hear each other's broadcast traffic). Instead of broadcasts tying up the bandwidth and processing of all devices on a network, we're lowering the number of broadcasts that will proliferate through our network and the number of devices that can hear them. It's akin to why each class at RIT is taught in a room by itself. If we had just one humongous auditorium where all classes were taught simultaneously, my students would have to listen and try to understand all the other professors and classes. That would take their attention away from me and my lessons.

Another reason why multiple networks are preferred to one big flat network is for security purposes. Routers provide security in the form of an access control list (ACL) to filter traffic by source IP address, destination IP address, protocols, and even ports. This allows you to control access to and from certain devices and resources much more effectively than if everything were on the same network. Multiple networks also enable hierarchical network design and make troubleshooting easier by allowing you to isolate problems to a specific network.

As autonomous systems, independent of ISPs, entities like RIT are able to maintain routing tables and exchange routing information with multiple ISPs. As traffic is ready to leave the AS, the routers decide which ISP and which ISP connection (assuming an organization has multiple connections to a single ISP for fault tolerance and load-balancing purposes) to send the traffic to for the most efficient packet delivery.

At home, we don't have to exchange any information about networks with our ISP. There's a default route in our router that basically says, "Send any traffic for anywhere but my local home network to the ISP's router." Why would we want the overhead of exchanging routes? If the connection to our ISP goes down, we're not sending any communication from our network anyway. Besides, our home routers don't have the memory or processing power for a million-plus routes! However, inside a company, within an AS, routers need a dynamic way to exchange information about the internal networks as well as to reach the edge router—the router that connects to the company's ISP for packets destined for external networks. This is where routing configuration and protocols come into play.

Static Routing

For *stub* networks (networks with only one path in and out, like from a house to an ISP) and *linear* networks (a small infrastructure with a few routers not arranged hierarchically), static routing makes sense. *Static routing* is where a network engineer programs the routes packets should take from a router to a destination network. This involves telling routers the next hop IP address—an IP address of the neighboring router—for a destination network. (Remember, a *hop* is each network/router through which a packet passes.)

Take a moment and flip back to Figures 2-5 and 2-6 in Chapter 2. Notice that R1 has only one way to get packets to the 10.10.4.0/24 network: through R2's left interface, which has an IP address of 10.10.2.99. That route and all the other routes in that topology are statically configured, because if an interface or router goes down, there's nothing else that can be done. There are no other paths into networks, and there is no hierarchy in the topology.

With linear topologies and stub networks, you don't need any overhead or the additional processing of a dynamic routing protocol.

Dynamic Routing

In cases where there are multiple ways in and out of a network, dynamic routing makes sense. *Dynamic routing* is a process that routers use to update routes in order to accommodate certain conditions, such as when a line goes down because of an electrical blackout. Dynamic routing protocols enable routers to work around such problems.

Dynamic routing protocols really shine when you manage a complex network. What if your routers look like Figure 5-5? Do you really want to try to set up all these routes statically? What happens when something changes? Can you imagine the administrative nightmare?

Dynamic routing protocols enable routers to talk to each other so that they know what's happening not only to the other directly connected routers but also to routers two or more hops away.

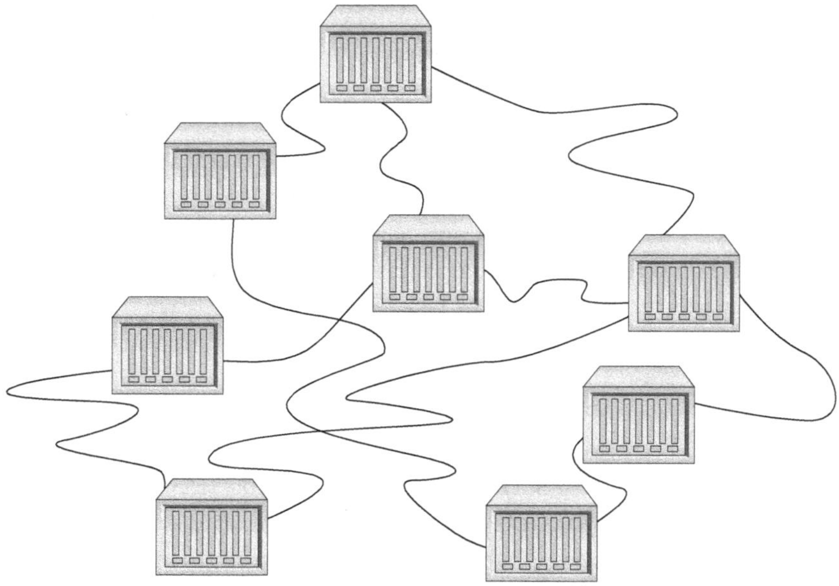

FIGURE 5-5 Lots of routers

Dynamic routing protocols have four main functions:

- Learning about networks and how to get to them from other routers.
- Telling the other routers about the networks they know about themselves.
- Picking the best route if there are multiple routes available to get to a destination network.
- Recovering from a link going down and selecting a new path (known as *fault tolerance*) and then restoring the original best path when the problem is fixed. For example, if an accident or construction prevents you from taking your normal route to work, you'll pick the next best way there. When the accident or construction is cleared, you'll return to taking the original best path.

Metrics are values that the routers use to determine the best way to get to a destination network when there are multiple paths available. Unlike the routers in our homes, an industry-level router often has multiple connections to get to a particular network. This is the beauty of routers combined with dynamic protocols. If a router suddenly loses a connection, it has alternative routes to the same network. It's the role of the metric to help the router decide which route to use first as well as which to use when something happens to the primary or best route.

Consider Figure 5-6, which shows a networked router with two routes to Network B: Route 1 has a metric of 1, and Route 2 has a metric of 10.

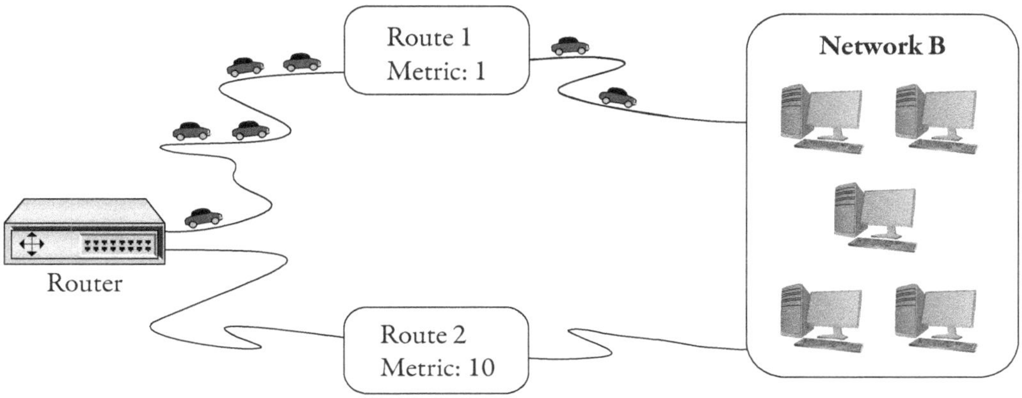

FIGURE 5-6 Two routes to the same network

NOTE For non-linear network topologies, when a router has multiple routes to the same destination network, the network engineer must assign different metrics for each route that is manually configured. With dynamic routing protocols, the routers automatically calculate the proper metric for each route. If routes to the same destination network have the same metric, the router will *load balance* the traffic, meaning it splits packets evenly across each available path (two paths = 50/50, three paths = 33/33/33, etc.).

The route with the lowest metric always wins. Thus, the router in Figure 5-6 will always use Route 1. If that route suddenly stopped working, the router would automatically switch to Route 2 (Figure 5-7). This is how the entire internet works! It's nothing more than a whole bunch of big, powerful routers connected to lots of other big, powerful routers. Connections go up and down from time to time, and routers (with multiple routes) constantly talk to each other, sharing when a connection goes down and automatically switching to alternate routes.

NOTE If a routing table has multiple valid routes for a particular IP address destination, it always chooses the route with the lowest metric, just like you'd opt to pay less money in tolls to get to a certain destination.

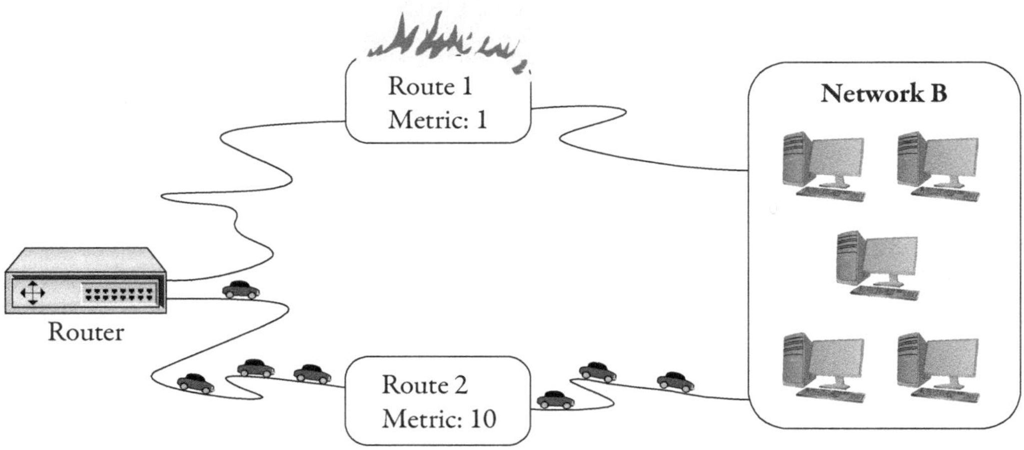

FIGURE 5-7 When one route no longer works, the router automatically switches to an alternate route.

Dynamic routing protocols use different criteria to calculate their own routing metric. As you learn about these protocols, you'll see how each calculates its own metrics differently. The need for these standardized approaches became critical as networks grew larger.

The explosive growth of the internet in the 1980s required a fundamental reorganization of its structure, and one big part of this reorganization was the call to make the "big" routers use a standardized dynamic routing protocol. Implementing this standard was much harder than you might think because the entities that govern how the internet works do so in a highly decentralized fashion. Even the organized groups, such as the Internet Society (ISOC), the Internet Assigned Numbers Authority (IANA), and the Internet Engineering Task Force (IETF), are made up of many individuals, companies, and government organizations from across the globe. Because of this decentralization, the reorganization process took a lot of time and many meetings.

What came out of this process was the organizational concept of the autonomous system. The network or collection of networks in an AS share a unified "policy" regarding how they exchange traffic with other ASes. These policies are usually economic or political decisions made by the entity that administers the AS, such as Rochester Institute of Technology or Finger Lakes Community College.

EXAM TIP To learn more about AS4385 (Rochester Institute of Technology), see *bgp.he.net/AS4385*. For more on AS394988 (Finger Lakes Community College), see *bgp.he.net/AS394988*.

Each AS is assigned a special globally unique Autonomous System Number (ASN) by the IANA. Originally, ASNs were 16-bit numbers, like RIT's ASN 4385. Today, ASNs can be 32 bits, like FLCC's ASN 394988, but they remain backward-compatible with existing 16-bit numbers, allowing older ASNs to coexist with newer assignments.

Dynamic routing protocols fall into two main categories: those used within an AS (IGPs), and those used between different ASes (EGPs).

IGP

An Interior Gateway Protocol (IGP) is a routing protocol that allows routers within an AS to communicate with each other, sharing information about the networks they're directly or indirectly connected to. After these messages are passed between the routers, each router forms an idea of the topology and determines the best way to get to it a destination network. Nowadays, the two main IGPs are Open Shortest Path First (OSPF) and Cisco's Enhanced Interior Gateway Routing Protocol (EIGRP).

OSPF

OSPF is an open standard and the most used IGP in the world. Most large enterprises use OSPF on their internal networks. OSPF converges dramatically fast. *Convergence* is achieved when all routers in an autonomous system see the same topology and each has its routing table updated with the current topology.

Routers running OSPF initially send out *Hello messages*, looking for other OSPF routers to form *neighborships* (neighbor relationships) with. It's the same way you'd introduce yourself to your neighbors when you move into a new house. OSPF neighbors are routers that exchange routing information with each other. Two routers, each with an interface connected to a common network, will become neighbors, provided they have compatible parameters.

After two adjacent routers form a neighborship through the Hello messages, they exchange information about routers and networks through *link-state advertisement* (LSA) messages. Each router stores LSAs in its *link-state database* (LSDB). Initially, each router in the neighbor pair lists its LSAs, and then requests the LSAs it doesn't have in its LSDB from the other router.

A router can't directly use LSAs to update its routing table. LSAs are like puzzle pieces, so a router needs to use math—specifically, the Dijkstra Shortest Path First (SPF) algorithm, which influenced the protocol's name—to get a view of the topology and figure out the best path to each destination network. These routes are then added to its routing table along with the next hop IP address that will receive the packet en route to the destination.

LSAs are sourced by each router and flooded (sent out of all ports except the port on which the LSA was heard) from router to router, as shown in Figure 5-8, which shows:

- R5 detecting a link coming up for a new LAN and sending an LSA about that link to R1, R6, and R8
- R1 sending the LSA to R2, which sends it to R3, which sends it to R4, which sends it to R7
- R6 sending the LSA to R7
- R8 sending the LSA to R9, which sends it to R7

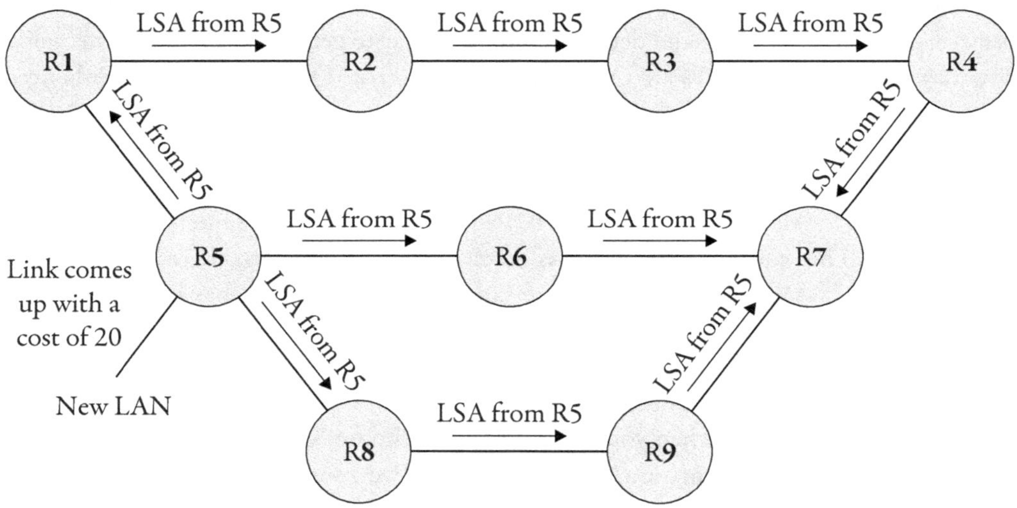

FIGURE 5-8 LSAs flooded between routers

Once all the routers communicate, they individually decide their own optimal routes, and convergence happens almost immediately. If a route goes down, OSPF routers quickly recompute a new route with stored LSAs.

OSPF computes the best path to each destination network based on the total cost of the path. The cost is inversely proportional to interface bandwidth, as faster interfaces like Gigabit or 10-Gigabit Ethernet will (after a change to a default setting) have lower costs, making them preferable for routing. The routers choose the route with the lowest total cost, even if that means more hops. In other words, a packet could go through more routers (hops) to get to a destination if that option is faster. If a packet goes through three hops where the routers are connected by fiber, for example, as opposed to two hops via a slow 1.544 Mbps link, the packet will get to its destination quicker. We make these decisions every day as humans, too. I'd rather drive more miles on the highway to get somewhere quicker than drive fewer miles on local streets, where the speed limit is much lower and I'll be slowed down by red lights and stop signs.

Notice in Figure 5-9 that R7 can send packets destined to the new LAN off R5 via R4, R6, or R9. Earlier, R7 heard LSAs about the new LAN from R4, R6, and R9. Knowing that any of those three routers can be the next hop for packets destined for the new LAN, R7 now needs to determine the best choice for the next hop. Will R7 send packets destined for the new LAN to R4, R6, or R9?

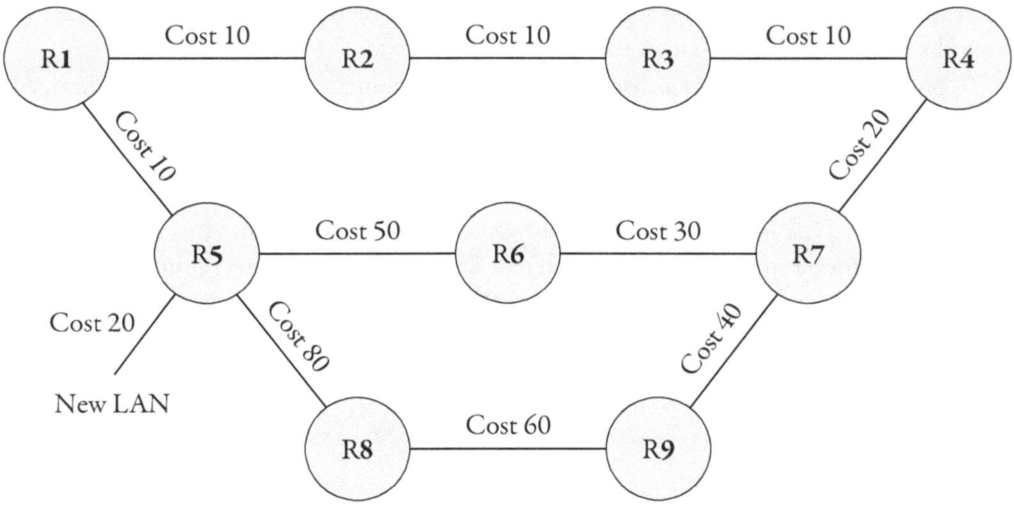

FIGURE 5-9 OSPF cost calculation

What is the "best" route? It's the one with the smallest cumulative cost, just like taking a road trip and paying the least possible amount in gas and tolls. A link's cost is an egress value, added to the cumulative cost as packets leave an interface. R7 has three options:

1. R7 to R4 to R3 to R2 to R1 to R5 is a cost of 80 (20 + 10 + 10 + 10 + 10 + 20).
2. R7 to R6 to R5 is a cost of 100 (30 + 50 + 20).
3. R7 to R9 to R8 to R5 is a cost of 200 (40 + 60 + 80 + 20).

Notice that option 1 has more hops than option 2, but a lower cost. In fact, it's the lowest of all three options, so R7 will install R4's IP address on the interface connected to R7 as the next hop IP address for packets destined for the new LAN.

In OSPF, an interface's cost is inversely proportional to its bandwidth, so slower interfaces have higher costs and faster interfaces have lower costs, making them preferable for routing. However, interface types including Fast Ethernet, Gigabit Ethernet, 10 Gigabit Ethernet, 40 Gigabit Ethernet, and 100 Gigabit Ethernet all have an OSPF cost of 1, which OSPF treats as equal, meaning it can't find the optimal route for the packets. The reason is that OSPF's formula for calculating cost was designed before the newer interface types came along, when you were basically limited to Serial interfaces (1.544 Mbps cost of 64), Ethernet interfaces (10 Mbps cost of 10), and Fast Ethernet interfaces (100 Mbps, cost of 1). Fortunately, there are commands to change the default cost in multiple ways, which will result in OSPF giving priority to the faster interfaces.

Beyond the cost calculation problem, OSPF networks face another scalability issue. Every time a link (or interface) goes up or down, a Type 1 (Router) LSA is sent, triggering every router to recalculate SPF. This processing-intensive operation can slow down convergence for networks with hundreds of routers and thousands of subnets.

To prevent this, OSPF uses *areas*, administrative groupings of interconnected routers. All OSPF networks use areas, even if there is only one area. A single-area OSPF deployment or the central (backbone) area in a multi-area deployment gets assigned an Area ID of 0 or 0.0.0.0. All traffic between areas must go through the backbone area. Now, when there are multiple OSPF areas, the Type 1 LSA triggers only the routers in the corresponding area to recalculate SPF, not every router in the network. A different LSA (Type 3, Summary) summarizes which networks are reachable and at what cost, and the routers can quickly update their routing tables based on this summary.

OSPF not only scales to large networks but also supports authentication and prevents loops. For good measure, every 30 minutes, OSPF refloods all LSAs to ensure nothing is stale or outdated.

EXAM TIP OSPF corrects link failures and creates convergence almost immediately, making it the routing protocol of choice in most large enterprise networks. OSPF version 2 is used for IPv4 networks, and OSPF version 3 includes updates to support IPv6.

EIGRP

Cisco's proprietary EIGRP uses both bandwidth and delay as metrics by default. Bandwidth is calculated from the slowest link on the route (you're only as quick as your slowest link); while delay for a link is calculated as a fixed value proportional to the interface bandwidth. EIGRP adds up all these values from a router to a destination network, and that number represents the delay value (smaller is better).

To select paths to destination networks and establish a loop-free topology, EIGRP uses the *diffusing update algorithm* (DUAL). Routers running EIGRP use a topology table with information on the advertised networks, neighbors, metrics, and values for metric calculation. Routers running EIGRP establish neighborship adjacencies and send peers their entire routing table initially but only updates thereafter.

EIGRP routers maintain *successor* routes (the actual route used for a destination network) and *feasible successor* routes (the second-best route for a destination). If a successor route is no longer valid, the feasible successor route immediately becomes the successor route. At the same time, routers send updates for that path, as the EIGRP metrics have changed. Each router then runs DUAL, and the successor and feasible successor routers may change since the metrics are now different.

EGP

An Exterior Gateway Protocol (EGP) is a routing protocol that allows routers from different ASes to communicate with each other and exchange routing information. The only EGP in use today is Border Gateway Protocol (BGP), which is used across the entire internet and has been since the mid-1990s.

NOTE The original EGP was . . . EGP. It was replaced with BGP in the 1990s. EGP couldn't handle the growing size and complexity of the internet, whereas BGP supports scalable, policy-based routing between autonomous systems.

BGP

BGP is the glue of the internet, connecting all ASes. The current version of BGP is BGP-4. BGP implements and supports *route aggregation*, a way to simplify routing tables into manageable levels. Rather than trying to keep track of every network on the internet, the backbone routers track the shortest common network ID(s) of all the routes managed by each AS.

EXAM TIP A company's edge routers will run both an IGP and an EGP (BGP).

For example, if all North American IP addresses start with 198.0.0.0 (using the subnet mask of 255.0.0.0), all routers from South America could have one entry point to routers in North America for all addresses that start with 198.0.0.0 (regardless of the values of other octets). Then, all North American routers will have more specific routes for each ISP. For example, one ISP could control all 198.133.0.0 (using the subnet mask of 255.255.0.0) addresses, and another ISP could control all 198.134.0.0 (using the subnet mask of 255.255.0.0) addresses. Then, each ISP will have more specific routes for each of its customer companies. For example, the first ISP could have customers with IP addresses starting with 198.133.1.0 (using the subnet mask of 255.255.255.0), 198.133.2.0 (using the subnet mask of 255.255.255.0), and so on.

EXAM TIP BGP usually implies eBGP (External BGP), but there's also an iBGP (Internal BGP). iBGP allows routers within the same AS to exchange external routing information, leading to more efficient routing and coordination. Without iBGP, only the edge routers connected to other ASes would know about the external BGP routes. iBGP also supports fault tolerance, load balancing, and policies to control traffic flows (and even block certain traffic) within an AS. Thus, iBGP doesn't function like an IGP, since it doesn't discover internal network topology or calculate paths within the AS.

BGP has many metrics, but its decision-making usually comes down to the following three:

LOCAL PREFERENCE If an AS has multiple ways out, this locally significant value (hence the name) is used to determine which exit point to use. Bigger is better. For example, in Figure 5-10, notice that there are two ways out of AS4385, one through R1 and one through R2. Since the Local Preference value for R2 (75) is greater than the Local Preference value for R1 (52), BGP chooses R2 as the outbound router instead of R1. Think of a room with two doors, on one of which is a sign reading "Use other door."

If there is a tie, the next metric BGP checks is Autonomous System Path.

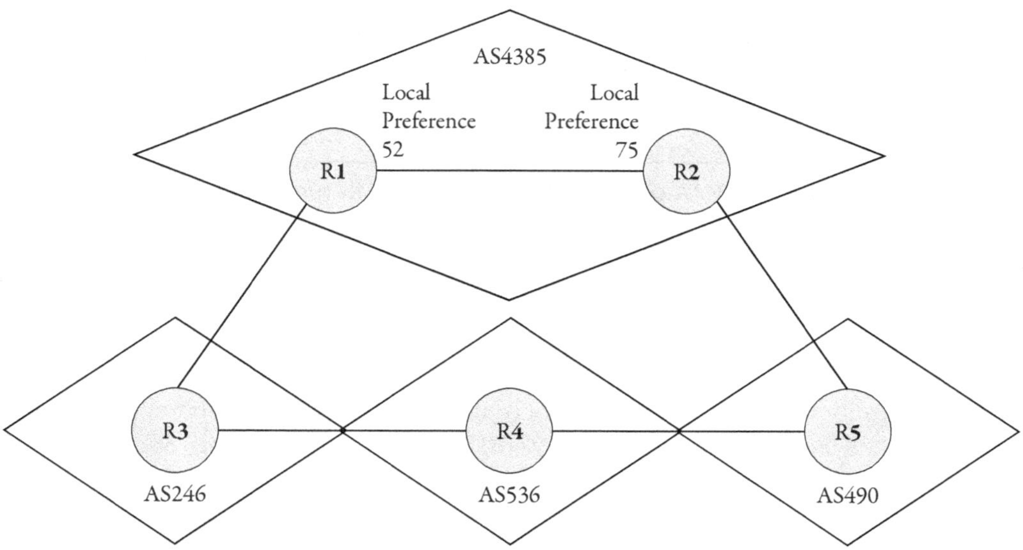

FIGURE 5-10 Local Preference

AUTONOMOUS SYSTEM PATH Autonomous System Path refers to how many ASes the packet must pass through. Lower is better. For example, as shown in Figure 5-11, to get to any of the 129.21.0.0/16 subnets, AS1 has two options:

1. AS1 to AS2 to AS4 to AS 4385 (three ASes)
2. AS1 to AS3 to AS4385 (two ASes)

Since option 2 involves traversing through two ASes, and option 1 involves traversing through three ASes, packets from AS1 destined for any of the 129.21.0.0/16 subnets will be sent to AS3 and not AS2. Think of the number of doors you have to go through to get to a room in a large office building. You'd probably want to open as few as possible.

If there is a tie, the next metric BGP checks is Multi-Exit Discriminator.

MULTI-EXIT DISCRIMINATOR MED is a value advertised to AS neighbors to indicate the preferred entry point into your network. Lower is better. In Figure 5-12, AS625 is telling R3 of AS78 to send packets into AS625 via R1 and not R2, since R1's MED is 12, which is lower than R2's MED, which is 14. Think of a building with multiple doors that you can enter through, one of which (R2) says "Use other door." The difference between this analogy and the one used for Local Preference is that this is for inbound traffic, while Local Preference is for outbound traffic.

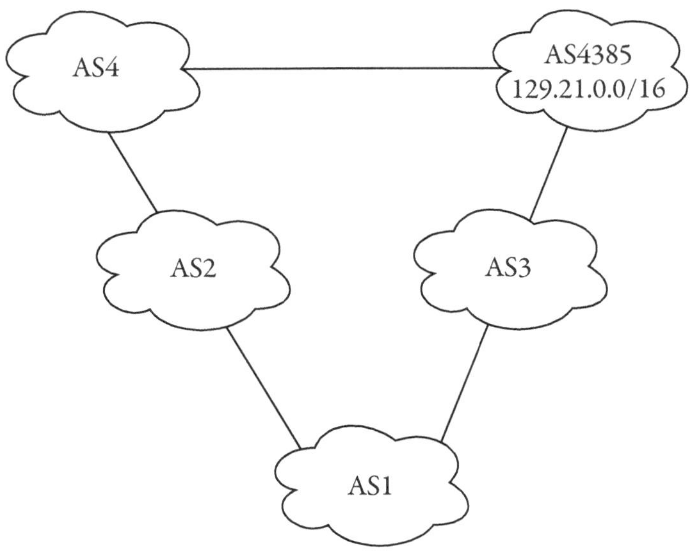

FIGURE 5-11 AS path

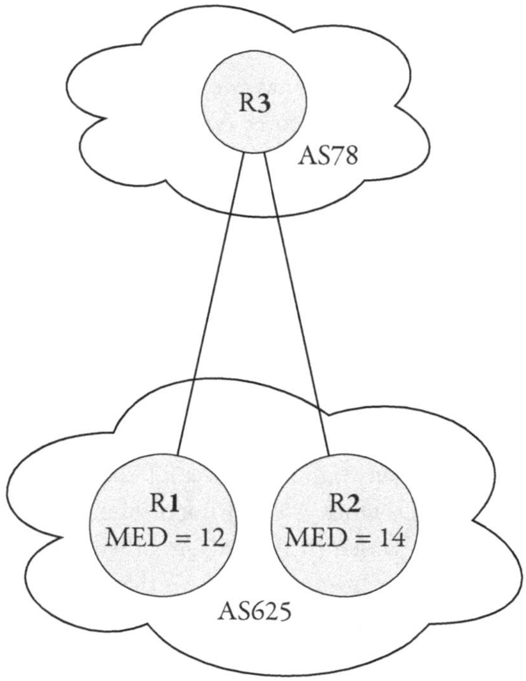

FIGURE 5-12 Multi-Exit Discriminator

NOTE BGP supports policies for limiting which and how other routers may access an ISP, but many times BGP (sometimes with DNS issues) is behind an attack or a misconfiguration that wreaks havoc for the internet as a whole. I wrote an article about it at *linkedin.com/pulse/weissmans-way-understanding-facebook-outage-jonathan-s-weissman*.

ADMINISTRATIVE DISTANCE

When a router has learned routes to the same destination network from multiple sources (such as different routing protocols or a combination of a routing protocol and static routes), it uses a value called *administrative distance* to determine which route to use. Administrative distance measures the trustworthiness of the routing information source and is locally significant. As you might have guessed, lower is better. The following table shows Cisco's AD chart, which contains routing protocols past and present not covered by the CompTIA Network+ Exam Objectives.

ROUTE SOURCE	DEFAULT DISTANCE VALUES
Connected interface	0
Static route	1
Enhanced Interior Gateway Routing Protocol (EIGRP) summary route	5
Border Gateway Protocol (BGP)	20
Internal EIGRP	90
Interior Gateway Routing Protocol (IGRP)	100
Open Shortest Path First (OSPF)	110
Intermediate System-to-Intermediate System (IS-IS)	115
Routing Information Protocol (RIP)	120
Exterior Gateway Protocol (EGP), a protocol with the same name as the category that was replaced by BGP	140
On Demand Routing (ODR)	160
External EIGRP	170
Internal BGP	200
Unknown (the router doesn't trust a route's source or install the route in the routing table with an administrative distance of 255)	255

Working with Routers

Understanding how routers work is one thing. Actually making them work is a different animal altogether. This section examines routing tables, router connections (physical and otherwise) and technologies, router redundancy, and Network Address Translation.

Routing Tables

Routing begins as packets come into the router for handling. The router immediately strips off the Layer 2 frame and queues the resulting packet based on when it arrived (unless it's using Quality of Service, in which case it can be prioritized by a wide array of factors—Chapter 15 takes a closer look at QoS).

The router inspects each packet's destination IP address and then sends the packet out the correct port. To perform this inspection, every router consults its routing table to determine exactly where to send the packets. This table is the key to understanding and controlling the process of forwarding packets to their proper destination. Figure 5-13 shows a routing table for a typical home router. Each row in this routing table defines a single route. Each column identifies one of two specific criteria. Some columns define which packets are for the route, and other columns define which port to send them out of.

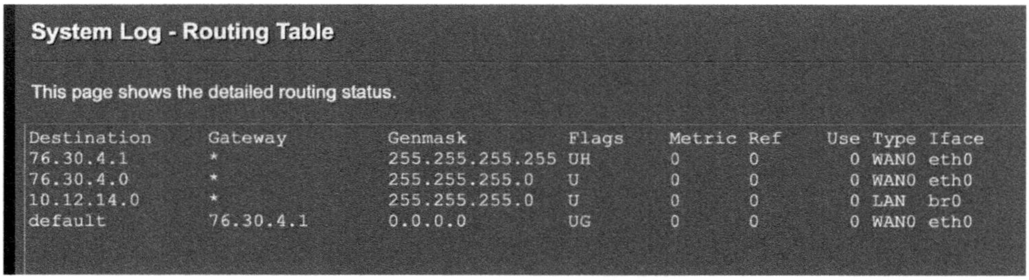

System Log - Routing Table

This page shows the detailed routing status.

Destination	Gateway	Genmask	Flags	Metric	Ref	Use	Type	Iface
76.30.4.1	*	255.255.255.255	UH	0	0	0	WAN0	eth0
76.30.4.0	*	255.255.255.0	U	0	0	0	WAN0	eth0
10.12.14.0	*	255.255.255.0	U	0	0	0	LAN	br0
default	76.30.4.1	0.0.0.0	UG	0	0	0	WAN0	eth0

FIGURE 5-13 Routing table for a home router

The router in this example has only two ports internally, shown in the `Type` and `Iface` (Interface) columns: one port that connects to an ISP (labeled `WAN0` and `eth0`, respectively) and another port that connects to the router's built-in switch (labeled `LAN` and `br0`, respectively; *br* stands for *bridge*, indicating a switching function). Due to the small number of ports, this router table has only four routes. Wait a minute! Four routes and only two ports? That's correct: there's *not* a one-to-one correlation of routes to ports, as you'll soon see. Let's inspect this routing table in more detail.

READING AND INTERPRETING ROUTING TABLE ENTRIES

From left to right, Figure 5-13 shows the following columns:

- **`Destination`** A defined network ID. Every network ID directly connected to one of the router's ports is always listed here.
- **`Gateway`** The IP address for the next hop router—in other words, where the packet should go. If the outgoing packet is for a network ID that's not directly connected to the router, the Gateway column specifies the IP address of a router that the packet should be sent to. That next router then handles the packet, and your router is done. If the network ID is directly connected to the router, you don't need a gateway. In that case, most routing tables put either `*`, `0.0.0.0`, or `On-link` in this column.
- **`Genmask`** The name this router and certain Linux distributions use for a subnet mask (introduced in Chapter 2), which defines a network ID.
- **`Flags`** Descriptors for the destination. For instance, `U` means that the route is up and working. `H` means this route is a host, or in other words, a complete 32-bit IP address (not broken up into a network ID) for a system on the network, not a subnet. `G` means this is the route to the gateway.

- **`Metric`, `Ref`, AND `Use`** Values used for picking the best route to a destination. Most small networks are simple enough that these values will all be `0`.
- **`Type` AND `Iface`** Which of the router's ports to use and what type of ports they are. This router uses the Linux names for interfaces, `eth0` and `br0`. Other routing tables use the port's IP address or some other description. Some routers, for example, use `Gig0/0/0` or `Gig0/0/1`.

The router uses the combination of the destination and subnet mask (genmask) to see if a packet matches a route. Since a routing table actually looks like a table, you might assume that the router starts at the top of the table and marches down until it finds the correct route. That's not accurate, though. The router compares the destination IP address on a packet to every route listed in the routing table and only then sends the packet out. If a packet matches more than one route, the router uses the most specific route.

The most important trick to reading a routing table is to remember that a zero (`0`) means "anything." For example, in Figure 5-11, the third route's destination network ID is 10.12.14.0. You can compare that to the subnet mask (255.255.255.0) to confirm that this is a /24 network. This tells you that any value between 1 and 254 is acceptable for the last value in the 10.12.14.0/24 network ID. So, if you had an incoming packet with a destination IP address of 10.12.14.26, the router would quickly determine that the packet matches the third route.

A properly configured router must have a route for any packet it might encounter. Routing tables tell you a lot about the network connections. From just this single routing table, for example, you can draw the diagram in Figure 5-14.

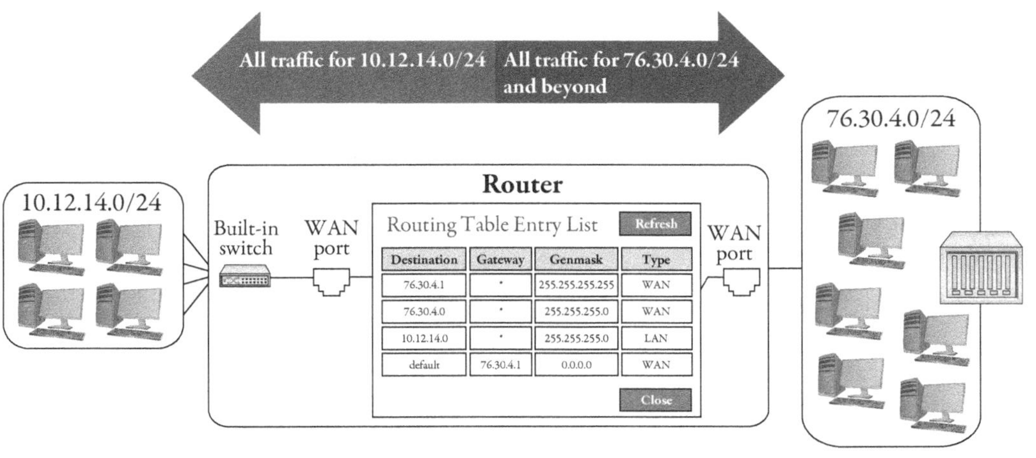

FIGURE 5-14 The network based on the routing table in Figure 5-13

Take another look at Figure 5-13. Notice the last route. How do you know the 76.30.4.1 port connects to another network? The fourth line of the routing table shows the default route for this router, and (almost) every router has one. In this case it's actually labeled `default`. You'll also commonly see the default destination listed as `0.0.0.0`. You can interpret this line as follows:

(Any destination address)	*(with any subnet mask)*	*(forward it to 76.30.4.1)*	*(using the WAN port)*
Destination	Gateway	Genmask	Type
Default	76.30.4.1	0.0.0.0	WAN

The default route is very important because it tells the router exactly what to do with every incoming packet *unless* another line in the routing table lists another more specific route. Interpret the other lines of the routing table in Figure 5-13 in the same fashion:

(Any packet for the 10.12.14.0/24 network)	*(don't use a gateway)*	*(just ARP on the LAN interface to get the MAC address and send it directly to the recipient)*	
Destination	Gateway	Genmask	Type
10.12.14.0	*	255.255.255.0	LAN

(Any packet for the 76.30.4.0/24 network)	*(don't use a gateway)*	*(just ARP on the WAN interface to get the MAC address and send it directly to the recipient)*	
Destination	Gateway	Genmask	Type
76.30.4.0	*	255.255.255.0	WAN

NOTE There are two places where you'll find routers that do not have default routes: isolated (as in not on the internet) internetworks, where every router knows about every connected network, and the monstrous "Tier One" backbone, where you'll find the routers that make the main connections of the internet.

EXAMINING ROUTING TABLES IN OTHER DEVICES

Routers aren't the only devices that use routing tables. In fact, every node (computer, printer, etc.) on the network also does. The main difference is that these routing tables also include rules for routing broadcast and multicast packets.

At first, this may seem silly—doesn't every computer have a single connection that all traffic has to flow through? Every packet sent out of your computer uses the routing table to figure out where the packet should go, whether directly to a node on your network or to your gateway. Consider the following example of a routing table in Windows. This machine connects to the home router described earlier, so you'll recognize the IP addresses it uses. (The results screen of the `route print` command is very long, even on a basic system, so I've deleted some output for brevity's sake.)

```
C:\>route print
IPv4 Route Table
===========================================================================
Active Routes:
Network Destination          Netmask       Gateway      Interface   Metric
            0.0.0.0          0.0.0.0    10.12.14.1    10.12.14.201      25
          127.0.0.0        255.0.0.0       On-link       127.0.0.1     306
          127.0.0.1  255.255.255.255       On-link       127.0.0.1     306
    127.255.255.255  255.255.255.255       On-link       127.0.0.1     306
         10.12.14.0    255.255.255.0       On-link    10.12.14.201     281
       10.12.14.201  255.255.255.255       On-link       127.0.0.1     281
       10.12.14.255  255.255.255.255       On-link    10.12.14.201     281
          224.0.0.0        240.0.0.0       On-link       127.0.0.1     306
          224.0.0.0        240.0.0.0       On-link    10.12.14.201     281
    255.255.255.255  255.255.255.255       On-link       127.0.0.1     306
    255.255.255.255  255.255.255.255       On-link    10.12.14.201     281
===========================================================================
Persistent Routes:
None
```

This table seems a bit more involved than the routing table for the typical home router you saw in Figure 5-13. My PC has only a single NIC, though, so it's not quite as complicated as it might seem at first glance.

NOTE Every operating system gives you tools to view a computer's routing table. Most techs use the command line or terminal because it's fast. To see your routing table, run **`ip route`** for Linux or **`netstat -r`** for both macOS and Windows (or, as you just saw, `route print` works as an alternative on Windows machines).

My computer has an IP address of 10.12.14.201/24, and 10.12.14.1 is its default gateway. The interface entries have actual IP addresses—10.12.14.201, plus the loopback interface of 127.0.0.1—instead of the word LAN. Following that is the metric.

NOTE The whole block of addresses that start with 127 is set aside for the loopback interface, but by convention, we use just one: 127.0.0.1.

Every address is compared to every line in the routing table before the packet goes out, so it doesn't matter if the default route is at the beginning or the end of the table. In this case, the top line defines the default route:

(Any destination address)	*(with any subnet mask)*	*(forward it to my default gateway)*	*(using my NIC)*	*(Metric of 25 to use this route).*
Network Destination	Netmask	Gateway	Interface	Metric
0.0.0.0	0.0.0.0	10.12.14.1	10.12.14.201	25

Anything that's not local goes to the router and from there out to the destination (with the help of other routers).

The next three lines tell your system how to handle the loopback address (127.0.0.1). The second line is straightforward, but examine the first and third lines carefully. According to the first route, any packet with a network ID of 127.0.0.0/8 will be sent to the loopback interface. The third line handles the broadcast traffic (more theoretical than actual) for the loopback address:

```
Network Destination          Netmask    Gateway    Interface    Metric
          127.0.0.0        255.0.0.0    On-link    127.0.0.1       306
          127.0.0.1  255.255.255.255    On-link    127.0.0.1       306
    127.255.255.255  255.255.255.255    On-link    127.0.0.1       306
```

TRY THIS: GETTING LOOPED

Ping any 127.0.0.0/8 address, and you'll see that it recursively loops 127.0.0.1. Even with your NIC disabled, this will work. Remember, the loopback interface has *nothing* to do with a NIC, although some people mistakenly think it does!

The next line defines the local connection:

(Any packet for the 10.12.14.0/24 network)	*(don't use a gateway)*	*(just ARP on the LAN interface to get the MAC address and send it directly to the recipient)*		*(Metric of 281 to use this route).*
Network Destination	Netmask	Gateway	Interface	Metric
10.12.14.0	255.255.255.0	On-link	10.12.14.201	281

The next line's easy; anything addressed to this machine should go right back to it through the loopback interface (127.0.0.1):

```
Network Destination          Netmask    Gateway   Interface  Metric
       10.12.14.201  255.255.255.255    On-link   127.0.0.1     281
```

The next line, a directed broadcast, is for broadcasting to the other devices on the same network:

```
Network Destination          Netmask    Gateway      Interface  Metric
       10.12.14.255  255.255.255.255    On-link   10.12.14.201     281
```

Directed here means this type of broadcast can be directed to a specific network (by setting all host bits to 1s, as discussed in Chapter 3).

The next two lines are for the multicast address range; Windows put these lines in automatically:

```
Network Destination     Netmask     Gateway      Interface     Metric
          224.0.0.0   240.0.0.0     On-link      127.0.0.1        306
          224.0.0.0   240.0.0.0     On-link   10.12.14.201        281
```

The bottom lines each define a limited broadcast:

```
Network Destination            Netmask   Gateway      Interface     Metric
    255.255.255.255    255.255.255.255   On-link      127.0.0.1        306
    255.255.255.255    255.255.255.255   On-link   10.12.14.201        281
```

Limited here means that the broadcast is limited to the current network and cannot be sent to other networks. After all, 255.255.255.255 is not network specific.

NOTE The RFCs (919 and 922, if you're curious) don't specify which interfaces a limited broadcast should be sent from if more than one is available.

Just for fun, let's add one more routing table. This one is from my Ubiquiti EdgeMax router, which is doing a great job of connecting me to the internet! I accessed the EdgeMax router remotely from my system using SSH, logged in, and then ran this command:

```
show ip route
```

Don't let all the output shown next confuse you. The first part, labeled Codes, is just a legend to let you know what the letters at the beginning of each row mean.

```
jonathan@cscprof:~$ show ip route
Codes: K - kernel, C - connected, S - static, R - RIP, B - BGP
       O - OSPF, IA - OSPF inter area
       N1 - OSPF NSSA external type 1, N2 - OSPF NSSA external type 2
       E1 - OSPF external type 1, E2 - OSPF external type 2
       > - selected route, * - FIB route, p - stale info
IP Route Table for VRF "default"
S     *> 0.0.0.0/0 [1/0] via 73.155.122.1, eth0
C     *> 73.155.122.0/23 is directly connected, eth0
C     *> 127.0.0.0/8 is directly connected, lo
C     *> 192.168.4.0/24 is directly connected, eth1
```

The last four lines are the routing table. The router has two active Ethernet interfaces called `eth0` and `eth1`. This is how the EdgeMax (which is based on Linux) names Ethernet interfaces.

Reading from the bottom, you see that `eth1` is directly connected (indicated by the `C` at the beginning of the line, though it also explicitly says this at the end of the line) to the network 192.168.4.0/24. Any packets that match 192.168.4.0/24 go out on `eth1`. On the next line up, you can see the entry for the loopback interface, `lo`, taking all packets matching 127.0.0.0/8. On the second line from the top, any packets for the connected 73.155.122.0/23 network go out on `eth0`. Finally, the top route gets an `S` for *static* because it was manually set, not inserted by a routing protocol like OSPF. This is the default route, indicated by 0.0.0.0/0.

You've now seen three different types of routing tables from three different types of devices. Even though these routing tables have different ways of listing the routes and showing the categories, they all perform the same job: moving IP packets to the correct interface to ensure they get to where they need to go.

TROUBLESHOOTING ROUTING TABLE ISSUES

Routers have some serious but rare potential problems. One place to watch is your routing table. For the most part, today's routers automatically generate directly connected routes, and dynamic routing takes care of itself. This leaves one possible culprit: static routes. These are the entries to investigate when packets aren't getting to the places you expect them to go. Look at the following sample static route:

```
Network Destination         Netmask        Gateway       Interface  Metric
        22.46.132.0   255.255.255.255   22.46.132.1    22.46.132.11       1
```

No packets for the network 22.46.132.0/24 are going out interface 22.46.132.11. Can you see why? Yup: the Netmask is set to 255.255.255.255, and no computers have exactly the IP address 22.46.132.0. It's very easy to enter the wrong network destination, subnet mask, gateway, and so on. If a new static route isn't delivering the packets, first assume you made a typo.

Also watch out for missing routes, which result either because you've forgotten to add them (if you're entering static routes) or, more commonly, because there's a convergence problem in the dynamic routing protocols. For the CompTIA Network+ exam, be ready to inspect a routing table to recognize these problems.

Furthermore, if no default route is set, packets destined for a network that the router doesn't know about will be dropped. Even with a default route set, however, there could be an incorrect next hop IP address for that default route, also preventing packets from reaching their destination.

Router Technologies Beyond Ethernet

Routers enable you to connect different types of network technologies. You now know that routers strip off all the Layer 2 data from the incoming packets, but thus far you've only seen routers that connect to different Ethernet networks—and that's just fine with routers. But routers can connect to almost anything that stores IP packets. Once you want to start making long-distance connections, Ethernet is not the only choice, with technologies like Data Over Cable Service Interface Specification (DOCSIS) for cable modems, Point-to-Point Protocol over Ethernet (PPPoE) for DSL modems, or passive optical network (PON) for fiber also in the mix. These technologies all work very differently than Ethernet. The only common feature between DOCSIS, PPPoE, PON, and Ethernet is that they all carry IP packets inside their Layer 2 encapsulations.

Most enterprise (that is, not home) routers enable you to add *modules* (hardware components that you physically install into the router) that contain interfaces. You buy the router and then snap in different types of modules depending on your needs. For the Cisco router shown in Figure 5-15, for example, you can buy and add a removable network interface module

FIGURE 5-15 Modular Cisco router

(NIM), also known as WAN Interface Card (WIC), that contains serial interfaces. If you want to connect to a Long Term Evolution (LTE) cellular network, you'd buy a cellular NIM.

Router Connections

When you take a new router out of the box, it's not good for very much. You need to plug into that shiny new router and start telling it what you want to do. One of the oldest (yet still very common) methods for doing so is to use a special serial connection. Figure 5-16 shows the classic Cisco console cable, more commonly called a *rollover* or *Yost cable.*

FIGURE 5-16 Cisco console cable

> **NOTE** The term *Yost cable* comes from its creator's name, Dave Yost. Go to *yost.com/computers/RJ45-serial* to view the Yost wiring standard.

Like routers, switches often have some form of configuration interface. Granted, you have nothing to configure on a basic switch, but in later chapters, you'll discover a few network features that you'll want to configure more advanced switches to use. Both routers and these advanced switches are called *managed devices*, but I'll use the term *router throughout this discussion for simplicity's sake.* The techniques shown here work for both.

When you first unwrap a new router, you plug the rollover cable into both its console port (Figure 5-17) and your PC's USB port. Nowadays, the rollover cable comes with a USB side, converted in the cable from serial. Alternatively, with a console cable that has serial pins on one side, you can use a USB-to-serial adapter.

FIGURE 5-17
Cisco console port

Next, you need to use a terminal emulation program to talk to the router. A common program is PuTTY (*chiark.greenend.org.uk/~sgtatham/putty*). Regardless of which emulator you use, these basic settings should get you connected:

- 9,600 baud
- 8 data bits
- 1 stop bit
- or flow control

NOTE Much initial router configuration harkens back to the methods used in the early days of networking, when massive mainframe computers were the primary computing platform available. Researchers used dumb terminals—machines that were little more than a keyboard, monitor, and network connection—to connect to the mainframe and interact. You connect to and configure many modern routers using software that makes your PC function like a dumb terminal. These programs are called *terminal emulators*; the screen where you type is called a *console*.

CISCO IOS

Now it's time to connect. Most Cisco products run *Cisco IOS* (Internetworking Operating System), Cisco's proprietary operating system. If you want to configure Cisco routers, you must learn IOS. Learning it in detail is a massive job and outside the scope of the CompTIA Network+ exam, but if you wish to become a "Cisco person," Cisco provides a series of certifications to support you. Although the CompTIA Network+ exam won't challenge you in terms of IOS, it's important to get a taste of how this amazing operating system works.

Once you've connected to the router and started a terminal emulator, you should see the initial router prompt:

```
Router>
```

NOTE A new Cisco router often won't have a password, but all good admins know to add one.

This is the IOS user EXEC mode prompt—you can't do too much here. To get to the fun, you need to enter *privileged EXEC mode*, also known as *enable mode*. Type **enable** and press ENTER. The prompt changes to the following:

```
Router#
```

From here, IOS gets intricate. For example, here are the commands to set the IP address for one of the router's ports:

```
Router# configure terminal
Router(config)# interface GigabitEthernet 0/0
Router(config-if)# ip address 192.168.4.10 255.255.255.0
Router(config-if)# no shutdown
Router(config-if)# ^Z
Router# copy running-config startup-config
```

Upon booting, a brand-new or factory reset router will show you the following prompt:

```
Would you like to enter the initial configuration dialog?
[yes/no]?
```

If you say yes, the most basic setup is handled for you based on your responses to the prompts. Nothing IOS related is covered on the CompTIA Network+ exam; however, as a network administrator or engineer, you won't learn about IOS or know what to do when something goes wrong or needs a change if you go through the initial configuration dialog. I recommend always saying no here and configuring the router manually.

LLDP and CDP

Both the open standard IEEE 802.1AB Link Layer Discovery Protocol (LLDP) and Cisco's proprietary Cisco Discovery Protocol (CDP) operate at Layer 2 of the OSI model and allow devices to share and learn information with each other, including hostnames, IP addresses, device types, hardware information, and software information.

On one hand, the information passed between devices greatly helps with network troubleshooting and monitoring. On the other hand, the information passed in these messages can be used by cybercriminals and pose a great security risk. Some network engineers will turn on one of these protocols when setting up a network but turn it off when the configuration is complete.

Important Commands

As a network tech, you'll run into Cisco equipment and need to know how to use the console to access routers from time to time. This section lists several commands that will come in handy.

`no shutdown` You must enable an interface on a router with the `no shutdown` command (in interface configuration mode in Cisco IOS). If you don't, the status of the interface will remain its default: `administratively down`.

`show interfaces` This command can provide important configuration information, status information, and statistics such as link state (up/down), speed/duplex, send/receive traffic, cyclic redundancy checks (CRCs), and protocol packet and byte counts.

`show running-config`, `show startup-config` The `show running-config` command allows you to view the *running-config* file, which is stored in dynamic RAM and contains the current configuration of the router, including unsaved configuration changes. The **`show startup-config`** command allows you to view the *startup-config* file, which is stored in NVRAM and will be used the next time the router boots. Note that this file doesn't contain any changes made to the *running-config* file that haven't been explicitly saved.

To copy the latest changes to the router's configuration from the *running-config* file to the *startup-config* file, execute **`copy running-config startup-config`**.

`show ip route` This command allows you to view the router's routing table, which is stored in dynamic RAM.

`show ip arp` This command allows you to view the router's ARP cache, where you can see hosts that have sent and received traffic from the router (Chapter 2's "Remote Communication" section explains why hosts and routers communicate).

NOTE All `show` commands are executed from privileged EXEC mode in Cisco IOS.

You should be familiar with these commands, but for everyday management, you'll typically access a router—especially one that's already configured—through a web interface or network management software.

WEB ACCESS AND OTHER CONNECTION METHODS

Most routers come with a built-in web interface that enables you to do everything you need on your router and is much easier to use than Cisco's command-line IOS. For a web interface to work, however, the router must have a built-in IP address from the factory, or you must enable the web interface after you've given the router an IP address. Bottom line? If you want to use a web interface, you have to know the router's IP address. If a router has a default IP address, you will find it in the documentation.

Never plug a new router into an existing network! There's no telling what that router might start doing. Does it have Dynamic Host Configuration Protocol (DHCP) configured on it? You might now have a rogue DHCP server. Are there routes on that router that match up to your network addresses? Then you might see packets disappearing into the great bit bucket in the sky. Always fully configure your router before you place it into a live production network.

Most network engineers use a laptop and a crossover cable (where the transmit and receive wires are swapped to connect similar devices directly) to connect to the new router. To get to the web interface, first set a static address for your computer that will place your PC on the same network ID as the router. If, for example, the router is set to 192.168.1.1/24 from the factory, set your computer's IP address to 192.168.1.2/24. Then connect to the router (some routers tell you exactly where to connect, so read the documentation first) and check the link lights to verify you're properly connected. Open a web browser and type in the IP address.

> **NOTE** Many SOHO routers are also DHCP servers, making the initial connection much easier. Check the documentation to see if you can just plug in without setting an IP address on your PC.

Assuming you've done everything correctly, you almost always need to enter a default username and password, which come with the router's documentation. If you don't have that information, plenty of websites list this data. Do a web search on "default username password" to find one.

Once you've accessed the web interface, you're on your own to poke around to find the settings you need. There's no standard interface—even between different versions of the same router make and model. When you encounter a new interface, take some time to inspect every tab and menu to learn about the router's capabilities. You'll almost always find some really cool features!

Be aware that most routers have even more ways to connect. Industry-level routers allow you to connect using the ancient Telnet protocol (which you should never use because it doesn't use cryptography, meaning it transmits everything in plaintext) or Secure Shell (SSH), which encrypts everything transmitted.

Router Redundancy

If clients aren't configured with the IP address of the default gateway, their outbound traffic will never be sent off their network, and inbound traffic from other networks won't be delivered to them. A *first hop redundancy protocol* (FHRP) allows two or more routers to provide backup for the default gateway IP address given to hosts. Let's say the default gateway's IP address given to hosts is 192.168.1.1, and a single router has that IP address statically configured on its interface on the LAN. If that router goes down, no host from the LAN will be able to send or receive traffic to or from different LANs. That's a single point of failure.

Now imagine two, three, or more routers having their own IP addresses bound to each of their LAN interfaces. The router interfaces could have the following addresses: 192.168.1.2, 192.168.1.3, 192.168.1.4, and 192.168.1.5. Each router would provide support for the default gateway address, a virtual IP (VIP) address, assigned to hosts: 192.168.1.1. Within a few seconds of a failure of an active router, a backup router would spring into action, keeping the VIP address functioning.

The more common FHRPs include the following:

- **Hot Standby Router Protocol (HSRP)** Cisco proprietary.
- **Virtual Router Redundancy Protocol (VRRP)** An open standard that's very similar to HSRP.
- **Gateway Load Balancing Protocol (GLBP)** Cisco proprietary protocol that allows for load balancing by default by having multiple active routers, as opposed to HSRP and VRRP, where only one router is active at a time unless multiple groups are configured.

NOTE HSRP and VRRP don't support load balancing by default, but you can work around this by configuring multiple (HSRP or VRRP) groups. However, that's not the easiest thing to pull off. Half of the clients will be configured to get one gateway IP address, while the other half will be configured to get a different one. There's just no easy way to do that. GLBP, though, is "plug and play load balancing" from the start.

Network Address Translation

Many regions of the world have depleted their available IPv4 addresses already, and the end is in sight everywhere else. Although you can still get an IPv4 address from an ISP, the days of easy availability are over. Network Address Translation (NAT) has extended the useful life of IPv4 by enabling devices using private addresses to communicate over the internet. NAT is extremely common and heavily in use, so it's important to understand how it works. Note that while many routers include NAT as a feature, NAT is a separate technology from routing itself.

The Setup

Say you have a LAN with five computers that need access to the internet. With classic TCP/IP and routing, several things must happen. First, you need to get a block of legitimate, unique, expensive IP addresses from an ISP. You could call up an ISP and purchase a network ID—say, 1.2.3.136/29. Second, you assign an IP address to each computer and to the LAN connection on the router. Third, you assign the IP address for the ISP's network, such as 1.2.4.1, to the WAN connection on the local router. After everything is configured, the network looks like Figure 5-18.

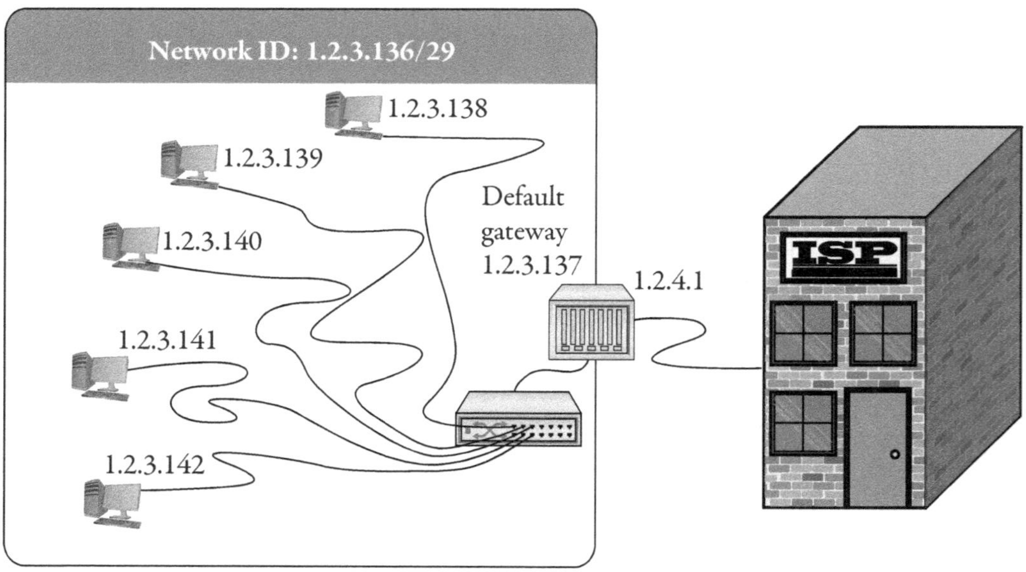

FIGURE 5-18 Network setup

EXAM TIP NAT replaces the source IP address of a computer with the source IP address from the outside router interface on outgoing packets. NAT is performed by NAT-capable routers.

All the clients on the network have the same default gateway (1.2.3.137). This router interface on the LAN side acts as the default gateway for all the client computers. This style of network mirrors how computers in LANs throughout the world connected to the internet for its first 20+ years, but the major problem of a finite number of IP addresses worsened as more and more computers connected.

Port Address Translation

Commonly, internal networks get one public IP address from an ISP, and of course networks today have many devices. So how does each device send traffic if the entire network is allocated a single public IP address? They use a block of private IP addresses for the hosts inside the network and connect to the internet through one or more public IP addresses.

The most common form of NAT that handles this one-to-many connection—called *Port Address Translation* (PAT)—uses port numbers (discussed in Chapter 4) to map traffic from specific machines in the network. Let's consider a simple example to make the process clear.

The JSW Corporation has a network that uses the private IP addressing space of 192.168.1.0/24. All the computers in the private network connect to the internet through a single router using PAT, with the global IP address of 203.0.113.52/24. Table 5-1 represents the NAT/PAT translation table, which is dynamically generated on the router running NAT.

TABLE 5-1 JSW Corporation using NAT

HOST	IP ADDRESS	SOURCE LOCAL SOCKET	SOURCE TRANSLATED SOCKET	DESTINATION REMOTE SOCKET
A	192.168.1.10	192.168.1.10:60536 TCP	203.0.113.52:60536 TCP	129.21.1.40:443 TCP
B	192.168.1.11	192.168.1.11:60246 TCP	203.0.113.52:60246 TCP	129.21.1.40:443 TCP
C	192.168.1.12	192.168.1.12:60246 TCP	203.0.113.52:60247 TCP	129.21.1.40:443 TCP

There are three hosts, labeled A through C. Each host's IP address starts with 192.168.1, as there are three network octets in this /24 network. The fourth octet is a host octet, with 8 host bits. Notice each host's IP address.

Now, let's say Host A and Host B both send traffic to 129.21.1.40, the IP address of the Rochester Institute of Technology web server. The source local socket, which combines the source IP address with a source port and includes the Layer 4 protocol (TCP in this case), is shown in Table 5-2. Notice that for the source translated socket, the private inside IP addresses are replaced with the single public outside IP address of 203.0.113.52. In this case, the source ports remain the same. Also notice that the destination remote socket is the same for Host A and Host B since they're both sending traffic to the same web server.

When traffic comes back to the network from the RIT web server, traffic destined for Host A and Host B will have a destination IP address of 203.0.113.52. However, the router running NAT will notice the destination ports, and use each of those as an index in the NAT table. Seeing port 60536 will trigger NAT to change the destination IP address to 192.168.1.10 and send the traffic out of the LAN interface as such. Seeing port 60246 will trigger NAT to change the destination IP address to 192.168.1.11 and send the traffic out of the LAN interface as such.

Imagine that at the same time Host A and Host B went to the RIT web server, Host C did as well. Also imagine that Host C, by some coincidence, used the same local port that Host B used, 60246. If the source port is used as an index (when it comes back as a destination port) to find the correct inside host IP address, and if each source translated socket uses the same, single public IP address, how can traffic for Host B and Host C now be differentiated? Easy! NAT will replace the Layer 4 source port number of Host C to make it unique, setting it to 60247 in this case. When traffic returns to port 60247, both the Layer 4 port and the Layer 3 IP address will be translated back to what they were, and traffic will be sent out of the router's LAN interface, reaching the appropriate inside host.

Sometimes NAT will change the source port, even without a conflict with what's in the table already. So, how does NAT work with ICMP, if ICMP is a Layer 3 protocol, which means there is no Layer 4 header (TCP or UDP) with port information? For ICMP messages that have queries and replies (ICMP Echo request/ICMP Echo reply, for example), the ICMP QueryID value will be treated like an actual TCP or UDP port number. ICMP messages that are one-way error messages have no ICMP ID. However, ICMP error messages contain the complete IP header and at least the first 8 bytes of the payload of the packet that caused the ICMP error message. In those cases, NAT will use the actual port number of the encapsulated TCP segment or UDP datagram.

NOTE NAT is not a security mechanism, nor has it ever been. See the following links for more details:

weberblog.net/why-nat-has-nothing-to-do-with-security

0day.work/an-example-why-nat-is-not-security

blog.ipspace.net/2011/12/is-nat-security-feature.html

f5.com/resources/white-papers/the-myth-of-network-address-translation-as-security

youtu.be/v26BAlfWBm8

Since the router is revising the packets and recording the IP address and port information already, why not enable it to handle ports more aggressively? Enter port forwarding, stage left.

Large-Scale NAT and Carrier-Grade NAT

Due to IPv4 address exhaustion, many ISPs are using Large-Scale NAT (LSNAT), which gives customers zero public IP addresses. Instead, the outside router interface gets a private IP address, which is turned into a public IP address as the provider's infrastructure. When the return traffic comes back to the provider, it is turned into the private IP address assigned to the router interface and sent to the customer site. Keep in mind, each customer site is using NAT, so in essence, each packet goes through NAT twice and has three different IP addresses (private on the customer network, private from the customer to the ISP, and public from the ISP to the internet) at each point in the journey!

A specific implementation of LSNAT is Carrier-Grade NAT (CGNAT), deployed by ISPs. To avoid a potential overlap with private IP addresses on the inside customer infrastructure, ISPs use the block of IP addresses from 100.64.0.0 through 100.127.255.255, which are reserved for CGNAT.

A non-CGNAT example of LSNAT is a large enterprise or cloud provider (for example, Amazon Web Services, Microsoft Azure, and Google Cloud Platform) that operates a private data center or virtual private cloud (VPC) for thousands of workloads (VMs, containers, etc.) that use private IP addresses. LSNAT allows these workloads to initiate outbound connections to the internet for software updates, API calls, and more. Since this is done entirely within the cloud infrastructure and internal to a single organization—not on a service provider access network—it's not considered CGNAT.

Port Forwarding

The obvious drawback to relying exclusively on PAT for NAT is that it only works for outgoing communication, not incoming communication. For traffic originating *outside* the network to access an *internal* machine, such as a web server or an FTP server hosted inside your network, you need to use other technologies.

With *port forwarding*, you can designate a specific machine with an address that can be described as private, inside, and local for various network services. Computers outside the network can request a service using the public IP address of the router and the port number of the desired service. The port-forwarding router will examine the packet, look at the list of services mapped to local addresses, and then send that packet along to the proper destination.

If you'd like users outside of your network to have access to an internal web server and an internal FTP server, for example, you can set up port forwarding rules for each. You'd do that with entries as shown in Table 5-2.

TABLE 5-2 Port forwarding

EXTERNAL PORT	INTERNAL PORT	PROTOCOL	IP ADDRESS	ENABLED
80	80	TCP	192.168.1.107	Yes
21	21	TCP	192.168.1.108	Yes

There's a web server running on 192.168.1.107 and an FTP server running on 192.168.1.108. External users can access these services by using a client to send traffic to the router's external IP address and the standard port number of the corresponding server service. The outside router interface reads in the packet, since the destination IP address is a match, but then the router looks in the port forwarding table and sends the traffic to 192.168.1.107 if the destination port is 80 and 192.168.1.108 if the destination port is 21. The external port and the internal port can be the same or different. A common misconception is that using a different external port provides security, but it doesn't. Security through obscurity—hiding something and thinking that the hiding makes it secure—isn't real security. Furthermore, someone could use port scanning and other techniques to discover any open ports/services on destination machines.

Of course, on infrastructures behind a CGNAT, port forwarding won't work. In this case, you'd need to pay your ISP a monthly fee (usually $15 to $20) for a static public IP address.

Chapter Review

Questions

1. What do routers use to forward packets?
   - **A.** Source IP address
   - **B.** Destination IP address
   - **C.** Source MAC address
   - **D.** Destination MAC address
2. What OSI model layer are routers found at?
   - **A.** 1
   - **B.** 2
   - **C.** 3
   - **D.** 4

3. Which of these routing protocols uses cost as its metric?
   A. OSPF
   B. EIGRP
   C. BGP
   D. All of the above
4. Which of these routing protocols is used between routers of different autonomous systems?
   A. OSPF
   B. EIGRP
   C. BGP
   D. All of the above
5. Which of these routing protocols has a feasible successor route in place that is promoted to the successor role immediately if the successor route fails?
   A. OSPF
   B. EIGRP
   C. BGP
   D. All of the above
6. Which of these is not a reason for using a dynamic routing protocol?
   A. Stub network
   B. Fault tolerance
   C. Load balancing
   D. Easy to set up
7. What command is used to show a router's routing table?
   A. `show ip route`
   B. `display routing table`
   C. `display ip route`
   D. `show routing table`
8. Which of these protocols is not used as a first hop redundancy protocol (FHRP)?
   A. VRRP
   B. GLBP
   C. ICMP
   D. HSRP

9. Which command brings up a router interface?
   A. `show running-config`
   B. `enable`
   C. `shutdown`
   D. `no shutdown`

10. Which address will not need NAT, before being used in a packet sent over the internet?
    A. 192.168.1.108
    B. 129.21.1.40
    C. 17.26.1.15
    D. 10.10.10.10

Answers

1. **B.** A router will forward a packet to the next hop interface based on the destination IP address in the IP packet. MAC addresses, found in frames, have nothing to do with routers making decisions on forwarding packets. The source IP address is where the packet comes from, and isn't something the router can use to determine the best path to the destination.
2. **C.** Routers are Layer 3 devices.
3. **A.** OSPF uses cost, which is a function of bandwidth.
4. **C.** BGP is the only exterior gateway protocol (EGP). Each of the others is an IGP (interior gateway protocol).
5. **B.** EIGRP uses successor routes and feasible successor routes.
6. **A.** A stub network, with only one way in or out, doesn't benefit from a dynamic routing protocol.
7. **A.** The command `show ip route` displays a router's routing table
8. **C.** ICMP is used for error and informational reporting. The others are used as an FHRP.
9. **D.** The `no shutdown` command brings up a router interface, since the default setting for an interface is `shutdown`.
10. **B.** All the others are RFC 1918 private IP addresses, while 129.21.1.40 is a public IPv4 address, not needing NAT. In fact, it's the IP address of the RIT web server.

Switching

IN THIS CHAPTER, YOU WILL LEARN HOW TO

- Describe how switches learn and make decisions
- Use VLANs to separate network traffic
- Explain switch technologies and features including link aggregation, duplex, speed, and jumbo frames
- Master Spanning Tree Protocol

In Chapter 4, we were in Layer 4, discussing ports, TCP, UDP, and more. In Chapter 5, we went down to Layer 3, discussing routing. Now, in Chapter 6, we'll go down one more layer, to Layer 2, with another deep dive. This time, we'll explore the wonderful world of switching.

Historical/Conceptual

Introduction to Switches

A Layer 2 switch connects devices on the same network together. Think of switches as the local streets of a city, connecting entities (such as homes, office buildings, banks, coffeehouses, and supermarkets) in the same vicinity. These entities are like the network's end devices. End devices, which include desktops, laptops, printers, cameras, and mobile devices, are the sources or destinations of traffic and are identified by IP addresses. Just like the streets of a city allow you to easily go from a bank to a coffeehouse, switches allow network traffic (for example, a document) to go from your computer to a network printer. And just like a set of streets can lead to another part of a city, switches connect to other switches, extending the network's reach. Of course, a network must have a switch connected to a router, which forwards traffic destined for other networks to another router and also receives traffic sent from routers on other networks.

EXAM TIP A switch that works at more than one layer of the OSI model is called a *multilayer switch* (MLS). An MLS that handles routing is often called a *Layer 3 switch* because it can understand and route IP traffic.

Test Specific

How a Switch Learns and Makes Decisions

When you first turn on a switch, it knows nothing about the devices connected to it or how to identify them. However, as computers directly connected to that switch send frames to it, the switch copies the source MAC addresses and quickly creates a table mapping them to ports of each connected computer. Armed with this table—known as a *source address table* (SAT), *MAC address table*, or *content addressable memory* (CAM) table—the switch can then determine where to send incoming frames. Figure 6-1 shows a switch in action.

For example, when a PC sends an Ethernet frame into a switch, the switch checks the destination MAC address against its SAT to see if it knows which port that MAC address is connected to. If the switch knows where the device with that MAC address is (that is, if it

Port	MAC address
1	None
2	28-4F-C2-31-22-B2
3	None
4	45-9D-84-D2-AA-10
5	F1-E2-A9-9C-41-BC
6	None
7	AD-83-F2-90-D2-39
8	None

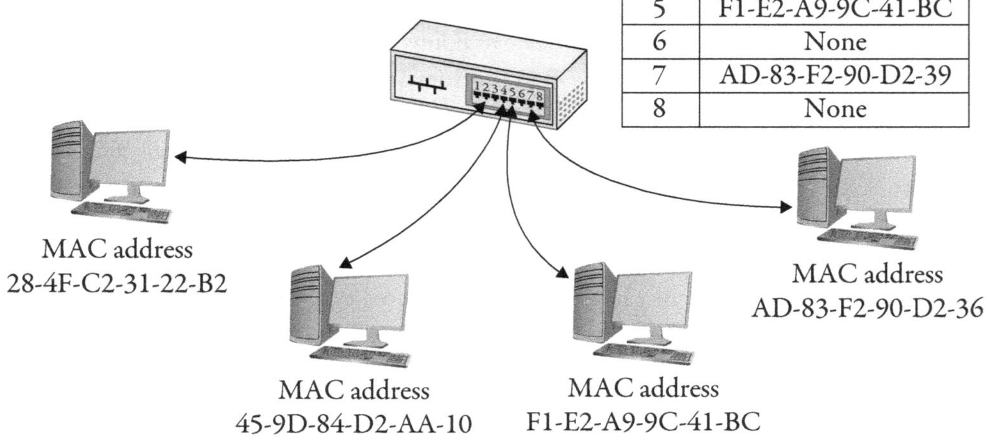

FIGURE 6-1 A switch in action

already has an entry in its SAT), it sends the frame out of just that port. If the switch doesn't know where the destination MAC address is, it *floods* the frame—sending the frame out of all ports except the interface on which it originated.

NOTE The term *port* in this chapter refers to a switch's physical ports, into which you plug connectors from Ethernet cables (just like it referred to a router's physical ports in Chapter 5). In Chapter 4, *port* referred to logical communication endpoints between communicating devices. Adding to this confusion, most network engineers use the word *port*, used in this chapter and the previous one, interchangeably with the word *interface*. However, *port* is the physical part of a router or switch, whereas *interface* is how the router's or switch's operating system logically accesses it.

So how does the switch learn where MAC addresses are in the first place? As Figure 6-2 shows, if Host A sends a frame for Host B into Port 1 on the switch, the switch says, "I can now associate the MAC address of Host A with the port on which I heard the frame" and notes that in its SAT.

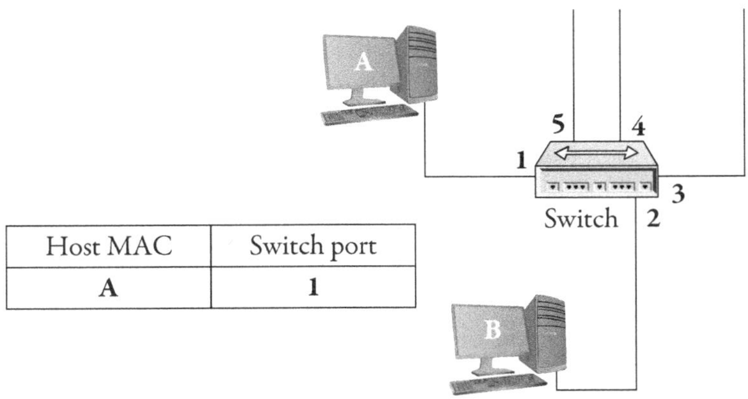

FIGURE 6-2 A switch learning Host A's MAC address

Since the switch doesn't know where Host B is, it floods the frame out of all the ports except Port 1, the one on which the frame originated. In Figure 6-2, these are Ports 2, 3, 4, and 5.

When Host B replies, as shown in Figure 6-3, the frame goes into the switch, and the switch learns that Host B can be found on Port 2. The switch then adds the MAC address of Host B and the port on which it heard the frame into its SAT.

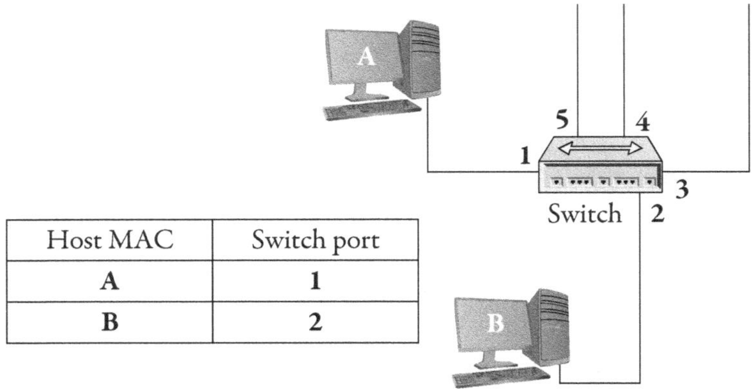

Host MAC	Switch port
A	1
B	2

FIGURE 6-3 A switch learning Host B's MAC address

The logic works the same for switches that are connected. Each switch maintains its own SAT. Say each host has sent some traffic. In Figure 6-4, Switch 2 has associated Hosts E, F, G, and H with Ports 1, 2, 3, and 4, respectively. However, as far as Switch 1 goes, Hosts E, F, G, and H are all accessible through Port 5, which connects to Switch 2. Hosts A, B, C, and D are known to Switch 1 on Ports 1, 2, 3, and 4, respectively. However, as far as Switch 2 goes, Hosts A, B, C, and D are accessible through Port 5, which connects to Switch 1.

If Host C sends a frame to Host E, it goes into Switch 1 on Port 3. Switch 1 consults its SAT and realizes Host E is accessible out of Port 5. Therefore, Switch 1 sends the frame out of Port 5, and it's picked up by Switch 2. Switch 2 now looks at the destination MAC address in the frame, which is still the MAC address of Host E. In the previous chapter, you learned that routers reframe packets at each hop. Switches, on the other hand, are transparent and don't change a single part of the frame. After consulting its SAT, Switch 2 sends the frame out of Port 1, where Host E gets it.

In addition to flooding unknown unicasts (when the switch doesn't know where a destination MAC address is), the switch will also flood multicasts and broadcasts out of all ports except the one on which the frame originated. Remember, ARP requests are always broadcasts. If there are 20 connected switches in a network, with 20 PCs connected to each switch, a single ARP request by one of the PCs will be sent to and read by the other 399.

NOTE Switches use the source MAC address in the frame to learn where hosts are and use the destination MAC address in the frame to determine where to send the frames to.

To examine the SAT in RAM, type **`show mac address-table`** (*MAC address table* is the name Cisco uses instead of SAT) in privileged EXEC (enable) mode on a Cisco switch.

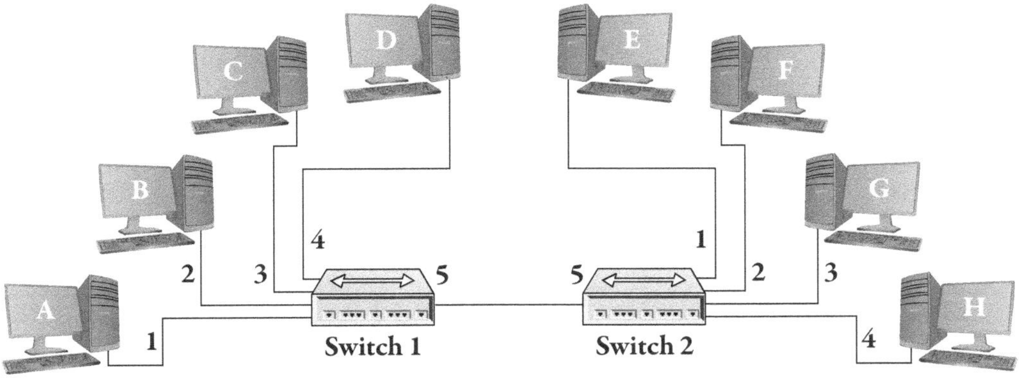

SW1 SAT

1	A
2	B
3	C
4	D
5	E
5	F
5	G
5	H

SW2 SAT

1	E
2	F
3	G
4	H
5	A
5	B
5	C
5	D

FIGURE 6-4 Two switches and their SATs

VLANs

All devices in a LAN are in the same broadcast domain. That means when one of them sends a broadcast frame, all of the other devices receive and process it. By default, all switch ports are in the same broadcast domain.

A *virtual local area network* (VLAN) enables you to create broadcast domains within a single switch. When a device in a VLAN sends a broadcast, that message stays within the VLAN. VLANs offer several benefits. Having fewer hosts receive and process broadcasts not meant for them improves efficiency, since there are fewer CPU processing requirements. It also improves security, since fewer hosts receive the traffic (whether multicast, broadcast, or unknown unicast) that the switches flood throughout the network, and you can configure security policies for specific VLANs to control access. Finally, using one or more switches with multiple VLANs allows for a more flexible network topology; users and their devices can be logically grouped by department or team instead of by physical location.

VLANs create isolated communication boundaries. Systems within a single VLAN and IP subnet can only communicate with one another, not with systems in other VLANs or subnets (unless they are connected through a Layer 3 device that enables this). Since Layer 3 devices only route traffic between subnets, not within them, if two systems in the same IP subnet are configured for different VLANs (not following the best practice of putting each subnet in its own VLAN), they can't communicate at all. This *incorrect VLAN assignment* situation should be on your troubleshooting checklist.

NOTE Technically, two devices in the same subnet but different VLANs *can* communicate if you connect a crossover cable to the switch port on each VLAN, but you'll need physical access to the switch for that. If an attacker has physical access to a switch, though, they'll probably use it for more nefarious purposes.

In Figure 6-5, three ports on the switch have been configured to tag incoming traffic as VLAN1 traffic, while two other ports have been configured to tag incoming traffic as VLAN2 traffic. The tagging the switch applies for incoming frames is known as *implicit tagging*, because the switch is simply noting which VLAN each frame belongs to rather than physically modifying the frame data as it does with explicit tagging (discussed shortly).

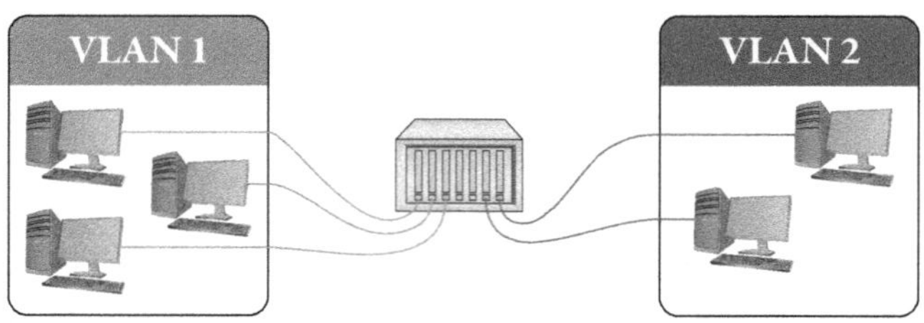

FIGURE 6-5 A switch with two VLANs

Imagine that the devices connected to the VLAN 1 ports are from the 10.1.0.0/16 subnet, while devices connected to the VLAN 2 ports are from the 10.2.0.0/16 subnet. Without the VLANs, you'd need separate physical switches for each subnet, but now, devices from different subnets can be placed in the same switch, and the networking still works as before.

Understanding VLAN assignment is important because VLANs are always in effect on a switch, and VLAN 1 is the default VLAN for all ports. That's a single broadcast domain. When thinking about what's in a VLAN or what "belongs" to one, keep in mind that it's not PCs, protocols, or applications; in the most technical sense, Layer 2 frames belong to a VLAN.

Configuring VLANs on a switch means creating new VLANs and assigning ports to them rather than leaving them associated with VLAN 1. Once you've configured a switch to support multiple VLANs, each VLAN is its own broadcast domain (and, as noted earlier, each VLAN should also be a separate IP subnet), just as if all of the VLANs were on separate switches, networks, and physical infrastructures. That's the reason for the word *virtual* in *Virtual Local Area Network*.

What if you had another switch with VLAN 1 and VLAN 2 members? You'd connect the switches, as shown in Figure 6-6.

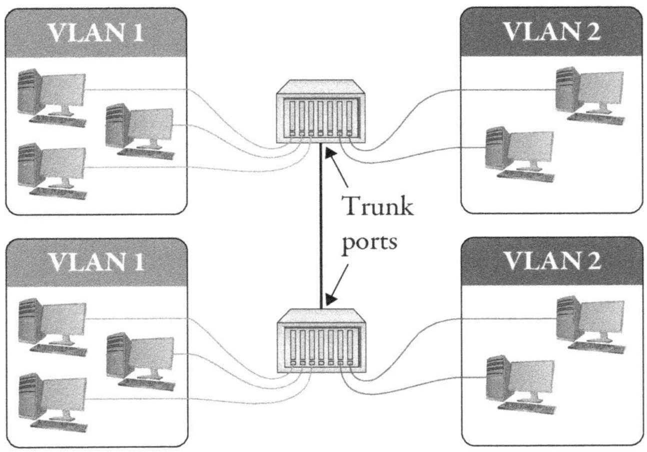

FIGURE 6-6 Two switches, each with a VLAN 1 and a VLAN 2

Trunking

When using VLANs between multiple switches, VLAN *trunking* allows traffic from more than one VLAN (all of them by default, but VLANs can be *pruned*, or removed, from trunk links automatically or manually) to traverse a single link between trunk ports on connected switches. A *trunk port* is a port on a switch connected to another switch, whereas an *access port* is a port on a switch connected to a PC.

Broadcast, multicast, and unknown unicast traffic are only sent out of all access ports associated with the same VLAN as the frame. Where there is a matching entry in the SAT, unicast traffic is sent out of an access port associated with the same VLAN as the frame.

VLAN trunking is done through *explicit tagging*, which involves actually encapsulating a 4-byte IEEE 802.1Q VLAN tag (unlike the implicit tagging described earlier) in the frame's Ethernet header. This tag contains multiple fields. The one most relevant here is the VLAN ID field, which identifies frames as belonging to a specific VLAN. The switch inserts the tag before sending the frame out of a trunk port, along a trunk link, to another switch's trunk port. The other switch then uses this tag to decide which ports to send the frame out of.

The switch removes tags before sending frames out of access ports, so devices connected to those ports never see tagged frames (with a couple of rare exceptions by certain VLAN-aware end devices). Tags are meant for adjacent switches, so they'll know how to forward the frames properly to the respective VLANs.

Layer 3/Multilayer Switch

A Layer 3 switch operates at both Layer 2 and Layer 3 and allows you to create *switched virtual interfaces* (SVIs), logical Layer 3 interfaces with IP addresses that are assigned to VLANs and act as default gateways for devices within those VLANs. The word *virtual* in *switched virtual interface* highlights that the default gateway is not a physical router port, but rather a logical Layer 3 interface assigned to the VLAN on a Layer 3 switch.

Additionally, Layer 3 switches allow you to configure physical routed ports using the `no switchport` command, converting a Layer 2 switch port into a Layer 3 interface for direct IP routing between networks or devices.

You'll need to enable routing on the switch with the Cisco global configuration mode `ip routing` command.

As shown in Figure 6-7, if devices in VLAN 100 (which will all be on the same subnet, say with a network ID of 10.1.0.0/16) and VLAN 200 (also all on the same subnet, say with a network ID of 10.2.0.0/16) want to communicate, they can do so through inter-VLAN routing provided by the switch. Each VLAN has an SVI that enables routing to other VLANs directly on the switch without needing an external router.

In this setup, the SVI should be configured on only one Layer 3 switch. Configuring the SVI on multiple switches without a redundancy protocol—like Hot Standby Router Protocol (HSRP) or Virtual Router Redundancy Protocol (VRRP)—can cause routing issues.

To connect this Layer 3 switch to the rest of the network, you can configure a routed port on the switch and assign it an IP address. This routed port connects to a router or core switch, with both ends in a separate subnet (such as 10.3.0.0/16), allowing for proper Layer 3 routing between the VLANs and the external network.

As mentioned earlier, VLAN 1 is the default VLAN. It's also the native VLAN, which means if a frame tagged with that VLAN needs to be sent across the trunk link, the VLAN tag is not explicitly added. When the frame gets to the other switch, the other switch, noticing that the frame is untagged, sends it only to the VLAN associated with the native VLAN, shared between both switches. This can lead to VLAN Hopping attacks, described in Chapter 17.

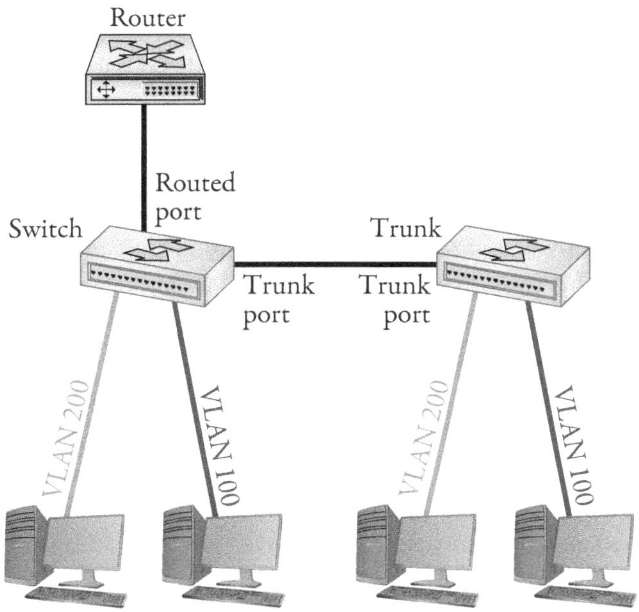

FIGURE 6-7 InterVLAN routing

VOICE VLAN

A *voice VLAN*, one optimized for voice data streams, prioritizes Voice over IP (VoIP) traffic over data traffic to ensure smooth voice communication. A voice VLAN can either use MAC addresses to determine which devices on the network are phones or use VLAN-based tags in the received frame. The switch can prioritize the voice traffic and deprioritize data traffic as specified.

In the networking sense, having separate connections to a switch from a user's phone and PC requires extra cables and ports. Instead, VoIP phones have a three-port switch built in, where one port connects to the phone component (this one is internal), one port connects to the user's PC, and one port connects the device itself to the corporate switch. Obviously, the voice traffic in the voice VLAN should have a higher priority than the PC's traffic in the data VLAN.

The connection between the phone and the corporate switch is a trunk link. The connection between the phone and the PC is an access link. All of the PC's traffic will be sent untagged from the phone to the corporate switch. The voice traffic, though, will be tagged and associated with the voice VLAN.

VLAN Database

Cisco switches store VLAN configurations in a separate VLAN database file (*vlan.dat*) on the device, rather than in the main configuration files (*running-config*, *startup-config*) like many other vendors do. This can cause confusion when administrators try erasing *startup-config* to reset the switch. In reality, the VLAN database remains intact unless explicitly deleted.

This is especially risky when you're using VLAN Trunking Protocol (VTP). If VTP is enabled and not properly secured with a password, connecting an untrusted or misconfigured switch with a higher revision number to the network could propagate blank or incorrect VLAN information (such as from a different internal or external infrastructure). This could overwrite active VLANs across a production environment, potentially taking entire networks down. Therefore, before deploying a used Cisco switch, you should erase both the switch's configuration and the VLAN database to avoid unintended consequences.

NOTE VTP simplifies and centralizes VLAN management by having switches themselves distribute VLAN configurations, eliminating manual configuration on each switch, thereby saving time and reducing errors.

The `show vlan` command outputs the VLAN database with ports mapped to their corresponding VLAN. Figure 6-8 shows the `show vlan` command and output for a switch with all ports associated by default to VLAN 1.

```
Switch#show vlan

VLAN Name                             Status    Ports
---- -------------------------------- --------- -------------------------------
1    default                          active    Gig1/0/1, Gig1/0/2, Gig1/0/3, Gig1/0/4
                                                Gig1/0/5, Gig1/0/6, Gig1/0/7, Gig1/0/8
                                                Gig1/0/9, Gig1/0/10, Gig1/0/11, Gig1/0/12
                                                Gig1/0/13, Gig1/0/14, Gig1/0/15, Gig1/0/16
                                                Gig1/0/17, Gig1/0/18, Gig1/0/19, Gig1/0/20
                                                Gig1/0/21, Gig1/0/22, Gig1/0/23, Gig1/0/24
                                                Gig1/1/1, Gig1/1/2, Gig1/1/3, Gig1/1/4
1002 fddi-default                     active
1003 token-ring-default               active
1004 fddinet-default                  active
1005 trnet-default                    active

VLAN Type  SAID       MTU   Parent RingNo BridgeNo Stp  BrdgMode Trans1 Trans2
---- ----- ---------- ----- ------ ------ -------- ---- -------- ------ ------
1    enet  100001     1500  -      -      -        -    -        0      0
1002 fddi  101002     1500  -      -      -        -    -        0      0
1003 tr    101003     1500  -      -      -        -    -        0      0
1004 fdnet 101004     1500  -      -      -        ieee -        0      0
1005 trnet 101005     1500  -      -      -        ibm  -        0      0

VLAN Type  SAID       MTU   Parent RingNo BridgeNo Stp  BrdgMode Trans1 Trans2
---- ----- ---------- ----- ------ ------ -------- ---- -------- ------ ------

Remote SPAN VLANs
------------------------------------------------------------------------------

Primary Secondary Type              Ports
------- --------- ----------------- ------------------------------------------
```

FIGURE 6-8 The `show vlan` command and output

Link Aggregation

In some situations, a connection between a switch and a device doesn't have enough data capacity to meet demand. This happens regularly in large data centers, where tremendous amounts of data must be moved between racks of storage devices to vast numbers of users. Sometimes the solution is simple, like changing from 1 Gigabit Ethernet to 10 Gigabit Ethernet or more. However, there are ways to achieve high-speed links between devices without having to upgrade the infrastructure.

One option is to join two or more connected ports between two switches logically so that the resulting bandwidth is treated as a single connection and the throughput is multiplied by the number of linked connectors. Think of it like many lanes on a highway that can be accessed at the same time. All the cables from the joined ports must go to the same device, such as another switch or a storage area network (SAN). That device must also support the logical joining of all the involved ports. This solution is called *link aggregation* (as well as *port bonding*, *port aggregation*, *NIC bonding*, and *NIC teaming*).

Cisco's implementation of link aggregation is known as EtherChannel. When a port in the EtherChannel configuration is incompatible with others in the same EtherChannel, that port goes into a suspended state, as shown in the following output:

```
Aug 15 19:07:05.490:% EC-5-CANNOT_BUNDLE2: Gi0/8 is not Compatible with Po1
and Will be suspended (trunk mode of Gi0/8 is dynamic, is Po1 trunk)

Aug 15 19:07:05.536:% EC-5-CANNOT_BUNDLE2: Gi0/25 is not Compatible with Po1
and Will be suspended (trunk mode of Gi0/25 is dynamic, is Po1 trunk
```

The Cisco proprietary protocol for accomplishing EtherChannel is Port Aggregation Protocol (PAgP). The open, IEEE standards-based protocol for link aggregation is Link Aggregation Control Protocol (LACP). PAgP and LACP both automate the negotiation, management, load balancing, and failure modes of aggregated ports.

Duplex

Modern switches enable you to manually control duplex settings for older hardware. Some truly ancient, wired devices operate at *half duplex*, meaning they can send or receive, but not at the same time. The standard today (and for decades) is *full duplex*, which allows a device to send and receive at the same time. The default switch port setting is auto (which is short for Ethernet auto-negotiation, defined in IEEE 802.3), which dynamically senses which setting should be used, but you can force a port to half duplex if necessary to support an old device.

Speed

A typical "Gigabit" switch automatically supports 1,000 Mbps (1 Gbps) connections, the slower 100 Mbps "Fast Ethernet" connections, and the super-slow 10 Mbps connections. In some rare circumstances, you might set a port manually to run at a specific speed instead of leaving the default setting of auto (similar to the duplex configuration just described).

Jumbo Frames

Some special-purpose networks, such as those optimized for reading and writing to storage devices (we'll take a closer look at these in Chapter 14), require a lot of throughput. An inexpensive way to boost their performance is to configure jumbo frames larger than the normal 1,518 byte Maximum Transmission Unit (MTU) limit (comprising the 18 byte Layer 2 frame header and trailer, as well as the 1,500 byte payload) specified by IEEE 802.3, because it helps improve the payload-to-overhead ratio. Jumbo frames are usually 9,000 bytes long (though technically anything over 1,500 qualifies), and they reduce the total number of frames moving through the network.

You can't just configure jumbo frames for all purposes, however, especially if you're connected to the internet. The rest of the wide area network (WAN) won't respect your hefty frames, and you'll just end up with fragmentation and dropped packets that hurt performance or prevent connections altogether.

Spanning Tree Protocol

Because you can connect switches together in any fashion, it's easy to create redundant connections—known as *switching loops*, *bridging loops*, or *network loops*—in a network. In this unwanted state, frames simply loop around switches with no end in sight. There's no mechanism like the time to live (TTL) in the IP header, as described in Chapter 3, to stop this loop. In the early days of switches, making a switching loop in a network setup would bring the network crashing down. A frame could get caught in the loop, so to speak, and not reach its destination, and effectively take down devices with the unending processing requirements.

The Ethernet standards body adopted Spanning Tree Protocol (STP) to eliminate the problem of accidental switching loops. For decades, switches have had STP enabled by default and can detect potential loops before they happen. Using special STP frames known as *bridge protocol data units* (BPDUs), switches communicate with other switches to prevent loops from happening in the first place.

NOTE While today we say *switching* loops instead of *bridging* loops (a term coined before the advent of switches), we still use the same term for the frames: *bridge protocol data units* (also coined before the advent of switches).

Despite their early bad reputation, thanks to STP, loops today are often intentionally designed into networks to allow for redundancy.

WIRELESS VS. WIRED BRIDGES

A *wireless bridge* is a current technology used to connect two wireless network segments, two wired network segments, or wireless and wired network segments in the same way that wired switches do. You can also use wireless bridges to provide access to other networked devices, such as printers. Wireless bridges come in two different flavors: point-to-point and point-to-multipoint. *Point-to-point bridges* can only communicate with one other bridge and are used to connect two wireless network segments. *Point-to-multipoint* bridges can talk to more than one bridge at a time and can connect multiple wireless network segments.

Before we go further in our discussion of STP, we need to go back in time and understand the *wired bridge*, a bridge connected to devices with cables. PCs were wired into hubs, which sent a frame to all connected ports except the port on which the frame originated (unlike switches, which use the MAC address table). Hubs in turn were wired into bridges. The MAC address table worked the same way for bridges as it does for switches. The switch eliminated the hub/bridge combination, as PCs are wired into the single switch. Think of a switch as a multiport bridge.

Since STP was designed when bridges were used—before switches—it has always used the term *bridge*. For decades, in the context of STP, *bridge* has always referred to a switch, so think "switch" when you see "bridge" in anything STP related.

STP Port States

Switch ports advance through multiple STP states, summarized in Table 6-1.

Configuration BPDUs establish the topology, where one switch is elected the *root bridge* and acts as the center of the STP universe. Each switch then uses the root bridge as a reference point to maintain a loop-free topology. There will be redundant links, for fault tolerance, that would ordinarily cause a switching loop, but certain ports will be placed in a "blocking" state and will not send or receive data frames. Ports in the blocking state will still hear the configuration BPDUs, which are sourced by the root bridge and forwarded downstream to the other switches every two seconds.

A switched network design relies upon STP or Rapid Spanning Tree Protocol (RSTP, discussed shortly) to provide fault-tolerant links on the network. If a link or device goes down, STP springs into action with another type of BPDU, called a *topology change notification* (TCN) BPDU, that enables the switches to rework themselves around the failed interface or device. The blocked ports, listening to the BPDUs, will realize they're needed and eventually move to a forwarding state. We'll come back to blocked ports shortly.

TABLE 6-1 STP port states

STP STATE	PORT CAN...	PORT CAN'T...	DURATION
Disabled (not an actual STP state)		• Receive BPDUs • Send BPDUs • Learn MAC addresses • Send and receive data	Until the port is brought up using the no `shutdown` command
Blocking	• Receive BPDUs	• Send BPDUs • Learn MAC addresses • Send and receive data	Indefinite (if a switching loop has been detected)
Listening	• Receive BPDUs • Send BPDUs	• Learn MAC addresses • Send and receive data	15 seconds, length of the forward delay timer, which causes a 15-second wait period in the listening and learning states
Learning	• Receive BPDUs • Send BPDUs • Learn MAC addresses	• Send and receive data	15 seconds, length of the forward delay timer, which causes a 15-second wait period in the listening and learning states
Forwarding	• Receive BPDUs • Send BPDUs • Learn MAC addresses • Send and receive data		Indefinite (as long as the port is up and a loop is not detected)

Administrators can manually change STP settings for a switch. A switch port directly connected to a PC, for example, should never participate in STP, and could be configured with a setting called PortFast that brings up the interface right away, without the normal latency introduced by STP. Another reason to configure switch ports with PortFast is to prevent TCN BPDUs being sent out of that switch every time a PC is powered on and off, which has severe side effects, like causing all switches to flush their MAC address table and relearn MAC addresses.

PortFast ports still participate in STP; they just skip the listening and learning phases and transition directly to forwarding. If a port configured for PortFast receives a BPDU, the port will revert to a normal STP port (without PortFast) and go through the standard STP process. This allows network booting devices to immediately get DHCP traffic without the 30-second delay while still providing protection if a switch is accidentally connected.

For additional security on PortFast ports, you can enable a feature called BPDU guard. Then, if the port receives a BPDU, BPDU guard will move the port into a status of *errdisable* ("error occurred, disabled"), and an administrator must manually bring it back up, avoiding the risk of switching loops.

Another mechanism, root guard, will move a port into a root-inconsistent state if BPDUs received on that port indicate that another switch is trying to become the root bridge. The root-inconsistent port will automatically return to its forwarding state once these BPDUs stop arriving. This helps define areas where the root bridge should never be located.

NOTE The terms used for the preceding STP features (*PortFast*, *BPDU guard*, *root guard*, and *errdisable*) apply specifically to Cisco switches. Other companies, notably Juniper, compete with Cisco and use different terms for the same functions.

The original STP, introduced by the IEEE as 802.1D, was replaced in 2001 by Rapid Spanning Tree Protocol (RSTP), 802.1w. RSTP offers significantly faster convergence time following a network change. STP could take up to 52 seconds to get back to a steady state, for example, whereas an RSTP network could return to convergence in 6 seconds or less.

NOTE Beyond faster convergence, modern networks can also choose between running multiple STP instances or a single instance. Per-VLAN Spanning Tree+ (PVST+) is an enhancement and replacement of Per-VLAN Spanning Tree (PVST). PVST+ runs a separate instance of STP/RSTP for each VLAN for performance benefits and ease of configuration. A single instance of STP/RSTP, Common Spanning Tree (CST), is the alternative.

Root Bridge Selection

All switches in the topology need to agree on a central reference—a root bridge—to make sure there are no loops. The root bridge selection process starts with each switch sending BPDUs that contain its bridge ID to other switches. The *bridge ID* is an 8-byte value that contains a *bridge priority* (2 bytes) and MAC address (6 bytes). The root bridge ID in the BPDU is set to the switch's bridge ID, so each switch is essentially saying, "I am the root bridge; prove me wrong."

NOTE You might also see the term *election* used to describe the selection process for a root bridge, root port, and designated port (the latter two are described next). I use these terms interchangeably in this chapter.

The bridge priority defaults to 32,768 and can be set from 0 to 65,535 (in multiples of 4,096). Each switch has a base MAC address, and each port on a switch has its own MAC address. The switch's base MAC address is used as part of the bridge ID.

One switch will have the lowest bridge ID, and that switch is acknowledged by all other switches as the root bridge. If two or more switches have the same priority, the MAC address is used as a tiebreaker. For example, in Figure 6-9, all the switches have the same default priority, but since Switch 1 has a lower MAC address than the other switches, it becomes the root bridge.

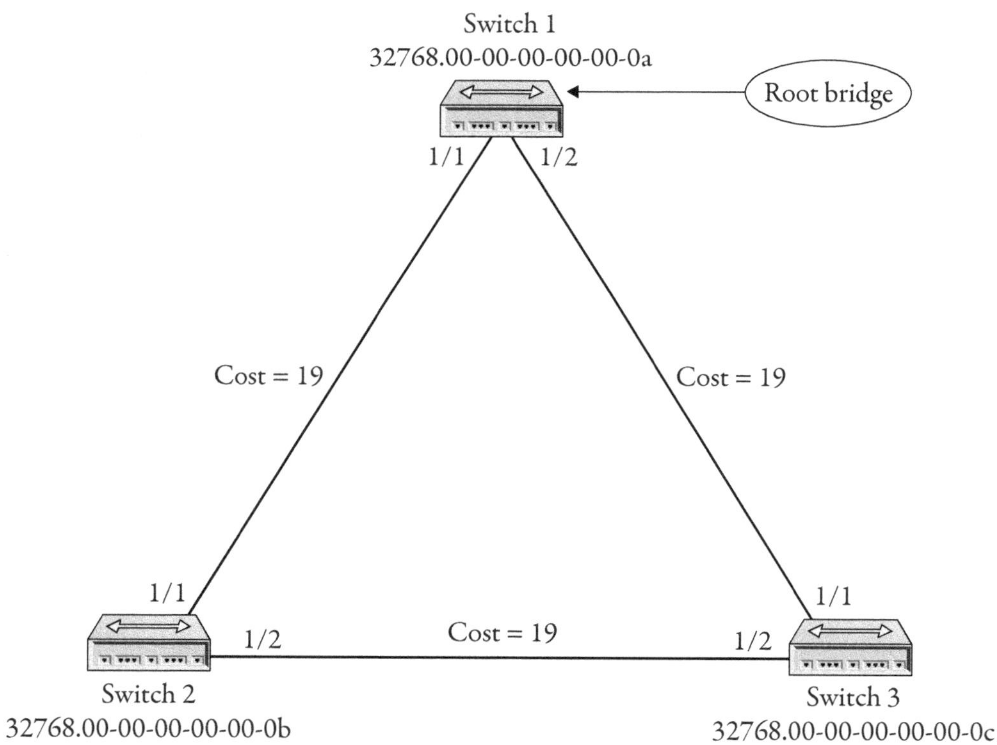

FIGURE 6-9 Root bridge selection

In some cases, having the switch with the lowest MAC address become the root bridge can cause problems, such as your network using slower links while faster ones sit unused because of a poorly positioned root bridge. Since the root bridge dictates how traffic flows at Layer 2, manually changing the bridge priority to force a well-positioned, high-speed switch to become the root bridge is a best practice.

As the STP process continues, each port of each switch is assigned one of the following *port roles*: root port, designated port, or blocked port.

Root Port Selection

At this point, all of the other switches must position themselves relative to the root bridge. To do so, each switch selects a *root port*, which represents that switch's quickest way back to the root bridge. (The root bridge will not have a root port.)

NOTE Root ports send traffic upstream, toward the root bridge.

Each switch selects its root port with a *root path cost*, the cumulative value of all links going toward the root bridge. The higher the bandwidth, the lower the cost (on a road trip, you'd rather pay less for tolls and gas than more!). The root bridge will send out BPDUs with a 0 value for the root path cost; since it is the root bridge, the cost to itself is 0. As each switch receives these BPDUs from the root bridge (after becoming the root bridge, this switch is the only source of BPDUs), it increments the root path cost by adding its root port's path cost to 0. It then sends the BPDU downstream, where the next switch again increments the root path cost upon receiving the BPDU.

For example, in Figure 6-10, Switch 1 is the root bridge and is sending BPDUs to Switch 2 and Switch 3. Switch 2's root path cost for Port 1 is 0 (BPDU from Switch 1) plus 19 (the path cost of the Switch 1–Switch 2 link). Switch 2's root path cost for Port 2 is 0 (BPDU from Switch 1) plus 19 (the path cost of the Switch 1–Switch 3 link), plus 19 (the path cost of the Switch 3–Switch 2 link), for a total of 38. Since 19 is lower than 38, Switch 1 chooses Port 1 as its root bridge.

Switch 3 makes a similar choice of Port 1.

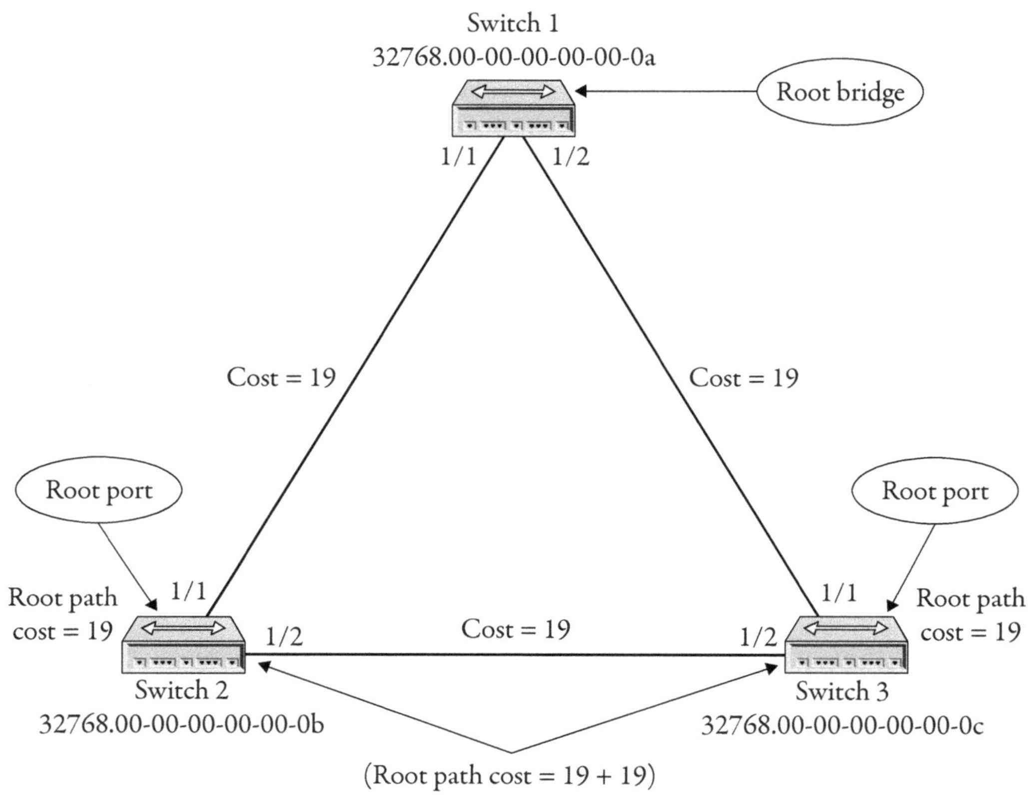

FIGURE 6-10 Root port selection

Designated Port Selection

The elimination of switching loops is now one election away. Each network segment (connection between switches) needs a single designated port. If two switches connect to a segment, both switches would send out the same frame, causing a switching loop. Now, only the designated port—the one with the lower cumulative root path cost to the root bridge—sends traffic onto that segment.

NOTE Designated ports send traffic downstream, away from the root bridge.

Refer to Figure 6-11. All ports of a root bridge are always elected designated ports for those respective segments. Quite simply, the root path cost for the port on the root bridge for each segment is 0. For the segment between Switch 1 and Switch 2, the root path cost for Switch 2 Port 1 (the other port on the segment) is 19. For the segment between Switch 1 and Switch 3, the root path cost for Switch 3 Port 1 (the other port on the segment) is 19. That takes care of the segment between Switch 1 and Switch 2 and the segment between Switch 1 and Switch 3. The segment between Switch 2 and Switch 3 still needs a designated port.

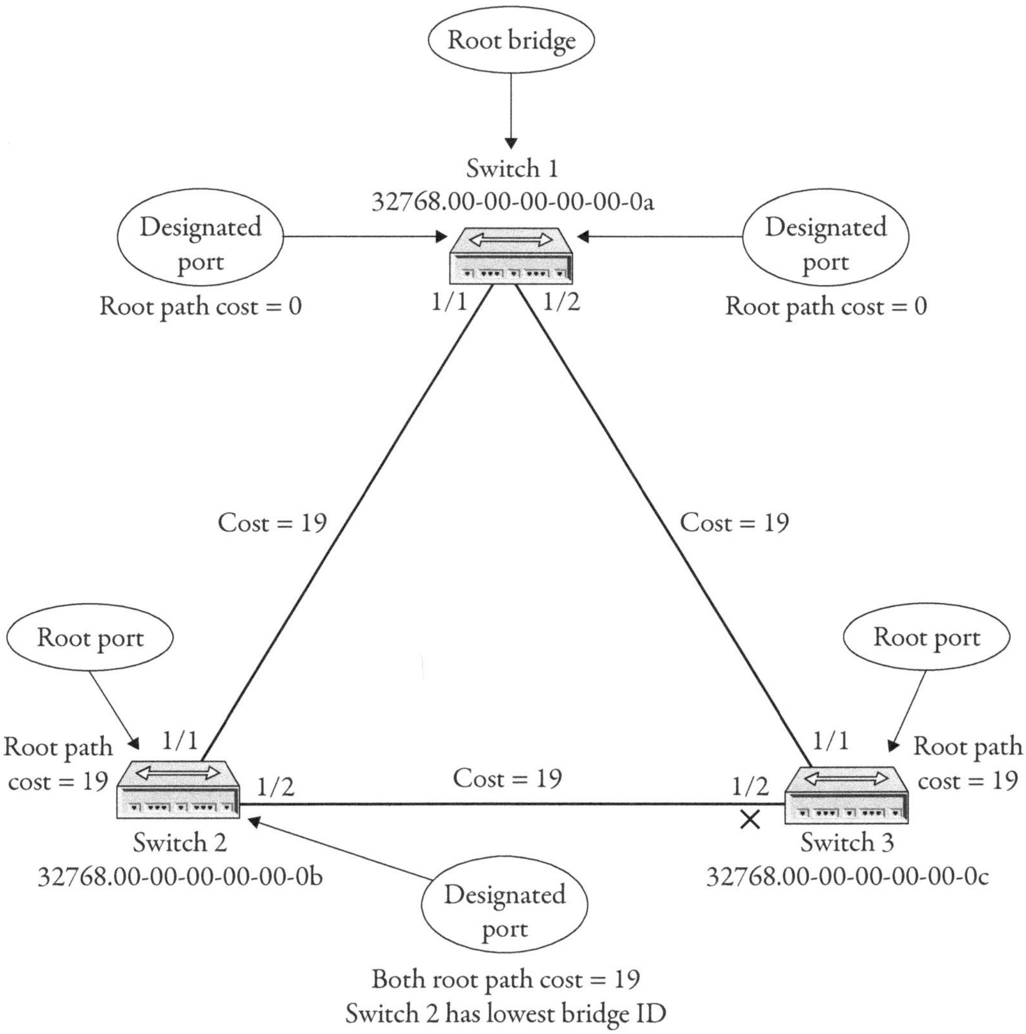

FIGURE 6-11 Designated port selection

Switch 2 Port 2 is the designated port for the segment between Switch 2 and Switch 3. The reason is quite interesting. Both Switch 2 Port 2 and Switch 3 Port 2 have a root path cost of 19. In this case, there is a tiebreaker: the lower sender bridge ID. Switch 2 sends BPDUs to Switch 3, and Switch 3 sends BPDUs to Switch 2. Since Switches 2 and 3 have the same priorities, we have to look at the next part of the bridge ID, which is the MAC address. Switch 2's MAC address is lower than Switch 3's MAC address, so it wins the tiebreaker and is elected the designated port for the segment between Switch 2 and Switch 3.

All ports on all switches have either been elected as a root port or a designated port—except for one. Switch 3 Port 2 is like the kid on the playground who hasn't been chosen for a team. Thus, that port becomes a *blocked port*, the final piece in the puzzle to prevent switching loops.

Topology Changes

When a switch port transitions between STP states (typically due to a link going up or down), STP may detect this as a topology change. This can trigger reconvergence and update the network topology, but it does not necessarily cause new root bridge or port elections unless the change affects STP path costs or priorities.

Interface Issues

By monitoring switch and router interfaces, you can address any issues as quickly as possible, reducing potential degradation or downtime. When you see increasing interface counters, for example, you need to take action.

The `show interfaces` command generates important output, such as the information highlighted in bold:

```
Switch#show interfaces
GigabitEthernet0/1 is up, line protocol is up (connected)
   Hardware is Lance, address is 00d0.97a0.c719 (bia 00d0.97a0.c719)
BW 100000 Kbit, DLY 1000 usec,
         reliability 255/255, txload 1/255, rxload 1/255
   Encapsulation ARPA, loopback not set
   Keepalive set (10 sec)
   Full-duplex, 1000Mb/s
   input flow-control is off, output flow-control is off
   ARP type: ARPA, ARP Timeout 04:00:00
   Last input 00:00:08, output 00:00:05, output hang never
   Last clearing of "show interface" counters never
   Input queue: 0/75/0/0 (size/max/drops/flushes); Total output drops: 0
   Queueing strategy: fifo
   Output queue :0/40 (size/max)
   5 minute input rate 0 bits/sec, 0 packets/sec
   5 minute output rate 0 bits/sec, 0 packets/sec
```

```
956 packets input, 193351 bytes, 0 no buffer
Received 956 broadcasts, 0 runts, 0 giants, 0 throttles
0 input errors, 0 CRC, 0 frame, 0 overrun, 0 ignored, 0 abort
0 watchdog, 0 multicast, 0 pause input
0 input packets with dribble condition detected
2357 packets output, 263570 bytes, 0 underruns
0 output errors, 0 collisions, 10 interface resets
0 babbles, 0 late collision, 0 deferred
0 lost carrier, 0 no carrier
0 output buffer failures, 0 output buffers swapped out
```

Let's go over some of the counters to monitor.

Cyclic Redundancy Checks

As Chapter 1 discussed, *cyclic redundancy check* (CRC) information reports on frames whose computed *frame check sequence* (FCS) trailer value did not match the value in the Ethernet trailer and, as a result, failed the integrity check. This information appears eight lines up in the preceding output.

Runts

Runts are frames that didn't meet the minimum size of 64 bytes (14 bytes for the Ethernet header, 46 bytes for the Ethernet payload, and 4 bytes for the Ethernet trailer). In the past, collisions (which were eliminated decades ago with full-duplex Ethernet) were likely causes of runts. Nowadays, bad wiring and electrical interference are the main culprits. You can see this information nine lines up in the preceding output.

Giants

Giants, as defined earlier in this chapter, are frames that exceed the maximum size of 1,518 bytes (14 bytes for the Ethernet header, 1,500 bytes for the Ethernet payload, and 4 bytes for the Ethernet trailer). They can be caused by a host configured with an MTU greater than 1,500 bytes or by a malfunctioning network interface card (NIC). You'll find this information nine lines up in the preceding output.

Drops

Drops are frames or packets discarded while entering or leaving an interface. This can result from a few situations, including network congestion (too much network traffic in general), buffer capacity being exceeded (too much traffic going through a single interface), access control lists (ACLs) that filter packets, and mismatched speeds (a device capable of higher speeds connected to a slower device where the faster device can't adjust the rate at which it sends data).

This information can be seen 15 lines up in the preceding output.

ACLs

One final point to keep in mind is that Layer 2 ACLs, if incorrectly configured, can cause issues with frames. Most discussions around ACLs relate to IP ACLs (coming up in Chapter 17) that can filter traffic to or from a router or standalone firewall by source IP address, destination IP address, and protocol in the IP packet, as well as by port in the Layer 4 TCP segment or UDP datagram.

Layer 2 ACLs work differently, filtering traffic inbound to a switch based on Ethernet frame fields (source MAC address, destination MAC address, or EtherType) and VLAN tags (Outer VLAN ID, Class of Service [COS], and VLAN Discard Eligibility Indication [DEI]).

VLAN range is not supported by Layer 2 ACLs, but a *VLAN ACL* (VACL) can permit or deny traffic within a VLAN or routed between VLANs.

Chapter Review

Questions

1. Which of these is not a way to describe the table switches have in RAM?
   A. SAT
   B. CAM
   C. MAC address table
   D. Routing table
2. Which of these addresses do switches use to learn where hosts are?
   A. Source MAC address
   B. Destination MAC address
   C. Source IP address
   D. Destination IP address
3. Which of these addresses do switches use to determine which port(s) to send frames out of?
   A. Source MAC address
   B. Destination MAC address
   C. Source IP address
   D. Destination IP address

4. What is an SVI?
   A. A collection of switches
   B. A switch port connected to a router port
   C. An IP address assigned to a VLAN
   D. A switch port connected to another switch port
5. What are PAgP and LACP?
   A. Protocols that allow different switch links to be bundled as one
   B. Multiple default gateways
   C. Switch management protocols
   D. STP mechanisms
6. Which of these is not an actual STP state?
   A. Blocking
   B. Disabled
   C. Listening
   D. Forwarding
7. In STP elections, which value is preferred?
   A. Bigger in all cases
   B. Smaller in all cases
   C. Sometimes bigger, sometimes smaller
   D. Smaller in just one, bigger in all the rest
8. Today's wired switch communication is what?
   A. Half-duplex
   B. Simplex
   C. Full-duplex
   D. Quarter-duplex
9. What is the goal of STP?
   A. To allow for efficient routing
   B. To allow for efficient switching
   C. To give out default gateway information
   D. To block switching loops

10. Which of the following is true?
    A. A voice VLAN and a data VLAN should be treated the same way.
    B. A voice VLAN should be prioritized over a data VLAN.
    C. A data VLAN should be prioritized over a voice VLAN.
    D. A voice VLAN and a data VLAN both exist in routers.

Answers

1. **D.** Routers have a routing table, as they are Layer 3 devices. Switches don't route; instead, they use the SAT/CAM/MAC address table to decide which port(s) a frame should be sent out of.
2. **A.** Switches learn where hosts are by inspecting incoming frames and looking at the source MAC address. Then, the switch associates the MAC address with the port the switch heard it on. Switches don't learn where hosts are by the destination MAC address, but can send traffic from the correct ports when the destinations have sent traffic before. Switches do not inspect IP addresses in packets.
3. **B.** Switches look at the destination MAC address in the frame and check the SAT for the outgoing port associated with that MAC address.
4. **C.** A switched virtual interface, an IP address assigned to a VLAN, is the default gateway for all devices on that VLAN/subnet.
5. **A.** PAgP is Cisco propietary, while LACP is open.
6. **B.** Disabled means the port is shut down, and thus cannot be participating in STP.
7. **B.** Smaller is the preference in all STP election phases.
8. **C.** Full duplex means the device can send and receive at the same time.
9. **D.** STP's goal is to block switching loops.
10. **B.** Voice, due to its time sensitivity, should always be prioritized over data.

DNS and DHCP

IN THIS CHAPTER, YOU WILL LEARN HOW TO

- Explain how name resolution through DNS works
- Differentiate between DNS resource record types
- Compare authoritative DNS servers and caching DNS servers
- Distinguish forward lookup zones and reverse lookup zones
- Describe how DHCP works
- Follow the DORA process of DHCP
- Differentiate between dynamic addressing and static addressing
- Define DHCP concepts, including lease, scope, exclusion, reservation, and relay agent

When you think of some of the most iconic duos of all time, certain ones come to mind. Abbott and Costello. Bert and Ernie. Batman and Robin. Snoopy and Woodstock. C-3PO and R2-D2. Lennon and McCartney. In the wonderful world of networking, two protocols that serve completely different purposes are often mentioned together thanks to their great importance as network services. In this chapter, we'll take a deep dive into the dynamic duo of DNS and DHCP.

Historical/Conceptual

Some websites, like the one for Rochester Institute of Technology (*www.rit.edu*), can be accessed by their IP address (129.21.1.40). Multiple websites hosted by a hosting company on the same machine can't be accessed by their IP address, however, because it's ambiguous which site is being requested. In these cases, you need the name of the website to resolve that ambiguity. But how does a request for a specific website get to the machine if the user can't specify the IP address? Domain Name System (DNS) has that covered. DNS implements name resolution to resolve a fully qualified domain name (FQDN) like *www.rit.edu* into an IP address like 129.21.1.40. Without name resolution, accessing resources, both locally and on the web, would be painful at best, and impossible at worst.

Take out your phone. How many phone numbers are stored there? Out of all these numbers, how many can you dial from memory? I don't know how we managed before smartphones, as I fully rely on my Favorites, Contacts, and Siri. Now imagine if you had to memorize the IP addresses of websites and network resources. Before DNS existed, you either had to access resources by IP addresses from memory or use a text file called *hosts* found on all operating systems. Originally published and manually updated by Stanford Research Institute for members of the Advanced Research Projects Agency Network (ARPANET), the hosts file contained hostnames and corresponding IP addresses.

Today's operating systems still have the hosts file, but it's not used for the same purpose. We don't collect pairs of web addresses and IP addresses and type them into the hosts file. That's not scalable. In addition, website IP addresses change. Isn't it easier to type *www.rit.edu* into a browser instead of memorizing that server's IP address of 129.21.1.40? If Google stored and indexed IP addresses instead of websites' FQDNs, search results would be incorrect, inconsistent, and unpredictable whenever those IP addresses changed.

Thankfully, Google also realizes that storing IP addresses is a flawed idea. When a website's IP address changes—due to a network reorganization, new ISP, or a company merger, for example—Google doesn't need to be notified, because the name stays the same. It's just like updating a friend's phone number in your Contacts list. You can ask Siri to call Bob and because Siri is still referencing that contact by name, not by number, the call will succeed. Likewise, an IP address for a server might change, but the name of that machine stays the same.

CURRENT APPLICATIONS FOR THE HOSTS FILE

These days, antimalware software uses the hosts file to send all requests to malicious domains to 127.0.0.1, where the request dies because your local machine doesn't host those malicious sites. Malware also uses the hosts file to write entries to send requests to legitimate sites, such as *www.linkedin.com*, to a malicious server. In addition, the hosts file maps the IPv4 loopback address (127.0.0.1) and the IPv6 loopback address (::1) to the name *localhost*.

The hosts file is used when:

- You have a small network of hosts without DNS and need to resolve by name rather than IP.
- You need to override DNS when infrastructure has changed and admins have not updated DNS.

- You need to do testing and override DNS by sending traffic to a new or testing server rather than the production one.
- There are domain considerations, such as if you need to direct traffic by FQDN to a remote network segment with its own Windows domain (so DNS servers do not share information each other). Or, as another example, you might need to move and recover resources between a failed Windows domain and a new one. With the failed DNS offline, you can add hosts entries to allow software to temporarily resolve to the old servers while the resources are moved to the new DNS domain.

At the same time, entries in the hosts file can interfere with the DNS name resolution processes (where entries were added before the new domain was set up), as well as with proper Active Directory (AD) domain operations, until they are removed.

The DNS client resolver cache on Windows contains entries preloaded from the hosts file and entries from recent DNS responses. As of Windows 2000, the operating system no longer checks the hosts file directly on each DNS query. Instead, its contents are loaded into the DNS cache when the DNS client service starts (or when changes are made and saved to the hosts file), and all lookups consult the cache first. This behavior is specific to Windows. Linux and macOS still check the hosts file dynamically for each query, typically before DNS resolution, according to system configuration (for example, *nsswitch.conf* on Linux).

Clearly, DNS is a necessary protocol for all networks. Now let's turn to this chapter's other major protocol.

Dynamic Host Configuration Protocol (DHCP) implements *dynamic addressing*—automatically assigning an IP address and other parameters, including subnet mask, default gateway, and DNS server IP addresses—whenever a computer connects to the network.

Back in the early days of networking, devices were manually configured with their static 32-bit IPv4 addresses, subnet masks, and more. That means a systems administrator had to walk over to every machine to access, change, and maintain the settings. Humans are very prone to errors. One mistake in the IP address or subnet mask, and the device might lose network connectivity. This approach wasn't very scalable either. Enter DHCP.

DHCP works like this: A client machine asks the DHCP server for an IP address. The server picks one from a pool of addresses and assigns it (along with the other parameters just mentioned) to the host, binding the logical IP address to the host's physical MAC address for some duration. This process is known as a *lease*. It's not too different from how you lease a car. Unlike a car lease, though, the client tries to renew the lease before it expires to avoid losing network connectivity.

Nowadays, static addressing is still prevalent, specifically for servers and router interfaces that can't rely on a DHCP server giving them dynamic IP addresses. If that DHCP server were to go down, these important resources would go down with it. However, statically assigning addresses isn't scalable for client machines in a network. That's why, just like DNS, DHCP is an essential network protocol.

We'll go into more detail on DHCP later in the chapter, but for now let's return to DNS for a deeper dive.

Test Specific

The DNS Structure and Query Resolution Process

A domain (like rit.edu, flcc.edu, and syr.edu) will have multiple DNS servers for responding to queries from other domains' DNS servers. For example, if I'm on the rit.edu domain and I want to go to the FLCC website, a query will be issued from the RIT DNS server to one of the FLCC DNS servers for the IP address of www.flcc.edu (as described in great detail shortly). In this case, the FLCC DNS servers give out information about resources on the flcc.edu domain to DNS servers from other domains (rit.edu).

In addition to the DNS servers that respond to queries from other domains' DNS servers, each domain will also have a different type of DNS server (usually two for each domain) to do the querying for internal clients. In this case, the RIT DNS server is issuing a query for an internal client to an external DNS server at flcc.edu.

The DNS servers that respond to queries from other domains' DNS servers have a *zone file* that lists all the hostnames on the domain and their corresponding IP addresses, along with other resource record types (discussed shortly).

> **NOTE** Both the hosts file/DNS resolver cache combination and the zone file map hostnames to IP addresses, but the former is on each device, while the latter is on the server. So, if the hosts file/DNS resolver cache combination is like your personal Contacts list on your phone, the zone file is more like directory assistance. If you don't find the phone number you need in your Contacts, you'll have to call directory assistance in order to reach your contact.

Each server is known as an authoritative name server for the domain, meaning it doesn't rely on a cache in RAM to give out answers, since it has the answers in the zone file. Chapter 4 discussed port numbers and how they relate to clients and servers. DNS clients send and receive traffic on a dynamic port number, while DNS servers send and receive traffic on port 53.

Imagine how busy the google.com domain is—it needs lots of DNS servers to support all the incoming DNS queries. In a case like this, a single domain will have a primary name server but several other secondary DNS servers, all of which are authoritative for the domain. The difference between the two server types is that the systems administrator makes changes to the zone file on the primary DNS server, and those changes are copied (upon request) to the secondary DNS servers in a process known as a *zone transfer*.

NOTE DNS generally uses UDP for queries because it is fast and has low overhead. If a server does not reply, the client resolver can retransmit the query or try another server. However, DNS will use TCP in three scenarios: for a zone transfer, because accuracy and integrity are important; when a DNS response exceeds 512 bytes; and with the modern encryption DNS protocols DNS over TLS (DoT) and DNS over HTTPS (DoH), both of which are covered in Chapter 17.

Zone Transfers

The primary DNS server needs to make sure that the secondary DNS server is updated with any changes to the zone file. Let's say you add a new computer called rochester to the jonathansweissman.edu domain, with the IP address 192.168.19.75. As a systems administrator, you would add this data to the primary DNS server, which will distribute this information through a zone transfer to the domain's secondary DNS servers. Timers in the SOA resource record, discussed shortly, will dictate how often the secondary DNS servers query the primary for updates (zone transfers are a pull technology, not push). In addition, if configured to do so, the primary DNS server can notify the secondary that the zone file has changed to trigger an update, with a message like "The zone file has changed; please ask me for the updates."

NOTE If a domain isn't divided into subdomains, the terms *domain* and *zone* are effectively synonymous, as there's only one zone file for that domain. Even if there are subdomains, a single zone file can still contain all DNS records for the entire domain and its subdomains, in which case the domain and zone remain one and the same. However, subdomains can also be delegated to separate DNS servers, each managing its own zone file.

For example, the domain weissman.edu could be divided into subdomains such as jonathan.weissman.edu, eva.weissman.edu, noah.weissman.edu, and jacob.weissman.edu, with each subdomain maintaining its own DNS zone. In such cases, the parent zone (weissman.edu) includes NS records that delegate authority to the DNS servers responsible for each subdomain.

Global Hierarchy

DNS works in a global hierarchical fashion. Consider the FQDN *www.flcc.edu* for the Finger Lakes Community College web server. In this example, the FQDN consists of the hostname of the machine, *www* (a common hostname for machines that run web server services); followed by the second-level domain (SLD), *flcc*; and, finally, the top-level domain (TLD), *.edu*. Most websites are set up in DNS such that if the user leaves *www* off the URL, the web server's IP address will be returned by one of various methods (more on this in the section "CNAME" later in the chapter). A URL starts with a transfer protocol (such as HTTP, HTTPS, or FTP), after which comes the FQDN, which in turn may be followed by a specific path including folders or even a filename. See if you can identify all of the parts of this URL (you can check it out online, too) from the preceding description: *https://www.rit.edu/directory/jswics-jonathan-weissman*.

If I'm at Rochester Institute of Technology connected to an RIT network and I type *www.flcc.edu* into my browser, my DNS client service will check my machine's *DNS resolver cache* in RAM for the corresponding IP address. If there's an entry for *www.flcc.edu*, my DNS client service will immediately start a TCP three-way handshake with the machine running the web server service.

If there's no such entry in the DNS resolver cache, my DNS client service will query an RIT DNS server (step 1 of Figure 7-1). Usually, there are two local DNS servers (for fault tolerance and load balancing) to get DNS information for the internal DNS clients. Each domain (in this case, flcc.edu) should also have two authoritative DNS servers, again for fault tolerance and load balancing, to handle external queries from other domains (such as rit.edu). We'll talk about this more in the section "Internal vs. External DNS" later in the chapter.

If the RIT DNS server has the IP address for *www.flcc.edu* cached from a previous client query, it will return that answer to my DNS client. Otherwise, the RIT DNS server begins some heavy lifting by asking the same query to one of the 13 root servers, also known as *root name servers*, that reside in the root zone (step 2 of Figure 7-1). The RIT DNS server picks one from multiple servers in a round-robin fashion.

ROOT DNS SERVERS

There are hundreds of root servers around the world, but they use only 13 IP addresses (initially there were 13 IPv4 addresses, but in 2008, each IPv4 address was assigned a corresponding IPv6 address). These addresses are preprogrammed into a company's internal DNS servers, which handle querying and caching for their clients. Using *anycast addressing* (in which multiple nodes share the same public IP address), DNS queries are routed automatically to the nearest root server via Border Gateway Protocol (BGP), the routing protocol the internet uses between autonomous systems. It's like finding the nearest gas station, bank, Dunkin', or Starbucks from your current location. This anycast setup allows for scalability, redundancy, and low-latency access, and keeps the original 13 root name server setup.

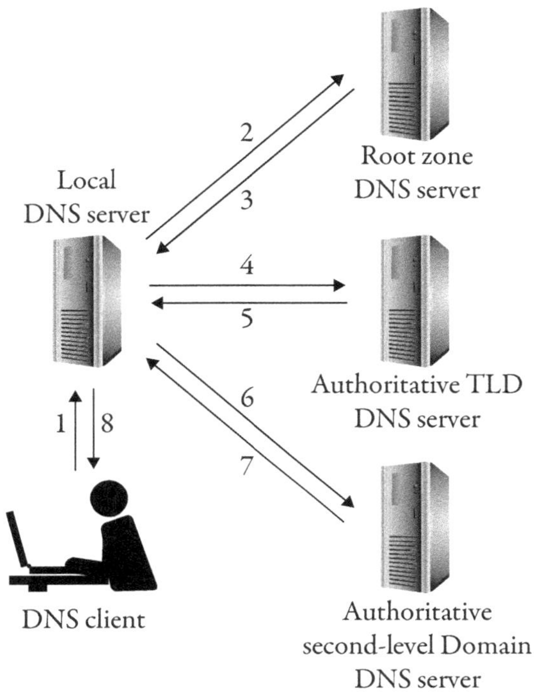

FIGURE 7-1 DNS in action

Why are there only 13 root name server IP addresses? When DNS was designed in the 1980s, DNS responses were limited to 512 bytes (the payload of UDP datagrams) to avoid IP fragmentation (when packets have to be broken up into smaller sizes) because back then networks were less reliable, had smaller buffers, and had lower bandwidths. As a result, only 13 root server names and their IP addresses could fit within a single DNS response. DNS responses that didn't fit into the 512-byte limitation were either truncated or resent over TCP (with more overhead).

Extension Mechanisms for DNS (EDNS) became commonplace in the 2000s and allowed DNS responses to exceed 512 bytes (usually up to 4,096 bytes) to support Domain Name Security Extensions (DNSSEC), IPv6 (discussed in Chapter 8), and larger resource records. DNSSEC and other security-related DNS extensions will be discussed in Chapter 17.

AUTHORITATIVE TLD DNS SERVERS

The selected root server will refer the RIT DNS server to the authoritative TLD DNS servers—in this case, those for the .edu TLD (step 3 of Figure 7-1)—and the RIT DNS server will issue the same query to one of these servers (step 4 of Figure 7-1), again selecting it in a round-robin fashion.

Note that each TLD has its own registry. If your query was for a .com TLD in this step, the referral would be for a .com authoritative TLD DNS server, not a .edu one. Each TLD has multiple machines working together to perform the authoritative name resolution. For each SLD in their TLD, these machines are only responsible for knowing the "point of contact"—specifically, the IP addresses of the authoritative DNS servers that have the zone files for each domain in the TLD. The response will be a referral to the authoritative DNS servers for flcc.edu (step 5 of Figure 7-1), and the RIT DNS server will select one of them, round-robin-style, to query (step 6 of Figure 7-1).

NOTE Notice how distributed and hierarchical DNS really is. The root servers only need to know the IP addresses of each TLD's authoritative DNS servers, not the IP address of every resource on the planet. The authoritative TLD DNS servers only need to know the IP addresses of each SLD's authoritative DNS servers, not the IP addresses of every resource in their TLD. The SLDs wouldn't want their resource records stored on the TLD servers anyway (due to security, liability, configuration, and other concerns), which is why they're stored in zone files on the SLD DNS servers.

It might seem that the root servers could be left out so that the corporate DNS servers point to the authoritative TLD DNS servers instead. That wouldn't work, though. Without root servers, whenever a new TLD is created, every single systems administrator would need to add information about it on their local DNS servers. With root servers, the local DNS servers just need information about these 13 logical IP addresses, which in turn will have the responsibility of knowing about any new TLDs.

If I'm at home and I type *www.flcc.edu* into my browser, my ISP's DNS server will go down the chain and get a response for me. If I'm using a public DNS server (such as Google's 8.8.8.8 or 8.8.4.4, Cloudflare's 1.1.1.1 or 1.0.0.1, or Quad9's 9.9.9.9), that server would do the heavy lifting. Once the response comes either to the RIT DNS server, to my ISP's DNS server, or to one of the public DNS servers (step 7 of Figure 7-1), that server caches the response so that it doesn't have to do the heavy lifting for subsequent queries. Then, it returns the response to the DNS client (step 8 of Figure 7-1). This response is also cached on the client machine, so the DNS client doesn't need to subsequently query a DNS server for the *www.flcc.edu* address.

In the case of parent and child domains, the referral process could go further. As an example, the rit.edu parent domain could contain the child domains (subdomains) cybersecurity.rit.edu (Department of Cybersecurity), ischool.rit.edu (School of Information), cs.rit.edu (Department of Computer Science), se.rit.edu (Department of Software Engineering), igm.rit.edu (School of Interactive Games and Media), and phd.rit.edu (Department of Computing and Information Sciences PhD).

Resources for rit.edu could be housed and controlled in the rit.edu parent domain, while resources specific to each department and school could be housed and controlled individually in the corresponding child domains. Then, administration and security could be delegated to multiple systems administrators at different levels. The Department of Cybersecurity, for example, wouldn't want the rit.edu systems administrators to control resources from cybersecurity.rit.edu, nor would the rit.edu systems administrators be able to administer and secure all resources from all child domains.

If a client queried a resource of the cybersecurity.rit.edu domain, let's say a web page at the fictitious FQDN *www.cybersecurity.rit.edu*, the query would hit the authoritative DNS server for the rit.edu domain the way the DNS hierarchy is set up. However, the rit.edu authoritative DNS server could do one of two things based on how the systems administrator configured it:

1. Give the querying DNS server a referral containing the authoritative DNS servers for the cybersecurity.rit.edu zone. The querying DNS server would go one more level down the hierarchy and hit one of those servers (iteration).
2. Query the authoritative DNS server for cybersecurity.rit.edu itself and return the response to the querying DNS server (recursion).

Steps 1 and 8 in Figure 7-1 use a *recursive* lookup process. The client's local DNS server puts the client on hold, acts as the client, and then returns the response to the client in the end. Steps 2–7 use an *iterative* lookup process. The client's local DNS server is querying three separate DNS servers in a step-by-step fashion, getting further along and closer to the final IP address each time.

DNS Caching and TTL

The Time To Live (TTL) field of the DNS message encapsulated in a UDP datagram specifies how long resource records should be cached. This is not to be confused with the TTL field in the IP header, which is a hop count rather than a duration. The systems administrator of the SLD (like flcc.edu) being queried sets the DNS TTL in the zone file.

On a Windows system, to see the DNS cache, execute the following command in Command Prompt:

```
ipconfig /displaydns
```

The TTL value is stored in seconds and counts down continuously for each resource record starting from when it was first cached. If you execute the preceding command again, you can see the TTL value gradually decreasing. When it reaches 0, the resource record is removed from RAM.

On a Windows system, to clear the DNS cache, execute the following command in Command Prompt:

```
> ipconfig /flushdns
```

The TTL and caching concepts also apply to DNS servers. The result of the recursive/iterative lookup process is stored in the local DNS server's DNS cache. If the server gets another request for that resource record before the TTL expires, it checks the cache first, only performing another recursive/iterative lookup if the entry is no longer cached.

As far as other operating systems go, macOS has a native DNS cache that's integrated into the OS itself. While Linux systems don't have a native DNS cache, they can do DNS caching if a dedicated service like systemd-resolved, dnsmasq, or nscd is installed and active.

DNS Resource Record Types

Part of the power and flexibility of DNS comes from how it uses various resource record types to do its job. Throughout this section, we'll use the `nslookup` ("name server lookup") utility to explore each record type.

NOTE The nslookup tool is useful for troubleshooting DNS issues because it bypasses the operating system's DNS resolver cache and sends queries directly to the configured DNS server. This makes it ideal for diagnosing whether a problem lies with cached results or upstream name resolution. You can use nslookup to troubleshoot IP addresses, hostnames, FQDNs, DNS servers, MX records, and more.

A more advanced tool, dig, is also cross-platform and provides detailed output, but it is not installed by default on Windows. Like nslookup, dig also bypasses the DNS resolver cache and performs direct DNS queries, making both tools effective for testing fresh resolution rather than relying on possibly stale cached data.

A

An IPv4 host address (A) resource record maps hostnames or FQDNs to IPv4 addresses, such as www.rit.edu to 129.21.1.40. Individual host machines get their own unique A resource record.

When you open a browser and enter *www.rit.edu*, your system asks your DNS server for that FQDN's A resource record. Assuming nothing is in cache anywhere, your DNS server then sends the same query to a root name server, an authoritative TLD DNS server, and finally the authoritative DNS server for the rit.edu domain. The response 129.21.1.40 is sent first from a rit.edu domain authoritative DNS server, and then from your DNS server back to you. For this specific FQDN, though, there's another resource record type, CNAME (discussed shortly), that comes into play.

On a Windows system, to see your DNS server(s), execute the following command in Command Prompt:

```
> ipconfig /all
```

The `DNS Servers` section will be listed toward the bottom of the output.

In Command Prompt, type **`nslookup`** and then hit ENTER. Now, `nslookup` will run interactive mode, which you can exit with CTRL-C. Your default DNS server's FQDN and IP address will be displayed. At the prompt, type the following and hit ENTER to set the query type (`q`) to `A`:

```
> set q=A
```

At the next prompt, type the FQDN of FLCC's website (including the dot at the end, for reasons I'll explain in the upcoming "MX" section) and hit ENTER:

```
> www.flcc.edu.
```

You'll see the corresponding IP addresses.

Keep `nslookup` running as is for the other resource record examples in this section.

AAAA

An IPv6 host address (AAAA) resource record maps hostnames or FQDNs to IPv6 addresses. For example, the response to the AAAA query for www.rit.edu will be 2620:8d:8000:0:aba:-ca:daba:217. If your machine is running both IPv4 and IPv6 (covered in the next chapter), your browser will issue separate queries for both the A resource record and the AAAA resource record for a website.

NOTE The resource record type is called AAAA, or "quad A," because IPv6 addresses are four times the length of IPv4 addresses (32 bits × 4 = 128 bits).

At the prompt, type the following and hit ENTER, to set the query type to AAAA:

```
> set q=AAAA
```

At the next prompt, type the following FQDN (including the dot at the end) and hit ENTER:

```
> www.google.com.
```

You'll see the corresponding IPv6 address.

CNAME

A canonical name (CNAME) resource record is an alias that maps a hostname or FQDN to another hostname or FQDN. For example, if you query for the A resource record of *www.rit.edu*, you'll be given a CNAME response of web01www01.rit.edu. The RIT web server's hostname is web01www01 (for whatever reason), but the RIT systems administrators knew this would be annoying for users to type, so they created a CNAME resource record to map any query for www.rit.edu to web01www01.rit.edu. The CNAME response plays the "think ahead game" and gives the A resource record for web01www01.rit.edu as well, which is 129.21.1.40. Therefore, in this case, you can access the same website by its actual hostname, its aliased hostname, and its IP address.

At the `nslookup` prompt, type the following and hit ENTER to set the query type to `A`:

```
> set q=A
```

At the next prompt, type the FQDN of RIT's website as follows (including the dot at the end) and hit ENTER:

```
> www.rit.edu.
```

You'll see the corresponding name of `web01www01.rit.edu` (which has the alias of `www.rit.edu`) and its IP address of `129.21.1.40`. Incidentally, RIT has an A record for rit.edu that maps to 129.21.1.40, which is used when the query omits `www`.

Syracuse University uses the CNAME record in a different way. Anytime a query for www.syr.edu hits the Syracuse University authoritative DNS servers, a CNAME response of syr.edu is returned, along with its corresponding A record of 128.230.18.63. This way, anyone who types www.syr.edu gets the A record for syr.edu. The systems administrator made an A record for the domain itself, not www.syr.edu, and with a CNAME record, all queries for www.syr.edu are turned into queries for syr.edu.

With the query still set to `A` from the previous example, at the prompt, type the FQDN of Syracuse University's website as follows (including the dot at the end) and hit ENTER:

```
> www.syr.edu.
```

You'll see the corresponding name of `syr.edu` (which has the alias of `www.syr.edu`) and its IP address of `128.230.18.63`.

In a different fashion, Nazareth University maps both the domain (naz.edu) and the FQDN (www.naz.edu) to the same IP address (204.128.145.15) in separate A records for each.

With the query still set to `A`, at the prompt, type the FQDN of Naz's website as follows and hit ENTER:

```
> www.naz.edu.
```

Now, at the prompt, type the following (omitting the `www`) and hit ENTER:

```
> naz.edu.
```

You'll notice both results show the same IP address and neither has an Aliases section, which proves that there is an A resource record for www.naz.edu and another A resource record for naz.edu.

Typing in `www` is necessary for certain domains. Pinging or going to the website of the branches of the US Armed Forces with a browser will work:

www.army.mil.

www.navy.mil.

www.af.mil.

www.marines.mil.

www.uscg.mil.

www.spaceforce.mil.

But for all six, leaving off the *www* will not work, because they have chosen not to populate the default/apex record for the domain (for example, the apex record for flcc.edu is flcc.edu). Most major sites or domains will populate it as a courtesy to their visitors, though.

These sites have likely omitted the apex record purposely, perhaps to avoid directing requests missing a server name to their main website. Other domains might simply have ignored an extra step in their setup.

Try it out for all of the above! For the pings, open a new Command Prompt session or exit the `nslookup` environment first, because you can't send pings from there.

MX

A mail exchanger (MX) resource record maps a domain to the FQDNs of that domain's mail servers. When your Simple Mail Transfer Protocol (SMTP) server has email to send to another domain, it issues a DNS query to your domain's DNS server for the MX resource record of the destination domain. For example, if I want to send an email to my RIT email account from my FLCC email account, my FLCC email server will issue a query to the FLCC DNS server, asking for the rit.edu domain's MX resource record. One of the answers coming back (RIT has multiple MX records and mail servers) will be mx03a-in01r.rit.edu.

The answer to the query for an MX resource record will always be an FQDN. Now, the FLCC SMTP server will need to issue a query for the A resource record for the IP address of mx03a-in01r.rit.edu to get its corresponding IP address of 129.21.3.76. In some cases and configurations, to cut down on the extra traffic that would be needed, the RIT DNS server does a recursive lookup for the A resource record itself and presents it, along with the reply to the MX query, to the FLCC DNS server, which in turn presents all this information to the FLCC SMTP server.

At the `nslookup` prompt, type the following and hit ENTER to set the query type to `MX`:

```
> set q=MX
```

At the next prompt, type the following (including the dot at the end) and hit ENTER:

```
> rit.edu.
```

You'll see the corresponding mail server FQDNs for the rit.edu domain.

When querying for an MX record, you can't provide an FQDN like www.rit.edu, since the domain's mail servers are for the domain itself, not for individual hosts on that domain. This is why it's necessary to add the dot at the end in this case.

All DNS names end with a dot. In the previous `nslookup` queries, leaving it off would have had no apparent effect on the output; however, it would have generated error responses under the hood. Windows will always try to append any DNS name without a dot with configured suffixes (relative to the domain you're on). For example, when you are connected to the rit.edu domain, an `nslookup` query for www.flcc.edu (without the dot at the end) would show up in Wireshark as a query for www.flcc.edu.rit.edu, which, of course, doesn't exist. Then, your machine would try it without the suffix, and that would work. Thus, you'd only see the "good output" in Command Prompt.

In this case, though, where the query isn't for an FQDN, you need the dot, because if you tried the previous MX query with a hostname (www.rit.edu., for example) or without a dot (rit.edu), you'd get the SOA record—which indicates that something is wrong, as explained in the next section.

SOA

A start of authority (SOA) resource record contains a zone's administrative information with the following fields:

PRIMARY NAME SERVER The FQDN of the primary (master) DNS server for the zone. This server holds the authoritative copy of the zone data, which secondary servers use to update their copies.

RESPONSIBLE MAIL ADDR The email address of the zone administrator listed in the SOA record. In this format, a dot (.) replaces the @ symbol to conform with DNS syntax (e.g., admin.rit.edu. corresponds to admin@rit.edu). This provides a contact point for DNS issues.

SERIAL A number that increments each time the zone file is updated. When a secondary DNS server checks the primary, it compares serial numbers. If the primary's serial is higher, the secondary performs a zone transfer to update its copy.

REFRESH The interval at which a secondary DNS server checks the primary server for updates to a zone (by comparing the SOA serial number). If the serial has changed, the secondary performs a zone transfer to update its copy.

RETRY The interval for which a secondary DNS server waits after a failed zone refresh attempt before trying again to contact the primary server for an updated zone. This retry process continues until the zone is successfully updated or the EXPIRE interval is reached.

EXPIRE The interval after which a secondary DNS server stops considering a zone authoritative if it hasn't been able to successfully refresh the zone from the primary server.

After this period, the secondary will no longer serve authoritative answers for the zone until it can successfully contact the primary again.

DEFAULT TTL ThThe TTL value applied to any resource record in a zone that does not have its own explicit TTL. When the primary DNS server performs a zone transfer to a secondary server, this default value ensures that all records on the secondary have a valid TTL, controlling how long they are cached by resolvers.

NOTE Despite the fact that `nslookup` labels the last column "Default TTL," some DNS servers (for example, Berkeley Internet Name Domain, or BIND) instead use the last field as a negative TTL caching value, which indicates how long to keep an "I can't find the answer to that query" response from a DNS server in cache.

At the `nslookup` prompt, type the following and hit ENTER to set the query type to SOA:

```
> set q=SOA
```

At the next prompt, type the following one at a time (including the dot at the end), hitting ENTER after each:

```
> flcc.edu.
> rit.edu.
> syr.edu.
```

Notice how the values for each SOA resource record vary.

PTR

A pointer (PTR) resource record maps IP addresses to their corresponding hostnames or FQDNs by doing the exact reverse of what DNS normally does: forming the value to query by taking an IP address, reversing the order of the four octets, and adding a unique TLD called in-addr.arpa. For example, a query for 129.21.1.40 becomes 40.1.21.129.in-addr.arpa and will be mapped to the corresponding FQDN, which will be sent in a DNS response. The octets must be reversed because IP addresses go from general (the network ID) to specific (the host ID), but FQDNs go from specific to general (the computer name, then the SLD, then the TLD).

One place you'll see PTR resource records in action is when you do a tracert/traceroute. Instead of just displaying the IP addresses, whenever possible, a PTR resource record will turn those IP addresses into FQDNs to make the output more meaningful. PTR resource records are also used to show FQDNs in logfiles. You can manually look up an IP address, but having logfiles do it automatically is more efficient.

You might have noticed that when you entered the `nslookup` environment, it showed the IP address of your primary DNS server. That's because a PTR query was issued in the background for the IP address of your primary DNS server, to which all queries will be sent by default (this can be changed, as explained shortly in the "NS" section).

At the `nslookup` prompt, type the following and hit ENTER to set the query type to `PTR`:

```
> set q=PTR
```

At the next prompt, type the following and hit ENTER:

```
> 129.21.1.40
```

Notice the FQDN of the RIT web server (as explained earlier in the "CNAME" section).

TXT

A text (TXT) resource record maps text (without any specifications or requirements) to a hostname or FQDN, or simply to more text. One great usage of the TXT resource record is for Sender Policy Framework (SPF), which allows receiving SMTP servers to check that incoming mail from a domain comes from a host authorized by that domain's administrators. Authorized sending hosts and IP addresses for a domain are specified in a specially formatted TXT resource record, which is checked by receiving SMTP servers. This can prevent email spoofing, spam, and phishing that forge "From:" addresses.

At the `nslookup` prompt, type the following and hit ENTER to set the query type to `TXT`:

```
> set q=TXT
```

At the next prompt, type the following (including the dot at the end) and hit ENTER:

```
> rit.edu.
```

Notice the section starting with `v=spf1` containing all the IP addresses that can send mail on behalf of the rit.edu domain.

A second great use of the TXT resource record is for DomainKeys Identified Mail (DKIM), which authenticates email and, like SPF, prevents email spoofing, spam, and phishing. In this case, the owner of a domain uses a public/private key pair just for signing outgoing messages. The public key is listed in a DNS TXT resource record, while the private key can be accessed by the DKIM-enabled outbound email server.

When an authorized domain user sends an email, the server uses the private key to generate a digital signature of the message, which becomes the message's header. The DKIM-enabled receiving email server examines the signature and claimed From: domain, and then retrieves the public key from the DNS system for that From: domain to verify the signature. A match proves that the email was sent from, and with the permission of, the claimed domain and that the message headers and content, including attachments, haven't changed in transit. The message might be deleted if the signature does not match.

With the query still set to `TXT`, at the prompt, type the following (the first part, `rit1608`) can only be gleaned from an email from that mail server) and hit ENTER:

```
> rit1608._domainkey.rit.edu.
```

Notice the section starting with `v=DKIM1` containing `p=` followed by the public key of the domain used for verification.

A third great use of the TXT resource record is for Domain-based Message Authentication, Reporting and Conformance (DMARC), which enables domain owners to protect their domains from email spoofing and other unauthorized-use attempts. Domain administrators publish a policy, with a DNS TXT resource record, that specifies what should happen if SPF and/or DKIM verification fail.

With the query still set to `TXT`, at the prompt, type the following and hit ENTER:

```
> _dmarc.rit.edu.
```

Notice the section starting with `v=DMARC1` containing fields and values used for protection and reporting.

One final usage of the `TXT` resource record is how some cloud service providers, such as Azure, validate ownership of custom domains. You are provided with data to include in your `TXT` record, and once you've done so, the domain is verified and can be used. The idea is that if you control the DNS, then you own the domain name.

SRV

A service (SRV) resource record maps a service to a hostname or FQDN and a port number. For example, SRV resource records can help clients find a domain controller running Lightweight Directory Access Protocol (LDAP) through Active Directory by mapping the LDAP service to the domain controller's hostname.

At the nslookup prompt, type the following and hit ENTER to set the query type to `SRV`:

```
> set q=SRV
```

At the next prompt, type the following one at a time, hitting ENTER after each:

```
> _ldap._tcp.ad.rit.edu.
> _kerberos._tcp.ad.rit.edu.
```

Notice that ports 389 (LDAP) and 88 (Kerberos) are associated with their corresponding services, as discussed in Chapter 4.

NS

A name server (NS) resource record maps a domain to the FQDNs of the authoritative DNS servers for that domain. When a root name server refers your DNS server to a TLD DNS server, it gives your DNS server the FQDNs of the authoritative TLD DNS servers. Your DNS server must then query for the A resource records of each of these servers before asking one of them the next question. Similarly, when an authoritative TLD DNS server refers your DNS server to the authoritative DNS server for the destination domain, your DNS server must then query for those A resource records to get their IP addresses before asking one of them the next question.

At the `nslookup` prompt, type the following and hit ENTER to set the query type to `NS`:

```
> set q=NS
```

At the next prompt, type the following one at a time, hitting ENTER after each:

```
> .
> edu.
> flcc.edu.
```

You'll see the 13 root name servers first, followed by the authoritative TLD DNS servers for the .edu domain, and finally the authoritative DNS servers for flcc.edu. Of course, to get the corresponding IP addresses, each of these FQDN answers needs to be queried for its corresponding A or AAAA record.

Authoritative vs. Non-Authoritative Responses

Let's revisit an earlier example. Change the query type to `A` and query for the IPv4 address of www.flcc.edu as follows:

```
> set q=A
> www.flcc.edu.
```

Since the DNS response is coming from your local DNS server (which is how DNS works), and not an authoritative DNS server of flcc.edu (which is what will send the response to your DNS server), you see `Non-authoritative answer:` before the response.

As discussed earlier in the chapter, *authoritative* means the response is coming directly from a DNS server that has the corresponding zone file, whereas *non-authoritative* means the response is coming from a DNS server that doesn't have the corresponding zone file itself but got the information from a DNS server that does. To see this in action, let's find an authoritative DNS server for flcc.edu and query it directly:

```
> set q=NS
> flcc.edu.
```

You should see multiple DNS servers listed. These are the authoritative DNS servers for the flcc.edu domain. Pick one of them for subsequent queries by running the `server` command followed by its FQDN like so (you could use the DNS server's IP address instead, but you'd need to change the query type back to `A` and query for its A resource record first):

```
> server ns.suny.edu.
```

With 64 institutions across New York, State University of New York (SUNY) is the largest public university system in the United States. The zone files for these institutions, which include FLCC, are hosted on SUNY servers. Notice the IP address of the server you selected is also shown now as a PTR query executed in the background, as explained earlier.

Now for the big moment—execute the following two commands as you did before:

```
> set q=A
> www.flcc.edu.
```

There is no `Non-authoritative answer:` label in the output anymore, because this time you queried the authoritative DNS server for flcc.edu directly.

ZONE TYPES

Forward lookup zones map FQDNs to IP addresses. All of the DNS resource records just discussed except for PTR are found in forward lookup zones. *Reverse* lookup zones, as their name implies, map IP addresses to FQDNs. The only resource records found in a reverse lookup zone are SOA, NS, and PTR.

Internal vs. External DNS

As a best practice, an organization should have a pair of public DNS servers (for external requests) and a separate pair of private DNS servers (for internal requests).

Internal versus external DNS relates to who is asking the queries and who is answering them. Public DNS servers must be authoritative for external hosts accessing internal resources, like a web server that the company wants the outside world to access. However, for clients inside that domain that need access to external resources, like another company's web page, private DNS servers act both as resolvers and as caching servers. Furthermore, these private DNS servers could host resource records for internal resources that shouldn't be accessed by external networks. From a security (availability) standpoint, having two separate servers protects you from a single point of failure.

SPLIT-HORIZON DNS

Split-horizon DNS is a mechanism that returns different IP addresses for the same resource, depending on where the query originates. For example, if resources.flcc.edu is an internal server and accessible from outside the network through a different address (either through port forwarding or dual NICs), then internal devices will get the server's private IP address, while external DNS servers issuing queries on behalf of their clients will get the server's public IP address.

Through split-horizon DNS, local machines can access corporate servers directly through the local infrastructure instead of having their traffic sent to the corporate router, minimizing latency.

You can also think about internal and external DNS in terms of the location of your DNS infrastructure. Instead of using an internal authoritative DNS server to resolve queries about resources in your domain, as you've seen so far, you could use a cloud-based DNS provider, putting your resource records on their servers and having those servers resolve queries for resources in your domain, for scalability, predictability, and security (i.e., to avoid a distributed denial of service, or DDoS, attack). This strategy isn't foolproof, however: Dyn, a former DNS service provider, was itself the target of a series of major DDoS attacks on October 21, 2016, and hundreds of sites—some of them major internet sites, no less—that depended on Dyn for DNS services became inaccessible.

DHCP Operations and Configuration

Now that you understand how DNS name resolution works, we can return to this chapter's other major protocol, DHCP, to explore how devices actually obtain the IP addresses that DNS helps resolve.

THE DORA Process

Earlier in the chapter, you learned that a client asks the DHCP server for an IP address and the server assigns one, but now we'll examine the specific messages exchanged during this process. Whenever I teach DHCP in a course, I have a Dora the Explorer doll nearby. At first, students have no idea what its purpose is. But once I start wondering aloud if there's a good acronym to remember the four DHCP messages sent initially (there are eight in total, the other four will be discussed shortly), they figure it out and crack up!

NOTE DHCP uses UDP for all messages. At the very beginning of the leasing process, the client doesn't have an IP address, so TCP and its three-way handshake are not even possible. The client sends messages during the leasing process with the unspecified address 0.0.0.0 (referred to as "quad zero").

DISCOVER

When a DHCP client boots up, it automatically sends out a DHCP Discover UDP datagram with a source IP address in the packet of 0.0.0.0 (the unspecified address) and a destination IP address in the packet of 255.255.255.255 (the flooded broadcast address). This DHCP Discover message asks, "Are there any DHCP servers out there?" See Figure 7-2.

The client can't send unicast traffic yet, as it doesn't have a valid IP address to use. DHCP servers send and receive traffic on port 67, while DHCP clients send and receive traffic on port 68. DHCP is unique among client services in that it uses a well-known port number (1–1023) rather than a dynamic port.

FIGURE 7-2
DHCP Discover

NOTE There's a good reason why DHCP clients use a fixed UDP port (68). If DHCP clients were to use dynamic ports like many other services, it could cause confusion across the network. For instance, if one DHCP client used a high-numbered port such as 60,000, and another device on the same network was running a different client service, like a web browser, listening on that same port, both devices would receive the DHCP broadcast sent to port 60,000.

Each operating system would then deliver the DHCP message to the application bound to that port, potentially causing non-DHCP applications to receive and misinterpret DHCP traffic. By standardizing port 68 for DHCP clients, DHCP servers know exactly where to send responses, and clients reliably listen there. When multiple DHCP clients coexist on the same network, they all listen on port 68, but each client uses its unique MAC address embedded in the DHCP messages to identify which responses are intended for it.

OFFER

A DHCP server is designed to respond to DHCP Discover requests with a DHCP Offer, which, depending on various factors, could either be unicast (to the address being offered) or broadcast. See Figure 7-3.

The DHCP server is configured to provide, in this DHCP Offer, an IP address, subnet mask, default gateway, and more to the client (see the upcoming "Options" section).

FIGURE 7-3 DHCP Offer

REQUEST

The DHCP client sends out a DHCP Request as a broadcast. See the left side of Figure 7-4.

FIGURE 7-4 DHCP Request and DHCP Ack

The client still can't unicast, but as an added benefit of broadcasting here, if multiple offers came from multiple servers, this broadcast lets one server know the client wants its IP address, and the other servers know the client doesn't want theirs. Those servers can then return their addresses to the pool for a future request instead of leaving them in an in-between state.

ACKNOWLEDGE

The DHCP server then sends a DHCP Ack (which like the DHCP Offer can be either unicast or broadcast) and starts the lease for the DHCP client, associating the DHCP client's MAC address with the IP address from the scope. See the right side of Figure 7-4.

At the end of the four-step DHCP dance—Discover, Offer, Request, and Ack (DORA)—the DHCP client has a DHCP lease.

NOTE DHCP servers in home routers always send Offers and Acks as broadcasts, but in most cases, standalone DHCP servers (dedicated machines running DHCP services) will send the Offers and Acks unicast to the address being offered. The client will open the frame and packet and notice the UDP datagram with a destination port of 68. The DHCP Offer or Ack will be inside the UDP datagram, with the MAC address of the client requesting the address. If it's that machine's MAC address, the machine will know the message is in the right place; otherwise, the message will be dropped.

DHCP Commands

Network techs sometimes must manually refresh a network host's DHCP lease, such as when a major change has been made to the network's configuration. To release and renew a network host's DHCP lease manually on a Windows system, you must execute two commands in Command Prompt:

- **`ipconfig /release`** releases the IP address back into the pool of addresses.
- **`ipconfig /renew`** causes the host to obtain a new DHCP lease or renews an existing lease without running `ipconfig /release` first.

To see DHCP-related information, execute **`ipconfig /all`** and notice the `DHCP Enabled`, `Autoconfiguration Enabled` (referring to APIPA), `Lease Obtained`, `Lease Expires`, and `DHCP Server` values. You'll also notice the configuration you received from the DHCP server in the `IPv4 Address`, `Subnet Mask`, `Default Gateway`, and `DNS Servers` values.

Options

The server, in addition to an IP address, gives the client other parameters for configuration, known as *options*. Some of the more common options, which are numbered, are:

- 1: Subnet mask
- 3: Default gateway

- 6: DNS servers
- 51: Time that the IP address is leased for

The DHCP client, in its DHCP Discover and DHCP Request, sends options of its own to the server. Some of the more common ones are:

- 61: Client identifier (MAC address)
- 12: Host name
- 60: Vendor class identifier (MSFT 7.0 for Microsoft Windows 10, for example)
- 55: Parameter request list (what options the client is requesting from the server, although the server sends only what it's configured for, not necessarily everything requested)

Options can be set at a server, scope, or reservation level (a *reservation*, discussed shortly, is a preset configuration for a specific client). This allows you to both generalize settings (for example, setting the same DNS servers for all scopes) and override them for specific devices (for example, specifying a default gateway or DNS server for a particular device).

Lease

A DHCP lease is set for a fixed amount of time, generally one to eight days. The number of available leases depends on the number of addresses in the scope.

Halfway (50 percent) into the lease, the DHCP client sends out a DHCP Request as a unicast to the DHCP server it got the address from (during DORA, the DHCP Request is a broadcast), trying to renew its lease. If that DHCP server doesn't respond, at 87.5 percent into the lease, the DHCP client will send out DHCP Requests as broadcasts in hopes that another DHCP server will renew its lease. If the lease fully elapses, the client gives itself an APIPA address (169.254.0.0/16; see the following note) and periodically sends out DHCP Discover messages in an effort to restart the DORA process.

LINK-LOCAL ADDRESSES AND GRATUITOUS ARPS

The single biggest DHCP issue is when a DHCP client fails to get a DHCP-assigned address. You'll know when this happens because the operating system will return an error telling you there's a problem (this commonly occurs when a device detects another, likely statically configured, device using the same IP address), and the DHCP client will have a rather strange address in the 169.254.0.0/16 network ID range. This special IP address is generated by a version of zero-configuration networking (Zeroconf) when a DHCP client fails to obtain a lease. Microsoft's implementation is called Automatic Private IP Addressing (APIPA).

All DHCP clients are designed to generate a link-local address automatically if they detect an IP address conflict or if they do not receive a response to multiple DHCP Discover messages. The client only generates the last two octets of a link-local address. A client sends a gratuitous ARP (an unsolicited broadcast of a sender's information) to see if another device already has the IP address the client is trying to give itself. If the ARP request gets an ARP reply, that means another device is currently using that address, and the client picks another IP address on the 169.254.0.0/16 subnet. Otherwise, the client starts using the IP address it gave itself. This at least allows the dynamic clients on a single network to continue to communicate with each other because they are on the same network ID.

Unfortunately, the link-local process cannot issue a default gateway (since no router interface will ever be configured with an IP address on 169.254.0.0/16), so you'll never get on the internet using APIPA. That provides a huge clue to a DHCP problem scenario: you can communicate with other computers on your network that also received link-local addresses after the DHCP server went down, but you can't get to the internet or access computers that retain the DHCP-provided address.

There are two ways to prevent an IP address conflict in the first place. First, DHCP servers can be configured to send one or more ICMP echo requests to the address that will be offered to the client. If one or more ICMP echo replies come back, a device is already using that IP address, so the DHCP server will pick a different IP address and perform the same check. If no ICMP echo replies come back, the server offers the IP address to the client. Second, depending on the OS, DHCP clients will send a gratuitous ARP during the DORA process with an offered IP address. If an ARP reply comes back, the client will send a DHCP Decline message to the server, because that IP address is already in use (and was likely configured statically, so the DHCP server wouldn't know that this is the case).

If, within the lease period (stored in a Registry key in Windows), the DHCP client is rebooted or powered on after a shutdown, a DHCP Request will be triggered to renew the lease.

Dynamic vs. Static Assignment

DHCP clients get IP addresses and more from DHCP servers through dynamic assignment. DHCP clients need to be configured to receive addresses dynamically.

A client that is not configured for dynamic assignment uses static assignment: the manual configuration of an IP address, subnet mask, default gateway, DNS servers, and more. Servers and router interfaces should be statically configured. You don't want their IP addresses potentially changing, which could be the case with dynamic addressing.

Furthermore, reservations (covered shortly), which allow a device to get the same dynamic IP address, still pose a problem. If the DHCP server(s) goes down, the servers and router interfaces that rely on the reservations won't be able to renew leases and will become inaccessible with link-local addresses, making static assignment a much better option. A system statically assigned an IP address can still send out DHCP Inform messages (asking for other information, like DNS server IP addresses) if the DHCP client service is running.

Exclusion Ranges

Exclusion ranges are IP addresses from the pool of addresses that the DHCP server is not to give out. For example, the static addresses manually configured on servers and router interfaces are excluded, so they won't be offered to DHCP clients.

Reservation

DHCP servers can be configured to set aside IP addresses (or other configurable parameters, as discussed earlier) for specific machines through a *reservation*. The best practice with servers, though, is to use static IP addresses so that they're reachable if the DHCP server goes down, as previously mentioned.

A better use case for a reservation is a lab, where, for example, you always want Computer #13 to get the IP address 192.168.1.13. Reservations have also been popular for firewall/proxy/router access control lists (ACLs), where specific IP addresses are reserved for permitted or denied devices. While devices like proxy servers have moved to user authentication to grant access, firewalls and routers are still heavily focused on IP-based access.

DHCP Message Types

There are eight DHCP message types. They are listed in RFC 2131 in all caps with no spaces (for example, DHCPDISCOVER), but in documentation, they are written in title case with a space between the words, as seen in this chapter (for example, DHCP Discover). We've covered most of these already, but for the sake of completeness, here is the full list:

- **DHCP Discover** The client tries to find available servers.
- **DHCP Offer** One or more servers respond to the client with offers containing an available IP address and configuration parameters.
- **DHCP Request** The client formally requests the offered configuration from one server, implicitly declining offers from others. This message is also used to confirm a previously allocated address after reboot or to extend an existing lease.
- **DHCP Ack** The server acknowledges the client's request and confirms that it may use the assigned IP address and other configuration parameters.
- **DHCP Nak** The server denies the client's request, typically because the requested IP address is invalid, expired, or no longer appropriate for the client's current subnet. (Nak means negative acknowledgment.)

- **DHCP DECLINE** The client, usually after detecting a conflict (through gratuitous ARPs, mentioned earlier), informs the server that the offered IP address is already in use.
- **DHCP RELEASE** The client notifies the server that it is relinquishing its IP address and canceling the remainder of the lease.
- **DHCP INFORM** This message type is used by a DHCP client that already has an IP address, typically one that has been manually configured rather than assigned via DHCP. The client sends a DHCP Inform message to request additional network configuration parameters, like DNS server addresses, domain name information, or NTP server details, from a DHCP server. In some cases, clients that have obtained their IP address through DHCP may also issue a DHCP Inform message to refresh specific configuration options without performing a full lease renewal. This allows clients to maintain up-to-date network settings without altering their current IP configuration.

DHCP Relay and IP Helper/UDP Forwarding

In small, single-subnet networks, such as small office/home office (SOHO) and home networks, it's a given that the DHCP server will be on that subnet along with the DHCP clients. However, in an internetwork, where there are multiple subnets, it's not practical to put a DHCP server or pair of DHCP servers on each subnet. If you have a pair of DHCP servers on a different subnet, though, how do clients without IP addresses reach them? They can't send any traffic to a remote DHCP server using IP routing, because they don't have a routable IP address, they don't know the IP address of a default gateway, and they don't know the IP address of a DHCP server. Furthermore, routers don't forward broadcasts, so the DHCP Discover messages wouldn't get to the right place.

The solution is to configure router interfaces (or servers) as DHCP relay agents, also known as IP helpers. In the Cisco IOS, the command for routers is `ip helper-address 1.2.3.4`, where `1.2.3.4` represents the IP address of a DHCP server. In fact, there could be multiple router interfaces on a single LAN acting as relay agents, whereas only one of them can wind up being a client's default gateway.

The DHCP client sends a DHCP Discover broadcast to all devices on that network, including the router interface acting as the relay agent, which was configured with the IP addresses of the DHCP servers. The DHCP relay agent performs a special kind of UDP forwarding, stripping away the DHCP Discover message and the UDP datagram from the broadcast packet and frame encapsulating them. Then the relay agent places the UDP datagram with the DHCP Discover message in a new IP packet. This packet, though, is a unicast packet, sent to the actual IP address of a DHCP server with a source IP address of that relay agent itself. In other words, the relay agent takes the broadcast traffic and turns it into unicast traffic rather than simply "forwarding the broadcast."

NOTE An IP helper can turn broadcasts into unicasts for eight protocols/ UDP port numbers (not just for a DHCP relay agent):

- Time (port 37; not NTP)
- TACACS/TACACS+ (port 49; for the UDP implementation only, as most TACACS+ implementations today use TCP)
- DNS (port 53)
- BOOTP/DHCP server (port 67)
- BOOTP/DHCP CLIENT (port 68)
- TFTP (port 69)
- NetBIOS Name Service (port 137)
- NetBIOS Datagram Service (port 138)

The client's MAC address is preserved in the DHCP Discover message payload. The DHCP server can determine the scope to use for an IP address in the DHCP Offer, because the relay agent placed its IP address in the Gateway IP Address field of the DHCP Discover payload as well.

The DHCP server replies to the client by using unicast transmission to send the DHCP Offer to the relay agent, which in turn sends it to the client. The DHCP Request and DHCP Ack follow the same process.

Common DHCP Issues

Several things can cause a DHCP deployment to go awry. This section outlines some of the most common issues you'll encounter.

Address Pool Exhaustion

Address pool exhaustion occurs when the DHCP server runs out of available host IP addresses to lease to clients. For example, on a /24 network, there are 254 usable host addresses, which means if all 254 addresses are currently leased, no other DHCP clients can get an IP address from the DHCP server. If a new client sends a DHCP Discover message, that client is out of luck.

Normally, the way IP networks are designed and provisioned, address pool exhaustion shouldn't be an issue. However, it can result from new network uses or changes in implementations. If a company sets up an imaging bench and runs through 50 to 100 devices a day, using a 7-day lease, it could exhaust its address pool. Issues could also arise when many visitors enter and exit a company in a short amount of time.

Incorrect Default Gateway

If the default gateway address for a client (configured statically or dynamically) is incorrect, the client won't be able to send traffic off of its subnet.

Incorrect IP Address

An incorrect IP address—that is, one that's not in the valid range of host addresses for the subnet—will cause all communication to fail. Once again, the host won't be able to reach any local device, including its default gateway.

Duplicate IP Address

One of the most obvious configuration errors occurs when you're duplicating machines and using static IP addresses. As soon as you configure a duplicate IP address—an IP address already assigned to a device on the same network—problems will arise. No two computers can have the same IP address on a broadcast domain. The fix for the problem is either to change the IP address on the new machine to an unused static IP address or to set it to use DHCP.

Incorrect Subnet Mask

An incorrect subnet mask will stop even local traffic from the client, since it will incorrectly deduce that destinations on the same subnet are on different subnets. Remote traffic will also fail, since the client won't be able to reach its default gateway, which now won't be on the same subnet (per the incorrect mask) as the client.

Incorrect DNS

A client with incorrect DNS server IP addresses won't be able to resolve FQDNs into their corresponding IP addresses, and thus won't be able to access devices by name. This issue may be subtler (such as causing only internal DNS names to fail) if the address is a valid DNS server, just not the right one.

Chapter Review

Questions

1. If a domain client on the flcc.edu domain needs a website's IP address, which DNS server is the client configured to use?
   A. One of the 13 root name servers
   B. An authoritative TLD DNS server
   C. An authoritative DNS server for the domain
   D. The DNS server for the client's domain

2. When a domain client's DNS server is resolving *www.rit.edu* to its corresponding IP address, when does the client's DNS server query the authoritative DNS server for the .edu TLD?
   A. Before querying one of the 13 root servers
   B. After querying one of the 13 root servers
   C. After querying the authoritative DNS server for rit.edu
   D. Never
3. How many total messages are sent just between the domain DNS client and the client's domain DNS server (directly from the domain client to its domain DNS server, and from the domain DNS server to its domain client, not including any other server), when the client needs a name resolved to its corresponding IP address? Assume there are no cached entries.
   A. 2
   B. 4
   C. 6
   D. 8
4. By default (without configuring your networked devices to use a public DNS server like Google's 8.8.8.8 or 8.8.4.4), when your devices at home need to resolve FQDNs to IP addresses, which server does most of the querying?
   A. The router in the home
   B. The ISP's DNS server
   C. The DNS server in the home
   D. One of the 13 root name servers
5. Which of the following should use DHCP rather than static configuration?
   A. DNS server
   B. Client machine
   C. Router
   D. DHCP server
6. Which of these DNS resource records is for a mail server?
   A. MX
   B. A
   C. AAA
   D. NS

7. When a DHCP server is on a different network than the DHCP client, how does the DHCP server know from which scope to give the client an address?
   A. The client will specify it.
   B. The client's MAC address will indicate it.
   C. The DHCP server will pick a random scope.
   D. The relay agent's IP address will indicate it.
8. From which devices do clients that are not statically configured learn who their DNS servers are?
   A. DNS server
   B. DHCP server
   C. Default gateway
   D. Systems administrator
9. During the DHCP DORA process, what address does the client use as the source IP address?
   A. Its IPv4 address
   B. A multicast address
   C. A broadcast address
   D. 0.0.0.0
10. During the DHCP DORA process, what address does the client use as the destination IP address?
   A. Its IPv4 address
   B. A multicast address
   C. A broadcast address
   D. 0.0.0.0

Answers

1. **D.** Clients always query their domain's DNS servers.
2. **B.** A root name server will give a referral to an authoritative TLD DNS server for the specified TLD.
3. **A.** Just the first and last steps are between the DNS client and its DNS server.
4. **B.** The ISP's DNS server gives the answer to the home DNS server, which caches it for future use by clients.
5. **B.** Client devices should use DHCP.

6. **A.** Mail Exchanger (MX) records are for mail servers.
7. **D.** The relay agent's IP address will be on the same network as the client.
8. **B.** DHCP servers pass out multiple configurable parameters to clients, including DNS server IP addresses.
9. **D.** The client uses 0.0.0.0, the unspecified address, during the DORA process because it doesn't have an actual IPv4 address to use.
10. **C.** The client uses 255.255.255.255, the flooded broadcast address, during the DORA process because it can't unicast at this point since it doesn't have an actual IPv4 address to use.

IPv6

IN THIS CHAPTER, YOU WILL LEARN HOW TO

- Discuss the fundamental concepts of IPv6
- Navigate the internet address hierarchy
- Comprehend the format and representation of IPv6 addresses
- Identify the different types of IPv6 addresses
- Recognize how Neighbor Discovery Protocol works
- Grasp the roles ICMPv6 and DHCPv6 play in IPv6
- Explain how SLAAC works
- Perform subnetting in IPv6
- Describe IPv6 practices
- Employ IPv6 in a TCP/IP network
- Implement transition/tunneling mechanisms

I'm serious, the decision to put a 32-bit address space on there was the result of a year's battle among a bunch of engineers who couldn't make up their minds about 32, 128, or variable length. And after a year of fighting, I said, I'm now at ARPA, I'm running the program, I'm paying for this stuff and using American tax dollars—and I wanted some progress because we didn't know if this is going to work. So, I said 32 bits, it is enough for an experiment, it is 4.3 billion terminations—even the Defense Department doesn't need 4.3 billion of anything and it couldn't afford to buy 4.3 billion edge devices to do a test anyway. So, at the time I thought we were doing an experiment to prove the technology and that if it worked we'd have an opportunity to do a production version of it. Well—[laughter]—it just escaped!—it got out and people started to use it and then it became a commercial thing. So, this [IPv6] is the production attempt at making the network scalable. Only 30 years later.

—VINT CERF, GOOGLE IPV6 CONFERENCE 2008 (*YOUTU.BE/MZO69JQOLB8?T=815*)

TCP/IP development took place in the early 1970s, when there were fewer than 1,000 computers in the entire world, but that didn't keep the networking developers from thinking big. They decided to go absolutely crazy (as many people thought at the time) and in 1980, standardized the TCP/IP protocol suite, which included the Internet Protocol version 4 (IPv4) 32-bit IP address space, creating over four billion IP addresses. That should have held us for the foreseeable future. It didn't.

First, there were many, and huge, wasted chunks of IP addresses due to classful addressing and a generally liberal approach to assigning IP addresses. Second, the internet reached a level of popularity way beyond the original developers' imaginations. By the early 1990s, the rate of consumption for IP addresses started to worry them, and the writing was on the wall for IPv4's 32-bit addressing.

As a result, in 1994, the Internet Engineering Task Force (IETF) started developing Internet Protocol version 6 (IPv6). The first IPv6 draft became an IETF standard in 1998. IPv6 extended IPv4's 32-bit IP address space to 128 bits, allowing up to 2^{128} (that's around 3.4×10^{38}) addresses.

Do you like to go to the beach? The IPv6 address space size is more than 10 million trillion times the total number of grains of sand on every single beach on Earth. Do you like seeing things on a really small scale? You could assign an IPv6 address to all atoms on the Earth's surface and then have enough left over to do the same thing for more than 100 other "Earths." What about from a perspective in time? If a new unique IPv6 address was assigned at every picosecond (one trillionth of a second) for one trillion years, there would still be lots of IPv6 addresses available!

NOTE IPv6 offers 340,282,366,920,938,463,463,374,607,431,768,211,456 IP addresses, to be specific. In words, that's 340 undecillion, 282 decillion, 366 nonillion, 920 octillion, 938 septillion, 463 sextillion, 463 quintillion, 374 quadrillion, 607 trillion, 431 billion, 768 million, 211 thousand 456. But you can just say 340 undecillion for short.

IPv6 has been the future of TCP/IP network addressing since the IETF published the IPv6 draft standard in 1995. Someday, we knew, we'd flip the switch from IPv4 to IPv6 and transform networking, the internet, and TCP/IP forever.

New companies, internet service providers (ISPs), many mobile devices, and, of course, tens of billions of Internet of Things (IoT) devices wouldn't exist today without IPv6. In fact, the exponential growth of both mobile devices and IoT devices required immediate usage of IPv6. On the flip side, IPv6 hasn't really taken off on enterprise networks because of the ol' "if it ain't broke, don't fix it" mentality, where companies running IPv4 see no need to move ahead with IPv6 when their IPv4 deployments are running as a well-oiled machine.

This chapter breaks down the exploration of IPv6 into four parts. First, you'll learn about how IPv6 addressing works and about the different types of IPv6 addresses. Second, you'll get a walkthrough of Neighbor Discovery Protocol (NDP) and all that it entails. Third, you'll see how stateless address autoconfiguration (SLAAC), DHCPv6, DNS, and subnetting come into the picture for IPv6. Finally, you'll get familiar with transition mechanisms for infrastructures that don't have both IPv4 and IPv6 connectivity (some are connected by IPv4 only and some by IPv6 only).

As you'll see in this chapter, IPv6 is not simply an enormous expansion of available addresses. Its creators took the opportunity to make the protocol more efficient and simplified than IPv4 in many ways.

Test Specific

IPv6 Addressing

Although they achieve the same function—enabling computers on IP networks to send packets to each other—IPv6 and IPv4 differ in just about every regard. Now's the time to learn about IPv6: there's little to no pressure and no looming deadlines. At some point in the future, that will change. When it does, you'll be ready!

IPv6 Address Allocation

At the very top of the internet hierarchy is Internet Corporation for Assigned Names and Numbers (ICANN). ICANN coordinates the maintenance and procedures of various databases dealing with DNS and IP addressing. Below ICANN is Internet Assigned Numbers Authority (IANA), which is a function of ICANN. IANA was established in 1998 through a United States Department of Commerce contract and was managed by ICANN until 2016, when an ICANN affiliate, Public Technical Identifiers (PTI), took over management responsibilities. Underneath ICANN and IANA are five Regional Internet Registries (RIRs) that oversee IP addresses for different parts of the world:

- African Network Information Centre (AFRINIC), based in Ebene, Mauritius, serves all of Africa.
- American Registry for Internet Numbers (ARIN), based in Chantilly, Virginia, serves Antarctica, Canada, the United States, and various Caribbean countries and territories.
- Asia Pacific Network Information Centre (APNIC), based in Brisbane, Australia, serves East, South, and Southeast Asia and Oceania.
- Latin America and Caribbean Network Information Centre (LACNIC), based in Montevideo, Uruguay, serves Latin America and various Caribbean countries.
- Réseaux IP Européens Network Coordination Centre (RIPE NCC), based in Amsterdam, Netherlands, serves Central and West Asia, Europe, and Russia.

NOTE See *arin.net/blog/author/jonathan-s-weissman* for my blog posts on IPv6 for ARIN.

Each RIR gets IPv6 allocations from IANA, which are usually a /23. You'll recall that in Classless Inter-Domain Routing (CIDR) notation, the number after the slash represents how many 1s are in the subnet mask (called *prefix length* in IPv6). That means RIRs get blocks of IPv6 addresses with the first 23 bits locked in from IANA.

Each ISP gets a /32 (usually) from its corresponding RIR. ISPs, in turn, will "subnet" the next 16 bits and give a /48 to each of their customer sites. The number of customer site networks is 2^{16} = 65,536 (since 16 bits are being "borrowed"). In other words, each ISP can have 65,536 customer sites with that allocation of addresses.

Similarly, every customer site that gets a /48 from its ISP will subnet that, borrowing the next 16 bits, to form a /64 for each network. That means each customer site can have 2^{16} = 65,536 (again, since 16 bits are being borrowed) networks. I can't think of a single company in the world, not even one of the major corporations, that needs 65,536 networks!

For homes, the ISPs usually allocate a /56, which means 2^8 = 256 (since 8 bits are being borrowed) networks. That means each home can have 256 different networks—yes, networks, not devices. A home with 256 networks is *not* a home!

Each local area network (LAN) or network, which IPv6 calls a *link*, gets a /64 from its corporate allocation or, in the case of a home, from the home router:

$$2^{64} = 18,446,744,073,709,551,616$$

That means each IPv6 network can theoretically (but not realistically) have over eighteen quintillion devices on it.

Each IPv6 device is a /128, just like how each IPv4 device is a /32.

IPv6 Address Notation

Up until now, you've been used to looking at IPv4's dotted decimal notation, with four base-10, or decimal, numbers (octets) separated by dots, like 192.168.1.75. IPv6 moves from 32 bits to 128 bits—and thus presents a whole new way to write addresses. At first, these addresses may look a little foreign. Instead of just making every address four times as long, the IPv6 designers worked out several ways to make the human-readable form of each address—its *notation*—short enough for techs to work with.

Since IPv6 has 128 bits, the octets are gone. IPv6 addresses are written like this:

2001:0db8:0000:0000:0800:200c:00cf:1234

Instead of a dot, IPv6 uses a colon as a separator. Each 16-bit group—called a *quartet* or *hextet*—is a hexadecimal number between 0000 and ffff.

EXAM TIP You'll see the hexadecimal characters a through f in IPv6 written both uppercase and lowercase. It doesn't matter to devices, but RFC 5952 insists they should be lowercase, and that's the convention used here. You might see the letters in uppercase on the CompTIA Network+ exam. It's all the same, so don't get thrown off.

An IPv6 address splits into two 64-bit sections: the first 64 bits are the *prefix*, analogous to the IPv4 network ID, which is shared by all devices on a particular link. The second 64 bits are the *interface ID*, analogous to the IPv4 host ID, which uniquely identifies an interface (IPv6 uses the term *interface* instead of IPv4's *device* or *host*).

NOTE Base 16, hexadecimal, was covered in Chapter 1.

A complete IPv6 address always has eight groups of four hexadecimal characters. If this sounds like you're going to type in really long IP addresses, don't worry: IPv6 offers two shortcuts.

First, you can drop leading zeroes from any group, so 00cf becomes cf, 0db8 becomes db8, and 0000 becomes 0. You can rewrite the preceding IPv6 address as follows:

2001:db8:0:0:800:200c:cf:1234

You can't omit *trailing* zeroes, however, as that would change the value of a number (in any numeral system).

Second, you can use a pair of colons (::) to represent one or more consecutive hextets of all zeroes. For example, using the :: rule, you can write this IPv6 address

2001:db8:0:0:800:200c:cf:1234

as

2001:db8::800:200c:cf:1234

Double colons are very handy, but you have to be careful when you use them. Take a look at this IPv6 address:

fe80:0000:0000:0000:00cf:0000:ba98:1234

which you can convert as follows:

fe80::cf:0:ba98:1234

Note that you *cannot* use a second :: to represent the last group of four zeroes—you can only use the double colon once per address! There's a good reason for this rule. If you used more than one, you wouldn't be able to tell how many sets of zeroes were in each group. RFC 5952 states that, if there are multiple possibilities, the largest grouping of consecutive all-zero hextets should get the double colon. If there are equal-size consecutive all-zero hextets, the one that comes first, left to right, should get the double colon notation (just like order of operations in math).

IPv6 uses the */x* prefix length convention to specify the number of bits in the network ID, similar to CIDR notation in IPv4. Here's how to write an IP address and prefix length for a typical IPv6 host:

fe80::cf:0:ba98:1234/64

The /64 prefix length indicates the network prefix is 64 bits. The address starts with fe80 followed by some number of hextets of all zeroes (0000). With the /64, and the fact that there are four hextets after the double colon, you know that there are three hextets not shown and the original address looked like this:

fe80:0000:0000:0000:cf:0:ba98:1234/64

The IPv6 loopback address (which has the same usage as the IPv4 loopback address of 127.0.0.1) takes full advantage of the double colon:

::1

Without the double-colon notation, the IPv6 loopback address looks like this:

0000:0000:0000:0000:0000:0000:0000:0001

NOTE Although the prefix length technically can vary (like in IPv4), /64 is used in nearly all cases because it supports multiple IPv6 features, including Stateless Address Autoconfiguration (SLAAC), discussed later in the chapter.

Link-Local Address

One of the biggest IPv6 concepts to wrap your mind around is that a host typically has multiple IPv6 addresses at the same time. When a computer running IPv6 first boots up, it gives itself a *link-local address.*

The link-local address is the equivalent of IPv4's link-local (Zeroconf/APIPA) address in the 169.254.0.0/16 block, which indicates dynamic addressing is configured but no DHCP server is available (as discussed in Chapter 7). But unlike their IPv4 counterpart, which you want to avoid like the plague, link-local addresses in IPv6 are always used for on-link (local) communications—quite an upgrade! Clients use them to reach their default gateway, and routers use them to send routing updates to each other.

The first 64 bits of a link-local address are always fe80::/10, followed by 54 zero bits. If you recall the hexadecimal-to-binary conversions from Chapter 1, f is 1111, e is 1110, 8 is 1000, and 0 is 0000, so fe80::/10 means that the first 10 bits are 1111111010. Remember, trailing zeroes can't be dropped, which is why the standard doesn't say fe8::/10, which would imply 0fe8::/10.

NOTE According to RFC 4291, this structure means every link-local address always begins with fe80:0000:0000:0000, or fe80::/64 in practice.

The interface ID, the second 64 bits of a link-local address, is generated in two ways. Most operating systems generate a 64-bit random number. Older operating systems (and also devices where this privacy is less critical) may instead use the device's MAC address to create a 64-bit number called an *Extended Unique Identifier, 64-bit* (EUI-64). The choice between random numbers and EUI-64 has important privacy implications.

Many people use a specific laptop on multiple networks. If EUI-64 is used, the MAC address of your laptop's NIC will be part of your IPv6 address. As a result, your laptop can be tracked, aggregated, and correlated across all the networks you've connected to. That unique identifier will also appear in network traces as well as logfiles. This is why randomized identifiers are used in most places instead of EUI-64.

Some operating systems use EUI-64 for link-local addresses, and that's fine, because those addresses never leave your link (LAN). With local communication, every communicating station needs the others' MAC addresses anyway. Some routers, like Cisco's, default to using EUI-64, and that's fine too. Unlike a laptop, the routers aren't moving around from one network to the next, so tracking the MAC address isn't a privacy issue.

Global Unicast Address

A system's IPv6 link-local address is a *unicast address*, a unique address exclusive to that system. To get on the internet, devices need a second unicast address known as a *global unicast address* (GUA), a fully routable public address that supports two-way connectivity between a device and the world (unless a firewall has something to say about it). We'll take a closer look at the different ways a device can get its GUA in the "IPv6 Deployment" section.

A GUA follows the 2000::/3 pattern, where the first three bits are 010. Since the fourth bit, in the 1s column, can be either a 0 or a 1, that means the first hex character in the IPv6 address for a GUA will be a 2 or a 3 (although only 2s have seen real-world usage to this point).

Open a command prompt, execute the **ipconfig** command, and see if you have an IPv6 address that starts with a 2. If so, you have a GUA. There are certain IPv6 addresses that start with a 2 that are not GUAs, though, like those used in translation/transition addresses, and even one range used for documentation (2001:db8::/32).

In addition to generating randomized interface IDs (instead of EUI-64), devices generate addresses to be used temporarily as source IPv6 addresses. Having different IPv6 GUAs over time helps ensure privacy and anonymity. Furthermore, multiple temporary addresses can be active at the same time, so existing connections can continue while a new temporary address is used for subsequent connections. In addition to this GUA, another, static GUA will be generated for incoming connections (incoming connections for a device that has an IP address that changes would be a problem).

A host can have multiple GUAs on one or more links. The host also has a link-local address for each link.

NOTE Not only does a device have multiple types of IPv6 addresses, but it uses multiple addresses of each type as well.

Multicast Addresses

IPv6 completely drops the IPv4 concept of a *broadcast address* (traffic sent to all devices on a LAN), but it maintains *multicast addresses*, where a single computer sends a message to a group of designated computers. Somewhat surprisingly, IPv6 multicast addresses are built up from independent parts.

If an IPv6 system sends out a multicast to the address ff02::2, for example, only routers read the message; everyone else ignores it. The first 2 in this address specifies the scope (local link), and the last 2 identifies the group (all routers) within that scope. (The group can be indicated by more than one hex character; this is just an example.) *Scope* defines how widely the message is propagated, while the *group* specifies which hosts should receive it. Another scope, site-local, is indicated by the fourth hex character's value of 5.

NOTE The Ethernet address (MAC address) for IPv6 multicast traffic is 33-33-*xx-xx-xx-xx*. Here's a bit of geeky trivia for you. Why 33-33? The physical address for Xerox Palo Alto Research Center (PARC), the birthplace of Ethernet and many other networking technologies used today, is 3333 Coyote Hill Road.

Every computer can receive the multicast traffic, but acts only on packets that are addressed to multicast groups to which it has joined.

Table 8-1 shows a few of the more useful IPv6 multicast addresses.

TABLE 8-1 Notable IPv6 multicast addresses

ADDRESS	FUNCTION
ff02::1	All-nodes multicast address
ff02::2	All-routers multicast address
ff02::5	OSPF routers
ff02::6	OSPF designated routers
ff02::a	EIGRP routers
ff02::1:2	DHCPv6 servers and relay agents

Looking at the first listing, ff02::1, you might be wondering how it differs from a broadcast. The answer lies more in the definition of *multicast* than in what really takes place. A computer must be configured as a member of a particular group to read a particular multicast. In the case of ff02::1, all systems on the network are members; a packet sent to that address will be much like a IPv4 broadcast. That same packet sent to ff02::2 will be read only by routers on the network. These addresses become important in the upcoming discussion of the Neighbor Discovery Protocol.

NOTE Multicasting in IPv4 relied on Internet Group Management Protocol (IGMP). In IPv6, multicasting relies on Multicast Listener Discovery version 2 (MLDv2).

Anycast Address

Like IPv4, IPv6 also supports anycast addressing. An *anycast address* is a bit of a strange animal because it's a single IP address shared by multiple hosts. Routers are configured to direct traffic destined for that address to the closest system based on the routing metrics set by the network designers.

A common use for anycast addresses is in content delivery networks (CDNs). These networks use servers placed in cities around the world to cache content—such as news sites or video from Netflix and YouTube—so that you can binge your favorite series from a data center just up the road. Since the CDN's servers share an anycast address, all the routers between you and the content provider will direct your request, via Border Gateway Protocol (BGP), to the CDN server in your city instead of one on the other side of the globe.

Neighbor Discovery Protocol

Neighbor Discovery Protocol (NDP), also known as Neighbor Discovery (ND), uses ICMPv6 (which is ICMP for IPv6, not the sixth version of ICMP) and consists of five control message types:

- Router Solicitation (RS, the IPv6 equivalent of a DHCP Discover)
- Router Advertisement (RA, the IPv6 equivalent of a DHCP Offer)
- Neighbor Solicitation (NS, the IPv6 equivalent of an ARP request)
- Neighbor Advertisement (NA, the IPv6 equivalent of an ARP reply)
- Redirect (how default gateway routers notify PCs of better routes to destinations)

NOTE Recall from Chapter 2 that ARP is a Layer 2 protocol that uses broadcasts for ARP requests. Since there is no broadcasting in IPv6, a replacement was needed.

All the NDP control message types are encapsulated in an ICMPv6 packet, which is encapsulated in an IPv6 packet, which in turn is encapsulated in a frame. To understand how this works in practice, let's see what happens when an IPv6 device needs to communicate with another device on the same network.

NOTE In the world of IPv4, you could filter some or all ICMP messages and still have a functional network. You just can't do that in IPv6. ICMPv6 is a way of life for IPv6; it's how IPv6 conducts business. No ICMPv6, no IPv6 networking!

Solicited-Node Multicast Address

Let's say an IPv6 device has to send a packet to 2001:db8:f00d:1::200/64. That's the destination IPv6 address that will be found in the packet's IPv6 header. The packet, of course, must be encapsulated inside a frame, and the source needs the destination's MAC address for the frame.

The source first checks its neighbor cache, the IPv6 equivalent of the IPv4 ARP cache. If the binding is there, it's used, just like the ARP cache is used for IPv4. If it's not, the source sends a Neighbor Solicitation (NS; discussed in the next section) message to the destination's solicited-node multicast address—in this case, ff02::1:ff00:200.

Let's back up a bit. Each interface's unicast address will always have a corresponding solicited-node multicast address. Like all multicast addresses, it starts with ff. The next hex character is a 0 for permanent, well-known multicast addresses (IANA assigns these), or a 1 for a multicast address for an organization's needs. The fourth hex character represents the scope, 2 (link-local scope, the most common one).

We're at ff02 so far.

The prefix for solicited-node multicast addresses is ff02:0:0:0:0:1:ff00::/104 (or ff02::1:ff*xx*:*xxxx*, where *x* represents hex characters that need to be filled in). There are 104 bits given (as indicated by the /104), so we need to fill in the other 24. To do so, we simply take the last six hex characters (24 bits) of the IPv6 address and put them there. That's it!

In **2001:db8:f00d:1::200/64**, the last six hex characters are 000200, although you don't see all of them in the compressed format. To see them clearly, look at the full format:

2001:db8:f00d:0001:0000:0000:00**00:0200**/64

The leading-zero shortcut takes away the 0 at the start of the eighth hextet, and the double-colon shortcut takes away the fifth, sixth, and seventh hextets, which are all 0s.

Now, if we start with this

ff02::1:ff*xx*:*xxxx*

and fill in the *x* positions with 000200, we get this (notice the bolding for the last six hex characters):

ff02::1:ff**00:0200**

Then, we can remove the leading 0 in the eighth hextet to wind up with this solicited-node multicast address:

ff02::1:ff00:200

IPv6 multicast addresses have corresponding Ethernet MAC addresses. A multicast MAC address corresponding to an IPv6 address always starts with 33:33, with the rest of the MAC address (the lower 32 bits) corresponding to the lower 32 bits of the IPv6 multicast address. For example:

33:33:00:00:00:01 is the MAC address for ff02::1 (all devices).

33:33:00:00:00:02 is the MAC address for ff02::2 (all routers).

To calculate the MAC address, we need to take the last 32 bits (eight hex characters) of the fully expanded form of the solicited-node multicast address:

ff02:0000:0000:0000:0000:0001:**ff00:0200**

and put them after 33:33: (notice the bolding):

33:33:**ff:00:02:00**

That is the MAC address placed in the frame, corresponding to the IPv6 solicited-node multicast address in the packet.

With the use of a Layer 2 multicast address now instead of a broadcast ARP request (which all devices read in after the Ethernet frame), the NIC can filter NS messages quickly and easily. The IPv6 header and the ICMPv6 packet don't need to be consulted.

Of course, it's possible (although not that likely) to have more than one interface with the same last six hex characters on a link. The interface ID is 64 bits long, so these interfaces will differ in their upper 40 bits of the interface ID. If so, these interfaces will have the same solicited-node multicast address and the same multicast MAC address. That's not an issue, because inside of the ICMPv6 NS message is a Target Address field, and the interface with an IPv6 address that doesn't match the value in that field will drop the NS message at that point.

Neighbor Solicitation

Hosts use Neighbor Solicitation messages not only to request a target system's MAC address from the solicited-node multicast address (as just described), but also to inform the target system of their own MAC address and to verify that the target system is still reachable.

Neighbor Advertisement

Two things happen when a host receives an NS message. The host adds the MAC address of the sending system to its *neighbor cache* (equivalent to the IPv4 ARP cache), and it sends a Neighbor Advertisement (NA) via unicast in response to the NS. The response tells the sending system the host's MAC address and confirms that this host—or advertiser—is reachable. The sending system also adds the host's MAC address to its own neighbor cache.

The IPv6 neighbor cache includes other information, including the neighbor's device type (host or router) and reachability state. A state of Reachable means that this device recently sent a packet. A Stale state means that it's been some time since this device sent a packet (the timer for this state varies by OS). The Permanent state is for multicast addresses. There is always a corresponding Layer 2 multicast MAC address for every Layer 3 multicast IP address.

On a Windows system, open Command Prompt and execute the following to see the neighbor cache:

```
netsh interface ipv6 show neighbors
```

To clear the neighbor cache, use the following command (you'll need to be running Command Prompt as an administrator to do this):

```
netsh interface ipv6 delete neighbors
```

To see other commands that will show you IPv6-related information, execute:

```
netsh interface ipv6 show
```

Then, continue the command. For example:

```
netsh interface ipv6 show addresses
```

In addition to a neighbor cache, IPv6 devices have a *destination cache*, which has no IPv4 equivalent. Items in the destination cache include Path Maximum Transmission Unit (PMTU), Destination Address, and Next Hop Address. The destination cache stores entries for both locally connected devices and devices on other links. The Next Hop Address for locally connected devices is the actual destination's IP address, while the Next Hop Address for remote destinations is the link-local address of the default gateway. IPv6 hosts have a default router list that's used for off-link destinations. The destination cache associates the off-link addresses with the corresponding default gateway.

On a Windows system, open Command Prompt and execute the following to see the destination cache:

```
netsh interface ipv6 show destinationcache
```

Use the following command to clear the destination cache (you'll need to be running as an administrator):

```
netsh interface ipv6 delete destinationcache
```

If you have a GUA (an IPv6 address that starts with a 2, as explained earlier in the chapter), ping `www.google.com` and `www.cisco.com`. You'll see their corresponding IPv6 addresses in Command Prompt. After that, see if you can find those addresses in the destination cache.

Router Solicitation

While NS and NA messages handle address resolution between hosts, IPv6 also needs a way for hosts to discover routers on the network. When an IPv6 host has an interface enabled, it sends a Router Solicitation (RS) to the all-routers multicast address of ff02::2 in hopes of receiving a Router Advertisement (RA) in response. This is the IPv6 equivalent of an IPv4 DHCP Discover message.

Router Advertisement

The RA can be sent either to the all-hosts multicast address of ff02::1 or to the host's link-local unicast address. The host's MAC address is included in the RS as well, so the router has all it needs. Routers also send unsolicited RAs at regular intervals.

RA messages let hosts know to go ahead with dynamic addressing. They contain a prefix, prefix length, default gateway, and other configuration information. A router can also be configured to send the IP addresses of DNS servers in an RA option.

There are many flags in the RA, including:

MANAGED ADDRESS CONFIGURATION FLAG (M FLAG) A 1 instructs a host to use a stateful DHCPv6 server for everything, including its GUA and other configuration information, just like an IPv4 host would use a DHCP server. However, the source IPv6 address in the RA becomes the host's default gateway address. DHCPv6 servers (stateful or stateless) never give out default gateway information. A host always uses the link-local address of the router sending the RA as its default gateway.

OTHER CONFIGURATION FLAG (O FLAG) A 1 instructs a host to get information other than an actual GUA (like DNS server IPv6 addresses) from a stateless DHCPv6 (DHCP for IPv6) server.

ADDRESS AUTOCONFIGURATION FLAG (A FLAG) A 1 (default) instructs a host to create its GUA with SLAAC (discussed shortly). The RA contains a 64-bit prefix, which will be followed by a 64-bit interface ID generated by the host during the SLAAC process.

NOTE The M and O flags are found in the main ICMPv6 flags section, while the A flag is found in an RA option for the prefix being advertised.

Redirect

A router uses a *redirect* packet to tell a host that there's a better router to use for traffic to a given destination. You don't see redirects used on a network segment with a single router, but they can come into play when multiple routers are available to hosts. Modern operating systems don't add this information to their routing tables as they did in the past, because attackers can use redirects to launch an on-path attack.

IPv6 Deployment

Understanding NDP is just one piece of the IPv6 puzzle. For a complete IPv6 deployment, you also need to understand how devices obtain their addresses and network configuration. In this section, you will see how SLAAC, DHCPv6, DNS, and subnetting come into the picture for IPv6.

SLAAC

One of the big ideas in IPv6 is to use autoconfiguration to make setting up most systems so easy that *it just works.* Big ideas like this aren't worth much without solid implementations that do what they say on the label, but IPv6 delivers on this promise for most users. This also means IPv6 has a slightly different relationship with DHCPv6. Let's look at how this autoconfiguration process works and where DHCPv6 fits into the picture.

IPv6 uses Stateless Address Autoconfiguration (SLAAC) to enable network clients to configure their own addresses. SLAAC leans on the neighbor discovery process supported by NDP. Hosts in an IPv6 network can create their own link-local and global unicast addresses. We looked at how hosts generate their link-local address earlier in the chapter, but NDP also plays a crucial role in the process. After hosts generate their link-local address, they perform *duplicate address detection* (DAD) to make sure it isn't already taken. DAD involves sending an NS to the solicited-node multicast address of the address the host is about to assign to itself. If an NA comes back, someone has it! Otherwise, it's free for the host to use.

Hosts can generate a GUA as soon as they get a crucial piece of the puzzle—the prefix (and prefix length, which should always be /64)—from the RAs that their router sends out. When hosts join a network, they send out an RS to request a fresh advertisement. When they receive it, hosts combine the prefix it contains with the same interface identifier they used for the link-local address—and then once again perform DAD to verify that it is open.

DHCPv6

You'd think with RAs that you wouldn't need DHCPv6 (which is DHCP for IPv6, not the sixth version of DHCP), and in many ways you'd be right. DHCPv6 is still important in IPv6, but it can be optional in some deployments.

DHCPv6 still works like traditional DHCP in that you have to configure a DHCPv6 server. This DHCPv6 server works in one of two modes: stateful or stateless. A *stateful* DHCPv6 server works very similarly to an IPv4 DHCP server: it tells the host the full 128-bit address it should use and keeps track of the addresses it has passed out. A *stateless* DHCPv6 server lets the host pick its own address via SLAAC. In fact, stateless DHCPv6 is needed to give clients using SLAAC other information, like DNS server IP addresses.

NOTE DHCPv6 servers, stateless or stateful, will never give clients a default gateway IP address. Clients always get this information from the RA. Why would the RA give clients its own IP address as a default gateway? The RA is coming from the gateway itself!

Since SLAAC is good at solving problems traditionally handled by DHCP in IPv4, far fewer networks need their own DHCPv6 server. DHCPv6 is super popular with ISPs, who use *prefix delegation*—specifically, *DHCPv6 Prefix Delegation* (DHCPv6-PD)—to assign IPv6 prefixes to customer routers. Inside most of those customer networks, SLAAC is just fine. You're more likely to find DHCPv6 servers, in stateless or stateful incarnations, in enterprise environments and networks with specific requirements, such as data centers.

IPv6 and DNS

Most DNS servers support IPv6 addresses nowadays, so setting up DNS is very simple. For SLAAC without DHCPv6, include the IPv6 DNS server in your RAs; for DHCPv6, be sure to properly configure your DHCPv6 server. Zone files use the AAAA resource record to map names to IPv6 addresses.

NOTE The AAAA record is named to reflect the size difference between IPv6 and IPv4 addresses. While an A record maps a hostname to a 32-bit IPv4 address, an AAAA record (commonly referred to as "quad-a") maps a hostname to a 128-bit IPv6 address, which is four times the size of an IPv4 address.

Subnetting

Subnetting in IPv6 is a lot quicker and easier than subnetting in IPv4 (described in Chapter 3).

An ISP will assign the first three hextets to an organization. Subnet the fourth hextet by simply incrementing by one!

For example, given 2001:1337:f00d, count in the fourth hextet:

2001:1337:f00d:0000::/64

2001:1337:f00d:0001::/64

2001:1337:f00d:0002::/64

...

2001:1337:f00d:0009::/64

2001:1337:f00d:000a::/64

2001:1337:f00d:000b::/64

...

2001:1337:f00d:000f::/64

2001:1337:f00d:0010::/64

2001:1337:f00d:0011::/64

That's it! No formulas, no magic number, no charts—just counting.

This is referred to as *the 3-1-4 rule*: three hextets assigned by the ISP or RIR, one hextet where the subnetting occurs, and four hextets representing the interface ID.

Connecting IPv4 and IPv6 Infrastructures: Compatibility Requirements

There's no reason for you *not* to try running IPv6 today—like right now! At the very least, you can explore the IPv6-only websites that are out there. At the most, you may very well become the IPv6 expert in your organization. You almost certainly have an operating system equipped for IPv6; the only trick is to connect to the rest of us fun-loving IPv6-enabled folks.

All modern operating systems support IPv6, and almost all routers support IPv6, though not all internet routers have that support enabled yet. Eventually, every router and every computer on the internet will support IPv6, but we're not yet there. Two critical parts of the internet are ready, however:

- All the root DNS servers support IPv6 resolution.
- All the Tier 1 ISP routers properly forward IPv6 packets.

The problem is that the routers and DNS servers between IPv6-enabled computers that wish to connect may not yet be IPv6-ready. How do you get past this IPv6 gap?

Dual Stack

The first option is to run a *dual stack*—having both IPv4 and IPv6 on your computers and routers at the same time. This capability is a critical part of the process enabling the world to migrate slowly from IPv4 to IPv6.

Transition Mechanisms

You can also leap over this gap by implementing an IPv4-to-IPv6 transition mechanism. You can do this using one of many IPv4-to-IPv6 tunneling standards, including the following:

4TO6 An IPv4-to-IPv6 tunnel works like any other tunnel, encapsulating one type of data into another. In this case, you encapsulate IPv4 traffic into an IPv6 tunnel to get to an IPv6-enabled router. To make this tunnel, you would download a tunneling client and install it on your computer. You would then fire up the client and make the tunnel connection—it's very easy to do.

6IN4 Also called IPv6-in-IPv4, 6in4 is one of the most popular IPv6 tunneling standards. 6in4 is one of only two IPv6 tunneling protocols that can go through IPv4 NAT (called *NAT traversal*).

NOTE Tunnel brokers are mostly used today for legacy support, education, and lab environments. As native IPv6 continues to roll out, they are becoming less necessary in real-world deployments. Read through this section specifically for items you'll find on the N10-009 exam.

Tunnel Brokers

Manually setting up an IPv6 tunnel is involved. You have to find someone willing to act as the far endpoint, you have to connect to their system somehow, and then you have to know the tunneling standard they use. To make life easier, *tunnel brokers* create the actual tunnel and (usually) offer a custom-made endpoint client for you to use, although more advanced users can often make a manual connection.

NOTE Your tunnel broker provides the tunnel protocol, so you rarely have a choice about which to use, and it's usually invisible to you.

Many tunnel brokers take advantage of one of two automatic configuration protocols, called Tunnel Setup Protocol (TSP) and Tunnel Information and Control (TIC) protocol. These protocols set up the tunnel and handle configuration as well as login. If it weren't for TSP and TIC, there would be no automatic third-party tunnel endpoint clients for you to use.

NOTE Hurricane Electric is currently the only major, active, and free public IPv6 tunnel broker. Based in Fremont, California, they have a huge IPv6 global transit network and offer IPv6 certifications and more. Check them out at *he.net*. To use Hurricane Electric as a tunnel broker, see *tunnelbroker.net*.

Overlay Tunnels

An *overlay tunnel* enables two IPv6 networks to connect over an existing IPv4 infrastructure, such as the internet. In more precise terms, the routers that connect the IPv6 networks to the IPv4 infrastructure encapsulate the traffic from the local network into IPv4 packets. Those IPv4 packets travel over the IPv4 infrastructure, and the router at the other end (which can also be a single host) of the tunnel strips the IPv4 encapsulation off the packet and sends the remaining IPv6 packet on its merry way.

NAT64

NAT64 is not the form of Network Address Translation (NAT) described in Chapter 5—Port Address Translation (PAT). IPv6 has no need or use for the classic NAT implemented in IPv4 to mitigate address exhaustion. The massive IPv6 address space just renders it unnecessary. This doesn't mean the idea of translating network addresses is dead and buried; it still plays an important role in the transition to IPv6.

NAT64 appends the 32 bits of an IPv4 address to the end of an IPv6 address that uses the 64:ff9b::/96 prefix for network traversal. Typically, you'll have a NAT64 gateway that handles the traffic between the IPv4 and IPv6 segments, doing the address translation on the fly and keeping track of who's who on either end.

With the first 96 of 128 bits locked in place, that leaves 32. IPv4 addresses are 32 bits, and that's exactly what goes after the first preset 96 bits.

NAT64, along with DNS64, was designed specifically to enable IPv6-only clients to access servers still running only IPv4. A NAT64 gateway can be installed in front of an IPv4 server to provide automatic translations (*stateless mapping*) or on the client side or at the ISP with manual translations (*stateful mapping*).

Transition mechanisms are meant to be ***transitional***. They aren't supposed to be there forever. The end goal is, of course, native IPv6 connectivity and GUAs for all!

Chapter Review

Questions

1. What is the /48 prefix of the address 2001:0480:b6f3:0001::0001?
   A. 2001:480:b6f3:1

   B. 2001:480:b6f3

   C. 2001:480:b6f3:1:0000::1

   D. 2001:480:b6f3:1:0000:0000:0000:1

2. Which of the following is a valid IPv6 address?
   A. 2001:bead:beef::1

   B. 2001:30f5::3d62::04ffe

   C. 192.168.1.4:ff45:129g:48fd:1

   D. 2001.0470.b33e.23f4.27de.d34a.aed2.1827

3. Which of the following is the shortest valid abbreviation for fe80:0000:0000:0000:00 10:0000:0000:0123??
   A. fe8::1::123

   B. fe80:0:0:0:10::123

   C. fe80::10:0:0:123

   D. fe80::10::123

4. What does a client use to talk to other devices on the same link?
   A. A link-local address
   B. A multicast address
   C. A global unicast address
   D. NAT
5. What does a client need to access IPv6 content on the internet?
   A. A link-local address
   B. A multicast address
   C. A global unicast address
   D. NAT
6. What contains information about what an IPv6 device needs to get a GUA?
   A. Neighbor Solicitation
   B. Neighbor Advertisement
   C. Router Solicitation
   D. Router Advertisement
7. What does an IPv6 device send to get a MAC address of a device it wants to communicate with?
   A. Neighbor Solicitation
   B. Neighbor Advertisement
   C. Router Solicitation
   D. Router Advertisement
8. If a Router Advertisement sends DNS information, what does the client need a DHCPv6 server for?
   A. Default gateway IP address
   B. DHCPv6 server IP address
   C. Prefix length
   D. Nothing
9. Where does an IPv6 client store MAC address information for IPv6 addresses?
   A. Destination cache
   B. Neighbor cache
   C. ARP cache
   D. DNS cache

10. What do tunnel brokers provide?
    A. A method for users on IPv4 networks to reach IPv6 destinations
    B. NAT
    C. Access to IPv6 DNS records
    D. A second connection for multihoming

Answers

1. **B.** The /48 prefix consists of only the first three groups of the address.
2. **A.** B is invalid because it has two sets of double colons. C is using IPv4 numbers. D is using periods instead of colons.
3. **C.** Leading zeroes can be left off. One or more consecutive hextexts of all zeroes can be represented with a double colon.
4. **A.** A link-local address is used for all local communication.
5. **C.** A client needs a global unicast address to access the IPv6 internet.
6. **C.** Hosts use Router Advertisements to get a GUA.
7. **A.** Neighbor Solicitation messages are sent to the destination's solicited-node multicast address.
8. **D.** DHCPv6 is not needed when the RA has DNS information.
9. **B.** The neighbor cache is the IPv6 equivalent of the IPv4 ARP cache.
10. **A.** Devices on an IPv4 network that are not connected with IPv6 to an ISP can use a tunnel broker to send and receive IPv6 traffic.

Cabling

IN THIS CHAPTER, YOU WILL LEARN HOW TO

- Describe the different types of cables and connectors and explain which is the appropriate type for a solution
- Given a scenario, troubleshoot common cable connectivity issues and select the appropriate tools
- Describe the IEEE networking standards

Every network must provide some method to get data from one system to another. In most cases, this method consists of some type of cabling running between systems, although most networks today incorporate wireless methods to move data as well. Stringing those cables brings up several critical issues you need to understand to work on a network. How do all these cables connect the computers? Does every computer on the network run a cable to a central point? Does a single cable snake through the ceiling, with all the computers on the network connected to it? These questions need answering!

Furthermore, manufacturers need standards so they can make networking equipment that works well together. While we're talking about standards, what about the cable itself? What type of cable is it? What quality of copper or fiber is it? How thick should it be? Who defines the standards for cables so they all work in the network?

This chapter answers these questions in two parts. First, you will tour the most common standardized cable types used in networking. Second, you will learn about the IEEE committees that create network technology standards.

NOTE In networking, *cable* refers to the actual physical object, like a Cat 6 cable, while *cabling* refers to the entire infrastructure consisting of multiple cables or to the cable installation process. Though you'll often see these terms used interchangeably (even by CompTIA), the distinction is more relevant in specific contexts such as *structured cabling*, which is the organized design and installation of a building or campus wiring system in which a *cable* is only a single component. Chapter 11 discusses structured cabling in depth.

Test Specific

Most networked systems link together using some type of cabling. Different types of networks over the years have used different types of cables, and you need to learn about all of these cables—and when to use them—to succeed on the CompTIA Network+ exam.

All cables used in the networking industry can be categorized in two distinct groups: copper and fiber-optic. Every style of cable has a distinct connector type that you need to know as well.

Copper Cables and Connectors

The most common form of cabling uses copper wire wrapped in some kind of protective sheathing, thus the term *copper cabling*. The two primary types of copper cables used in the industry are coaxial and twisted pair, both of which sport a variety of connector types.

Coaxial Cables

A *coaxial* cable consists of a central copper conductor wire surrounded by an insulating material, which, in turn, is surrounded by a braided metal shield. The cable is referred to as coaxial (*coax* for short) because the center wire and the braided metal shield share a common axis or centerline (Figure 9-1).

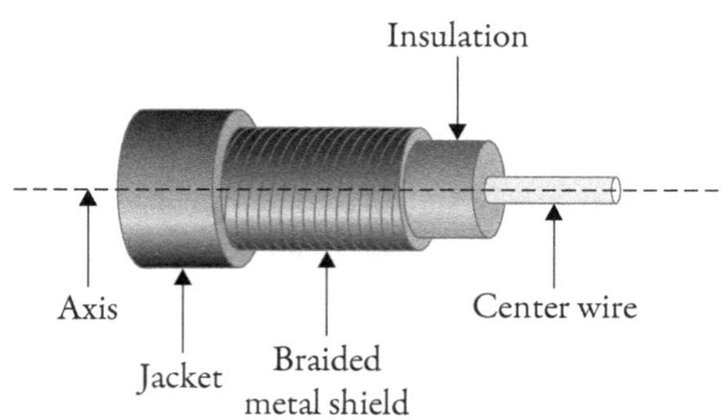

FIGURE 9-1 Cutaway view of coaxial cable

Many devices in the typical office environment—including lights, fans, copy machines, and refrigerators—generate magnetic fields. When a metal wire encounters these magnetic fields, it generates an electrical current. This extra current, called *electromagnetic interference* (EMI), can cause errors, poor performance, or outages because NICs can easily misinterpret it as a signal. To prevent EMI from affecting the network, the outer mesh layer of a coaxial cable shields the center wire (on which the data is transmitted) from interference (Figure 9-2).

FIGURE 9-2
Coaxial cable showing braided metal shielding

Early bus topology networks (where a single cable, the *bus*, connected all the computers in a line) used coaxial cable to connect computers together. Back in the day, the most popular cable used special bayonet-style connectors called *BNC connectors* (Figure 9-3).

NOTE Techs all around the globe argue over the meaning of BNC. A solid percentage says with authority that it stands for "British Naval Connector." An opposing percentage says with equal authority that it stands for "Bayonet Neill–Concelman," after the stick-and-twist style of connecting and the purported inventors of the connector.

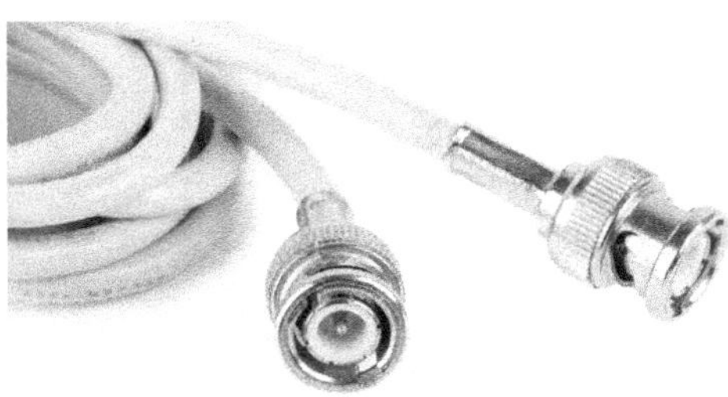

FIGURE 9-3
BNC connector on coaxial cable

Today, you'll find coaxial cables used primarily to enable a cable modem to connect to an internet service provider (ISP). That's the typical scenario for using coaxial cable: connecting a computer to the cable modem enables that computer to access the internet. This cable is the same type used to connect televisions to cable boxes or to satellite receivers. These cables use an *F connector* (or *F-type connector*) that screws on, making for a secure connection (Figure 9-4).

FIGURE 9-4
F-type connector on coaxial cable

EXAM TIP Coaxial cables are also very popular for use with satellite dishes, over-the-air antennas, and even some home video devices.

Cable modems connect using one of two coaxial cable types. *RG-59* was used primarily for cable television rather than networking. Its thinness and the introduction of digital cable motivated the move to the more robust *RG-6*, the predominant cable used today (Figure 9-5).

FIGURE 9-5
RG-6 cable

All coax cables have a *Radio Guide (RG) rating*. The US military developed these ratings to provide a quick reference for the different types of coax. The only important measure of coax cable is its *Ohm rating*, a relative measure of the cable's resistance (or more precisely, characteristic impedance; see the following note). You may run across other coax cables that don't have acceptable Ohm ratings, although they look just like network-rated coax. Both RG-6 and RG-59 cables are rated at 75 Ohms. RG-6 was designed to handle the higher frequencies and bandwidth that modern digital television, satellite, and internet signals need, while RG-59 was designed for older, lower-frequency analog signals.

NOTE *Impedance* describes a set of characteristics that define how much a cable resists the flow of electricity. This isn't simple resistance, though. Impedance is also a factor in how long it takes the wire to get a full charge—the wire's *capacitance*—and other metrics.

Given the popularity of cable for both television and internet in homes today, sometimes you'll need to split a single coaxial cable. A coaxial splitter like the one shown in Figure 9-6 handles this quite easily.

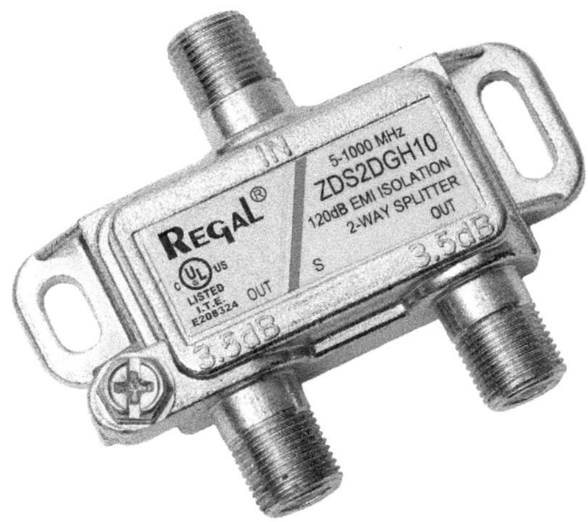

FIGURE 9-6
Coaxial splitter

You can also connect two coaxial cables together easily using a barrel connector when you need to add some distance to a connection (Figure 9-7).

FIGURE 9-7 Barrel connector

Table 9-1 summarizes the coaxial standards.

TABLE 9-1 Coaxial cables

RATING	OHMS	USE	CONNECTOR
RG-59	75	Cable TV	F Type
RG-6	75	Cable TV	F Type

Twinaxial Cables

A *twinaxial* cable is a type of coaxial cable that contains two central copper conductors wrapped around a single shield (Figure 9-8). You'll see it used as a substitute for short fiber connections, generally between equipment within a rack, like switches. For such uses, it's substantially cheaper than fiber and its associated hardware. Twinaxial cable used this way is called a *direct attached copper* (DAC) *cable.*

FIGURE 9-8 Twinaxial cable

Twisted-Pair Cables

The most common type of cabling used in networks consists of twisted pairs of cables, bundled together into a common jacket. Each pair in the cable works as a team to either transmit or receive data. Using a pair of twisted wires rather than a single wire to send a signal reduces a specific type of interference, called *crosstalk*. The more twists per foot, the less crosstalk. Two types of twisted-pair cabling are manufactured: shielded and unshielded.

SHIELDED TWISTED PAIR A *shielded twisted-pair* (STP) cable consists of twisted pairs of wires surrounded by shielding to protect them from EMI. There are six types (see Table 9-2), differentiated by which part gets shielding, such as the whole cable or individual pairs within the cable. Figure 9-9 shows a typical piece of STP with the cladding partly removed so you can see the internal wiring.

TABLE 9-2 STP standards

NAME[1]	DESCRIPTION
F/UTP	Foil shields the entire cable; inside, the wires are just like UTP.
S/UTP	A braid screen shields the entire cable; inside, the wires are just like UTP.
SF/UTP	A braid screen and foil shield the entire cable; the wires inside are just like UTP.
S/FTP	A braid screen shields the entire cable; foil shields each wire pair inside.
F/FTP	A foil screen shields the entire cable; foil shields each wire pair inside.
U/FTP	No overall shielding; each pair inside is shielded with foil screens.

[1] Before the slash: Overall shielding; After the slash: Pair shielding; F: Foil S: Braid (Screen); UTP: Pairs themselves are unshielded; FTP: Each pair is shielded with foil.

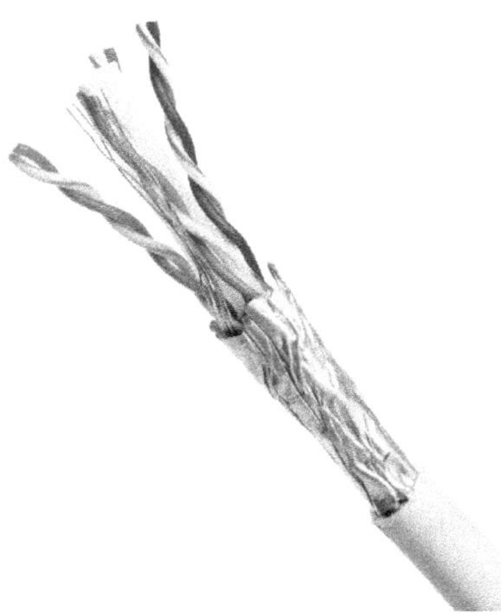

FIGURE 9-9
Shielded twisted pair

EXAM TIP You don't need to memorize the STP variations for the CompTIA Network+ exam. You will, however, see them in the field once you become a network tech. The typical scenario in which you'd deploy STP rather than UTP is in high-EMI environments, where troubleshooting has revealed that the unshielded cable couldn't handle the noise.

UNSHIELDED TWISTED PAIR An *unshielded twisted-pair* (UTP) cable consists of twisted pairs of wires surrounded by a plastic jacket (Figure 9-10). This jacket does not provide any protection from EMI, just a slightly protective skin, so when installing UTP cabling, you must be careful to avoid interference from fluorescent lights, motors, and so forth. UTP costs much less than STP but, in most environments, performs just as well.

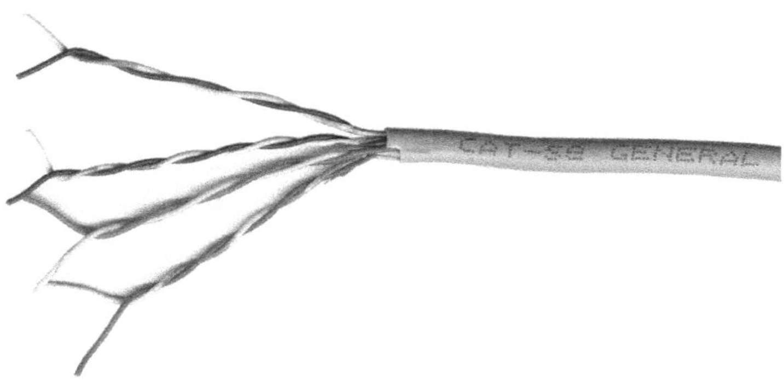

FIGURE 9-10 Unshielded twisted pair

Twisted-pair cabling has been around since the 1970s. Over the years, as evolving technologies called for higher data speeds, manufacturers increased the number of twists per foot, used higher-gauge cable, and added shielding to accommodate the demand. To help network installers determine the right cable for the right network technology, the cabling industry developed a variety of grades called *category (Cat) ratings*. Cat ratings are officially rated in megahertz (MHz), indicating the highest frequency the cable can reliably carry. Table 9-3 shows the most common categories along with their TIA status (see the subsequent note for more information).

NOTE Several international groups set the standards for cabling and networking in general. Ready for alphabet soup? At or near the top is the International Organization for Standardization (ISO). The American National Standards Institute (ANSI) is both the official US representative to ISO and a major international player. ANSI checks the standards and accredits other groups, such as the Telecommunications Industry Association (TIA).

TABLE 9-3 Cat ratings for twisted-pair cables

CAT RATING	MAX FREQUENCY	MAX BANDWIDTH	STATUS WITH TIA
Cat 3	16 MHz	16 Mbps	Recognized
Cat 4	20 MHz	20 Mbps	No longer recognized
Cat 5	100 MHz	100 Mbps	No longer recognized
Cat 5e	100 MHz	1 Gbps	Recognized
Cat 6[1]	250 MHz	10 Gbps	Recognized
Cat 6a[2]	500 MHz	10 Gbps	Recognized
Cat 7	600 MHz	10+ Gbps	Not recognized
Cat 7a[3]	1000 MHz	40–100 Gbps	Not recognized
Cat 8	2000 MHz	25–40 Gbps	Recognized

[1] Cat 6 cables can use the full 100-meter length when used with 10/100/1000BASE-T networks. With 10GBASE-T networks, Cat 6 is limited to 55 meters.

[2] Cat 6a cables can use the full 100-meter length with networks up to 10GBASE-T.

[3] Cat 7a cables can theoretically support 40 Gbps at 50 meters and 100 Gbps at 15 meters.

New installs should use the latest and greatest, which is Cat 6a. Note that Cat 7 is not recognized by TIA. For exceptionally high-speed infrastructures over smaller distances, like data centers, consider Cat 8.

UTP cables handle a certain frequency or cycles per second, such as 100 MHz or 1,000 MHz. You could take the frequency number in the early days of networking and translate that into the maximum throughput for a cable. Each cycle per second (or hertz) basically accounted for 1 bit of data per second. A 10 million cycle per second (10 MHz) cable, for example, could handle 10 million bits per second (10 Mbps). The maximum amount of data that a cable can transmit per second is called the *bandwidth*, and higher-frequency cables can generally support higher bandwidth.

EXAM TIP The CompTIA Network+ exam is only interested in your knowledge of Cat 5, Cat 5e, Cat 6, Cat 6a, Cat 7, and Cat 8 cables. (In the field, you'll see category represented in both lowercase and uppercase, so Cat 6a or CAT 6a.)

For current networks, developers have implemented *bandwidth-efficient encoding schemes*, which means they can squeeze more bits into the same signal if the cable can handle it. Thus, the Cat 5e cable can handle a throughput of up to 1,000 Mbps, even though it's rated to handle a frequency of only up to 100 MHz.

Because most networks can run at speeds of up to 1,000 Mbps, most new cabling installations use Cat 6 cables, although many installations use Cat 6a or Cat 7 to future-proof the network.

Make sure you can look at twisted pair and know its Cat rating. There are two places to look. First, twisted pair is typically sold in boxed reels, and the manufacturer will clearly mark the Cat level on the box. Second, look on the cable itself—the category is usually printed on it.

TRY THIS: SHOPPING SPREE!

Just how common has Cat 6 or Cat 6a become in your neighborhood? Run down to your local hardware or office-supply store and shop for UTP cables. Does the store carry Cat 6? Cat 6a? What's the difference in price? If it's not much more expensive to go with the better cable, it's a sign that the expected shift in networking standards has occurred and you might want to upgrade your network.

The old landline telephones plugged in with a *registered jack* (RJ) connector. Telephones used *RJ11* connectors, designed to support up to two pairs of UTP wires. Current wired networks use the four-pair *8 position 8 contact* (8P8C) connectors, which most techs and manufacturers erroneously refer to as *RJ45* connectors (Figure 9-11). There was an *RJ45S* connector, used in telephones and with slightly different keying, that looked very similar to an 8P8C connector, though, so the theory is that the name carried over from technicians installing that new UTP cabling. Also, RJ11 cords usually use *6 position 4 conductor/contact* (6P4C) connectors.

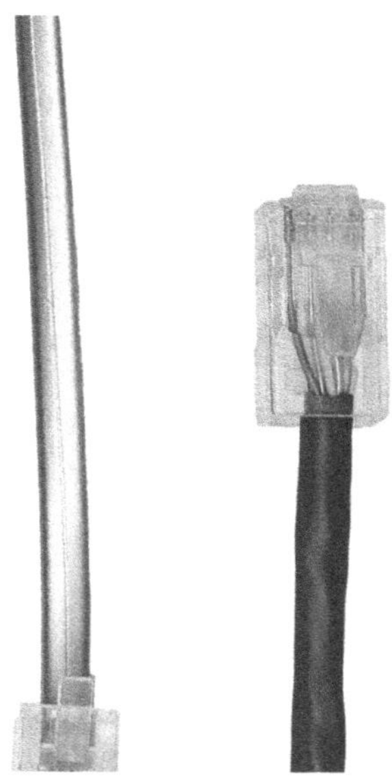

FIGURE 9-11
RJ11 (left) and 8P8C/"RJ45" (right) connectors

EXAM TIP CompTIA follows the common usage for networking cable connectors. You will *not* see 8P8C on the exam; you will *only* see RJ45.

Fiber-Optic Cables and Connectors

A *fiber-optic cable* transmits light rather than electricity, making it attractive for both high-EMI areas and long-distance transmissions. Whereas a single copper cable cannot carry data more than a few hundred meters at best, a single piece of fiber-optic cable will operate, depending on the implementation, for distances of up to tens of kilometers.

When a signal progresses down a piece of wire, it becomes steadily weaker. This process, known as *attenuation*, is much less of a factor for fiber-optic cables than it is for copper cables. Since fiber-optic cables experience significantly less signal loss over large distances, they're the ideal selection for high-bandwidth and long-distance applications.

A fiber-optic cable has four components: the *core*, which is the glass fiber itself; the *cladding*, the part that makes the light reflect down the fiber; *buffer* material to give strength; and the *insulating jacket* (Figure 9-12).

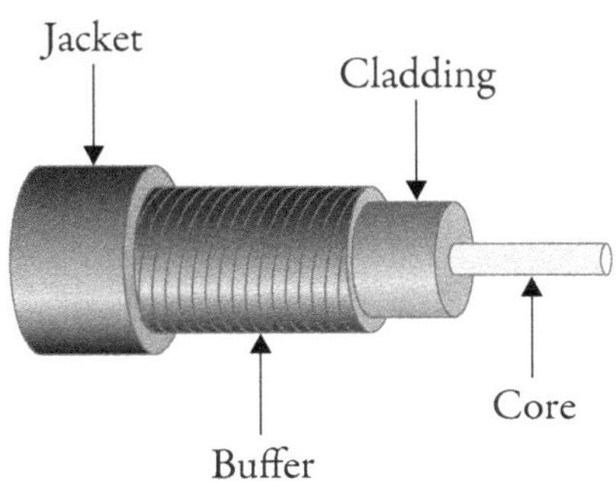

FIGURE 9-12 Cross-section of fiber-optic cable

Fiber-optic cables are manufactured with many different core and cladding diameters. Cable manufacturers use a two-number designator to define fiber-optic cables according to their core and cladding measurements. Common fiber-optic cable sizes are 9/125 µm, 50/125 µm, and 62.5/125 µm. Almost all network technologies that use fiber-optic cable require pairs of fibers. One fiber is used for sending, the other for receiving. In response to the demand for two-pair cables, manufacturers often connect two fibers together to create *duplex* fiber-optic cables (Figure 9-13).

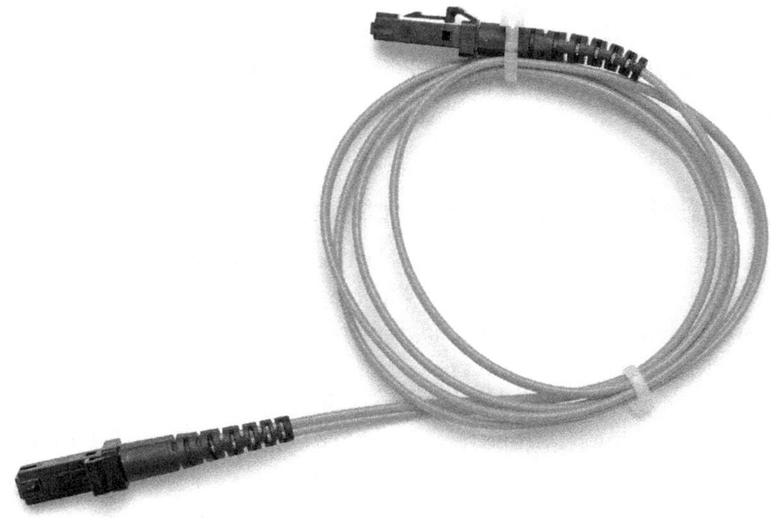

FIGURE 9-13 Duplex fiber-optic cable

NOTE The *u*-shaped symbol (μ) stands for *micro*, so μm is a *micrometer* (sometimes referred to as *micron*), or 1/1,000,000 of a meter.

Light can be sent down a fiber-optic cable as regular light or as laser light. The two types of light require totally different fiber-optic cables. Network technologies that use fiber optics use light-emitting diodes (LEDs) to send light signals. A fiber-optic cable that uses LEDs is known as *multimode fiber* (MMF).

NOTE MMF can use a form of laser called a *vertical-cavity surface-emitting laser* (VCSEL), which differs substantially from the lasers used in SMF. You'll find VCSELs in computer mice and laser printers, among other uses. And in case you're curious, VCSELs are *not* on the CompTIA Network+ exam.

A fiber-optic cable that uses lasers is known as *single-mode fiber* (SMF). Using laser light and SMF prevents a problem unique to MMF optics called *modal distortion*—where signals sent at the same time don't arrive at the same time because the paths differ slightly in length—and enables a network to achieve phenomenally high transfer rates over incredibly long distances.

NOTE A *nano*—abbreviated as *n*—stands for 1/1,000,000,000, or one-billionth. Here you'll see it as a nanometer (nm), one-billionth of a meter. That's one tiny wavelength!

Fiber optics also defines the wavelength of light used, measured in nanometers. Multimode cables transmit 850 nm or 1,300 nm wavelengths, whereas single mode transmits either 1310 nm or 1550 nm, depending on the laser.

NOTE The ANSI/TIA-568.3-D standard defines the nomenclature for fiber. The multimode standard prefix is OM (single mode is OS). OM1 and OM2 are used in shorter runs with LEDs. OM3, OM4, and OM5 can use lasers and run at higher bandwidths, thus providing faster speed and greater distances.

The ANSI/TIA 598-C standard provides guidelines for color-coding various fiber types. SMF is yellow. OM1 and OM2 are both orange. OM3 and OM4 sport aqua, and OM5 appears in a spectacular lime green.

Fiber-optic cables come in a broad choice of connector types. There are over one hundred different connectors, but the four you need to know for the CompTIA Network+ exam are ST, SC, LC, and MT-RJ. Figure 9-14 shows the first three; Figure 9-15 shows an MT-RJ connector.

FIGURE 9-14 From left to right: ST, SC, and LC fiber-optic connectors

FIGURE 9-15 MT-RJ fiber-optic connector

Although all fiber connectors must be installed in pairs, the ST and SC connectors traditionally have unique ends. The LC and MT-RJ connectors are always *duplex*, meaning both the send and receive cables are attached. You can certainly find SC connectors or sleeves to make them duplex too, so don't get too caught up on which can be which.

Multiple-fiber Push-On (MPO) connectors incorporate multiple optical fibers. They are usually for data center connections where the multiple fibers of backbone cable must be consolidated. These connectors allow applications to reach higher speeds by transmitting and receiving optical signals over multiple fibers.

We'll revisit fiber-optic connectors in Chapter 11 when we discuss the implementation of specific networking standards.

NOTE Most technicians call common fiber-optic connectors by their initials—such as ST, SC, or LC—perhaps because there's no consensus about what those initials mean. ST probably stands for *straight tip*, although some call it *snap and twist*. But SC and LC? How about *subscriber connector*, *standard connector*, or *Siemon connector* for the former, and *local connector* or *Lucent connector* for the latter? If you want to remember the connectors for the exam, try these: *snap and twist* for the bayonet-style ST connectors, *stick and click* for the straight push-in SC connectors, and *little connector* for the . . . little . . . LC connector.

Fire Ratings

Have you ever seen the movie *The Towering Inferno?* It was one of the better disaster movies of the 1970s. Steve McQueen stars as the fireman who saves the day when a skyscraper goes up in flames because of poor-quality electrical cabling. The burning insulation on the wires ultimately spreads the fire to every part of the building. Although no cables made today contain truly flammable insulation, the insulation is made from plastic, and if you get any plastic hot enough, it will create smoke and noxious fumes. The risk of burning insulation isn't fire—it's smoke and fumes.

To reduce the risk of your network cables burning and creating noxious fumes and smoke, Underwriters Laboratories and the National Electrical Code (NEC) joined forces to develop cabling *fire ratings*. The two most common fire ratings are PVC and plenum. PVC stands for polyvinyl chloride, and *plenum* refers to the space between the acoustical tile ceiling in an office building and the actual concrete ceiling above. A PVC-rated cable has no significant fire protection; if you burn one, it creates lots of smoke and noxious fumes. A plenum-rated cable creates much less smoke and fumes, but it costs three to five times as much as PVC-rated cable. Most city ordinances require the use of plenum cable for network installations. The bottom line? Get plenum!

A third type of fire rating, known as *riser*, designates the proper cabling to use for vertical runs between floors of a building. *Riser-rated* cable provides less protection than plenum cable, though, so most installations today use plenum for runs between floors. PVC can be used for riser applications but not in plenum spaces.

> **EXAM TIP** Look for a troubleshooting scenario question on the CompTIA Network+ exam that asks you to choose between plenum and PVC cable. If it goes in the wall, make it plenum!

IEEE Networking Industry Standards

The *Institute of Electrical and Electronics Engineers* (IEEE) defines industry-wide standards that promote the use and implementation of technology. In February 1980, a committee called the 802 Working Group took over from the private sector the job of defining network standards. (Because 802 is 2/80 reversed, some say that's how the committee got its name. The IEEE, though, says 802 was simply the next number in sequence, which is a great coincidence!) The IEEE 802 committee defines frames, speeds, distances, and types of cabling to use in a network environment. Concentrating on cables, the IEEE recognizes that no single cabling solution can work in all situations and, therefore, provides a variety of cabling standards.

IEEE committees define standards for a wide variety of electronics. A committee's name is often used to refer to the standards it publishes. The IEEE 1284 committee, for example, set standards for parallel communication, so you'll see parallel cables marked "IEEE 1284 compliant," as in Figure 9-16.

FIGURE 9-16 Parallel cable marked IEEE 1284 compliant

Although the IEEE 802 committee's original plan was to define a single, universal standard for networking, it quickly became apparent that no single solution would work for all needs. The 802 committee split into smaller subcommittees, with names such as IEEE 802.3 (Ethernet—wired networks) and IEEE 802.11. Table 9-4 shows the currently recognized IEEE 802 (Wireless LAN—Wi-Fi) subcommittees and their areas of jurisdiction. The missing numbers, such as 802.2 and 802.12, were used for committees that disbanded long ago. Each subcommittee is officially called a Working Group, except the few listed as a Technical Advisory Group (TAG).

TABLE 9-4 Some IEEE 802 subcommittees

IEEE 802.1	Higher Layer LAN Protocols (with many subcommittees, like 802.1X for port-based network access control)
IEEE 802.3	Ethernet (with a ton of subcommittees, such as 802.3ae for 10 Gigabit Ethernet)
IEEE 802.11	Wireless LAN (WLAN); specifications, such as Wi-Fi, and many subcommittees
IEEE 802.15	Wireless Personal Area Network (WPAN)
IEEE 802.18	Radio Regulatory Technical Advisory Group
IEEE 802.19	Wireless Coexistence Working Group
IEEE 802.24	Vertical Applications Technical Advisory Group

Chapter Review

Questions

1. Which group(s) do all cables used in networking fall into?
   - **A.** Copper
   - **B.** Fiber-optic
   - **C.** Both A and B
   - **D.** Neither A nor B
2. What is the primary use for coaxial cables today?
   - **A.** Connecting a cable modem to an ISP
   - **B.** Connecting a PC to a switch
   - **C.** Connecting a switch to another switch
   - **D.** Connecting a switch to a router
3. What connector is used for a coaxial cable?
   - **A.** F-type
   - **B.** ST
   - **C.** SC
   - **D.** LC
4. What is the most common type of cable found in networks?
   - **A.** Coax
   - **B.** Fiber
   - **C.** Twisted pair
   - **D.** Riser
5. What is the term for how twisted pair cables are rated?
   - **A.** Resistance
   - **B.** Ohm
   - **C.** Grade
   - **D.** Cat

6. Which type of UTP should be used for new installs (no data center involved)?
   A. Cat 5
   B. Cat 5e
   C. Cat 6
   D. Cat 6a
7. Which of the following isn't true regarding fiber-optic cables?
   A. They transmit light rather than electricity.
   B. They're not well suited for high-EMI areas.
   C. They can go long distances.
   D. They're always used between a PC and a switch.
8. Which one of these is not a fiber connector?
   A. SF
   B. ST
   C. SC
   D. LC
9. Which of the following is a duplex fiber-optic connection?
   A. LC
   B. RJ45
   C. ST
   D. SC
10. Which type of cable should be used in a wall?
    A. PVC
    B. Plenum
    C. Riser
    D. Cat 7

Answers

1. **C.** All networking cables will either be copper or fiber-optic.
2. **A.** Coaxial cables today are seen connecting cable modems to ISPs.
3. **A.** The F-type connector is used for coax cable.
4. **C.** Twisted-pair cables are the most common type used in networks.
5. **D.** Twisted-pair cables are assigned various grades called category (Cat) ratings.
6. **D.** Always go with the latest for new installs, and Cat 6a is the latest grade recognized by TIA. For data centers, consider Cat 8 (not listed).
7. **B.** Since fiber-optic cables use light rather than electricity, they're very well suited for high-EMI areas. They're less commonly used to connect PCs but very commonly used with servers. You see fiber-optic cables in high-security environments and healthcare due to their resistance to EMI and electronic eavesdropping.
8. **A.** There is no SF fiber connector.
9. **A.** Of the options given, only the LC connector is designed for duplex fiber-optic.
10. **B.** Plenum-rated cable creates less smoke and fumes than PVC and riser. Cat 7 itself has nothing to do with fire concerns.

Ethernet

IN THIS CHAPTER, YOU WILL LEARN HOW TO

- Define and describe Ethernet
- Explain the various 802.3 standards, including their media and transceivers
- Identify components of Ethernet frames
- Explain early Ethernet implementations
- Describe ways to enhance and extend Ethernet networks
- Compare the varieties of 100 Mbps (Fast) Ethernet
- Discuss copper- and fiber-based Gigabit Ethernet
- Identify Ethernet varieties beyond Gigabit Ethernet

In the beginning, there were no networks. Computers were isolated, solitary islands of information in a teeming sea of proto-geeks who banged out binary messages with wooden clubs and wore fur pocket protectors. Okay, maybe it wasn't that bad, but if you wanted to move a file from one machine to another, you had to use *Sneakernet*, which meant you saved the file on a disk, laced up your tennis shoes, and ran over to the other system.

All that walking no doubt had lots of health benefits, but frankly, proto-geeks weren't all that into health benefits—they were into speed, power, and technological coolness in general. (Sound familiar?) It's no wonder, then, that geeks everywhere agreed on the need to replace walking with some form of networking technology that connects computers together to transfer data at very high speeds.

This chapter explores the networking technology that eventually took control of the industry: Ethernet. We'll start with basic terminology and then look at two early forms of Ethernet before discussing ways of enhancing and expanding Ethernet networks. We'll then look at the improvements in Ethernet since the early 10BASE-T standard. You'll read about the 100 Mbps standards and the Gigabit Ethernet standards. Finally, we'll look at Ethernet standards that exceed Gigabit speeds.

Historical/Conceptual

Ethernet Origins

In 1973, Xerox answered the challenge of moving data without sneakers by developing *Ethernet,* a networking technology standard based on a bus topology in which a single coaxial cable (the bus) connected all computers, enabling them to transfer data at a rate of up to three million bits per second (3 Mbps). Although slow by today's standards, this early version of Ethernet was a huge improvement over manual transfer methods and served as the foundation for all subsequent versions of Ethernet.

Ethernet remained a largely in-house technology within Xerox until 1979, when Xerox decided to look for partners to help promote it as an industry standard. Xerox worked with Digital Equipment Corporation (DEC) and Intel to publish what became known as the Digital/Intel/Xerox (DIX) standard. The DIX standard improved on the original Ethernet standard, increasing speed to a screaming 10 Mbps.

These companies then did something visionary: they transferred (one might also say gave away) control of the DIX standard to the Institute of Electrical and Electronics Engineers (IEEE), which, in turn, created the 802.3 (Ethernet) working group that controls the Ethernet standard to this day. Transferring control to IEEE made Ethernet an open standard, which enabled anyone to make interchangeable Ethernet equipment, made Ethernet much cheaper than any alternative technology, and certainly contributed to Ethernet winning the marketplace.

802.3 Standards

The 802.3 working group defines wired network standards that share the same basic frame type and network access method and have their own identifiers. Here's a small selection:

- **802.3I** 10 Mbps Ethernet using twisted pair cabling (1990)
- **802.3AB** Gigabit Ethernet over twisted pair (1999)
- **802.3BY** 25 Gigabit Ethernet over fiber (2016)
- **802.3BS** Terabit Ethernet: 200 Gigabit Ethernet and 400 Gigabit Ethernet (2017)
- **802.3CM** 400 Gigabit Ethernet over multimode fiber (2020)
- **802.3CU** 100 Gigabit and 400 Gigabit Ethernet over single-mode fiber using 100 Gbps lanes (2021)
- **802.3DF** 800 Gigabit Ethernet (2024)
- **802.3DJ** 1.6 Terabit Ethernet (still being developed; expected to be completed in 2026)

Because the technologies share essential components, you can communicate among them just fine. The implementation of the network might be different, but the frames remain the same.

Ethernet's designers faced the same challenges as the designers of any network: how to send data across the wire, how to identify the sending and receiving computers, and how to determine which computer should use the shared cable at what time. The engineers resolved these issues by using data frames that contain MAC addresses to identify computers on the network and by using a process called CSMA/CD (discussed shortly) to determine which machine should access the wire at any given time. You saw some of this in action in Chapter 1, but now I'll introduce you to several additional concepts and terms.

NOTE The source for all things Ethernet is but a short click away on the internet. For starters, check out *ieee802.org*.

Test Specific

Ethernet Frames

As you learned in Chapter 1, every network technology breaks down data transmitted between computers into segments or datagrams and places them into packets, which in turn are encapsulated by *frames*. Using frames addresses two networking issues. First, frames prevent any single machine from monopolizing the shared bus cable. Second, they make the process of retransmitting lost data more efficient.

EXAM TIP Some techs use the terms *frame* and *packet* interchangeably (and incorrectly), but this book uses the terms strictly. You'll recall from Chapter 1 that frames at Layer 2 contain source and destination MAC addresses, while packets at Layer 3 contain source and destination IP addresses.

The process you saw in Chapter 1 of transferring a document between two computers illustrates these two issues. First, if the sending computer sends the document as a single huge frame, the frame will monopolize the cable, preventing other machines from using it until the entire file gets to the receiving system. Using relatively small frames enables computers to share the cable easily: each computer listens on the *network segment*, sending a few frames of data whenever it detects that no other computer is transmitting. Second, in the real world, bad things can happen to good data. When errors occur during transmission, the sending system must retransmit the frames that failed to reach the receiving system in good shape. If a document was transmitted as a single massive frame, the sending system would have to retransmit the entire frame—in this case, the entire document. Breaking the file up into smaller frames enables the sending computer to retransmit only the damaged frames. These benefits—shared access and more efficient retransmission—are the reason all networking technologies use frames.

In Chapter 1, you saw a generic frame. Let's take what you know of frames and expand on that knowledge by inspecting the details of an Ethernet frame (see Figure 10-1).

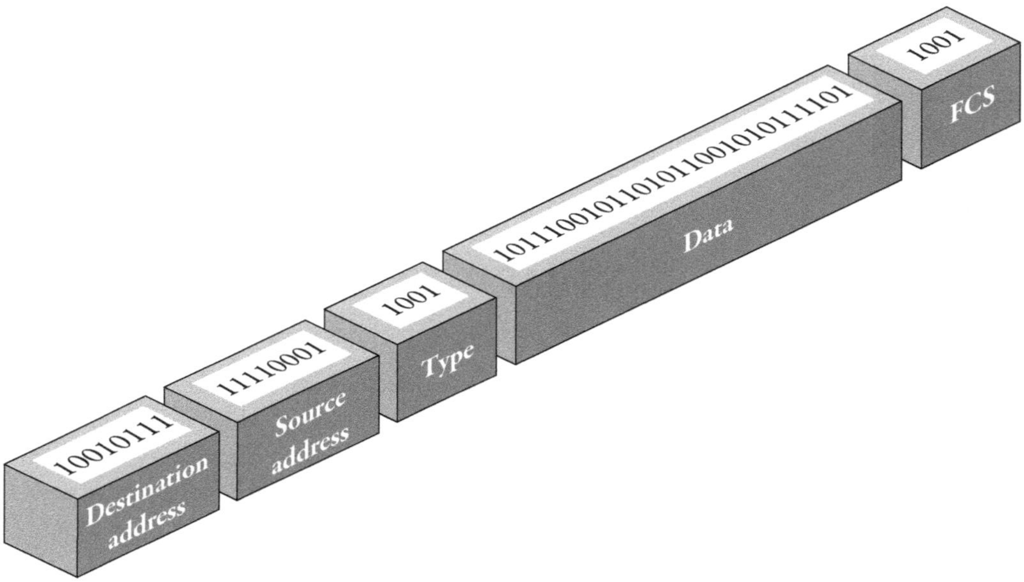

FIGURE 10-1 A basic Ethernet frame

Transmission of a frame starts with a preamble and can also include some extra filler called a *pad*. A basic Ethernet frame contains five fields following the preamble: the destination address, the source address, the type of the data, the data itself, and a frame check sequence. Let's look at each piece:

PREAMBLE A preamble is an 8-byte (64-bit) sequence that precedes every Ethernet frame. It consists of 7 bytes (56 bits) of alternating 1s and 0s (101010...) followed by 1 byte (8 bits) called the *start frame delimiter* (SFD), which ends in two 1s (10101011). The purpose of the preamble is to allow the receiving NIC to synchronize its clock with the incoming signal, essentially giving it time to "wake up" and prepare for the incoming frame. The SFD tells the receiving NIC exactly when the actual frame data begins. The sending NIC automatically adds the preamble to the frame before transmission.

DESTINATION ADDRESS/SOURCE ADDRESS Each NIC on an Ethernet network must have a unique identifying address. Ethernet identifies the NICs on a network using special 48-bit (6-byte) binary addresses known as MAC addresses. The destination address is the MAC address of the frame's recipient, and the source address is the MAC address of the sending system.

EXAM TIP The CompTIA Network+ exam might describe MAC addresses as *48-bit binary addresses* or *6-byte binary addresses*.

Back in the early days of Ethernet, on a bus network, all the connected computers could see all traffic. The destination address in the frame enabled NICs to examine each frame and process only frames intended for them. The source address in the frame enabled the recipient to respond accurately.

TYPE An Ethernet frame may carry one of several types of data. The Type field helps the receiving computer interpret the frame contents at a very basic level to determine which protocol the frame encapsulates. In most cases, it will be ARP, an IPv4 packet, or an IPv6 packet.

The Type field does *not* tell you if the frame carries higher-layer data, such as an email message or web page. You have to dig deeper into the frame's Data field (from the IP packet to the TCP segment or UDP datagram) to find that information.

DATA The Data field contains the payload for the protocol specified in the Type field: ARP data, IPv4 packets, or IPv6 packets.

PAD The minimum Ethernet frame is 64 bytes (which includes the header, data/payload, and trailer), but not all of that has to be actual data. If an Ethernet frame has fewer than 64 bytes of data to haul, the sending NIC automatically adds extra data—a pad—to bring the size up to the minimum 64 bytes. Padding is still used in today's modern Ethernet standards.

FRAME CHECK SEQUENCE (FCS) The FCS enables Ethernet nodes to recognize when bad things happen to good data. Machines on a network must be able to detect when data has been damaged in transit. To detect errors, the computers on an Ethernet network attach a special code to each frame. As discussed in Chapter 1, when creating an Ethernet frame, the sending machine runs the data through a special mathematical formula called a *cyclic redundancy check* (CRC) and attaches the result, the FCS, to the frame as the trailer. The receiving machine opens the frame, performs the same calculation, and compares its answer with the one included with the frame. If the answers do not match, the receiving machine drops the frame.

Early Ethernet Standards

Contemplating the physical network brings up numerous questions. What kind of cables should you use? What should they be made of? How long can they be? For these answers, turn to the IEEE 802.3 standard, both true bus and star-bus versions.

Bus Ethernet

The original Ethernet networks employed a *true bus* topology, meaning every computer on a network connected to the same cable, the bus. Every version of Ethernet designed since the early 1990s uses a hybrid *star-bus* topology. At the center of these early networks was a *hub*, which was a multiport repeater that interpreted the 1s and 0s coming in from one port and repeated that signal out to the other connected ports (whereas repeaters, which preceded hubs, extended the length of a network cable by regenerating weak signals and only had two ports.) (but not the port that originally sent it), as shown in Figure 10-2.

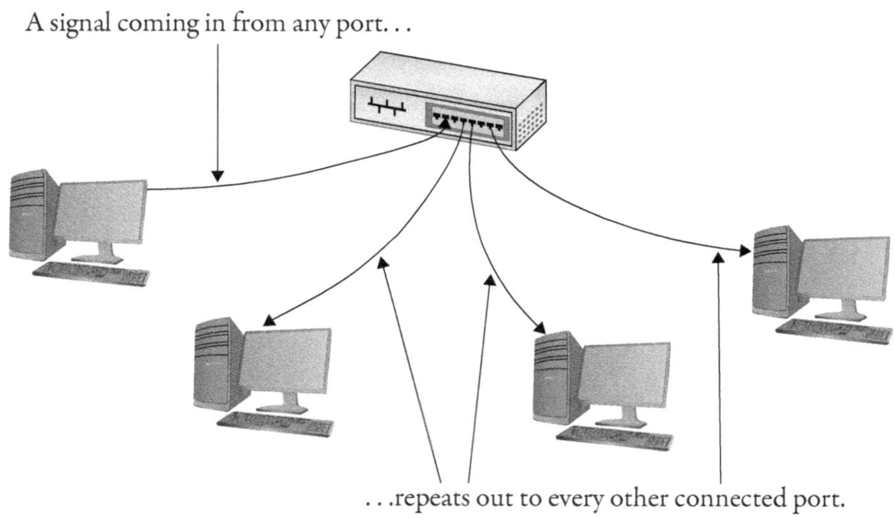

FIGURE 10-2 Ethernet hub

10BASE-T

In 1990, the IEEE 802.3 committee created a version of Ethernet called *10BASE-T* that rapidly became the most popular network technology in the world, replacing competing and now long-gone competitors like IBM's Token Ring and Apple's LocalTalk. The classic 10BASE-T network consisted of two or more computers connected to a central hub. The NICs connected with wires as specified by the 802.3 committee.

The name 10BASE-T follows roughly the same naming convention used for earlier Ethernet cabling systems. The number *10* refers to the speed: 10 Mbps. The word *BASE* refers to the signaling type: baseband. The letter *T* refers to the type of cable used: twisted pair. 10BASE-T used unshielded twisted-pair (UTP) cabling.

EXAM TIP A *baseband* network means that only a single signal travels over the wires of the network at one time, occupying the lowest frequencies. All Ethernet networks are baseband. Contrast this with *broadband*, which allows multiple signals to flow over the same wire at the same time, modulating to higher frequencies. The latter is how cable television and cable internet work.

UTP

Officially, 10BASE-T required the use of two-pair Cat 3 (or higher) UTP cable. One pair of wires sent data to the hub, while the other pair received data from the hub. Even though 10BASE-T only required two-pair cabling to connect devices to the hub, everyone installed four-pair cabling as a future-proofing strategy (Figure 10-3). Not surprisingly, this came in handy shortly thereafter.

Most UTP cables (then and now) come with stranded Kevlar fibers to add strength, enabling installers to pull on the cable without much risk of ripping it apart.

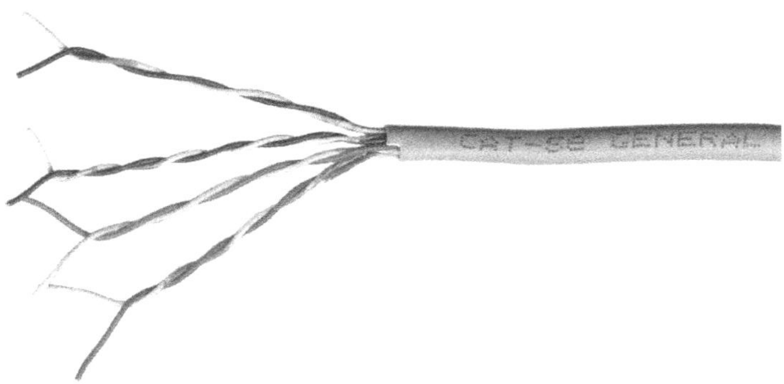

FIGURE 10-3 A typical four-pair Cat 5e UTP cable

10BASE-T also introduced the networking world to the *RJ45 connector* (Figure 10-4), discussed in the previous chapter. Each pin on the RJ45 connects to a single wire inside the cable, enabling devices to apply voltage to individual wires. The pins on the RJ45 are numbered from 1 to 8, as shown in Figure 10-5.

FIGURE 10-4 Two views of an RJ45 connector

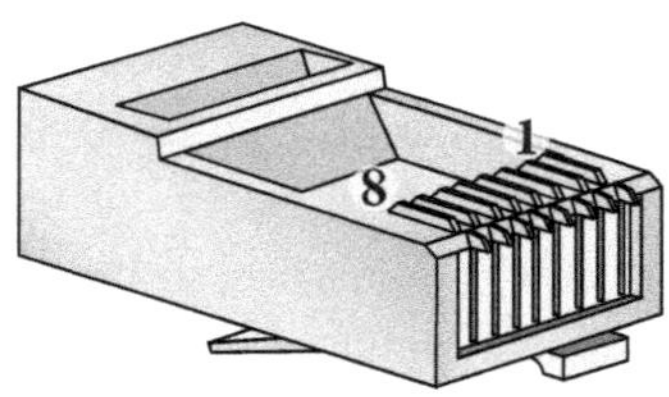

FIGURE 10-5 The pins on an RJ45 connector are numbered 1 through 8.

The 10BASE-T standard designates some of these numbered wires for specific purposes. As mentioned earlier, although the cable has four pairs, 10BASE-T used only two of the pairs. 10BASE-T devices used pins 1 and 2 to send data, and pins 3 and 6 to receive data. Despite having separate send and receive wires, a 10BASE-T device connected to a hub could not send and receive simultaneously; it ran in *half-duplex* mode, communicating in only one direction at a time. Later advances (as you'll see shortly) enabled NICs to send and receive at the same time, thus running in *full-duplex* mode.

An RJ45 connector is attached to the end of a UTP cable in a process (some call it an art) called *crimping*. The tool used for this process is called a *crimper*. Each wire inside a UTP cable must connect to the proper pin inside the crimp. Manufacturers color-code each wire within four-pair UTP to help ensure the same wires connect to the same pins at both ends. Each pair of wires consists of a solid-colored wire and a striped wire: blue/blue-white, orange/orange-white, brown/brown-white, and green/green-white (Figure 10-6).

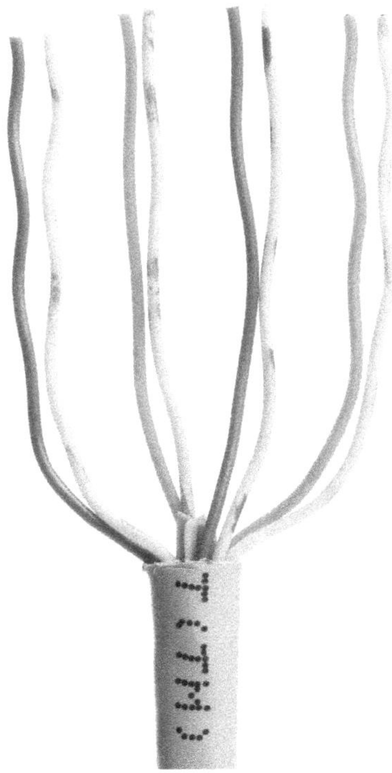

FIGURE 10-6 Color-coded pairs (note the alternating solid and striped wires)

NOTE As noted in Chapter 9, the real name for RJ45 is *8 position 8 contact (8P8C)* modular plug. The term *RJ45* is so prevalent, however, that nobody calls it by its real name.

The Telecommunications Industry Association/Electronics Industries Alliance (TIA/EIA) originally defined the industry *termination standard* for correct crimping of four-pair UTP. Figure 10-7 shows the TIA/EIA 568A and TIA/EIA 568B color-code standards. Note that the wire pairs used by 10BASE-T (1 and 2, 3 and 6) come from the same color pairs (green/green-white and orange/orange-white).

The current standard for twisted-pair Ethernet cabling, known as ANSI/TIA-568, continues to include the same wiring schemes originally known as TIA/EIA-568A and TIA/EIA-568B. The name changed after the EIA ceased operations in 2011, leaving the TIA to maintain the standard under American National Standards Institute (ANSI) oversight. While the technical specifications remain the same, the official name now omits *EIA*. Many textbooks, tools, and industry professionals still use the older *TIA/EIA* terminology out of habit.

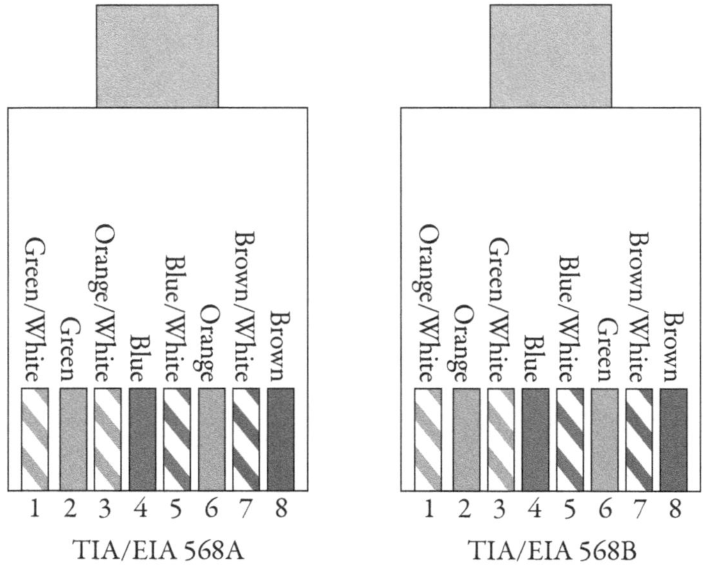

FIGURE 10-7 TIA/EIA 568A and 568B standards

Both 568A and 568B define the wire color order in Ethernet cables. If both ends of a cable use the same standard (either 568A or 568B), it's a straight-through cable, typically used to connect different devices (like PC to switch). If one end uses 568A (green pair first) and the other 568B (orange pair first), it's a crossover cable, traditionally used for similar devices (like switch to switch, router to router, or even PC to PC). Most modern equipment, however, supports Automatic Medium-Dependent Interface Crossover (Auto-MDI/MDI-X, coming up later in the chapter), which makes crossover cables largely obsolete.

The ability to make your own Ethernet cables is a real plus for a network tech. With a reel of cable, a bag of RJ45 connectors, a moderate investment in a crimper, and a little practice, you can kiss those mass-produced cables goodbye! You can make cables in custom lengths and save time and money by replacing broken RJ45 connectors, which otherwise would require you to throw out the entire cable.

EXAM TIP An easy trick to help you remember the difference between 568A and 568B is the word *go*. The green and orange pairs are swapped between 568A and 568B, whereas the blue and brown pairs stay in the same place!

For the CompTIA Network+ exam, you will be tested on the TIA/EIA 568A or 568B color codes. Memorize them. You'll see the standards listed as EIA/TIA 568A, TIA/EIA568A, T568A, or just 568A. Know the A and B, and you'll be fine.

10BASE-T LIMITS AND SPECIFICATIONS

Like any other Ethernet standard, 10BASE-T had limitations, both on cable distance and on the number of computers. The key distance limitation for 10BASE-T was the distance between the hub and the computer. The twisted-pair cable connecting a computer to the hub could not exceed 100 meters in length. A 10BASE-T hub could connect no more than 1,024 computers, although that limitation rarely came into play. It made no sense for vendors to build hubs that large—or more to the point, that *expensive.*

10BASE-FL

Just a few years after the introduction of 10BASE-T, a fiber-optic version called *10BASE-FL* was released. As you know from the previous chapter, fiber-optic cabling transmits data using pulses of light instead of electrical current. Using light instead of electricity addresses the three key weaknesses of copper cabling. First, optical signals can travel much farther. The maximum length for a 10BASE-FL cable was up to 2 kilometers, depending on how you configured it. Second, fiber-optic cable is immune to electrical interference, making it an ideal choice for high-interference environments. Third, the cable is much more difficult to tap into, making fiber a good choice for environments with security concerns. 10BASE-FL used *multimode* 62.5/125 µm (OM1) fiber-optic cabling and employed either a *subscriber connector* (SC) or *straight tip* (ST) connector.

NOTE Multimode fiber (MMF) comes in varying core sizes and capabilities. You'll see these as *optical multimode* (OM) types, such as OM1, OM2, OM3, and OM4. The key is to match the fiber to the technology.

Figure 10-8 shows a typical 10BASE-FL card. Note that it uses two fiber connectors—one to send and one to receive. All fiber-optic networks use at least two fiber-optic cables. Although 10BASE-FL enjoyed some popularity for a number of years, most networks today are using the same fiber-optic cabling to run far faster network technologies.

So far you've seen two different flavors of star-bus Ethernet, 10BASE-T and 10BASE-FL. Even though they used different cabling and hubs, they both used Ethernet frames. As a result, interconnecting flavors of Ethernet was (and still is) common. A *media converter* (Figure 10-9) allows you to connect the different cable types.

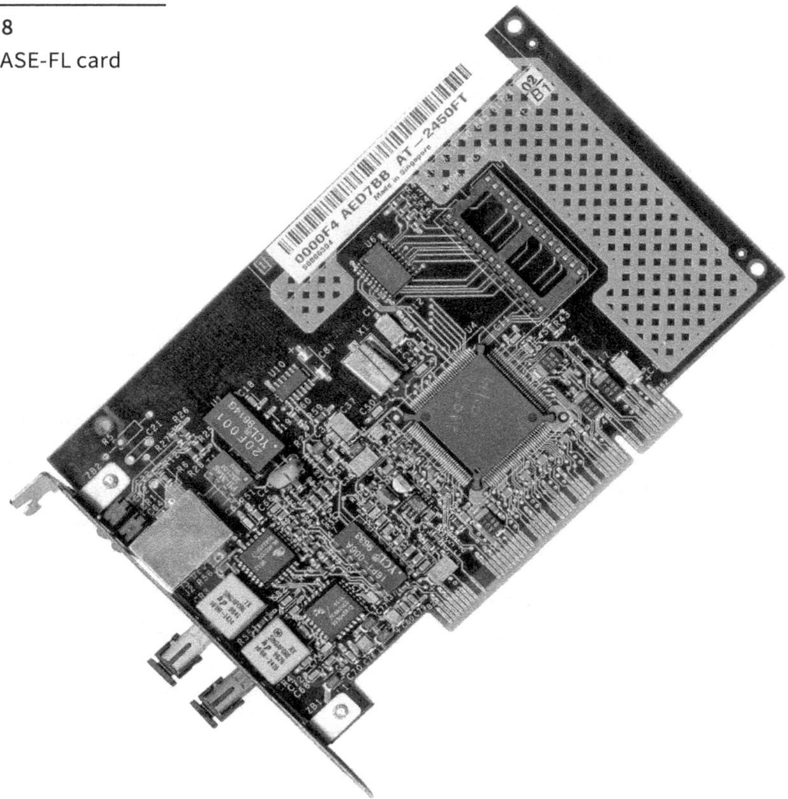

FIGURE 10-8
Typical 10BASE-FL card

FIGURE 10-9
Typical copper-to-fiber Ethernet media converter (photo courtesy of TRENDnet)

Table 10-1 summarizes the 10 Mbps Ethernet standards.

TABLE 10-1 10 Mbps Ethernet summary

STANDARD	DISTANCE	NODE LIMIT	CABLE TYPE	CONNECTORS
10BASE-T	100 m	1,024 per hub	Cat 3+ UTP	RJ45
10BASE-FL	2 km	1,024 per hub	OM1 MMF	ST/SC

CSMA/CD

One of the issues with bus communication is that devices essentially share the same cable. This applies to both true bus networks and hybrid star-bus networks. The NICs need some way to determine which machine should send data at which time. Ethernet designers came up with a clever way to handle the issue of potential collisions.

Ethernet networks used a system called *carrier-sense multiple access with collision detection* (CSMA/CD) to determine which computer should use a shared cable at a given moment. *Carrier sense* meant that each node using the network examined the cable before sending a data frame (Figure 10-10). If another machine was using the network, the node detected traffic on the segment, waited a random number of slot times (a few microseconds to milliseconds depending on the network speed), and then rechecked. If it detected no traffic, the node sent out its frame.

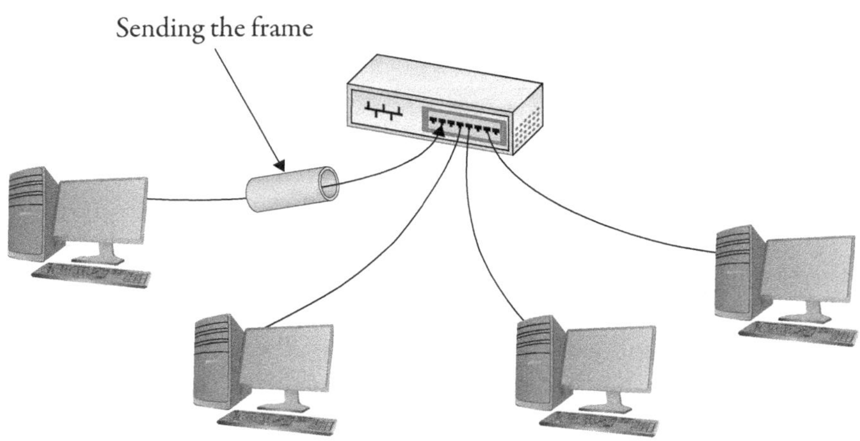

FIGURE 10-10 No one else is talking—send the frame!

EXAM TIP CSMA/CD was a network access method that mapped to the IEEE 802.3 standard for Ethernet networks. It's disabled in modern full-duplex networks.

Multiple access meant that all machines had equal access to the wire. If the line was free, any Ethernet node could send a frame. From Ethernet's point of view, it didn't matter what function the node performed: it could have been a desktop system running a Windows operating system or a file server running a Windows Server operating system or Linux. As far as early Ethernet was concerned, a node was a node was a node, and access to the cable was assigned strictly on a first-come, first-served basis.

So what happened if two machines, both listening to the cable, simultaneously decided that it was free and tried to send a frame? A collision occurred, and both transmissions were lost (Figure 10-11). A collision is like two people talking at the same time: the listener hears a mixture of two voices and can't understand either one.

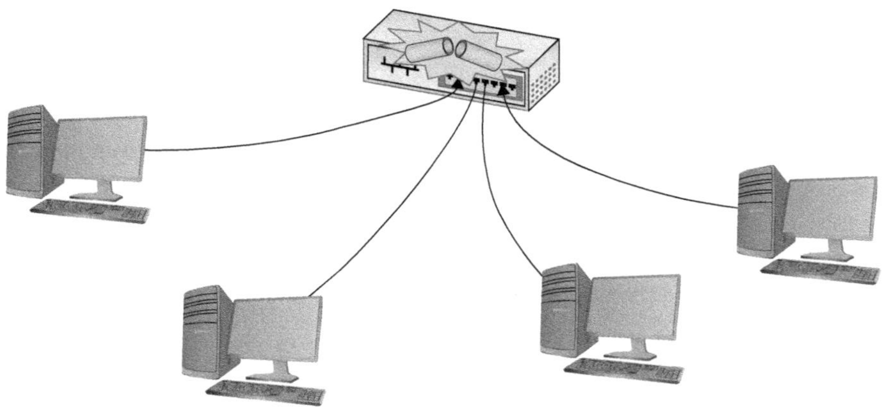

FIGURE 10-11 Collision!

When two NICs sent at the same time, they'd sense the collision because each NIC would be transmitting its own frame and receiving another station's frame simultaneously. When they detected a collision, both nodes stopped transmitting.

They then each generated a random number (using a binary exponential backoff algorithm) to determine how long to wait before trying again. If you're imagining each machine rolling its magic electronic dice and waiting for that number of seconds, you're not too far off, except that the wait time was much shorter than one second (Figure 10-12). Whichever node generated the lowest random number began its retransmission first, winning the competition to use the wire. The losing node, seeing that traffic, waited for the wire to be free again before attempting to retransmit its data.

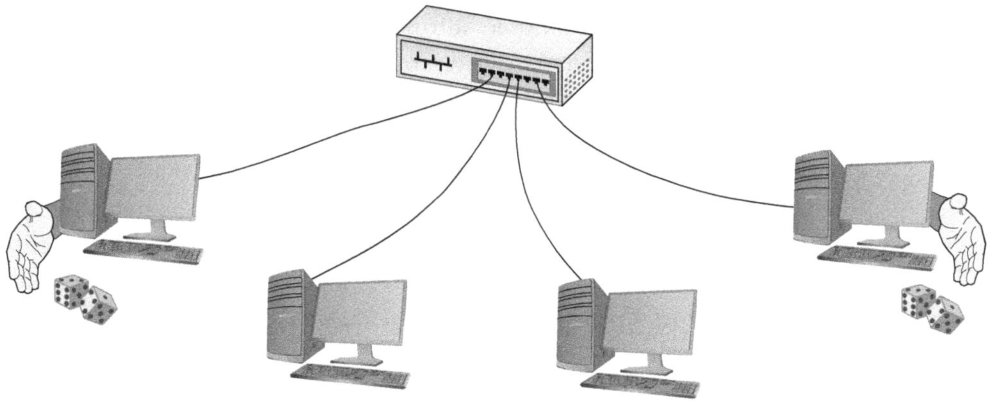

FIGURE 10-12 Rolling for timing

Collisions were a normal part of the operation of early Ethernet networks, because every device shared a bus. A group of nodes that can all send frames at the same time, resulting in collisions, is called a *collision domain*. Better technology (full-duplex) eliminates collisions today.

Enhancing and Extending Ethernet Networks

While plain-vanilla 10BASE-T Ethernet performed well enough for first-generation networks (which did little more than basic file and print sharing), by the early 1990s networks used more-demanding applications, such as Lotus Notes, SAP business management software, and Microsoft Exchange, which quickly saturated a 10BASE-T network. Fortunately, the IEEE kept expanding the standard, giving the network tech in the trenches a new tool that provided additional bandwidth: the switch.

Additionally, more companies and organizations adopted Ethernet, leading to a demand for larger networks, both geographically and in the number of nodes that could interconnect. Hubs were cranky and creaky; switches brought much better scalability.

The Trouble with Hubs

A classic 10BASE-T network with a hub could have only one message on the wire at any time. When two computers sent messages at the same time, the hub dutifully repeated both signals. The nodes recognized the collision and, following the rules of CSMA/CD, attempted to resend. With more computers came more collisions, lowering the effective transmission speed for the whole network. A busy network became a slow network because all the computers shared the same collision domain.

EXAM TIP Adding another hub or two to an early Ethernet network enabled you to add more devices but also extended a collision domain, increasing the number of collisions. Using a *bridge* to connect such network segments created multiple collision domains, reducing the number of devices in each and thereby reducing the number of collisions. A bridge acted like a repeater to connect two or more network segments but then went a step further by filtering and forwarding traffic between them based on the MAC addresses of the computers on each. Its placement between two segments preserved bandwidth, making larger Ethernet networks possible.

You'll see the term *bridge* used to refer to modern devices, such as wireless access points that bridge wired and wireless networks. While these devices perform a similar function—connecting network segments—the underlying technology is fundamentally different.

Switches to the Rescue

An Ethernet *switch* looks like a hub because all nodes plug into it (Figure 10-13), but it doesn't function like a hub. Switches have extra capabilities that enable them to take advantage of MAC addresses, effectively creating point-to-point connections between two conversing computers. This gives every conversation between two computers the full bandwidth of the network. Switches were covered in detail in Chapter 6.

FIGURE 10-13 Hub (top) and switch (bottom) comparison

Sometimes one switch just isn't enough. Once an organization uses every port on its existing switch, adding more nodes requires adding more switches. Other reasons that might motivate an organization to add more switches are physical distance requirements and fault tolerance. If every node on the network connects to the same switch, that switch becomes a single point of failure—in other words, if it fails, everybody drops off the network.

Modern switches can automatically detect the type of device connected to each port. This means that when another switch is plugged in, there's no need to worry about crossover cables (as mentioned earlier) or dedicated uplink ports, as was the case years ago. You can simply plug a cable into any port, and the connection will work. This flexibility is made possible by a feature called Auto-MDI/MDI-X, which enables the switch to automatically configure its transmit and receive pins to match the connected device (PC, router, or switch) accordingly.

Problems with Switches

The simple switches described in this chapter generally function flawlessly for years without the tech having to do anything more than wipe dust off the top. Very occasionally, however, you'll run into a switch that has problems, and these often fall into two categories:

- Obvious physical damage
- Dead ports

Diagnosing either problem follows a similar pattern. First, you recognize that a switch might have problems because a device you've plugged in can't connect to the network. Second, you examine the switch for obvious damage. Third, you look for link lights. If they're not flashing or indicate a duplex or speed mismatch, you try a different port. Fourth, you look at your cables. If anything looks bent, broken, or stepped on, you should replace it. A bad cable, improper cable type, or incorrect termination/pinout can cause problems that point to a "failed" switch instead of the true culprit. The bad cable could be behind a wall or in a ceiling, sometimes damaged by construction (like a nail, screw, or the guy who cut out a section of ceiling wires that were "in the way"). Finally, you use the tried-and-true method of replacing the switch or the cable with a known-good device.

100-Megabit Ethernet

The quest to break 10 Mbps network speeds in Ethernet started in the early 1990s. By then, 10BASE-T Ethernet had established itself as the most popular networking technology (although other standards, such as IBM's Token Ring, still had some market share). The 802.3 committee's goal was to implement a new speed standard that made no changes to the Ethernet frames. This would allow different speeds of Ethernet to interconnect, assuming you had equipment that could handle the speed differences and a media converter if the connections differed. This standardization ensured communication and scalability.

100BASE-T

Network hardware makers, all focused on the prize of leading the new Ethernet standard, proposed a large number of potential standards to replace 10BASE-T. The result was two twisted-pair Ethernet standards: *100BASE-T4* and *100BASE-TX*. 100BASE-T4 used Cat 3 cable, whereas 100BASE-TX used Cat 5 and Cat 5e. By the late 1990s, 100BASE-TX became the dominant 100 Mbps Ethernet standard. 100BASE-T4 disappeared from the market and has been long forgotten. In fact, we never say *100BASE-TX* anymore, but simply *100BASE-T*.

NOTE 100BASE-T is known as *Fast Ethernet*. The term still sticks to the 100 Mbps standards, even though there are now much faster versions of Ethernet.

Upgrading a 10BASE-T network to 100BASE-T was not a simple process. First, you needed Cat 5 cable or better. Second, you had to replace all 10BASE-T NICs with 100BASE-T NICs. Third, you had to replace the 10BASE-T hub or switch with a 100BASE-T hub or switch. Making this upgrade cost a lot in the early days of 100BASE-T, so people clamored for a way to make the upgrade a little easier and less expensive. This was accomplished via multispeed, auto-sensing NICs and hubs or switches.

Figure 10-14 shows a typical multispeed, auto-sensing 100BASE-T NIC from the late 1990s. When this NIC first connected to a network, it negotiated automatically with the hub or switch to determine the other device's highest speed. If they both supported 100BASE-T, then you got 100BASE-T. If the hub or switch supported only 10BASE-T, the NIC used 10BASE-T. All of this happened automatically.

FIGURE 10-14 PCI 100BASE-T NIC

Distinguishing a 10BASE-T NIC from a 100BASE-T NIC without close inspection was impossible. You had to examine the card for some indication of its speed; for example, some NICs had extra link lights to show the speed (see Chapter 6 for more on link lights). Of course, you could always install the card and see what the operating system said it saw.

You'll have trouble finding a true 10BASE-T or 100BASE-T NIC any longer because multispeed NICs have been around long enough to have replaced any single-speed NIC. All modern NICs are multispeed and auto-sensing.

100BASE-FX

Most Ethernet networks use unshielded twisted-pair (UTP) cabling, but quite a few use fiber-based networks instead. In some networks, using fiber simply makes more sense for the three reasons noted earlier in the chapter, namely:

- The 100-meter distance limitation of UTP-based networks is inadequate for networks covering large buildings or campuses.
- UTP's lack of electrical shielding makes it a poor choice for networks functioning in locations with high levels of electromagnetic interference.
- UTP cabling (and copper cabling in general) is easier to tap, making it an inappropriate choice for high-security environments.

Thus, the IEEE 802.3 standard provides for a flavor of 100 Mbps Ethernet using fiber-optic cable called *100BASE-FX.*

The 100BASE-FX standard saw quite a bit of interest for years, as it combines the high speed of 100 Mbps Ethernet with the reliability of fiber optics. Outwardly, 100BASE-FX looks exactly like its predecessor, 10BASE-FL, using multimode fiber-optic cabling and SC or ST connectors. But 100BASE-FX offers improved data speeds over 10BASE-FL and equally long cable runs, supporting a maximum cable length of 2 kilometers.

EXAM TIP There's no scenario today where you would *install* 100BASE-networking components, except perhaps to make use of donated equipment. At the same time, you'll definitely *see* legacy 100BASE- gear installed and functioning in many organizations.

Table 10-2 summarizes the two 100 Mbps Ethernet standards just discussed.

TABLE 10-2 100 Mbps Ethernet summary

STANDARD	DISTANCE	NODE LIMIT	CABLE TYPE	CONNECTORS
100BASE-T	100 m	1,024 per hub/switch	Cat 5+ UTP	RJ45
100BASE-FX	2 km	1,024 per hub/switch	OM1 MMF	SC/ST (multimode fiber only)

100BASE-SX

100BASE-SX was a short-distance, LED-based alternative to 100BASE-FX. It ran on OM1 or OM2 fiber at 850 nm (nanometers) and used ST, SC, or LC connectors. It was completely backward-compatible to 10BASE-FL, so was touted as a viable upgrade from the even older tech. 100BASE-SX is long gone.

Full-Duplex Ethernet

Early 100BASE-T NICs, just like 10BASE-T NICs, could send and receive data, but not at the same time. The IEEE addressed the half-duplex limitation shortly after adopting 100BASE-T as a standard. By the late 1990s, most 100BASE-T cards could auto-negotiate for full-duplex so that a NIC could send and receive at the same time.

NOTE Full-duplex doesn't increase network speed directly, but it doubles network bandwidth (only in the sense of simultaneous send/receive, not raw NIC speed). Imagine a two-lane road with traffic moving in opposite directions in each lane. If one lane is closed, a traffic cop manages the flow of traffic from each direction in a single lane, allowing traffic from only one direction and then from the other. That's half-duplex: the bandwidth is in one direction, transmitting or receiving. When the lane is reopened, traffic can again flow in both directions simultaneously. That's full-duplex: the bandwidth is in effect for both directions at the same time, transmitting and receiving.

All NICs today run in full-duplex mode. The NIC and the attached switch determine full- or half-duplex during the auto-negotiation process. Most of the time, you simply let the NIC complete its negotiation. Every operating system has some method to force the NIC to a certain speed/duplex, as shown in Figure 10-15. A switch can also force speed and duplex settings and deal with issues when there is a mismatch.

Fast Ethernet makes sense for *local area networks* (LANs)—where computers are interconnected in a defined space (like a home or office) and share small data, such as documents and spreadsheets. Plenty of LANs around the world continue to soldier on at 100 Mbps speeds. A lot of network-connected devices, such as printers, function just fine on it as well. Still, Fast Ethernet is dead in new installations, so let's turn to the current standards.

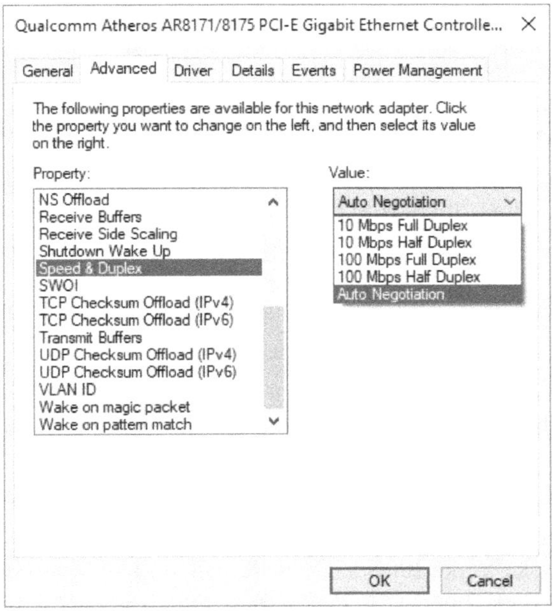

FIGURE 10-15 Forcing speed and duplex in Windows

Gigabit Ethernet

By the end of the 1990s, Fast Ethernet was not enough for networking needs. In response, the IEEE created *Gigabit Ethernet*, which today is the most common type of Ethernet found on new NICs.

The IEEE approved two different versions of Gigabit Ethernet. The most widely implemented solution, published under the IEEE *802.3ab* standard, is called *1000BASE-T*. The other version, published under the *802.3z* standard and known as *1000BASE-X*, is divided into a series of standards, with names such as 1000BASE-SX and 1000BASE-LX.

Unlike earlier standards, 1000BASE-T uses all four twisted pairs in the UTP or STP cable simultaneously to support full-duplex gigabit transmission. Like 10BASE-T and 100BASE-T, 1000BASE-T has a maximum cable length of 100 meters on a segment. 1000BASE-T connections and ports look exactly like the ones on a 10BASE-T or 100BASE-T network.

NOTE The term *Gigabit Ethernet* is more commonly used than *1000BASE-T* (1,000 megabits is 1 gigabit).

The 802.3z standards require a bit more discussion. Let's look at each of these solutions in detail to see how they work.

EXAM TIP 1000BASE-T Gigabit Ethernet requires Auto-MDI/MDI-X. Ports automatically detect the cable type (straight-through or crossover) and configure transmit/receive pairs, eliminating the need for crossover cables.

1000BASE-SX

Many networks upgrading to Gigabit Ethernet use the *1000BASE-SX* standard for short-distance, campus/building installations. 1000BASE-SX uses multimode fiber-optic cabling to connect systems, with a generous maximum cable length of 220 to 500 meters (dependent on manufacturer and fiber type); the exact length is left up to the various manufacturers. 1000BASE-SX uses an 850 nm wavelength LED to transmit light on the fiber-optic cable. 1000BASE-SX devices look like 100BASE-FX devices, and although both standards can use several types of connectors, 1000BASE-SX devices commonly use LC (which are smaller than SC), while 100BASE-FX devices frequently use SC. (See "SFF Fiber Connectors" for details on LC connectors.)

EXAM TIP The *wavelength* of a particular signal (laser, in this case) refers to the distance the signal has to travel before it completes its particular shape and starts to repeat. The different colors of the laser signals feature different wavelengths.

1000BASE-LX

1000BASE-LX is the long-distance carrier for Gigabit Ethernet. 1000BASE-LX uses lasers on single-mode cables to shoot data at distances up to 5 kilometers—and some manufacturers use special repeaters to increase that to distances as great as 70 kilometers! The Ethernet folks are trying to position this as the Ethernet backbone of the future, and already some large carriers are beginning to adopt 1000BASE-LX. You may live your whole life and never see a 1000BASE-LX device, but odds are good that you will encounter connections that use such devices soon. 1000BASE-LX connectors look like 1000BASE-SX connectors.

SFF Fiber Connectors

Around the time that Gigabit Ethernet emerged, two problems began to surface with ST and SC connectors. First, ST connectors are relatively large, twist-on connectors, requiring the installer to twist the cable when inserting or removing it. Twisting fiber-optic cables can cause the delicate fibers to fracture. Also, some techs have a problem with ST connectors if the connectors are too closely packed: they can't get their fingers around them.

NOTE Technically, "SC connector" is a redundant expression like "IP protocol" and "NIC card," but unlike those examples, it's the standard industry term.

SC connectors snap in and out, making them much more popular than ST connectors. SC connectors are also large, however, and the folks who make fiber networking equipment wanted to pack more connectors onto their boxes.

This brought about two new types of fiber connectors, known generically as *small form factor* (SFF) connectors, both of which were introduced in Chapter 9. The first, the *Mechanical Transfer Registered Jack* (MT-RJ), became popular with big companies like Cisco and is still quite common. The second, the *local connector* (LC), is shown in Figure 10-16. LC-type connectors are very popular, particularly in the United States, and many fiber experts consider them the predominant fiber connector.

LC and MT-RJ are the most popular types of SFF fiber connectors, but there are many others, such as Multi-Fiber Push-On (MPO) and MTP (a brand name variant of MPO). The fiber industry has no standard beyond ST and SC connectors, which means that different makers of fiber equipment may have different connections. Table 10-3 summarizes common Gigabit Ethernet standards.

FIGURE 10-16 LC-type connector

TABLE 10-3 Gigabit Ethernet summary

STANDARD	DISTANCE	CABLE TYPE	CABLE DETAILS/ WAVELENGTH	CONNECTORS
1000BASE-T	100 m	Cat 5e/6 UTP	Four-pair/full-duplex	RJ45
1000BASE-SX	220–500 m	OM2 or better multi-mode fiber (although OM1 works for short distances)	850 nm	Variable, commonly LC
1000BASE-LX	5 km	OS1 or OS2 single-mode fiber	1,300 nm	Variable, commonly LC and SC

Mechanical Connection Variations

Aside from the various connection types, fiber connectors vary in the connection point. The standard connector type today is called a *physical contact (PC) connector* because the two pieces of fiber touch when inserted. These connectors replace the older *flat-surface connector* that left a little gap between the connection points due to imperfections in the glass. PC connectors are highly polished and slightly spherical, reducing the signal loss at the connection point.

Two technologies have dropped in price and have replaced PC connectors in some implementations. *Ultra-physical contact (UPC) connectors* are polished extensively for a superior finish and reduce signal loss significantly over PC connectors. *Angled physical contact (APC) connectors* add an 8-degree angle to the curved end, which helps reduce signal reflections at the fiber interface, improving overall optical performance and lowering signal loss further. Plus, their connection does not degrade from multiple insertions, unlike earlier connection types.

So, when you purchase fiber cables today, you'll see the connector type and the contact type, plus the type of cable and other physical dimensions. A typical patch cable, for example, would be an SC/UPC single-mode fiber of a specific length.

Gigabit Ethernet Implementation

Because Ethernet frames don't vary among the many flavors of Ethernet, network hardware manufacturers have long built devices capable of supporting more than one flavor right out of the box.

As noted previously, you can also use dedicated *media converters* to connect any type of Ethernet cabling together. Most media converters are plain-looking boxes with a port or dongle on either side with placement between two segments. Options include the following:

- Single-mode fiber (SMF) to UTP/STP
- Multimode fiber (MMF) to UTP/STP

- Fiber to coaxial
- SMF to MMF

Eventually, the Gigabit Ethernet folks created a standard for modular ports called a *gigabit interface converter* (GBIC). With many Gigabit Ethernet switches and other hardware, you can simply pull out a *transceiver*—the connecting module, commonly referred to as an *optic*—that supports one type of Gigabit Ethernet and plug in another. You can replace an RJ45 GBIC, for example, with an SC GBIC, and it'll work just fine. In this kind of scenario, electronically, the switch or other gigabit device is just that—Gigabit Ethernet—so the physical connections don't matter. Ingenious!

Switches and other network equipment today use a much smaller modular transceiver, called a *small form-factor pluggable* (SFP). Hot-swappable like the GBIC transceivers, the SFPs take up a lot less space, support all the same networking standards, and became the preferred choice in modern switches due to their compact size.

EXAM TIP A *transceiver* or *optic* is a removable module that enables connectivity between a device and a cable. A *media converter* enables connection between two different types of networks, such as copper and optical fiber.

Ethernet Evolutions

Most wired networks today feature Gigabit Ethernet, which remains cost-effective, backward-compatible, and fast enough for typical LAN workloads. Nevertheless, developers and manufacturers continue to push well beyond these limits.

10-Gigabit Ethernet

Developers continue to refine and increase Ethernet networking speeds, especially in the LAN environment and in backbones. *10 Gigabit Ethernet* (10 GbE), as its name indicates, offers speeds of up to 10 gigabits per second. Fiber-optic cabling is common for long-distance links, while copper is often used for shorter connections in data centers.

10 GbE has a number of fiber standards and two copper standards. While designed with fiber optics in mind, copper 10 GbE can still often pair excellent performance with cost savings. As a result, you'll find a mix of fiber and copper in data centers today.

FIBER-BASED 10 GBE

When the IEEE members formalized 10 GbE specifications, their first challenge was maintaining Ethernet frame integrity to ensure backward compatibility with existing networks.

The second challenge was designing a physical layer capable of reliably transmitting frames at 10 Gbps. They could use the traditional Physical layer mechanisms defined by the Ethernet standard, but a high-speed fiber network that can run at multiple Optical Carrier (OC) rates, called *Synchronous Optical Network* (SONET), was already in place and being used for wide area networking (WAN) transmissions. What to do?

The IEEE decided to create a whole set of 10 GbE standards that could use traditional LAN Physical layer mechanisms, plus a set of standards that could interoperate with high-speed optical WAN networks, like SONET. To make the 10 Gbps jump as easy as possible, the IEEE also recognized the need for different networking situations. Some implementations require data transfers that can run long distances over single-mode fiber, for example, whereas others can make do with short-distance transfers over multimode fiber. This led to a lot of standards for 10 GbE.

The 10 GbE standards are defined by several factors: the type of fiber used, the wavelength of the laser or lasers, and the Physical layer signaling type. These factors also define the maximum signal distance.

The IEEE uses specific letter codes with the standards to help sort out the differences, so you know what you're implementing or supporting. All the standards have names in the format 10GBASE-*xy*, where the *x* stands for the type of fiber (usually, though not officially) and the wavelength of the laser signal, and the *y* stands for the Physical layer signaling standard. The *y* code is always either *R* for LAN-based signaling or *W* for SONET/WAN-based signaling. The *x* code differs a little more, so let's take a look.

10GBASE-S*y* uses a short-wavelength (850 nm) signal over multimode fiber. The maximum fiber length is 400 meters, although this length will vary depending on the type of multimode fiber used. (OM1 offers a super-short 33-meter range, for example, whereas with OM4 the distance extends to 400 meters.) *10GBASE-SR* is used for Ethernet LANs, and *10GBASE-SW* is used to connect to SONET devices.

STANDARD	FIBER TYPE	WAVELENGTH	PHYSICAL LAYER SIGNALING	MAXIMUM SIGNAL LENGTH
10GBASE-SR	Multimode	850 nm	LAN	33–400 m
10GBASE-SW	Multimode	850 nm	SONET/WAN	33–400 m

10GBASE-L*y* uses a long-wavelength (1,310 nm) signal over single-mode fiber. The maximum fiber length is 10 kilometers, although this length will vary depending on the type of single-mode fiber used. *10GBASE-LR* connects to Ethernet LANs and *10GBASE-LW* connects to SONET equipment. 10GBASE-LR is the most popular and least expensive 10 GbE media type.

STANDARD	FIBER TYPE	WAVELENGTH	PHYSICAL LAYER SIGNALING	MAXIMUM SIGNAL LENGTH
10GBASE-LR	Single-mode	1,310 nm	LAN	10 km
10GBASE-LW	Single-mode	1,310 nm	SONET/WAN	10 km

10GBASE-E*y* uses an extra-long-wavelength (1,550 nm) signal over single-mode fiber. The maximum fiber length is 40 kilometers, although this length will vary depending on the type of single-mode fiber used. *10GBASE-ER* works with Ethernet LANs and *10GBASE-EW* connects to SONET equipment.

STANDARD	FIBER TYPE	WAVELENGTH	PHYSICAL LAYER SIGNALING	MAXIMUM SIGNAL LENGTH
10GBASE-ER	Single-mode	1,550 nm	LAN	40 km
10GBASE-EW	Single-mode	1,550 nm	SONET/WAN	40 km

The 10 GbE fiber standards do not define the type of connector to use, instead leaving that to manufacturers (see the upcoming section "10 GbE Physical Connections").

THE OTHER 10 GBE FIBER STANDARDS

Manufacturers have shown both creativity and innovation in taking advantage of both existing fiber and the most cost-effective equipment. This has led to a variety of standards that are not covered by the CompTIA Network+ exam objectives, but that you should know about nevertheless. The top three as of this writing are 10GBASE-L4, 10GBASE-RM, and 10GBASE-ZR.

The *10GBASE-L4* standard uses four lasers at a 1,300-nanometer wavelength over legacy fiber. On multimode cable, 10GBASE-L4 can support up to 300-meter transmissions. The range increases to 10 kilometers over single-mode fiber.

The *10GBASE-LRM* standard uses the long-wavelength signal of 10GBASE-LR but over legacy multimode fiber. The standard can achieve a range of up to 220 meters, depending on the grade of fiber cable.

Finally, some manufacturers have adopted the *10GBASE-ZR* "standard," which isn't part of the IEEE standards at all (unlike 10GBASE-L4 and 10GBASE-LRM). Instead, the manufacturers have created their own set of specifications. 10GBASE-ZR networks use a 1,550-nanometer wavelength over single-mode fiber to achieve a whopping 80-kilometer range. The standard can work with both Ethernet LAN and SONET/WAN infrastructure.

COPPER-BASED 10 GBE

It took until 2006 for IEEE to come up with a standard for 10 GbE running on twisted-pair cabling. It's called, predictably, *10GBASE-T* and looks and works exactly like the slower versions of UTP Ethernet (although it's more complex electrically). The only downside is that 10GBASE-T running on Cat 6 has a maximum cable length of only 55 meters. The Cat 6a standard extends that distance to 100 meters.

NOTE The 802.3bz standard (2014) specifies support for Ethernet over twisted pair between 1 Gbps and 10 Gbps, notably 2.5 Gbps (*2.5 GBASE-T* running over Cat 5e or better cable) and 5 Gbps (*5 GBASE-T* running over Cat 6 or better cable). These intermediate standards allow for network upgrades without replacing cabling entirely. You'll see both standards in the wild, but not on the CompTIA Network+ exam.

Table 10-4 summarizes the 10 GbE standards.

TABLE 10-4 10 GbE Summary

STANDARD	DISTANCE	CABLE TYPE	CABLE DETAILS/ WAVELENGTH	CONNECTORS
10GBASE-SR/SW	33–400 m	Multimode fiber	OM3 minimum (OM1/ OM2 very short distances), 850 nm	Vendor-dependent, LC common, SC occasionally, MPO/MTP in high-density applications
10GBASE-LR/LW	10 km	Single-mode fiber	OS2 recommended, 1,310 nm	LC most common, SC occasionally
10GBASE-ER/EW	40 km	Single-mode fiber	OS1 or OS2 depending on vendor, 1,550 nm	LC most common, SC occasionally
10GBASE-T	55/100 m	Copper UTP	Cat 6 (up to 55 m), Cat 6a (up to 100 m), four-pair, full-duplex	RJ45

10 GBE PHYSICAL CONNECTIONS

This hodgepodge of 10 GbE types might have been the ultimate disaster for hardware manufacturers. All types of 10 GbE send and receive the same Ethernet frames; only the physical medium is different. Imagine a single switch that had to come out in seven different versions to match all these types! Instead, the 10 GbE industry simply chose not to define the connector types and devised a very clever, very simple concept called *multisource agreements* (MSAs), which define standard physical form factors, electrical or optical interfaces, and mechanical specifications for transceivers. A transceiver based on an MSA plugs into your 10 GbE equipment, enabling you to convert from one media type to another media type.

CHARACTERISTICS OF FIBER TRANSCEIVERS

Up to this point, the book has described the most common forms of fiber-optic networking, where fiber is installed in pairs in which one cable sends and the other receives. This duplex configuration remains the most widely used fiber-based networking solution. All the transceivers used in these technologies have two connectors, a standard *duplex* format. A typical transceiver used in 10 GbE is called the *enhanced small form-factor pluggable* (SFP+), shown in Figure 10-17.

FIGURE 10-17
SFP+ transceiver (photo courtesy of D-Link)

Manufacturers have developed technology that uses *wavelength division multiplexing* (WDM) to differentiate optical signals on a single fiber, enabling single-strand fiber transmission. *Bidirectional (BiDi) transceivers* (Figure 10-18) have only a single optical port designed inside to send on one wavelength, such as 1,310 nm, and receive on a different wavelength, such as 1,550 nm. A corresponding BiDi transceiver must be installed on the other end of the fiber for this setup to work.

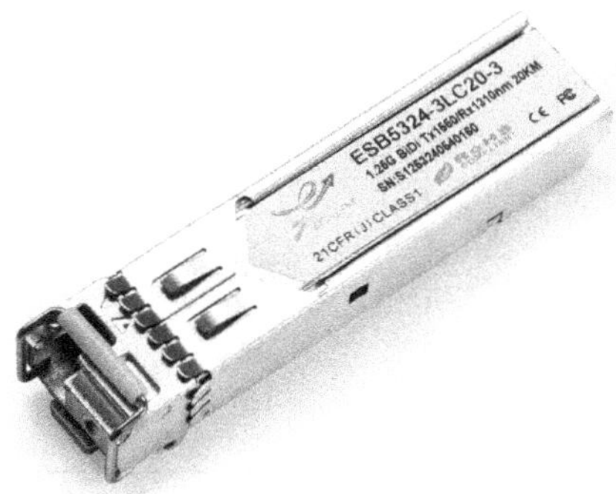

FIGURE 10-18
BiDi transceiver

BiDi technology has a couple of notable advantages over its dual-fiber predecessors. First, it costs less to deploy in a new network. You can establish the same level of network performance using half the number of fiber runs. Second, you can use existing fiber runs to rapidly double a network's capacity. Replace the duplex transceivers with twice the number of BiDi transceivers and plug in the fiber.

Gigabit BiDi transceivers typically use SFP optics. Most 10 GbE BiDi transceivers use SFP+ connectors. 40 GbE BiDi transceivers use *quad small form-factor pluggable* (QSFP) optics.

BACKBONES

The beauty and the challenge of the vast selection of Ethernet flavors is deciding which one to use in your network. The goal is to give your users the fastest network response time possible while keeping costs reasonable. To achieve this balance, most network administrators find that a multispeed Ethernet network works best. In a multispeed network, a series of high-speed (relative to the rest of the network) switches maintain a backbone network. No computers, other than possibly servers, attach directly to this backbone. Figure 10-19 shows a typical backbone network. Each floor has its own switch that connects to every node on the floor. In turn, each of these switches also has a separate high-speed connection to a main switch that resides in the office's computer room.

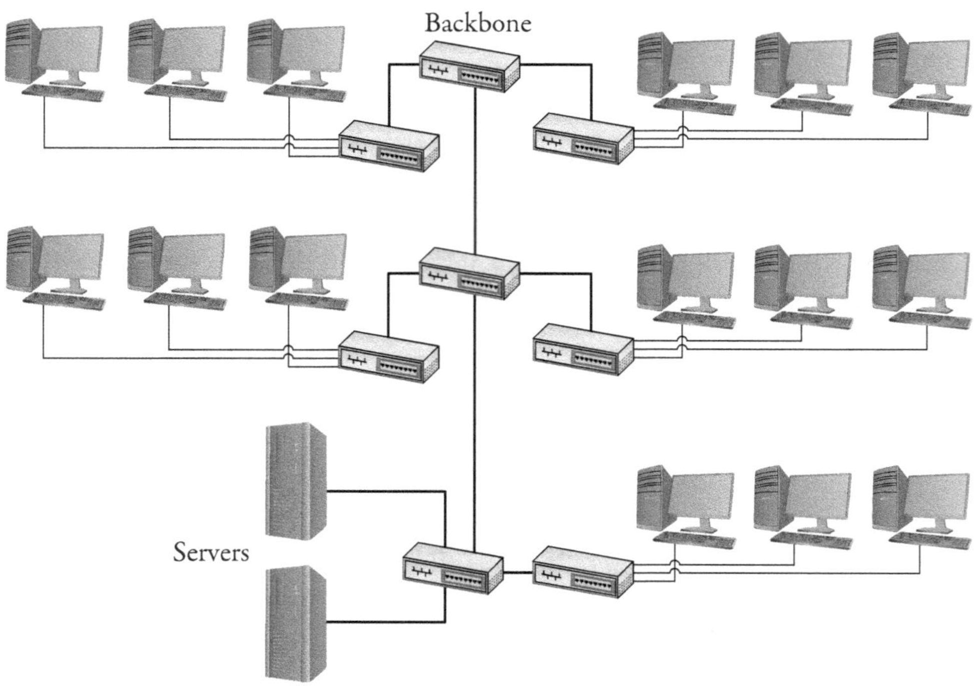

FIGURE 10-19 Typical network configuration showing backbone (pun intended)

To make this work, you need switches with separate, dedicated, high-speed ports like the ones shown in Figure 10-20. These floor switches connect via dedicated high-speed ports (often fiber) to a main backbone switch in the computer room.

FIGURE 10-20 Switch with dedicated, high-speed ports

> **SHOPPING FOR SWITCHES**
>
> Cisco, one of the industry leaders for Ethernet switches, has a great website for its products. Imagine that you're setting up a network for your school or business (keep it simple and pick a single building if you're in a large organization). Decide what type of switches you'd like to use, including both the backbone and local switches. If you're really motivated, decide where to locate the switches physically. Don't be afraid to try a fiber backbone—almost every Cisco switch comes with modular ports (such as SFP or SFP+) to enable you to pick the type of Ethernet you want to use for your backbone.

40GBE, 100GBE, AND TERABIT ETHERNET

Way back in 2010, the IEEE 802.3ba committee approved the *40 Gigabit Ethernet* (40GbE) and *100 Gigabit Ethernet* (100GbE) standards. Both standards, in their many varieties, use the same frame as the relatively slower earlier versions of Ethernet, so with the right switches, you've got perfect interoperability. The 40 GbE and 100 GbE standards are primarily used when lots of bandwidth is needed, such as connecting servers, switches, and routers.

Common 40 GbE runs on OM3 or better multimode fiber, uses laser light, and uses various four-channel connectors. A typical connector, called an *enhanced quad small form-factor pluggable* (QSFP+), essentially takes four SFP+ transceivers and combines them into a single, wider transceiver. Other 40 GbE standards run on single-mode fiber and support distances up to 10 kilometers. Still other 40 GbE connections run on Cat 8 UTP for a maximum of 30 meters. This is *40GBASE-T.*

In contrast, 100 GbE standards employ both MMF and SMF with various connectors. A typical connector is the *QSFP28*, which has four channels of 25 Gb each. You'll sometimes see this connector referred to as a *QSFP100* or *100G QSFP*.

Terabit Ethernet refers to Ethernet standards that support speeds beyond 100 GbE. These standards include 200 GbE, 400 GbE, and 800 GbE and employ both MMF and SMF with various connectors:

- **200 GBE** QSFP-DD, QSFP56, microQSFP, OSFP, MPO/MTP (MPO-12), LC, QSFP112, SFP-DD112, DSFP, OSFP, MPO(MPO-12)
- **400 GBE** MPO/MTP(MPO-32), MPO/MTP(MPO-16), MPO/MTP(MPO-12), LC, QSFP-DD, QSFP112, OSFP
- **800 GBE** QSFP–DD800 OSFP, MPO/MTP(MPO-16)

But wait, there's more: 1.6 Terabit Ethernet (TbE) is expected to be standardized in July 2026!

The highest connection speeds often appear first in network backbones or data centers, where server-to-switch or switch-to-switch connections are usually the bottleneck. Those speeds then sometimes move out the rest of the network. This is the same pattern we've seen since the move from 10 Mbps to 100 Mbps, and from 100 Mbps to 1 Gbps.

Chapter Review

Questions

1. Which of the following is transmitted before an Ethernet frame?
   A. MAC address
   B. Length
   C. Preamble
   D. CRC

2. When used for Ethernet, unshielded twisted pair uses what type of connector?
   A. RG-58
   B. RJ45
   C. RJ11
   D. RS-232
3. With 1000BASE-T, what is the maximum distance between the switch and the node?
   A. 1,000 meters
   B. 400 meters
   C. 100 meters
   D. 150 meters
4. What standard does IEEE 802.3ab define?
   A. 1000BASE-LX
   B. 1000BASE-T
   C. 100BASE-T
   D. 1000BASE-SX
5. How many wire pairs does 1000BASE-T use?
   A. 1
   B. 2
   C. 3
   D. 4
6. Which of the following connector would you typically find with a 40 GbE installation?
   A. LC
   B. SFP
   C. QSFP+
   D. XSFP+
7. What is the maximum distance for 1000BASE-LX without repeaters?
   A. 1 mile
   B. 2,500 meters
   C. 20,000 feet
   D. 5,000 meters

8. What is a big advantage to using fiber-optic cable?
   A. Fiber is common glass; therefore, it's less expensive.
   B. Fiber is not affected by electromagnetic interference.
   C. Making custom cable lengths is easier with fiber.
   D. All that orange fiber looks impressive in the network closet.
9. What is the standard connector for the 10 GbE fiber standard?
   A. ST
   B. SC
   C. MT-RJ
   D. There is no standard.
10. Which of the following is not considered Terabit Ethernet?
   A. 100 GbE
   B. 200 GbE
   C. 400 GbE
   D. 800 GbE

Answers

1. **C.** Before an Ethernet frame is transmitted, the preamble synchronizes NICs.
2. **B.** UTP cable uses an RJ45 connector for twisted-pair Ethernet. RG-58 was the type of coaxial cable used with the old 10BASE-2 standard. RJ11 is the standard four-wire connector used for regular phone lines. RS-232 is a standard for serial connectors.
3. **C.** The maximum distance is 100 meters.
4. **B.** IEEE 802.3ab is the 1000BASE-T standard (also known as Gigabit Ethernet).
5. **D.** 1000BASE-T uses all four pairs for full-duplex signaling.
6. **C.** 40 GbE installations over fiber typically use QSFP+ connectors.
7. **D.** 1000BASE-LX can go for 5,000 meters (5 kilometers).
8. **B.** Because fiber uses glass and light, it is not affected by and is preferred in EMI-heavy environments.
9. **D.** There is no standard connector; the 10 GbE committee has left this up to the manufacturers.
10. **A.** Terabit Ethernet includes standards with speeds faster than 100 GbE.

Installing a Physical Network

IN THIS CHAPTER, YOU WILL LEARN HOW TO

- Describe structured cabling and the process of installing structured cable
- Identify the network components and devices needed for structured cabling
- Given a scenario, use the appropriate tool or protocol to solve networking issues
- Install a network interface card (NIC)

Armed with the knowledge of previous chapters, you're ready to construct a physical network. This might seem easy; after all, the most basic network is nothing more than a switch with cables snaking out to all of the network PCs (Figure 11-1).

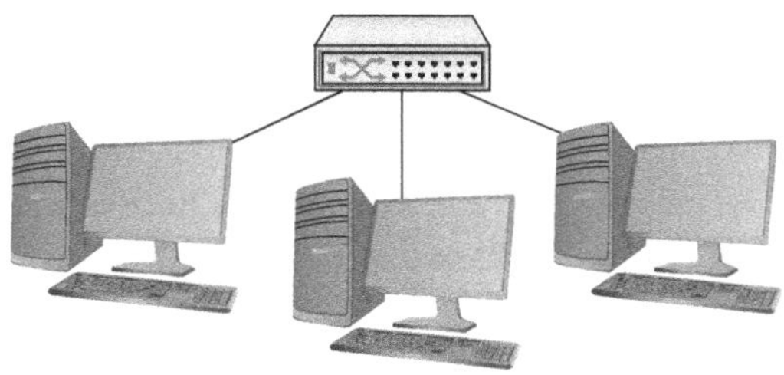

FIGURE 11-1 What an orderly-looking network!

On the surface, this network is correctly set up, but if you tried to run it, you'd face some serious practical issues. In the real world, you need to deal with physical obstacles like walls and ceilings. You also need to deal with people, who are incredibly adept at destroying physical networks. They unplug switches, trip over cables, and rip connectors out of NICs with incredible consistency unless you protect the network from their destructive ways. Although the simplified switch-and-a-bunch-of-cables type of network can function in the real world, it clearly has some problems that must be addressed before it can work safely and efficiently (Figure 11-2).

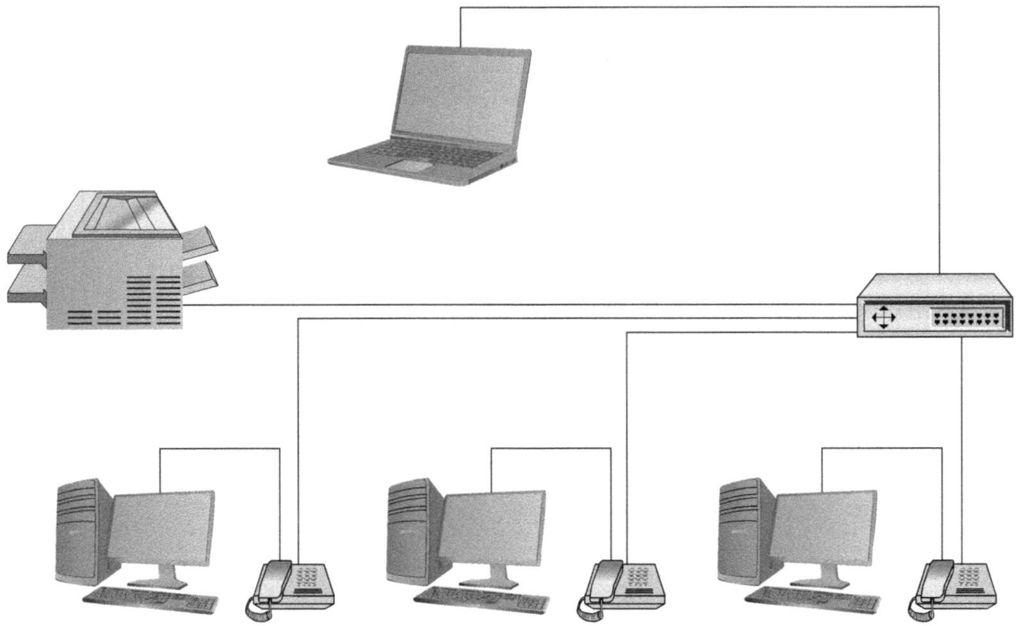

FIGURE 11-2 A real-world network

This chapter translates the abstract discussion of network technologies from previous chapters into the concrete reality of physical networks by walking you through the process of installing an entire network system from scratch. It starts by introducing you to *structured cabling*, the critical set of standards used all over the world to install physical cabling in a safe and orderly fashion. It then delves into the world of larger networks—those with more than a single switch—and shows you some typical methods used to organize them for peak efficiency and reliability. Then, you'll take a quick tour of the most common NICs used in PCs and learn how to install them. Finally, you'll get tips on troubleshooting cabling and other network devices, including an introduction to some fun diagnostic tools.

Historical/Conceptual

Understanding Structured Cabling

If you want a functioning, dependable, real-world network, you need a solid understanding of a set of standards and proprietary systems collectively called *structured cabling*. In the United States, the Telecommunications Industry Association (TIA) gives professional cable installers detailed standards on every aspect of a cabled network, from the type of cabling to use to the position of wall outlets. The European Union has adopted some of the TIA standards but publishes versions with various bodies such as Europe Norm (EN) and CENELEC.

The CompTIA Network+ exam requires you to understand the basic concepts involved in designing a network and installing network cabling and to recognize the components used in a real network. The CompTIA Network+ exam does not, however, expect you to be as knowledgeable as a professional network designer or cable installer. Your goal is to understand enough about real-world cabling systems to communicate knowledgeably with cable installers and to perform basic troubleshooting. Granted, by the end of this chapter, you'll have enough knowledge to try running your own cable (I certainly run my own), but consider that a bonus.

The idea of structured cabling is to create a safe, reliable cabling infrastructure for all the devices that may need interconnection. Certainly, this applies to computer networks, but also to telephone, video, and anything that might need low-power, distributed cabling.

You should understand three main aspects of structured cabling: cable basics (media types, connectors, and standards), network components (such as how cabling is routed through walls and terminated), and external connections (where your network links to outside services).

NOTE Most networks today have a wireless component in addition to a wired infrastructure. The switches, servers, and workstations rely on wires for fast and stable networking, but laptops, phones, tablets, and the other mobile devices found in a modern network are supported wirelessly. This chapter focuses on the wired infrastructure; wireless is covered in the next chapter.

Structured Cabling Basics: A Star Is Born

This exploration of the world of connectivity hardware starts with the most basic of all networks: a switch, some UTP cable, and a few PCs—in other words, a physical star network (Figure 11-3). The *star* topology, also called *hub and spoke*, uses a central connection box for all the networked computers and offers fault tolerance: if one of the cables breaks, all the other computers can still communicate.

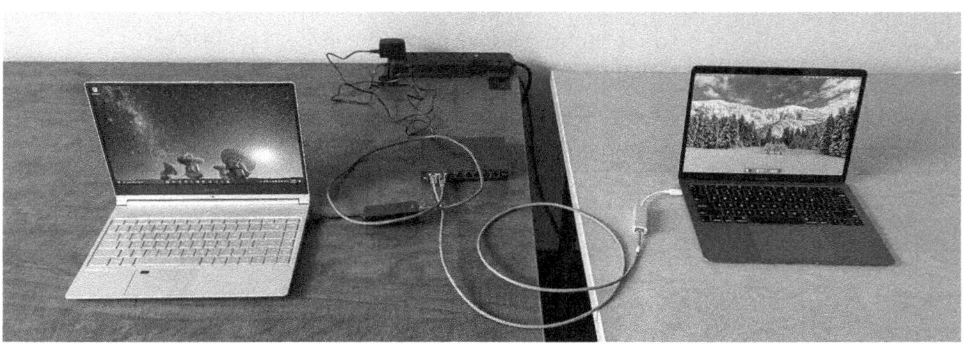

FIGURE 11-3 A switch connected by UTP cable to two PCs

Often, enterprise networks combine the star topology with a wireless infrastructure. This is known as a *hybrid* topology.

No law of office decor prevents you from installing a switch in the middle of your office and running cables on the floor to all the computers in your network. As mentioned in the chapter opener, this setup works, but it falls apart spectacularly when applied to a real-world environment. Network techs will encounter three problems. First, the exposed cables running along the floor are just waiting for someone to trip over them, damaging the network and giving that person a wonderful lawsuit opportunity. Possible accidents aside, simply moving and stepping on a cable will cause it to fail over time due to the connector detaching from the cable jacket or pins failing. Second, the presence of other electrical devices close to the cable can create interference that confuses the signals going through the wire. Third, this type of setup limits your ability to make changes to the network. Before you can do so, you must figure out which cables in the huge rat's nest connected to the switch go to which machines. Imagine *that* troubleshooting nightmare!

Gosh, you're probably thinking, *there must be a better way to install a physical network.*

A better installation would provide safety, protecting the star from vacuum cleaners, clumsy coworkers, and electrical interference. It would have extra hardware to organize and protect the cabling. Finally, the new and improved star network installation would feature a cabling standard with the flexibility to enable the network to grow according to its needs and then to upgrade when the next great network technology came along.

As you've no doubt guessed, I'm not just theorizing here. In the real world, the people who most wanted improved installation standards were the ones who installed cable for a living. In response to this demand, TIA and other standards bodies developed standards for cable installation. The ANSI/TIA-568 standards you learned about in Chapter 9 are only some of the standards lumped together under the umbrella of structured cabling.

Installing structured cabling properly takes a startlingly high degree of skill. Thousands of pitfalls await inexperienced network techs who think they can install their own network cabling. Pulling cable requires expensive equipment, a lot of hands, and the ability to react to problems quickly. Network techs can cost employers a lot of money—not to mention lose their good jobs—by attempting to do it themselves without the proper knowledge.

If you are interested in learning more about structured cabling, the Building Industry Consulting Service International (BICSI; *bicsi.org*) provides a series of widely recognized certifications and training courses for the cabling industry.

Test Specific

Structured Cabling: Network Components

Successful implementation of a basic structured cabling network requires three essential ingredients: a telecommunications room, horizontal cabling, and a work area. Let's zero in on one floor of Figure 10-19 from the previous chapter. All the cabling runs from individual PCs to a central location, the *telecommunications room* (Figure 11-4). What equipment goes in there—a switch or a telephone system—is not important. What matters is that all the cables concentrate in this one area. This room, like others with important hardware and equipment, should be *lockable* to ensure that only authorized individuals with proper credentials and permissions can enter.

All cables run horizontally (for the most part) from the telecommunications room to the PCs. This cabling is called, appropriately, *horizontal cabling*.

EXAM TIP A single piece of cable that runs from a work area to a telecommunications room is called a *run*.

At the opposite end of the horizontal cabling from the telecommunications room is the *work area*, often simply an office or cubicle that potentially contains a PC and a telephone. Figure 11-5 shows both the horizontal cabling and work areas.

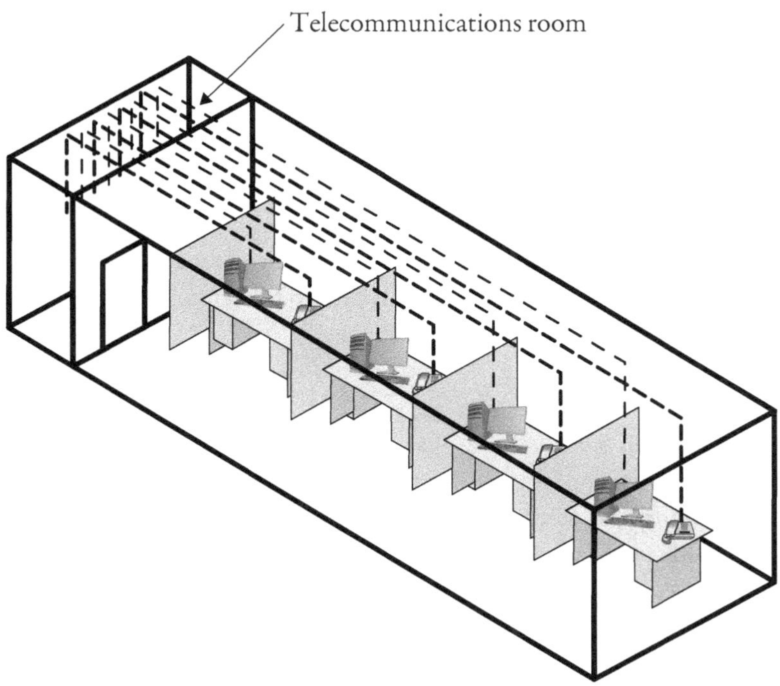

FIGURE 11-4 Telecommunications room

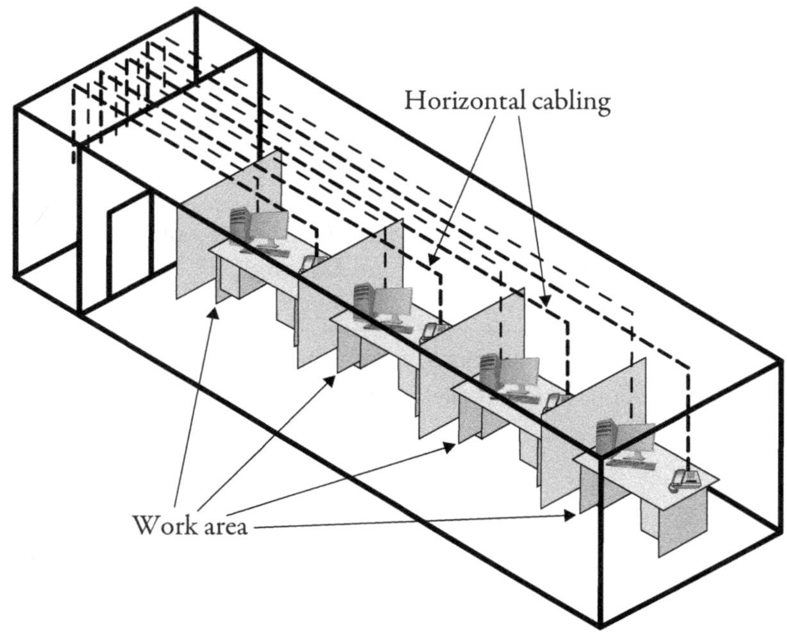

FIGURE 11-5 Horizontal cabling and work area

Vertical cabling, also called *backbone cabling*, runs between floors in a multistory building rather than from the ceiling to individual work areas.

Each of the three parts of a basic star topology network—the telecommunications room, the horizontal cabling, and the work area(s)—must follow a series of strict standards designed to ensure that the cabling system is reliable and easy to manage. ANSI/TIA-568 covers connectors, patch panels, and labeling, providing a broader view of what structured cabling entails, so let's tackle horizontal cabling first and then return to the telecommunications room. We'll finish up with the work area.

HORIZONTAL CABLING

A horizontal cabling run is the cabling that extends more or less horizontally from a work area to the telecommunications room. In most networks, this cable is Cat 6 or better UTP for copper-based standards, such as 1000BASE-T. (Fiber-based standards, such as 1000BASE-SX, would use multimode fiber-optic cabling, also in a star topology.) When you move into structured cabling, the ANSI/TIA-568 standards define several other aspects of the cable, such as the type of wires, number of pairs of wires, and fire ratings.

Type of Wires

All UTP cables come in one of two types: solid core or stranded core. Each wire in *solid core* UTP is a single solid wire. With *stranded core*, each wire is a bundle of tiny wire strands. Both cable types have benefits and downsides. Solid core is a better conductor, but it is stiff and will break if handled too often or too roughly. Stranded core is not quite as good a conductor, but it will stand up to substantial handling without breaking. Figure 11-6 shows a close-up of solid and stranded core UTP.

FIGURE 11-6 Solid and stranded core UTP

ANSI/TIA-568 specifies that horizontal cabling should always be solid core. Remember, this cabling is going into walls and ceilings, safe from the harmful effects of shoes and vacuum cleaners. The ceilings and walls enable you to take advantage of the better conductivity of solid core without the risk of cable damage. As we'll discuss shortly, stranded core cable also has an important function in a structured cabling network.

Number of Pairs

Pulling horizontal cables into your walls and ceilings is a time-consuming, messy process that you want to avoid repeating if possible. For this reason, most cable installers recommend using the highest Cat rating you can afford. Many years ago, I'd also have mentioned that you should use four-pair UTP, but today, that's assumed. Four-pair UTP is so common that it's difficult, if not impossible, to find two-pair UTP. Cat 6, Cat 6a, Cat 7, and so on, all use four-pair UTP.

You'll find even larger bundled UTP cables in legacy telephone installations. These cables hold 25 or even 100 pairs of wires (Figure 11-7). These cables are not used for Ethernet.

FIGURE 11-7 A 25-pair UTP cable

Bandwidth and Speed Requirements

Network installations today favor at least Cat 6. Higher-rated cabling (Cat 6a, 7, etc.) is installed either as a hedge against new network technologies that may require a more advanced cable or simply to adopt the faster 10+ Gigabit standards.

THE TELECOMMUNICATIONS ROOM

The heart of the basic star topology network is the telecommunications room, where all the horizontal runs from all the work areas come together. The concentration of all this gear in one place makes this room potentially one of the messiest parts of the network. Even if you do a nice, neat job of organizing the cables when first installing them, networks change over time—people move computers, work areas are added, network topologies are added or improved, and so on. Unless you impose some type of organization, this conglomeration of equipment and cables turns into a nightmarish mess.

NOTE The telecommunications room is also known as the *intermediate distribution frame* (IDF), as opposed to the main distribution frame (MDF), which we will discuss later in the chapter.

Fortunately, the ANSI/TIA-568 structured cabling standards define the use of specialized components in the telecommunications room that make organizing a snap. In fact, it might be fair to say that there are too many options! To keep it simple, we're going to stay with the most common telecommunications room setup and then take a peek at some other common options.

Equipment Racks

The central component of every telecommunications room is one or more *equipment racks*, which provide a safe, stable platform for all the different hardware components. All equipment racks are 19 inches wide, but they vary in height from two- to three-foot-high models that bolt onto a wall (Figure 11-8) to the more popular 73.5-inch high, or 42U, free-standing racks (Figure 11-9).

FIGURE 11-8 A short equipment rack

FIGURE 11-9
A free-standing rack

RACK MEASUREMENTS

Equipment racks evolved out of the railroad signaling racks from the 19th century. The components in a rack today obviously differ a lot from railroad signaling, but the 19-inch width has remained the standard for well over 100 years.

Height for rack-mounted equipment is measured in *units* (U), where one unit equals 1.75 inches. Thus, a device that fits in a 1.75-inch space is called a 1U; a device designed for a 3.5-inch space is a 2U; and a device that goes into a 7-inch space is called a 4U. Most rack-mounted devices are 1U, 2U, or 4U. A typical full-size rack is called a *42U rack* to reflect the total number of Us it can hold.

You can mount almost any network hardware component into a rack. All manufacturers make rack-mounted switches that mount into a rack with a few screws. These switches are available with a wide assortment of ports and capabilities. There are even rack-mounted servers, complete with slide-out keyboards, and rack-mounted uninterruptible power supplies (UPSs) to power the equipment (Figure 11-10). A UPS provides backup power to the devices on the rack. (See "Problems in the Telecommunication Room" later in this chapter for more details.)

The key when planning a rack system is to determine what sort of rack-mounted equipment you plan to have and then get the rack or racks for your space. For example, if your

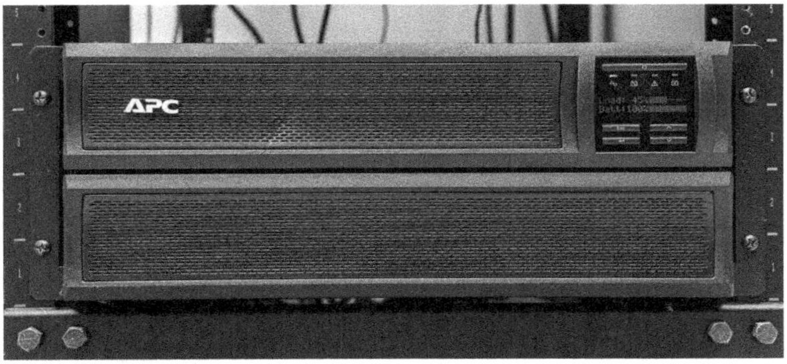

FIGURE 11-10 A rack-mounted UPS

rack will have only patch panels (see the next section), switches, and routers, you can get away with a *two-post rack*, which is bolted to the floor. The pieces are small and easily supported. Sometimes communications-specific cabinets are shorter than server cabinets (which need to support the server depth) and will use a two-post rack.

If you're going to install big servers, on the other hand, then you need to plan for a *four-post rack* or a *server rail rack*. A four-post rack supports all four corners of the server. The server rail rack enables you to slide the server out so you can open it up. This is very useful for swapping out dead drives for new ones in big file servers.

Bigger installations incorporate a *power distribution unit* (PDU) for centralized power management (Figure 11-11). On the surface, a PDU works like a power strip, providing multiple outlets for components, drawing electricity directly from a wall socket or indirectly from an UPS. Advanced models provide remote monitoring, circuit protection, and load balancing.

NOTE We'll revisit UPSs, PDUs, generators, and other elements of *facilities and infrastructure support* in future chapters when we explore techniques for keeping data-center infrastructure up and running (called *high availability*) and handling potential disasters.

When planning how many racks you need in your rack system and where to place them, consider proper airflow. You shouldn't cram servers and gear into every corner. Even with good air-conditioning systems, bad airflow can cook components.

There are blocking panels for racks so that the entire front of the rack is filled in, and with proper room design (with hot and cold aisles, to be discussed in Chapter 14), you actually want the only path for the air to move being through the servers.

FIGURE 11-11 A PDU in a server rack

Finally, make sure to secure the telecommunications room to protect your valuable equipment. Get a lock! Figure 11-12 shows a server lock on a rack.

FIGURE 11-12 A lock on a rack-mounted server

Server enclosure manufacturers incorporate all sorts of locking mechanisms. In addition to physical locks, you'll see keypad locks, biometric locks, smart card locks, and more. The terms *locking racks* and *locking cabinets* refer to a chassis (rack or cabinet) plus a door with a locking mechanism.

EXAM TIP Expect a question on the CompTIA Network+ exam about *physical security access prevention methods*, which might feature locking racks and cabinets. We'll cover many more physical security concepts in Chapter 17.

Patch Panels and Cables

Ideally, once you install horizontal cabling, you should never move it. The solid core cables used in UTP horizontal cabling are stiff. They can handle some rearranging, but if you insert a bundle of cables directly into your switches, every time you move a cable to a different port on the switch or move the switch itself, you'll jostle the cable. You don't have to move a solid core cable many times before one of the individual copper conductors breaks, and there goes a network connection!

Luckily, you can easily avoid this problem by connecting the horizontal cables to a *patch panel*, a box with a row of female ports in the front and permanent connections in the back (Figure 11-13).

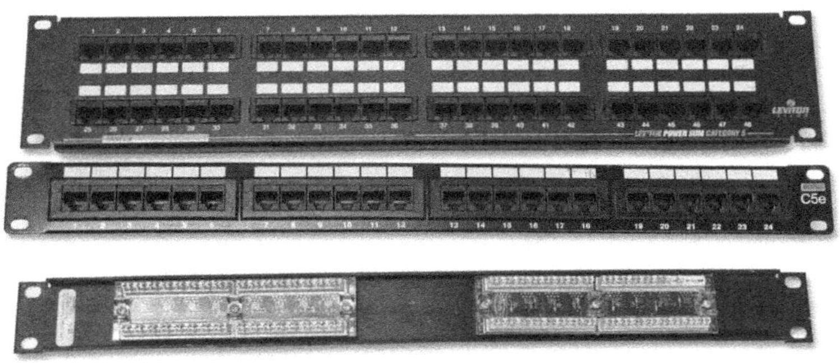

FIGURE 11-13 Typical patch panels

The most common type of patch panel today uses a special type of connector called a *110 block*, also called a *110-punchdown block*. UTP cables connect to a 110 block using a *punchdown tool* (shown in Figure 11-14).

FIGURE 11-14 Punchdown tool

Figure 11-15 shows the punchdown tool punching down individual strands.

FIGURE 11-15 Punching down a 110 block

The punchdown block has small, metal-lined slots for the individual wires. The punchdown tool has a blunt end that forces the wire into the slot. The metal in the slot slices the cladding enough to make contact.

NOTE Make sure you insert the wires according to the same standard (TIA-568A wiring or TIA-568B wiring) on both ends of the cable. If you don't, you might end up swapping the sending and receiving wires (known as *Transmitter (TX)/Receiver (RX) transposed*) and inadvertently creating a crossover cable.

At one time, the older 66-punchdown block patch panel (a *66 block*), found in just about every commercial telephone installation (Figure 11-16), saw some use in PC networks. The 110 block introduces less crosstalk than 66 blocks, so most high-speed network installations use the former for just telephone service and LANs. (Crosstalk, or signal interference between wire pairs in the same cable, will be discussed more later in the chapter.) Given their large installed base, it's still common to find a group of 66-block patch panels in a telecommunications room separate from the network's 110-block patch panels.

FIGURE 11-16
A group of 66-block patch panels

Not only do patch panels prevent the horizontal cabling from being moved, but they are also your first line of defense in organizing the cables. All patch panels have space in the front for labels, which are the network tech's best friend. Simply place a label on the patch panel to identify each cable, and you'll never have to experience the sinking feeling of standing in the telecommunications room of your nonfunctioning network, wondering which cable is which. If you want to be a purist with your labels, there is an official (and rather confusing) ANSI/TIA naming convention called *ANSI/TIA-606-C*, but many real-world network techs use their own internal codes (Figure 11-17).

FIGURE 11-17 Typical patch panels with labels

Patch panels are available in a wide variety of configurations that include different types and numbers of ports. You can get UTP, STP, or fiber ports, and some manufacturers combine several different types on the same patch panel. Panels are available with 8, 12, 24, 48, or even more ports.

UTP patch panels, like UTP cables, come with Cat ratings, which you should be sure to check. Don't blow a good Cat 6 cable installation by buying a cheap patch panel—get a Cat 6 patch panel! A Cat 6 panel can handle the 250 MHz frequency used by Cat 6 and offers lower crosstalk and network interference. A higher-rated panel is backward compatible, so you can use a Cat 6 or even Cat 6a rack with Cat 5e cabling. Most manufacturers proudly display the Cat level right on the patch panel (Figure 11-18).

FIGURE 11-18
Cat level on patch panel

Once you have installed the patch panel, you need to connect the ports to the switch through *patch cables*, which are short, straight-through UTP cables. Patch cables use stranded core rather than solid core, so they can tolerate much more handling. You can make your own patch cables, but most people buy premade ones in different colors for easier organization (yellow for accounting, blue for sales, or whatever scheme works for you). Most prefabricated patch cables also come with a reinforced (booted) connector specially designed to handle multiple insertions and removals (Figure 11-19).

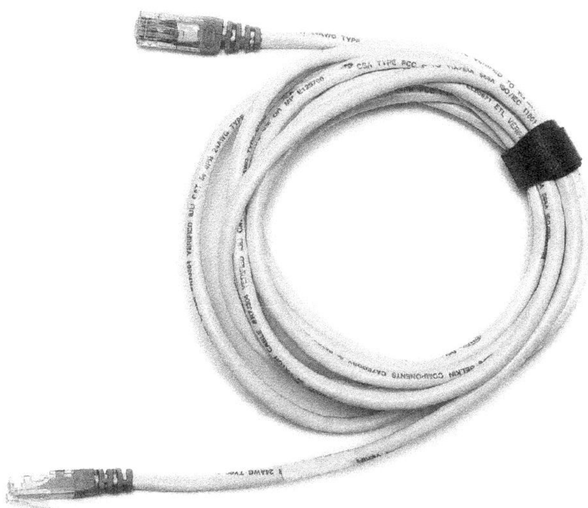

FIGURE 11-19 A typical patch cable

EXAM TIP Networks that include audio and video have a second set of wires for the A/V connections running to the telecommunications room. These runs of coaxial or fiber connect to a *patch bay*, a dedicated block with A/V connections rather than twisted pair and fiber network connections. Expect a question on the CompTIA Network+ exam that explores patch bays.

Alternative Cable Connection Points

Although you'll most likely encounter 110 blocks today, some cable installations—especially outside the United States—incorporate proprietary cable interconnects. The *BIX block*, for example, is a proprietary networking interconnect developed by Nortel Networks. (BIX stands for *Building Industry Cross-connect*.) Similar in function to a 110-punchdown block, a BIX block is installed on a wall rather than in a rack. Figure 11-20 shows BIX blocks and connectors. BIX is not used for new installs today but exists as legacy equipment for older telecom installs (mainly in Canada, where Nortel was widely deployed), as well as government and institutional buildings that have older infrastructures and haven't upgraded to modern cabling standards.

The *Krone LSA-PLUS* proprietary European telecommunication connector—*Krone block*—offers another alternative to the 110-punchdown block. Developed by the German telecommunications company The Krone Group in the 1970s, Krone connectors enable networking as well as audio interconnections. Figure 11-21 shows a couple of Krone blocks. While Krone blocks are still used in some regions, they are largely legacy in Ethernet LAN installations.

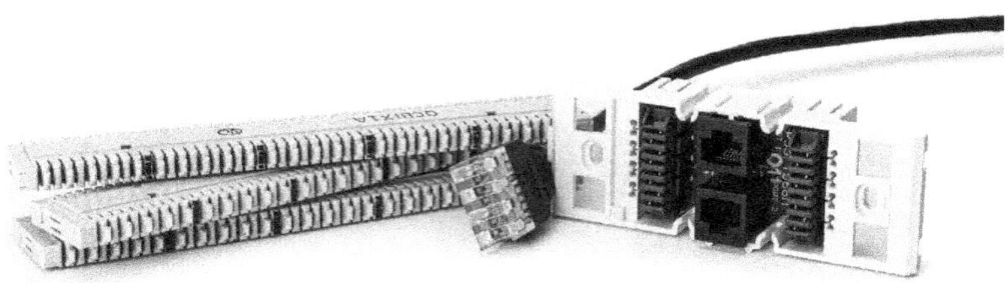

FIGURE 11-20 BIX blocks and connectors

FIGURE 11-21 Krone blocks

Telecommunications Room Alternatives

A telecommunications room doesn't have to be a special room dedicated to computer equipment. You can use specially made cabinets with built-in equipment racks that sit on the floor or attach to a wall, or you can use a storage room if the equipment can be protected from the other items stored there. Fortunately, the demand for telecommunications rooms has been around for so long that most office spaces have premade telecommunications rooms, even if they are no more than closets in smaller offices.

At this point, the network is taking shape (Figure 11-22). The horizontal cabling is installed, and the telecommunications room is configured. Now it's time to address the last part of the structured cabling system: the work area.

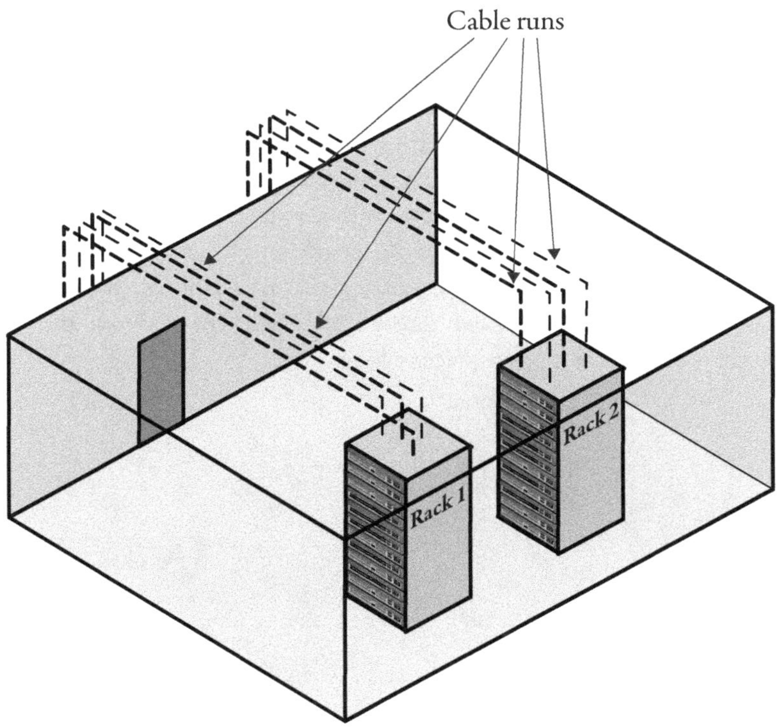

FIGURE 11-22 The network taking shape, with racks installed and horizontal cabling runs

THE WORK AREA

From a cabling standpoint, a work area is nothing more than a wall outlet that serves as the termination point for horizontal network cables: a convenient insertion point for a PC and a telephone. (In practice, of course, the term *work area* includes the office or cubicle.) A wall outlet itself consists of one or two female jacks to accept the cable, a mounting bracket, and a faceplate. You connect the PC to the wall outlet with a patch cable (Figure 11-23).

The female RJ45 jacks in these wall outlets also have Cat ratings. You must buy Cat-rated jacks for wall outlets to go along with the Cat rating of the cabling in your network. In fact, many network connector manufacturers use the same connectors in the wall outlets that they use on the patch panels. These modular outlets significantly increase ease of installation. Make sure you label the outlet with each connector's purpose (Figure 11-24). A good outlet will also have some form of label that identifies its position on the patch panel. Proper documentation of your outlets will save you an incredible amount of work later.

The last step is connecting the PC to the wall outlet. Here again, most folks use a patch cable. Its stranded core cabling stands up to the abuse caused by moving PCs, not to mention the occasional kick.

In Chapter 10, you learned that most Ethernet networks specify a limit of 100 meters between a switch and a node. Interestingly, though, the ANSI/TIA-568 specification allows only UTP cable lengths of 90 meters. What's with the missing 10 meters? Hint: The answer lies in the discussion we've just been having. Ding! Time's up. The answer is . . . the patch cables! Patch cables add extra distance between the switch and the PC, so ANSI/TIA-568 compensates by reducing the horizontal cabling length.

The work area may be the simplest part of the structured cabling system, but it is also the source of many network failures. When a user can't access the network and you suspect a broken cable, the work area is the first place to look.

FIGURE 11-23 Typical work area outlet

FIGURE 11-24 A properly labeled outlet

Structured Cabling: Beyond the Star

Thus far you've seen structured cabling as a single star topology on a single floor of a building. Let's now expand that concept to an entire building and learn the terms used by the structured cabling folks, such as the demarc and NIU, to describe this much more complex setup.

NOTE Structured cabling goes beyond a single building and even describes methods for interconnecting multiple buildings. The CompTIA Network+ certification exam does not cover interbuilding connections.

You can hardly find a building today that isn't connected to both the internet and the telephone company. In many cases, this is a single connection, but for now, let's treat them as separate connections.

As you saw in Chapter 10, a typical building-wide network consists of a high-speed backbone that runs vertically through the building and connects on each floor to multispeed switches, which in turn service the individual PCs on that floor. A legacy telephone cabling backbone that helped distribute phone calls to individual telephones might run alongside the network cabling. While every telephone installation varies, most commonly you'll see one or more strands of 25-pair UTP cables running to a 66 block in the telecommunications room on each floor (Figure 11-25).

DEMARC

Connections from the outside world—whether network or telephone—come into a building at a physical location called a *demarcation point* (demarc), which marks the dividing line of responsibility for the functioning of the network. You take care of the internal functioning, and the company that supplies the upstream service must support connectivity and function on the far side of the demarc.

EXAM TIP You might get a question about the location of a demarc on the CompTIA Network+ exam. You'll find the demarc located in the *service-related entry point* for a network.

The best way to think of a demarc is in terms of responsibility. If something breaks on one side of the demarc, it's your problem; on the other side, it's the ISP's problem.

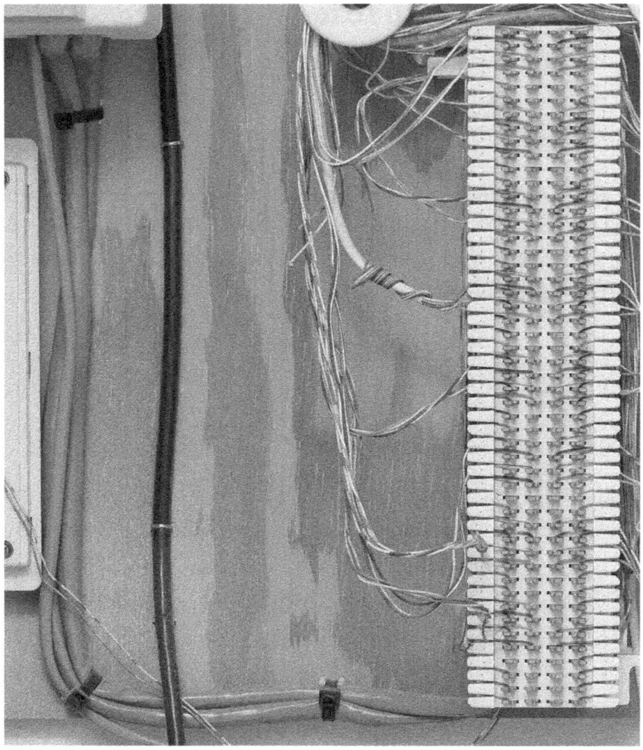

FIGURE 11-25 A group of 25-pair UTP cables running to a local 66 block

In a private home, the equipment (cable modem, optical network terminal, etc.) supplied by your ISP is a *network interface unit* (NIU) that serves as a demarc between your home network and your ISP, and most homes have a network interface box like the one shown in Figure 11-26.

NOTE One challenge ISPs face is the need to diagnose faults in the system. Early systems used an NIU called a *smartjack* to set up a *remote loopback*—a test that sends a signal from one end of the connection and loops it back to verify the circuit is working properly. This test was critical when you were at one end of the connection and the other connection was blocks or even miles away.

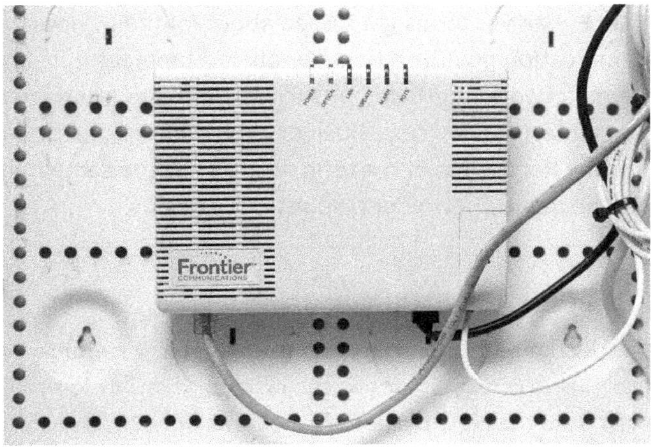

FIGURE 11-26 Typical home network interface box for home fiber internet service

In an office environment, the demarc is usually more complex, given that a typical building simply has to serve a much larger number of computers. Figure 11-27 shows the demarc for a midsize building with both internet and legacy telephone connections coming in from the outside.

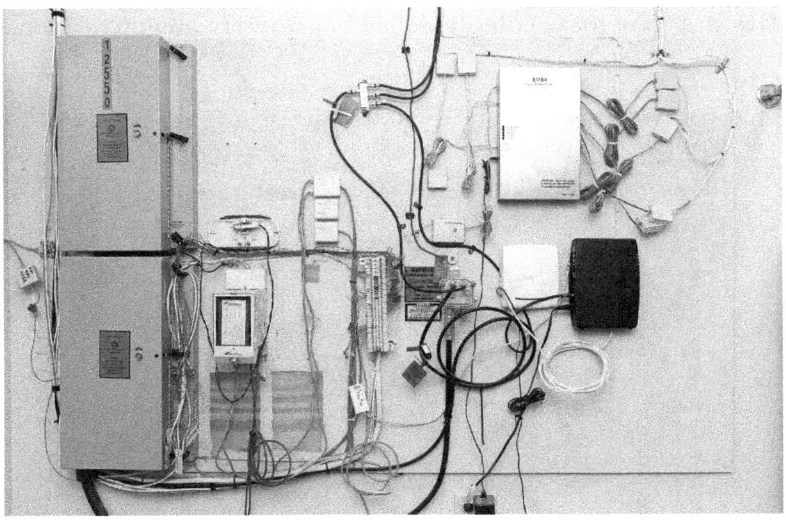

FIGURE 11-27 Messy office demarcs for internet and legacy phone

NOTE Various terms get tossed about for the devices that often mark the demarcation point in a home or office. Manufacturers and technicians call them network interface units (NIUs), network interface boxes (NIBs), network interface devices (NIDs), or even demarcs, just to muddy the waters further. Regardless of the term used, it's all the same thing—the box marking the point where your responsibility begins.

CONNECTIONS INSIDE THE DEMARC

After the demarc, network and telephone cables connect to the *customer-premises equipment* (CPE), a box the customer owns that acts as the primary distribution tool for the building. Any cabling that runs from the NIU to the CPE is the *demarc extension*. The cabling connects to a powerful switch or other network box, which usually connects to a patch panel, which in turn leads to every telecommunications room in the building. This main patch panel is called a *vertical cross-connect*. Figure 11-28 shows an example of a *fiber distribution panel* (fiber patch panel) acting as a vertical cross-connect for a building.

The demarc and LAN cross-connect equipment is stored in a room known as a *main distribution frame* (MDF). This name distinguishes the room from the multiple *intermediate distribution frame* (IDF) rooms—that is, telecommunications rooms—that serve individual floors.

The ideal scenario where every building has a single demarc, a single MDF, and multiple IDFs is only that: an ideal. Every structured cabling installation is unique and must adapt to the physical constraints of the building. One building may serve multiple customers, creating

FIGURE 11-28 LAN vertical cross-connect

the need for multiple NIUs that each serve a different customer. A smaller building may combine a demarc, MDF, and IDF into a single room. With structured cabling, the idea is to appreciate the terms while also appreciating that it's the actual building and the needs of the customers that determine the system's design.

Installing Structured Cabling

A professional installer always begins a structured cabling installation by first assessing the site and planning the installation in detail before pulling a single piece of cable. As the customer, your job is to work closely with the installer. That means locating floor plans, providing access, and even putting on old clothes and crawling alongside the installer to comb through ceilings, walls, and closets. You must understand the installation process to help the installer make the right decisions for your network.

Structured cabling requires a lot of planning. You need to know if the cables from the work areas can reach the telecommunications room. Is the distance less than the 90-meter limit dictated by the ANSI/TIA-568 standard? How will you route the cable? What path should each run take to get to the wall outlets? Just because a cable looks like it can reach doesn't mean that it will. Ceilings and walls often include hidden surprises like firewalls—big, thick, concrete walls that require a masonry drill or a jackhammer to punch through. Let's look at the steps that go into proper planning.

Getting a Floor Plan

First, you need a blueprint of the area. If you ever contact an installer who doesn't start by asking for a floor plan, fire that person immediately and get an installer who does. A good floor plan is the key to proper planning; it shows you the location of closets that could serve as telecommunications rooms, alerts you to any firewalls in your way, and gives you a good overall feel for the scope of the job ahead.

If you don't have a floor plan—which is often the case with homes or older buildings—you'll need to create your own. Get a ladder and a flashlight; you'll need them to poke around in ceilings, closets, and crawlspaces as you map out the location of rooms, walls, and anything else relevant to the installation. Figure 11-29 shows a typical do-it-yourself floor plan.

EXAM TIP A floor plan, as part of an organization's physical network diagram, is a key component of organizational documents. You might see it listed as one of the correct options for important documentation on the CompTIA Network+ exam.

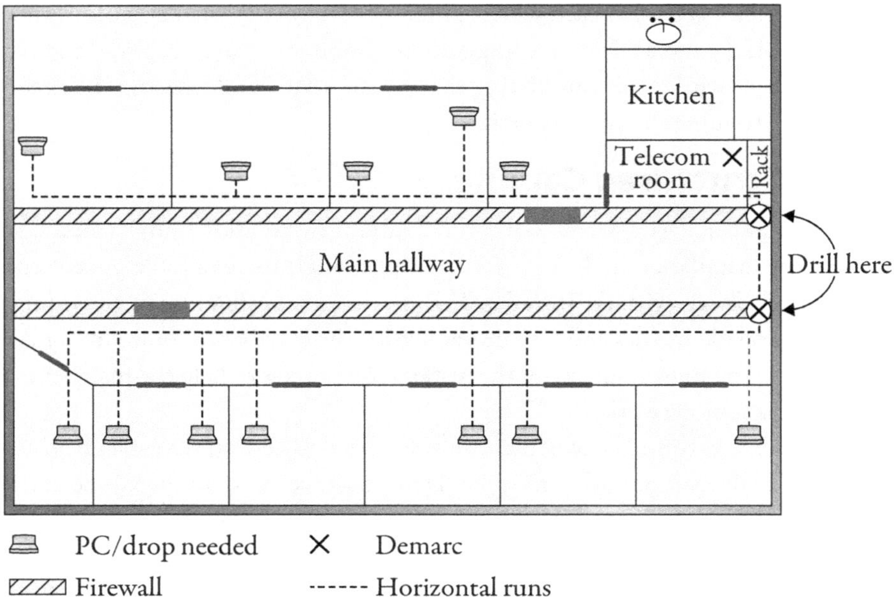

FIGURE 11-29 A network floor plan

Mapping the Runs

Now that you have your floor plan, you need to create *cable maps and diagrams* to document the cable runs. Here's where you survey the work areas, noting the locations of existing or planned systems to determine where to place each *cable drop*, the point where the cable comes out of the wall in the work area. You should also talk to users, management, and other interested parties to try to understand their future plans. Installing a few extra drops now is much easier than installing them a year from now when those two unused offices are suddenly occupied by users who immediately need networked computers!

This is the point when cost first raises its ugly head. Face it: cables, drops, and the people who install them cost money! While costs vary in different locales, a common price for a network installation is around US $50–150 per drop. Find out how much you want to spend and make some calls. Most network installers price their network jobs by quoting a per-drop cost.

EXAM TIP Watch out for the word *drop,* as it has more than one meaning. It's used to refer to a single run of cable from the telecommunications room to a wall outlet, as well as to define a new run coming through a wall outlet that does not yet have a jack installed.

While you're mapping your runs, you must make another big decision. Do you want to run the cables in the walls or outside them? Many companies sell wonderful external *raceway* products that adhere to your walls, making for a much simpler, though less neat, installation than running cables in the walls (Figure 11-30). Raceways make good sense in older buildings or when you don't have the guts—or the rights—to go into the walls.

FIGURE 11-30 A typical raceway

Determining the Location of the Telecommunications Room

While mapping the runs, you should decide on the location of your telecommunications room. Keep these six factors in mind:

- **DISTANCE** The telecommunications room must be in a spot that won't require cable runs longer than 90 meters. In most locations, as long as the telecommunications room is placed in a central location, keeping runs under 90 meters isn't difficult.
- **POWER LOAD** Many of the components in your telecommunications room need power, so make sure you provide enough! If possible, put the telecommunications room on its own dedicated circuit; that way, when someone blows a circuit in the kitchen, it doesn't take out the entire network.
- **HUMIDITY** Electrical components and water don't mix well. (Remind me to tell you about the time I installed a rack in an abandoned bathroom and the toilet later exploded.) Remember that dryness also means low humidity. Avoid areas with the potential for high humidity, such as a room near a pool or a janitor's closet with mop buckets full of water. Of course, any well air-conditioned room should be fine—which leads to the next big issue . . .
- **FIRE SUPPRESSION** When a fire is detected, tanks disperse fire suppression elements that quickly reduce oxygen levels to stop combustion and extinguish flames.

Halon, once a common choice, is no longer produced due to environmental concerns. Modern systems use clean agents (FM200, Novec 1230) or inert gases (nitrogen, argon), which extinguish fires without leaving residue or damaging electronics.

- **TEMPERATURE** Telecommunications rooms tend to get warm, especially if you add a couple of server systems and a UPS. Ensure the room is air-conditioned, maintains stable temperatures (18–27°C), and prevents hot spots around racks. Figure 11-31 shows how I monitor the temp of my equipment rack.
- **ACCESS** Access involves two different issues. First, it means preventing unauthorized access. Think about the people you want and don't want to mess around with your network, and act accordingly. In my small office, the equipment closet literally sits eight feet from me, so I don't worry too much about unauthorized access. You, on the other hand, may want to consider locking your telecommunications room if you're concerned that unscrupulous or unqualified people might try to access it.

  The second issue to keep in mind when choosing your telecommunications room is expandability. Can this telecommunications room grow with your network? Will it be able to service any nearby additional office space your company may acquire? If your company decides to take over the floor above you, can you easily run vertical cabling from this room to another telecommunications room on that floor? While the specific issues will be unique to each installation, keep expansion or scalability in mind as you design—your network *will* grow, whether or not you think so now!

NOTE These issues also apply to data centers, covered in Chapter 14.

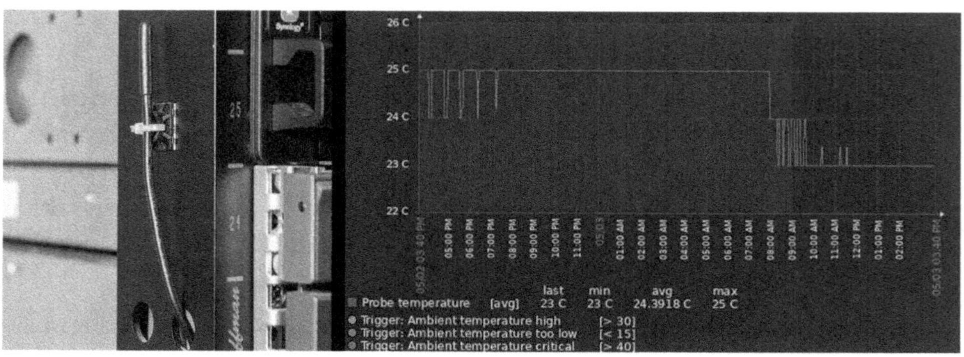

FIGURE 11-31 Temperature probe (left) with a graph of the temperature (right)

With your cable runs mapped and your telecommunications room established, now you're ready to start pulling cable!

Pulling Cable

Pulling cable is easily one of the most thankless and unpleasant jobs in the entire networking world. It may not look that hard from a distance, but the devil is in the details. First of all, if you want to get the job done quickly, you need two people—three is even better. Most pullers start from the telecommunications room and pull toward the drops. In an office area with a drop ceiling, pullers often feed the cabling along the run by opening ceiling tiles and stringing the cable via hooks or *cable trays* above the ceiling (Figure 11-32). Professional cable pullers have an arsenal of interesting tools to help them move the cable horizontally, including telescoping poles, coiled flat steel wire (called *fish tape*) for snaking through conduit, special nylon pull ropes.

FIGURE 11-32 Cable trays over a drop ceiling

Cable trays are standard today, but a previous lack of codes or standards for handling cables led to a nightmare of disorganized cables in drop ceilings all over the world. Any cable puller will tell you that the hardest part of installing cables is having to work around all the old cable installations in the ceiling (Figure 11-33).

Local codes, TIA, and the National Electrical Code (NEC) all have strict rules about how you pull cable in a ceiling. Hooks and trays provide better cable management, safety, and protection from electrical interference. The faster the network, the more critical good cable management (Figure 11-34) becomes.

FIGURE 11-33 Messy cabling nightmare

FIGURE 11-34 Nicely run cables

Running cable horizontally requires relatively little effort compared to running it down from the ceiling to a pretty faceplate at the work area, which often takes a lot of skill. In a typical office area with sheetrock walls, the installer first decides on the position for the outlet, generally using a stud finder to avoid cutting on top of a stud. After cutting the hole (Figure 11-35), most installers drop a line to it using a weight tied to the end of a nylon pull rope (Figure 11-36). They can then attach the network cable to the pull rope and pull it down to and then through the hole. The installer then puts in an outlet box or a low-voltage *mounting bracket* (Figure 11-37) that acts as a holder for the faceplate.

FIGURE 11-35 Cutting a hole

FIGURE 11-36 Locating a dropped pull rope

FIGURE 11-37 Installing a mounting bracket

Back in the telecommunications room, the installer consolidates and organizes the many cables leading to each work area to prepare for the next stage: making connections. A truly professional installer takes great care in organizing the equipment closet. Figure 11-38 shows a typical installation using special cable guides to bring the cables down to the equipment rack.

FIGURE 11-38 Guiding the ends of the cables to the rack

Making Connections

Making connections consists of connecting both ends of each cable to the proper jacks. It also includes a very important step: testing each cable run to ensure that every connection meets the requirements of the network that will use it. Installers also use this step to document and label each cable run—a critical task too often forgotten by inexperienced installers, and one you need to verify takes place!

CONNECTING THE WORK AREAS

In the work area, the installer terminates a cable run by attaching an RJ45 jack to the end of the wire and mounting the faceplate to complete the installation (Figure 11-39). Note the back of the jack shown in Figure 11-39. This jack uses the popular 110-punchdown connection, just like the one shown earlier in the chapter for patch panels. All 110-punchdown connections have a color code that tells you which wire to punch into which connection on the back of the jack.

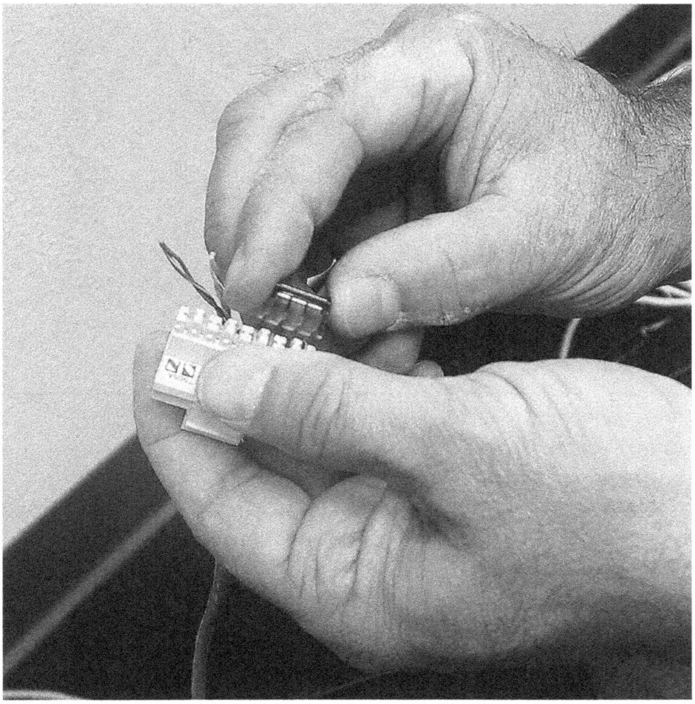

FIGURE 11-39 Punching down a jack

ROLLING YOUR OWN PATCH CABLES

Although most people prefer to purchase premade patch cables, making your own is fairly easy. To do so, use stranded core UTP cable that matches the Cat level, twist rate, and conductor quality to minimize crosstalk and ensure proper performance. Stranded core cable also requires specific crimps, so don't use crimps designed for solid core cable. Crimping is simple enough, although getting it right takes some practice.

Figure 11-40 shows the two main tools of the crimping trade: an RJ45 crimper with a built-in cable stripper and a pair of wire snips/cutters. Professional cable installers naturally have a wide variety of other tools as well.

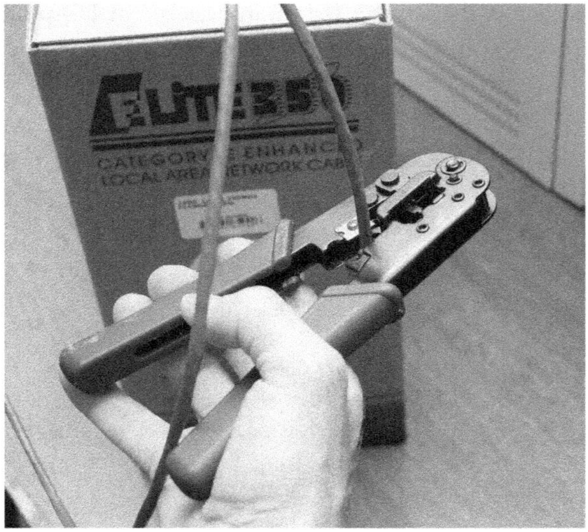

FIGURE 11-40 Crimper and snips/cutters

If you have some crimps, cable, and a crimping tool handy, follow these steps for properly crimping an RJ45 onto a UTP cable:

1. Cut the cable square using RJ45 crimpers.
2. Strip around a half-inch of plastic jacket from the end of the cable (Figure 11-41) with a dedicated cable stripper or the one built into the crimping tool.
3. Slowly and carefully insert each individual wire into the correct location according to either TIA-568A wiring or TIA-568B wiring (Figure 11-42). Unravel as little as possible.

FIGURE 11-41 Properly stripped cable—it doesn't hurt to leave room for mistakes!

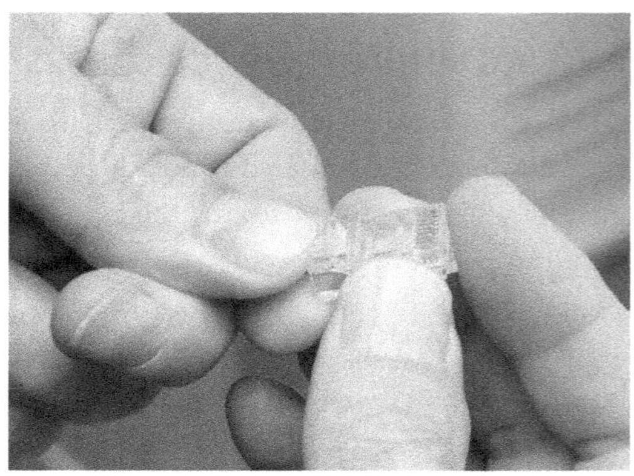

FIGURE 11-42 Fully seat the wires to the front of the connector so the copper reaches the pins.

4. Insert the crimp into the crimper and press (Figure 11-43). Don't worry about pressing too hard; the crimper has a stop to prevent you from using too much pressure.

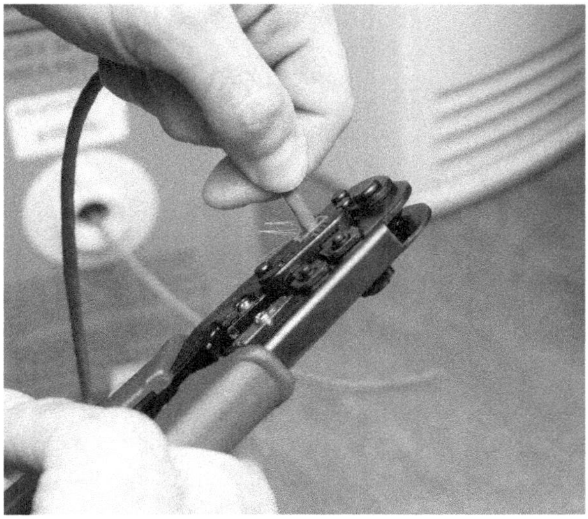

FIGURE 11-43 Crimping the cable

Figure 11-44 shows a nicely crimped cable. Note how the plastic jacket goes into the crimp.

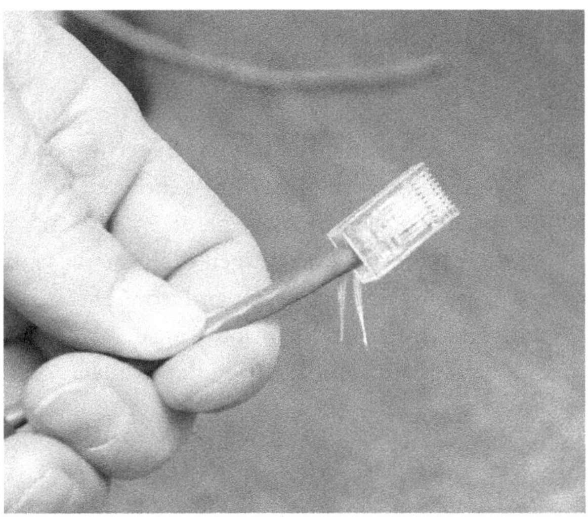

FIGURE 11-44 A properly crimped cable

A good patch cable should include a boot, which protects the clip and provides strain relief for the cable jacket. Figure 11-45 shows a boot being slid onto a newly crimped cable. Don't forget to slide each boot onto the patch cable *before* you crimp both ends!

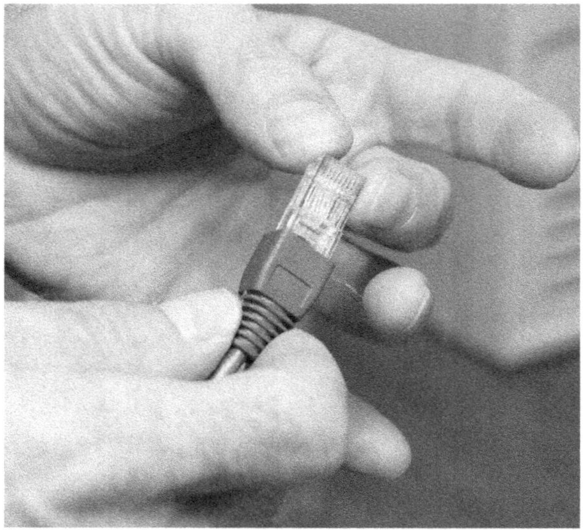

FIGURE 11-45 Adding a boot

After making a cable, you need to test it to make sure it's properly crimped. Read the section "Testing the Cable Runs" on page 316 to learn how.

CONNECTING THE PATCH PANELS

There are three things you need to account for when connecting the cables to patch panels. The first is patch cable management. Figure 11-46 shows the front of a small network's equipment rack—note the complete lack of cable management!

Managing patch cables means using the proper cable management hardware. Plastic D-rings guide the patch cables neatly along the sides and front of the patch panel. *Cable managers* are rectangular cylinders with slots in the front; you run the patch cables into the open ends of the box and thread the individual cables through the fingers on their way to the patch panel, keeping them neatly organized.

Creativity and variety abound in the world of cable management hardware, and there are as many different solutions to cable management as there are ways to screw it up. Figure 11-47 shows a rack using good cable management; these patch cables are well secured with cable management hardware, making them much less susceptible to damage from mishandling. Plus, it looks much nicer!

FIGURE 11-46 Bad cable management

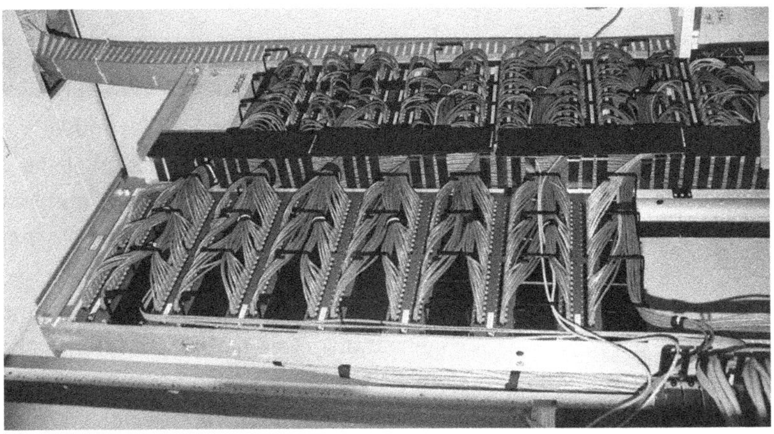

FIGURE 11-47 Good cable management

The second consideration is the overall organization of the patch panel as it relates to the organization of your network. Organize your patch panel so it mirrors the layout of your network. You can organize according to the physical layout so that the different parts of the patch panel correspond to different parts of your office space—for example, the north and south sides of the hallway. Another popular option is to match your patch panels to the logical layout of the network so that the different user groups or company organizations have their own sections of the patch panel.

Finally, proper patch panel cable management means documenting everything clearly and carefully. This way, any competent technician can follow behind you and troubleshoot connectivity problems. Good techs draw diagrams!

Testing the Cable Runs

In theory, your horizontal cabling system is now installed and ready for you to connect a switch and some systems. Before you do this, though, you must test each cable run. While you might think that all you need to do is verify that each jack has been properly connected—and this *is* an important and necessary step—you must also verify that your cable run can handle the speed of your network.

The basic Layer 1 network connection issues fall into three categories: signal degradation, lack of connection, and interference. A host of factors can cause overall degradation, which in turn slows or stops network communication. A lack of connection has many potential causes, as we'll discuss shortly, but the effect is that the networked device(s) can't communicate. Interference is any disruption on a wired or wireless medium that intentionally or inadvertently prevents valid signals from being read by an intended recipient.

MEASURING SIGNAL LOSS

Signal loss in networking—for both electrical signals in copper wires and light signals in fiber cables—is measured in decibels. Unfortunately for a lot of network techs, a decibel is tough to grasp without a lot of math. I'll skip the technical details and give you a shorthand way to understand the numbers to troubleshoot a cable connectivity scenario with decibel loss.

When a signal is traveling from one end of a cable to another, what you really care about is how much of the information being transmitted makes it to the end; that's what we think of as *signal strength*. In a simple sense, if you have some interference, some imperfections in the cable or fiber, you'll get some loss from beginning to end. Most people think about that loss in terms of percentage or general measures like "a little" or "a lot of" loss.

The problem when you apply that same concept to networking is that the percentages lost can be gigantic or really, really small. When you start talking about a 10,000 percent loss or a .00001 percent loss, most folks' eyes glaze over. The numbers are simply too big or small to make intuitive sense.

Technicians use the term *decibel* to describe those numbers in a more digestible format. For example, a 3 dB loss represents about half the signal power, while 10 dB represents roughly one-tenth.

Copper- and fiber-based network runs have different causes for loss of connectivity, interference, and degradation, and thus require different tools to resolve. We'll look at copper, then fiber.

Copper and fiber networks experience different types of signal degradation and require different tools to troubleshoot. While professional cable certification tools are expensive, often exceeding $5,000, basic testers for continuity and wiring verification are sufficient for most network admins. These tools also help diagnose existing network problems.

NOTE The test tools described here also enable you to diagnose network problems.

ADDRESSING COPPER CHALLENGES

Most network admins staring at a scenario with a potentially bad copper cable want to know the following:

- How long is this cable? If it's too long, the signal will degrade to the point that it's no longer detectable on the other end.
- How much noise is there? Every signal—copper, fiber, and wireless—has noise. Too much noise, and the signal will degrade, slowing down or stopping the network. You'll see this in action with cable internet connections.
- Are any of the wires broken or not connected in the crimp (*open*)? If a wire is broken or a connection is open, it no longer has *continuity* (a complete, functioning connection). Are there bent pins on the RJ45 or in the jack?
- Is there any place where two bare wires touch? This creates a short. Shorts can result when cables are damaged, but also from two cables being improperly crimped into the same position.
- If there is a break, where is it? It's much easier to fix if the location is detectable.

- Are all of the wires terminated in the right place in the plug or jack? Does each termination match to the same standard? In other words, is this an *incorrect pinout* scenario with *transmitter (TX)/receiver (RX) transposed*?
- Is there electrical or radio *interference* from outside sources? UTP is susceptible to electromagnetic interference (EMI), as introduced in Chapter 4.
- Is there an *improper termination* order on one end of the connection (mixed wires instead of the proper pair order)? This common problem in UTP installations is called a split pair.

To answer these questions, you must verify that both the cable and the terminated ends are correct. Making these verifications requires a *cable tester*. Various models of cable testers can answer some or all of these questions, depending on how much you want to spend. At the low end of the cable tester market (under $100) are *continuity testers* (Figure 11-48), which, as the name implies, test only for continuity. Many of these testers require you to insert both ends of the cable into the tester. Of course, this can be a bit of a problem if the cable is already installed in the wall!

Better testers can run a *wire map* test that goes beyond mere continuity, testing that all the wires on both ends of the cable connect to the right spot. A wire map test will pick up shorts, crossed wires, and more. Figure 11-49 shows a MicroScanner diagnosing a wire map problem.

FIGURE 11-48 Continuity tester

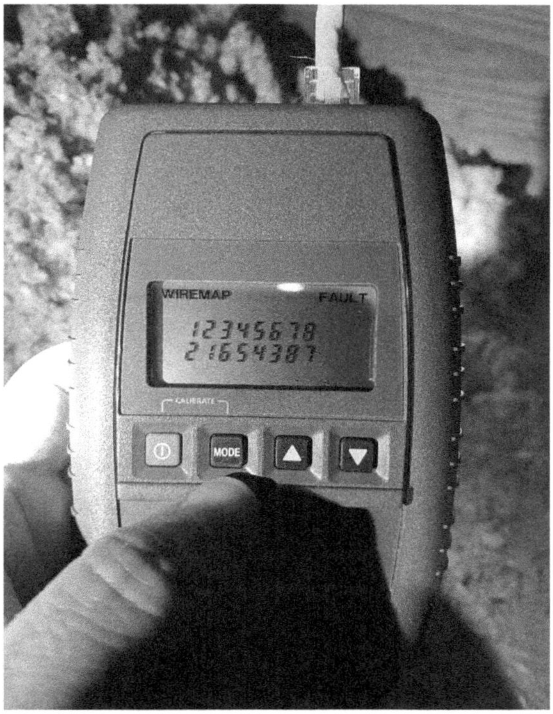

FIGURE 11-49 MicroScanner readout

NOTE Many techs and network testing folks use the term *wire map* to refer to the proper connectivity for wires, as in, "Hey Bob, check the wire map!"

To check continuity, you can also use a *multimeter*, a device to test AC and DC voltage and current as well as continuity and resistance. Some advanced models can test other components such as transistors and capacitors. Set the multimeter (Figure 11-50) to continuity mode (if it has one) or to its lowest Ohm range. In the latter mode, a reading of 0 Ohms indicates continuity and infinite Ohms indicates no connection.

Medium-priced testers (~$400) test continuity and wire map and include the additional capability to determine the length of a cable; they can also approximate the location of a break or short in a cable pair. This type of cable tester (Figure 11-51), known as a *time-domain reflectometer* (TDR), usually comes with a small loopback device to insert into the far end of the cable, enabling the TDR to work with installed cables. This is the type of tester you want to have around!

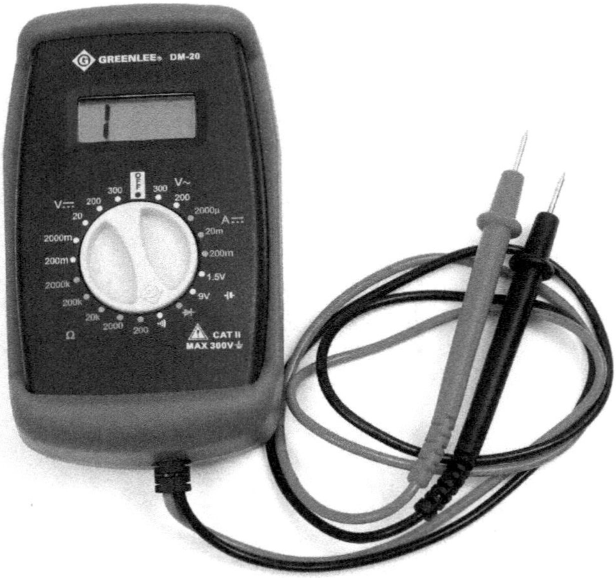

FIGURE 11-50 Multimeter

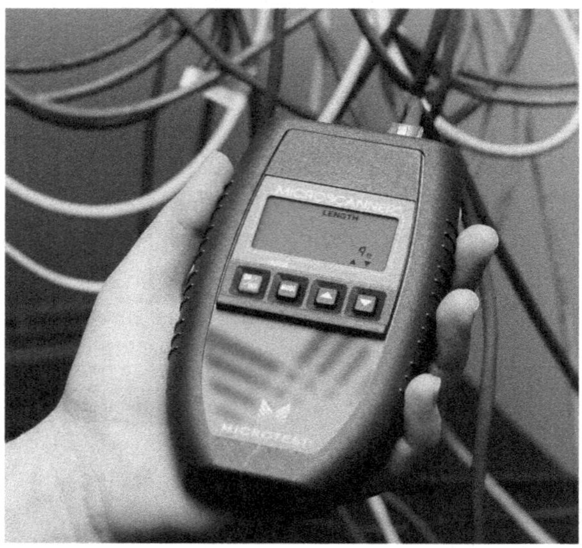

FIGURE 11-51 A vintage MicroScanner TDR

If you want a device that fully tests a cable run to the very complex TIA standards, the price shoots up fast. These higher-end testers can detect things the lesser testers cannot, such as crosstalk and attenuation.

Crosstalk

When you send a signal down one pair of wires in today's four-pair UTP cables, the other pairs pick up some of the signal, as shown in Figure 11-52. This kind of interference, known as *crosstalk*, poses a threat to properly functioning cable runs.

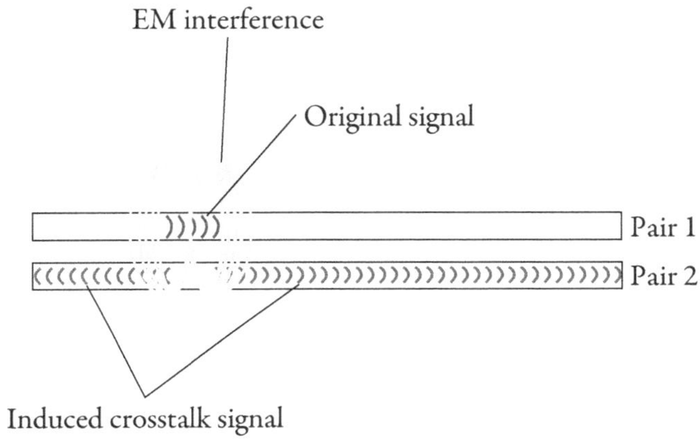

FIGURE 11-52 Crosstalk

Crosstalk is why each pair of wires is twisted at a separate rate, and why pairs are twisted around each other. The twist rates are part of the cable certification and reduce the chance that signal leaking from one pair will affect another pair for very long. Improper twisting causes crosstalk, and this can be a problem at cables' ends, especially self-crimped cables, where people may untwist too much wire.

Every piece of UTP in existence generates crosstalk. Worse, when you crimp the end of a UTP cable to a jack or plugs, crosstalk increases. A poor-quality crimp creates so much crosstalk that a cable run won't operate at its designed speed. You should always verify cables with a *speed tester*. Detecting crosstalk involves sending a normal-strength signal down one pair of wires in a cable. An electronic detector, connected on the same end that's emanating the signal, listens on the other three pairs and measures the amount of interference, as shown in Figure 11-53. This is called *near-end crosstalk* (NEXT).

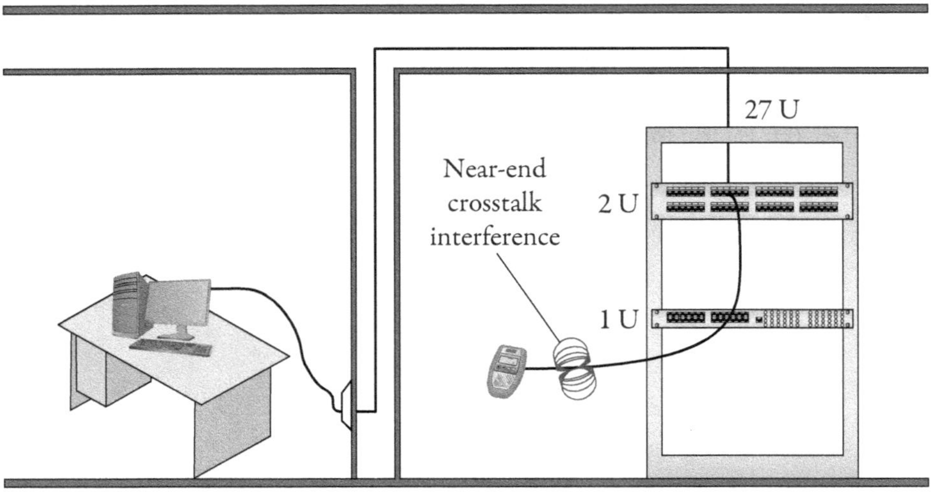

FIGURE 11-53 Near-end crosstalk

If you repeat this test, sending the signal down one pair of wires but this time listening at the far end of the connection, you test for *far-end crosstalk* (FEXT), as shown in Figure 11-54.

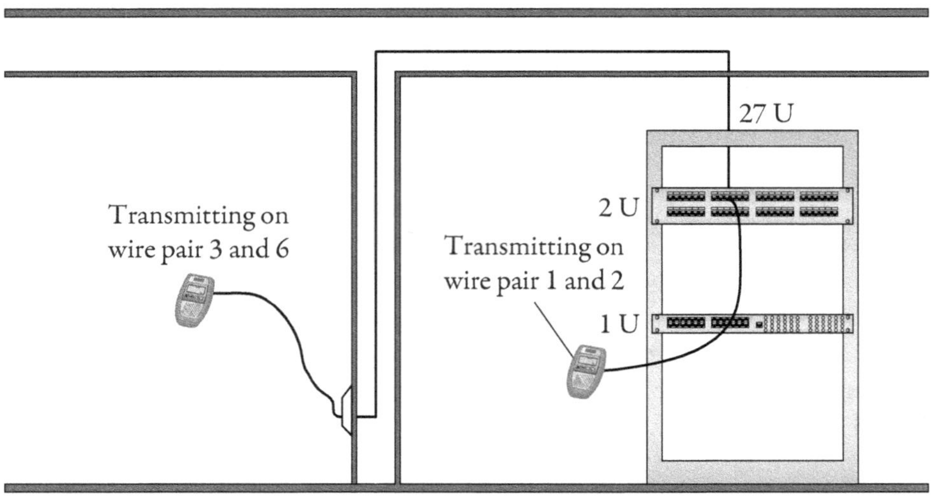

FIGURE 11-54 Far-end crosstalk

NOTE Both NEXT and FEXT are measured in decibels.

Attenuation

If that's not bad enough, as a signal progresses down a piece of wire, it becomes steadily weaker; this is called *attenuation*. As a cable run gets longer, the attenuation increases, and the signal becomes more susceptible to crosstalk. A tester must send a signal down one end of a wire, test for NEXT and FEXT on the ends of every other pair, and then repeat this process for every pair in the UTP cable.

EXAM TIP Every network—copper or otherwise—experiences data loss or lag over distances and with enough traffic. Ethernet network frame traffic has *latency*, a delay between when the sending machine sends a message and when the receiving machine can start processing it.

Add in a lot of machines, and the network will also experience *jitter*, the variation in packet arrival times. Small amounts of jitter are normal, but excessive jitter may cause choppy audio or video in real-time applications like VoIP or video conferencing. Modern network technologies are designed to handle typical latency and jitter without impacting file transfers.

This process of verifying that every cable run meets the exacting ANSI/TIA-568 standards requires very powerful testing tools, generally known as *cable certifiers* or just certifiers. Cable installers can use certifiers to perform the high-end testing and generate a report for the customer to prove compliance with ANSI/TIA-568 standards. Cable certifiers cost a lot and are thus reserved for cable installation experts rather than network techs.

ADDRESSING FIBER CHALLENGES

Challenges with fiber cable runs are similar to those for copper cable runs, but there are also some very specific differences. Just like with copper, signal loss is important and measured in decibels. But the causes of loss can differ a lot. Also, the many competing standards can catch techs running fiber by surprise.

SIGNAL DEGRADATION AND LOSS

Just like with copper wire, various imperfections in the media—the glass fiber, in this case—cause signal loss over distance. A lot of factors come into play:

- *Damaged cables* or *open connections* obviously stop signals. The typical small form-factor pluggable (SFP) can have problems. When looking for a bad SFP, you'll need to check both the connector and the cable going into that connector. Either or both could cause the signal loss.

- A *visual fault locator* is a tool that checks for polarity and cable continuity in a fiber-optic cable. Any faults, like bends or breaks, are easily identifiable with the help of a laser, like the one I use for pointing during class.
- A *dirty connector* can cause pretty serious signal loss with fiber. It's important not to smudge the glass!
- Remember that in fiber-optic cables, the part that carries the signal is really tiny—only a few microns. When you're connecting two pieces of fiber, even a small *connector mismatch* in either the cladding (the outside) or the core (the inside) can cause serious losses.
- In multimode fiber, *modal dispersion* can cause the signal to spread over long distances, while all fiber types experience attenuation over distance.
- Every piece of fiber has a certain *bend radius limitation*. If you bend a fiber-optic cable too much, you get *light leakage*, as shown in Figure 11-55, where part of the signal escapes the cable rather than arriving at the end—not a good thing!

PHYSICAL OR SIGNAL MISMATCH

Fiber networks have many connectors and a pretty wide variety of signal types that use them. These variations come into play in several ways. First, just because you can connect to a particular SFP doesn't mean the signal will work. Plugging an incorrect transceiver into a switch

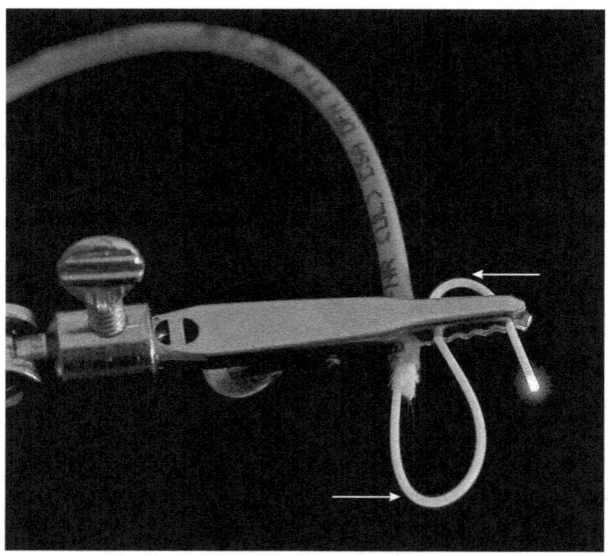

FIGURE 11-55 Light leaking out at the bends

port (10GBASE-SR transceiver into a port that only supports 10GBASE-LR, for example) is a transceiver mismatch. The transceiver will fit in the port, but the link won't come up.

Likewise, you can find fiber connectors like SC or LC that will attach to single-mode or multimode fiber. This can lead to *cable issues*. Using an *incorrect cable*—for example, a single-mode cable into a switch that expects multimode—will create a *cable mismatch* or *fiber mismatch*, meaning your network—at least that portion of it—won't work.

Finally, different runs of fiber use different wavelength signals. You might be able to plug an LC connector into a switch just fine, for example, but if the signal starts at 1,310 nm and the switch expects 1,530 nm, that *wavelength mismatch* will stop the transmission cold.

FIBER TOOLS

A fiber technician uses many tools (Figure 11-56) and demonstrates a skill level bordering on artistry. Putting an ST, SC, LC, or other connector on the end of a piece of fiber is very challenging, although easier terminations have been developed over the years.

A fiber-optic run has problems that are both similar to and different from those of a UTP run. Fiber-optic runs don't experience crosstalk or interference (as we usually think of it) because they use light instead of an electrical current.

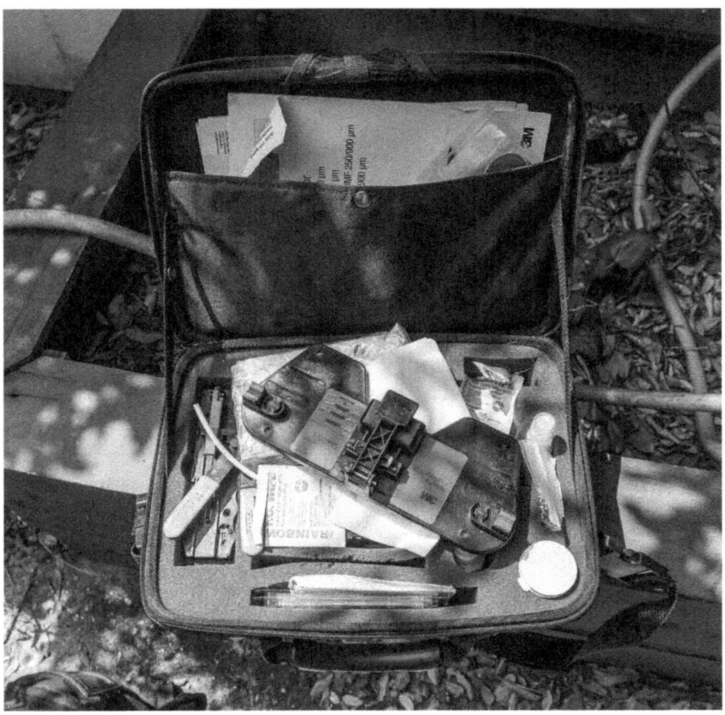

FIGURE 11-56 Fiber splicing kit in the field

Fiber-optic cables still break, however, so a good tech always keeps an *optical time-domain reflectometer* (OTDR) handy (Figure 11-57) for just such scenarios. OTDRs determine continuity and, if there's a break, tell you exactly how far down the cable to look for it.

FIGURE 11-57 An OTDR (photo courtesy of Fluke Networks)

The three big issues with fiber are light leakage, attenuation, and dispersion, along with practical issues like maintaining the proper bend radius and keeping connectors clean.

ANSI/TIA-568 has very complex requirements for testing fiber runs, and the cabling industry sells fiber certifiers to ensure a cable meets these performance standards.

> **EXAM TIP** One of the common tools for fiber-optic cable installers is a *fusion splicer*, which enables the tech to combine two fiber-optic cables with minimal signal loss and back reflection.

The process of installing a structured cabling system is rather involved, requires a great degree of skill, and should be left to professionals. By understanding the process, however, you can tackle most of the problems that come up in an installed structured cabling system. Most importantly, you'll understand the lingo used by installers so you can work with them more efficiently.

NICs

Now that the network is completely in place, it's time to turn to the final part of any physical network: the NICs. A good network tech must recognize different types of NICs by sight and know how to install and troubleshoot them. Let's begin by reviewing the differences between UTP and fiber-optic NICs.

All modern LAN NICs use the RJ45 connector. The cable runs from the NIC (Figure 11-58) to a switch.

FIGURE 11-58 Typical UTP NIC

NOTE Motherboards these days include an onboard NIC, which of course invalidates the acronym NIC because a card is no longer involved. But just as we'll probably never stop using *RJ45* when the correct term is *8P8C*, we'll keep using *NIC*. Let's just pretend that now it stands for *network interface chip* or *connection*.

Fiber-optic NICs come in many models and can support multiple standards. Figure 11-59 shows a typical fiber-optic network card.

FIGURE 11-59 A typical NIC supporting fiber (copyright © Intel Corporation)

Buying NICs

I always purchase name-brand NICs. For NICs, I recommend sticking with big names, such as Intel. The NICs are better made, have extra features, and are easy to return if they turn out to be defective.

Plus, replacing a missing driver on a name-brand NIC is easy, and you can be confident the drivers work well. The type of NIC you should purchase depends on your network. Try to stick with the same model of NIC. Every different model you buy means another set of drivers, so using the same NIC model makes driver updates easier, too.

PHYSICAL CONNECTIONS

I'll state the obvious here: if you don't plug the NIC into the computer, the NIC won't work! If you're buying a NIC, physically inserting it into one of the PC's expansion slots is the easiest part of the job. Most PCs today have two types of expansion slots. The older expansion slot is the Peripheral Component Interconnect (PCI) type (Figure 11-60).

The PCI Express (PCIe) expansion slots are now widely adopted by NIC suppliers. PCIe NICs are usually ×1 or ×4 (Figure 11-61) and are widely supported by NIC manufacturers. You might add a PCIe NIC if your PC only has an onboard copper-based NIC and you want to connect to a fiber network. Make sure the NIC supports the correct fiber type, transceiver, and speed.

FIGURE 11-60 PCI NIC

FIGURE 11-61 PCIe NIC

If you're not willing to open a PC case, you can get NICs with USB connections (Figure 11-62). USB NICs are handy to keep in your toolkit. If you walk up to a machine that might have a bad NIC, test your suspicions by inserting a USB NIC and moving the network cable from the potentially bad NIC to the USB one. (USB NICs are also commonly used with super-thin laptops that don't come with built-in Ethernet ports.)

FIGURE 11-62
USB NIC

DRIVERS

A modern OS might have a driver included for the NIC. If not, installing a NIC's driver into a Windows, macOS, or Linux system is easy: just insert a driver disc when prompted by the system. Many current systems don't sport optical drives, so installing a new NIC requires access to the internet. Have a spare machine and copy drivers to a USB flash drive, then install drivers from there.

Every operating system has some method to verify that the computer recognizes the NIC and is ready to use it. Windows systems have the Device Manager; Ubuntu Linux users have the Network applet under the Administration menu; and macOS users get the Network utility in System Preferences. Most operating systems have multiple methods to show that the NIC is in good working order. Learn the various ways to verify the NIC for your OS, as this is the ultimate test of a good NIC installation.

Understanding Link Lights

All NICs and switches made today have some type of light-emitting diodes (LEDs) that give information about the state of the link to whatever is on the other end of the connection. Even though you know they're LEDs, get used to calling them *link lights*, as that's the term all network techs use. NICs and switches can have between one and four different link lights, and the LEDs can be any color. These lights give you clues about what's happening with the link and are one of the first items to check whenever you think a system is disconnected from the network (Figure 11-63).

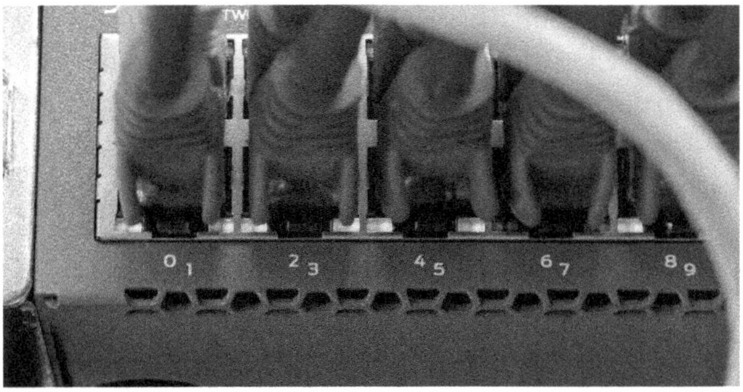

FIGURE 11-63 Switch with link lights off for port 7 and on for ports 1, 3, 5, and 9

A link light displays connectivity. If a PC can't access a network and is acting disconnected, always check the link lights first. Multispeed devices usually have a link light that tells you the speed of the connection. In Figure 11-64, the left link light for port 2 is lit, but the right link light is not, signifying that the other end of the cable is plugged into a 100BASE-T NIC. Port 1, on the other hand, has both link lights lit. It's clearly Gigabit.

FIGURE 11-64 Multispeed lights

Another light is the *activity light*, which turns on when the card detects network traffic, so it intermittently flickers when operating properly. The activity light is a lifesaver for detecting problems, because the connection light will sometimes lie to you. If the connection light says the connection is good, try copying a file or doing something else to create network traffic. If the activity light does not flicker, there's a problem.

On many NICs, a properly functioning link light is on and steady when the NIC is connected to another device. Being on with no flickering indicates a good connection. On NICs that use a single LED to display both the link and activity status, on the other hand, the single LED *should* flicker with activity. That's how the NIC in Figure 11-63 works. Read the online documentation from the NIC manufacturer's website to properly interpret their steadiness or flickering.

No standard governs how NIC or switch manufacturers use their lights, and, as a result, they come in an amazing array of colors and layouts. When you encounter a NIC or switch with a number of LEDs, try to figure out what each one means. Although different NICs and switches have various ways of arranging and using their LEDs, the functions are always the same: link, activity, and speed.

Diagnosing and Repairing Physical Cabling Issues

"The network's down!" is easily the most terrifying phrase a network tech will ever hear. Networks fail for many reasons, and the first thing to know is that good-quality, professionally installed cabling rarely goes bad. Chapter 18 covers principles of network diagnostics and support that apply to all networking scenarios, but this section will discuss how to troubleshoot common cable connectivity issues when you're faced with a scenario that points to a problem with your physical network.

A key clue that you may have a physical problem is that a user gets a "No server is found" error or tries to use the operating system's network explorer utility (like Network in Windows) and doesn't see any systems besides their own. First, try to eliminate software errors. If one application fails, try another. If the user can't browse the internet but can get email, odds are good that the problem is with software, not hardware—unless someone unplugged the email server!

Multiple systems failing to access the network often points to hardware problems. This is where knowledge of your network cabling helps. If all the systems connected to one switch suddenly no longer see the network, but all the other systems in your network still function, you not only have a probable hardware problem but also a suspect: the switch.

Check Your Lights

If you suspect a hardware problem, first check the link lights on the NIC and switch. If they're not lit, you know the cable isn't connected somewhere. If you're not physically at the system in question (if you're on a tech call, for example), you can have the user check the connection status through the link lights or through software. Every operating system has some onscreen way to tell you if it detects that the NIC is disconnected. In Windows 10, for example, the notification area displays a stylized globe with a small, crossed-out circle when a NIC is disconnected (Figure 11-65), versus a connected computer icon when it's properly connected (Figure 11-66).

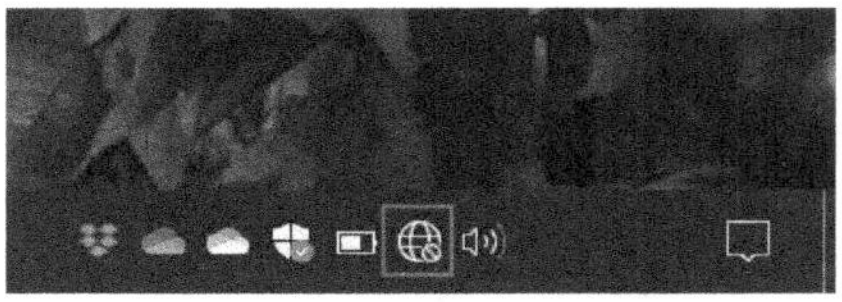

FIGURE 11-65 Disconnected NIC in Windows

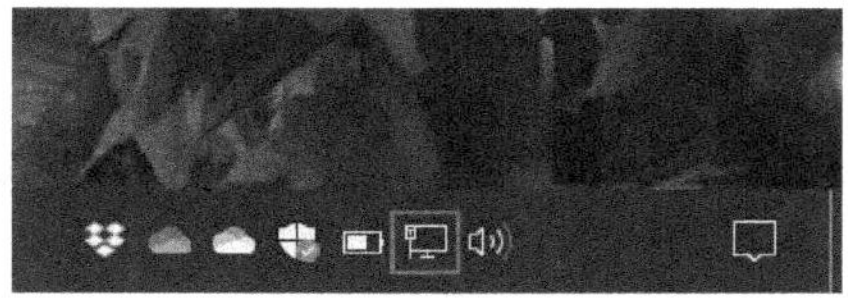

FIGURE 11-66 Connected NIC in Windows

If a problem system has no connection, eliminate the possibility of a failed switch or other larger problem by checking to make sure other people can access the network, and that other systems can access the shared resource (server) that the problem system can't see. Make a quick visual inspection of the cable running from the back of the PC to the outlet.

Finally, if you can, plug the system into a known-good outlet and see if it works. A good network tech always keeps a long patch cable for just this purpose. If you get connectivity with the second outlet, you should begin to suspect bad wiring in the structured cable running from the first outlet to the switch. Alternatively, it could be a bad connector. Assuming the cable is installed properly and has been working correctly before this event, a simple continuity test will confirm your suspicion in most cases.

Check the NIC

Be warned that a bad NIC can also generate this "can't see the network" problem. Use the utility provided by your OS to verify that the NIC works. If you've got a NIC with diagnostic software, run it—this software checks the NIC's circuitry. The NIC's female connector is a common failure point, so NICs that come with diagnostic software often include a loopback test, sending data out of the NIC and checking to see if it comes back. A true external loopback requires a *loopback adapter* or *loopback plug* inserted into the NIC's port (Figure 11-67). If a NIC is bad or has a bad port, replace it. Using the same model can simplify driver installation, but modern operating systems generally detect and install drivers for new NICs automatically.

NOTE Onboard NICs in laptops are often difficult to replace. Failures are usually caused by electrical issues, driver problems, or motherboard defects rather than repeated plugging and unplugging.

FIGURE 11-67 A loopback adapter or plug

Test Your Cables

The vast majority of network disconnect problems occur at the work area. If you've tested those connections, though, and the work area seems fine, it's time to consider deeper issues.

With the right equipment, diagnosing a bad horizontal cabling run is easy. Anyone with a network should own a midrange tester with TDR such as the Fluke MicroScanner. With a little practice, you can easily determine not only whether a cable is disconnected but also where the disconnection takes place. Sometimes patience is required, especially if the cable runs aren't labeled, but you will find the problem.

When you're testing a cable run, always include the patch cables as you test. This means unplugging the patch cable from the PC, attaching a tester, and then going to the telecommunications room. Here you'll want to unplug the patch cable from the switch and plug the tester into that patch cable, making a complete test, as shown in Figure 11-68.

Testing in this manner gives you a complete test from the switch to the system. In general, a broken cable must be replaced. Fixing a bad patch cable is easy, but what happens if the horizontal cable is to blame? In these cases, I call my local installer. If a cable's bad in one spot, the risk of it being bad in another is simply too great to try anything other than total replacement.

Finally, if a coupler is used to extend a run, inspect it carefully. UTP couplers, which have two female ports, can introduce signal loss if damaged or of low quality. Fiber and coaxial couplers exist as well, but in professional installations, couplers are generally avoided unless absolutely necessary, as each connection can degrade signal quality.

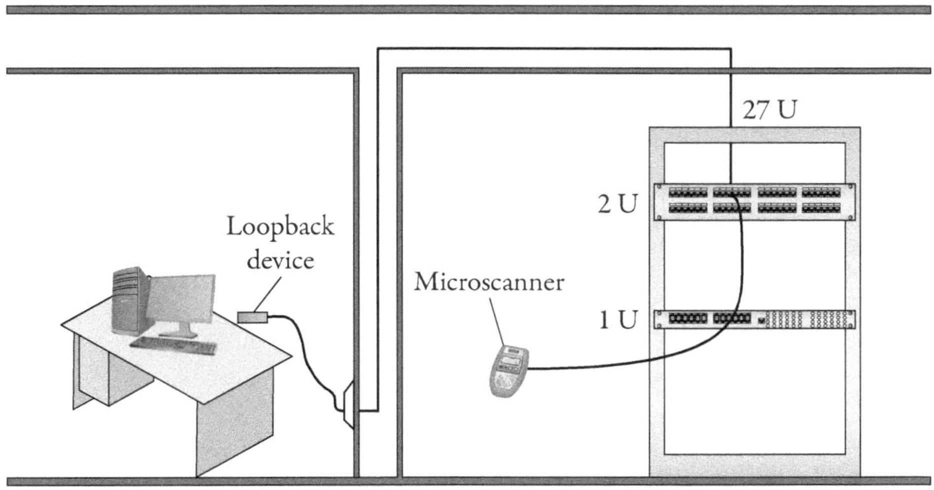

FIGURE 11-68 Loopback adapter in action

PROBLEMS IN THE TELECOMMUNICATIONS ROOM

Even a well-organized telecommunications room is a complex maze of equipment racks, switches, and patch panels. The most important issue to remember as you work is to keep your diagnostic process organized and documented. For example, if you're testing a series of cable runs along a patch panel, start at one end, and don't skip connections. Place a sticker as you work to keep track of where you are on the panel.

Your biggest concerns in the telecommunications room are *facilities and infrastructure support* concerns, such as power and air quality.

All those boxes in the rack need good-quality power. Even the smallest rack should run off a good UPS. Make sure you get one that can handle the amount of wattage used by all the equipment in the rack.

A UPS provides several benefits. First, it acts as an inverter. It stores power as direct current in its battery, then inverts that power to alternating current as the servers and other boxes in the rack system require. A network-manageable UPS also acts as a *power monitoring tool* so it can report problems when there's any fluctuation in the electrical supply. Some UPS models actively stabilize voltage, protecting against spikes, sags, and brownouts. Basic standby UPS devices may provide only minimal surge protection.

A UPS enables you to shut down in an orderly fashion. Larger-capacity UPS units may even support short-term operation of servers during brief outages. For extended power loss, a generator is required.

NOTE You can purchase two different types of UPSs—online and standby. An online UPS continuously powers the load through its inverter while simultaneously charging the internal battery. If the telecommunications room loses power, the computers stay powered up without missing a beat, at least until the battery runs out.

A *standby power supply* (SPS) supplies power directly from AC under normal conditions. When an outage occurs, internal circuitry switches the load to battery power. This switchover typically takes a few milliseconds, which is fast enough for most devices but can occasionally affect highly sensitive equipment.

Pay attention to how often your UPS kicks in. Don't assume the power coming from your physical plant (or power company) is okay. If your UPS comes on too often, it might be time to install a *voltage event recorder* (Figure 11-69), which, as its name implies, plugs into your power outlet and tracks the voltage over time. These devices often reveal interesting issues.

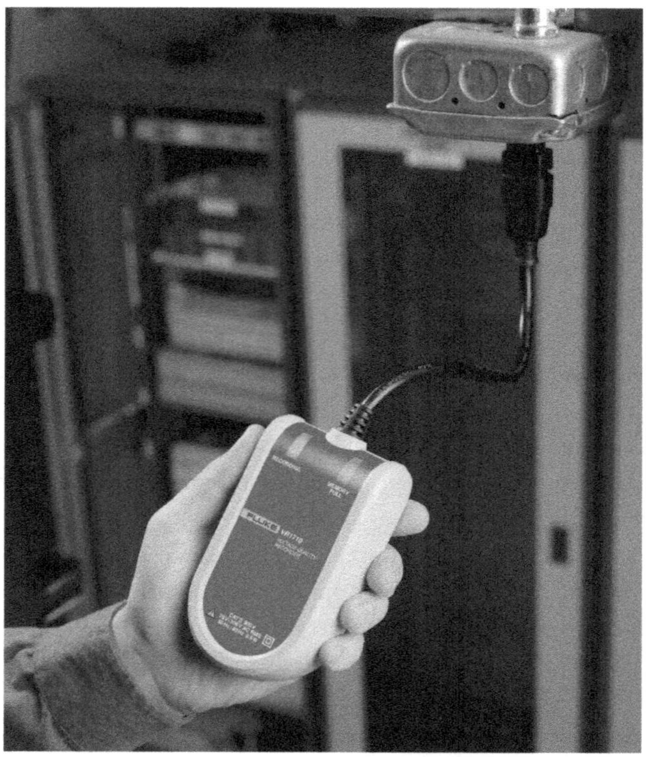

FIGURE 11-69 A voltage event recorder (photo courtesy of Fluke Networks)

The temperature in the telecommunications room should be maintained and monitored properly. If you lose the air conditioning, for example, and leave systems running, the equipment will overheat and shut down—sometimes with serious damage. To prevent this, all serious telecommunications rooms should have a UPS with a *temperature monitor*.

Likewise, you need to control the level of humidity in a telecommunications room. For just a few hundred dollars, you can install *environmental monitors* that keep a constant watch on humidity, temperature, and more. The devices cost little in comparison to the equipment in the telecommunications room that you're protecting.

TONERS

It would be nice to say that all cable installations are perfect and that over the years they won't tend to grow into horrific piles of spaghetti-like, unlabeled cables. In the real world, though, you might eventually find yourself having to locate or *trace* cables. Even in the best-planned networks, labels fall off ports and outlets, mystery cables appear behind walls, new cable runs are added, and rows and columns on patch panels are miscounted. Sooner or later, most network techs will have to be able to pick out one particular cable or port from a stack.

When the time comes to trace cables, network techs turn to a device called a toner for help. *Toner* is actually a generic term for two separate devices that are used together: a tone generator and a tone probe. The *tone generator* connects to the cable using alligator clips, tiny hooks, or a network jack, and it sends an electrical signal along the wire at a certain frequency. The *tone probe* emits a sound when it is placed near a cable connected to the tone generator. These two devices are often referred to by the brand-name Fox and Hound (Figure 11-70), a popular model of toner made by the Triplett Corporation.

To trace a cable, connect the tone generator to the known end of the cable in question, and then position the tone probe next to the other end of each cable that might be the right one. The tone probe makes a sound when it's placed next to the right cable. Some toners have one tone probe that works with multiple tone generators. Each generator emits a separate frequency, and the probe sounds a different tone for each one. Good-quality tone and probe kits typically cost around $100–$150, while higher-end digital tracers run several hundred dollars. Cheaper kits exist, but they're often unreliable. If you're responsible for supporting a network, investing in a dependable toner is worth it.

A good, medium-priced cable tester and a good toner are the most important tools for folks who must support, but not install, networks. As a final tip, be sure to bring along a few extra batteries—there's nothing worse than sitting on the top of a ladder holding a cable tester or toner that has just run out of juice!

FIGURE 11-70
Fox and Hound

TAPS

Cable can be tested with a device known as a *tap* that has three ports. The cable goes into the tap in one port. In another port you'd put another device like an oscilloscope, multimeter, or network analyzer. The last port continues the cable's propagation. The signal gets sent out where it would normally go, but in addition, it is duplicated to the port connected to a device that performs some analysis. Now you can analyze the signal—including voltage levels, timing, noise, interference, protocol behavior, and more—in real time without interrupting the normal data flow. In fiber networks, taps work a little differently. They often use an optical splitter that diverts a small percentage of the light signal to the monitoring port while letting the majority continue through the main link. This design enables non-intrusive monitoring of high-speed fiber connections while preserving signal integrity.

Chapter Review

Questions

1. Aside from outright breakage, what's the primary worry with bending a fiber-optic cable too much?
   - A. Attenuation
   - B. Bonding
   - C. Light leakage
   - D. Near-end crosstalk
2. When a signal is sent down one pair of wires in a four-pair UTP cable, what can happen to the other pairs?
   - A. They remain completely isolated.
   - B. They pick up some of the signal, causing crosstalk.
   - C. They reverse the signal direction.
   - D. They boost the signal on the transmitting pair.
3. What does a flickering activity light on a NIC indicate?
   - A. The NIC is not connected.
   - B. The NIC is receiving or sending network traffic.
   - C. The NIC is malfunctioning.
   - D. The network cable is unplugged.
4. A(n) ________________ organizes and protects the horizontal cabling in the telecommunications room.
   - A. Rack
   - B. Patch panel
   - C. Outlet
   - D. 110 jack
5. Which of the following would never be seen in an equipment rack?
   - A. Patch panel
   - B. UPS
   - C. PC
   - D. All of the above may be seen in an equipment rack.

6. What are patch cables used for? (Select two.)
   - **A.** To connect different telecommunications rooms.
   - **B.** To connect the patch panel to the switch.
   - **C.** As crossover cables.
   - **D.** To connect PCs to wall outlets.
7. Which of the following network technologies uses UTP cabling in a star topology?
   - **A.** Crosstalk
   - **B.** Fiber optics
   - **C.** 1000BASE-SX
   - **D.** 1000BASE-T
8. On your first day on the job, you get a call from the owner complaining that her network connection is down. A quick check of the central switch verifies that it's in good working order, as is the boss's PC. As luck would have it, your supervisor calls at just that time and tells you not to worry; she'll be by in a jiffy with her TDR to help root out the problem. What is she talking about?
   - **A.** Tune-domain resonator, her network tone generator
   - **B.** Time-detuning resonator, her network tester
   - **C.** Time-domain reflectometer, her network tester
   - **D.** Time-detail resource, her network schematic
9. What two devices together enable you to pick a single cable out of a stack of cables? (Select two.)
   - **A.** Tone aggregator
   - **B.** Tone binder
   - **C.** Tone generator
   - **D.** Tone probe
10. Rack-mounted equipment has a height measured in what units?
    - **A.** Mbps
    - **B.** MBps
    - **C.** Inches
    - **D.** U

Answers

1. **C.** Bending a fiber-optic cable too much can cause light leakage and thus loss or degradation of signal.
2. **B.** Crosstalk occurs when a signal in one pair of a UTP cable induces a voltage in another pair. Twisting the pairs at specific rates helps reduce this interference.
3. **B.** A flickering activity light shows that the NIC is actively transmitting or receiving data.
4. **B.** A patch panel organizes and protects the horizontal cabling in the telecommunications room.
5. **D.** All these devices may be found in equipment racks.
6. **B** and **D.** Patch cables are used to connect the patch panel to the switch and the PCs to the wall outlets.
7. **D.** 1000BASE-T uses UTP cabling in a star topology.
8. **C.** TDR stands for time-domain reflectometer, the generic term for a decent network tester that can determine locations of cable breaks, among other things.
9. **C** and **D.** A tone generator and tone probe work together to enable you to pick a single cable out of a stack of cables.
10. **D.** Rack-mounted equipment uses a height measurement known as a unit (U).

Wireless Networking

IN THIS CHAPTER, YOU WILL LEARN HOW TO

- Explain wireless networking standards
- Secure a Wi-Fi network
- Implement Wi-Fi
- Troubleshoot Wi-Fi
- Explain cellular networking
- Explain satellite networking

Every type of network covered thus far in the book assumes that your PCs connect to your network with some kind of physical cabling. Now it's time to cut the cord and look at the many technologies that collectively changed the way we use the internet: wireless networking.

Historical/Conceptual

You need to be careful when talking about wireless networking. Wireless is everywhere. It's in our phones and in our laptops. It's at home, work, and school. Wireless is so transparent and handy that we tend to forget that it isn't a single technology. There are a number of technologies that collectively make up wireless networking.

Let's start with the basics. Instead of a physical set of wires running among networked PCs, servers, printers, or what have you, a *wireless network* uses radio frequency (RF) waves to enable these devices to communicate with each other. Wireless technologies provide incredible flexibility and mobility.

NOTE Because the networking signal is freed from wires, you'll sometimes hear the term *unbounded media* to describe wireless networking.

For all their disconnected goodness, wireless networks have more similarities than differences with wired networks. Except for the first two OSI layers, wireless networks use the same protocols and everything else in Layers 3 through 7 as wired networks. What differs is the type of media—radio waves instead of cables—and the protocols for transmitting and accessing data. Different wireless networking solutions have come and gone in the past, but the wireless networking market these days is dominated by *Wi-Fi*, a family of protocols based on IEEE 802.11 standards.

This chapter looks first at the standards for modern wireless networks and then turns to implementing those networks. It concludes with a discussion on troubleshooting Wi-Fi and looks at two other types of wireless networking, cellular and satellite.

Test Specific

Wi-Fi Standards

Wi-Fi is by far the most widely adopted wireless networking type today, especially for accessing the internet. You'd be hard-pressed to find a location, workplace, or home that doesn't have Wi-Fi. Millions of private businesses and homes have wireless networks, and most public places, such as coffee shops and libraries, offer internet access through wireless networks.

NOTE Contrary to popular belief, Wi-Fi doesn't stand for *wireless fidelity* (like *Hi-Fi* stands for *high fidelity*). Wi-Fi doesn't stand for anything. According to Wi-Fi Alliance founding member Phil Belanger, who oversaw the name selection, it's just a name they chose. The marketing agency Interbrand presented the Wi-Fi Alliance with 10 options, and Wi-Fi was the winner. When board members had a problem with Wi-Fi not standing for anything, the organization added the tagline "The Standard for Wireless Fidelity," which was promptly abandoned. Belanger pointed out that since the organization had never developed standards (but rather interoperability certification and branding for the IEEE 802.11 standard) and Wi-Fi wasn't short for anything, the tagline was misleading from the start.

Wi-Fi technologies have been around since the late 1990s, supported and standardized under the umbrella IEEE 802.11 standard. Since then, the 802.11 standard has been continually updated through amendments with names like 802.11ac (and those names now have names themselves, like Wi-Fi 5). It's important for you to understand all these 802.11 amendments in detail, as well as the original 802.11 standard.

802.11

The *802.11* standard defines both how wireless devices communicate and how to secure that communication. The original 802.11 standard, now often referred to as *802.11-1997*, is no longer used, but it established the baseline features common to all subsequent Wi-Fi standards.

The 802.11-1997 standard defined certain features, such as a wireless NIC, special configuration software, and the capability to run in multiple styles of networks. In addition, 802.11-1997 defined how transmissions work, including radio signal frequencies, transmission methods, and collision avoidance. We'll look at all of these features and others throughout this section.

HARDWARE

Wireless networking hardware serves the same function as hardware used on wired PCs. Wireless NICs take data passed down from the upper OSI layers, encapsulate the data into frames, send the frames out on the network media in streams of 1s and 0s, and receive frames in streams of 1s and 0s sent from other computing devices. The only difference is that instead of charging up a network cable with electrical current or firing off pulses of light, these devices transmit and receive radio waves.

NOTE Wireless 802.11 frames have different fields and values than 802.3 Ethernet frames, although both encapsulate ARP frames and IP packets.

Wireless networking capabilities of one form or another are built into many modern computing devices. Almost all portable devices have built-in wireless capabilities. Desktop computers can easily go wireless by adding an expansion card. Figure 12-1 shows a wireless PCI Express (PCIe) Ethernet card.

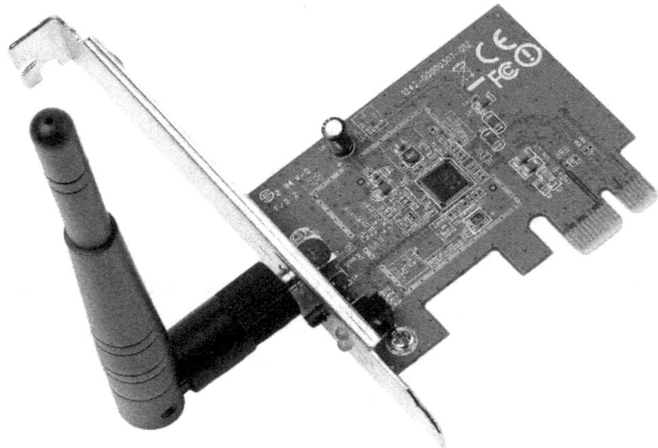

FIGURE 12-1 Internal PCIe wireless NIC

You can also add wireless network capabilities using USB wireless network adapters, an example of which is shown in Figure 12-2. The USB NICs have the added benefit of being *placeable*—that is, you can move them around to catch the wireless signal as strongly as possible, akin to moving the "rabbit ears" on old pre-cable television sets.

Is the wireless network adapter in all your devices the only hardware you need to create a wireless network? Well, back in the day people would sometimes connect a few laptops directly together (for example, to play games), and the answer was yes. Nowadays, however, that's not needed or even preferred. Furthermore, when you need to extend the capabilities of a wireless network—say, connecting a wireless network segment to a wired network—you need additional equipment. This typically means a wireless access point.

FIGURE 12-2 External USB wireless NIC

A *wireless access point* (WAP) is a device designed to provide networking and internet communications to wireless mobile devices. It receives wireless signals from one device and sends them to another. You can think of it as the switch of the wireless network, where wireless devices send traffic via the WAP rather than directly to one another. A WAP also can interconnect wireless devices with wired networks.

NOTE Many manufacturers drop the word *wireless* and simply call them *access points*. Furthermore, many sources abbreviate both forms, so you'll see both *WAP* and *AP*.

A basic WAP works at Layer 2 of the OSI model (although it also has Layer 1 components for wireless signal transmission). Many WAP manufacturers combine multiple devices into one box, however, to create a WAP with a built-in switch and/or router, all rolled into one and working at several OSI layers. The eero device shown in Figure 12-3 is an example of this type of combo device.

FIGURE 12-3
An eero device that acts as a WAP, switch, and router

SOFTWARE

Every wireless network adapter needs two pieces of software to function with an operating system: a device driver to talk to the wireless NIC and a configuration utility. Installing drivers for wireless networking devices is usually automatic these days, but you should always consult your vendor's instructions before popping that card into a slot.

You also need a utility for configuring how the wireless hardware connects to other wireless devices. Every operating system has built-in wireless clients for configuring these settings. Figure 12-4 shows the Windows 10 Wi-Fi configuration page in the Settings app. Using this utility, you can determine the *link state* (whether your wireless device is connected) and the *signal strength* (how well your wireless device is connecting to other devices). You can also configure items such as your wireless networking *mode*, security encryption, power-saving options, and so on. I'll cover each of these topics in detail later in this chapter.

You typically configure WAPs through browser-based setup utilities, especially outside an enterprise environment. There are command-line-based utilities as well. Cisco, for example, still includes console ports and supports a command line interface (CLI) on most devices to help support mass configuration, although now that is supported through WLAN controllers. The section "Implementing Wi-Fi" covers the configuration process a bit later in this chapter. For now, we'll turn to the different modes that wireless networks use.

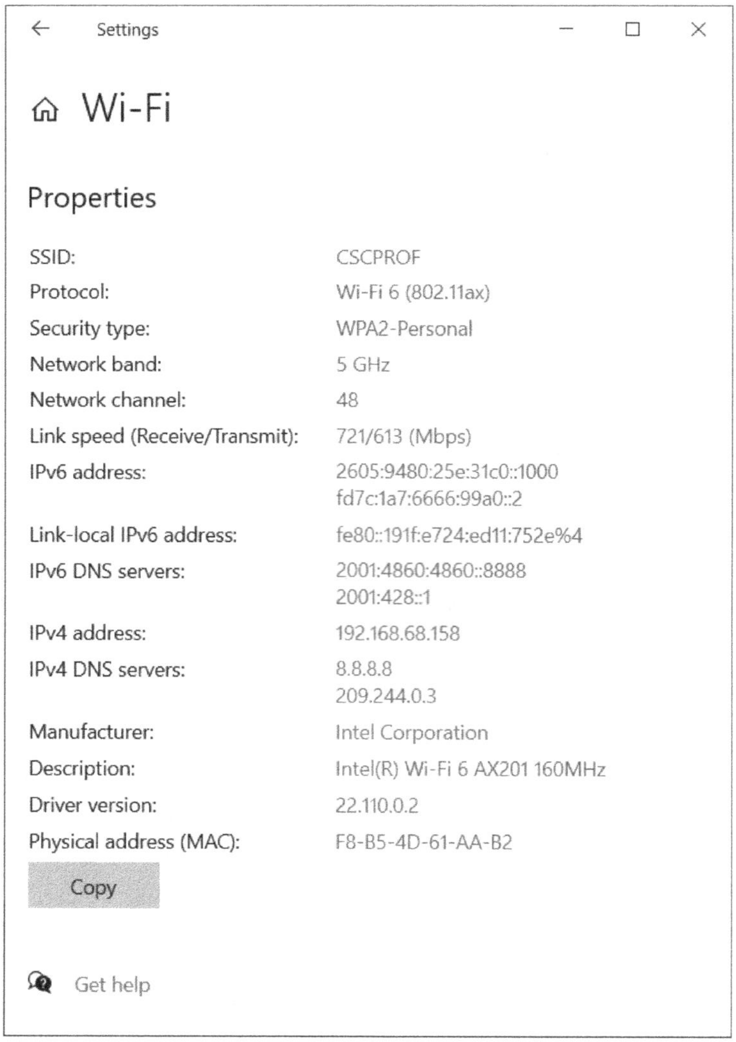

FIGURE 12-4 Wireless client configuration utility

NETWORK TYPES

There are four types of wireless network topologies: mesh networks, ad hoc, point-to-point, and infrastructure.

Mesh Networks

In a *mesh network*, each node connects to multiple nodes, which forms a self-healing, resilient network. Network traffic can pass through intermediary nodes before reaching the destination. This setup is very reliable, scales well, and can cover large areas. Examples include city-wide wireless mesh networks for public Wi-Fi as well as Google Nest Wi-Fi. These networks, however, require complex management and configuration, and latency can increase if traffic passes through many nodes.

Ad Hoc

In an *ad hoc* (sometimes called *peer-to-peer*) network, each wireless node is in direct contact with every other node in a decentralized free-for-all, as shown in Figure 12-5.

Two or more wireless nodes communicating in ad hoc mode form an *independent basic service set* (IBSS). This is a basic unit of organization in wireless networks. If you think of an IBSS as a wireless workgroup, you won't be far off the mark.

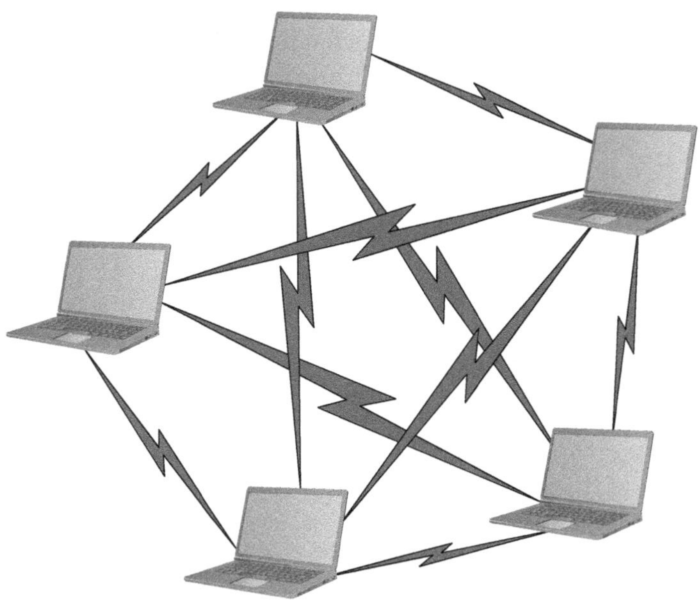

FIGURE 12-5 Wireless ad hoc mode network

Ad hoc mode networks work well for small groups of computers (fewer than a dozen or so) that need to transfer files or share printers. They're also good for temporary networks, such as study groups or business meetings. Even so, nowadays small groups of computers can connect through a WAP, which is quicker, easier, and more secure.

Hardly anyone uses an ad hoc mode network for day-to-day work, simply because you can't use it to connect to other networks, unless one of the machines is running Internet Connection Sharing (ICS) or some equivalent service. With their limited range, scalability, and performance, they're not the best choice to meet wireless needs.

Point-to-Point

A *point-to-point* network consists of a dedicated wireless link for exactly two devices, like a wireless bridge that connects two buildings across a street block. While this setup provides reliably high bandwidth and is more cost-effective than fiber cables, it connects only two nodes and requires a clear line of sight.

Infrastructure

A wireless network running in *infrastructure* mode uses one or more WAPs to connect the wireless network nodes centrally, as shown in Figure 12-6. This configuration is like the physical star topology of a wired network and creates a *wireless local area network* (WLAN). This network type is used in businesses and homes to connect laptops, tablets, printers, and more. Although the WAP represents a single point of failure, infrastructure deployments are easy to manage, scale well, and can be hardened for security.

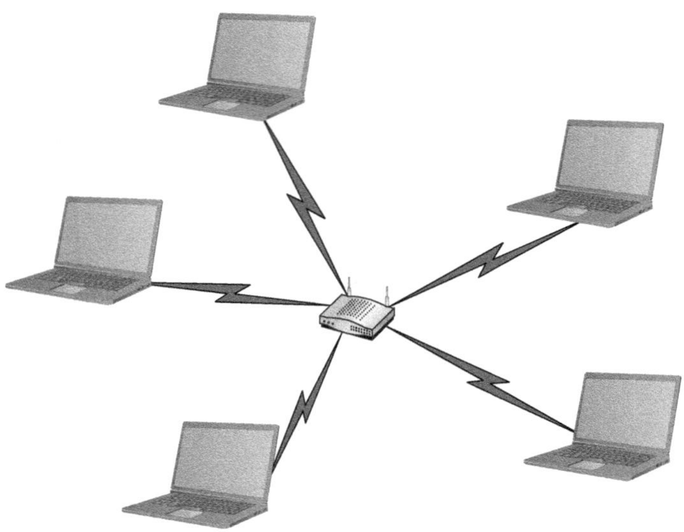

FIGURE 12-6 Wireless infrastructure mode network

You also use infrastructure mode to connect wireless network segments to wired segments. If you plan to set up a wireless network for many computing devices, or you need to have centralized control over the wireless network, use infrastructure mode.

A single WAP servicing a given area is called a *basic service set* (BSS). Adding more access points to extend the service area creates an *extended service set* (ESS).

> **NOTE** The early name for an infrastructure mode wireless network with more than one WAP was *extended basic service set*, but many techs drop the word *basic*. Accordingly, you'll see both EBSS and ESS, and either is correct.

Wireless networks running in infrastructure mode require a little more planning—such as where to place the WAPs to provide adequate coverage—than ad hoc mode networks (where the computers are just next to each other), and they provide a stable environment for permanent wireless network installations. Infrastructure mode is better suited to business networks or networks that need to share dedicated resources, such as internet connections and centralized databases. (See "Implementing Wi-Fi" later in this chapter for more details.)

RANGE

Wireless networking range is hard to define. You'll see most descriptions listed with qualifiers such as "*around* 150 feet" and "*about* 300 feet." Wireless range is greatly affected by environmental factors, such as interference from other wireless devices and solid objects.

The maximum ranges listed in the sections that follow are those presented by wireless manufacturers as the *theoretical* maximum ranges. In the real world, you'll achieve these ranges only under the most ideal circumstances. Cutting the manufacturer's listed range in half is often a better estimate of the true effective range.

BSSID, SSID, AND ESSID

Wireless devices connected into a network, whether ad hoc or infrastructure, require some way to identify that network. Frames bound for computers within the network need to go where they're supposed to go, even when you have overlapping Wi-Fi networks. The jargon gets a little heavy here, especially because marketing has come into the mix. Stay with me.

The *basic service set identifier* (BSSID) defines the most basic infrastructure mode network—a BSS of one WAP and one or more wireless clients. With such a simple network, the Wi-Fi folks didn't see any reason to create some new numbering or naming scheme, so they made the BSSID the same as the MAC address for the WAP. Simple! Ah, but what do you do about ad hoc networks that don't have a WAP? The nodes that connect in an IBSS randomly generate a 48-bit string of numbers that looks and functions just like a MAC address, and that BSSID goes in every frame.

You could, if required, discover the MAC address for the WAP in a BSS and manually type that into the network name field when setting up a wireless computer. But that causes two problems. First, people don't want to remember strings of 48 binary digits, even if translated out as 6 hexadecimal octets, like A9–45–F2–3E–CA–12. People want names. Second, how do you connect two or more computers together into an IBSS when the BSSID has to be randomly generated?

The Wi-Fi folks created another level of naming called a *service set identifier* (SSID), a standard name applied to the BSS or IBSS to help the connection happen. The SSID—sometimes called a *network name*—is up to a 32-bit identification string that's inserted into the header of each frame processed by a WAP. Every Wi-Fi device must share the same SSID to communicate in a single network. By default, a WAP advertises its existence by sending out a continuous *SSID broadcast*. It's the SSID broadcast that lets you see the wireless networks that are available on your wireless devices.

To really see the power of 802.11 in action, let's take it one step further into a Wi-Fi network that has multiple WAPs: an ESS. How do you determine the network name at this level? You use the SSID, but you apply it to the ESS as an *extended service set identifier* (ESSID). In an ESS, every WAP connects to a central switch or set of switches to become part of a single broadcast domain.

With multiple WAPs in an ESS, clients connect to whichever WAP has the strongest signal. As clients move through the space covered by the broadcast area, they change WAP connections seamlessly, a process called *roaming*.

When you configure a wireless device to connect to an ESS, you're technically using the ESSID rather than just the SSID, but most Wi-Fi manufacturers try to make it simple for you by just using the term *SSID*.

TRANSMISSION FREQUENCY

One of the biggest issues with wireless communication is the potential for interference from other wireless devices. To solve this, different wireless devices must operate in specific transmission frequencies. Knowing these wireless frequency ranges will help you troubleshoot interference issues from other devices operating in the same wireless band. The original 802.11 standards use either 2.4 GHz or 5.0 GHz radio frequencies.

TRANSMISSION METHODS

The original IEEE 802.11 wireless standard defined methods by which devices may communicate using *spread-spectrum* radio waves, which transmit data in small, discrete chunks over the different frequencies available within a certain frequency range.

The 802.11 standard defines three different spread-spectrum transmission methods: *direct-sequence spread-spectrum* (DSSS), *frequency-hopping spread-spectrum* (FHSS), and *orthogonal frequency-division multiplexing* (OFDM). DSSS sends data out on different frequencies at the same time, whereas FHSS sends data on one frequency at a time, constantly shifting (or *hopping*) frequencies. DSSS uses considerably more *bandwidth* than FHSS—around 22 MHz as opposed to 1 MHz. Compared to FHSS, DSSS is capable of greater data *throughput capacity* (the maximum rate at which a communication system can successfully transmit data), but it's also more prone to interference. OFDM is the latest of these three methods, better at dealing with interference, and is used on all but the earliest 802.11 networks.

CHANNELS

Every Wi-Fi network communicates on a *channel*, a portion of the available spectrum. The *channel width* (also known as *bandwidth*) determines the amount of frequency space on the radio spectrum that a wireless signal takes up. More data can be sent over wider channels, leading to faster speeds (good for clean environments), but narrow channels have more stability and less interference (good for congested areas). The 2.4 GHz band has widths of 20 MHz and 40 MHz. The 5 GHz band has widths of 20 MHz, 40 MHz, 80 MHz, and 160 MHz. The 5 GHz band has widths from 20 MHz to 320 MHz.

For the 2.4 GHz band, the 802.11 standard defines 14 channels of 20 MHz each (the channel width), but different countries limit exactly which channels may be used. In the United States, for example, a WAP using the 2.4 GHz band may use only channels 1 through 11. These channels have some overlap, so two nearby WAPs shouldn't use close channels like 6 and 7; many WAPs use channels 1, 6, or 11 for this reason. You can fine-tune a network by changing the channels on WAPs to avoid overlap with other nearby WAPs. This capability is especially important in environments with many wireless networks sharing the same physical space. See the section "Configuring a Consumer Access Point" later in this chapter for more details on channel utilization.

EXAM TIP You might get a question on the CompTIA Network+ exam about *regulatory impacts* on Wi-Fi channels. Governments strictly regulate which bands and channels Wi-Fi systems can use, as well as how much power devices can output. A specific example is 802.11h, a 2003 amendment for the IEEE 802.11 standard that appears in the exam objectives. Originally developed for Europe's 5 GHz band regulations, 802.11h now applies to many other countries and includes two main features. *Dynamic Frequency Selection* (DFS) detects any channel interference from radar systems, medical devices, and the like and automatically switches the network to a clear channel. *Transmit Power Control* (TPC) reduces the amount of RF output power to mitigate potential interference and stay within the established limits.

The 5.0 GHz and 6.0 GHz bands offer many more channels (around 40 each) than the 2.4 GHz band. However, different countries have wildly different rules for which channels may or may not be used. The versions of 802.11 that use the 5.0 and 6.0 GHz bands use automatic channel switching, so we don't need to worry about channels from a setup standpoint in these cases.

Band steering is the process in which dual-band devices are "steered away" from the 2.4 GHz frequency band in favor of a more capable and effective 5 GHz or 6 GHz band.

CSMA/CA

Because only a single device can use any network at a time in a physical bus topology, network nodes must have a way to access the network media without stepping on each other's frames. Wired Ethernet networks originally used *carrier-sense multiple access with collision detection* (CSMA/CD), introduced in Chapter 10, but Wi-Fi networks use *carrier-sense multiple access with collision avoidance* (CSMA/CA). Let's compare the two methods.

EXAM TIP Wired Ethernet networks used CSMA/CD. Wi-Fi networks use CSMA/CA.

How do multiple devices share network media, such as a cable? The process is fairly simple. Each device listens in on the network media by measuring the level of voltage currently on the wire. If the level is below the threshold, the device knows that it's clear to send data. If the level rises above a preset threshold, the device knows that the line is busy, and it must wait before sending data. Typically, the waiting period is the length of the current frame plus a short, predefined silence period called an *interframe gap* (IFG). So far, so good—but what happens when two devices both detect that the wire is free and try to send data simultaneously? As you might remember from Chapter 10, frames transmitted on the network from two different devices at the same time will corrupt each other's signals, causing a *collision*. Collisions are a fact of wireless networking life, and network nodes deal with them both reactively and proactively.

Modern wired networks use switches running in full-duplex mode (discussed in Chapter 4), so they don't have to worry about collisions. CSMA/CD is disabled with full-duplex mode. Wireless networks don't have this luxury.

With CSMA/CD, each sending node detected the collision and responded by generating a random timeout period, known as a *backoff*, during which it wouldn't try to send any more data on the network. Once the backoff period expired (remember that we're talking about only milliseconds here), the node went through the whole process again. This approach may not have been very elegant, but it got the job done.

CSMA/CD won't work for wireless networking because wireless devices simply can't detect collisions, for two reasons. First, radio is a half-duplex transmission method. Wireless devices cannot listen and send at the same time. Second, the hidden node problem is an issue on wireless networks. Consider wireless node A and wireless node B both sending a message to the WAP. In this case, each wireless node is in range of the WAP but not each other. Thus, when each "listens," neither detects the other. Since the WAP is in range of both wireless nodes, when A and B transmit to it simultaneously, a collision occurs.

Wireless networks needed another way to deal with potential collisions. The CSMA/CA access method, as the name implies, proactively takes steps to avoid collisions instead of addressing them reactively like CSMA/CD.

The 802.11 standard defines two methods for collision avoidance: *Distributed Coordination Function* (DCF) and *Point Coordination Function* (PCF). DCF, the only method currently implemented, specifies rules for sending data onto the network media. For instance, if a wireless network node detects that the network is busy, DCF defines a backoff period on top of the normal IFG wait period before a node can try to access the network again. DCF also requires that receiving nodes send an acknowledgment (ACK) for every frame that they process. The ACK also includes a value that tells other wireless nodes to wait a certain amount of time before trying to access the network media. This duration is based on how long the data frame takes to reach its destination based on its length and data rate. If the sending node doesn't receive an ACK, it retransmits the data frame until it gets a confirmation that the packet reached its destination.

NOTE Current CSMA/CA devices use the Distributed Coordination Function (DCF) method for collision avoidance. Optionally, they can use Request to Send/Clear to Send (RTS/CTS) messages to minimize collisions.

The 802.11-1997 standard, summarized in Table 12-1, was the very oldest wireless standard. Additions to 802.11 over time have improved speeds and taken advantage of other frequency bands.

TABLE 12-1 802.11-1997 summary

STANDARD	FREQUENCY	SPECTRUM	SPEED	RANGE	BACKWARD COMPATIBILITY
802.11-1997	2.4 GHz	DSSS	2 Mbps	~300'	802.11

NOTE As you read about the many speeds listed for 802.11, keep in mind that wireless networking has a tremendous amount of overhead and latency. WAPs send out almost continuous streams of packets that do nothing more than advertise their existence or maintain connections. Wireless devices may sometimes stall due to processing or timeouts.

All this overhead means that only a percentage of the total throughput speed is achieved in real data bits getting to the applications that need them. The *actual* rate of useful data transmission is called the *goodput* of the wireless network.

802.11b

The first widely adopted Wi-Fi standard—*802.11b*—supported data throughput of up to 11 Mbps and a range of up to 300 feet under ideal conditions. The main downside to using 802.11b was its frequency. The 2.4 GHz frequency is a crowded place, so you were more likely to run into interference from other wireless devices. Table 12-2 gives you the 802.11b summary.

TABLE 12-2 802.11b summary

STANDARD	FREQUENCY	SPECTRUM	SPEED	RANGE	BACKWARD COMPATIBILITY
802.11b	2.4 GHz	DSSS	11 Mbps	~300'	n/a

802.11a

The *802.11a* standard differed from the other 802.11-based standards in significant ways. Foremost was that it operated in a different frequency range, 5.0 GHz—much less crowded than the 2.4 GHz range, reducing the chance of interference from devices such as telephones and microwave ovens. Too much signal interference can increase *latency*, making the network sluggish and slow to respond. Running in the 5.0 GHz range greatly reduces this problem.

NOTE Despite the *a* designation for this extension to the 802.11 standard, 802.11a was available on the market *after* 802.11b.

The 802.11a standard also offered considerably greater throughput than 802.11b, with speeds up to 54 Mbps. Range, however, suffered somewhat and topped out at about 150 feet. Despite the superior speed of 802.11a, it never enjoyed the popularity of 802.11b. Table 12-3 gives you the 802.11a summary.

TABLE 12-3 802.11a summary

STANDARD	FREQUENCY	SPECTRUM	SPEED	RANGE	BACKWARD COMPATIBILITY
802.11a	5.0 GHz	OFDM	54 Mbps	~150'	n/a

802.11g

The *802.11g* standard offered data transfer speeds equivalent to 802.11a—up to 54 Mbps—and the wider 300-foot range of 802.11b. More importantly, 802.11g was backward compatible with 802.11b because they both used the 2.4 GHz band, so the same 802.11g WAP could service both 802.11b and 802.11g wireless nodes.

If an 802.11g network had only 802.11g devices connected, the network ran in *native mode* (at up to 54 Mbps), whereas when 802.11b devices connected, the network dropped down to *mixed mode* (all communication ran up to only 11 Mbps). Table 12-4 gives you the 802.11g summary.

TABLE 12-4 802.11g summary

STANDARD	FREQUENCY	SPECTRUM	SPEED	RANGE	BACKWARD COMPATIBILITY
802.11g	2.4 GHz	OFDM	54 Mbps	~300'	802.11b

Later 802.11g manufacturers incorporated *channel bonding* into their devices, enabling the devices to use two channels for transmission. Channel bonding is not part of the 802.11g standard, but rather proprietary technology pushed by various companies to increase the throughput of their wireless networks. Both the NIC and WAP, therefore, had to be from the same company for channel bonding to work.

802.11n

The *802.11n* standard brought several improvements to Wi-Fi networking, including faster speeds and new antenna technology implementations. The Wi-Fi Alliance backnamed 802.11n to *Wi-Fi 4*.

> **EXAM TIP** With the announcement of 802.11ax in 2018, the Wi-Fi Alliance added a fun marketing term, Wi-Fi 6, and then *retroactively* named earlier standards Wi-Fi 4 (as noted here) and Wi-Fi 5 (which you'll read about next). You might see either the standard names (such as 802.11n) or the Wi-Fi Alliance names (such as Wi-Fi 4) on the CompTIA Network+ exam.

The 802.11n specification requires all but handheld devices to use multiple antennas to implement a feature called *multiple input/multiple output* (MIMO), which enables the devices to make multiple simultaneous connections called *streams*. With up to four antennas, 802.11n devices can achieve excellent speeds. They also implement channel bonding, combining two 20 MHz channels into a single 40 MHz channel to increase throughput even more. (The official standard supports throughput of up to 600 Mbps, although practical implementation drops that down substantially.)

Many 802.11n WAPs employ *transmit beamforming*, a multiple-antenna technology that helps get rid of *dead spots*—places where the radio signal just does not penetrate at all—or at least mitigate them. The antennas adjust the signal once the WAP discovers a client to optimize the radio signal.

Like 802.11g, 802.11n WAPs can support earlier, slower 802.11b/g devices. The problem with supporting these older types of 802.11 is that 802.11n WAPs need to encapsulate 802.11n frames into 802.11b or 802.11g frames. This adds some overhead to the process. Adding any 802.11b devices to the network causes some slowdown overall, primarily because the faster devices have to wait for the slower devices to communicate.

To handle these issues, 802.11 WAPs transmit in three different modes, also known as *connection types*: legacy, mixed, and greenfield.

Legacy mode means the 802.11n WAP sends out separate packets just for legacy devices. This is a terrible way to utilize 802.11n but was added as a stopgap measure if the other modes didn't work. In *mixed mode*, also often called *high-throughput* or *802.11a-ht/802.11g-ht*, the WAP sends special packets that support the older standards yet also improve the speed of those standards via 802.11n's wider bandwidth. *Greenfield mode* is exclusively for 802.11n-only wireless networks; the WAP processes only 802.11n frames. Dropping support for older devices gives greenfield mode the best goodput but removes backward compatibility.

Table 12-5 summarizes 802.11n.

TABLE 12-5 802.11n summary

STANDARD	FREQUENCY	SPECTRUM	SPEED	RANGE	BACKWARD COMPATIBILITY
802.11n	2.4 GHz[1]	OFDM (QAM)	100+ Mbps	~300'	802.11b/g/n[2]

[1] Dual-band 802.11n devices could function simultaneously at both 2.4 and 5.0 GHz bands.

[2] Many dual-band 802.11n WAPs supported 802.11a devices as well as 802.11b/g/n devices. This was not part of the standard, but something manufacturers implemented.

802.11ac

802.11ac is a natural expansion of the 802.11n standard, incorporating even more streams, 80 MHz and 160 MHz channels, and higher speed. To avoid device density issues in the 2.4 GHz band, 802.11ac uses only the 5.0 GHz band. (See "Existing Wireless Networks" later in this chapter for more on dealing with device density.) The Wi-Fi Alliance backnamed 802.11ac to *Wi-Fi 5*. Table 12-6 summarizes 802.11ac.

TABLE 12-6 802.11ac summary

STANDARD	FREQUENCY	SPECTRUM	SPEED	RANGE	BACKWARD COMPATIBILITY
802.11ac	5.0 GHz	OFDM (QAM)	Up to 1 Gbps	~300'	802.11a

Current versions of 802.11ac include a version of MIMO called *multiuser MIMO* (MU-MIMO). MU-MIMO enables a WAP to transmit to multiple users simultaneously.

NOTE For a transmitting method, the 802.11n and 802.11ac devices use a version of OFDM called *quadruple-amplitude modulated* (QAM).

802.11ax

In 2021, IEEE released the *802.11ax* standard, which brings improvements in high-density areas, like stadiums and conference halls. Marketed as *Wi-Fi 6* (operating at the 2.4 GHz and 5 GHz bands) and *Wi-Fi 6E* (operating at the 6.0 GHz band), 802.11ax implements *orthogonal frequency-division multiple access* (OFDMA) to increase overall network throughput by as much as 400 percent and decrease latency by 75 percent compared to 802.11ac. Table 12-7 summarizes 802.11ax.

TABLE 12-7 802.11ax summary

STANDARD	FREQUENCIES	SPECTRUM	SPEED	RANGE	BACKWARD COMPATIBILITY
802.11ax	2.4 GHz, 5.0 GHz, 6.0 GHz	OFDMA (1024-QAM)	Up to 10 Gbps	~300'	802.11a, 802.11b, 802.11g, 802.11n, 802.11ac

The range of 802.11ax is similar to previous Wi-Fi standards of ~300 feet because of limitations on power by the US Federal Communications Commission (FCC). That doesn't tell the whole story, though. Improvements in the standard mean the *throughput* at that range is vastly superior to its predecessors.

802.11be

The 802.11be standard, known as Extremely High Throughput (EHT), was approved in September 2024 and formally published in July 2025. Marketed as Wi-Fi 7, it operates across the 2.4 GHz, 5 GHz, and 6 GHz bands and builds on Wi-Fi 6/6E with major enhancements.

In early 2023, before the standard was even finalized, stable draft versions were already available and Wi-Fi 7–branded devices began emerging. This standard is designed to support a greater number of simultaneous connections while delivering faster communication speeds, lower latency, and improved efficiency and stability.

Applications that stand to benefit most include virtual reality (VR), augmented reality (AR), cloud computing, high-definition video streaming, and connectivity in crowded public venues such as stadiums.

However, there is little reason to purchase a Wi-Fi 7 router unless you also own one or more Wi-Fi 7–capable devices. While the standard is backward compatible, older devices cannot take advantage of its new capabilities. With up to four times the throughput of Wi-Fi 6/6E (802.11ax) and as much as a 20 percent boost in peak performance, 802.11be represents a major leap forward in wireless networking.

Table 12-8 summarizes 802.11be.

TABLE 12-8 802.11be summary

STANDARD	FREQUENCIES	SPECTRUM	SPEED	RANGE	BACKWARD COMPATIBILITY
802.11be	2.4 GHz, 5.0 GHz, 6.0 GHz	EHT-OFDMA	Up to 46.1 Gbps	~300'	802.11a, 802.11b, 802.11g, 802.11n, 802.11ac, 802.11ax

802.11bn

The successor to the successor of the current Wi-Fi standard, *802.11bn/Wi-Fi 8*—also known as *Ultra High Reliability* (UHR)—is already being planned for May 2028! With its potential speeds of 100 Gbps, you'll see wireless transmission exceed copper Ethernet's maximum transmission speed of 40 Gbps. Stay tuned for further details.

WPS

By around 2006, 802.11 was everywhere and was starting to get popular for non-PC devices, such as printers, scanners, and speakers. The challenge with these devices was that they lacked any kind of interface to make it easy to configure the wireless settings.

To address this issue, the wireless industry created a special standard called *Wi-Fi Protected Setup* (WPS). WPS works primarily in two modes (push button and PIN); other modes like USB and NFC were defined in the specification but are rarely used. With the push button method, you press a button on one device (all WPS-compatible devices have a physical or virtual push button) and then press the WPS button on the other device. That's it. The two devices automatically configure themselves on an encrypted connection.

The PIN method is for connecting a PC to a WPS device (usually a WAP). You press the button on the WAP, locate the SSID on your device, and then enter an eight-digit PIN as the WPA personal shared key (more on WPA shortly). All WPS WAPs have the PIN printed on the device.

WPS is very easy to use, but it's susceptible to different forms of *WPS attacks*. By design, the WPS PINs are short, so bad actors focus their attacks on hacking the PINs to gain access to the network and launch further attacks on network devices. Keeping these actors off the network is the first step, so next we'll look at ways of securing Wi-Fi networks.

Wi-Fi Security

Originally, one of the biggest problems with wireless networking devices was that right out of the box they provided *no* security. Vendors went out of their way to make setting up their devices easy, so usually the only thing you had to do to join a wireless network was to turn on your wireless devices and let them find each other. Thankfully, most initial setup wizards for wireless networking devices now require you to configure encryption and change the default password.

We need to use a number of techniques to make a wireless network secure, to *harden* it from malicious things and people. Wireless security is network hardening. Network hardening techniques that apply to all kinds of networks will be discussed in Chapter 17.

NOTE All the methods used in wireless network security—authentication, encryption, MAC filtering—can be considered network hardening techniques.

You also need to consider that your network's data frames float through the air on radio waves instead of zipping safely along wrapped up inside network cabling. What's to stop an unscrupulous network tech with the right equipment from grabbing those frames out of the air and reading that data?

Wi-Fi has gone through numerous security techniques and authentication and encryption protocols and implementations since the original 802.11 rollout. This section starts with a brief review of encryption, then examines the ever-evolving security protocols, finishing with a discussion on a few other more or less effective security measures.

Data Encryption

Encrypting data packets enables wireless network security. *Encryption* electronically scrambles data packets and locks them with an encryption key before transmitting them onto the wireless network. The receiving network device must possess the decryption key to unscramble the packet and process the data. Thus, a hacker who grabs any data frames out of the air can't read them without the decryption key. Enabling wireless encryption through WPA2 or WPA3 (discussed shortly) provides a good level of security to data packets in transit.

WEP

The granddaddy of wireless security, *Wired Equivalent Privacy* (WEP) used a 64- or 128-bit encryption algorithm to scramble data packets. WEP sounded great on paper, but in practice it proved to be a horrible failure. Even with the strongest encryption enabled, WEP wasn't a particularly robust security solution. In fact, today WEP can be cracked in under a minute with just a regular laptop and open source software. The bottom line with WEP? Don't ever use it today.

WPA

Needless to say, the Wi-Fi developers scrambled to find a fix for the flaws in WEP. A full replacement called *802.11i* (discussed in the upcoming "WPA2" section) was designed to address the problems with WEP and to provide proper authentication. But the standard took a while to complete, so the wireless industry implemented an intermediate fix, *Wi-Fi Protected Access* (WPA), that adopted some features of the still-in-development 802.11i standard to address some of the weaknesses of WEP. WPA supports authentication using *Extensible Authentication Protocol* (EAP).

EAP

EAP was designed to resolve one of the great challenges to authentication: getting the two ends of the authentication process to handle the many different types of authentication options. Even though *Point-to-Point Protocol* (PPP) pretty much owned the username/password authentication business for a time, proprietary forms of authentication using smart cards or tokens, certificates, and so on began to show up on the market, threatening to drop practical authentication into a huge mess of competing standards.

EAP is a single standard that allows two devices to authenticate. Despite the name, EAP is not a protocol in the classic sense, but rather a PPP wrapper that EAP-compliant applications can use to accept one of many types of authentication. Although EAP is a general-purpose authentication wrapper, its only substantial use is in wireless networks. EAP comes in various types, but only seven types are commonly used today:

- **EAP-PSK** Easily the most popular form of authentication used in wireless networks today, EAP-PSK (Pre-shared key) is nothing more than a shared secret code that's stored on both the wireless access point and the wireless client, and encrypted through the powerful Advanced Encryption Standard (AES, covered in Chapter 17 and shown in the Encryption Type field in Figure 12-7).
- **EAP-TLS** EAP with Transport Layer Security (TLS) defines the use of a *Remote Authentication Dial-In User Service* (RADIUS) server as well as mutual authentication, requiring certificates on both the server and every client. On the client side, a smart card may be used in lieu of a certificate. Although its client-side certificate requirement is an administrative challenge, EAP-TLS is very robust and used by the most secure wireless networks. EAP-TLS is used only on wireless networks, but TLS is used on over 95 percent of websites today. RADIUS will be described momentarily.
- **EAP-TTLS** EAP-TTLS (Tunneled TLS) is similar to EAP-TLS but can use a single server-side certificate. EAP-TTLS, selected in Figure 12-7, is very common for more secure wireless networks.
- **EAP-MS-CHAPV2** More commonly known as Protected EAP (PEAP), EAP-MS-CHAPv2 uses a password function based on MS-CHAPv2 with the addition of an encrypted TLS tunnel similar to EAP-TLS. This is the most common implementation

of EAP, since it can interface with an Active Directory domain controller that has the credentials for users already in place.

- **EAP-MD5** This is a very simple version of EAP that uses only MD5 hashes (MD5 was broken in 2008) to transfer authentication credentials. EAP-MD5 is weak and the least used of all the versions of EAP described.
- **LEAP** Lightweight EAP (LEAP) is a proprietary EAP authentication used almost exclusively by Cisco wireless products. LEAP is an interesting combination of MS-CHAP authentication between a wireless client and a RADIUS server.
- **EAP-FAST** EAP-FAST (Flexible Authentication via Secure Tunneling) is Cisco's replacement for LEAP. All current operating systems support EAP-FAST (assuming the right software is installed).

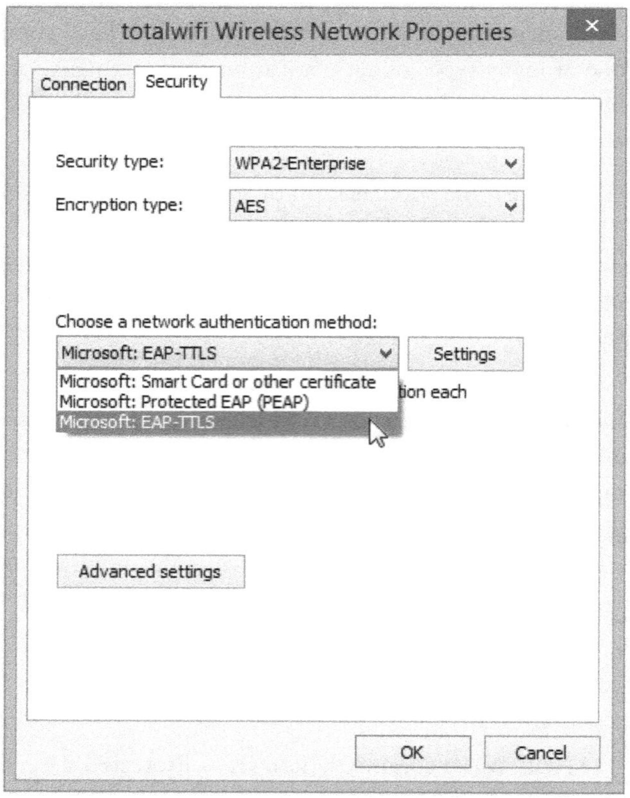

FIGURE 12-7 Setting the EAP authentication scheme

802.1X

EAP was a huge success and almost overnight provided a one-stop-shop methodology for those who needed point-to-point authentication. EAP was so successful that there was a cry to develop an EAP solution for Ethernet networks. This solution is called 802.1X. Whereas traditional EAP is nothing more than an authentication method wrapped in PPP, 802.1X gets rid of the PPP (Ethernet is not a point-to-point protocol) and instead puts the EAP information inside an Ethernet frame.

802.1X is a port-based authentication network access control mechanism for both wired and wireless networks. In other words, it's a complete authentication standard designed to force devices to go through a full process of authentication, authorization, and accounting (AAA, covered in Chapter 17) to be able to send traffic into a physical switch port or through an access point.

Before 802.1X, someone could just plug a cable into a switch and get access to a network, potentially sending and receiving traffic they shouldn't. 802.1X prevented them from even getting in the door until they were authenticated and authorized.

WPA-Enterprise uses 802.1X to provide a very robust authentication system using a RADIUS server and EAP. A *RADIUS server* either stores usernames and passwords or, more commonly today, consults Active Directory for authentication. It functions like a typical server, but the remote aspect of it requires you to learn new jargon.

NOTE Although RADIUS stands for *Remote Authentication Dial-In User Service*, dial-in isn't a requirement or even the way it operates today.

Here's how it works. The client wired or wireless computer, called a *supplicant*, contacts the *authenticator*—which is a switch for wired connections (see Figure 12-8) or an access point for wireless infrastructures (see Figure 12-9)—and requests permission to access the network. The authenticator collects the supplicant's username and password and then contacts the *authentication server* (the RADIUS server) to see if the supplicant appears in the server's security database. If the supplicant appears and the username and password are correct, the authentication server sends a message back to the supplicant, through the WAP, with an Access-Accept message and an Authenticator section that proves the packet came from the authentication server. Then the remote user gets access to the network resources.

EAP over LAN (EAPOL) frames carry the EAP messages from the supplicant to the authenticator on wired connections, while *EAP over Wireless* (EAPOW) frames carry the EAP messages from the supplicant to the authenticator over a wireless infrastructure. After the authenticator decapsulates the EAP message, it reencapsulates the EAP with RADIUS and sends it on to the authentication server.

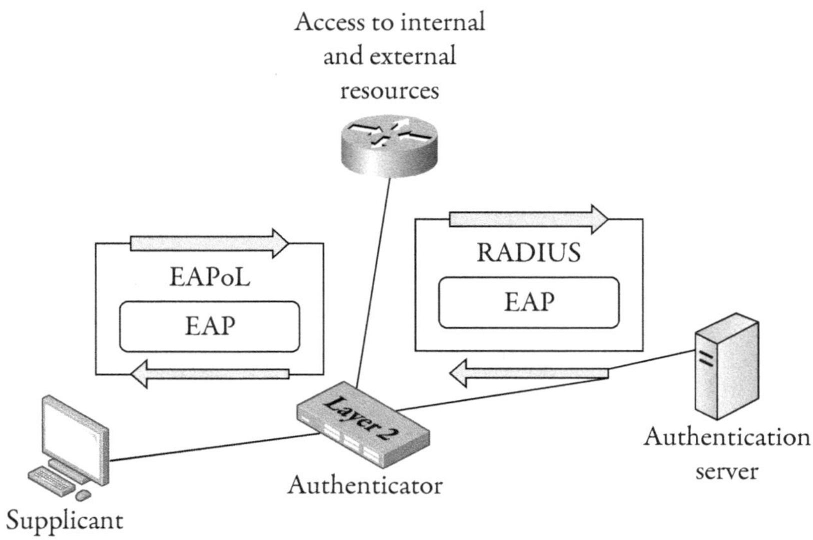

FIGURE 12-8 802.1X wired

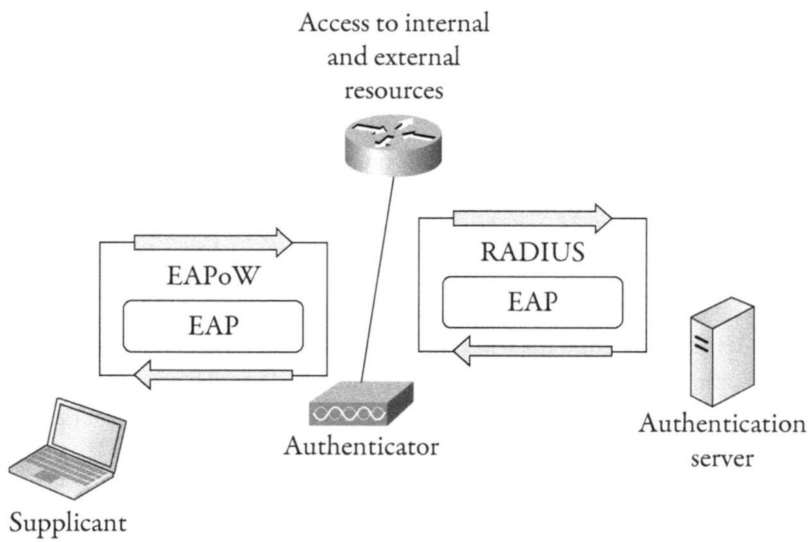

FIGURE 12-9 802.1X wireless

TKIP

WPA enhances wireless security by using the Temporal Key Integrity Protocol (TKIP), which provides dynamic encryption key generation (issuing unique keys for each user and session) and an encryption key integrity-checking feature (ensuring that keys and packets haven't been tampered with).

TKIP works on top of the existing WEP encryption scheme. It's not a complete replacement for WEP and still uses RC4 for cipher initialization. TKIP added a 128-bit encryption key that seemed unbreakable when first introduced. Within four years of its introduction, however, researchers showed methods by which hackers could bypass WPA security almost as easily as WEP. Even with the enhancements offered by EAP, 802.1X, and TKIP, it was clear that a more robust solution was needed to secure wireless networks.

NOTE The term *TKIP-RC4* was used in technical, academic, and cybersecurity contexts. It emphasizes the fact that WPA's TKIP relies on RC4 for encryption. Consumer-facing materials, like the Wi-Fi Alliance documentation or router manuals, used either the term *WPA with TKIP* or *WPA-TKIP*.

WPA2

Wi-Fi Protected Access 2 (WPA2) implemented the full IEEE 802.11i standard to add much-needed security features, including 802.1X. 802.11i also replaced TKIP-RC4 with the much more robust *CCMP-AES*, a 128-bit block cipher that's much tougher to crack.

NOTE CCMP stands for *Counter Mode Cipher Block Chaining Message Authentication Code Protocol*. Whew! That's why we commonly just use the initials CCMP. As mentioned earlier, AES stands for *Advanced Encryption Standard*.

Implementing the full 802.11i standard took time because most of the installed Wi-Fi hardware couldn't be updated to handle AES encryption. WPA held the title of "most secure wireless option" for several years.

Eventually, enough devices could support AES that the full 802.11i standard was implemented as *Wi-Fi Protected Access 2* (WPA2). A "WPA2-compliant device" is just a marketing term for a device that fully supports the 802.11i standard. WPA2 is not hack proof, but it offers a much tougher encryption standard that stops the casual hacker cold.

The most common way to set up WPA2 encryption is to use a simple version called *WPA2 Pre-shared key* (PSK), or *WPA2-Personal*. Basically, with the PSK version, you create a secret key that must be added to any device that is going to be on that SSID. There is no user authentication with WPA2-PSK; rather, the authentication is for any device that knows the PSK. Even with the other EAP methods, not all of them are tied to user identity.

WPA2 attacks can happen, especially with wireless networks using WPA2-Personal passphrases. The attacks use sophisticated methods that make assumptions about the passphrases themselves, as well as the fact that certain passphrases are used quite often. The most important thing to do to prevent these attacks from succeeding is to use long passphrases (16 or more characters), thus making the network hard to crack. Otherwise, you need authentication. If you want authentication, you move into what most wireless folks will call an enterprise setup. For example, when you use a RADIUS server for authentication with WPA2 to create an amazingly secure wireless network, it gets a fancy name: *WPA2-Enterprise*.

EXAM TIP You might be asked a question that explores the two encryption options for WPA2-Personal, AES or TKIP. WPA2-Enterprise also has the same two options. Definitely use AES. TKIP is deprecated, and you shouldn't ever use it today.

WPA3

Wi-Fi Protected Access 3 (WPA3) addresses weakness in WPA2's direct use of the Wi-Fi password to encrypt network traffic. WPA3 replaces WPA2's PSK with Simultaneous Authentication of Equals (SAE), a key exchange based on the Diffie–Hellman key exchange algorithm that generates unique encryption keys between each client and WAP. This makes it difficult for an attacker to break the encryption key and capture Wi-Fi traffic right out of the air. The Wi-Fi Alliance announced and started certifying devices that use WPA3 in 2018, although industry adoption has been slow.

EXAM TIP WPA3 appears in the CompTIA Network+ exam objectives list for the first time.

Additional Security Measures

Wireless networks have tried other techniques to secure networks beyond protocols for authentication and encryption. All seem plausibly effective in principle, but in practice, some fail, and some help. We'll look at SSID broadcast disabling, MAC address filtering, isolation of networks, captive portals, and geofencing.

SSID BROADCAST DISABLING

An early "security" suggestion was to disable the SSID broadcast. The theory was that only people who knew the SSID could connect, thus excluding the bad guys. This *security through obscurity* concept fails miserably at providing any security at all. Any wireless sniffing device will almost immediately discover "hidden" SSIDs. In practice, disabling SSID broadcast only makes it harder for legitimate users to access a wireless network.

MAC ADDRESS FILTERING

Most WAPs support *MAC address filtering*, a method that enables you to limit access to your network based on the physical addresses of wireless NICs. MAC address filtering creates a type of "accepted users" list—an *access control list* (ACL)—to restrict access to your wireless network. This is a common mitigation technique for undesired access to a network. A table called a *whitelist* is stored in the WAP and specifies the MAC addresses that are permitted to participate in the wireless network. Any network frames that don't contain the MAC address of a node in the whitelist are rejected.

EXAM TIP A WAP's access control list has *nothing* to do with the ACL in NTFS; it's just the same term used for two different things.

Many WAPs also enable you to deny specific MAC addresses from logging on to the network, creating a *blacklist*. This works great in close quarters, such as apartments or office buildings, where your wireless network signal goes beyond your perimeter. You can check the WAP and see the MAC addresses of every node that connects to your network. Check that list against the list of your computers, and you can readily spot any interlopers. Putting an offending MAC address in the "deny" column effectively blocks that system from piggybacking onto your wireless connection.

EXAM TIP MAC address filtering with a whitelist means you allow only specific computers to join the network. When you deny specific computers, you create a blacklist. Whitelisting and blacklisting are both labor-intensive processes, but whitelisting far more so.

Although MAC address filtering works, both whitelisting and blacklisting require way too much work for a network administrator and thus offer little practical security. Plus, a hacker can very easily *spoof* a MAC address—make the NIC report a legitimate address rather than its own—and access the network. Worse, a hacker doesn't have to connect to your network to grab your network traffic out of thin air! Avoid MAC address filtering; it offers no real security.

NETWORK ISOLATION

You can set up *wireless client isolation* or *guest network* isolation on better wireless access points to protect the rest of your network. Both features work similarly, blocking access to other wireless clients and the wired network while allowing internet access. In a typical Wi-Fi setup, every wireless client is part of the same WLAN and can communicate with all the others. Isolation blocks this feature, making it ideal for the public portion of a wireless network. Figure 12-10 shows an access point configured for a guest network.

CAPTIVE PORTALS

Many public facilities (such as airports) employ *captive portals* to control access to their public Wi-Fi networks *and* control the amount of bandwidth each user can use. An attempt to connect to the network opens a web browser that insists you follow the Terms of Service (ToS) and Acceptable Use Policy (AUP). Depending on how the organization sets it up, that captive

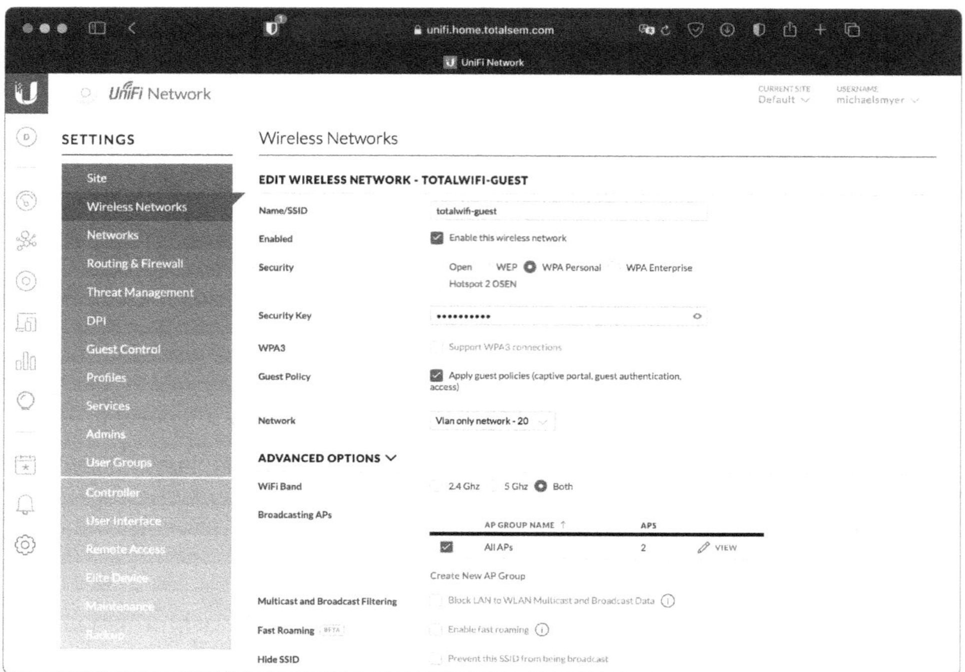

FIGURE 12-10 Guest network setting

portal can result in a seemingly slow connection. The reason is that all outbound traffic is initially intercepted and redirected to the captive portal page for acceptance of the ToS or for authentication. Once you have successfully authenticated through the portal, however, your device's traffic is allowed through and your connection speed shouldn't be impacted. If the underlying router or firewall is underpowered for the network size, you may experience slower performance, but this is the result of the network infrastructure and not the portal itself. Also keep in mind that higher security standards in your web browser can block captive portal content and thus your access to the network.

GEOFENCING

Geofencing uses various wireless methods—Wi-Fi, Bluetooth, cellular networks, Global Positioning System (GPS)—to create a perimeter or boundary around a specific physical area. Geofencing can be used to trigger alerts in several ways. Someone with an unauthorized smartphone stepping inside the boundary, for example, can raise a flag. Likewise, a person with a smartphone specifically tied to a system walking outside the boundary can stop the phone's access to the system.

The widespread use of mobile devices, which constantly move between multiple wireless networks, makes geofencing challenging. With a user's location constantly changing and signals fluctuating across networks, internet-connected devices (for example, smart lights) must continuously detect and track smartphones to determine whether to turn on or off. Geofencing is a moving target that requires systems that can adapt in real time to maintain accurate location-based control.

Enterprise Wireless

A simple BSSID or ESSID is incredibly easy to set up. You can buy a few cheap WAPs from your local store, connect them to a switch, use a web interface to configure each one, and start connecting clients. Inexpensive Small Office/Home Office (SOHO) WAPs and wireless routers have been around so long—almost as long as 802.11 itself—that this is what "wireless network" means for many of us.

But as wireless networks become more important, complex, and busy, the cheap SOHO boxes just aren't going to work anymore. When you want dependable, robust, secure, administrable wireless networks, you need enterprise-class wireless equipment. In general, an enterprise wireless device differs from a SOHO device in five areas: robust device construction, enterprise wireless administration, VLAN pooling, and Power over Ethernet.

Robust Device Construction

If you compare a typical SOHO WAP to an enterprise WAP, you'll notice immediately that the enterprise WAP is made of better materials (often metal instead of plastic). Enterprise WAPs for the most part will also be more configurable. For example, most enable you to swap out antennas and radios, so you can upgrade them to the latest technologies without having to replace them altogether. Figure 12-11 shows an enterprise WAP.

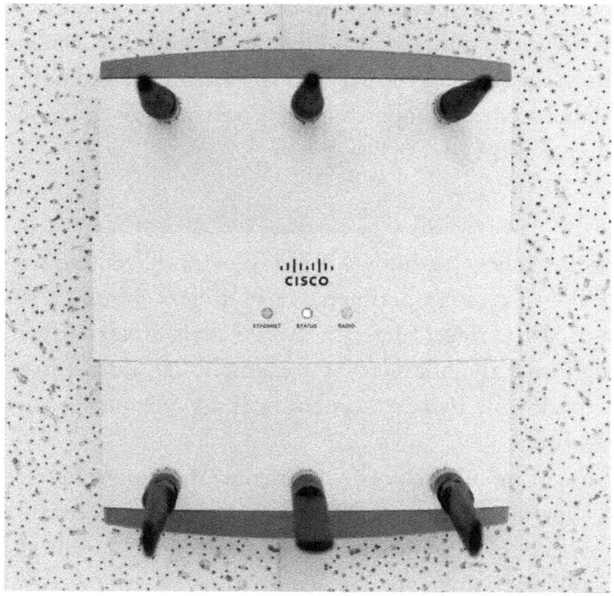

FIGURE 12-11 Enterprise WAP

Enterprise Wireless Administration

An enterprise wireless infrastructure is almost certainly going to consist of a large number of WAPs, which is almost impossible to administer when you have to access each one individually. Imagine something as simple as changing the password on a WPA2-encrypted ESSID on a wireless network with 50+ WAPs, as shown in Figure 12-12. The job would take forever!

The wireless industry long ago appreciated the complexity of enterprise-level wireless networks and created tools to make administration easier. The important point to any wireless network is that all of the WAPs, at least on a single SSID, connect to a single switch or group of switches. What if we could offload the jobs of management and monitoring to a device that's designed to handle a number of WAPs simultaneously? Enter the *wireless LAN controller* (Figure 12-13).

NOTE Wireless LAN controllers have a number of other names, such as *wireless switch* and *wireless LAN switch*.

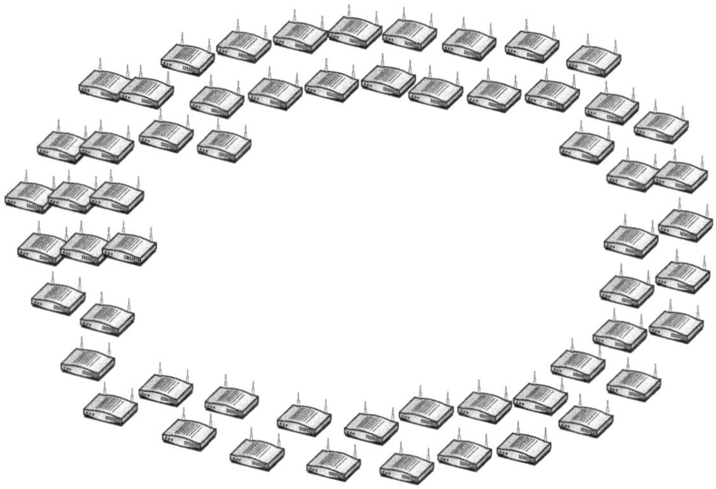

FIGURE 12-12 Configuring WAPs (the ring arrangement is for illustrative purposes only)

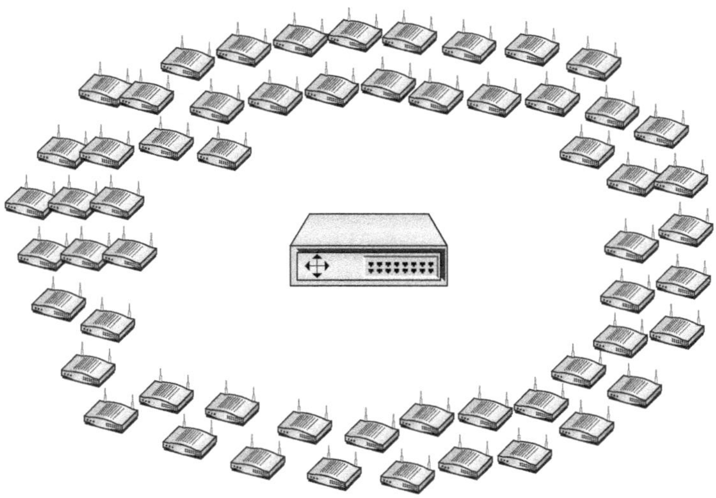

FIGURE 12-13 Wireless LAN controller

Any WAP that you can access directly and configure singularly via its own interface is called an *autonomous* AP. A WAP that can only be configured by a wireless controller is called a *lightweight* AP. For years, these centralized configuration methods were proprietary for each wireless manufacturer, making for little or no cross-brand interoperability. This incompatibility was a common wireless issue back in the day. Today, most manufacturers use the *Lightweight Access Point Protocol* (LWAPP) to ensure interoperability. Given LWAPP's broad acceptance, most WAPs will accept commands from any wireless controller.

NOTE Although it's not covered in the CompTIA Network+ objectives, you should know that a lot of companies have adopted cloud-based AP control options. Companies big and small offer cloud AP solutions to organizations. Cisco's Meraki solution, for example, features Cisco APs provisioned and managed through the Meraki dashboard, a web-based multisite management tool.

The advantages of cloud-based wireless management mirror advantages in other aspects of networking, such as removing the need for dedicated hardware, applications, and technicians. You'll read a lot more about cloud solutions in all aspects of networking in Chapter 13.

VLAN Pooling

One of the big challenges to larger enterprise networks is the large number of clients that might be on a single SSID at any given moment. As the number of devices grows, so does the number of broadcasts on the network. The traditional method to reduce this congestion is to divide the WLAN into multiple broadcast domains and use routers to interconnect them. In many cases, though, the needs of the wireless network demand a single broadcast domain. In this scenario, the WLAN controller assigns wireless clients to one of many VLANs in either a round-robin or hash-based fashion. This is called *VLAN pooling*.

Fewer broadcasts for wireless clients means less latency and faster communications. Furthermore, wireless clients can now move across a campus, like my phone and laptop do at Rochester Institute of Technology and Finger Lakes Community College, and keep the same VLAN and IP address.

Power over Ethernet

WAPs need electrical power, but they're invariably placed in strange locations (like ceilings or high up on walls) where providing electrical power is not convenient. No worries! Many WAPs support one of the *Power over Ethernet* (PoE) standards, enabling them to receive their power from the same Ethernet cables that transfer their data. As long as both the WAP and the switches to which they connect support PoE, you don't have to do anything other than plug in Ethernet cables; PoE works automatically. PoE-compatible WAPs and switches cost more, but the convenience of PoE for wireless networks makes it worthwhile.

The original PoE standard—*802.3af*—came out in 2003 and was met with great enthusiasm from the industry. PoE switches support a maximum of 15.4 watts of DC power per port. In 2009,

802.3af was revised to output as much as 25.5 watts per port. This PoE amendment to 802.3 is called *802.3at*, PoE plus, or PoE+. In 2018, the IEEE upgraded PoE again with the *802.3bt* standard. Switches that support PoE++ (or 4PPoE) can provide one of two power upgrades, with Type 3 supplying up to 51 watts per port and Type 4 supplying up to 71.3 watts per port.

Using an *incorrect standard* with PoE can cause multiple problems. If a device receives less power than it requires, it might operate improperly or shut down intermittently. Mismatched standards can also prevent proper negotiation between devices, which can make them unpowered or unstable. To ensure reliable operation, it is important to match the PoE standard of the power source to the requirements of the device.

You can monitor power consumption through the switch's command line interface. A `power budget exceeded` error indicates the PoE devices connected to a switch are trying to consume more power than is available. As a result, devices could malfunction, crash, or shut down; network availability can be compromised; and devices could overheat. Make sure you track power consumption, optimize devices with higher or lower power needs, and upgrade power supplies.

The `show power inline` command displays the PoE configuration. Figure 12-14 shows the output of this command for a switch before any configuration.

```
Switch#show power inline
Available:390.0(w)  Used:0.0(w)  Remaining:390.0(w)

Interface Admin  Oper       Power   Device              Class Max
                            (Watts)
--------- ------ ---------- ------- ------------------- ----- ----
Gig1/0/1  auto   off        0.0     n/a                 n/a   30.0
Gig1/0/2  auto   off        0.0     n/a                 n/a   30.0
Gig1/0/3  auto   off        0.0     n/a                 n/a   30.0
Gig1/0/4  auto   off        0.0     n/a                 n/a   30.0
Gig1/0/5  auto   off        0.0     n/a                 n/a   30.0
Gig1/0/6  auto   off        0.0     n/a                 n/a   30.0
Gig1/0/7  auto   off        0.0     n/a                 n/a   30.0
Gig1/0/8  auto   off        0.0     n/a                 n/a   30.0
Gig1/0/9  auto   off        0.0     n/a                 n/a   30.0
Gig1/0/10 auto   off        0.0     n/a                 n/a   30.0
Gig1/0/11 auto   off        0.0     n/a                 n/a   30.0
Gig1/0/12 auto   off        0.0     n/a                 n/a   30.0
Gig1/0/13 auto   off        0.0     n/a                 n/a   30.0
Gig1/0/14 auto   off        0.0     n/a                 n/a   30.0
Gig1/0/15 auto   off        0.0     n/a                 n/a   30.0
Gig1/0/16 auto   off        0.0     n/a                 n/a   30.0
Gig1/0/17 auto   off        0.0     n/a                 n/a   30.0
Gig1/0/18 auto   off        0.0     n/a                 n/a   30.0
Gig1/0/19 auto   off        0.0     n/a                 n/a   30.0
Gig1/0/20 auto   off        0.0     n/a                 n/a   30.0
Gig1/0/21 auto   off        0.0     n/a                 n/a   30.0
Gig1/0/22 auto   off        0.0     n/a                 n/a   30.0
Gig1/0/23 auto   off        0.0     n/a                 n/a   30.0
Gig1/0/24 auto   off        0.0     n/a                 n/a   30.0
```

FIGURE 12-14 The `show power inline` command and output

EXAM TIP Look for a *cable connectivity* troubleshooting scenario that involves PoE or PoE+ on the CompTIA Network+ exam. The failure of a wireless network that relies on PoE/PoE+ might not have anything to do with wireless components. Just like a loss of electricity means all the lights go out, any break in the cable or problem with the PoE switch will cause all connected WAPs to fail.

Implementing Wi-Fi

Installing and configuring a Wi-Fi network requires several discrete steps. You should start with a site survey to identify any obstacles (existing wireless networks, interference, and so on) you need to overcome and to determine the best location for your access points. You'll need to install one or more access points and then configure both those and the wireless clients. Finally, you should put the network to the test, verifying that it works as you intended.

Performing a Site Survey

As mentioned, the first step of installing a wireless network is the *site survey*, which will reveal any obstacles to creating the wireless network and help you determine the best possible location for your access points. The main components for creating a site survey are a floor plan of the area where you'll be installing the network and a site survey tool, such as NETSCOUT's AirMagnet Survey Pro (Figure 12-15). *Wireless survey tools* can identify any other wireless networks in the area and integrate them into a drawing of your floor plan with the interference sources clearly marked. With this information, you can get the right hardware and the proper network coverage.

EXISTING WIRELESS NETWORKS

Discovering any wireless network signals other than your own in your space enables you to set both the SSID and channel to avoid overlapping networks. One part of any good site survey is a *Wi-Fi analyzer*, also known as a *wireless analyzer*, a device that finds and documents all existing wireless networks in the area. Wi-Fi analyzers are handy tools for diagnosing wireless network issues as well. You can get dedicated, hand-held wireless analyzers or you can run site survey software on a laptop or wireless mobile device. Wireless survey tools like the AirMagnet Survey Pro just shown always include an analyzer as well. Figure 12-16 shows a screenshot of Acrylic Wi-Fi, a free and popular Wi-Fi analyzer.

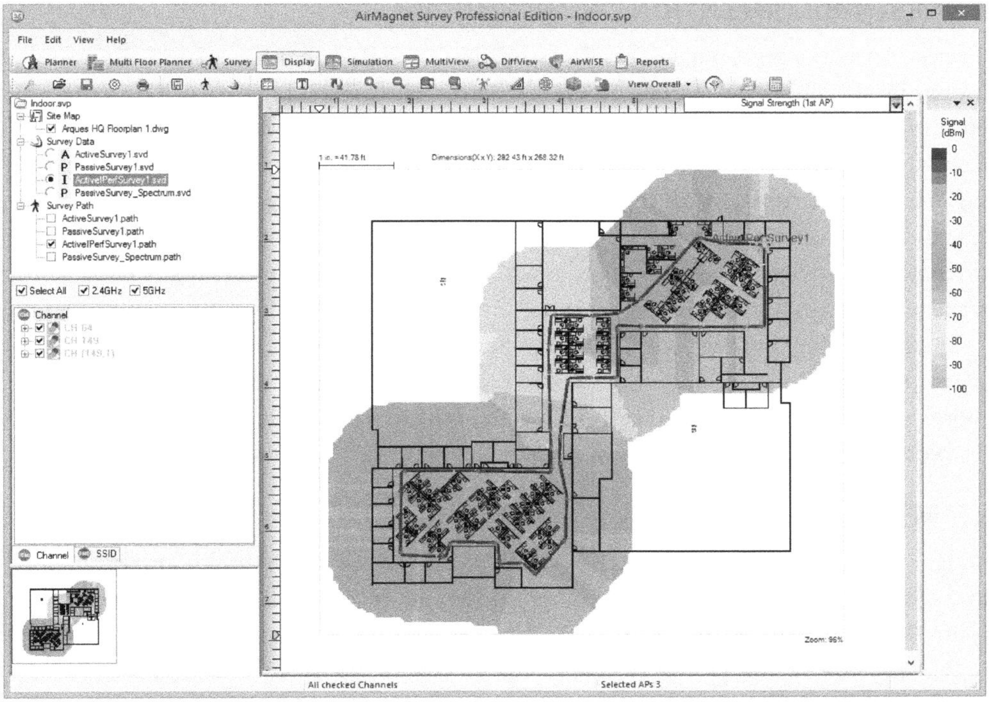

FIGURE 12-15 AirMagnet Survey Pro

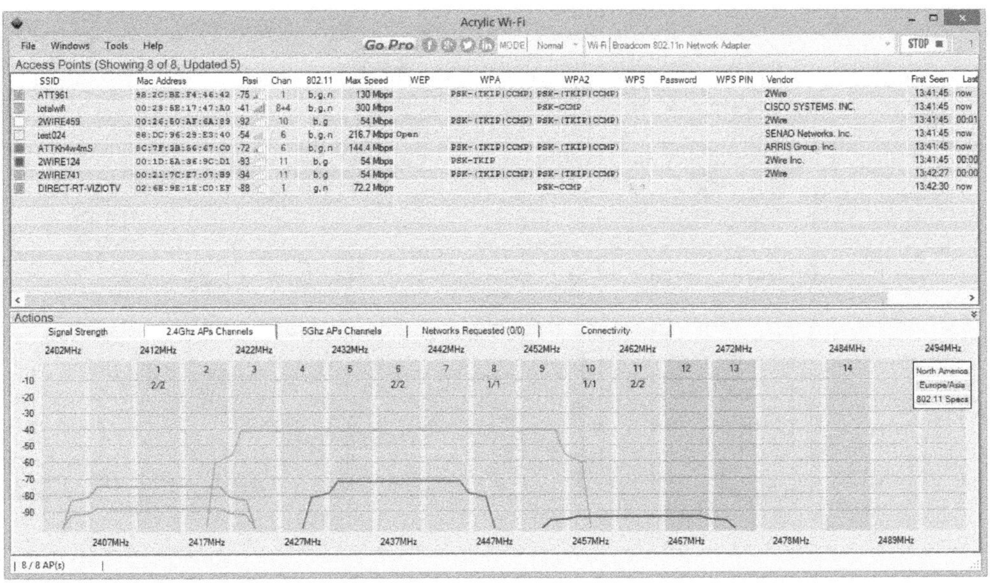

FIGURE 12-16 Acrylic Wi-Fi

CONGESTION/CONTENTION

Wireless networks send out radio signals on the 2.4, 5.0, or 6.0 GHz spectrum using one of a number of discrete channels. In early wireless networks, a big part of the setup was to determine the channels used nearby in order to avoid them. In modern wireless networks, we rarely adjust channels manually anymore. Instead, we rely on powerful algorithms built into WAPs to locate channels with the least *congestion/contention* automatically. The bigger challenge today is the presence of many existing Wi-Fi networks with lots of clients, creating high-device-density environments. You need a wireless solution that handles many users running on the few wireless frequencies available.

There are plenty of tools like AirMagnet Survey Pro to support a *wireless survey*. All good survey utilities share some common ways to report their findings. One of the most powerful reports is a *heat map*, a graphical representation of the RF sources on your site that uses different colors to represent the intensity of the signal. Figure 12-17 shows a sample heat map.

INTERFERENCE SOURCES

It might seem like overkill in a small network, but any network beyond a simple one should have a sketched-out site survey with any potential interference sources clearly marked (Figure 12-18). Refrigerators, reinforced walls, metal plumbing, microwave ovens—all of these

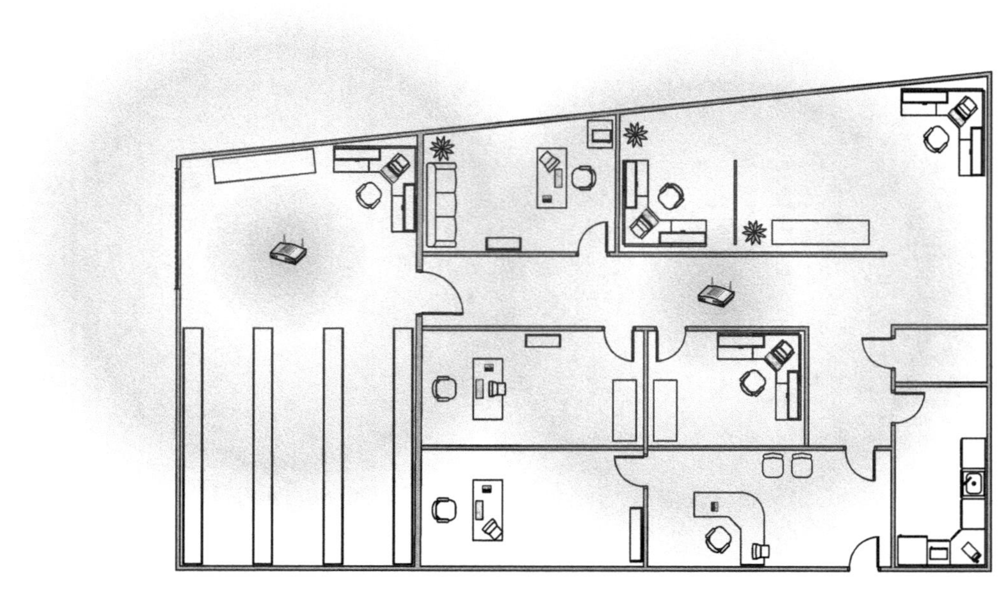

FIGURE 12-17 Site survey with heat map

can create horrible dead spots where your network radio wave can't easily penetrate. With a difficult or high-interference area, you might need to move up to 802.11ax equipment with three or four antennas just to get the kind of coverage you want. Or you might need to plan a multiple WAP network to wipe out the dead zones. A proper site survey gives you the first tool for implementing a network that works.

Installing the Client

Because every Wi-Fi network needs clients (otherwise, what's the point?), you need to install Wi-Fi client hardware and software. Pretty much every type of mobile device (smartphones, laptops, tablets, and so forth) comes with a built-in client, usually part of the operating system.

Desktop systems are a different story. Most desktops don't have built-in wireless, so you'll need to install a wireless NIC. You have a choice between installing a PCIe card or a USB device. With a PCIe NIC, power down the PC, disconnect from the AC source, and open the case. Following good CompTIA A+ technician procedures, locate a free slot on the motherboard, remove the slot cover, remove the NIC from its antistatic bag, install the NIC, and affix the retaining screw. See Figure 12-19. Often, you'll need to attach the antenna. Button

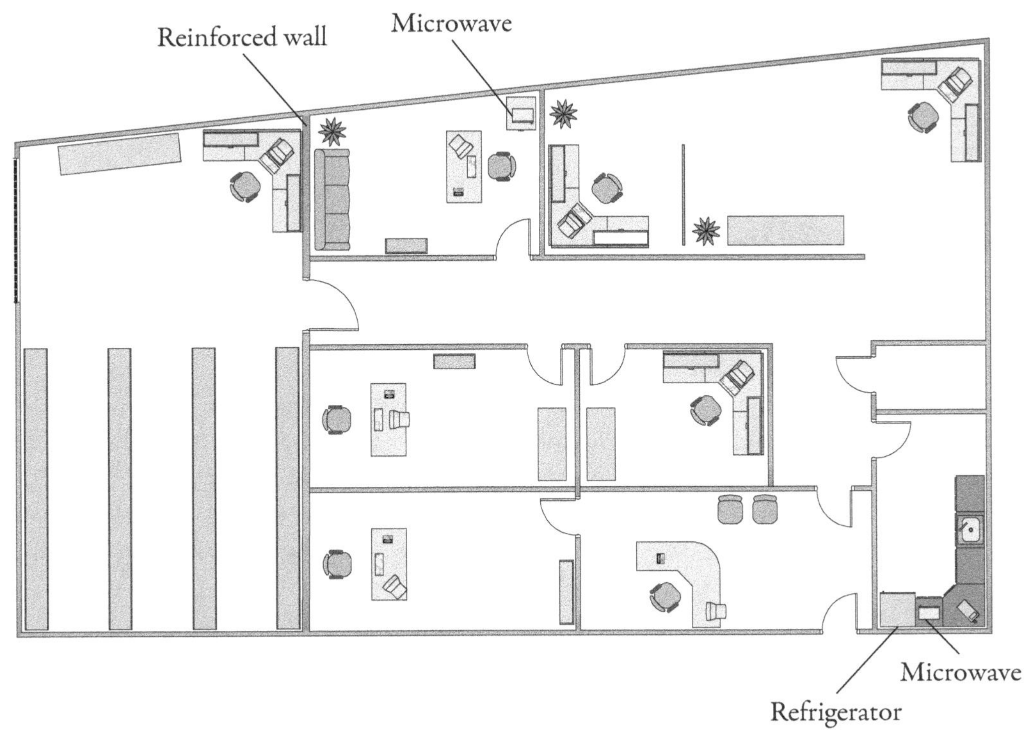

FIGURE 12-18 Site survey with interference sources noted

everything up, plug it in, and start the computer. If prompted, put in the disc that came from the manufacturer (or use your wired NIC to go to the manufacturer's website) and install drivers and any other software necessary.

With a USB NIC, you should install the drivers and software before you connect the NIC to the computer. This is standard operating procedure for any USB device, as you most likely recall from your CompTIA A+ certification training (or from personal experience).

FIGURE 12-19 Wi-Fi NIC installed

Setting Up an Ad Hoc Network

Although ad hoc networks are rare and not easily supported by modern operating systems, they are on the CompTIA Network+ exam. Plus, you might end up dealing with some legacy gear and need to set one up somewhere, so let's look at the process.

Configuring NICs for ad hoc mode networking requires you to address four things: SSID, IP addresses, channel, and sharing. (Plus, of course, you have to set the NICs to function in ad hoc mode!) Each wireless node must be configured to use the same network name (SSID). Of course, no two nodes can use the same IP address. If everything worked correctly, you will have a TCP/IP connection between the machines with no WAP. Figure 12-20 shows enabling support for ad hoc networks on a wireless NIC.

EXAM TIP You might notice the rather antique quality of the screenshot in Figure 12-20. That's because modern operating systems only grudgingly support ad hoc networks, and only via complicated command-line command strings. Except for on the CompTIA Network+ exam, ad hoc mode is dead.

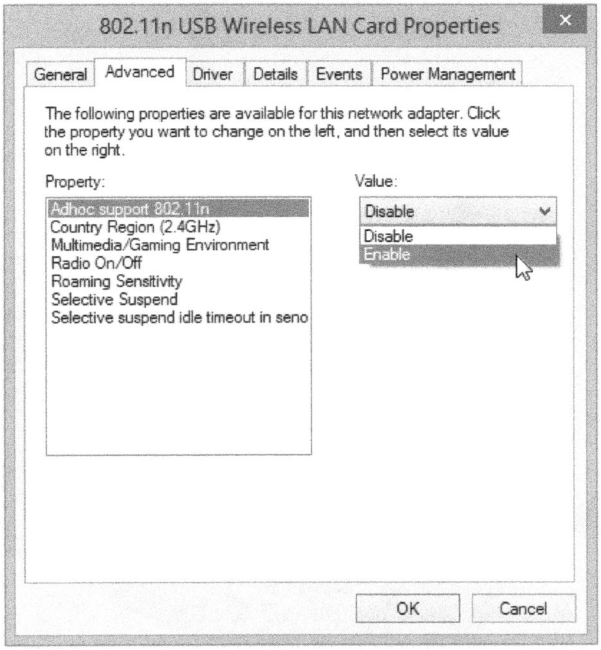

FIGURE 12-20 Enabling support for ad hoc networks on a wireless NIC

Setting Up an Infrastructure Network

With your site survey in hand and Wi-Fi technology selected, you're ready to set up a wireless network in infrastructure mode. You need to determine the optimal location for your WAP, configure it, and then configure any clients to access it. Seems straightforward, but the devil, as they say, is in the details.

PLACING THE ACCESS POINTS/ANTENNAS

All wireless access points have antennas that radiate the 802.11 signal to the clients, so the optimal location for a WAP depends on the area you want to cover and whether you care if the signal bleeds out beyond the borders. You also need to use antennas that provide enough signal and push that signal in the proper direction and alignment. There are some interesting options here, and you should know them both for modern networking and for the CompTIA Network+ exam.

Antenna placement on the WAPs is also very important. WAP antennas come in many shapes and sizes. In the early days it was common to see WAPs with two antennas. Some WAPs have only one antenna, and some (802.11n, 802.11ac, and 802.11ax) have more than two (Figure 12-21). Even a WAP that doesn't seem to have antennas is simply hiding them inside the chassis.

FIGURE 12-21 An ASUS AX6000 Wi-Fi 6 gaming router with four external antennas

There are three basic types of antennas common in 802.11 networks: omnidirectional, directional, and patch. Each offers different solutions for coverage of specific wireless network setups. In addition, the signals emanating from the antennas have a feature called *polarization* that you need to consider.

Omnidirectional

In general, an *omnidirectional antenna* radiates signal outward from the WAP in all directions. For a typical network, you want blanket coverage and would place a WAP with an omnidirectional antenna in the center of the area (Figure 12-22). This has the advantage of ease of use—anything within the signal radius can potentially access the network. The standard straight-wire antennas that provide the most omnidirectional function are called *dipole antennas*.

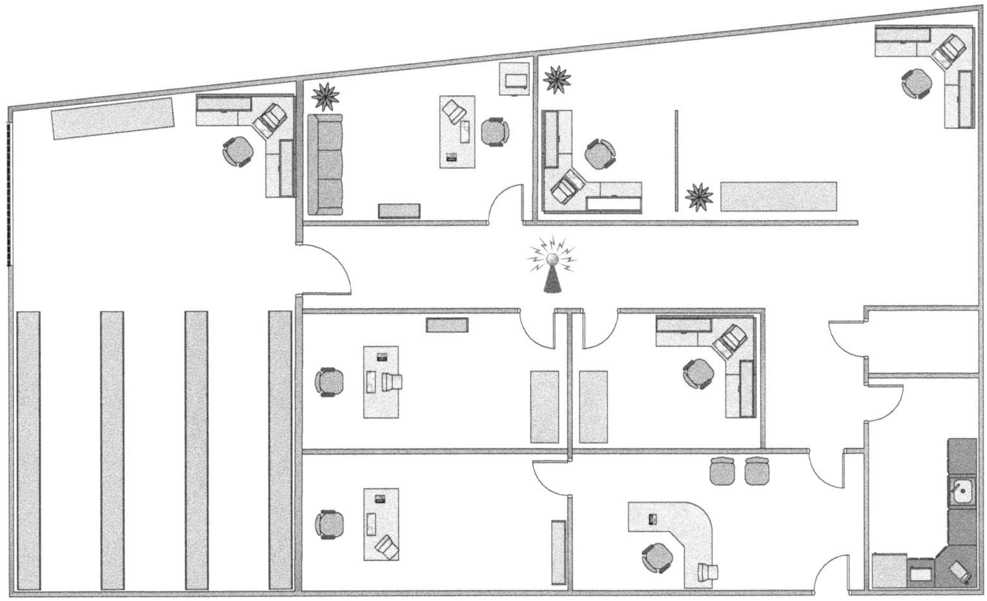

FIGURE 12-22 Office layout with WAP in the center

The famous little black antennas seen on older WAPs are all dipoles. A dipole antenna has two radiating elements that point in opposite directions. But if you look at a WAP antenna, it looks like it only points in one direction (Figure 12-23). If you open one of these antennas, however, you'll see that it has two opposing radiating elements (Figure 12-24).

FIGURE 12-23 Typical WAP dipole antenna—where are the two elements?

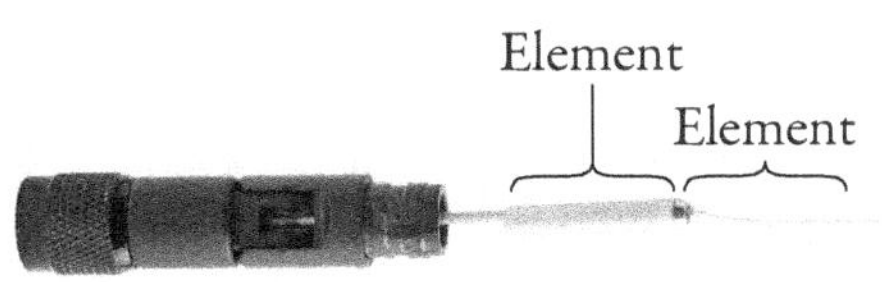

FIGURE 12-24 Same antenna from Figure 12-23 opened, showing the two elements

A dipole antenna doesn't radiate in a perfect ball. It is more of a doughnut shape, as shown in Figure 12-25. Note that this shape is great for outdoors or a single floor, but it doesn't send much signal above or below the WAP.

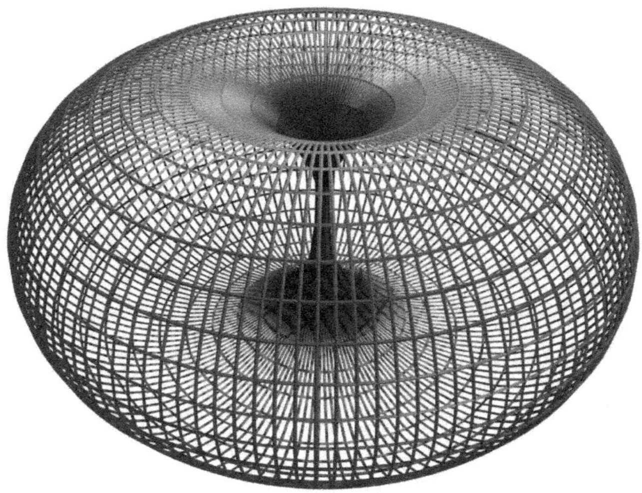

FIGURE 12-25 Dipole radiation pattern

The omnidirectional and centered approach does not work for every network, for three reasons. First, if the signal exceeds the size of the network space, it bleeds out—a lot, in some cases, particularly if your specific space requires you to position the WAP off-center. This presents a security risk as well because someone outside your network space could lurk, pick up the signal, and compromise your network. Second, if your network space exceeds your WAP signal, you'll need to get some sort of signal booster. Third, any obstacles will produce glaring dead spots in network coverage. Too many dead spots make a less-than-ideal solution. To address these issues, you might need to turn to other solutions.

An antenna strengthens and focuses the RF output from a WAP. The ratio of increase—what's called *gain*—is measured in decibels (dB). The gain from a typical WAP is 2 dB, enough to cover a reasonable area, but not a very large room. Increasing the signal requires a bigger device antenna. Some WAPs, especially outdoor models, have removable antennas. To increase the signal range for a single WAP using omnidirectional antennas, simply replace the factory-installed antennas with higher-gain models.

Directional

When you don't necessarily want to broadcast to the world, you can use one or more *directional antennas*, also known as *unidirectional antennas*, to create a nicely focused network. As the name implies, a directional antenna focuses a radio wave into a beam of sorts. Directional antennas come in multiple flavors, such as parabolic (dish), and Yagi, to name just a few. A *parabolic antenna* looks like a satellite dish. A *Yagi antenna* (named for one of its Japanese inventors), often called a *beam antenna*, can enable a focused radio wave to travel a long way, even miles (Figure 12-26). If you need to connect in a narrow beam (down a hallway or from one faraway point to another), directional antennas are the way to go.

FIGURE 12-26 Yagi antenna

Patch Antennas

Patch antennas are flat, plate-shaped antennas that generate a half-sphere beam. Patch antennas are always placed on walls. The half-sphere is perfect for indoor offices where you want to fill the room with a strong signal but not broadcast to the room behind the patch (Figure 12-27).

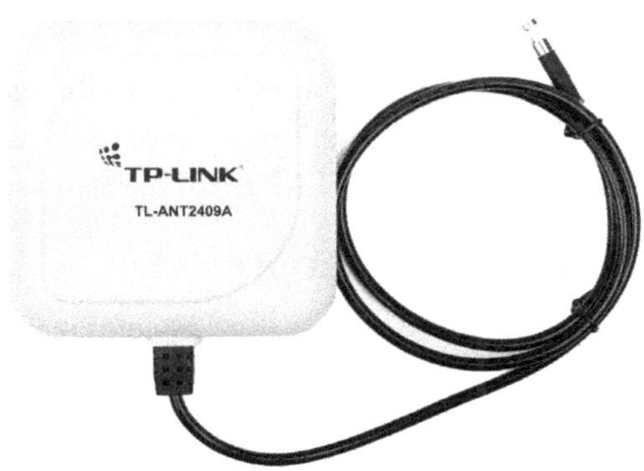

FIGURE 12-27 Patch antenna

Polarization and Antenna Alignment

All radio signals have a property called *polarization*, which describes the orientation of the radio waves. The polarization of a Wi-Fi signal depends on the antenna, though linear polarization (meaning the waves all oscillate in the same direction) is the most common. In addition, these polarized antennas and emitted signals can be oriented in several ways, such as vertically, horizontally, and slanted (like a 45-degree angle).

When you adjust a Wi-Fi antenna or rotate the device it is attached to in physical space, you effectively change the orientation of its signal. Aligning the receiving antenna with the polarization of the transmitter—known as *common polarization*—creates the strongest signal. The greater the misalignment between receiver and transmitter—known as *cross-polarization*—the weaker the signal. Cross-polarization can lower a network's effective range and throughput.

Let's look at a scenario to show the impact of misalignment more clearly. Erica, a network tech, wants to connect two buildings in her organization via Wi-Fi. With both antennas aligned vertically, the connection will be strong and solid. On the other hand, if she sets one antenna to vertical and the other to horizontal (a 90-degree difference), the signal strength will drop by 18 decibels. Every 3 dB equates to a doubling (or halving) of power, so –18 dB represents a 98.4 percent loss in power.

The math isn't important for the CompTIA Network+ exam, but the outcome is. In a worst-case cross-polarization scenario like Erica's network, the connection would be 1/64 the signal strength of the same configuration using common (aligned) polarization. Ouch!

EXAM TIP When setting up WAP antennas, know the concepts of cross-polarization and common polarization. When setting up a typical home or SOHO Wi-Fi network, don't worry about polarization at all.

Optimal Antenna Placement

Optimal antenna placement varies according to the space to fill and security concerns. You can use the site survey and the same wireless analyzer tools to find dead spots, odd corners, and so on. Use the right kind of antenna on each WAP to fill in the space.

CONFIGURING A CONSUMER ACCESS POINT

Consumer WAPs often have a browser-based setup utility combined with routing and switching features. Typically, you open a web browser on one of your network client workstations and enter the access point's IP address, such as 192.168.1.1, to bring up the configuration page.

You need to supply an administrative password, included with your access point's documentation, to log in (Figure 12-28).

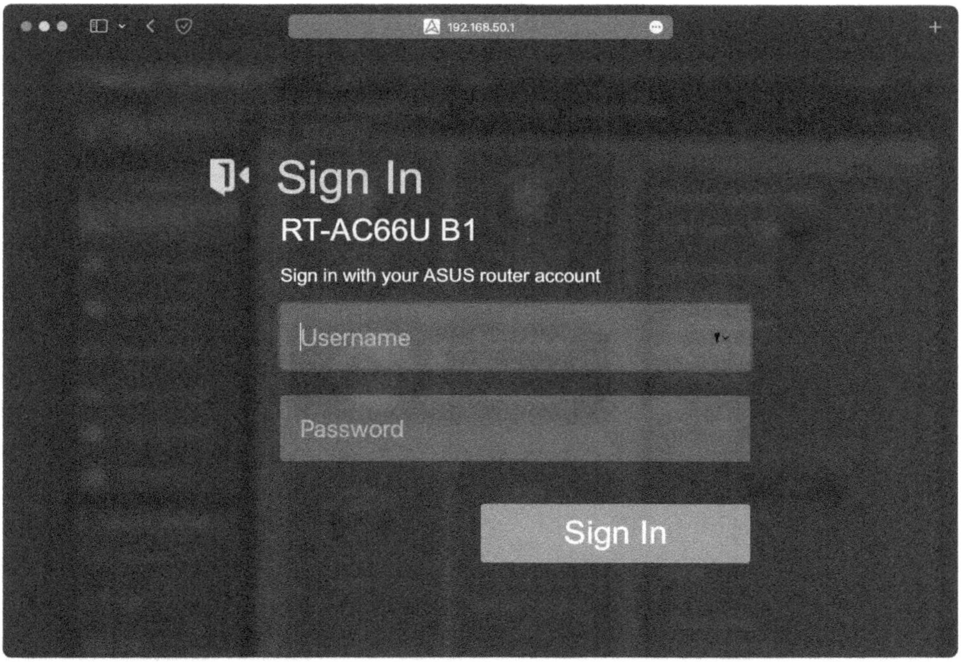

FIGURE 12-28 Security login for ASUS WAP

Once you've logged in, you'll see configuration screens for changing your basic setup, access point password, security, and so on. Different access points offer different configuration options. Figure 12-29 shows the home screen (Network Map in the menu) for an ASUS WAP/router.

Configuring the SSID and Beacon

The SSID option is usually located somewhere obvious on the configuration utility. On the ASUS model shown in Figure 12-29, this option is right on the home screen. Configure your SSID to something unique.

The primary way we locate wireless networks is by using our clients to scan for SSIDs. All wireless networks have a function to turn off the SSID broadcast. You can choose not to broadcast the SSID, but this only stops casual users—sophisticated wireless intruders have tools to detect networks that do not broadcast their SSIDs. Turning off SSID broadcast forces users to configure the connection to a particular SSID manually.

FIGURE 12-29 ASUS WAP home screen

Aside from the SSID, broadcast traffic includes the *beacon*, essentially a timing frame sent from the WAP at regular intervals. The beacon frame enables Wi-Fi networks to function, so this is important. Beacon traffic also makes up a major percentage of network traffic because most WAPs have beacons set to go off every 100 ms! You can adjust the rate of the beacon traffic down and improve your network traffic speeds, but in doing so you lower the speed at which devices can negotiate to get on the network, among other things. Figure 12-30 shows the Beacon Interval setting on an ASUS WAP.

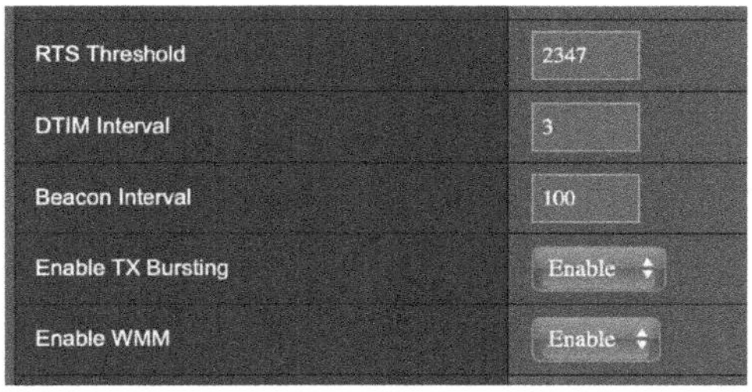

FIGURE 12-30 Setting for the beacon interval

Configuring MAC Address Filtering

As discussed earlier in the chapter, you can use MAC address filtering to build a list of wireless network clients that are permitted or denied access to your wireless network based on their unique MAC addresses. Figure 12-31 shows the MAC address filtering configuration screen on the ASUS WAP. (In this case, I'm not using MAC filtering for security, but to make sure my Apple TV only uses the 5.0 GHz band.) Simply enter the MAC address of a wireless client that you want to allow or deny access to your wireless network.

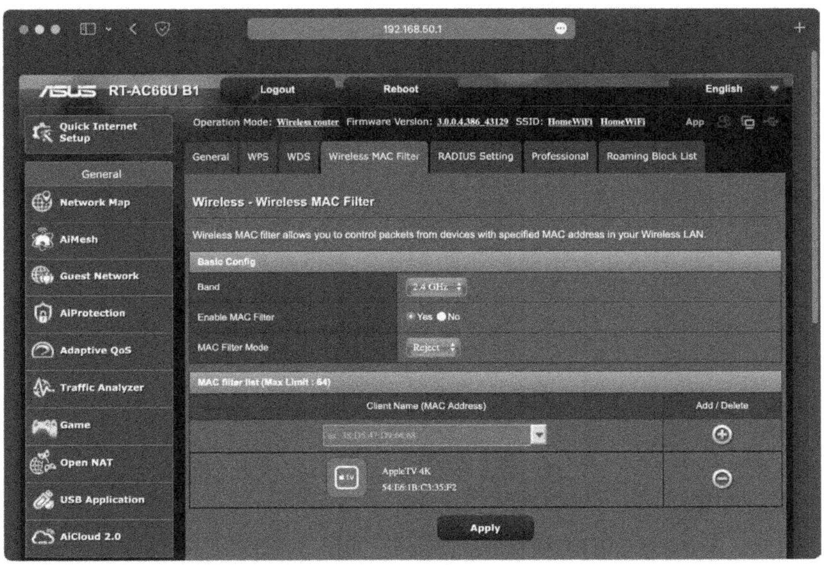

FIGURE 12-31 MAC address filtering configuration screen for an ASUS WAP

Configuring Encryption

Enabling encryption ensures that data frames are secured against unauthorized access. To set up basic encryption, select an authentication method at the WAP and create a strong password—a *pre-shared key* (PSK). Then configure all connected wireless clients on the network with the same key. Figure 12-32 shows the WPA2-Personal authentication and the pre-shared key settings screen for an ASUS WAP.

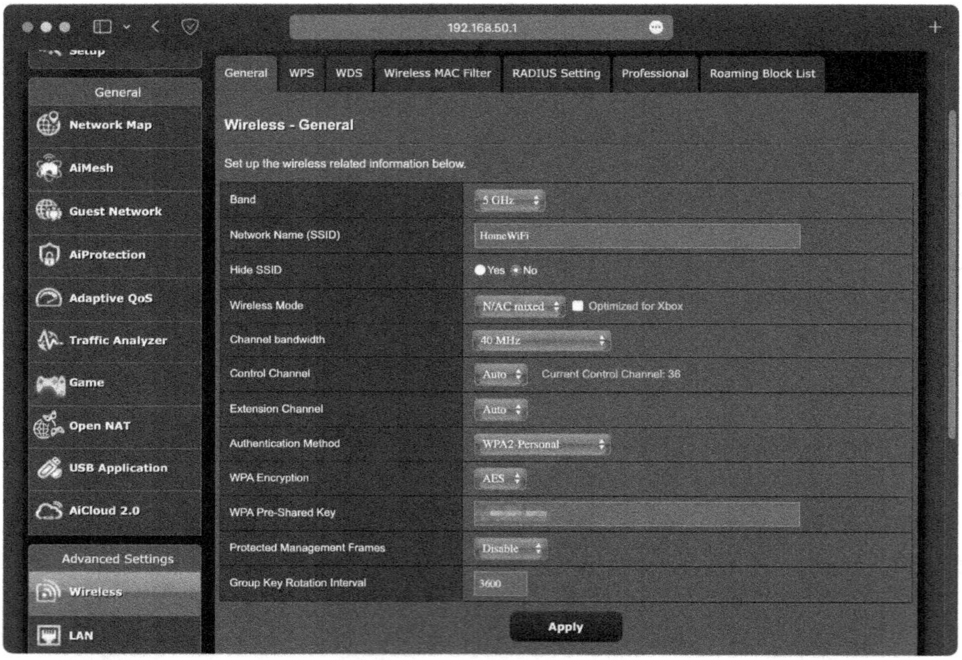

FIGURE 12-32 Security settings screen on an ASUS WAP

Most WAPs also support WPA2-Enterprise, allowing authentication using a RADIUS server (Figure 12-33). Always use the strongest encryption you can and choose a strong password if using WPA2-Personal.

Configuring Channel and Frequency

With most home networks, you can simply let the WAP automatically select the channel for each band, but in an environment with overlapping Wi-Fi signals, you'll want to set the channel manually. Using a wireless analyzer, view the current *wireless channel utilization* and then set your channel to one that doesn't conflict in the WAP configuration screens. Figure 12-34 shows the 5.0 GHz channel menu in an ASUS WAP.

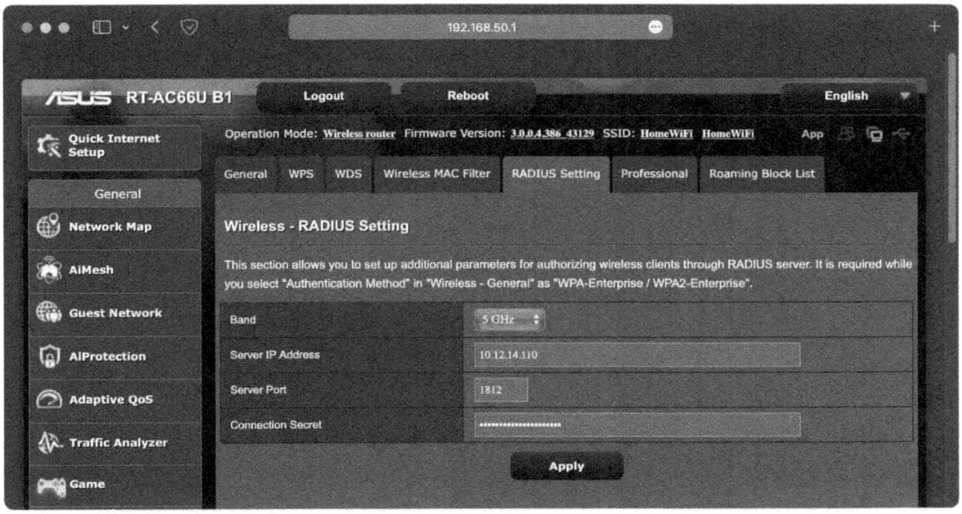

FIGURE 12-33 RADIUS settings

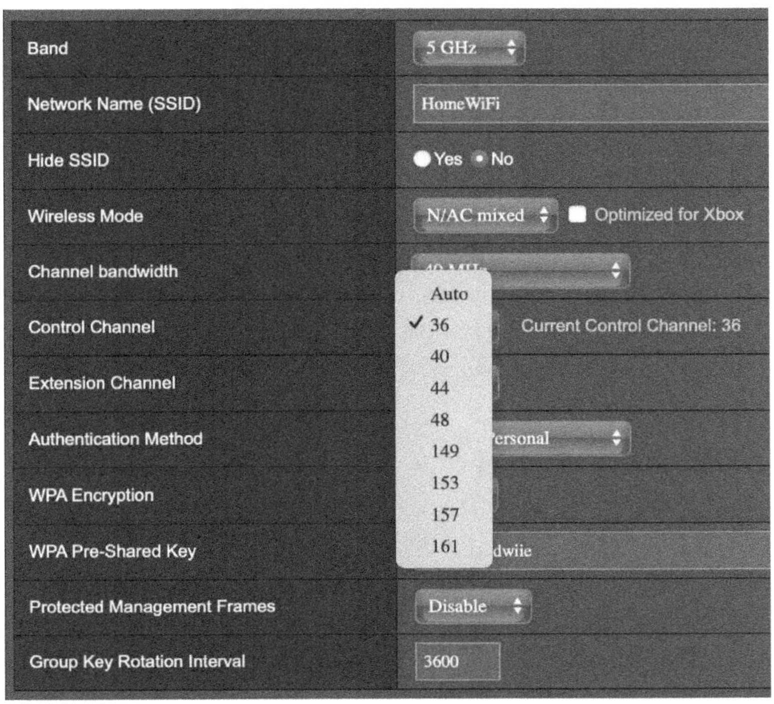

FIGURE 12-34 Changing the channel for the 5.0 GHz band

With dual-band WAPs, you can configure the SSID and security separately for 2.4 GHz or 5.0 GHz. This is useful if you want to force older 2.4 GHz devices onto their own SSID with a unique PSK. If you're not using one band, you can disable the radio. Figure 12-35 shows disabling the 2.4 GHz radio on an ASUS WAP.

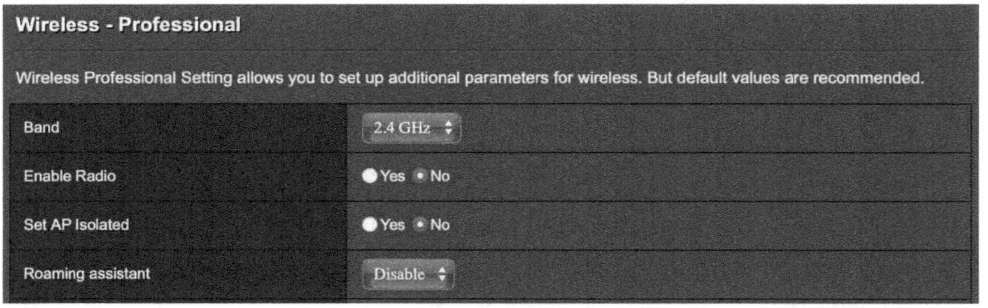

FIGURE 12-35 Disabling the 2.4 GHz radio

CONFIGURING THE CLIENT

Infrastructure mode networks require that the same SSID be configured on all clients and access points. Normally, the client picks up a broadcast SSID and all you need to do is type in the PSK. With non-broadcasting networks, on the other hand, you need to type in a valid SSID as well as the PSK (Figure 12-36).

Once you successfully connect a device to a wireless network, the client will store the settings for that network in a profile. From now on, whenever the client sees a particular SSID, the device will automatically try to connect to that SSID using the encryption and key stored in the profile. Of course, if the wireless network changes in any way—for example, if the encryption password is changed—the device won't be able to access it unless you delete the profile and reacquire the network.

Extending the Network

Creating a basic service set network with a single WAP and multiple clients works in a relatively small area, but you can extend a Wi-Fi network in a few ways if you have difficult spaces—with lots of obstructions, for example—or need to communicate beyond the ~300-foot range of the typical wireless network. Most commonly, you'd add one or more WAPs to create an extended service set. You can also install a wireless bridge to connect two or more wired networks.

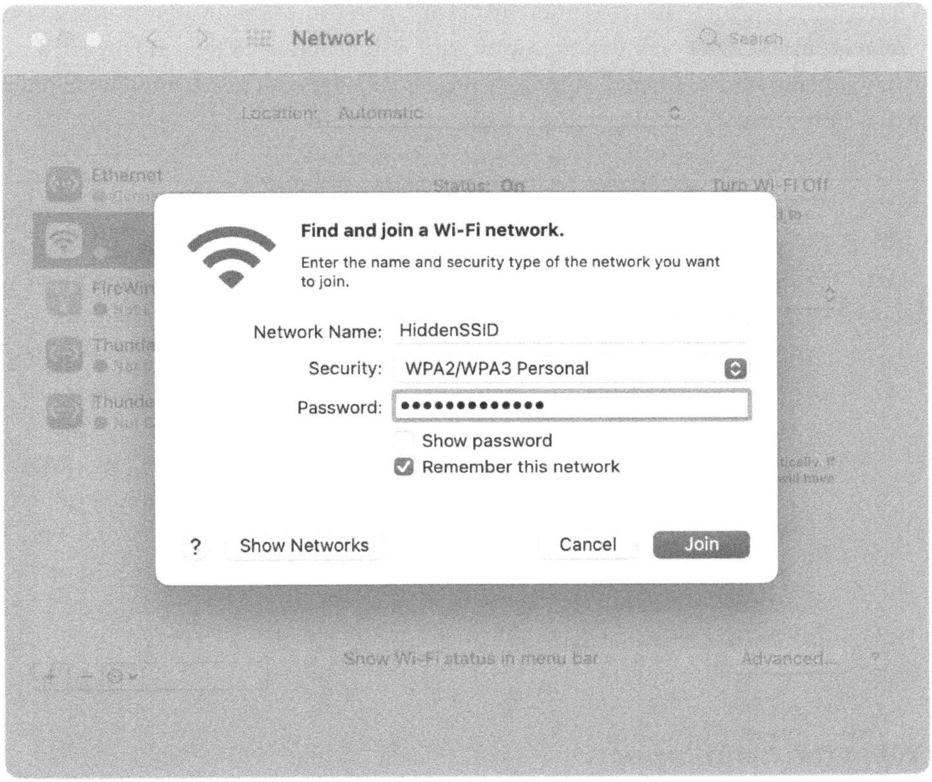

FIGURE 12-36 Typing in an SSID manually

Many companies make *wireless range extenders*, devices that pick up your Wi-Fi signal and rebroadcast it. Some look like a WAP; other models plug directly into an electrical outlet. Current wireless range extenders require very little setup and can extend your network between floors and into dead spots.

ADDING A WAP

To add a WAP to a Wi-Fi network, you'll need to run a cable from a switch on the network to where you want to install it. Configuration is straightforward. Both WAPs require the same ESSID, and if the WAPs are near each other, use separate channels.

ADDING WIRELESS BRIDGES

Dedicated *wireless bridges* connect two wired networks together or join wireless and wired networks together in the same way that wired switches do.

Wireless bridges come in two different flavors: point-to-point and point-to-multipoint. *Point-to-point* bridges can only communicate with a single other bridge and are used to connect two wired network segments. *Point-to-multipoint* bridges can talk to more than one other bridge at a time and can connect multiple network segments.

NOTE Several Wi-Fi equipment manufacturers produce *mesh* networking gear in the consumer space to enable users to set up a multi-WAP network with ease. A typical mesh network product comes with three WAPs and a smartphone app. Creating a relatively secure network means opening the app, connecting to the first WAP, and then plugging in and connecting subsequent WAPs in the set. To add more coverage, just buy more mesh WAPs and apply the same process.

All mesh networks come preconfigured with security, such as WPA2. The lack of rigorous, manual control over security settings, on the other hand, makes mesh networks okay for the home but not suitable for a work environment. You won't find this sort of consumer gear on the CompTIA Network+ exam, but it is in the Weissman household in the form of a TP-Link Deco Mesh Wi-Fi System!

Verifying the Installation

Once you've completed the initial installation of a Wi-Fi network, test it. Move some traffic from one computer to another using the wireless connection. Never leave a job site without verifying the installation.

Troubleshooting Wi-Fi

Wi-Fi networks are pretty magical when they work right, but their lack of wires often makes them vexing to troubleshoot when they don't.

As with any troubleshooting scenario, the first step in troubleshooting a Wi-Fi network is to break down tasks into logical steps. First, figure out the scope of the wireless networking problem. I like to break wireless problems into three symptom types:

- You can't get on the Wi-Fi network. Your client (or clients) may or may not think it's connected, but you can't access shared resources (web pages, remote folders, and so on).
- Your wireless connections are way too slow. Your clients are accessing shared resources.
- Your wireless connection is doing weird things.

No Connection

Wi-Fi networks want to connect the client devices. You rarely if ever get an error on a device that says, "You may not speak to WAP52 that is supporting SSID CSCPROF." Instead, you get subtler errors, such as repeated prompts for passwords or Automatic Private IP Addressing (APIPA)/zeroconf addresses.

EXAM TIP Be prepared for scenario questions that quiz you about the limits of the wireless standards. This includes throughput speeds (11, 54, and 100+ Mbps), frequencies, distances, and channel usage. See the discussions in the section "Wi-Fi Standards" earlier in the chapter for the limitations of each standard.

CHANNEL PROBLEMS

If you're working with one of the older 802.11 versions using the 2.4 GHz channel, you may have problems with channels. One issue is channel overlap, where 2.4 GHz channels overlap with their nearest channel neighbors, causing interference. For example, channel 3 overlaps with channels 1, 2, 4, and 5, so configuring an SSID and setting each WAP only one channel apart will cause connection problems. As noted previously, try to stick to using channels 1, 6, and 11 only.

EXAM TIP Use wireless scanning tools to check for wireless channel utilization and discover overworked WAPs, saturated areas, and the like so that you can deploy WAPs to optimize your network.

SECURITY TYPE MISMATCHES

A *security type mismatch* indicates one of two things: either you've connected manually to a wireless network and set up the incorrect encryption type—an *encryption protocol mismatch*—or you've automatically accessed a particular SSID and entered the *incorrect passphrase*. Entering the wrong encryption type is rare, since it happens only during manual setup, but entering the wrong passphrase is the classic no-errors-but-won't-work issue. In older operating systems, you often would get only one chance to enter a key, and if you failed, your only clue was that your client got an APIPA/zeroconf address. Modern operating systems are clearer, displaying a message like `wrong passphrase`. Pretty much every wireless NIC is set to DHCP, and if you don't have the right password, your client won't get past the WAP to talk to anything on the network, including the DHCP server.

SIGNAL/POWER LEVELS

802.11 is a low-power radio and has a limited range. If the WAP doesn't have enough power, you'll have signal attenuation, and your device won't be able to access the wireless network (CompTIA blandly calls this *insufficient wireless coverage.*). All the 802.11 standards have distance limitations; exceeding those limitations will reduce performance. Certainly, a quick answer is to move closer to the WAP, but there are several issues that cause power levels to drop too low to connect beyond the obvious "you're too far away" from the WAP.

Manufacturers use scales called *received signal strength indication* (RSSI) to show the signal between a WAP and a receiver. Every manufacturer uses different RSSI numbers, but they usually show as "how many bars" you have. Running the Wi-Fi Scan feature of the AirPort Utility app on my iPhone, for example, shows my WLAN RSSI as –29 dBm, whereas my neighbor's WLAN shows as –40 dBm (Figure 12-37). (We live close together in my neighborhood.) The closer to 0 dBm, the better the signal. The little symbol for Wi-Fi strength shows full strength to my WLAN.

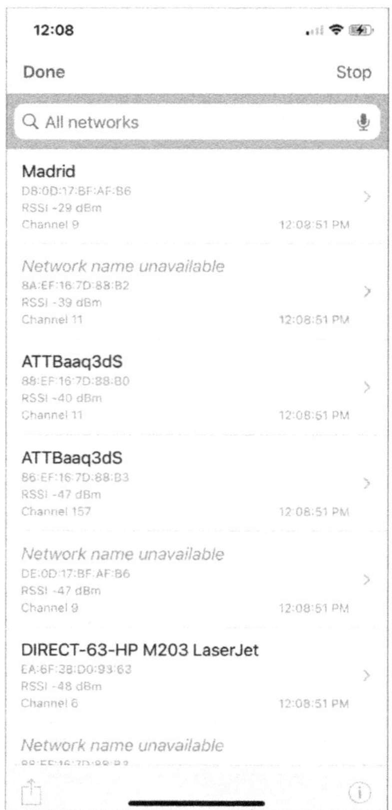

FIGURE 12-37 AirPort Utility showing RSSI strengths measured in decibel-milliwatts (dBm)

NOTE Interference can also cause signal loss, but I choose to treat this as a separate issue later in this section. For now, we're talking about simple signal loss due to insufficient power.

If your WAP lacks enough signal power, what CompTIA calls *signal degradation* or *loss*, you have a few choices besides simply moving closer to the WAP:

AVOID PHYSICAL ISSUES A physical issue is what it sounds like: something physical in the way keeps the signal from reaching its destination. When installing a network, you must watch out for concrete walls, metal (especially metal studs), and the use of special RF-blocking window film. The solution is planning your WAP placement more carefully, but keep in mind that even in the best-planned environment it's common to have to move WAPs in order to clear dead spots. We'll cover more about physical issues later in this chapter.

TURN UP THE POWER Some wireless devices make it easy to increase the power (Figure 12-38). It's tempting to think "cranking it up to 11" à la Spinal Tap will fix all your Wi-Fi problems, but the unfortunate reality is more complex. If you have one WAP and live in the country, go ahead and crank the transmit power as high as it will legally go. But in a crowded urban environment, this can make Wi-Fi worse. Nearby WAPs will see your stronger signal and turn their own power up to compensate.

It's like being in a crowded restaurant. If everyone is talking at a moderate to low volume, everyone can converse without problems. But if people at one table start to get boisterous, the people at the table next to them have to get louder to be heard over the noise. This cascades until everyone in the restaurant is practically shouting just so someone a few feet away can hear them.

USE A BETTER ANTENNA Too many 802.11 installations ignore the antennas, dropping in WAPs using their default antennas. In most cases, the omnidirectional antennas that come with WAPs are very good—which is why they're so often the default

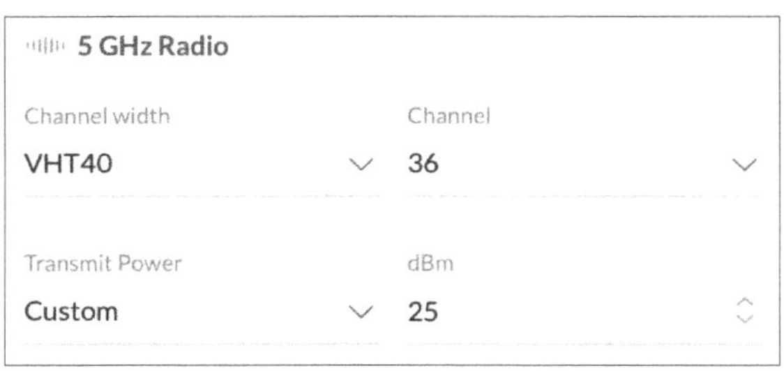

FIGURE 12-38 Transmit power configuration for an Ubiquiti WAP

antennas—but sometimes they're simply the incorrect antenna type and need to be replaced. If you're losing signal, consider whether the antenna is wrong for the wireless setup. Watch for scenarios on the CompTIA Network+ exam where replacing an omnidirectional antenna with one or more directional antennas makes an easy fix. Also, look for incorrect antenna placement, where moving a few inches away from an obstacle can make a big difference in performance.

EXAM TIP The *effective radiated power* (ERP) is the signal strength coming out of an antenna. With a nondirectional antenna, the signal in any direction will be the same. Use the *effective isotropic radiated power* (EIRP) to measure the relative signal strength coming out of a directional antenna, comparing the "strong" end signal with an omnidirectional antenna.

UPGRADE TO A NEWER 802.11 VERSION The MIMO features in 802.11n, 802.11ac, and 802.11ax are absolutely amazing in their ability to overcome dead spots and similar issues that would require aggressively tweaking WAP locations and antenna types on earlier versions of 802.11. While MIMO and MU-MIMO aren't intended only to increase signal distance, it's almost certain you'll see a scenario where simply updating WAPs to 802.11ac or 802.11ax will automatically fix otherwise tricky problems.

Slow Connections

Slow wireless connections are far more difficult to troubleshoot than no connection at all. Unlike a disconnection, where you have obvious and clear clues, a slowdown is just . . . slow. In these situations, you are clearly connected to an SSID, you have a good IP address, and the client itself runs well, but data transfer is slow. Web pages load slowly, applications time out, and you sense a general, hard-to-measure, irritating slowness.

NOTE There are plenty of reasons for a device to run slowly that have nothing to do with wireless. Don't forget issues such as insufficient RAM or the presence of malware.

In general, you can trace the cause of this slowness to one of several issues: you have too many devices overworking your WAPs; there are physical problems with signals going between your WAP and your clients; or there is too much RFI on the network.

OVERWORKED WAPS

An individual WAP has a very specific amount of bandwidth that depends on the version of 802.11 and the way it is configured. Once you hit the maximum bandwidth, you're going to have network slowdowns as the overworked WAP tries to handle all the incoming wireless connections.

We overwork WAPs in many ways, but one of the most common is by attaching too many devices to a single SSID over time, known as *device saturation*. This creates *overcapacity* issues, such as slow speeds and inability to connect to the network. Avoid device saturation by adding more capacity. Careful placement of extra WAPs in high-demand areas is a huge step in the right direction. Usually the best, but most expensive, method is to upgrade your hardware: leaping from the 802.11n to the 802.11ac standard alone makes a massive difference in eliminating device saturation.

Jitter is a variation in packet arrival times, often caused by congestion or an overworked WAP. As Chapter 11 discussed, jitter shows up as choppy conversations over a video call, strange jumps in the middle of an online game, or pretty much anything else that feels like the network has missed some data.

Latency is when data stops moving for a moment due to a WAP being unable to do the work. This manifests as a Word document that stops loading, for example, or an online file that stops downloading.

Worse than jitter and latency, *packet loss* is when packets never reach their destination, leaving gaps in the communication. Packet loss is also caused by overworked WAPs, as well as network congestion, wireless interference, faulty hardware (bad cables or NICs), software or configuration issues (mismatched MTU sizes or routing errors), and even security measures like firewalls that intentionally drop certain packets.

Speaking of 802.11ac, the biggest single issue causing device saturation is the imbalance of many devices using the 2.4 GHz band versus few devices using the 5.0 GHz band. In almost every midsize or larger wireless network, the 2.4 GHz band is filled to capacity, even with careful use of multiple channels. This *bandwidth saturation* is a huge issue with 802.11 networks, and there's no answer other than to move to the 5.0 GHz band using primarily 802.11ac or 802.11ax.

EXAM TIP Expect a scenario question on the CompTIA Network+ exam about specific statistics or sensors to use to ensure wireless network availability. Some of the performance metrics—specifically *network metrics*—you'll need to look for are bandwidth, latency, and jitter.

PHYSICAL ISSUES

Any physical item placed on or near the straight-line path between a WAP and a wireless client can cause problems with a wireless signal. The problem depends on what's in the way and how it affects the radio signals as they encounter it. Physical issues fall into three categories:

ABSORPTION Nonmetallic building materials, such as brick, sheetrock, and wood, *absorb* radio signals, greatly reducing or in some cases completely eliminating a Wi-Fi signal.

REFLECTION Metallic materials like pipes, radiators, metal doors, and windows frames will *reflect* (or bounce) radio waves, sending them in unsuspected directions and keeping them from getting to their target device.

REFRACTION Glass is notorious for its ability to bend, or *refract*, radio waves as they pass through it. Even if there's a straight line from a WAP to a client, a glass door between them can cause problems.

The result of all these physical problems is *attenuation*, the progressive loss of radio signal strength as the radio wave passes through different mediums—even elements like air and rain.

Be careful here: different materials may cause more than one of these effects. A concrete wall may both absorb and reflect radio waves, whereas a metal framed door with glass inserts may both reflect and refract them. Because attenuation effects are different in every case, they're tricky to predict during a site survey, requiring serious troubleshooting after the installation of a wireless network. A solid concrete wall is easy to predict as a problem and to work around with strategic WAP placement, but an office full of thick-walled, metal-framed room dividers might not be as easy to identify during a survey and won't emerge as a physical problem until users start complaining about slow connections.

When a tech suspects a physical issue with a wireless network, the first step is to conduct another site survey. Look for physical barriers that block signals to hosts in critical locations. Often a quick visual inspection is all that's needed to identify obstacles that can be moved or to determine where WAPs or antennas should be repositioned or added. Additionally, the tech can deploy WAPs with multiple antennas, creating multipath signals to improve coverage and reliability in areas affected by physical obstructions.

INTERFERENCE

Radio frequency interference (RFI) is an equally big problem as physical obstacles when it comes to wireless network slowdowns. The 802.11 standard is impressive in its ability to deal with noisy RF environments, but there's a point where any environment gets too noisy for 802.11. Interference comes from a number of sources, but we can break them down into two basic categories: RFI from non-Wi-Fi sources and RFI from Wi-Fi networks.

Non-Wi-Fi sources of RFI include CFL and LED lighting; low-power RF protocols like Bluetooth, Zigbee, and Z-Wave; cordless phones; and microwaves. In general, these devices can work nicely with 802.11 networks, but too many devices, especially when they're too close to 802.11 equipment, can cause problems. The only way to eliminate this type of interference is to shut down or move the devices.

RFI can also be caused by devices that predate the regulation of those channel ranges, which mostly affects the 2.4 GHz band.

When it comes to 802.11-based interference, we're looking mainly at other WAPs generating signals that interfere with ours. The most common problem is that the limited number of channels means it's easy to have two WAPs on the same channel physically near each other. The extreme limitation of three *non-overlapping channels* in 2.4 GHz is one reason why it's common to abandon the band in modern network designs.

To identify and measure interference, use some form of RF scanner. A *spectrum analyzer*, for example, such as those used in wired and wireless networks, can measure electrical signals for frequency, power, harmonics, distortion, and more. We measure RFI with the *signal-to-noise ratio* (SNR), essentially comparing the signal strength and the overall interference in the space. Figure 12-39 shows the popular AirMagnet Wi-Fi Analyzer PRO reporting SNR. Use a channel that's not overwhelmed.

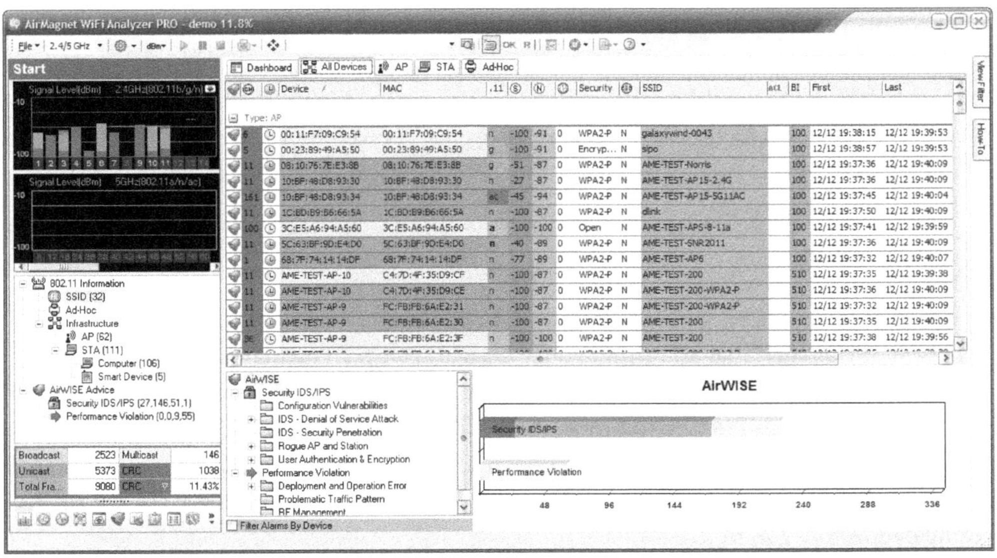

FIGURE 12-39 SNR on AirMagnet

Weird Connections

There are a number of situations where devices are connected to a wireless network and run at a good speed, but something is wrong—in some cases, dangerously wrong from a security perspective. Let's look at a few of these situations.

OPEN NETWORKS

Open (unencrypted) 802.11 networks are the bane of users and administrators. The two biggest challenges are avoiding unintentionally logging into an open network with an SSID identical (or similar) to one you have in another location, and providing security in an open network environment.

It's very common for your wireless device to access open networks with WAPs that use manufacturer default SSID names, such as Linksys or D-Link. The danger is that once the bad guys have created a profile to connect to one of these default, open SSIDs, they know they can automatically connect to any others like it.

The second issue with any open wireless is that all the data is transferred in the clear. It's easy for bad guys to listen in on your transmissions. Ways to avoid this include using a VPN or Tor (The Onion Router), a browser/network combination that uses a peer-to-peer infrastructure to scramble web traffic through relays/nodes that have multiple layers—like an onion—of encryption worldwide.

However, the eavesdropping issue has declined greatly in recent years because almost 95 percent of websites today use TLS, which encrypts web traffic. Thus, encrypting already encrypted web traffic would be superfluous, unless you're a journalist, activist, dissident, or otherwise well-known figure. In those cases, using a VPN would provide extra levels of privacy and anonymity because metadata that can identify a person, device, or location can be aggregated even when TLS is used.

WRONG SSID

It's easy to access the wrong SSID. Some 802.11 clients are notorious for moving their list of discovered SSIDs such that you think you're clicking one SSID when you're actually clicking another. The only fix is to practice diligence when logging on to a new SSID. For example, who hasn't seen SSIDs like the infamous "attwifi"? This SSID is AT&T's attempt to use all its devices as hotspots. Sadly, it's simple enough to create an evil twin SSID (described in the upcoming section "Rogue Access Points") to mimic the attwifi SSID and get otherwise unsuspecting people to log in to it.

Manually entering an SSID can obviously result in a typo. Luckily, in these cases your typo won't accidentally land you onto another SSID. You'll just get an error.

UNTESTED UPDATES/INCOMPATIBILITIES

802.11 is an ever-evolving standard, and manufacturers learned a long time ago to work hard to ensure their devices could evolve with it. This means that anyone supporting any 802.11 network will find themselves continually updating client firmware/software and WAP firmware. These updates are almost always good, but you need to stay aware of problems.

First, always research and test any update—especially firmware updates, which aren't very easy to reverse. Untested updates that go into your production network can potentially wreak havoc. If possible, run updates on a test network first.

Most commercial (and even some home WAP/wireless routers) now support two firmware slots. When you upgrade, your new firmware is loaded into the spare slot, leaving the current version in place if you need to revert to it. Before this practice, it was absurdly hard to revert to a prior version.

Incompatibilities are related to untested updates in that they tend to appear at the same time an update appears. Make sure you are extremely clear on the backward compatibility of different 802.11 versions. Also be aware that there might be incompatibilities even in the same type of network. Say that a few years ago, you bought what you thought was a dual-band (2.4 and 5.0 GHz) 802.11n WAP. You also invested serious money in upgrading your 802.11n NICs in a few clients to accept dual band. Sadly, it wasn't until you were installing the new WAP that you read in the instructions that it supported only one of the two bands at a time and was totally incompatible with your new, expensive wireless NICs. Ouch! Too bad you didn't test the WAP before you tried to run it in your production environment.

ROGUE ACCESS POINTS

Rogue access points (rogue APs) are simply unauthorized access points, and they've tortured every wireless network since the day Linksys came out with the first cheap wireless router back in the early 2000s. Not all rogue APs are evil; sometimes it's just a user who installs a WAP in a handy location to connect to the wired network.

Some rogue APs are far more nefarious, acting as a backdoor to a network or an on-path attack, grabbing usernames and passwords, among other items.

The most infamous form of rogue AP, an *evil twin*, intentionally mimics an existing SSID (like attwifi, mentioned previously) to get people to connect to it instead of the proper AP. The cybercriminals can now infiltrate to and exfiltrate from a device (for example, to inject malware and steal sensitive information) that connects to their rogue AP. Evil twins work best in unsecured networks such as those you see in airports and hotels. Small and midsize businesses that implement proper wireless and wired network security disable network drops in the lobby and use MAC address restrictions.

A rogue AP is connected to your network, not just an AP you can see from your location. An evil twin may or may not be on the network, like in a coffee shop where users just want to get online and might not notice that they're on the wrong network. An evil twin on a corporate network is harder to manage since it can potentially steal credentials and other sensitive internal information.

CLIENT DISASSOCIATION ISSUES

Association describes the connection between an AP and a wireless client, a part of the typical 802.11 process. Association problems that result in very slow connection times or forced *disassociation* (the abrupt loss of the Wi-Fi connection) can be accidental or intentional.

A few years ago, a popular Wi-Fi manufacturer upgraded their AP firmware, which worked great for most users. Some users, however, immediately started complaining that the association process—which previously happened in a couple of seconds—took minutes and often failed altogether. Obviously, this association problem was unintentional. Another firmware upgrade fixed the issue but didn't quite fix the disgruntled users!

More common, especially in public Wi-Fi settings, is a *deauth attack* (*deauth* is short for *deauthentication*) designed to force a device off a legitimate AP and onto the attacker's AP. The attacker can then try to capture usernames and passwords. WPA3 requires support of IEEE 802.11w-2009, which, among other security features, prevents unencrypted deauth frames from knocking clients off networks.

Chapter 17 goes into more detail on deauth and other attacks, including evil twin and on-path attacks.

NOTE You can view the event log for an AP to see details about every wireless client connected, such as the *AP association time*—how long they've been connected—and the amount of bandwidth used. You can often also see how many retries a client has made. Short association time and a lot of retries might point to something nefarious happening.

ROAMING MISCONFIGURATION

When wireless clients roam from one access point to another, the hope is that the process will be transparent and seamless. However, there are numerous misconfiguration issues that can cause a connection to drop or weaken during this process. SSIDs, channels, and security settings can all be misconfigured, as can the roaming aggressiveness setting, which dictates when a client will try to find another AP based on current signal strength. At the Lowest setting, clients find new APs if the current signal strength is very low, while at the Highest setting they try to find new APs even if the current signal strength is good. Other values include Medium-Low, Medium (the default), and Medium-High. Roaming too frequently or failing to switch when the signal is weak can cause dropped connections, slower throughput, higher latency, or interruptions in real-time applications like streaming or video calls.

Satellite

Living in the countryside may have its charms, but you'll have a hard time getting high-speed internet out on the farm. Satellite may be your only option. Satellite access comes in two types: one-way and two-way. *One-way* means that you download via satellite, but you must use a PSTN/dial-up modem connection for uploads. *Two-way* means the satellite service handles both uploads and downloads.

NOTE Companies that design satellite communications equipment haven't given up on their technology. The standard HughesNet products advertise download speeds up to 100 Mbps and upload speeds up to 3 Mbps. The SpaceX Starlink service advertises download speeds from 25 to 220 Mbps (most users get over 100 Mbps), and upload speeds between 5 and 20 Mbps.

Satellite requires a small satellite antenna, identical to the ones used for satellite television. This antenna connects to a satellite modem, which in turn connects to your PC or your network (Figure 12-40).

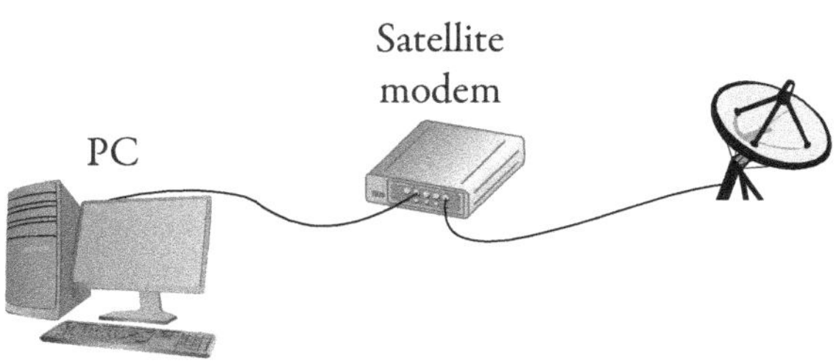

FIGURE 12-40 A satellite connection

Cellular WAN

Anyone with a smartphone enjoys the convenience of wireless cellular technology. Who doesn't love firing up their iPhone or Android phone and surfing the internet from anywhere? As cell phone technology converges with internet access technologies, competent techs need to understand what's happening behind the scenes.

Unless you have 802.11 wireless turned on, smartphone data moves through cellular wireless networks with towers all over the world (Figure 12-41). You can also connect through cellular modems and hotspots rather than tethering to your phone.

FIGURE 12-41 A cellular tower

Understanding how wireless cellular technology works also means tackling an alphabet soup of standards. Mobile data services started in the mid-1980s and, as you might imagine, have gone through a dizzying number of standards and protocols, all of which have been revised, improved, abandoned, and reworked. Instead of trying to advertise these fairly complex and intimidating technologies, the industry instead came up with the marketing term *generations*, abbreviated to the letter *G* and preceded by a number: 2G, 3G, 4G, and 5G.

These terms are used by salespeople and TV commercials to push mobile cellular services, but they aren't generally used within the industry, and certainly not at a deeply technical level. As we go through the following standards that you may see on the exam and encounter in real life, I'll mention both the technical name and the generation where applicable:

- GSM and EDGE
- CDMA
- HSPA+
- LTE
- 5G

GSM and EDGE

The *Global System for Mobile Communications* (GSM), the first group of networking technologies widely applied to mobile devices, relied on a type of multiplexing called *time-division multiple access* (TDMA). TDMA enabled multiple users to share the same channel more or less at the same time, and the switch from one user to another happened so quickly that no one noticed.

NOTE There's no *C* on the end of *GSM* because it originates from the French term *Groupe Spécial Mobile*.

GSM introduced the handy and now ubiquitous *subscriber identity module (SIM) card* in smartphones (Figure 12-42). The SIM card identifies the phone, enabling access to the cellular networks, and stores various other information.

FIGURE 12-42 Original SIM card

The GSM standard was considered a 2G technology. The standard continued to improve over the years, getting new names and better data speeds. One of the last of these, *Enhanced Data rates for GSM Evolution* (EDGE), offered data speeds up to 384 Kbps.

CDMA

Code-division multiple access (CDMA) came out not long after GSM, but it used a spread-spectrum form of transmission that was totally incompatible with GSM's TDMA. Rather than enabling multiple users to share a single channel by splitting the channel into time slices, spread-spectrum transmission changed the frequencies used by each user.

CDMA was considered superior to GSM, and US carriers adopted CDMA en masse, which created some problems later since the rest of the world went with GSM. Not only that, but CDMA lacked some key features, such as SIM cards.

The original CDMA was considered a 2G technology.

HSPA+

In the late 1990s, the International Telecommunication Union (ITU) forwarded a standard called International Mobile Telecommunications-2000 (IMT-2000) to address shortcomings in mobile technology. IMT-2000 defined higher speeds, support for full-time internet connections, and other critical functions. The standard also pushed support for multimedia messaging system (MMS), allowing you to send cat pictures in your text messages, and IP-based telephony.

Both GSM and CDMA made improvements during the late 1990s to the mid-2000s to address IMT-2000, publicizing them under probably the most confusing marketing term ever used: *3G*. Ideally, 3G meant a technology that supported IMT-2000, although the industry was very lax in how the term was used. In fact, the terminology during this time period was so confusing that many technologies were given decimal generations to try to clarify the situation. For example, GSM EDGE was called 2.9G due to its lack of full IMT-2000 support.

Evolved High-Speed Packet Access (HSPA+) was the final 3G data standard, providing theoretical speeds up to 168 Mbps, although most HSPA+ implementations rarely exceeded 10 Mbps.

LTE

Devices and networks using *Long Term Evolution* (LTE) technology rolled out world-wide in the early 2010s and now dominate wireless services. Marketed as—and now generally accepted as—a true *4G* technology, LTE networks feature speeds of up to 300 Mbps download and 75 Mbps upload. All LTE services use SIM cards such as the one shown in Figure 12-43. Notice how much smaller this *nano-SIM* is than the original, standard SIM in Figure 12-42.

Smartphones have LTE radios built in, but it's easy to add LTE to almost any device. Need LTE on a laptop or a desktop? No problem: get an LTE NIC and just plug it into a convenient USB port (Figure 12-44).

FIGURE 12-43 Modern nano-SIM

FIGURE 12-44 Cellular wireless NIC on USB stick

5G

The successor to 4G, called *5G*, offers substantially upgraded technology and dramatically increased speeds over its predecessor. Cellular companies started rolling out 5G in 2019.

5G operates at three bands: low runs at 600 to 800 MHz (similar to 4G), medium at 2.5 to 3.7 GHz, and high at 25 to 39 GHz. The higher the frequency, the faster the possible throughput speeds and the shorter the range. Depending on the radios installed by the carriers and those in the portable devices that use 5G, the expected speed ranges are 30 Mbps up to 1 Gbps.

The high-band 5G implementation requires dense saturation of transmitters/receivers and antennas, so it will work best in high-density settings, such as stadiums. Additionally, the exceptional speeds offered by 5G make it a viable replacement for other technologies in mobile devices such as laptops and tablets, as well as a major selling point for the latest smartphones.

> **WHICH CONNECTION?**
>
> With so many connection options for homes and small offices, making a decision can be a challenge. Your first question concerns availability: which services are available in your area? Second, how much bandwidth do you need? The latter is a question of great debate. Most services are more than happy to increase bandwidth if you find that your current level is too slow. I usually advise clients to start at a relatively slow level and then increase if necessary. After all, once you've tasted the higher speeds, going slower is hard, but the transition to faster is relatively painless and always rewarding.

Chapter Review

Questions

1. What is the progressive loss of radio signal passing through different media called?
   - **A.** Attenuation
   - **B.** EAP
   - **C.** RFI
   - **D.** SNR
2. Which technology enables use of a WAP without directly connecting the WAP to an AC power outlet?
   - **A.** AES
   - **B.** PoE
   - **C.** Powered Wi-Fi
   - **D.** TKIP

3. Which of the following is known as a basic service set in infrastructure mode?
   A. A WAP
   B. A WPA
   C. A RADIUS server
   D. A TKIP
4. Which 802.11 standard is the latest and greatest?
   A. 802.11ac
   B. 802.11a
   C. 802.11b
   D. 802.11ax
5. When setting up WPA2-PSK on a wireless network, should you choose TKIP or AES?
   A. Only AES
   B. Only TKIP
   C. Both AES and TKIP
   D. Neither. You should implement RADIUS.
6. To achieve maximum Wi-Fi coverage in a room, where should you place the WAP?
   A. Place the WAP on the north side of the room.
   B. Place the WAP in the center of the room.
   C. Place the WAP near a convenient electrical outlet.
   D. It doesn't matter where you place the WAP.
7. What hardware enables wireless PCs to connect to resources on a wired network segment in infrastructure mode? (Select two.)
   A. An access point
   B. A router
   C. A hub
   D. A wireless bridge
8. What do you call a wireless network in infrastructure mode with more than one access point?
   A. BSS
   B. EBSS
   C. WBSS
   D. ExNet

9. What type of server supports EAP-encrypted passwords in accordance with the 802.1X standard?
   A. WAP server
   B. WEP server
   C. RADIUS server
   D. NAS server
10. Which of the following is the most secure method of wireless encryption?
   A. WEP
   B. WPA2
   C. WPA3
   D. WPA4

Answers

1. **A.** Attenuation is the term describing the progressive loss of radio signal passing through different media.
2. **B.** Power over Ethernet (PoE) enables a wireless access point (WAP) to use electricity from a PoE switch rather than connect to an AC power outlet directly.
3. **A.** A single wireless access point (WAP) is a basic service set. Wi-Fi Protected Access (WPA) is a data encryption scheme. A RADIUS server provides authentication via a username and password. Temporal Key Integrity Protocol (TKIP) is used by the WPA encryption scheme to encrypt the data.
4. **D.** 802.11ax, Wi-Fi 6, was officially endorsed by the IEEE in 2021.
5. **A.** Although WPA2 supports both TKIP and Advanced Encryption Standard (AES), TKIP is deprecated, and AES is far more secure.
6. **B.** To achieve maximum coverage, place the WAP in the center of the room.
7. **A** and **D.** A wireless access point or wireless bridge enables you to connect wireless PCs to a wired network segment.
8. **B.** A wireless network in infrastructure mode with more than one access point is called an extended basic service set, or EBSS.
9. **C.** A RADIUS server provides authentication through a username and password encrypted with Extensible Authentication Protocol (EAP).
10. **D.** WPA3 offers the highest security. There is no WPA4.

PART III

Modern Operations and Cloud Architectures

IN THIS PART:

- CHAPTER 13: Virtualization and Cloud Computing
- CHAPTER 14: Data Centers
- CHAPTER 15: Devices, Access, Management, and Monitoring
- CHAPTER 16: Processes and Procedures

Virtualization and Cloud Computing

IN THIS CHAPTER, YOU WILL LEARN HOW TO

- Describe virtualization, virtual networking, and cloud computing concepts
- Explain how network virtualization and cloud computing work in modern networks

Let's pretend you have an incredible idea for a new company. Oh my gosh; it's such a good idea! We can make millions! Let's do it! So, let's set up that website! Here we go. . . .

Hang on there! Not that long ago, you had to go through a fairly onerous process of buying a beefy system, getting a static IP address from an ISP, installing and configuring the operating system, installing and configuring the web server software, and registering the website's domain. Then, of course, you had to build the website. You didn't have any other choices.

Building a website these days is easy if you don't need a lot of control. You pick a point-and-click service that will register a domain for you, and then choose a template, fill in some information about your company, and even add a store to sell things! You can build a robust, functioning website without thinking about servers, operating systems, or IP addresses.

For your awesome new company, though, you'll need more control than that. But you don't have to go hardware shopping, kill your back racking servers, and operate all that gear. You pick an online cloud provider like Amazon Web Services, Microsoft Azure, or Google Cloud and quickly set up a server that lives in someone else's rack.

How did we get from a process requiring so much manual effort to being able to set up websites and app servers by clicking a few buttons? Well, this is a combination of the two technologies you'll discover in this chapter: virtualization and the cloud. As you will soon see, virtualization and the cloud aren't at all the same thing, but they sure play well together!

One caveat before we start: these examples of super-easy websites and app hosting explore only one aspect of the power of virtualization and the cloud. There's so much more, but hopefully this is enough to pique your interest to delve into this chapter with gusto!

This chapter begins with virtualization and cloud computing concepts to create a framework for discussion. Then it dives into how virtualization shapes many aspects of modern networking. To wrap up, it covers practical applications of network virtualization and cloud computing. Let's get started.

Test Specific

Virtualization and cloud computing bring a host of jargon and specific concepts into play. Techs need to understand the fundamentals underlying the technologies to know how best to deploy them in current networking scenarios. We'll look first at virtualization and then cloud computing.

Virtualization

From the first day some nerdy type decided to take a PC and turn it into a server, *hardware underutilization*—a server or desktop PC not being used to its full capability—has been a problem. Consider a file server in an office LAN or a web server hosting a single website. In both cases, not enough users are accessing the server (Figure 13-1).

FIGURE 13-1 Underutilization

No matter what a server is serving, traditionally there's a substantial amount of hardware underutilization. Sure, we've all experienced trying do something on the internet and receiving a "Server busy" message or similar *overutilization* error, but in the vast majority of cases, underutilization is the problem.

So how do we fix it? Well, we need the servers to do more with the hardware they have. Luckily for us, PC processors, using roughly the same set of functions that enables your CPU to multitask many applications at once, can instead multitask a bunch of *virtual machines* (VM), software emulations of physical computers. *Virtualization* enables one physical machine, called the host, to simultaneously run multiple VMs, each with its own operating system. A VM runs in protected space (just like programs run in protected space) and is allocated portions of the physical machine's resources (RAM, CPU, drive space, peripherals, etc.). See Figure 13-2.

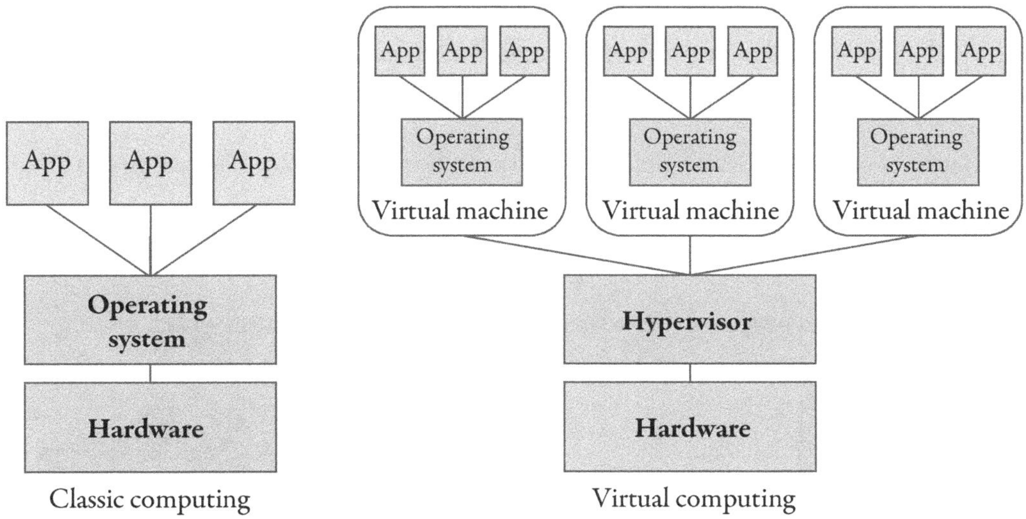

FIGURE 13-2 Classic computing versus computing with virtualization

You can install and run an OS in this virtual environment as if it were its own physical computer.

The Hypervisor

The program used to create, run, and maintain the VMs is called a *hypervisor*. At the core of the operating system is the kernel, the intermediary between a computer's software and hardware, which has complete control over everything including memory management, resource allocation, filesystems, network sockets, and more. Traditionally, the kernel was known as a *supervisor*. You can think of the hypervisor as the supervisor of the supervisors of the VMs.

A VM is stored as a set of files that the hypervisor can load and save with changes. The CPU, RAM, hard drive, and other physical hardware are virtualized for the guest operating systems that run through a hypervisor. A hypervisor must handle every input and output that an OS would request of normal hardware. With a good hypervisor like VMware Workstation Pro, you can easily add and remove virtual hard drives, virtual network cards, virtual RAM, and so on. (Workstation Pro became free for personal use in May 2024, eliminating the need for VMware Workstation Player, which had been used up to that point.) Virtualization even goes so far as to provide a virtualized BIOS (Basic Input/Output System)/UEFI (Unified Extensible Firmware Interface) and system setup utility for every VM.

NOTE The host system allocates real RAM and CPU time to every running VM but can only handle a finite number of simultaneous VMs before performance degrades. A single hypervisor on a single system will happily run as many VMs as its RAM, CPU, and drive space allow (RAM is almost always the main limiting factor). A VM that's shut down is just a set of files sitting on a hard drive.

Figure 13-3 shows a Mac using a hypervisor called Oracle VM VirtualBox to run an Ubuntu Linux guest OS on a VM.

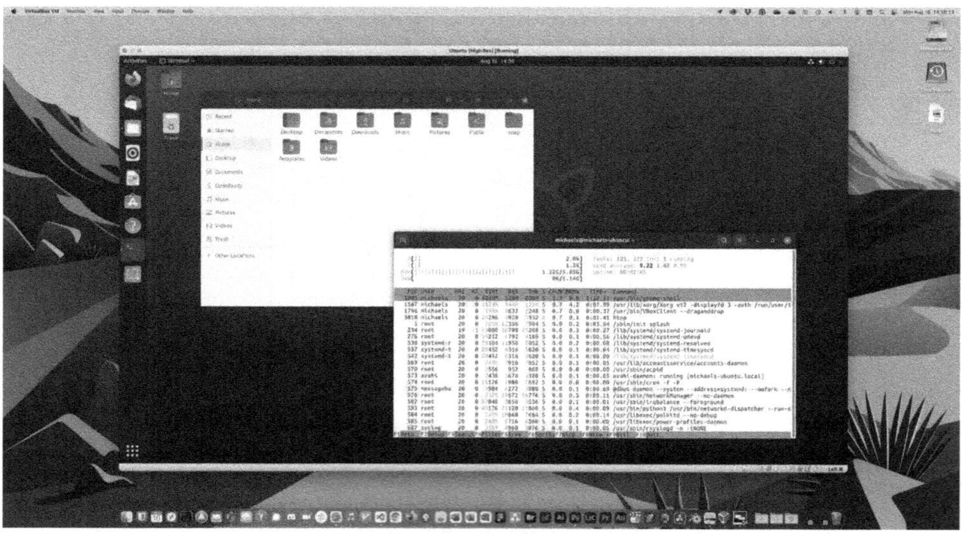

FIGURE 13-3 VirtualBox running Linux

There are two types of hypervisors (Figure 13-4).

VMware Workstation Pro requires an underlying OS, like Windows 11, so it functions essentially like a very powerful desktop application. Hypervisors that operate in this fashion are called Type 2 hypervisors.

What if you could remove the OS altogether and create a bare-metal implementation of virtualization? VMware introduced ESX in 2001 to accomplish this goal. ESX is a hypervisor that's powerful enough to replace the host OS on a physical box, turning the physical machine into nothing but a host for VMs. Hypervisors that operate in this fashion are called Type 1 hypervisors. You power up the server, and the server loads ESX. In short order, a very rudimentary interface appears where you can input essential information, such as a master password and a static IP address.

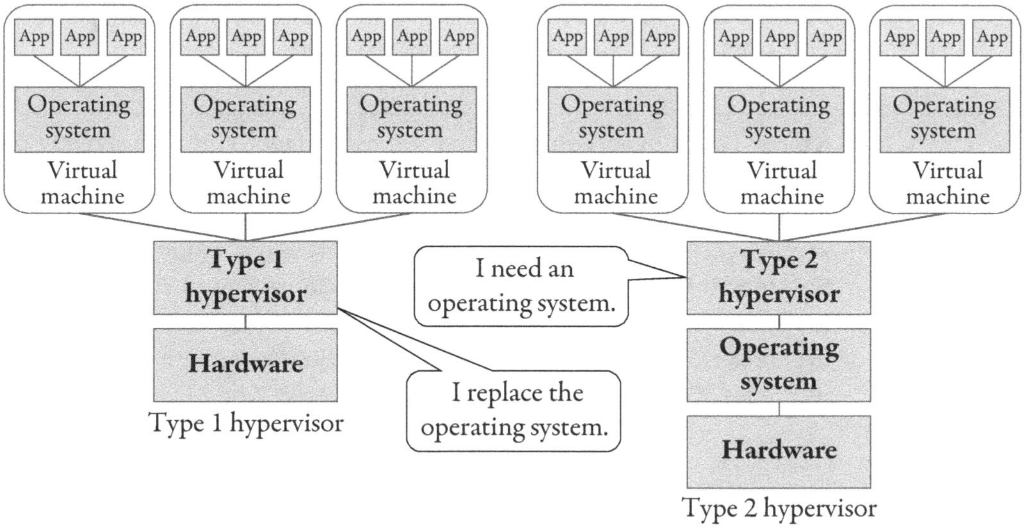

FIGURE 13-4 Hypervisor types

VMware came out with a free version of ESX, called ESXi, in 2008. This strategic move allowed administrators to use, publicize, and get comfortable with ESXi at no cost. There is a paid version of ESXi as well, which is highly recommended for production networks. Although there are still some ESX machines out there, in 2010 VMware discontinued development on ESX and strongly urged its customers to move over to ESXi, which is the only platform now supported by VMware vSphere (explained next). In November 2023, Broadcom acquired VMware for US$69 billion. In February 2024, VMware discontinued the free version of ESXi, moving its services to a subscription model.

NOTE For all you acronym lovers, ESX officially means nothing. Unofficially, it stands for "Elastic Sky," which is probably why it officially means nothing.

Don't let ESXi's size fool you: it's small (because it only has one job, hosting VMs) but mighty. Powerful hypervisors like ESXi are not administered directly at the box. Instead, you use tools such as VMware's vSphere Client, so you can create, configure, and maintain VMs on the hypervisor server from the comfort of a client computer running this program. Once the VM is up and running, you can close the vSphere Client, but the VM will continue to run happily on the server. So, you have two different ways to virtualize: using hypervisors such as

VMware Workstation Pro to manage VMs on a single machine or using powerful hypervisors such as ESXi to manage VMs on other machines, like those in a data center.

NOTE Type 1 hypervisors include Microsoft Hyper-V (it runs directly on hardware and the system boots into it first, while the Windows Server OS becomes a management partition), VMware ESXi, Virtual Environment, and XenServer. Type 2 hypervisors include VMware Workstation Pro, Parallels Desktop for Mac, and Oracle VM VirtualBox. Kernel-based Virtual Machine (KVM) and bhyve are kernel modules that convert the host OS to a Type 1 hypervisor. Since Linux systems have applications vying with each other for resources, KVM and bhyve can also be considered Type 2 hypervisors.

Virtualization is an incredibly powerful tool that's as ubiquitous as oxygen. Nearly every website is installed in a VM running on a server. The chances of you ever hitting a website that uses classical web hosting are almost nil. And there are many great advantages to it (some of which I'll expand on later in the chapter):

- Having each VM running on the same hardware eliminates hardware dependency issues.
- To make a copy of a VM, you can simply copy the files and folders it comprises. Alternatively, you can set a *checkpoint* (also known as a *snapshot*) to capture a VM's current state—including its data and configuration—and later revert to it if necessary.
- Consolidating servers from many physical machines into VMs reduces a data center's power consumption, carbon footprint, and business expenses (expensive hardware, for example). You can even expand data centers with VMs on an as-needed basis and restore them to their original size when those additional resources are no longer needed.
- Some hypervisors can perform *dynamic load balancing*, directing requests to VMs that are not as busy as others, and even dynamically allocate more resources to busier VMs.
- Instead of spending hours or days to replace or fix a physical machine affected by a disaster, you can provision (set up) and deploy a VM in minutes by replicating or cloning the affected machine. This rapid recovery reduces downtime and is a huge benefit for an organization's availability.
- Installing, updating, and maintaining virtual environments is more efficient, allowing the IT staff to be more productive.
- A developer can easily deploy a VM to test programs and patches in a certain environment.
- You can troubleshoot software on various platforms with multiple VMs much more easily than doing so through multiple physical machines running various OSs.

- You can configure a VM's security settings to prevent malware attacks or software glitches on it from affecting other VMs. Furthermore, you can restore an earlier saved copy of that VM if it gets compromised.

Next, we'll explore three primary aspects of virtualization to provide a framework for understanding: abstraction, flexibility, and scaling.

Abstraction

Modern networks separate form from function on many levels, actions that are defined by the jargon word *abstraction*. It's a loaded term that has meanings in both English and computing, so let's break it down with some examples, and then provide a working definition.

Abstract means existing in thought or as an idea but without a physical or concrete existence. It also means to remove or separate.

In computing terms, the hypervisor *abstracts* the physical hardware of the computer to the VM. The VM thinks it's the only show in town and that it's running directly on top of the hardware, but it isn't. The hardware of the VM has no physical or concrete existence. Of course, there is real physical hardware that's abstracted, but it's implemented in the form of files to the VM, not actual hardware. The hardware is removed and separate from the VM.

Virtualization is a specific kind of abstraction: a pattern that involves creating a virtual (software) version of something. We used to only create virtual (sometimes called *logical*) versions of real, physical things. But virtualization proved to be such a fruitful idea that we've kept right on virtualizing things that are already virtual. To keep your bearings, remember that most kinds of virtualization replace an existing component with a layer of software that is effectively indistinguishable to any programs, devices, or users that interact with it.

I hope a few examples drive these points home:

- Virtual memory replaces direct access to physical RAM with a layer of software that enables the OS to move a running program's memory to the swap file and back dynamically without the program's awareness.
- Hardware virtualization replaces all the physical devices an OS needs with software versions that the hypervisor controls. The hypervisor can use this control to redistribute the host's hardware resources among running VMs on the fly.
- One form of storage virtualization replaces a system's hard drive with a software block-storage device that can send reads and writes to other places, such as to a file or to a storage server accessible over the network.
- Network virtualization, the star of this particular show, creates software versions of networking functions—such as DNS, firewalls, and intrusion detection systems—that used to require dedicated network hardware boxes. The network OS interacts with network functions just as it always did. Those functions—now software—in turn work with a hypervisor that interfaces with real hardware. Figure 13-5 shows this relationship shift.

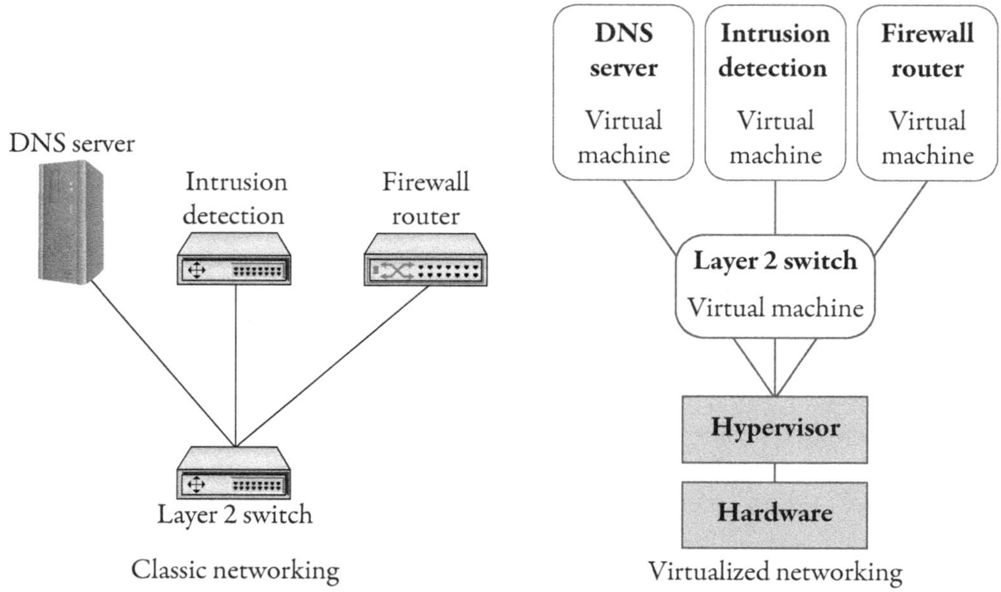

FIGURE 13-5 Classic versus virtualized networking

- Cisco makes an Adaptive Security Virtual Appliance (ASAv), a virtual ASA firewall, that can be deployed on ESX, AWS, Azure, and other platforms.
- Taken to one extreme, you can use virtualization to create a fully functional network. A hypervisor can use a virtual network, in the form of a virtual switch (discussed later in the chapter), to enable multiple VMs it hosts to communicate without the frames ever leaving the host machine.

NOTE With *containerization*, an operating system creates a self-contained environment for an application. This environment includes all the software the application needs to run as if it were the only application running on a clean OS. Containerization isn't listed in the CompTIA Network+ objectives, but you'll see it in the real world. It's a bit like hardware virtualization but essentially virtualizes the OS instead of the whole computer.

Containers use fewer resources than VMs, but they're stuck with the same OS as their host and are less isolated from each other. When you see terms like Docker, Kubernetes, k8s, k3s, LXC, and OCI, it indicates a container technology; terms like *cloud-native* and *microservices* are also closely associated with containerization.

Flexibility

Replacing hardware components with software generally adds flexibility in how you use that virtual hardware. (You do get a performance decrease due to the added layer of software.) Most commonly, you'll see added flexibility in input and output devices, location of devices, and resource allocation.

REROUTE AN INPUT OR OUTPUT

When you create a new VM from scratch, you'll need to install an OS in it. Easy, right? On boring old physical computers, you stick the installation media in a physical USB slot or optical drive. A VM has no such physical ports or drives. It has virtual equivalents that you can route input to from either the host's physical slot/drive or from a disk image file saved on the host. Figure 13-6 shows a VirtualBox installation selecting an ISO image to install Windows 11.

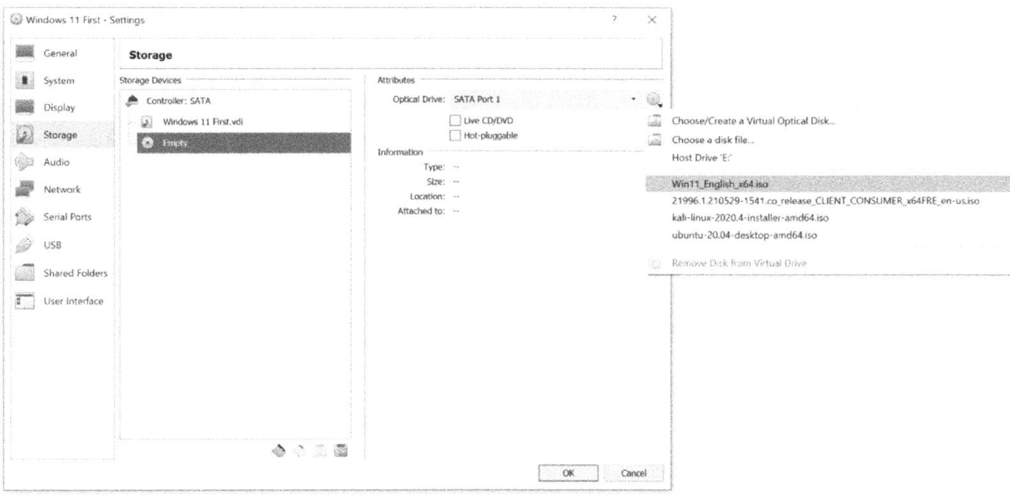

FIGURE 13-6 Selecting an ISO image for OS installation into a VM

Outputs can also get in on the game. If an application has no option for exporting a PDF but does have a print option, a virtual printer can save the output as a PDF without wasting ink or paper. A virtual printer can also capture a document you print while you're out and about and use the internet to print out a hard copy back at your home or office.

RELOCATE COMPONENTS

Virtualization makes it possible to move systems and their parts around in all kinds of creative ways. With a classic server, you have a dedicated hardware box for the server hardware and operating system. That box contains the mass storage needed for the OS, applications, and data. What do you do if the server gets swamped with requests and needs more powerful hardware? In this scenario, you'd build another stand-alone server, install the OS and applications in the dedicated mass storage, and then migrate the data. That's a time-consuming process.

However, virtual machines dramatically simplify the upgrade process. The VM is just a set of files. If it needs a faster processor or more RAM, just allocate more of the host's physical resources to the VM or move the files to an upgraded machine.

Virtualization can also separate components that normally appear together. You can, for example, collect the hard drives that would normally live in each server case and relocate them to a small number of powerful centralized storage servers. This storage virtualization using a storage area network (SAN) leads to the next point.

DIVIDE AND COMBINE RESOURCES

Virtualization enables you to pool resources and reallocate them as needed. Virtualizing a component such as RAM, a CPU, or a hard drive makes it possible to divide that resource up and give each VM its own portion. It also means the inverse. A virtualized hard drive backed by multiple physical drives, for example, can function as a single drive larger than anything you could buy off the shelf.

Scaling

The benefits of aggressive virtualization become readily apparent at scale. Virtualizing servers and network hardware in a SOHO environment adds complexity without any obvious gains. Scale up to data center size, on the other hand, and virtualization provides tangible benefits. (We'll talk more about scalability later in the chapter.)

If you're running a data center that hosts 100,000 physical servers, every server will have more or less fixed needs like rack space, power, network interface cards (NICs), cables, fans, and more—regardless of whether the server has a single CPU core and 256 MB of RAM or 32 cores and 64 GB of RAM. Powerful physical servers can host many VMs of different sizes (dozens if they are all small), making it possible to host 100,000 equivalent VMs using a fraction of these per-physical-machine resources. And this is just a start. A data center operator can analyze resource use and move VMs around to balance hardware use around the clock more efficiently or to power down idle systems. Even tiny tweaks can save millions of dollars a year at data center scale.

Just because new ideas often meet large-scale needs doesn't mean they aren't useful for the rest of us! Some ideas filter directly down into smaller networks, while others form the backbone of cloud computing services (which make extensive use of data centers) that customers can use.

Virtual Networking

Classic networking follows the same paradigm as classic computing. A dedicated computing device with a dedicated operating system performs each network function. Switches do switching; routers do routing. Even multilayer devices such as SOHO routers that perform switching, routing, and wireless networking are simply complex machines run by a dedicated OS.

Virtualization is transforming networking, so that *software* performs the classic network functions. You saw an early version of this transformation with switches and virtual local area network (VLAN) capability in Chapter 6. VLAN-capable switches use a software layer to create and modify VLANs.

This section explores sophisticated virtualization in networking, starting with virtual networking within VM hosts and then virtualization in switching and routing. We'll break out of the VM host and finish with *network function virtualization*. It'll take some backstory to clarify the last term, so let's get to it.

Virtual Networking Inside the VM Host

A hulking server hosting a few dozen VMs can have the same kind of complex networking requirements you'd have on a physical network that hosts a few dozen important servers. Some of the VMs may need to share a private network to collaborate; some may need to serve requests from the open internet; others may need to be isolated from the network. And the server needs to rapidly reconfigure the network as VMs come and go.

Virtual networking inside the host is one way to meet these needs. Hypervisors tend to come with their own basic networking capabilities, such as built-in switching. If you have networking needs that the built-in features don't cover, you can run other network functions as VMs (on the same hypervisor as any VMs they support, when you can).

VIRTUAL NETWORK INTERFACE CARDS

Let's say you install VMware Workstation Pro on a Windows machine and open Network and Sharing Center on the host system. To do that on a Windows 10 host system, click the Start button or type **sharing** in the search box. Click **Manage Advanced Sharing Settings**, then **Network And Sharing Center** in the address bar, and finally **Change Adapter Settings** on the left. Look at all of your interfaces. Besides your physical interfaces, you now have two new VMware Network Adapters, each of which is a virtual network interface card (vNIC).

In bridged networking, the host system and VM are on the same LAN, meaning the physical NIC is on the same subnet as the VM, so no virtual adapter is needed on the host system.

Network Address Translation (NAT) networking uses a virtual router running NAT between the host system and the VM, which will be on a different network than the host system. However, your host system is already configured for a default gateway on your physical router that doesn't know about another virtual network behind VMware's NAT router.

Therefore, to allow the host system to send traffic to the VM in NAT networking, VMware creates a vNIC, VMware Network Adapter VMnet8, for the host system. This virtual adapter has an IP address on the subnet of the VM running in NAT networking, which allows the host system to send traffic directly to the VM (and vice versa) without the need of a physical or virtual router.

Host-only networking, which allows the VM to communicate with just the host system, also uses a vNIC—this one called VMware Network Adapter VMnet1—on the host system. As in NAT networking, the VM is on a different network than the host system. To communicate with the VM in host-only networking, the host system uses the vNIC, because again, the host's default gateway doesn't know about the existence of this remote network that the VM is on.

NOTE When properly configured, there's no difference between a virtual NIC and a physical NIC. Virtual NICs have MAC addresses just like physical NICs. You set up everything about a vNIC—IP address, subnet mask, and so on—exactly as you do with a physical NIC.

VIRTUAL SWITCHES

A *virtual switch* (vSwitch) is software that does the same Layer 2 switching a hardware switch does, supporting features like VLANs, as shown in Figure 13-7. It allows multiple VMs to access the internet by bridging the host machine's single NIC. As with a physical Ethernet switch, each VM's vNIC gets a legitimate, unique MAC address to which the Layer 3 IP address will be associated.

The big difference from a physical switch is what it means to "plug" into the vSwitch. In bridged mode, the VMs and the host's NIC connect to the same vSwitch. Think of the physical NIC as the uplink port on a hardware switch. This makes vSwitches powerful components for networking your VMs—but just like physical networks, we need more than just Layer 2 switching. That's where virtual routers and firewalls come in.

NOTE Hardware switches are still a part of any "virtual" network; don't let that confuse you. Just because you can replace some hardware boxes with VMs doesn't mean you can eliminate all networking hardware! You still need a way to move network traffic between servers and up to the internet.

DISTRIBUTED SWITCHES

A *distributed switch* is automatically installed on every server in a cluster of servers, allowing you to configure and manage them as one group. Distributed switching means you don't have

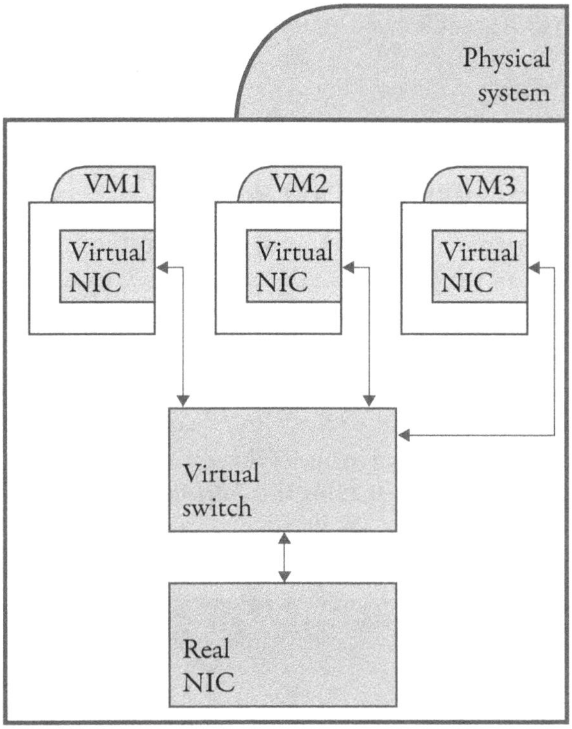

FIGURE 13-7 Virtual switch

to manually create matching port groups or settings or worry about a server losing all of its networking configuration when moved. You can also aggregate port usage across all virtual switches. Every hypervisor supports some form of central configuration for critical switch functions, such as VLAN assignment and trunking.

VIRTUAL ROUTERS

Similar to how VMs enable you to easily reallocate computing resources when demand changes, *virtual routers* let you dynamically reconfigure networks. This way, the network can keep up when VMs are moved from host to host to meet demand or optimize resources. As with any other VM, you can allocate more resources to virtual routers as traffic grows instead of having to buy bigger, better physical routers.

VIRTUAL FIREWALLS

Like virtual routers, *virtual firewalls* are a good option in circumstances where inserting physical hardware would be hard, costly, or impossible.

NOTE A great firewall/router VM combination is pfSense.

Virtual Networking Outside the VM Host

There's no rule that says virtual networking must stay inside the hypervisor. The same virtual network functions you can run as VMs in the cloud (see "Cloud Computing" later in this chapter) can also run as VMs on servers in your own network—or even inside your router if it runs inside a hypervisor.

For instance, my network's VPN concentrator is a VM running on my Dell R340 server (Figure 13-8). When a client connects to the VPN, their traffic is directed to a physical port on my router that is directly connected to one of the server's NICs. My hypervisor bridges this NIC to the VPN concentrator VM, enabling this "virtual" concentrator to handle real traffic between my physical network and remote clients.

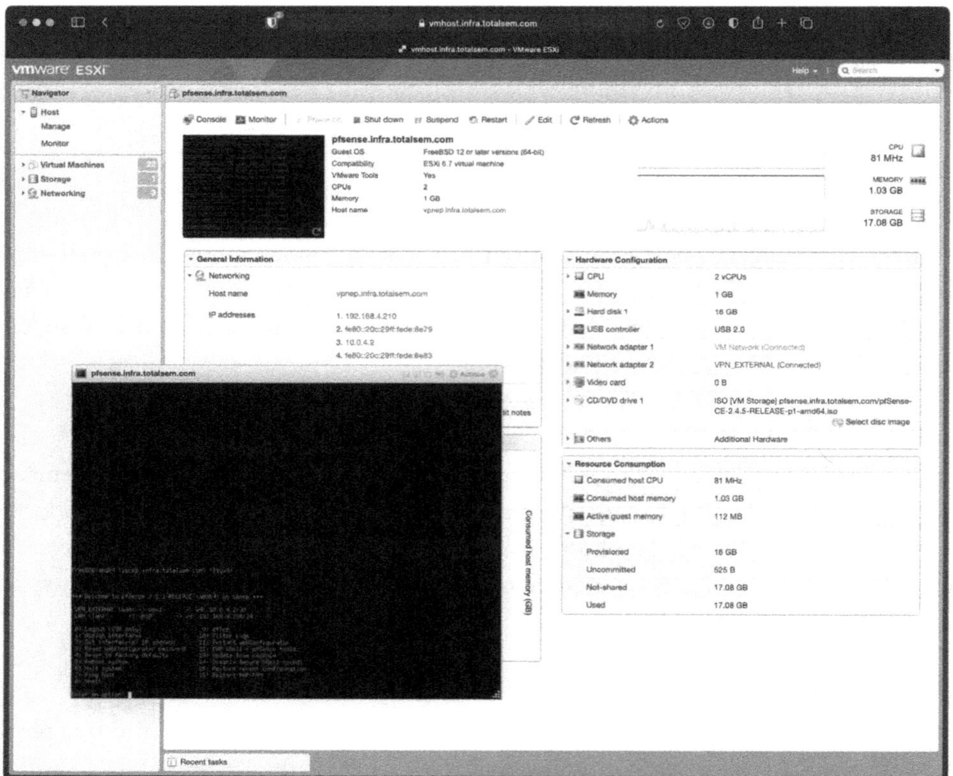

FIGURE 13-8 pfSense VM acting as a VPN concentrator

If everyone who uses the VPN only needed access to servers hosted in the cloud, I could just as easily have set up a VPN concentrator as a VM running on AWS or Microsoft Azure. To integrate those cloud servers with my local network, I'd just set up a persistent tunnel from the office router to the concentrator.

This example illustrates a broader approach called network function virtualization.

Network Function Virtualization

With *network function virtualization* (NFV), VMs take the place of network appliance hardware, like routers, switches, load balancers, firewalls, gateways, and more. Separating the services from the physical hardware devices (routers, switches, etc.) allows you to quickly spin up new services on an as-needed basis, without having to worry about purchasing and deploying new hardware. This turns months of work into hours and saves a lot of money in the process!

NFV ARCHITECTURE

The various parts of the virtual network are programmed and automatically provisioned through software with a hypervisor or software-defined networking (discussed next). An NFV architecture consists of three parts:

- **A centralized virtual network infrastructure** *Network function virtualization infrastructure* (NFVI) represents all hardware and software used to build the NFV environment. NFVI allows you to tie several NVF objects together for consolidated management of all objects.
- **Software implementations for network functions** *Virtualized network functions* (VNFs) represent these applications and are deployed on an NFVI.
- **A framework for NFV management and orchestration** Known as *management, automation, and network orchestration* (MANO), this framework allows for the management and orchestration of NFVI and VNFs.

Big ISPs embrace virtual components and functions for a couple of reasons. For one, they give the ISP a way to consolidate the strange, proprietary, and often incompatible boxes (from many different vendors, for many different technologies) in their network into a small number of standard servers that are compatible with everything else in a normal data center. Second, since these functions are no longer limited to the original box, the ISP can adjust how much RAM or how many processors they can use in real time based on what their users are doing—or shift traffic around misbehaving components.

Saying the "ISP" adjusts the resources, though, doesn't necessarily mean a person is sitting there clicking a mouse or flipping a switch. Real-time tweaks to networks like this—at this scale—are managed by fancy automation and orchestration tools. In NFV, this responsibility falls to the *NFV orchestrator*—a software conductor that does the work of creating, configuring, scaling, pausing, shutting down, and deleting the VNFs that run on the NFVI.

NOTE Just as the cool ideas developed for managing large data centers and cloud networks have trickled down into tools and practices used all around the industry, expect NFV (or at least parts of it) to turn up in smaller networks and projects as the concept continues to mature.

NFV VS. SOFTWARE-DEFINED NETWORKING

Virtual networking can already be a little hard to picture, especially something as loaded with jargon as NFV, so I want to take a moment to explain how network function virtualization—which uses software versions of network functions—differs from the similar-sounding software-defined networking.

Traditionally, hardware routers and switches were designed with closely integrated parts: a *control plane* that decides how to move traffic (a MAC address table on a switch and routing protocols on a router, for example), a *management plane* for device management and monitoring (SSH and SNMP, for example), and a *data plane* that deals with forwarding the actual packets within frames (ACLs, NAT, and QoS, for example).

NOTE Some sources use the term *layer*, some use *plane*, and others mix them. I've used them interchangeably to make sure you're comfortable seeing both.

Software-defined networking (SDN) cuts the control layer of individual devices out of the picture and lets an all-knowing program (running on a server, probably in the cloud) called a *network controller* dictate how both physical and virtual network components move traffic through the network (Figure 13-9). SDN requires components (think routers, switches, and firewalls) with a data layer (also called the *infrastructure layer*) designed to take instructions from the network controller instead of their own control plane.

While it's important that SDN allows for a master controller (such as the one shown in Figure 13-9, though large networks may also distribute the controller's workload over multiple servers), the truly revolutionary idea behind SDN is that the network controller is *programmable*. Programmers can write code (or use software designed by others) that controls how the entire network behaves.

To manage the complexity that comes with separating the infrastructure and control planes, SDN deals with planes as well. The most important are the management (or administration) plane and the application plane. The *management plane* is responsible for setting up network devices to get their marching orders from the right controller. The *application plane*, which sits on top of this entire framework, is where the software controlling the network runs. Applications that run at this layer often do jobs like load balancing, monitoring and optimizing the flow of traffic, enforcing security policy, and protecting against threats.

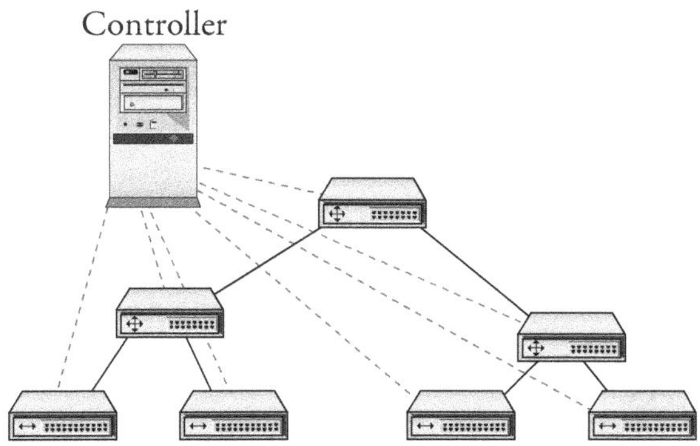

FIGURE 13-9 A controller controls traffic to all the routers and switches.

Even though the term isn't in the name, SDN is yet another example of virtualization. The control plane is virtualized to outsource its role to the network controller. In NFV, in contrast, the *entire* network function is virtualized. NFV and SDN are separate but complementary ways to manage networks with software. You can use the two approaches independently, but an NFV architecture usually also takes advantage of SDN.

Cloud Computing

Cloud computing moves the specialized machines used in classic and virtualized networking "out there somewhere," using the internet to connect an organization to other organizations to manage aspects of the network. Some people like to point out that the cloud is just someone else's computer, and they're at least half right. But it's also been possible to rent someone else's computer from a traditional hosting service for decades, and the cloud is a bit more than a new name for this old idea. Cloud computing also doesn't necessarily mean *someone else's* computer; some organizations build their own cloud just for internal use. The cloud is more like a cafeteria of computing and networking resources—an à la carte data center enhanced by layers of powerful services and software.

NOTE Check out the not-recent but still relevant article at *zdnet.com/article/stop-saying-the-cloud-is-just-someone-elses-computer-because-its-not/* in which Mary Branscombe tells it like it is: "So all of this means the cloud is 'a hyperscale, automated computer farm run by someone who's better at automation and security than you, and can buy electricity and servers and network connectivity more cheaply than you because they buy so much of it and if you want all the benefits of cloud you have to design things to achieve that.'"

The Service-Layer Cake

Service is the key to understanding the cloud. At the hardware level, it's hard to differentiate the cloud infrastructure from the servers and networks that make up the internet as a whole. We use the cloud's servers and networks through layers of software that add great value to the underlying hardware by making it simple to perform complex tasks or manage powerful resources.

End users mostly interact with the service-layer cake's sweet software icing—web applications like Dropbox, Google Drive, Gmail, and Netflix. The rest of the cake, however, is thick with cool services that programmers, techs, and admins can use to build and support their applications and networks.

NOTE The absolutely massive catalog of services available from large cloud service providers can seem like a hodge-podge of unrelated products sometimes. The early cloud ecosystem existed almost exclusively to supply building blocks for these web applications. Economies of scale have enabled CSPs to create new ways to use, and sell, their computing resources to scratch all kinds of IT itches for their customers.

It's common to categorize cloud services into one of three *service models* that broadly describe the type of service provided to whoever pays the bill. I'll relate each of these service models to popular providers, but it's not a perfect mapping, because most CSPs offer many services that fit into different categories in the model. Service models are, however, a good shorthand to differentiate between services that meet the same general need in very different ways. Let's slice the cake open to take a closer look at these three service models (Figure 13-10), starting from the bottom.

FIGURE 13-10 A tasty three-layer cake

INFRASTRUCTURE AS A SERVICE

Large-scale global *infrastructure as a service* (IaaS) providers use virtualization to minimize idle hardware, protect against data loss and downtime, and respond to spikes in demand. Companies can use big IaaS providers, like Amazon Web Services (AWS), to launch new virtual servers using an operating system of choice on demand for pennies an hour. The beauty of IaaS is that you no longer need to purchase expensive, heavy hardware. You are using Amazon's powerful IaaS.

Think about certain times of the year when there's an increase in online shopping (Black Friday, pre-Christmas, etc.). An online retailer might need to temporarily extend their current data center infrastructure to handle that spike in traffic. Instead of investing in hardware, software, and more that they won't need all year round, the retailer can use AWS, for example, to provide many of the services needed to drive popular, complex web applications—unlimited data storage, database servers, caching, media hosting, and more—all billed by usage. When the busy period ends, the retailer can delete those virtual machines and stop paying for those extra services. There will be some residual fees for OS licenses and disk data storage, but the retailer saves on access costs and the like.

What else can you do with IaaS? You can launch a few virtual servers (Figure 13-11) to host an internal application like a support ticket database, create a private network for communication between the servers, and support VPN connections from a few branch offices to the user-facing application server. Or you can migrate a file server that has run out of drive bays to the cloud, giving you effectively unlimited data storage (Figure 13-12) billed by how much you store, how long you store it, and how often it gets transferred or downloaded.

The hitch is that, while you're no longer responsible for the hardware, you're still responsible for configuring and maintaining the OS and software of any VMs you create. This can give you a lot of flexibility to tune it for your needs, but it also requires knowledge of the underlying OS and time to manage it.

PLATFORM AS A SERVICE

Web applications are built by programmers. Programmers do one thing really well: they program. The problem is that a web application needs a lot more than just a programmer; it needs people to manage the infrastructure: system administrators, database administrators, general network support, and more. A web application also needs more than just hardware and an operating system. It needs development, monitoring, and database tools, and potentially hundreds of other resources and services. Getting a web application up and running is a big job.

With IaaS, you could set up a server and install IIS or SQL Server to host a website or database, but you would still need to manage the underlying server. In contrast, a *platform as a service* (PaaS) provider offers a complete web application deployment and management system, including operating systems, frameworks, libraries, software development kits (SDKs), editors, debuggers, and compilers. As far as the programmer is concerned, the PaaS is just a place to deploy and run their application. PaaS also often integrates with technologies like web development tools that can publish directly to a site.

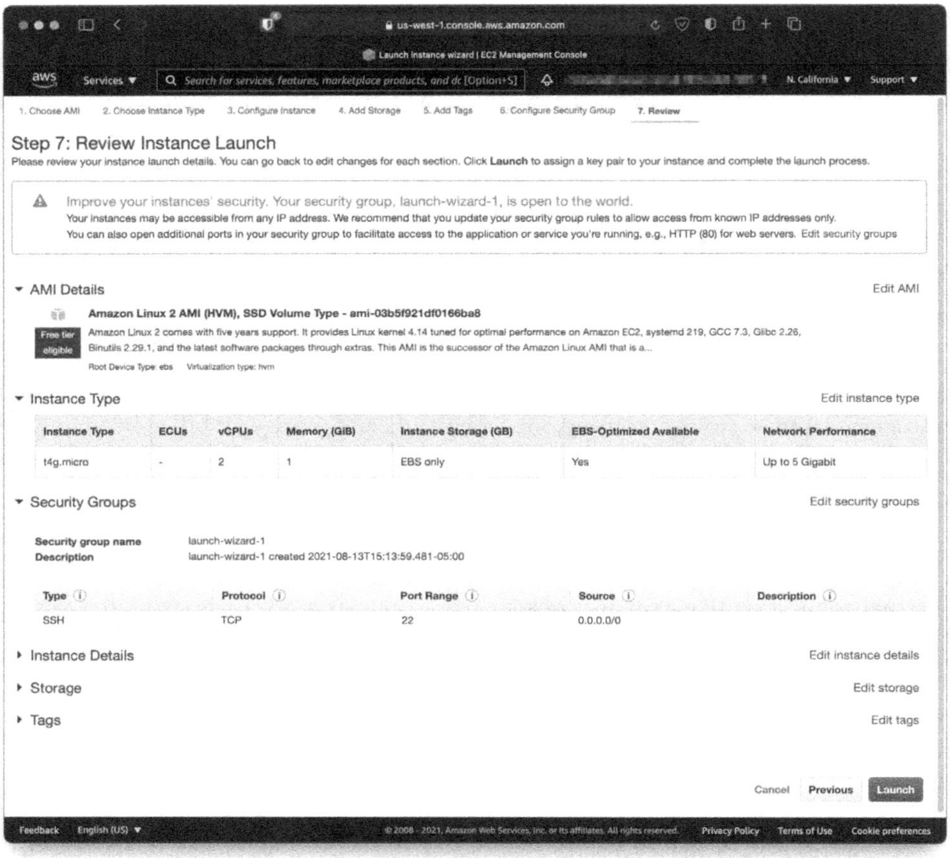

FIGURE 13-11 Creating an instance on AWS Elastic Compute Cloud (EC2)

PaaS providers build their platform on some form of infrastructure (which could be provided by an IaaS) and manage it for you. The underlying infrastructure is completely invisible to the developer, so they don't need to think about its complexity, much less how to control it.

Say you set up a development website on your server that you want to be able to test, promote to production, and roll back if there are problems. That's all your responsibility to manage. Instead, you could use Azure, AWS, and other PaaS tools and just tell them that you want a website with certain functions. You'll automatically get two or more "slots" for development and production along with pipeline tools to allow you to easily promote the development site to production or roll it back.

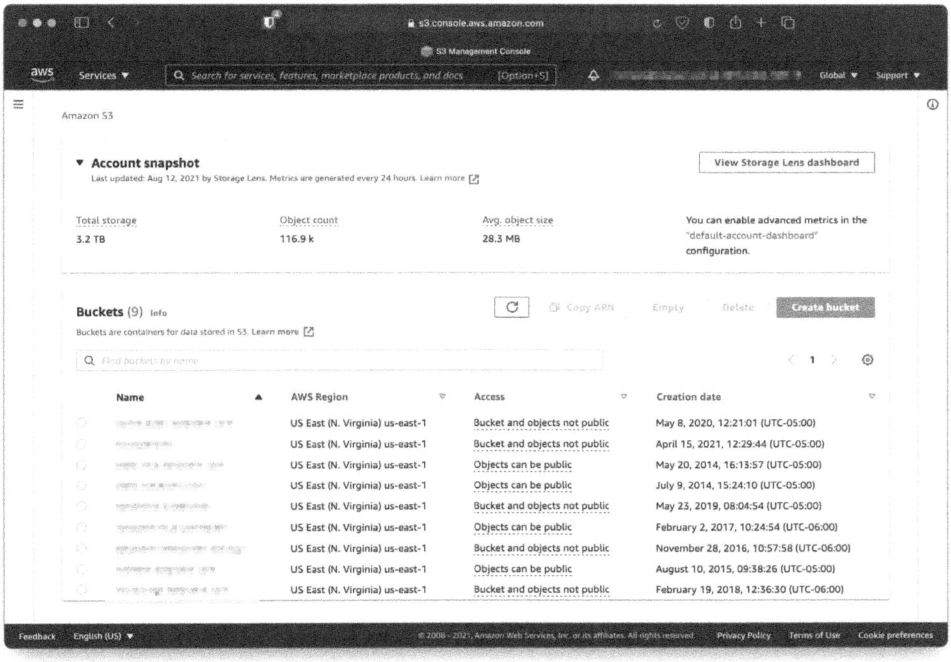

FIGURE 13-12 The Amazon S3 interface

Since it is PaaS, you only have to manage the website, not the server. PaaS also takes care of scaling and load balancing multiple instances of a website. You have similar options for databases: you can tell Azure that you want a database, and it will create one, without you needing to worry about—or even see—the underlying server.

NOTE There are other kinds of PaaS beyond PaaS for web application development, and the concept of a platform provides a good way to communicate whether the box a provider is selling contains metaphorical LEGO bricks or IKEA furniture parts. In other words, a PaaS targeting web apps will bundle different features than one targeting smartphone apps.

Heroku, one of the earliest PaaS providers, creates a simple interface on top of AWS's EC2, further reducing the complexity of developing and scaling web applications. Heroku's management console (Figure 13-13) enables developers to increase or decrease the capacity of an application with a single slider, or easily set up add-ons that add a database, monitor your logs, track performance, and more. It could take days for a tech or developer unfamiliar with the software and services to install, configure, and integrate a set of these services with a running application. PaaS providers help cut this down to minutes or hours.

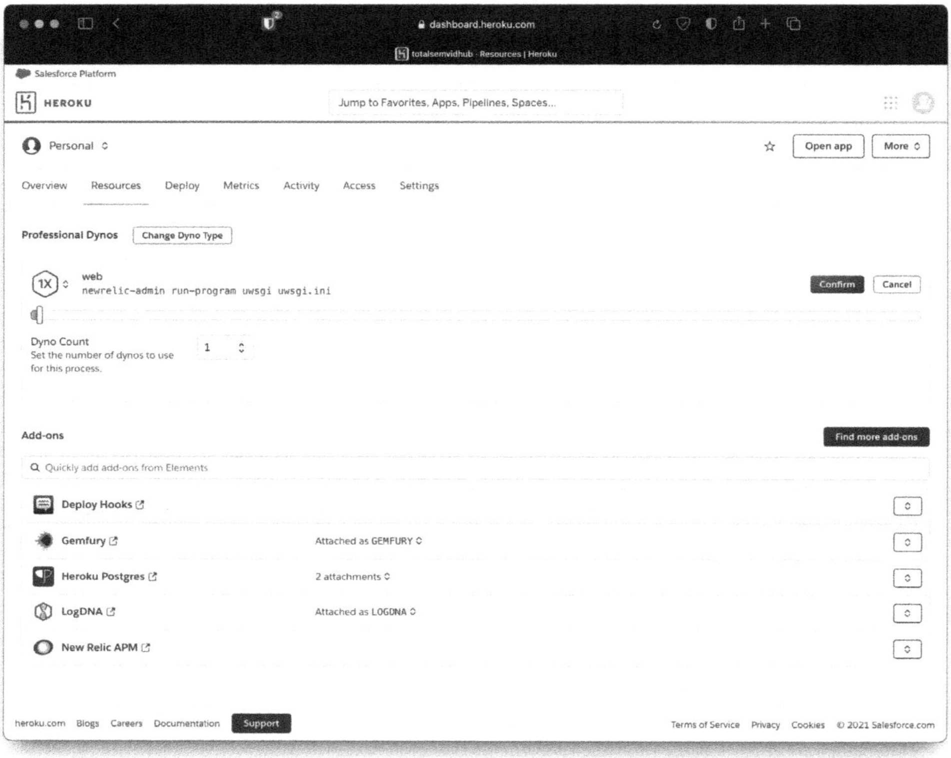

FIGURE 13-13 Heroku's management console

SOFTWARE AS A SERVICE

Software as a service (SaaS) sits at the top layer of the cake, replacing applications once distributed and licensed via physical media (such as CD-ROMs in retail boxes) with subscriptions to equivalent applications from online servers. In the purest form, the application runs on the server; users don't install it—they just access it with a client (often a web browser).

Remember the days of downloading Microsoft Office or buying it on disc, then having to download and install updates? A few years later, that version became obsolete, and you had to repeat the whole process! Now, with Microsoft Office 365, you use a browser to access the latest and greatest of the Office suite in the cloud, with security patches applied immediately. Furthermore, you don't have to uninstall the previous version to install the current one.

Google offers a similar set of cloud tools with Google Docs, Sheets, and Slides at no cost for consumers and different price points for enterprise-level features, options, tools, and settings.

NOTE Microsoft Office is still available as a standalone, non-subscription product. Microsoft leaves no stone unturned!

With the SaaS model, you can access applications wherever you have an internet connection, often without having to carry data with you (it can be stored in the cloud as well) or regularly update software. At the enterprise level, the subscription model of many SaaS providers makes it easier for organizations to budget software expenses and to keep hundreds or thousands of computers up to date with office software, messaging software, payroll processing software, database management software, management software, and much more.

The flexibility of using public, third-party SaaS often comes at the cost of having strict control of your data, however. While security might not be crucial for drafting a blog post using Google Drive, many companies are concerned about sensitive intellectual property or business secrets traveling through untrusted networks and being stored on servers they don't control.

In addition to Office 365 and the G Suite, specific examples of SaaS include web-based email (like Gmail and Yahoo!), cloud storage (Dropbox and Box), collaboration (Slack), and customer relationship management (Salesforce) platforms.

Cloud Deployment Models

Organizations have differing needs and capabilities, of course, so there's no one-size-fits-all cloud *deployment model* that works for everyone. When it comes to cloud computing, organizations must balance cost, control, customization, and privacy. Some organizations also have needs that no existing cloud provider can meet. Each organization makes its own decisions about these trade-offs, but the result is usually a cloud deployment that can be categorized in one of four ways: public, private, hybrid, and virtual private cloud.

PUBLIC CLOUD

Most folks usually just interact with a *public cloud*, a term used to describe software, platforms, and infrastructure delivered through networks that the general public can use. Companies like Amazon, Google, and Microsoft own the underlying hardware, but their services interconnect so seamlessly that we often think of "the cloud" as a single entity rather than separate platforms. For example, Netflix can build its application using IaaS offerings from multiple providers simultaneously.

You can think of a public cloud provider like a restaurant. Every diner in the restaurant orders and eats their own meal, but all the food comes from one kitchen. Likewise, all public cloud provider customers use their own VMs and software through the cloud, but all that infrastructure comes from the same provider.

PRIVATE CLOUD

If a business wants some of the flexibility of the cloud, needs complete ownership of its data, and can afford both, it can build an internal cloud the business actually owns—a *private cloud*. A security-minded company with enough resources could build an internal IaaS network in an onsite data center. Departments within the company could create and destroy VMs as needed and develop SaaS to meet collaboration, planning, or task and time management needs, all without sending the data over the open internet. A company with these needs but without the space or knowledge to build and maintain a private cloud can also contract a third party to maintain or host it.

What differentiates a private cloud from other owned and on-premises data centers and servers is that it automates tools and processes like VM and database creation instead of relying on manual IT services and management techniques.

A private cloud environment is akin to a cafeteria where employees can eat breakfast, lunch, and dinner. No one from outside the organization can eat at the cafeteria, and employees serve themselves, buffet-style, at each meal.

HYBRID CLOUD

Not all data is crucial, and not every document is a secret. Needs that an organization can only meet in-house might be less important than keeping an application running when demand exceeds what it can handle onsite. A hybrid cloud involves combining public and private clouds, allowing communication between them. Using a hybrid cloud model can mean not having to maintain a private cloud powerful enough to meet peak demand: an application can grow into a public cloud instead of grinding to a halt, a technique called *cloud bursting*. However, a hybrid cloud isn't just about letting one web application span two types of clouds; it's also about integrating services across them.

Say Bob runs a national chain of sandwich shops and is looking into drone-delivered lunch. He already has an order-tracking application in his private cloud, and he'll need to integrate a new application there to calculate routes and track drones. But he'll also need to integrate a third-party weather application in the public cloud to avoid sending drones out in a blizzard, and a flight-plan application running in a hybrid cloud to avoid collisions with other aircraft. The sum of these integrated services and applications is the hybrid cloud that will power Bob's drone-delivered lunch.

Microsoft's Azure Stack is a great example of a hybrid cloud. It provides software to run an on-premises virtualization environment that you can manage as if it were in Azure. You can migrate those VMs to and from—or burst into—the cloud. Since you own the resources on your premises, customers can keep their business data private while leveraging the cloud for other services and manage all of it through a single interface.

VIRTUAL PRIVATE CLOUD

Companies use private IP addresses, subnets, and VLANs (all discussed in previous chapters) to isolate their resources. Company users access the virtual private cloud (VPC)—a private cloud that exists inside of a public cloud—through a virtual private network (VPN), which simplifies the connection between a VPC and the company's on-premises infrastructure. We'll talk more about VPNs a little later in the chapter.

Think of a VPC like a special events room in a restaurant reserved for private parties. Regular customers cannot access that room, the special event menu, or the service staff for the event; only members of the private party can use these dedicated resources. Likewise, only authorized users can access the cloud resources reserved for them in a VPC.

A VPC has significant benefits over a private cloud. First, new infrastructure and resources can easily be added as needed. It's more difficult to set up, configure, and especially pay for these resources within a private cloud. Secondly, cloud providers have the expertise to run the networking, applications, websites, and more with greater speed and efficiency. They build their infrastructure using the latest and greatest hardware and software, which they maintain and upgrade constantly. Similarly, these cloud providers don't want any breaches from cybercriminals, so they build cybersecurity into their infrastructures that wouldn't be possible in a private cloud infrastructure.

Cloud gateways allow devices inside a VPC to communicate over the internet and fall into two categories. Instances (VMs within your cloud infrastructure) with public IP addresses access the internet through an *internet gateway*, while instances with private IP addresses use a *NAT gateway*. Of course, NAT gateway instances can only communicate outbound; inbound communication from external devices can't reach them.

Virtualization's Role in Cloud Computing

We've already seen a big financial reason for virtualization's role in cloud computing: it helps the many massive data centers that constitute the cloud scale up efficiently. But virtualization's role is more foundational than dollar signs.

IaaS providers let their customers "create" as many servers as they need on-demand, "destroy" those same servers as soon as they are done, and bill them only for the time and resources they used. This arrangement works because the providers can set up everything the customer selects in real time and then release the resources for another customer just as quickly.

Human techs couldn't possibly reconfigure networks and systems with the speed and accuracy it would take to make this model work for one customer, let alone keep it humming along smoothly for hundreds of thousands or even millions of them. The software-based flexibility of virtualized components enables a cloud provider to integrate all of them with its own management systems to automate thousands of tasks across the globe-spanning infrastructure we call *the cloud*.

Infrastructure as Code

Infrastructure as code (IaC) does away with manual processes by managing and provisioning the cloud infrastructure entirely through configuration files or scripts. This makes it easier to modify and deploy configurations, guarantee consistency across provisioned environments, and modularize an infrastructure. This section will discuss three aspects of IaC: automation, source control, and orchestration.

Automation

When an application managed by a small number of people runs on a single server, manually configuring and tweaking that server can be the most cost-effective and convenient approach. But if that application scales up to the point where several teams work on it and it runs on many servers spread around the world, that same convenience becomes a liability.

Over time, human error and miscommunication tend to snowball until software that works fine on one server is a source of hard-to-troubleshoot bugs on another. The broad solution to this problem is to replace manual tasks with *automation*—using code to provision and maintain systems (installing software updates, for example) consistently and accurately.

Multistep tasks that you perform frequently are a good place to start, but it can be even more useful to automate infrequent tasks since you're more likely to forget the steps to complete them. A little automation is better than nothing, but that's where IaC comes into play. By defining an application's or service's infrastructure (the servers and network components) in configuration files or scripts, organizations can more easily reproduce that infrastructure across multiple environments.

While this automation helps scale up the application to run on more servers, some of the big benefits of the IaC philosophy are just as important for small apps and teams:

- The ability to reproduce the necessary infrastructure makes it easy for people working on the application to create a *development environment* or *test environment*—separate temporary copies of the infrastructure used to develop new features and test out updates.
- You can save the infrastructure configuration files in a version control system alongside the rest of the application's code, making it easier to ensure the infrastructure and application are compatible.
- You can also carefully review changes before rolling them out, helping catch configuration mistakes before they are applied to real, working systems.

Ansible is a common suite of software tools that automates IT processes through the use of IaC. Ansible can deploy virtual networking devices, install software, and implement security—all without human intervention! To do so, Ansible uses a *playbook* composed of

YAML-based files that tell Ansible exactly what configurations, settings, and more to apply to servers, routers, switches, VMs, and other devices.

As you might imagine, many infrastructures share several common tasks. Instead of making a playbook from scratch, Ansible can use *templates*—or blueprints for *reusable tasks*—to help build a playbook.

In a data center, changes to hardware and software are ongoing. Sometimes they're intentional, but not always. Undocumented and unapproved changes put a system's functionality and security at great risk. For example, if your configurations change enough over time, known as *configuration drift*, your systems and security may no longer be in *compliance* with regulatory laws, making your data vulnerable and even putting you at risk of being sued. In addition to its legal meaning, *compliance* can refer simply to alignment with the desired configuration. For example, upgrading an application only to have it revert to its default settings would mean it is no longer compliant with the desired configuration. This kind of configuration drift should be identified early and corrected.

Configuration drift can also create compatibility issues between primary data center hardware and software and their counterparts in backup sites or systems. If the primary systems gradually change while backups remain static, it could prevent successful failover during an outage.

Fortunately, IaC can automate *upgrades*, synchronizing software versions across all devices, and generate *dynamic inventories* so that you know what you have and where it is. With these two pieces in place, configuration drift is less of a threat.

Source Control

IaC relies on *source control* to ensure that the automation performs as intended. *Version control*, commonly implemented through the Git distributed version control system (DVCS), tracks different versions of files so that you can roll back to previous versions at any point.

An entire project is stored in a *central repository*, which developers can check out to work on files. When finished, they reupload the repository with their changed files. Git identifies *conflicts*, finding instances where different developers have made contradictory changes. This happens when more than one developer checks out the files simultaneously and makes changes to the same codebase, resulting in incompatible and potentially problematic files. When Git identifies a conflict, the developers can roll back one of the changes, merge them, or implement some other solution to resolve it.

Another feature implemented by a DVCS is *branching*, which allows multiple developers to work on different parts (branches) of the code without causing any conflicts. After developing, testing, and completing code in a branch, the developer commits all of the changes, merges them into the main branch, and deletes their branch if they no longer need it.

Orchestration

Orchestration combines automated processes into bigger, multifaceted processes called *pipelines* or *workflows*. Orchestration streamlines development, testing, deployment, and maintenance.

Some of the best-run applications use a specific kind of orchestration called *continuous integration/continuous deployment* (CI/CD). When developers check in changes to the application's code, they trigger an automatic multistep pipeline that builds the application, sets up a temporary copy of the infrastructure the app needs, and runs a bunch of automated checks to ensure it works. If these checks fail, the developers have to go back to square one. If they pass, the pipeline starts deploying the new version.

Deployment can be as simple as uploading the new code to each server, but these pipelines tend to incorporate lessons learned the hard way from botched prior deployments that knocked the service offline or deleted important data. The result can be a methodical sequence in which the pipeline eases into the update by backing up data, spinning up new copies of the infrastructure running the latest code, rotating them into use, and monitoring for any signs that deployment should stop and the update should be rolled back. In either case, this pipeline orchestrates tasks across multiple systems and services to meet the high-level goal of rolling out application updates in a safe, consistent manner.

Another common kind of orchestration focuses on keeping a running service or application healthy. This usually involves monitoring a service and its components to identify any trouble—maybe a host froze, crashed, or is just responding slowly. When the monitoring system fires off a warning, it can trigger a pipeline that starts up a replacement host and swaps it into service as soon as it is ready.

NOTE Since organizations that depend on containerization can have hundreds or thousands of running containers to manage at any time, they often use *container orchestration* tools (such as Kubernetes) to automate most aspects of configuring, deploying, monitoring, and adapting the cluster as conditions change. Container orchestration is closely related to the IaC-style orchestration described here, but its scope is narrower.

Putting Network Virtualization and Cloud Computing to Work

It can be hard to really sink your teeth into enterprise networking if you don't have access to racks full of enterprise-grade equipment. So, if you have the opportunity to get some hands-on learning in an environment like that, take it!

Virtualization and cloud computing have both really changed the game when it comes to what you can do with just a computer, an internet connection, and a little time. Creating an account with an IaaS provider like AWS or Azure enables you to set up lab networks that wouldn't even fit in most apartments or houses (unless you happen to live in a data center).

NOTE Don't rule out playing around with cloud resources just because you don't have any money to spare. Many cloud platforms have free service tiers (at least for some basic services) or offer free credits when you create a new account. You may also be able to get free credits through any class, school, club/boot-camp/training, professional organization, or employer you're associated with. It doesn't hurt to ask.

A word of caution though: only set up a cloud account if you understand the risks and are prepared to manage them. Once you connect a cloud account to a credit or debit card, spinning up a high-end resource and forgetting to shut it down can be a costly mistake. Make sure that you understand the costs up front, that you tear down the resource as soon as you're done, that your account has a strong password, and that you close the account when you're done learning. Don't let someone break in and rack up a bank-account-draining bill at your expense.

Cloud Resource Management

Now, let's circle back to a few topics from the earlier discussion on cloud computing to cover the nuts-and-bolts stuff you need to know about how cloud resources work. Specifically, I want to outline a few practical things you should know about scalability, elasticity, and security in the cloud.

SCALABILITY

One of the cool things virtualization enables us to do (especially in the cloud) is to adjust computing resources based on demand, known as *scalability*. This includes both scaling up (adding more resources for a machine) and scaling out (adding more machines). With PaaS, you can scale both ways for an application. Not all cloud providers provide easy scaling options for something like PaaS, although Azure and AWS both do. With Azure's IaaS and PaaS, you can manually resize the virtual server to scale it up or down. Doing so requires only a restart of the server (or web app), not a reinstallation of the server or the transfer of data.

NOTE Whether to scale up or scale out depends on the application or service. Some apps are RAM-intensive and benefit from scaling up to larger instances, while CPU-bound applications often work better scaling out across multiple smaller instances. Applications designed for distributed computing can easily scale out, while legacy applications may only support scaling up.

While cloud providers continuously scale their underlying data centers, scalability from a customer perspective focuses on load balancing.

ELASTICITY

Elasticity refers to automation on scaling operations, so that if the load on an application exceeds a certain percentage, scaling automatically increases capacity (either up or out, but typically out), and when load drops below a certain percentage, scaling automatically reduces resources.

To revisit the Black Friday example mentioned earlier, a company will add resources to the frontend web apps to handle load, and after Cyber Monday, the resources they are paying for will automatically go back down. With only manual scaling options, the company would be paying for those increased Black Friday resources until they remember to relinquish them, incurring unnecessary costs. Some cloud providers may support scaling without support for elasticity, but the big providers like Azure and AWS support both.

SECURITY IMPLICATIONS

Using a particular cloud provider means you are putting complete faith and trust in them. Security implications are important. For example, insider threats at the cloud provider could be more damaging than insider threats at your own organization, so you need assurance that the cloud provider has internal controls to prevent insider threats. Before you choose a cloud provider, you need to explore various security implications and get answers from potential providers regarding how they handle security. For example, is the cloud provider prepared to respond if it's hit with a denial of service (DoS) attack? How do the providers intend to encrypt your data? How quickly will they react to patch vulnerabilities and deal with threats? Will they comingle your data (put it on the same server as another company's data) or even use shared RAM? If so, how do they keep the data segregated? Who owns what in the cloud? Standards covering cloud providers are lacking, so it is up to you to investigate a potential cloud provider's security posture.

Like almost all of networking, cloud computing has a long list of security implications. This section explores five areas of importance to cloud computing: account security, privacy, multitenancy, intrusion, and logging. Chapter 17 takes a deeper look at security issues.

Account Security

When you (or your organization) sign up with a cloud provider, you get at least one extremely powerful account—like root on steroids—that someone could use to steal your organization's data, delete all of its infrastructure, or rack up a huge bill mining cryptocurrency. As with any other system, apply the *principle of least privilege*, giving the cloud provider only the information it needs to perform its job and not a drop more.

Cloud providers have authorization systems that enable you to set up separate credentials with explicit, limited permissions for the humans, servers, apps, tools, and services that need to manage your cloud account's resources. Setting up separate credentials for every distinct use case makes it easier to keep track of each's purpose, restrict the permissions to limit the damage a compromised credential could do, and revoke a credential if it gets compromised without disrupting other users.

NOTE Cloud providers generally have one or more ways to log, monitor, and fire alerts based on account activity and changes to resources.

Privacy

The cloud provider (or someone working for it) may have access to your data. These providers have some rules and practices in place to limit the likelihood that someone on their end goes browsing through your data, but those assurances may not be enough if your organization has sensitive data. In this case, your organization might choose to use the cloud provider but encrypt all the data it stores there, or use a private cloud model (entirely, or just for the sensitive resources).

Multitenancy

Multitenancy is the ability to support multiple customers on the same infrastructure at the same time—and it's both a blessing and a curse. The blessing, and one of the great benefits of cloud computing, is that if you need a teeny-tiny server that does almost no work, you can pay for a likewise teeny-tiny fraction of the resources of a huge server for a few pennies a day. The curse, though, is that you have neighbors, and you don't get much say in who they are.

Your server may run well on a quiet system with polite neighbors, or struggle for CPU time on a system where every neighbor keeps demanding more server resources. And then there's the question of *malicious* neighbors (or perhaps just nice neighbors who have been hacked). Hypervisors do a good job of isolating one VM from another, but this isn't perfect (and containers are less isolated).

A steady stream of new exploits could enable a bad neighbor to snoop on your app or service. This isn't a big deal if you're just hosting some cat videos, but it can be a huge problem if you work with tightly regulated data such as patient medical records. In the latter case, the regulations may require you to pay a little more for *dedicated* instances (potentially using more secure facilities, networks, or hardware) that spare you from sharing the same infrastructure with other tenants. Of course, you don't see these issues with AWS or Azure, where physical security is treated as a high priority, as is isolation of customers from each other, monitoring of loads, data security, and network security.

Intrusion

Just like in an internal network, outright intrusion is a risk in the cloud. Even if everyone in your organization is trained about how to keep the LAN secure, integrating cloud resources with your LAN creates new risks. This is especially true if your organization focuses on securing the network perimeter and defaults to trusting every device inside the network.

Imagine a scenario, for example, where your organization maintains an always-on connection to enable servers or users to access cloud resources. Someone who compromises the least-secure device on either end may be able to use it as a jumping-off point to attack devices on the other end.

Logging

All kinds of devices and servers produce logs. These logs can be great when you're debugging or looking into a security incident, but they may also contain sensitive information. Your organization may, for example, need to set up policies and invest some effort to make sure the logs you need are collected from the devices and services that produce them and retained without violating customer privacy.

Desktop Virtualization

I've talked a lot about how cool it is to use virtualization and cloud networking for managing servers and the applications that run on them, but they aren't the only way to benefit from the *everything-as-a-service* trend that virtualization and cloud computing started. *Desktop virtualization* enables you to move user workstations into the cloud and manage them as flexibly as other cloud infrastructure.

Desktop virtualization isn't really a new idea—it's just the latest form of a kind of virtualization we've been doing for a while now. Desktop virtualization replaces direct access to a system's local desktop environment with a client that can access an OS running in a VM. You could technically run that VM on the same device, but benefits like flexible management come from centralizing the desktop VMs on a smaller number of servers—a pattern called *virtual desktop infrastructure* (VDI). This server/client VDI pattern is roughly what cloud providers bundle up and sell as desktop virtualization. The connections are securable with things like the VMware Horizon solution.

EXAM TIP A *virtual desktop* is a VM running a desktop OS used as a replacement for a desktop environment on a physical workstation.

Even though you can accomplish the same goals with in-house VDI, cloud services have some distinct benefits. For example, desktop virtualization makes it possible to onboard new employees even when there's no space on the internal servers. The ability to host virtual desktops closer to users all around the world, even when you don't have an office nearby, can also help them have a smooth experience because of the reduction in lag. Some services also have distinct options or features.

Figure 13-14 shows a virtual desktop running in the AWS desktop virtualization service: Amazon WorkSpaces. If you want to support these workspaces for your users, they'll need a way to log in. AWS and other providers typically have some kind of directory service you can use to manually set up accounts—and that's what I used to configure the account for this desktop, as shown in Figure 13-15. If you have many users, you'll likely end up leaning on your existing directory service (such as Active Directory), which may be running in the cloud or hosted on your LAN.

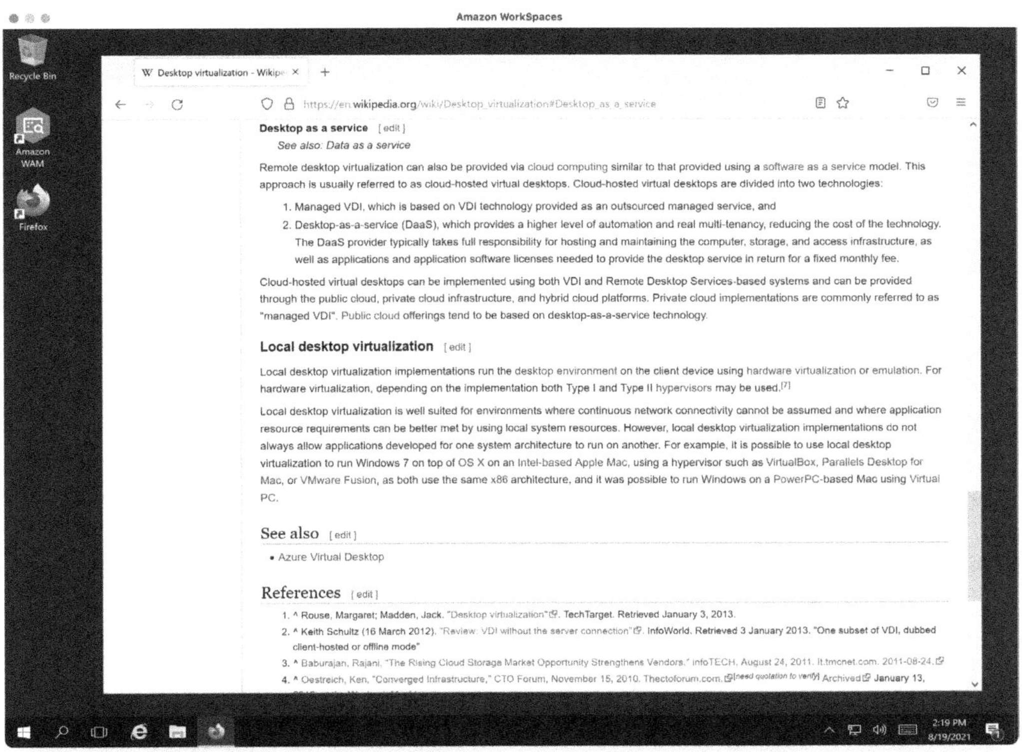

FIGURE 13-14 Amazon WorkSpaces virtual desktop

WorkSpaces is a building-blocks-style desktop virtualization, so I also need to set up one or more virtual networks for my virtual desktops. This is enough for very simple needs, though you may also need to configure your firewall to allow traffic from whatever protocols your client uses. There isn't a hard-and-fast rule here—Azure uses Microsoft's own proprietary Remote Desktop Protocol (RDP), while AWS uses a different proprietary protocol named PC-over-IP (PCoIP).

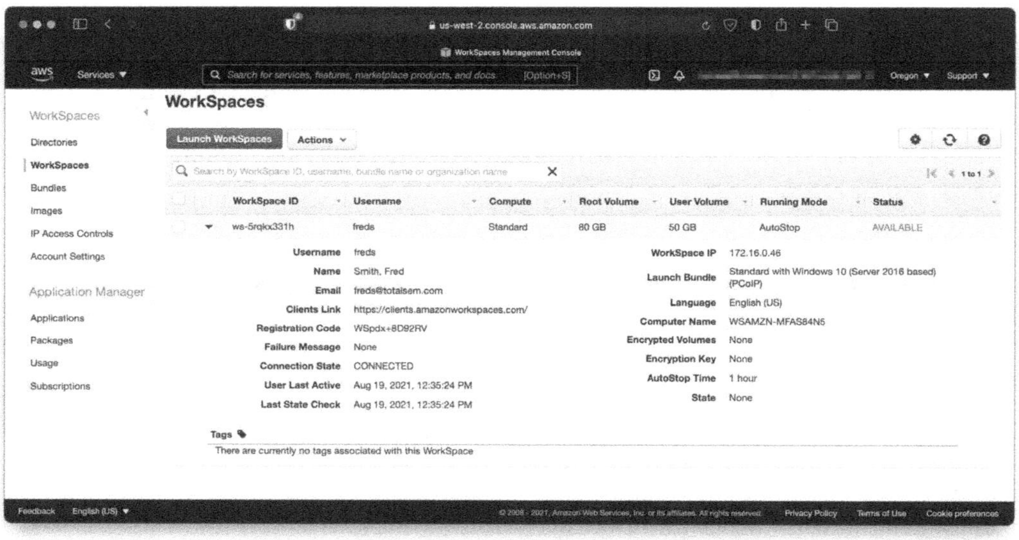

FIGURE 13-15 WorkSpaces configuration in Management Console

You'll have a bit more work to do if your desktops need to be able to connect to internal resources, or you want to allow only devices on your LAN to access a desktop. The next section shows how I can interconnect this virtual network with my LAN to meet needs like these.

Interconnecting Local and Cloud Resources

Unless your organization manages to chug along just fine without any cloud resources—or only needs to use resources that can be publicly accessible—it'll probably have to support interconnecting resources running locally with those running in the cloud. This chapter mentioned that the security implications of an always-on connection are problematic. Let's look also at two *cloud connectivity options* that the exam objectives focus on: a VPN and a private Direct Connect connection to the cloud provider.

VIRTUAL PRIVATE NETWORKS

The most convenient way to connect a network to the public cloud is through a VPN, which creates an encrypted tunnel between two networks over another, less-secure network. A *site-to-site VPN* can establish a permanent tunnel (often using IPsec) between a local network and a virtual network in the cloud.

VPN tunnels are relatively simple to set up because they use off-the-shelf technology like IPsec. This makes them easy to integrate with existing site-to-site WAN infrastructure or even an SD-WAN service (coming up in Chapter 14).

There are many reasons you might want or need to interconnect these networks, but they all boil down to making it easier for a device on one side to access a resource on the other. To work on this chapter from Amazon WorkSpaces as shown earlier, for example, WorkSpaces needed access to my file server. Figure 13-16 shows the VPN tunnel set up between my network's router and the AWS Virtual Private Cloud network to which my virtual desktop is attached. Once I have the tunnel set up and the routes propagate, I can copy down my working files as shown in Figure 13-17.

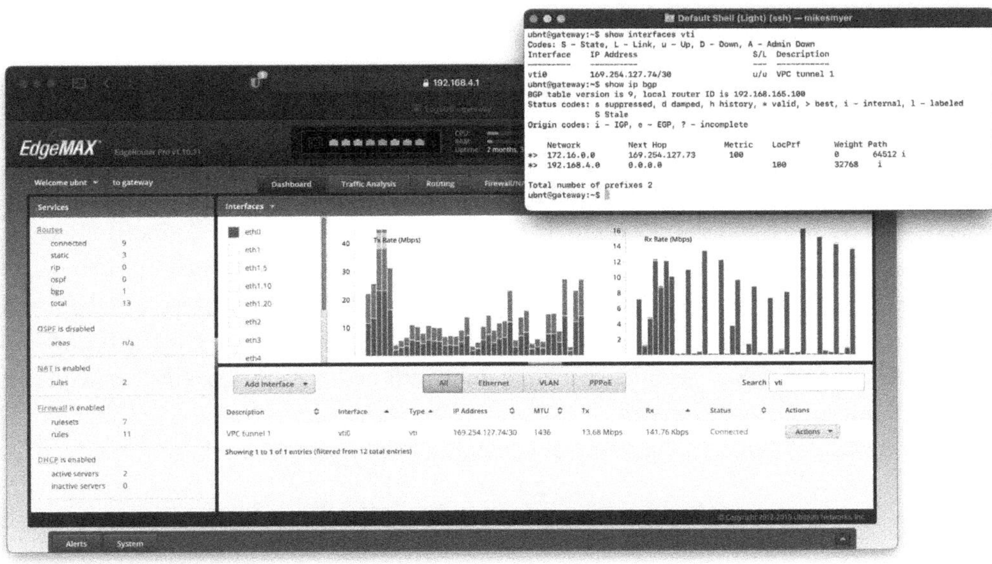

FIGURE 13-16 VPN activity on my network's router and its BGP routing table

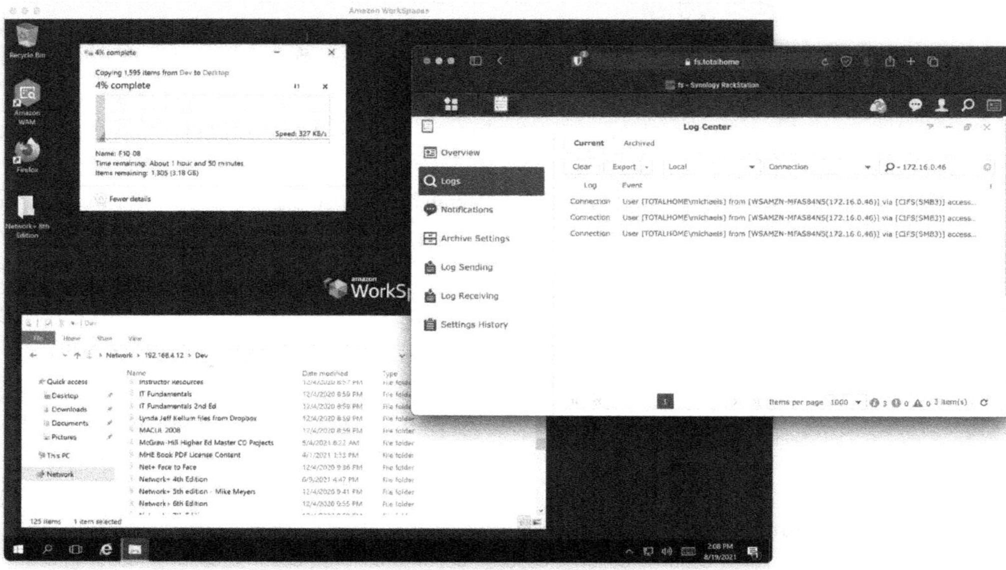

FIGURE 13-17 Transferring files from my on-premises file server to my virtual desktop

DIRECT CONNECT

VPNs are easy to set up, but big-time organizations often need big-time pipes. Providers such as AWS, Azure, and Google Cloud offer *private direct connections*—private direct links between your network and the cloud provider's—to meet this need. These connections, called *Direct Connect*, take one of two forms: a physical port on the cloud provider's switch, which enables you to run fiber between your equipment and the cloud provider's, or a leased line that you contract through a third party. The main thing to keep in mind is that the traffic for a private direct connection never goes over the public internet. It's a private line between your data center and your cloud provider.

Chapter Review

Questions

1. Which of the following describes virtual machines taking the place of network appliance hardware?
   A. Network Function Virtualization
   B. Elasticity
   C. Flexibility
   D. Orchestration
2. Which of the following is not true regarding a virtual private cloud (VPC)?
   A. New resources can easily be added.
   B. It's more difficult to set up than a private cloud.
   C. The services run more efficiently in a VPC than a private cloud.
   D. The upgrades to software, hardware, and cybersecurity are done more often than in a private cloud.
3. Which of the following can't be virtualized?
   A. Switch
   B. Router
   C. Firewall
   D. None of the above (they all can be virtualized)
4. Which cloud gateway would be used by a VPC with instances that have public IP addresses?
   A. Internet gateway
   B. NAT gateway
   C. VPC gateway
   D. VM gateway
5. Which of the following are cloud connectivity options?
   A. NFV
   B. VPN
   C. Public cloud
   D. Direct Connect

6. If you want to start a new photo-sharing service but you don't own any servers, how can you quickly create a new server to run the service?
   A. Public cloud
   B. Private cloud
   C. Hybrid cloud
   D. VPC
7. Which of the following represents an infrastructure on the organization's premises that can be accessed just by employees of that organization?
   A. Public cloud
   B. Private cloud
   C. Hybrid cloud
   D. VPC
8. Which of the following takes the place of programs being installed on and run from a machine?
   A. Infrastructure as a service
   B. Platform as a service
   C. Desktop as a service
   D. Software as a service
9. Which of the following would a company use when it expects extra traffic?
   A. Infrastructure as a service
   B. Platform as a service
   C. Desktop as a service
   D. Software as a service
10. Which of the following facilitates software development?
   A. Infrastructure as a service
   B. Platform as a service
   C. Desktop as a service
   D. Software as a service

Answers

1. **A.** Network Function Virtualization (NFV) implements routers, switches, load balancers, firewalls, gateways, and more through virtualization.
2. **B.** Setting up a VPC is a lot easier than setting up a private cloud
3. **D.** Switches, routers, firewalls, and even NICs can all be virtualized.
4. **A.** If a VPC's instances have public IP addresses, an internet gateway is used. If a VPC's instances have private addresses, a NAT gateway is used. The other choices are nonexistent.
5. **B** and **D.** Cloud connectivity options include VPN and Direct Connect.
6. **A.** Using the public cloud will enable you to quickly create the servers you need.
7. **B.** A private cloud is physically and logically internal to an organization.
8. **D.** Software as a Service (SaaS) involves running programs remotely through a browser.
9. **A.** Infrastructure as a Service (IaaS) allows organizations to temporarily extend their data center into the cloud.
10. **B.** Platform as a Service (PaaS) incorporates everything a programmer needs to develop an application.

Data Centers

IN THIS CHAPTER, YOU WILL LEARN HOW TO

- Describe classic data center architecture and design
- Describe modern data center architecture and design
- Explain high availability concepts and procedures
- Explain best practices for documentation in the data center

Ah, the data center—those mythical buildings that store all the data that powers our internet sojourns. Virtually every public server—from web, game, and email servers to DNS and certificate servers—sits in a data center, ready to respond to requests from client systems (Figure 14-1).

FIGURE 14-1 We live in data centers!

Test Specific

In a nutshell, a *data center* is a networked group of servers in a dedicated space—a building or part of a building—that provides data storage, web hosting, application hosting, cloud services, and more for remote client organizations.

A data center is so much more than just a big building full of servers, however. It requires all the networking hardware—including routers, switches, firewalls, and storage systems—to secure and effectively connect the many servers to the internet. The data center also provides the environmental controls and physical security to protect the servers and ensure uptime. Finally, it contains the tools necessary to protect itself from catastrophes such as fire and natural disasters (Figure 14-2).

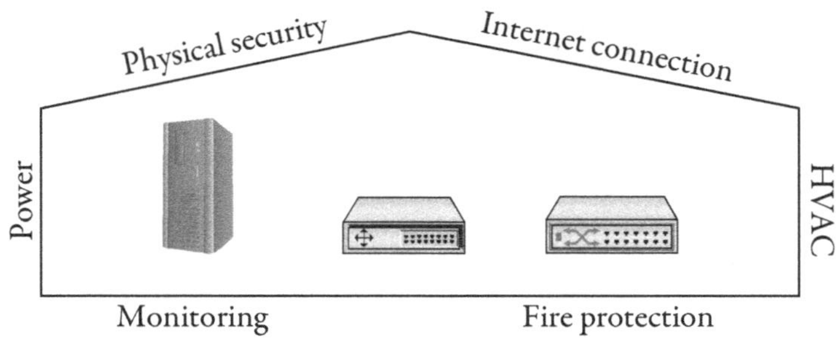

FIGURE 14-2 Data centers support the servers they contain.

This chapter introduces you to what it takes to build and maintain a modern data center. We'll begin by observing classic data center architecture and design, exploring terms such as *tiers*, *traffic flows*, *spine and leaf*, and the concept of *data storage*. Next, you'll see how the modern data center has evolved with *software-defined networking*, *Virtual Extensible Local Area Networks* (VXLANs), *zero trust architecture* (ZTA), *Secure Access Secure Edge* (SASE), and *Security Service Edge* (SSE). Third is an interesting tour of *high availability*—making sure the resources offered by the data center's servers are available when clients request them. The chapter closes by covering infrastructure support and documentation.

Classic Data Center Architecture and Design

Data centers, as a location to connect, protect, and support servers, aren't a new concept. Arguably, the earliest generations of mainframe-based data centers date back to the late 1960s, but for purposes of this discussion, it makes sense to start with data centers populated with internet-connected, PC-based servers from the 1990s. In smaller organizations, the data center typically is located at the same facility as the users it supports. In larger enterprises with multiple locations (aka branch offices), the data center is a separate, dedicated building, connected to the enterprise's locations through dedicated connections. These external connections in the early years had names like T1/E1, OCx, ATM, and frame relay. Today these connections are usually Ethernet, Multiprotocol Label Switching (MPLS), or software-defined wide area network (SDWAN), as shown in Figure 14-3.

All these external connections are useless unless all the servers in the data centers have the internal connections necessary to get to them. In other words, the data center needs a well-planned and proven architecture to ensure a reliable and efficient flow of data from the servers out to the clients.

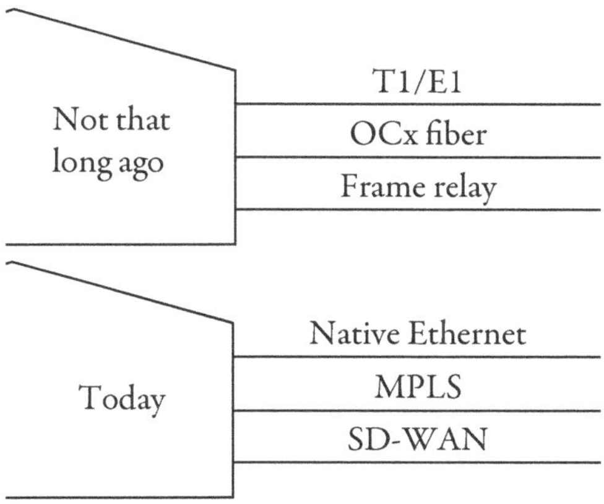

FIGURE 14-3 Data center connection technologies

Three-Tiered Architecture

In a simple world where a data center consists of a couple of servers, there isn't much in the way of architecture. You have servers, a switch, a router, and an ISP connection that might look something like Figure 14-4.

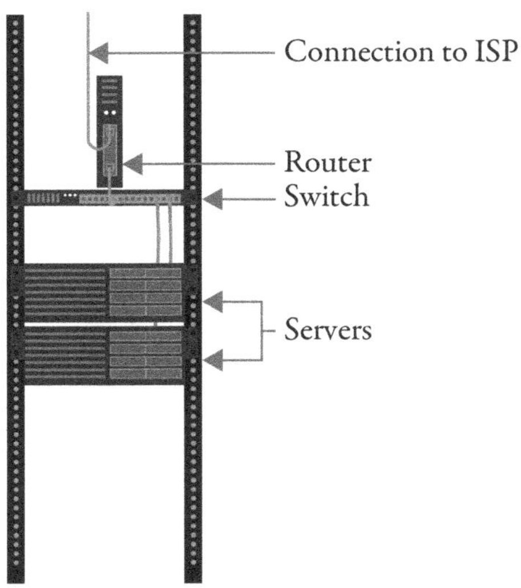

FIGURE 14-4 Simple data center

As the number of servers in your data center begins to grow, you need to have a structured approach to organizing your servers, switches, and routers, as well as many support systems (air conditioning systems and power especially). After decades of different architectures, the architecture most commonly adopted by traditional data centers is Cisco's *three-tiered architecture*, which consists of an access layer, distribution layer, and core layer (Figure 14-5).

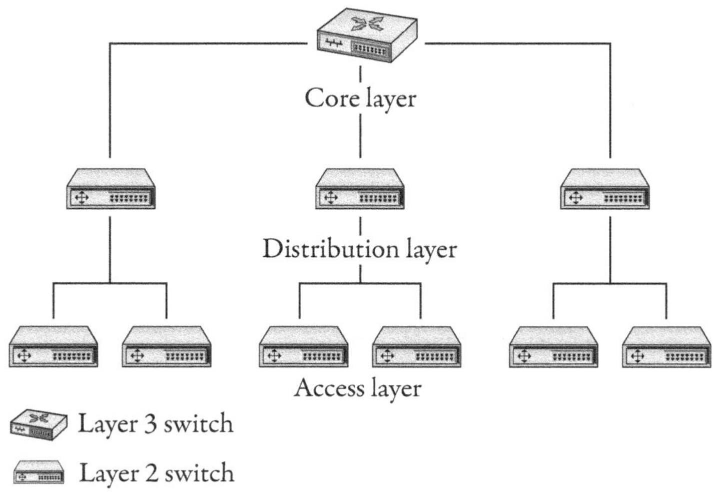

FIGURE 14-5 Three-tiered architecture

ACCESS LAYER

The *access layer*—also referred to as the *edge layer*—acts as the primary connection between the data center and the users (keep in mind that "users" in data centers are servers). The access layer comprises the cables and the access switches closest to the systems. A common implementation of access switches is *top-of-rack switching*, in which every equipment rack has one Layer 2 switch (or two for redundancy) sitting at the top of the rack, connecting to all the systems on the rack (Figure 14-6). Top-of-rack switches are *coresident* in the rack with servers, as compared to switches that reside in a separate rack.

Top-of-rack switches—*dedicated switches*—help keep cable runs short and well organized. Despite its name, top-of-rack switching does not require that the switches be physically at the top of the rack (although they usually are).

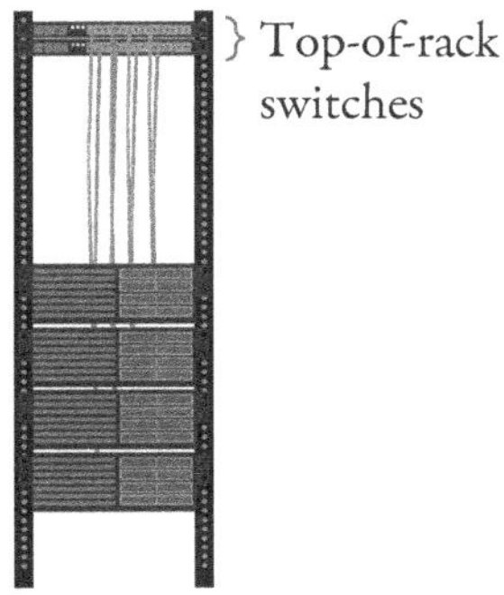

FIGURE 14-6 Typical rack with switch

DISTRIBUTION LAYER

Data centers have tens, hundreds, or in some cases thousands of racks in a single facility. With top-of-rack switches on all the racks, you need to provide a method to interconnect and distribute data to all the systems, acting as the connection between the access layer and the core layer. The *distribution layer* provides that connectivity. Distribution layer switches are usually multilayer switches and conduct forwarding from Layer 2 on the access side to Layer 3 for the core side. Cisco best practices recommend always having two distribution switches for each access layer switch to provide redundancy in case of switch or cable failures. Every group of modules connected to the same distribution switches, including the distribution layer switches, is known as a *pod* (Figure 14-7).

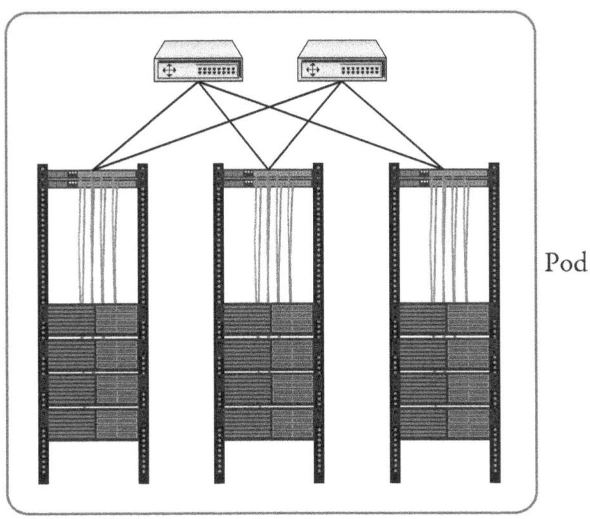

FIGURE 14-7 Distribution layer

CORE LAYER

The *core layer* ties together all the switches at the distribution layer and acts as the point of connection to the external connections (which are not part of this layer), including the internet. All systems at this level run exclusively at Layer 3 of the OSI model (the Network layer). These interconnections operate at the highest speed and bandwidth and are therefore defined as the *backbone*.

The core layer is only about moving data as quickly as possible. Therefore, this layer lacks VLAN tagging, filtering, services, or anything else that would slow down data transmission.

Data starts its journey from the client's access layer and then moves to the client's distribution layer. From there, it may be routed through the core layer to the destination's distribution layer before finally arriving at the destination's access layer.

Just as with distribution, Cisco best practices recommend always having two core switches accessible to each access switch for redundancy.

NOTE Cisco's three-tiered architecture isn't limited to a data center. For a campus environment, edge switches make up the access layer in the users' offices, floors, and buildings. The edge switches are connected to distribution layer switches (at the building level or server room level), which in turn are connected to the core layer to get back out to the servers' distribution and access layers. The access layer focuses on security (802.1X and other items) and traffic control (like QoS tagging, which marks packets to prioritize network traffic, ensuring that critical applications receive the necessary bandwidth and low latency).

Collapsed Core Architecture

A *collapsed core* architecture collapses the distribution and core layers into a combined layer, turning the three-tiered architecture into a two-tiered architecture. Modern switches are robust enough to provide the functionality of both the distribution and core layers, and this architecture can save significant costs for a small or medium organization. A collapsed core also reduces configuration and management complexity and simplifies the use of certain network protocols, reducing the chance of issues and making troubleshooting easier. In some buildings, the distribution and core layers are already in the same room, in which case a collapsed core just makes sense.

There are reasons why large and some medium organizations might not adopt the collapsed core architecture, though. With two layers, adding devices can hinder scalability (the ability to grow). Specifically, adding a new floor or building of devices would require a significant number of cables and processing capacity that might exceed the switch's capabilities.

Furthermore, since there are fewer redundant devices, the infrastructure might not be as resilient in the event of a failure.

Spine-and-Leaf Architecture

A *spine-and-leaf architecture* uses two types of switches: spine switches (which function as the network backbone, similar to core layer switches) and leaf switches (which connect to end devices, similar to access layer switches). Every spine switch connects to every leaf switch in a two-tiered *mesh* topology (Figure 14-8). The mesh topology removes the need for dedicated connections between the spine switches, because traffic moves seamlessly from spine to leaf to spine, regardless of how many spine or leaf switches are on the network.

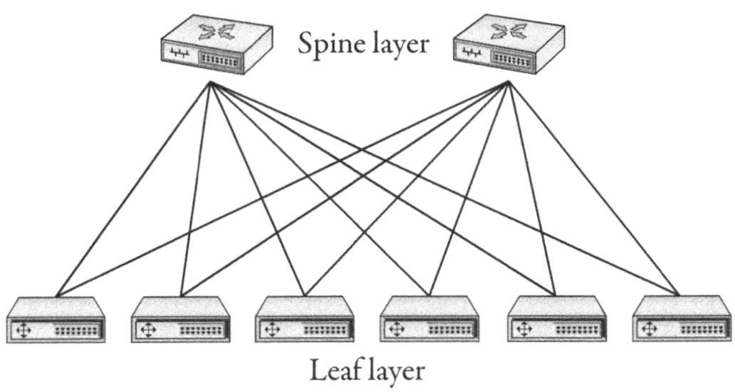

FIGURE 14-8 Spine-and-leaf architecture

NOTE Spine-and-leaf configurations have multiple, interconnected top-of-rack structures.

The spine-and-leaf architecture has some real benefits compared to the three-tiered architecture. First, spine-and-leaf architecture reduces the number of hops between devices; every step from the spine to leaf is a single hop, which reduces latency and creates completely predictable connections. Also, there's no longer a concern for loops, making Spanning Tree Protocol (STP; discussed in Chapter 6) unneeded. Virtual servers today rely heavily on data from other servers in the same data center, adding far more east-west traffic than a three-tiered architecture can easily handle. Spine-and-leaf architecture handles east-west traffic with ease. It also uses protocols such as *Equal-Cost Multipath* (ECMP) to provide load balancing across the paths so that no single connection gets overwhelmed. Finally, spine-and-leaf architecture makes adding capacity simpler than in a three-tiered architecture thanks to its mesh topology.

Traffic Flows

All the switches, cables, and routers that populate a typical data center have a single job: to move a lot of data. To help those who design data centers, the industry has established common terms to define the movement of the data into, out of, and around the data center, or *traffic flows*.

NORTH-SOUTH

North-south traffic describes data moving into and out of the data center. Breaking down this term even more, *northbound traffic* leaves the data center and *southbound traffic* enters the data center. Network devices involved in north-south traffic include edge routers, edge firewalls, and load balancers.

EAST-WEST

East-west traffic is defined as any traffic that moves between systems within the data center. Unlike north-south traffic, there is no separate east traffic or west traffic. It's all just east-west. Examples are backup traffic, intrusion detection system (IDS) alerts, and logs. Network devices involved in east-west traffic include internal routers, internal firewalls, and switches. Figure 14-9 shows traffic flows.

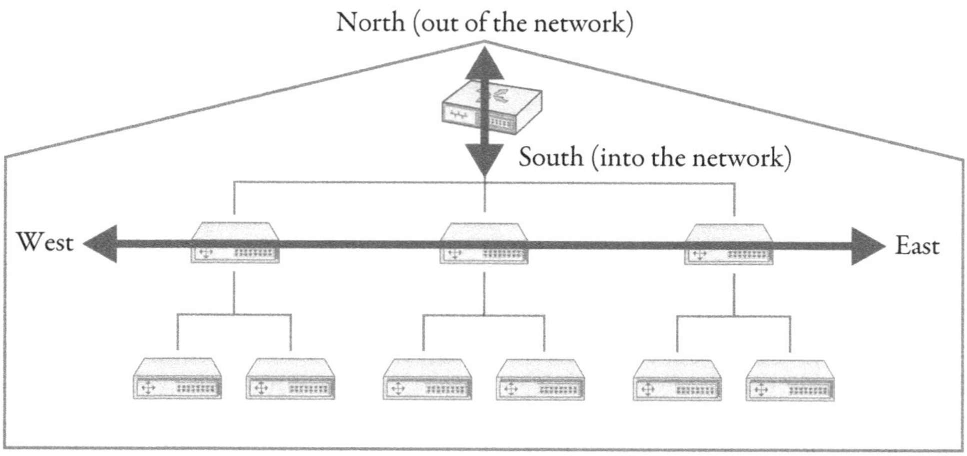

FIGURE 14-9 Traffic flows

Data Storage

All that data moving north, south, east, and west sometimes needs to rest someplace, and that's where data storage comes into play. For the most part, all data storage in a classic data center focuses on the mass storage devices that store the terabytes or petabytes of ones and zeroes that make up the data. *Mass storage devices* in a traditional data center include *hard drives* and *tape backups*. Tape backups are rare (or completely gone), making hard drives and solid-state drives (SSDs) the main technologies used to store data in data centers.

So, where are all these mass storage devices located in the data center, and what are their jobs? To be sure, every system is going to have a boot drive, in most cases a single M.2 drive mounted to the motherboard, but that drive does no more than boot the operating system. For the actual data storage, most traditional data centers use a *storage area network* (SAN), a network that connects individual systems to a centralized bank of mass storage (Figure 14-10).

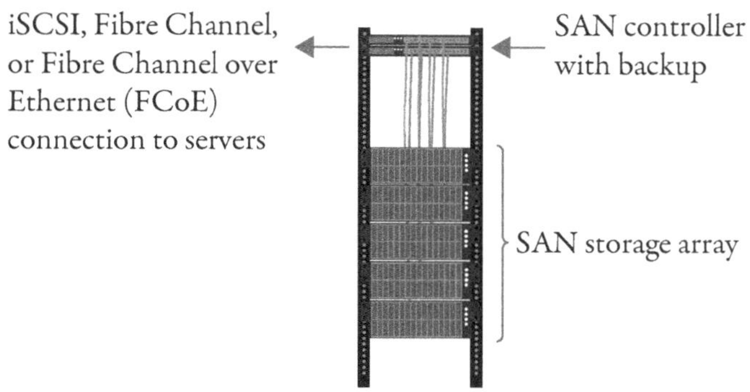

FIGURE 14-10 SAN in action

But don't think of a SAN as simply a networked hard drive! You might remember from CompTIA A+ that hard drive storage is broken up into tiny sectors known as *blocks*. You might also remember that to access the hard drive, you must plug it into an interface like SATA, which your operating system uses to read and write to blocks on the disk. A SAN is a *pool of mass storage devices*, presented over a network as any number of logical disks. The interface it presents to a client computer pretends to be a hard disk and enables the client's OS to read and write blocks over a network.

Think of a drive accessed through the SAN as a *virtual disk*. Much as the hypervisor convinces the operating system it runs on its own hardware, the SAN convinces the OS it is interacting with a physical hard drive. Just like with a traditional hard disk, we must format a virtual disk before we can use it. But unlike a traditional hard disk, the virtual disk the SAN presents could be mapped to several physical drives in various physical locations or even to other forms of storage.

One of the benefits of using a SAN is that, by just reading and writing at the block level, it avoids the performance costs of implementing its own filesystem. The SAN leaves it up to the client computers to implement their own filesystems—these clients often use specialized shared filesystem software designed for high volume, performance, reliability, and the ability to support multiple clients using one drive.

When it comes to the infrastructure to support a SAN, there are currently two main choices:

- *Fibre Channel* (FC) is, for the most part, its own ecosystem designed for high-performance storage. It has its own cables, protocols, and switches, all increasing the costs associated with its use. While more recent developments like *Fibre Channel over Ethernet* (FCoE) make FC a little more flexible within a local wired network, long-distance FC is still clumsy without expensive cabling and hardware.
- *Internet Small Computer System Interface* (iSCSI) is built on top of TCP/IP, enabling devices that use the SCSI protocol to communicate across existing networks using cheap, readily available hardware. Because the existing networks and their hardware weren't built as a disk interface, performance can suffer. Part of this performance cost is time spent processing frame headers. We can ease some of this cost by using *jumbo frames*, which are usually 9,000 bytes long (though technically anything over 1,500 qualifies), to reduce the total number of frames moving through the network.

NOTE The physical connections between the systems and the SAN are usually fiber optic.

Moving a server's data storage physically apart from the server adds some risk. If the SAN fails, the server won't function. To address this risk, most SAN solutions provide more than one connection or path between the server and the SAN, an approach called *multipathing*. If either connection fails, the other connection keeps the server connected to the SAN. A SAN is developed with high availability in mind, so in addition to multipathing it often includes features such as redundant controllers and power supplies, plus shared memory. (See "High Availability in the Data Center" later in the chapter for more details.)

Data Center Location

So, where does the data center physically exist? That answer varies based on where and how an organization stands in terms of growth. A tiny company might leave all its data sitting on a single computer in the founder's garage. As a company grows and its data requirements grow, it faces choices. Does it build an *on-premises data center*, a dedicated data center at the company's site?

SAN VS. NAS

We install special Host Bus Adapter (HBA) storage cards in devices and use Fibre Channel (FC) or iSCSI networking cables instead of SAS/SCSI cables and dedicated switches to connect those HBAs to disk enclosers within a storage area network (SAN). The SAN allocates a portion of its storage and presents it as a virtual disk to the HBA, which is identified by its World Wide Node Name (WWNN).

Centralizing storage in a SAN provides more flexibility for allocating storage to servers as opposed to multiport *direct-attached storage* (DAS) trays or enclosures. DAS is limited by cable length and the number of servers it can connect to directly.

When using a SAN with VMware, the same "disks" can be connected to multiple servers, allowing each server to access the disk simultaneously. This enables software like VMware vMotion to move running VMs between servers by transferring only the memory state, since all servers can access the VM's disk files on the SAN.

Unlike a SAN that presents storage as virtual disks at the block level, *network attached storage* (NAS) is a disk enclosure connected directly to the data network that shares folders with client systems using protocols like Network File System (NFS) and Server Message Block (SMB).

You can think of a NAS as a smart external hard drive connected to your network: it doesn't need a full server to work, but it acts like one by providing shared folders. NAS devices can be small for home use or very large for enterprise environments with lots of storage.

To compare a SAN to a NAS, let's use another analogy. Think of a SAN as a private storage warehouse that provides raw materials, blocks of data, that systems can use to build whatever they need. It doesn't organize the data into files or folders but offers space for systems to manage at a low level. On the other hand, a NAS is more like a shared filing cabinet on the network. It organizes data into folders and files that users and applications can access directly, without needing to manage the storage structure themselves. While both provide centralized storage, a SAN is optimized for performance and flexibility at the infrastructure level, while a NAS is designed for easy file sharing and user access.

An organization can also achieve similar functionality by placing a server in front of a SAN, connecting it to the SAN, and sharing folders over the network. However, this approach requires more hardware than a typical NAS device. NAS software often includes features resembling server clusters, such as data deduplication, which some SANs also support.

For many organizations, the next step is to build a rack in an empty room and load it with a few servers and mass storage devices—in essence, building a mini data center. That is perfectly fine for small organizations, but as data and server needs progress even further, a true data center is required. It's time to take the servers and move them into a proper, secure, reliable, classic data center.

But where to place this beast? On-premises data centers are wildly expensive in terms of both the building and the associated maintenance and upkeep. Back in the day, there really weren't any other viable choices. Over time, however, clever entrepreneurs (or folks who had already built data centers and had extra capacity) began to offer public, third-party data centers where anyone could place their own servers, a process known as *colocation*.

After creating a data center, most organizations start thinking about building and maintaining a secondary or backup data center. Top of mind is replicating data between the two locations in case of an issue with the main data center. This topic is covered in more detail in Chapter 16.

As an organization grows beyond a single site into multiple locations, or *branch offices*, there's usually a central location (often corporate headquarters) that contains its single data center. This data center serves the branch offices, which store very little data themselves.

The Modern Data Center

The first few decades of traditional data centers were populated with dedicated, monolithic hardware. Servers served one website or one function, such as DNS. Routers and switches were dedicated boxes that performed only a single job, routing or switching. Monolithic devices worked well back in the day, but the introduction of virtualization and software-defined networking (SDN) changed the data center dramatically, creating the *modern data center*. Virtual extensible local area networks, zero trust architecture, and SASE and SSE further bring the data center into the future.

Virtualization

Virtualization redefined the architecture of the data center. Where once physical servers ran single copies of web servers and other individual applications, physical servers today are nothing more than hypervisors, running 2, 3, or perhaps even 20 virtual servers each. There might be a few nonvirtual systems, but these apply almost always to very special situations such as SAN controllers. If you have a server in a data center today, it most likely is virtualized.

SDN and SD-WAN

In the previous chapter, we discussed how SDN works. Now, we'll discuss something that sounds and behaves similar, the *software-defined wide area network* (SD-WAN), as it relates to data center architecture.

A traditional WAN infrastructure depends on hardware, like routers, cables, and physical machines. Configuration and management are controlled at the devices themselves. An SD-WAN is based on software and virtualizes the hardware components. A software overlay provisions, manages, and secures the connections. Unlike a traditional WAN that requires making changes to routers one by one, an SD-WAN uses a centralized controller that allows for the simultaneous configuration and management of many WAN connections with centralized policies.

APPLICATION AWARENESS

An SD-WAN is *application aware*, cognizant of how applications work and what requirements need to be in place for them. As a result, it can automatically create policies to manage traffic. Once these policies are in place, the SD-WAN continuously monitors both the applications and the network to ensure efficiency, optimization, and security.

ZERO-TOUCH PROVISIONING

A centralized console performs *zero-touch provisioning*, a process that prepares the virtual SD-WAN routers, switches, mobile devices, and even network services automatically, alleviating the need to configure each device and service individually. Not only does this speed up time for provisioning a device or service, but having multiple devices using the same configuration files also cuts down on errors.

TRANSPORT AGNOSTICISM

An SD-WAN is *transport agnostic*, which means that it can use any method of transport, for example, Multiprotocol Label Switching (MPLS), Ethernet, broadband internet, cable, Digital Subscriber Line (DSL), Long Term Evolution (LTE), or even leased lines. Furthermore, you can group transports in terms of similar applications that require a certain bandwidth or security posture, geographical locations, and more.

CENTRAL POLICY MANAGEMENT

Having a *central policy management* system in place allows administrators to gain deep visibility into network traffic—specifically how applications are being used, what traffic is going through which devices, and what actions users are performing—through a *single pane of glass* (SPOG), the SD-WAN interface that aggregates data from multiple sources in one view. Networking and security are controlled from the SPOG interface as well.

Virtual Extensible Local Area Networks

A *virtual extensible local area network* (VXLAN) is an Internet Engineering Task Force (IETF) standard that allows multiple organizations to share a physical network without exposing their own organizational traffic to the others. Using certain ports from certain switches, administrators can create a virtual network that appears as a single physical network to the connected devices, each of which can only see traffic from its own VXLAN. Instead of being restricted by the traditional 4,094 VLANs limit, this standard supports up to 16 million VXLANs.

VXLAN achieves this through Layer 2 encapsulation, placing Layer 2 Ethernet frames inside of Layer 4 UDP datagrams, which are then transported over a Layer 3 IP network. In this overlay network, the VXLAN header sits between the UDP header and the Ethernet frame, and an outer IP header encapsulates all of it. The IP header and its payload are then encapsulated in a frame and sent to a switch. This preserves the Layer 2 information, unlike a traditional VLAN, where the router strips away the Layer 2 information from incoming traffic.

The VXLAN header has a 24-bit virtual network identifier (VNI) that identifies the VXLAN. VXLAN tunnel endpoints (VTEPs), whose IP addresses are in the outer packet, handle packet encapsulation and decapsulation. The UDP datagram that follows the outer IP header uses destination port 4789.

VXLAN applications include forming network segments that span multiple data centers, enabling service providers and cloud providers to keep traffic from each organization separate, and allowing an organization to isolate sensitive traffic from public traffic.

A Data Center Interconnect (DCI) connects multiple data centers using VXLANs, ensuring seamless communication and data transfer.

Zero Trust Architecture

Zero trust architecture (ZTA) takes nothing for granted, strictly verifying any people and devices attempting to access network resources, regardless of whether they are inside or outside of the network. In the past, insiders were trusted by default, which meant that if an attacker got network access, they could wreak havoc.

However, traditional definitions of "insider" and "outsider" no longer apply, since companies now have data distributed across many locations, including cloud-based environments, making the network perimeter much less clear. This shift makes ZTA's continuous verification approach essential for securing modern infrastructures.

ZTA relies on three fundamental and interconnected security principles: policy-based authentication to evaluate access requests, granular authorization to control what users can do, and least privilege access to limit exposure.

POLICY-BASED AUTHENTICATION

Policy-based authentication, also known as *policy-based access control* (PBAC), is when policies are crafted and enforced to permit or deny access to resources based on factors including users, groups, devices, geographical locations, day, time, actions being performed, and resource security classification.

AUTHORIZATION

Certain types of actions can be given *authorization*, based on certain policy matches. A user from a certain department might be able to access a server during working hours Monday through Friday, but not on weekends, for example.

LEAST PRIVILEGE ACCESS

Least privilege access means applying the principle of least privilege so that a user, process, device, or system has access only to what's needed to perform the job or task at hand, and no more.

SASE and SSE

Secure Access Secure Edge (SASE, pronounced "sassy") is a cloud-based framework and architecture that provides networking and security, connecting users, devices, data, and applications. Normally, traffic would be routed through data centers for security policy enforcement, but with SASE, security policies and controls are right there in the cloud, closer to the users and their devices. As a result, accessing data and applications is more efficient. SASE verifies user and device identity—and potentially additional factors such as location, day, and time—for security and access control.

The SD-WAN infrastructure, described earlier, connects sites and networks to an organization's data centers and on-premises networks, but SASE connects users and networks to geographically distributed cloud-based services. Thus, a data center would simply be another service in the topology.

In 2021, Gartner, an organization that performs technology-based research and consulting, created Security Service Edge (SSE), a subset of SASE that deals only with the security aspect.

SSE has four primary components:

- Zero trust architecture.
- Secure Web Gateway (SWG), which performs content filtering, browser security, DNS monitoring, and data loss prevention (DLP).
- Cloud Access Security Broker (CASB), which provides a deep analysis of communications to and from cloud-based applications.
- Firewall as a Service (FWaaS), a cloud-based firewall deployment as opposed to a physical on-premises firewall. Whereas SWG security focuses on web traffic and web-based applications, FWaaS security targets an entire network infrastructure. Protection mechanisms include URL filtering, DNS security, and intrusion prevention systems (IPSes).

High Availability in the Data Center

If there's one thing a data center must do well, it's providing the right data to the right host at the right time, without ever dropping or failing. Unfortunately, things fail in life: CPUs melt, rodents chew cables, and power supplies die. Therefore, it's important to ensure systems keep working without interruption or downtime; in other words, to make sure critical systems have *high availability* (HA). Some of HA's core concepts have been covered previously in the book and even in this chapter, such as multipathing within a SAN; as the concepts come into play here, I'll point to where you read about them before. HA in this section explores load balancing, redundancy, and facilities and infrastructure support.

HA Approaches

HA approaches include *active-active* and *active-passive.* Active-active HA involves multiple devices running simultaneously, all actively handling traffic or workloads. This setup provides load balancing, improved resource utilization, and seamless failover (the ability for backup systems to detect when a master has failed and then to take over).

In active-passive HA, a single active device handles all traffic, while one or more passive standby devices remain in an idle/hot-standby state. If the active node fails, the passive nodes take over. Failover can potentially be slower than in active-active deployments, but active-passive HA requires simpler synchronization and less resource usage during regular operations.

Use active-active deployments when you need maximum performance, scalability, and near-zero downtime. They're best suited for applications that have high traffic or workloads that can be distributed across multiple devices, like web servers, databases with clustering, and cloud services. All devices actively dealing with traffic will optimize resource use and ensure quick replies to clients. However, keep in mind that active-active deployments are more complex to implement and maintain, especially with data consistency and synchronization.

Use active-passive deployments when your priorities are simplicity, cost effectiveness, and reliability, and when the workload can tolerate a short failover delay. They're best suited for critical systems that have a clear primary system and a standby that's ready to take over, as well as environments where active-active synchronization is unnecessary or challenging. During regular workloads, active-passive deployments use fewer resources since the passive devices aren't processing traffic.

Load Balancing

Load balancing means sharing among two or more systems the effort to enable some process to work. Special-purpose load balancers help apportion the work among the various servers. You saw this concept earlier in the discussion of spine-and-leaf data centers, which rely on protocols like ECMP to balance the work among the various switches so that no single connection gets swamped. Load balancing in its many forms is one pillar of HA.

Redundancy

Redundancy means using additional equipment and connection options to ensure HA on many levels. Again, failover is key; if one device or connection goes down, another detects the failure and takes its place. With *redundant hardware/clusters*, you put into place primary switches, routers, firewalls, and other network gear, then have at the ready backup machines to step up in case the primary machine fails.

If you're going to use multiple devices to do one job, there must be a way to make them look like a single device to the rest of the network. The common approach is having them share a single external MAC address or IP address while using their own internal MACs or IPs to communicate with each other. You'll see this concept repeatedly.

Building with HA in mind extends to more than just servers; you can protect a default gateway, for example, by adding redundant backups. Protocols that support HA and redundancy for routers are referred to as *first hop redundancy protocols* (FHRPs). They include the open standard *Virtual Router Redundancy Protocol* (VRRP) as well as the Cisco-proprietary *Hot Standby Router Protocol* (HSRP) and *Gateway Load Balancing Protocol* (GLBP). The nice thing about VRRP, HSRP, and GLBP is that, conceptually, they perform the same function: they group multiple routers together into a single virtual router with a single *virtual IP* (VIP) address that clients use as a default gateway. This includes making redundant firewalls on the redundant routers! GLBP takes things a step further, providing full load balancing as well.

Clustering, in the traditional sense, means to connect multiple pieces of equipment, such as servers, such that they appear to the user and the network as one logical device providing data and services to the organization. Clusters usually share high-speed networking connections, as well as data stores and applications, and provide redundancy if a single member of the cluster fails.

NOTE Clustering solutions are typically examples of *active-active* HA in that all members of the cluster are active at the same time.

VRRP and HSRP are examples of *active-passive* HA in that only one router is active at a time; all other routers are passive until the active router fails.

Redundancy applies to connections as well as systems. What's an absolutely critical connection point for a data center? *Connection to the internet* should never be a single point of failure for a data center (or for any organization, for that matter). It's common for a data center to use multiple ISPs so that if one service goes down, the other ISP provides continued internet connectivity. Sometimes the other ISP is a hot standby, so the internet connection switches—a failover. In other setups, the secondary ISP is actively engaged, available for excess traffic, and ready to be the sole service if necessary. Employing multiple ISPs is a measure of fault tolerance.

It's very common for ISPs to share lines, especially when they are servicing the same physical location. It's therefore critically important to ensure *path diversity*, where the lines out of your ISP follow *diverse paths* to other routers. A common method for path diversity in smaller centers, for example, uses a fiber connection for the primary path and a very fast cellular connection as a failover. Using both a fiber ISP and a different cable ISP is another option for path diversity.

NOTE Redundancy with switches was covered in Chapter 6.

Facilities and Infrastructure Support

Data centers require proper support for facilities and infrastructure, which means ensuring that proper power; clean, cool air for components; and emergency procedures are in place. All of these add to HA and, in the case of the last item, disaster recovery.

POWER

Rack-mounted equipment has several special power needs. At an absolute minimum, start with a proper power source. A single small rack can get away with a properly grounded, 20-amp dedicated circuit. Larger installations can require larger, dedicated power transformers supplied by the local power grid.

NOTE Different rack manufacturers have specific rules and standards for rack electrical grounding. Refer to the specific manufacturer's installation instructions and consider hiring professional installers when placing your racks.

When you get down to individual racks, it's always a good idea to provide each rack with its own rack-mounted *uninterruptible power supply* (UPS)—a battery backup and power conditioner. You then connect a *power distribution unit* (PDU)—a rack-mounted set of outlets for devices—to that UPS. If you're using *power converters* for devices that require DC rather than AC, always use a single power converter per rack.

The more demanding equipment room also necessitates more robust power and *battery backup*. A single, decent UPS might adequately handle brief power fluctuations for a single rack, for example, but won't be able to deal with a serious power outage. For that kind of *power redundancy*—keeping the lights on and the servers rolling—you'd need to connect to the equipment room *power generators*, devices that burn some petroleum product to produce electricity when the main grid goes dark.

ENVIRONMENT

Racks with servers, switches, routers, and such go into closets or server rooms, and they dump heat. You must monitor and control the environment within this space for both temperature and humidity. Network components work better when cool rather than hot.

Rack placement should *optimize the airflow* in a server area. All racks should be placed so that components draw air in from a shared cool row and then exhaust the hot air into a hot row.

The *heating, ventilation, and air conditioning* (HVAC) system should recirculate and purify the hot air into cool air in a continuous flow. What's the proper temperature and humidity level? The ideal for the room, regardless of size, is an average temperature of 68 degrees Fahrenheit and around 50 percent humidity. A proper *fire suppression system*—one that can detect fire, cut power to protect sensitive equipment, displace oxygen with fire-suppressing gases, alert relevant staff, and activate sprinklers in a pinch—is an absolute must for any server closet or room. You need to extinguish any electrical spark quickly to minimize server or data loss.

EMERGENCY PROCEDURES

A data center must have proper emergency procedures in place before the emergencies happen. This is essential risk management. Here are five crucial aspects to cover:

- Building layout
- Fire escape plan
- Safety/emergency exits
- Fail open/fail close
- Emergency alert system

Exit plans need to cover *building layout*, *fire escape plans*, and the locations of *emergency exits*. Exit signs should be posted strategically so people can quickly exit in a real emergency.

Secured spaces, such as server rooms, need some kind of default safety mechanism in case of an emergency. Emergency exits like stairways also require safety mechanisms like fail-safe locks. Locked doors need to *fail open* (doors default to open in case of emergency) or *fail closed* (doors lock in case of emergency). Fail-safe locks, such as maglocks, require power to stay locked. When the power goes out, they automatically open. The contrasting locks are called *fail secure*. They're locked by default and require power to open. If the power goes out, they stay locked.

Finally, nothing beats a properly loud *emergency alert system* blaring away to get people moving quickly. Don't forget to have annual fire drills and emergency alert mixers to make certain all employees know what they need to know.

Documenting the Data Center

A properly organized data center requires extensive documentation that describes every aspect of the organization, from physical layout to electrical structure, from networking standards and installations to climate control systems. This documentation includes both the people necessary to maintain, repair, and replace every piece of equipment, as well as every applicable government standard. At least annually, the data center (and its documentation) should be reviewed and audited for efficiency and compliance. As you might imagine at this point, properly documenting a data center is a major *continuous* undertaking and not a task to shirk.

This section will consider the following scenario. The Wapi Lava Corporation (WLC), based in Pocatello, Idaho, has a midsize data center (nicknamed "Hot Flo") in the basement of a downtown building. WLC chose the city of Pocatello because of the availability of inexpensive electricity, good connectivity with the West Coast and solid links to the Midwest, and very low probability of natural disasters.

Good data center documentation contains all sorts of diagrams that map out physical and logical systems. These documents include dimensions, standards followed, locations, connectivity, technology manufacturers and model numbers, licensing, essential personnel, and more.

NOTE The fictitious Wapi Lava Corporation is named after the Wapi Lava Field, a very inactive volcanic site around 30 miles outside the city of Pocatello. It hasn't erupted in more than 2,000 years. (It's pronounced *WAH-pie*.)

Network Diagrams

It's important to create, store, and modify network diagrams showing Layer 1, Layer 2, and Layer 3 components (based on the OSI model covered in Chapter 1) when anything changes. Layer 1 is represented in the network diagrams by the physical cables connecting networking devices, Layer 2 is represented by switches, and Layer 3 is represented by routers.

While Layers 5, 6, and 7 are not usually represented in a network diagram, some organizations include Layer 4 TCP/UDP port information for firewall flow configuration options. Other diagrams could include details related to other configuration options, shares created on servers, or applications on servers (for example, SQL).

PHYSICAL NETWORK DIAGRAMS

Physical network diagrams map out physical aspects of the data center, including floor plans and documents describing the physical components and connectivity in the centralized wiring rooms on each floor.

Physical network diagrams rely on a few standard tools for layout, such as Microsoft Visio, Wondershare Edraw, or my current favorite, diagrams.net. Figure 14-11 shows some of the icons available in diagrams.net.

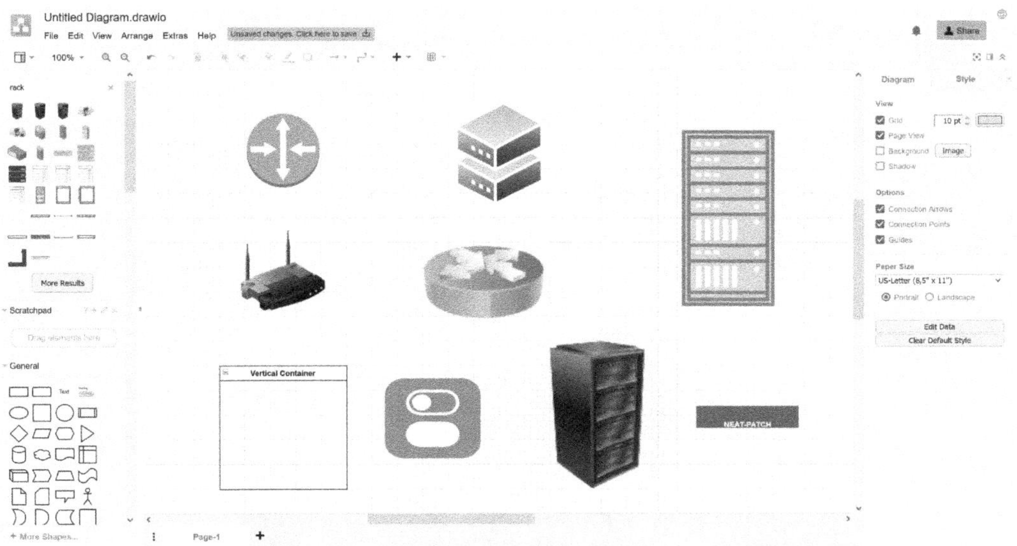

FIGURE 14-11 Icon options in the diagrams.net app

Floor Plans

A data center floor plan includes room dimensions and locations, as well as locations and detailed information about racks, hot and cold aisles, raised floors, ceiling heights, air conditioning units, ductwork, and more. Floor plan documentation can take many pages, illustrations, and discussion.

Figure 14-12 shows the basic layout of the lower level of Hot Flo. Note the three major sections. There is a wiring room in the west (left), a network operations center in the center, and the server farm in the east (right).

The wiring room is the *intermediate distribution frame* (IDF) that serves as the wiring focal point for all the devices on that floor. This is also called a *telecommunications* room, like you read about in Chapter 11. The *network operations center* (NOC) houses network engineers and technicians who maintain the applications housed in the data center, such as databases and web servers. Most of the lower level is the *server farm*, with row upon row of racks holding stacks of servers. Each rack is topped with two switches.

Figure 14-13 drills down further into the server farm area, showing the hot aisles (where heat can go away from the servers) and cold aisles (where the air conditioning vents pump cold air for thirsty servers).

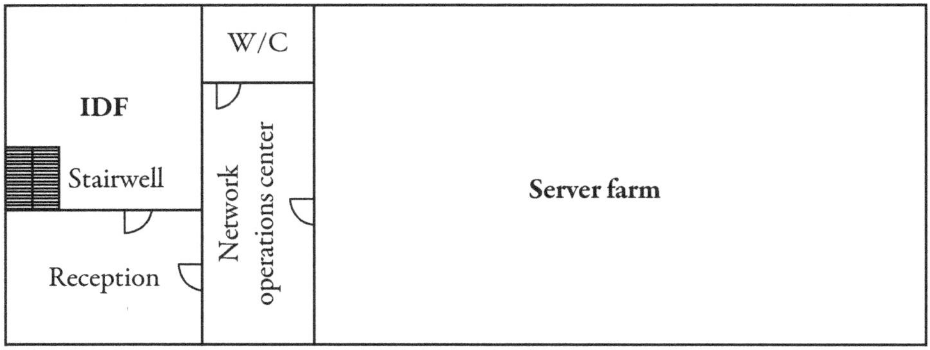

FIGURE 14-12 Basic layout of Hot Flo's lower floor

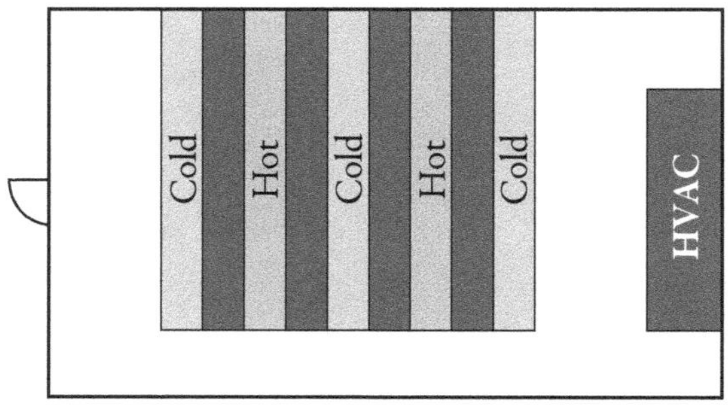

FIGURE 14-13 Floor plan details of server farm

Figure 14-14 shows the upper-floor layout—although without individual offices mapped—with both a telecommunications room for the floor and a *main distribution frame* (MDF) that holds all the equipment that enables Hot Flo's connection to the outside world.

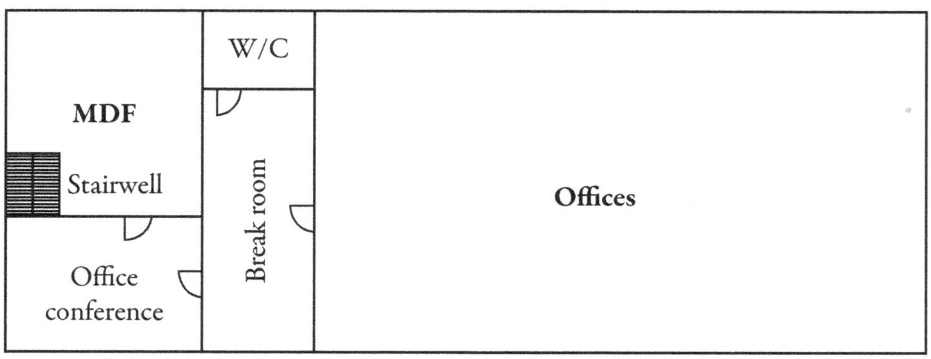

FIGURE 14-14 Upper-level floor plan of Hot Flo

MDF/IDF Documentation

The MDF provides connectivity to the outside world and the IDFs provide network connectivity within each floor. They require unique and detailed documentation of the overall layout and connections, plus specific rack diagrams for their various components. Figure 14-15 shows the MDF documentation, providing details about the demarc connection; the rack holding the patch panels and switches providing further connectivity within the data center; and the UPS providing clean power to the rack components. Each component's make and model are clearly labeled.

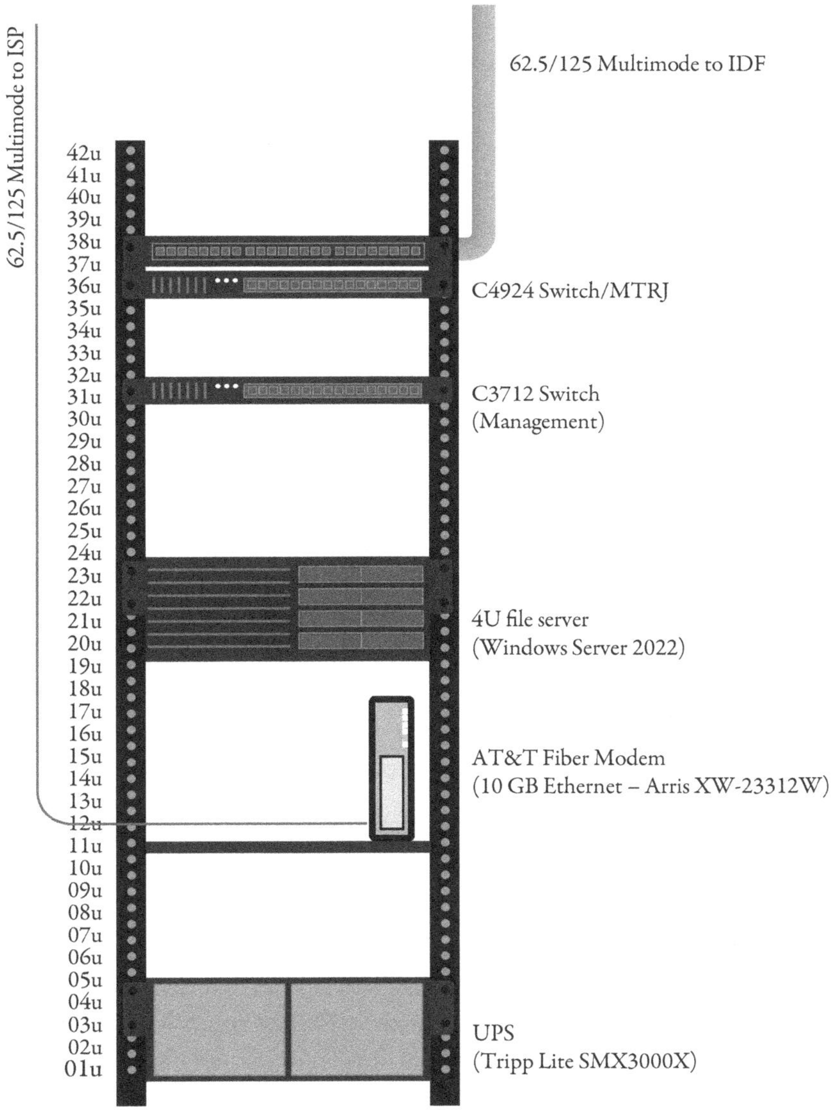

FIGURE 14-15 Basic MDF layout

MDF racks are accompanied by further documentation detailing firmware versions, service and upgrade records, assigned technicians, vendor contacts, and so on.

LOGICAL NETWORK DIAGRAMS

Essential network documentation includes *logical network diagrams*, line drawings that show how the many devices in the network are connected. These diagrams deal with how the communication flows between devices and focuses more on aspects like subnets and protocols than on physical layout. Figure 14-16 shows the server farm portion of the Hot Flo data center. Accompanying the logical drawing would be pages of additional documentation, including specific wiring standards used, vendor information, and so on.

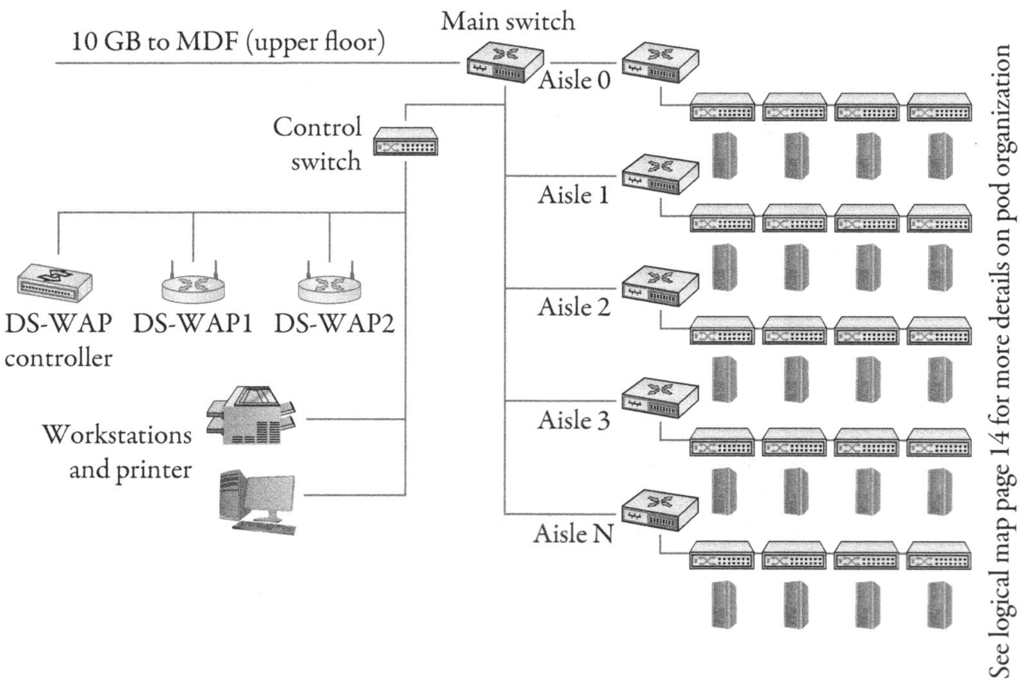

FIGURE 14-16 Logical network diagram showing Hot Flo's server farm

RACK DIAGRAMS

Drilling down for more details, each rack (in the server farm and the IDFs and MDF) has a detailed *rack diagram* with a ton of details. Figure 14-17 shows one such rack. Each rack component's location and make and model is labeled. Appended to this illustration is further documentation showing the current firmware version, date of purchase, upgrade history, service history, technician in charge of servicing, vendor contact, licensing information, and more.

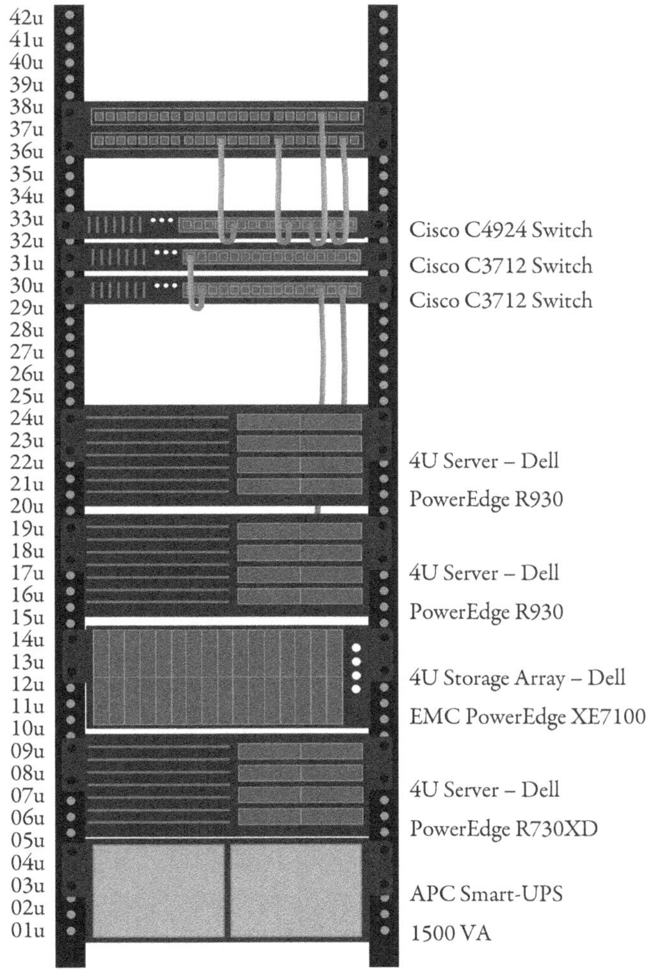

FIGURE 14-17 Rack diagram

CABLE MAPS AND DIAGRAMS

Cable maps and diagrams can show any number of types of wiring, from the full electrical map in Figure 14-18 to a detailed layout of the physical space with drops to each workstation and full cable runs. The detailed additional documents provide absolutely essential network documentation for the data center.

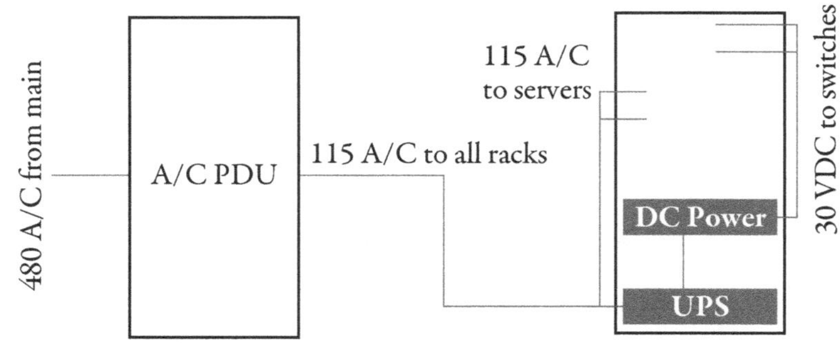

FIGURE 14-18 Wiring diagram showing the electrical components in Hot Flo's server farm

Asset Inventory

Asset inventory is crucial to make sure you know what hardware, software, licensing, and warranty support are in use. What brand and model are the routers and switches running in the data center? What operating system versions are they running? What about your servers? Which OSs are they running? What services and software are installed? Are you licensing any hardware or software? Who is the vendor? How can they be contacted? How quickly can they help if needed? Are your routers, switches, and servers under warranty?

Baseline Configurations

Once the data center is up and running and efficiently humming along, the *baseline configuration* documents all of its components. This is a *network baseline* rather than a *performance baseline*. Whereas the latter examines throughput, bandwidth, and the like, a baseline configuration describes all the pieces—including portable computers, servers, switches, and routers—as well as all the software packages installed on them. The baseline configuration also includes network topology and placement of devices in the organization.

The baseline configuration provides the foundation for future upgrades. After any upgrades, the organization should update it to the new baseline.

NOTE This definition of baseline configuration reflects the best practices outlined in NIST Special Publication 800-128, *Guide for Security-Focused Configuration Management of Information Systems*.

Assessments

Periodically, every data center should be assessed for overall efficiency and effectiveness. Is every component performing up to expectations? Does the current performance meet the organization's goals? Does everything in the network comply with current national or international laws and regulations?

The assessments can be conducted by an external party or an internal division. The benefit of the former is that, theoretically at least, an external party has no preconceptions about or bias toward any specific system or individuals. The benefit of the latter is that an internal division is much more familiar with how data center operations are supposed to work to accomplish the organization's goals.

Site Surveys

A periodic *site survey* assesses everything about the data center. It starts with an overall assessment and then drills down into each category. The *site survey report* should include the following categories:

- Layout and space utilization
- Infrastructure installed
- Expectations for the organization
- Future requirements
- Concerns about current performance

Category-level inspections should cover exhaustive details. For layout and space utilization, for example, examiners should inspect—and create detailed reports for—at least the following:

- General layout
- Space utilization
- Thermal management
- Electrical distribution
- Cabling types and paths
- Racks, cabinets, server locations
- Labeling compliance with ANSI/TIA 606-C

Every category the site survey team examines should be equally granular.

The site survey report provides not only a picture of the data center's current state but also recommendations for improvements in any number of areas. The site survey is an essential piece of data center maintenance and development.

Chapter Review

Questions

1. Which of the following is not part of the three-tier hierarchical model?
   - A. Core
   - B. Distribution
   - C. Access
   - D. Transmission
2. Which of the following data center implementations represents how data flows into and out of a data center?
   - A. North-south traffic flow
   - B. Spine-and-leaf architecture
   - C. Three-tiered architecture
   - D. Top-of-rack switching
3. How many tiers are in the spine-and-leaf architecture?
   - A. 1
   - B. 2
   - C. 3
   - D. 4
4. Which of the following is true regarding a SAN and a NAS?
   - A. SANs read and write at the block level.
   - B. NASes read and write at the block level.
   - C. NASes are more efficient.
   - D. SANs attach to a switch and appear as available network storage.
5. Which of the following is not a characteristic of an SD-WAN?
   - A. Application aware
   - B. Zero-touch provisioning
   - C. Transport agnostic
   - D. Local policy management

6. What is the purpose of a VXLAN?
   A. To allow multiple organizations to share a physical network without exposing organizational traffic between networks.
   B. To separate voice and data traffic.
   C. To allow a data center to connect to an on-premises infrastructure.
   D. To send traffic over a VPN.
7. Which of the following is not part of ZTA?
   A. Policy-based authentication
   B. Authorization
   C. Least privilege access
   D. High availability
8. Which of the following is true regarding SASE and SSE?
   A. SSE is a subset of SASE.
   B. SASE is a subset of SSE.
   C. SSE is used in data centers, while SASE is used on-premises.
   D. SASE is used in data centers, while SSE is used on-premises.
9. What's the difference between a physical and logical network diagram?
   A. Physical diagrams have routers, while logical diagrams have switches.
   B. Physical diagrams are printed out and stored, while logical diagrams exist as files.
   C. Physical diagrams deal with hardware, while logical diagrams deal with software.
   D. Physical diagrams deal with hardware, while logical diagrams deal with traffic flow and communications pathways.
10. Which of the following is not a device found on a network diagram?
   A. Switch
   B. Router
   C. Network link
   D. Configuration options

Answers

1. **D.** The three-tiered architecture connects three layers—access, distribution, and core—in the classic data center.
2. **A.** North represents the direction of data coming into the data center, while south represents the direction of data exiting from a data center.
3. **B.** The spine-and-leaf architecture consists of two tiers.
4. **A.** A SAN reads and writes at the block level.
5. **D.** SD-WANs have a central policy management system, not local policy management.
6. **A.** A VXLAN allows multiple organizations to share a physical network, but it keeps the traffic separate for each network.
7. **D.** A ZTA makes sure each request is verified, which has nothing to do with high availability.
8. **A.** SSE is a subset of SASE, dealing just with the security component.
9. **D.** Physical diagrams deal with hardware, while logical diagrams deal with traffic flow and communications pathways.
10. **D.** Configuration options could be on a diagram, but they are not devices.

Devices, Access, Management, and Monitoring

IN THIS CHAPTER, YOU WILL LEARN HOW TO

- Access networking devices and the network
- Perform network access and management tasks
- Perform network monitoring tasks

Networking professionals need to access devices and underlying networks to perform both management and monitoring tasks. Are these professionals working locally or remotely? How do they establish the connections? How can they do so securely? These are some of the questions this chapter will answer.

Test Specific

This chapter starts off with specialty devices, moves on to access and management tasks, and concludes with network monitoring tasks.

Devices

In addition to routers, switches, and other common devices, you'll encounter several specialty devices on networks.

Load Balancers

Popular web servers need to support hundreds of thousands to, in some cases, millions of requests per day. Web servers need to send text, images, videos, and more to web browser clients as quickly as possible. Multiple servers, therefore, are needed to provide the same service. How do the requests get spread across these parallel servers? That's where a load balancer comes into play.

Load balancers, which can be either hardware based or software based, send requests to the servers in an efficient way that maximizes speed and capability, making sure that no single server is overburdened. If a server goes down, the load balancer doesn't redirect traffic to it, and when a new server comes up, the load balancer adds it to the group. To decide which server to send traffic to, sometimes the load balancer uses a round-robin algorithm, simply going through all servers one by one. Alternatively, it might send traffic to the server with the fewest current connections to clients. More advanced criteria include sending traffic to a server based on a hash of the client's IP address.

Proxies

A proxy is a server that sits between clients and external servers, essentially pocketing client requests for server resources and making those requests itself. The client computers never touch the outside servers and thus stay protected from any unwanted activity. The biggest reasons for using a proxy are to filter requests based on content (either in the request or in the return data) and to perform caching.

Let's see how a proxy works using HTTP, one of its earliest applications. Since a proxy relies on redirecting client requests to a proxy server, you first must tell the browser not to use the usual DNS resolution to determine the web server and instead to use a proxy. Every browser allows you to set the IP address of the proxy server, as shown in Figure 15-1.

Once you configure the proxy server, HTTP requests move from the browser directly to the proxy. The URL of the target web server is built into every HTTP request, so the web proxy knows where to get the requested data. In the simplest case, the proxy server simply forwards the requests using its own IP address and then forwards the returning packets to the client, as shown in Figure 15-2.

This basic use of a proxy server prevents the web server from knowing where the browser is located.

As mentioned earlier, another big benefit of using a proxy is caching. A proxy keeps a copy of the served resource, giving clients a much faster response. However, caching presents a challenge: the proxy must ensure its cached copy accurately reflects the current version of the web page. To ensure accuracy, a good proxy uses querying tools to check the real web page and update the cache.

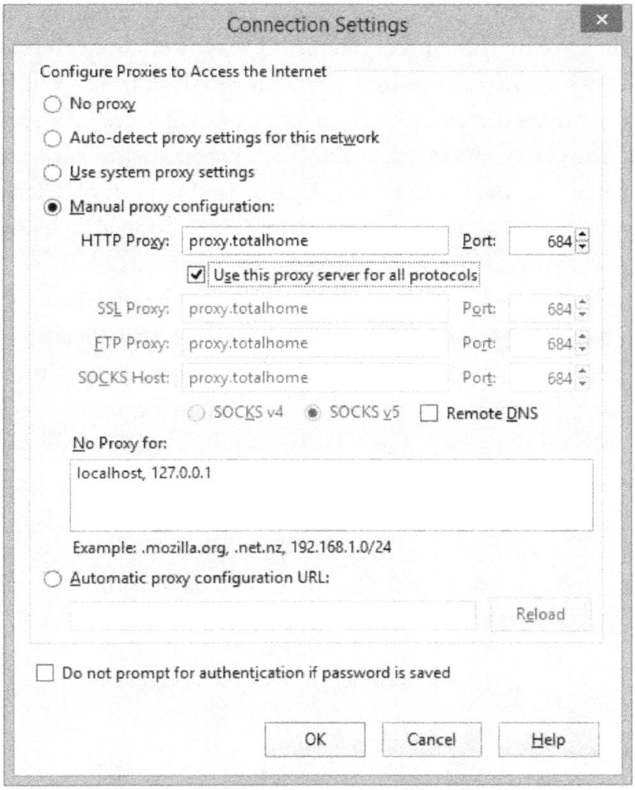

FIGURE 15-1 Setting a proxy server in Mozilla Firefox

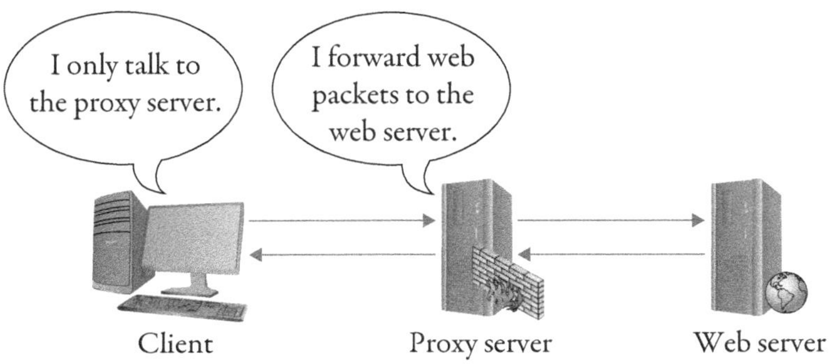

FIGURE 15-2 A web proxy at work

A *forward proxy* server acts on behalf of clients, getting information from various sources and handing it to the clients. The sources (servers) don't know about the clients; they see only the proxy server. A *reverse proxy*, in contrast, acts on behalf of its servers. Clients contact the reverse proxy, which gathers information from its associated servers and hands that information to the clients. The clients don't know about the servers behind the scenes; they interact only with the reverse proxy. The reverse proxy is also another layer of defense to protect a web server. It can inspect the request to ensure there are no injection attacks and uses authentication to restrict access to specific users, IP addresses, or other criteria.

A proxy might also be used to inspect the contents of the resource, looking for inappropriate content, malware, or just about anything else its creators specify. HTTP proxy servers are the most common type of proxy, but any TCP application can take advantage of a proxy. Numerous proxy programs—such as Squid, shown in Figure 15-3—are available. Proxy serving takes some substantial processing, so many vendors sell proxy servers in an integrated hardware solution, such as Broadcom's Symantec Secure Web Gateway Appliance.

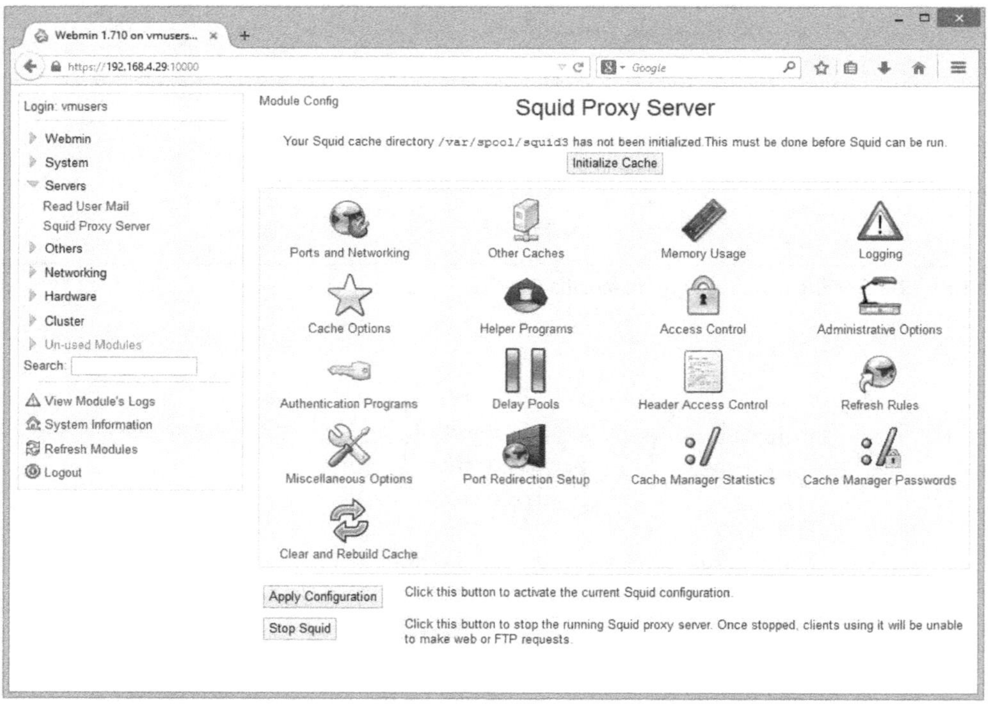

FIGURE 15-3 Squid Proxy Server

Firewalls

Firewalls follow rules to *filter* (block) certain traffic, meaning they don't let specified packets into or out of a network. In other words, firewalls permit or deny both inbound and outbound traffic. Firewalls can filter by source IP addresses, destination IP addresses, protocols, ports, and other criteria.

Firewalls sit on the border between the trusted inside and the untrusted outside. One side of the firewall is under the administrator's control. The other side is connected to the big bad unknown. Firewalls help prevent unauthorized access to or from a system or a network. This includes malware—sent by cybercriminals or downloaded unknowingly by users—that might attack your computer. The firewall logs network activity in both directions for a potential forensic investigation. Malware is restricted inbound to protect the organization's resources, and outbound to prevent it from communicating back to an attacker and opening up a reverse shell (as well as to prevent the organization from being accused of originating an attack when worms propagate). Like proxies, firewalls can restrict employees from visiting certain websites (such as Facebook and YouTube) and from downloading malware.

A firewall can be either a dedicated physical hardware device or software running on a host. Hardware-based firewalls are also referred to as *network-based firewalls*. One side is the network that the firewall is trying to protect, and the other is the untrusted outside. This type of firewall can be strategically placed between the corporate edge router, which connects to the ISP, and the internal network, as shown in Figure 15-4.

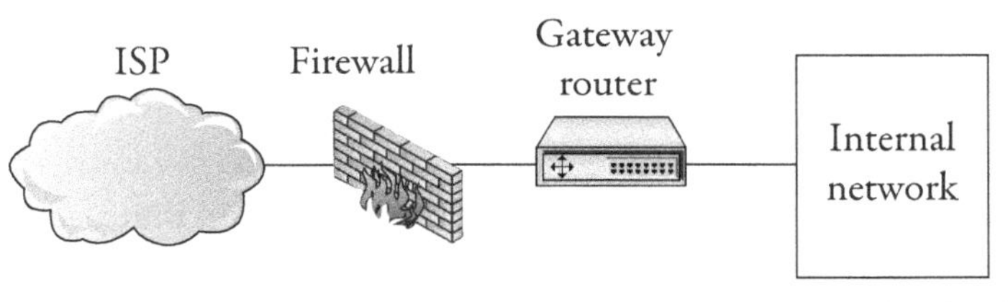

FIGURE 15-4 A hardware-based firewall

Network-based firewalls can also be placed on one side of an internal corporate router that doesn't connect to the ISP, but rather to other internal protected networks. In that case, the untrusted outside would be not only the internet, but other internal networks as well. This configuration still leaves a network vulnerable to malicious traffic originating from within its own boundaries.

Using software-based firewalls, also known as *host-based firewalls*, is one way to mitigate this vulnerability. Host-based firewalls only protect a single system. They can reduce the risk of an attack spreading from one machine to another.

NOTE Besides host-based firewalls, another way to deal with malicious traffic originating on the same network is with an intrusion detection system (IDS) and an intrusion prevention system (IPS), discussed later in this chapter.

Operating systems have host-based firewalls built in, as shown in Figure 15-5.

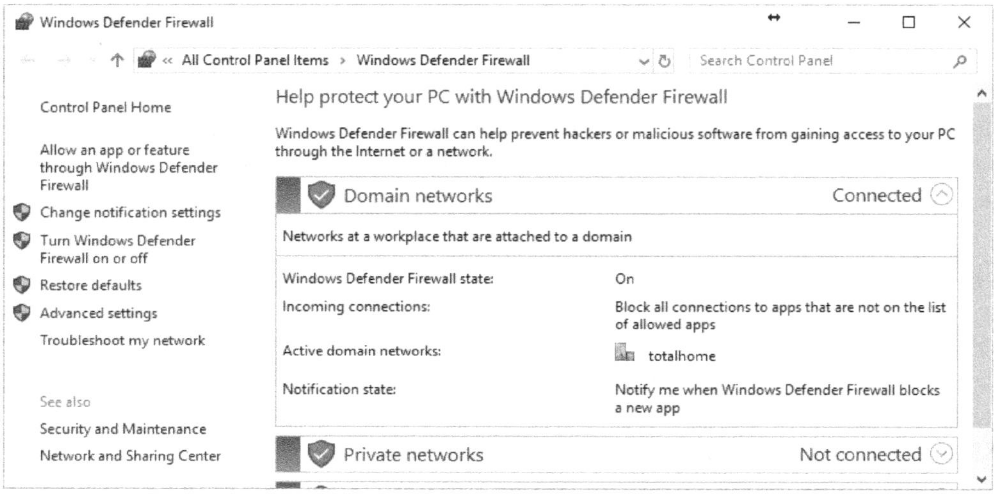

FIGURE 15-5 Windows Defender Firewall in Windows 10

In this case, the trusted inside is just the local machine, and the untrusted outside is not only the internet and other networks, but also all devices on the current network. The border of untrusted to trusted is essentially the device's network interface card (NIC). Anything on the other side of the NIC, as far as a host-based firewall is concerned, is the untrusted outside.

Regardless of whether they are network-based or host-based, firewalls use multiple techniques to filter traffic.

STATELESS VS. STATEFUL PACKET FILTERING

With *packet filtering*, the firewall looks at each packet that enters or leaves a network and permits or denies it based on user-defined rules, like source IP address, destination IP address, protocol, and port. Packets that the firewalls don't filter are allowed to enter or exit the network.

EXAM TIP Filter means to block. When firewalls filter certain packets, they block them.

Packet filtering can be broken down into two subcategories. *Stateless* packet filtering, which is sessionless, means each packet is treated as an isolated piece of communication. This requires less memory and time, resulting in low overhead and high throughput. However, this firewall technique cannot make complex decisions based on a communication stage, only on access control lists (ACLs) referencing IP addresses, protocols, and ports. If an attacker spoofs an IP address, a stateless packet filter can be fooled.

NOTE When ACLs are applied on routers to check traffic, the terms *inbound* and *outbound* are defined from the router's perspective, not the network's. Therefore, an inbound ACL would filter traffic going into the router (which is *outbound* from the network), and an outbound ACL would filter traffic going out of the router (and *inbound* to the network).

Stateful packet filtering, on the other hand, uses sessions, can understand stages of a TCP connection, and can detect an attacker who tries to spoof an IP address. For TCP-based traffic, after a connection has been established, packets can flow between the hosts without further checking. Windows Defender Firewall is stateful, and by default will not allow any unsolicited traffic in.

ALG

An application layer gateway (ALG) is a stateful tool that applies security mechanisms to specific applications like HTTP, TLS, FTP, DNS, and VoIP. Instead of just looking at IP addresses, transport protocols, and ports, ALGs examine Layer 7 to see if application protocols are being used properly. They can filter offensive or disallowed commands in the data stream.

DPI

An ALG performs deep packet inspection (DPI) to examine the contents of the data being sent to determine, for example, if it's in the right format and contains no malware. DPI looks into the actual protocols and their behavior instead of relying on just headers from the lower layers. Other uses of DPI include snooping and censoring. In fact, some ISPs use it to scan the contents of a packet and reroute or drop packets that meet certain criteria. ISPs in some countries use DPI to look for keywords and web addresses for censorship purposes. DPI can also be used for traffic management, such as prioritizing high-bandwidth communications, like those involving Zoom or YouTube, over regular HTTP traffic.

DCI

DPI has evolved into deep content inspection (DCI), which examines an entire file or email attachment, looking for new generations of malware, spam, data exfiltration, keywords, and other content. In other words, DCI reassembles objects, like PDFs and images, that are transmitted across multiple packets. DCI even decodes and decompresses files. DCI's analysis is much more comprehensive than DPI's examination of partial data at Layer 7.

UTM APPLIANCE VS. NGFW/LAYER 7 FIREWALL

Industry experts disagree about the distinction, if any, between a unified threat management (UTM) appliance and a next-generation firewall (NGFW)/Layer 7 firewall. Some say there's no difference between the two, calling them the same technologies with the same capabilities marketed and promoted differently by different companies and industries (mid-market vs. enterprise/carrier grade).

Others say NGFWs are simply components of UTMs. In this line of thought, NGFWs are firewalls with IPS (described next) and application intelligence, whereas UTM appliances have those features plus more, including email security, URL filtering, wireless security, web application firewalls, and VPNs.

IDSs and IPSs

Even after firewalls using stateless packet filters and ACLs weed out undesirable network traffic, there will still be malicious packets inside the network. Two issues are at work here. First, firewalls are just a single part of a more complex defense-in-depth architecture; malicious packets can, and will, regularly evade them. Second, malicious traffic originating from within the network is never checked by a network-based firewall, which sits on the perimeter of the network, because the malicious traffic is already inside!

Think of the firewall as a TSA agent at the airport inspecting your boarding pass and ID as you go through security on the way to your gate. They're checking the equivalent of the source IP address (who you are and where you live), the destination IP address (to whom and where you're flying to), the protocol (your airline), and the port (your flight number). Like a firewall, the agent is using a set of preconfigured rules and might ask you questions about yourself, the flight, or the destination. An intrusion detection system (IDS) or intrusion prevention system (IPS) is like the security guard on the other side by the gates where travelers wait to board their planes.

A passenger could start causing problems after passing the initial screening—getting loud and violent about a flight delay, for example. They might even try entering areas restricted to airport employees. The TSA agent (the firewall) who looked at their boarding pass can't help at this point. The problem exists beyond that location now. The security guard (the IDS or IPS) must now step in. IDSs and IPSs require more logic and learning capabilities than firewalls, and they have to make decisions about where certain lines have been crossed and take appropriate actions.

The TSA agent is still a very necessary component, however. If everyone was simply let through to the gates, the airport security guards would be overwhelmed and unable to monitor all potential passengers. The firewall weeds out traffic that shouldn't go in the network, but the IDS or IPS adds a new dimension for anything that made it past the first screening.

IDSs and IPSs help mitigate the two issues mentioned at the start of this section. An IDS operates *out of band*, meaning it receives copies of network traffic for monitoring rather than directly handling or forwarding traffic. In contrast, an *in-band* device sits directly in the path of network traffic and can actively allow or block traffic. The IDS receives copies of network traffic (see the bottom of Figure 15-6) through *port mirroring*, also known as *Switched Port Analyzer* (SPAN). A switch configured with SPAN sends copies of all traffic from its ports to the port connected to the IDS. This allows the IDS to monitor all network traffic—both internal data flowing between company servers and clients as well as external internet traffic.

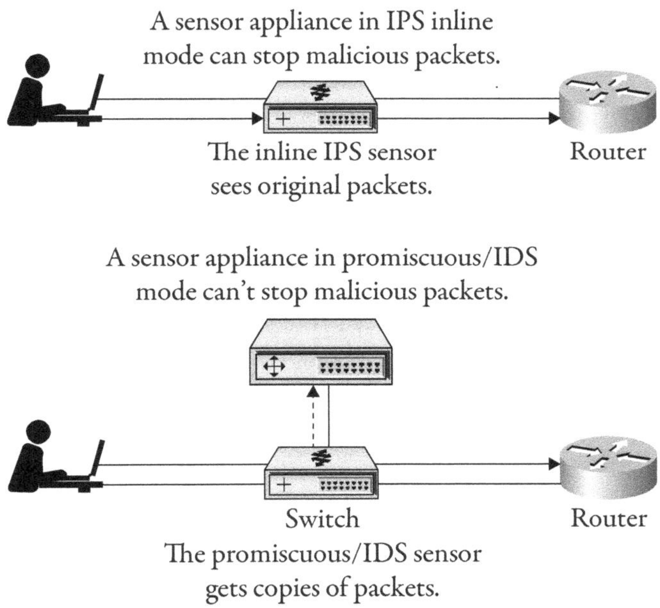

FIGURE 15-6 IPS vs. IDS

To understand why port mirroring is necessary, consider how switches normally operate. When a PC sends a frame into a switch, the switch associates the source MAC address in the Ethernet frame with the port on which the frame arrived, storing this information in its MAC address table. If the switch then receives a frame destined for that MAC address, it sends the frame only to the associated port.

NOTE Don't confuse the table described here with an ARP cache. The MAC address table maps MAC addresses to ports, while the ARP cache maps IP addresses to MAC addresses.

A switch floods broadcasts, standard multicasts, and unknown unicasts (a destination unicast MAC address that's not in the MAC address table) out of all ports except the port on which the message originated.

Let's say a company wants to implement an IDS to inspect traffic flowing through a switch for security, or even for troubleshooting and debugging purposes. It could install an IDS on a system and plug it into the switch. However, the switch would not send frames to the port that the IDS is connected to. Port mirroring changes everything. A switch can be instructed to send transmitted frames, received frames, or both in relation to a certain switch port to another port, where an IDS will be receiving them. Using a protocol analyzer (discussed later in the chapter) like Wireshark or tcpdump, you could examine these packets captured by the IDS.

Local SPAN sends traffic from parts of a single switch to one or more ports on the same switch. Remote SPAN trunks the SPAN traffic to other switches, as the traffic will be sent to an IDS not connected to the local switch. You probably wouldn't want to send all traffic in both directions from a certain VLAN to a specific port, as that could overload the SPAN destination port. The general rule is to capture what you need and as little as possible of anything else.

When SPAN ports get overloaded, packets could be dropped before reaching the IDS. Frames with errors will be lost, too. To mitigate this risk, the company could connect the IDS to a network *tap*, a dedicated hardware device usually placed between the network-based firewall and a switch. With this topology, the IDS can see all incoming and outgoing traffic, guaranteeing complete packet visibility, regardless of bandwidth or errors.

NOTE *Bottlenecking* is when the flow of data, processing, or resources slows down or even stops entirely, causing availability issues on a network. This would be a reason for using a tap instead of a SPAN deployment for an IDS. Bottlenecking can also occur on a system—for example, when the CPU or GPU slows down and affects other components.

An IPS is inline (see the top of Figure 15-6), so traffic must pass through it. This means the IPS could potentially bring the network down, causing a denial of service (DoS). Unlike the out-of-band IDS, an IPS adds latency as well. However, an IPS can stop malicious traffic as soon as it sees it, whereas an IDS can't. Both an IDS and an IPS can automatically notify other devices, such as a firewall, to block certain traffic earlier based on observed packets.

The obvious question is, if an IPS can do what an IDS can do but better, why does an IDS still exist today? The answer is that an IDS is like a window into your network traffic. It sits, listens, and collects data that can be used for monitoring, analysis, and forensic investigation. You can think of an IDS as a visibility device, whereas an IPS is a control device. Packets collected by the IDS can be subsequently analyzed to gain insight into past or even possible future violations when lots of traffic and events are linked together.

Both IDSs and IPSs are vulnerable to *false positives*, which is when benign traffic is flagged as malicious and generates incorrect alerts, and *false negatives*, which is when malicious traffic is flagged as benign and thus doesn't trigger the appropriate alerts. IDSs and IPSs need to be constantly tuned to minimize both false positives and false negatives. Since IDSs are out of band, a false positive won't stop legitimate traffic in its tracks, which is another reason why they're combined with IPSs to form a great defense-in-depth setup.

An IDS can also be programmed to alert an administrator instead of telling a firewall to block certain traffic. This option is preferred by administrators who want to be able to take action on their own instead of letting the IDS make a decision for them.

IDSs and IPSs, like firewalls, can be either host based or network based. In fact, thus far, we've been talking about network-based IDS (NIDS) and network-based IPSs (NIPS). A host-based IDS (HIDS) or a host-based IPS (HIPS) resides on a particular computer and monitors activity just on that host system. It benchmarks and monitors the access, creation, modification, and deletion of key system files as well as the Windows registry. Unlike a network-based IDS or IPS, a host-based one can deal with encrypted traffic that will have been decrypted on the host for processing. It can also detect attacks that may even elude a network-based IDS or IPS. As you can imagine, a HIDS or HIPS slows a system down. The difference between the two is that a HIDS doesn't stop network traffic in its tracks, whereas a HIPS does.

Just like network-based systems can catch malicious traffic that either evaded the network-based firewall or originated from within the network, host-based systems can catch malicious traffic that either evaded the host-based firewall or originated from the inside of the machine.

Signature-based IDSs and IPSs act just like anti-malware software, trying to detect attacks by looking for patterns (for example, certain instructions on a host machine or certain protocol behaviors). The obvious problem is that unknown patterns can't be detected, and adversaries are constantly changing their code to avoid simple signature detection. Furthermore, the signature database needs to be updated constantly. Anomaly-based IDSs and IPSs compare and establish baselines to identify potentially malicious activity. The latest anomaly-based systems can detect malicious insiders as well as machines or accounts that have been compromised by outsiders.

One of the most popular IDSs used today is Snort, which is supported on many hardware platforms and operating systems, including Windows, Linux, and macOS. Even though Snort runs on a host machine, it is considered a network-based system, since it monitors network traffic.

These network security devices—firewalls, proxies, IDSs, and IPSs—all require configuration and ongoing management. Network professionals need secure ways to access and manage this infrastructure, whether on-site or remote. The next section examines the tools and technologies that enable secure remote access and network management.

Access and Management

Remote connections have been around for a long time, even before the internet existed. Their biggest drawback was the cost to connect. If you were on one side of the continent and had to connect to your LAN on the other side of the continent, the only connection option was a telephone. Or, if you needed to connect two LANs across the continent, you ended up paying outrageous monthly charges for a private connection. The introduction of the internet gave people wishing to connect to their home or work networks a very inexpensive connection option, but there was one problem: the whole internet was, and still is, open to the public. People wanted to stop using dial-up and expensive private connections and use the internet instead, but they wanted to be able to do it securely.

QoS Policies

Just about any router you buy today has the capability to block packets based on port number or IP address, but these are simple mechanisms mainly designed to protect an internal network. What if you need to control how much of your bandwidth is used for certain devices or applications? In that case, you need *quality of service* (QoS) policies to prioritize traffic based on certain rules. These rules control how much bandwidth a protocol, PC, user, VLAN, or IP address may use.

On many routers and switches, you can implement QoS through bandwidth management, such as *traffic shaping*, where you control the flow of packets into or out of the network according to packet type or other rules.

Traffic shaping is very important when you must guarantee a device or application a certain amount of bandwidth and/or latency, such as with VoIP or video. Traffic shaping is also very popular in places such as schools, where IT professionals need to control user activities, such as limiting web usage or blocking certain risky applications (peer-to-peer file sharing, for example).

VPNs

Several standards use encrypted tunnels between a computer or a remote network and a private network through the internet, resulting in a virtual private network (VPN). A VPN creates an encrypted tunnel between two networks over another, less secure network, as shown in Figure 15-7.

An encrypted tunnel requires endpoints—the ends of the tunnel where the data is encrypted and decrypted—which can be either software running on a computer or a dedicated device, as shown in Figure 15-8.

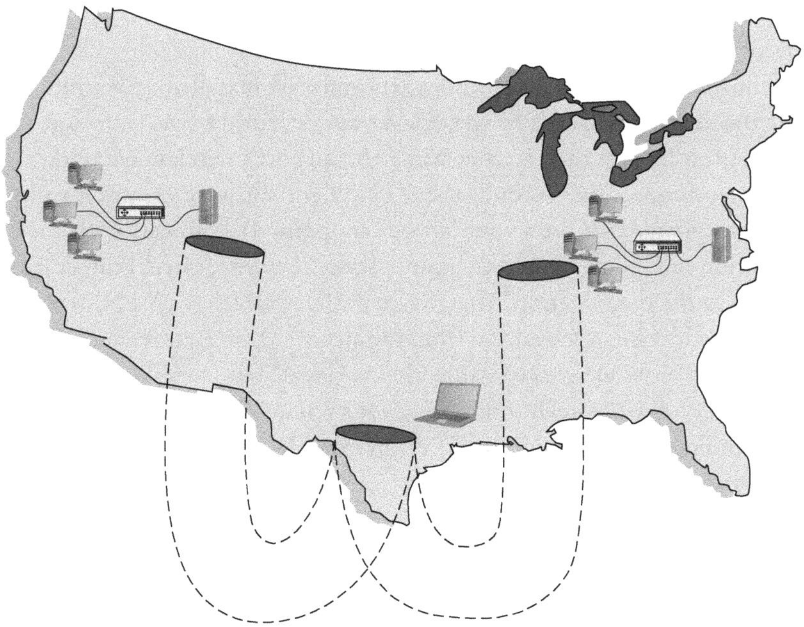

FIGURE 15-7 VPN connecting computers across the United States

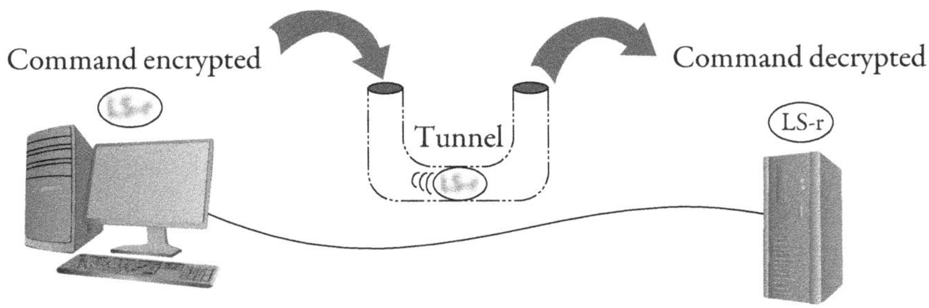

FIGURE 15-8 Typical tunnel

CLIENT-TO-SITE VPNS

In a *client-to-site VPN*, a remote computer needs to function like it's on one of the internal corporate networks as far as IP addressing goes. You would want the laptop you're using in the Newark Liberty International Airport (in Newark, New Jersey) airport lounge, for example, to have the same network ID as the computers in one of the LANs back in your organization in Rochester, New York. But there's no simple way to do this. If it's a single client trying to access a network, that client is going to take on the IP address from its local DHCP server. In the case of your laptop in the airport, your network ID and IP address come from the DHCP server in the airport, not the DHCP server back at work.

To make the VPN work, you need VPN client software installed on your local machine—the laptop at the airport—and VPN server software or hardware at your organization. You connect your laptop first to the internet using the airport's wireless network, which is just a normal Internet connection. Second, the VPN client software creates a tunnel interface (think of this as a virtual NIC) on your laptop (endpoint 1), connects with the VPN server at the organization (endpoint 2), and then, in essence, creates a virtual direct cable from the tunnel interface to the organization. That "virtual direct cable" is a VPN tunnel. The laptop now has two IPv4 addresses. One is local from the airport DHCP server and is associated with your physical (wired or wireless) NIC. The other is "local" but works with the office network and is associated with the tunnel interface, not your physical NIC.

When the traffic is sent through the VPN, an inner IP packet is placed inside an outer IP packet. Here's what each contains:

OUTER PACKET (USED FOR ROUTING)

- Source IP: Airport DHCP assigned address to physical NIC
- Destination IP: VPN server at organization

INNER PACKET (ENCRYPTED AND ENCAPSULATED IN THE OUTER PACKET)

- Source IP: Organization DHCP assigned address to tunnel interface (VPN client address)
- Destination IP: Internal organization resource

The airport router routes your packet to the VPN server at your organization. The VPN server will decapsulate and decrypt the inner packet and send it on its way to a resource in the organization as if it originated from that location on the organization's network.

For return traffic—coming from the organization to the airport—the process is reversed:

OUTER PACKET (USED FOR ROUTING)

- Source IP: VPN server at organization
- Destination IP: Airport DHCP assigned address to physical NIC

INNER PACKET (ENCRYPTED AND ENCAPSULATED IN THE OUTER PACKET)

- Source IP: Internal organization resource
- Destination IP: Organization DHCP assigned address to tunnel interface (VPN client address)

Most likely, on a public Wi-Fi you'll be behind a NAT, so that address will be translated into the outside public IP address of the airport router leading toward its ISP.

Let's consider another scenario. Say you're at a Starbucks in Rochester, NY using the Wi-Fi and enjoying a coffee while checking your balance at citibank.com. This time, however, you're using a personal VPN provider. Instead of your IP packet going from your machine to the Starbucks access point to the Citibank web server in New York City, it is encrypted and encapsulated in an outer IP packet, sent to the access point, and then sent to your VPN provider, possibly in San Francisco. The VPN server there decrypts and decapsulates your inner IP packet and sends it to the Citibank web server from that network in San Francisco. It's as if you're in San Francisco on that VPN provider network sending the traffic to Citibank.

The return traffic from Citibank's web server goes back to San Francisco, and in turn the VPN server sends it to your Rochester Starbucks location. Anyone sniffing your packets will not be able to decrypt the traffic. The only entity that will decrypt, in this case, is your VPN server because it has the necessary key.

VPNS AND PUBLIC WI-FI

Many experts say VPNs are not necessary for public Wi-Fi anymore (unless you're a journalist, dissident, or political figure, where anonymity is vital) since over 95 percent of the web, especially sites that require logins or contain personally identifiable information (PII), use TLS. In that case, the traffic the browser sends and receives is encrypted to and from the web server. Encrypting that in a VPN would be encrypting already encrypted traffic.

For more, check out the following articles, which go back a number of years to show you how long the safety of public Wi-Fi has been discussed:

wired.com/story/hotel-airport-wifi-safe/

eff.org/deeplinks/2020/01/why-public-wi-fi-lot-safer-you-think

vice.com/en/article/you-probably-dont-need-a-vpn/

nytimes.com/2021/10/06/technology/personaltech/are-vpns-worth-it.html

tomsguide.com/news/you-may-no-longer-need-vpn

washingtonpost.com/technology/2022/09/26/public-wifi-privacy/

With a personal VPN provider, the packet structure is identical—an encrypted inner packet encapsulated in an outer packet. The key difference is the destination: instead of accessing internal corporate resources, you're accessing public websites (like Citibank) through the VPN server. To observers, your traffic appears to originate from the VPN server's location (San Francisco), providing anonymity.

Here's how the IP addressing goes for your traffic from Starbucks to Citibank's web server:

OUTER PACKET (USED FOR ROUTING)

- Source IP: Starbucks assigned address
- Destination IP: VPN server

INNER PACKET (ENCRYPTED AND ENCAPSULATED IN THE OUTER PACKET)

- Source IP: VPN client address
- Destination IP: Citibank web server

Most likely, on a public Wi-Fi, you'll be behind a NAT, so that address will be translated into the outside public IP address of the Starbucks router leading toward their ISP.

The Starbucks router routes your packet to the VPN server in San Francisco. In San Francisco, the VPN server will decapsulate and decrypt the inner packet and send it on its way, as if it originated from that location on the company's network. After the VPN server strips off the outer packet, the inner packet with the source IP address on that network is sent. That's the IP address in the reply packet found in the destination IP address field. Now your VPN server encapsulates and encrypts that IP packet in an outer one with the source IP address of the VPN server and the destination IP address of the Starbucks router outside interface. After NAT, that outside public address is translated into your private inside address. Your VPN interface, implemented through software, sees the packet.

Here's how the return traffic coming back to you in Starbucks from the Citibank web server is addressed:

OUTER PACKET (USED FOR ROUTING)

- Source IP: VPN server
- Destination IP: Starbucks assigned address

INNER PACKET (ENCRYPTED AND ENCAPSULATED IN THE OUTER PACKET)

- Source IP: Citibank web server
- Destination IP: VPN client address

That's what a VPN is: a private tunnel that uses a public infrastructure. Tunnel endpoints are where the tunnel starts and ends—in this case, your laptop and the VPN server. Yes, a VPN will introduce latency with the added travels of your inner packet, but it's an essential trade-off for security.

VPN clients used to be a hassle, since most companies forced employees to use Internet Protocol Security (IPSec) VPNs rather than Point-to-Point Tunneling Protocol (PPTP) or Layer 2 Tunneling Protocol (L2TP) VPNs. Business travelers had problems since the destination ports were typically blocked at client offices and hotels. Firewalls allowed traffic to destination ports 80 and 443, but blocked the extra ports and protocols required by IPSec. Options included expensive tethering to your cellphone or forgoing the use of a VPN altogether.

The solution arrived with the release of F5's SSL VPN client, and other vendors quickly followed suit. SSL VPNs (now using TLS, though often still incorrectly called SSL VPNs) were game changers because they operated on port 443. Since VPN clients connected to VPN servers on port 443, the traffic was allowed out of most networks. VPNs now worked wherever people went, with no extra network configuration required.

CLIENTLESS VPNS

A *clientless* VPN runs through a web page or portal and doesn't require any special client software. All major vendors have a clientless option.

When F5 first introduced its VPN solution, it provided browser-based Java applications that allowed users to perform essential functions such as email, remote desktop (RDP/ICA), and file access without installing a client. Later, F5 added a Java-based "SSL VPN client" that enabled a full-tunnel connection rather than just application access. Although still technically clientless, this approach had practical limitations compared to a dedicated VPN client, particularly in terms of performance and compatibility.

SPLIT-TUNNEL VS. FULL-TUNNEL VPNS

Originally, a VPN tunneled all traffic (*full tunnel*) by default. *Split tunnel* was a solution to remove load from the VPN channel, and in many cases to speed up traffic that didn't need to be encrypted (for example, traffic not destined for the corporate network). A split-tunnel VPN connection creates a secure connection to a remote network but routes other internet traffic through the local network. In other words, when you open a browser and go to google.com, the request would go through the local connection, not the VPN one. In a full-tunnel VPN, in contrast, all traffic goes through the remote connection. This offers security in exchange for performance; that is, full-tunnel internet connections are slower than split-tunnel internet connections.

Split-tunnel deployments also remove the load on the company's internet-facing connection, which was traditionally underpowered. Since split tunnels emerged, some companies have opted to continue to do full tunnels for security reasons. Many companies today scan and validate all internet-bound traffic, and possibly all incoming web content and file downloads, by enforcing full tunnels through proxy servers or web filters. This introduces latency, since traffic must go through the VPN (shared with the other VPN clients at the *concentrator*, the device that manages VPN connections) and exit through the company's internet connection (shared with all employees). This means that on a 1 Gbps company connection, remote users' traffic must first travel to the company's network and then back out to the internet through the same link. Because that 1 Gbps connection is shared among employees and VPN clients, actual throughput for each user may be significantly lower than 1 Gbps.

A proper split tunnel will send only internal traffic to the tunnel (keeping the traffic load small), but many organizations have opted to do it backward, specifically whitelisting traffic that won't go through the tunnel (known as a *forced tunnel with exceptions*). Conference tools like Zoom and Microsoft Teams (especially Microsoft Teams Phone) and software updates via Windows Update have forced companies that only want to use a full tunnel to implement exceptions (similar to a split tunnel, but still tunneling too much traffic and making rules complicated to implement) in order to prevent traffic from going through the tunnel.

SITE-TO-SITE VPNS

Site-to-site VPNs make resources in one location available in other locations. They can be intranet based or extranet based. An intranet-based VPN links different branches of a single corporation to each other and to headquarters, while an extranet-based VPN establishes a connection with a third party, such as a partner, supplier, provider, or customer. The extranet VPN also allows for sharing certain parts of the networks while preventing access to private intranets of the individual companies. In site-to-site VPNs, the tunnel endpoints are either the outside interfaces of the corporate routers or VPN appliances on the inside networks.

Site-to-site VPNs are easy to set up, cost effective, and easy to move between locations, unlike the traditional leased lines, which are secure but expensive and difficult to relocate. Site-to-site VPNs do require a trade-off of some security for the flexibility they offer, and their endpoints (where devices on the joined networks are set up) can be targeted for attacks. This type of VPN is still quite secure, however, because of encryption and security exchange options.

The packet structure for site-to-site VPNs is similar to client-to-site VPNs, but with routers as both endpoints. Site A's router encrypts and encapsulates traffic destined for Site B. Site B's router decrypts and decapsulates the traffic and forwards it to the appropriate local subnets. Return traffic follows the reverse process, with Site B's router encrypting outbound packets and Site A's router decrypting and forwarding them to their intended local destinations.

Here's a look at the addressing for the inner and outer packets in a site-to-site VPN from the source:

OUTER PACKET (USED FOR ROUTING):

- Source IP: Router at Site A
- Destination IP: Router at Site B

INNER PACKET (ENCRYPTED AND ENCAPSULATED IN THE OUTER PACKET)

- Source IP: Client network address at Site A
- Destination IP: Internal company resource at Site B

Here's a look at the addressing for the inner and outer packets in a site-to-site VPN from the destination:

OUTER PACKET (USED FOR ROUTING):

- Source IP: Router at Site B
- Destination IP: Router at Site A

INNER PACKET (ENCRYPTED AND ENCAPSULATED IN THE OUTER PACKET)

- Source IP: Internal company resource at Site B
- Destination IP: Client network address at Site A

IPsec Tunneling Protocols

Many VPN technologies use IPsec tunneling for VPNs. IPsec is a suite of protocols used for authenticating and encrypting packets. In transport mode, only the payload of the IP packet is protected. In tunnel mode, the entire IP packet (including the IP header and payload) is protected.

AH/ESP

The Authentication Header (AH) protocol and the Encapsulating Security Payload (ESP) both perform integrity and authentication, but ESP also offers confidentiality through encryption. As a result, AH wasn't used much and is obsolete today.

IKE

The Internet Key Exchange (IKE) protocol allows for securely negotiating encryption keys and security parameters between VPN connection endpoints. The current deployment is IKEv2, which replaced IKEv1.

NOTE When IKE was first released, it was known just as IKE. Since IKEv2 is much more common than the first version, which was renamed IKEv1, some people say "IKE" to refer to IKEv2.

Many enhancements make IKEv2 the standard for current IPsec deployments:

- IKEv1 uses a two-phase negotiation process with complex message exchanges, but IKEv2 combines these phases into one efficient phase.
- While IKEv1 has limited and optional support for NAT traversal and Dead Peer Detection (which allows a VPN device to detect when the remote peer is no longer responding, helping the system quickly terminate or reestablish the connection), IKEv2 has those features built in, which enhances reliability in a NAT environment and improves connection monitoring.
- Unlike IKEv1, IKEv2 supports IKEv2 Mobility and Multihoming Protocol (MOBIKE), which enables seamless VPN connections even when a user's IP address changes when moving between networks.
- IKEv2 has removed support for outdated algorithms and thus offers stronger security than IKEv1.
- IKEv2's error handling and extensibility capabilities make it more robust and flexible than IKEv1.

GRE

For VPNs, Generic Routing Encapsulation (GRE) is often paired with IPsec to provide a flexible and secure tunneling solution. GRE itself is a tunneling protocol that allows for the encapsulation of many different network layer protocols (for example, IPv4, IPv6, multicast traffic, and broadcast traffic) over a point-to-point Layer 3 connection.

However, GRE does not provide encryption or authentication, which makes it vulnerable to interception; this is why it is often coupled with IPsec, which adds encryption, integrity, and authentication. This combination, known as *GRE over IPsec*, allows organizations to send complex traffic types (like dynamic routing protocols or multicast traffic) securely across untrusted networks like the internet. It's especially useful in site-to-site VPNs that require protocol flexibility and security.

PAST VS. PRESENT PROTOCOLS

Old and obsolete VPN protocols that should no longer be used include Point-to-Point Tunneling Protocol (PPTP) and Layer 2 Tunneling Protocol (L2TP), as their encryption is weak or outdated. Modern VPNs should use IPsec or TLS (often still called *SSL VPNs*, even though SSL has been replaced by TLS). Some people also create quick VPNs by tunneling all traffic through SSH on port 22, but this method doesn't offer the same strong encryption, key management, or performance features as dedicated VPN protocols, so it's not recommended for regular use.

NTP

Network Time Protocol (NTP) is used to synchronize the clocks of devices across a network, which is essential for services like Kerberos authentication, accurate log correlation, and digital certificate validation. NTP operates over UDP port 123, and a simpler version, Simple Network Time Protocol (SNTP), is often used for lightweight clients. NTP uses a hierarchical system called *strata*, where stratum 0 devices, like atomic clocks and GPS receivers, are the most accurate sources of time.

Stratum 1 servers connect directly to stratum 0 devices and provide time to stratum 2 clients, and so on, down to stratum 15. Devices beyond stratum 15 are considered unsynchronized. While NTP typically uses a client-server model, it also supports peer-to-peer connections between devices at the same stratum for redundancy and cross-checking accuracy.

PTP

Precision Time Protocol (PTP) offers extremely high-precision time synchronization, usually down to microseconds or beyond. Time-critical applications, including industrial automation, telecom, and financial trading, benefit from PTP. The drawback is that PTP doesn't provide much native security, so it must be supplemented with other security measures. Thus, PTP is often used in local and controlled infrastructures, not over the internet.

NTS

Network Time Security (NTS) is an extension to NTP that offers strong encryption and authentication through TLS. Time synchronization through untrusted networks, like the internet, benefit from NTS. The drawback, compared to PTP, is that NTS's timing precision is less accurate (milliseconds). Therefore, NTS is often used when time synchronization goes across untrusted/outside infrastructures.

Port Scanners

A port scanner is a tool that sends packets to a destination machine in order to identify the state of that machine's ports. This process, known as port scanning, helps you verify the security of systems under your control. From a cybercrime perspective, however, it allows attackers to find programs or services with vulnerabilities that can be exploited.

NOTE While there are many port scanning tools, some with specialized purposes, Nmap stands above the rest. Check it out at *nmap.org*.

Ports can be classified as open, closed, or filtered, as discussed in Chapter 4. Nmap scan classification states also include unfiltered, open|filtered (open or filtered), and closed|filtered (closed or filtered).

Port scanners can send many different types of scans. You simply select an appropriate one, or a combination of different scan techniques, for the task at hand. In addition to port state, port scanners can also potentially identify a target machine's operating system or versions of programs running on that machine.

Think of a burglar casing out the neighborhood, testing doorknobs and windows to see if they're unlocked. Technically, there's nothing illegal about that (trespassing notwithstanding). The legality of port scanning is similarly murky. Although there are three well-known legal cases against people who performed port scans, these instances are rare and there's still no conclusive answer. Legal precedent suggests that the intent to follow up the port scan with an attack is where the legal system might catch up to you.

SSH

Secure Shell (SSH) is a protocol used by system administrators and other IT professionals for remote management of systems and applications, software patch deployment, command execution, file management, and various administrative tasks. It allows an SSH client to remotely sign in to a system running an SSH server. During the session, SSH encrypts all communication between the client and server, preventing on-path attacks (formerly known as *man-in-the-middle attacks*), such as eavesdropping or session hijacking.

SSH debuted in 1995. Before then, and in some unfortunate cases still today, the notorious Telnet protocol was used for the same purpose, but with one major difference: Telnet provides no encryption. All client-to-server and server-to-client communication occurs in plaintext, allowing an on-path attacker to capture credentials, commands, and other sensitive data directly from the network traffic.

SSH uses the Diffie–Hellman Key Exchange (DHKE) algorithm—as does TLS (discussed in Chapter 17)—to establish a shared secret between the SSH client and server. This shared secret is not used directly for encryption; instead, it is input into a Key Derivation Function (KDF) that generates the symmetric session keys used to encrypt and authenticate all communication in both directions, including credentials. This process ensures confidentiality, integrity, and protection against eavesdropping and on-path attacks.

The SSH server's public key is transmitted to the client the first time the client connects and is then stored locally for future verification (in the *known_hosts* file). During the DHKE process, the server creates a hash of key exchange values and digitally signs that hash using its private key. The client independently computes the same hash and verifies the server's signature using the server's public key. If the verification succeeds, meaning the computed hash matches the decrypted signature hash, the client can trust that it is communicating with the legitimate server and that the symmetric session keys derived from the shared secret are authentic.

SSH supports strong client authentication using public/private key pairs. The client generates a key pair and places its public key in the server's *authorized_keys* file. When the client attempts to connect, the server sends a session-specific challenge (a random value) that must be signed with the client's private key. The server verifies the digital signature using the stored public key. If the verification succeeds, the server confirms the client's identity, proving possession of the private key without ever transmitting it over the network

This key-based authentication is more secure than simple username/password login. Private keys are never sent over the network; only the signed challenge is transmitted. Keys can be thousands of bits long, making them extremely difficult to crack, and you can optionally protect them with a passphrase. Only the machine possessing the private key can initiate the connection. Despite these advantages, password authentication is still common on devices like routers due to its convenience.

SSH can also create encrypted tunnels by forwarding ports from a local machine to a remote server (for example, forwarding a local port to port 3389 for Remote Desktop Protocol). While this enables secure remote access, compromised SSH credentials or endpoints can allow attackers to exploit these tunnels. Endpoint security remains critical to fully secure SSH connections.

RDC

You can use a terminal emulation program to create a *remote terminal*, a connection on a remote computer that enables you to control that computer as if you were logged in and sitting in front of it. Terminal emulation has been a part of TCP/IP from its earliest days in the form of Telnet. Because Telnet predates graphical user interfaces (GUIs), it's a text-based utility. As operating systems became graphical, demand arose for terminal tools that supported GUI-based remote connections.

Microsoft's proprietary protocol Remote Desktop Protocol (RDP) was influenced by the company's 1990s partnership with Citrix. RDP defines how screen updates, keyboard presses, mouse input, and more are transmitted between the client and server. The client application is known as Remote Desktop Connection (RDC), which is used to connect to a server using RDP. RDC provides the GUI for the user to start an RDP session.

NOTE Check out *cloudflare.com/learning/access-management/rdp-security-risks/* and *bleepingcomputer.com/news/security/logins-for-13-million-windows-rdp-servers-collected-from-hacker-market/* for more onRDP vulnerabilities.

Using a data-heavy application over a VPN could be very slow. With RDP, however, the application runs on the RDP/terminal server that's in the data center, near the servers storing the data. As a result, data access and processing become much quicker, so it feels almost like you're in the office. One minor caveat is that unless you map drives through the client, you won't be able to access or save files on the local machine from within the RDP session. You can, however, access remote desktops and remote apps, which look and feel as if you're running the apps locally.

REMOTE DESKTOP GATEWAY

Microsoft's Remote Desktop Gateway is a tunneling mechanism that encapsulates and encrypts an RDP session with TLS, potentially alleviating the need for a VPN. Companies no longer have to worry about the security risks of putting RDP servers on the internet since this server takes care of the first level of authentication (including multifactor authentication).

JUMP BOX/HOST

A jump box/host can access and manage devices in a zone that has a different (higher) security posture than the zone in which the current client computer or device is located. In most cases, it functions as a secure intermediary server (usually a hardened terminal server) that allows trusted administrators to initiate SSH or RDP sessions.

The device itself usually runs either a minimal Linux environment with SSH clients or a Windows OS with GUI tools but is strictly locked down, accessible only by authorized administrators. It's typically isolated from public networks, monitored for session activity, and configured with tight inbound and outbound access controls. This setup helps reduce lateral movement risk and improves auditing of administrative access. Because only administrators can sign in to it, the jump box represents a single point of control that has built-in logging, accounting, and auditing capabilities.

Here are some examples of what a jump box does (acting as a hardened intermediary system that administrators use to securely access resources in another, typically more sensitive or less trusted, network zone):

- Provides secure administrative access from a trusted internal network to servers located in a DMZ
- Enables authorized remote administrators on a public network to securely reach the internal network through a controlled gateway
- Acts as a protected management point that administrators use to access core data center systems such as Active Directory, file servers, and application servers
- Hosts remote desktop services to serve as a central, monitored access point for managing internal systems

In-Band vs. Out-of-Band Management

Letting unauthorized people have access to your switch management configuration interface is a scary prospect. In cases where you configure the switch over the network (in-band management), anyone who knows the IP addresses of the managed devices will be able to access them if they can provide a valid username and password combination.

In band refers to using the switch's network to manage it. To reduce exposure, it's common to dedicate one port on every managed device as a management port. You can only configure the interface by directly connecting to that port. Then, by connecting all of those dedicated ports into a switch that's totally separate from the rest of the network, you prevent unauthorized access to those ports. The management port on each device is also considered in-band management, as it's still using a switch's or router's network interfaces, albeit in a more secure fashion. In most cases, in-band management is done over a dedicated VLAN.

Out-of-band (OOB) management allows administrators to access a router or switch without relying on the device's network interfaces. This is critical when the network is down or misconfigured.

A *console port* (Figure 15-9; discussed in Chapter 5) is a physical port on a router or switch that provides direct, local access to the device's operating system. You connect a computer to the console port using a serial (or USB) console cable. Because this connection does not traverse the network, you can always access the device even if its network interfaces are offline.

Historically, an AUX port was used for remote out-of-band access via a dial-up modem. You could connect to the device over a phone line if the network was unavailable. Modern networks have mostly replaced AUX ports with USB console ports or dedicated management interfaces, but the principle is the same: providing a way to access the device out of band, without relying on normal network connectivity.

USB console ports and dedicated management interfaces allow administrators to access devices locally (by connecting a laptop directly) or remotely via a console server. The console server aggregates multiple console/USB ports and connects to a separate management network, so administrators can manage devices remotely while still bypassing the production network. In all cases, these connections are out of band because they do not rely on the device's main network interfaces, ensuring access during network outages or failures.

Let's bring it all together now.

In-band management is accessing the device over its production network (through SSH, for example), which requires the network to be operational. Out-of-band management is accessing the device via console, AUX, USB console, or dedicated management interfaces, and works even if the network is down.

Console ports are always direct/local. AUX, USB console, and dedicated interfaces can provide remote out-of-band access when connected through a console server or separate management network.

FIGURE 15-9 A console port

After connecting a router or switch to your PC, you use terminal emulator software, such as PuTTY (*chiark.greenend.org.uk/%7Esgtatham/putty/*), to send commands to the router and view its output on your monitor (see Figure 15-10).

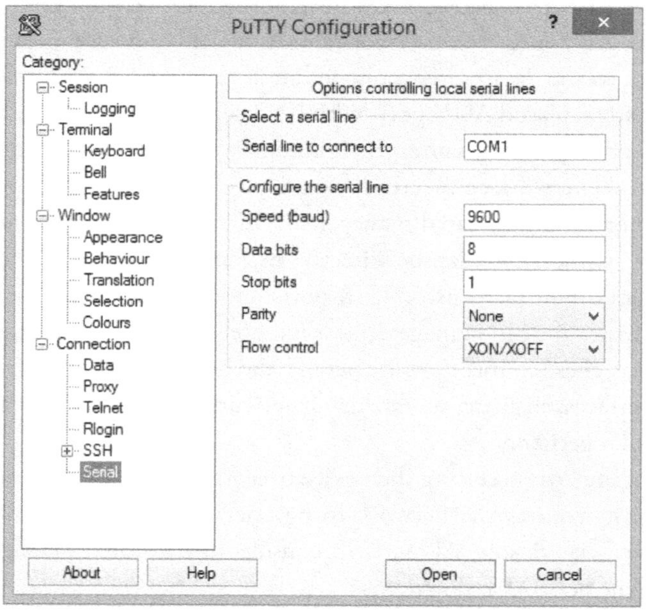

FIGURE 15-10 Configuring PuTTY

Terminal servers provide out-of-band management for multiple devices via serial connections. Administrators connect securely to the terminal server, then access the console ports of the devices. Modern devices often use networking cables with serial adapters at one or both ends to simplify cabling and reduce cost.

You can use the terminal server to connect to the power distribution units (PDUs) to control the power on each PDU port. Cutting power to one port will force a device that's stuck to reboot. This setup often runs on a separate network to ensure security and availability. In many cases, a switch might be located far away, so it's important to have some method of remote management. Switches with web management interfaces often provide a well-protected HTTPS/management URL that administrators can use to log into the switch via a web browser (another example of out-of-band management).

Monitoring

A modern network doesn't behave properly without intervention from network technicians. Techs need to install network management tools and then deploy other tools to monitor, troubleshoot, and optimize networks over time. Because IP networks dominate today, we have a standard set of free tools to accomplish these goals.

The biggest trick to network monitoring is to appreciate that even the smallest network has a dizzying amount of traffic moving through it every second. Not only that, but this traffic is flowing through various points in the network, from a single NIC interface in a system to a massive router on the edge of your infrastructure.

SNMP

Simple Network Management Protocol (SNMP) is the de facto network management protocol for TCP/IP networks. SNMP has gone through three major versions. SNMP version 1 (SNMPv1) was introduced in 1988 and defined basic management operations using community strings for authentication. SNMPv2c retained the community-string authentication of SNMPv1 while adding protocol enhancements such as bulk retrieval and improved error handling.

AUTHENTICATION AND ENCRYPTION

Both SNMPv1 and SNMPv2c use community strings for authentication. A community string functions like a plaintext password and is sent with SNMP requests (`Get` or `Set`) as well as with `Traps`, which are unsolicited notifications from agents to the SNMP manager. Sending these values in plaintext is a significant security risk.

SNMPv3 improves security with the User-based Security Model (USM), which uses hashed authentication (MD5, SHA1, or SHA2) instead of sending plaintext passwords. SNMPv3 also provides message encryption (DES or AES) to ensure confidentiality and adds advanced access controls and security policies to simplify management of many devices.

ARCHITECTURE

SNMP consists of three components:

- An *SNMP manager* is the component within a network management system (NMS) that communicates with SNMP agents. It collects and monitors information from managed devices, providing most of the processing and memory resources. The manager polls devices at regular intervals to gather data on network connectivity, device status, and events.
- A managed device—including routers, switches, and servers—is what the NMS is polling as it monitors these devices. For example, the NMS might poll a router interface to determine traffic counters or operational status, which could indicate abnormal activity or potential security issues.
- An agent is software on managed devices that responds to requests from the SNMP manager that can send a `Trap` about any significant events.

With these three components in mind, let's dig into how they work and interrelate with each other.

Management Information Base

The SNMP manager monitors information from managed devices using a management information base (MIB). SNMP is an extensible protocol, allowing vendors to define custom MIBs to expose device-specific data. The MIB organizes data in a hierarchical, tree-like structure, with each object identified by a unique object identifier (OID). Examples of queryable information include CPU load on a server, memory usage, interface statistics, temperature sensors, or even printer status (such as paper remaining).

Object Identifiers

An OID uniquely identifies a specific object within a MIB. Each SNMP operation, whether reading or setting data, refers to the object by its OID, allowing the SNMP manager to access or modify the corresponding value.

Queries

In a properly configured SNMP-managed network, the SNMP manager polls agents on managed devices to collect data about network status and device performance. The manager stores this information for analysis or monitoring. SNMP operations are carried out using protocol data units (PDUs), which encapsulate the specific function being performed. Four core PDUs commonly discussed are:

- **`Get`** Requests the value of a specific MIB object from an agent
- **`Set`** Changes the value of a specific MIB object on an agent

- **Response** Returns the requested data or confirmation of a `Set` operation from the agent to the manager
- **Trap** Sends an unsolicited notification from the agent to the manager to report significant events

NOTE An SNMP PDU is not related to the PDU discussed in Chapter 1 in the context of the OSI model (protocol data unit), nor the PDU discussed in Chapter 11 and earlier in this chapter (power distribution unit). Repurposing an excellent term is a typical tech sector practice.

When an SNMP manager wants to query an agent, it sends a `GetRequest` to retrieve the value of a specific OID or a `GetNextRequest` to retrieve the next OID in the MIB hierarchy. The agent responds with a `Response` PDU containing the requested information, as shown in Figure 15-11.

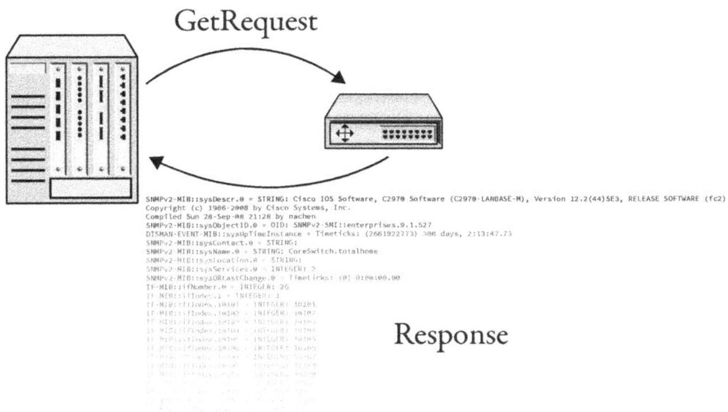

FIGURE 15-11 A simple SNMP process

An NMS can instruct an SNMP agent to modify the value of a MIB object using a `SetRequest` PDU. This allows the manager to change configuration or operational parameters on the managed device.

Traps

An SNMP agent can send a `Trap` to the NMS to report significant events, such as interface failures or threshold breaches. `Traps` are unsolicited messages, meaning the agent can notify the NMS without any prior request. In contrast, the SNMP manager component of the NMS can send `Get` or `Set` requests to the agent to retrieve or modify information.

You've just had a lot of jargon dropped on you, so let's consider a scenario that will make the process and terms a little more understandable. The CSCPROF Art Department has a high-end color laser printer for producing brochures. Their CompTIA Network+ certified technicians maintain that laser printer, meaning they replace toner cartridges, change paper, and install the printer maintenance kits. (They're also CompTIA A+ certified, naturally.)

To manage this printer, nicknamed "Anakin," the techs use an SNMP network management system. At regular intervals, the NMS sends a `GetRequest` to the printer agent about the number of pages printed. According to the `Response` sent from the printer agent to the NMS, the techs can determine if the printer needs maintenance (that is, if it's at the point in its usage cycle where the printer maintenance kit parts need to be replaced).

At irregular intervals, the printer agent must tell the techs that the printer is out of toner or out of paper. Although this information could come from the `Get/Response` interaction, it makes more sense that it come from the printer agent without a query. Anakin needs to yell "Help!" when he's out of toner. Otherwise, the techs have to deal with irate artists, and that won't be pretty. Anakin yells for help by sending a Trap to the NMS.

The CSCPROF network techs don't sit at the SNMP manager, waiting for Anakin the printer to send messages about toner or ink. Instead, the manager software can send alerts, such as SMS text messages or emails, directly to the techs when their intervention is required.

NOTE There are many additional SNMP utilities to automate tasks. For example, the *snmpwalk* utility instructs the SNMP manager to perform a series of `GetNextRequest` PDUs through the MIB tree.

Packet Capture

IP packets, which exist at Layer 3 of the OSI model, are encapsulated inside of Layer 2 frames. On wired LANs, they are Ethernet frames. On wireless LANs, they are 802.11 frames. In the context of capturing and analyzing network traffic, even though the lowest unit to capture and analyze is the frame, the process is still called *packet sniffing*. A protocol analyzer/packet capture program, also known as a *packet sniffer*, intercepts and logs all the 1s and 0s moving in and out of a NIC, then displays them in binary, hexadecimal, and a human-readable format.

NOTE The terms *frame* and *packet* are often used interchangeably. However, this is incorrect. Frames are found at Layer 2 and encapsulate packets, while packets are found at Layer 3 and encapsulate ICMP packets, TCP segments, UDP datagrams, and more. You should use the proper terms!

All of the fields of every single frame, packet, segment, datagram, and upper-layer data protocols will be shown with their names and corresponding data values. For example, in the IP packet, you'll see the source IP address with a value like 192.168.1.113 and the destination IP address with a value like 192.168.1.107. You'll also see the content as it's listed in an RFC or other specifications.

EXAM TIP Various names are used to describe utilities that analyze packets: *packet sniffer, packet analyzer, protocol analyzer,* and *network analyzer.* There's so much overlap here! That can be attributed to the fact that so many protocol analyzers come with sniffers as well. Bottom line: don't rely on the name of the monitoring tool to determine all it can do. Read the tech specs.

A packet sniffer can provide much insight into network traffic for multiple purposes:

- **ANALYSIS AND SECURITY MONITORING** It can provide analysis for troubleshooting, information about cyberattack attempts, and details on malicious insider and outsider activities.
- **INTELLIGENCE GATHERING** It can collect enough intelligence for pentesters and cybercriminals alike to carry out a cyberattack. This information could include client/server communications, actual data, network protocol implementation (including proprietary protocols), suspicious content, and login details or cookies (in the event of plaintext transmission).
- **NETWORK MANAGEMENT** It can help monitor and manage bandwidth, network usage, transmitted data, administration (items that have been added, removed, or changed), and security (effectiveness of firewalls, IDS/IPS implementations, filters, proxies).
- **REPORTS AND COMPLIANCE** It can collect information to generate a network statistics report or help document regulatory compliance by logging traffic at both the perimeter and endpoint levels.

While there are a few dozen packet sniffers, some with specialized purposes, Wireshark stands above the rest (see Figure 15-12).

According to its website (*wireshark.org/*):

Wireshark is the world's foremost and widely-used network protocol analyzer. It lets you see what's happening on your network at a microscopic level and is the de facto (and often de jure) standard across many commercial and non-profit enterprises, government agencies, and educational institutions. Wireshark development thrives thanks to the volunteer contributions of networking experts around the globe and is the continuation of a project started by Gerald Combs in 1998.

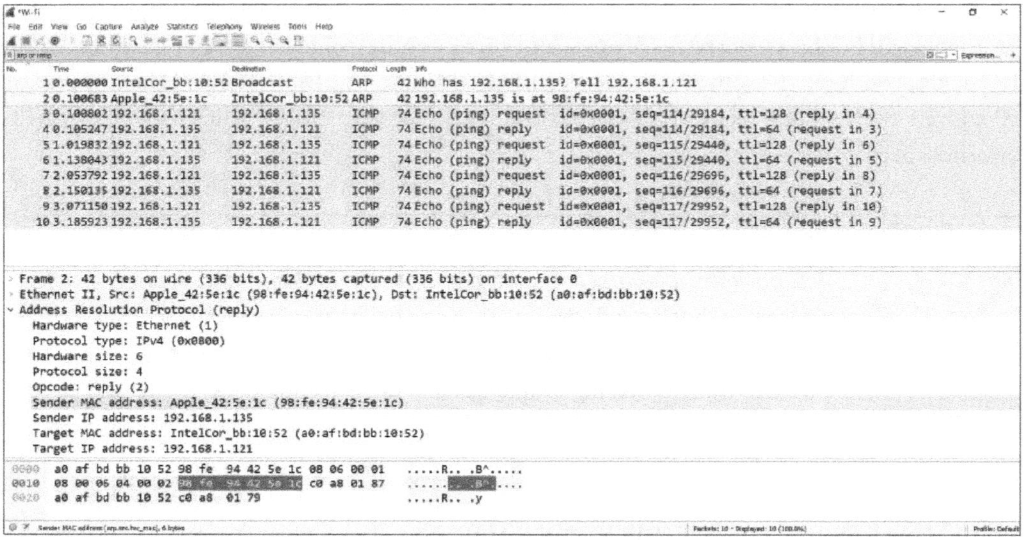

FIGURE 15-12 Wireshark in action

Sometimes a GUI tool like Wireshark won't work because a server has no GUI installed. In situations like this, tcpdump is the go-to choice. This great command line tool not only enables you to monitor and filter packets in the terminal but can also create files you can open in Wireshark for later analysis. Even better, it's installed by default on most UNIX/Linux systems.

Flow Data

Packet flow monitoring relies on a set of tools related to general packet sniffers and analyzers to track traffic flowing between specific source and destination devices. Cisco developed the concept of packet flow monitoring and subsequently included the functionality in routers and switches. The primary tool is called NetFlow, and what is being collected and analyzed is known as *flow data*. Packet capture and flow data are the tools needed for a successful *traffic analysis*.

NOTE While Cisco's NetFlow pioneered the idea of traffic flows that can be collected and analyzed, just about every other flow monitoring competitor (like sFlow, NetStream, and IPFIX) builds on that concept.

NetFlow has been around for quite a while and has evolved into a powerful tool that just about every owner of Cisco equipment uses. NetFlow is similar to SNMP and is based on the idea of flows that you define to track the type of traffic you wish to see. A single flow is a stream of packets from one specific place to another. Each of these flows is then cached in a *flow cache*. A single entry in a flow cache normally contains information such as destination and source addresses, destination and source ports, the source on the device running that flow, and the total number of bytes of that flow. Keep in mind that actual data is not included, just summary data/metadata about the communication. Analyzing the flow data enables administrators to build a clear picture of the volume and flow of traffic on the network, which in turn enables them to optimize the network by adding capacity or other options where needed.

NOTE To use NetFlow, you must enable it on each router or switch. If a device doesn't support NetFlow, you can use stand-alone probes that monitor maintenance ports on the unsupported device and send the information to the NetFlow collector.

Most of NetFlow's heavy lifting is handled by the NetFlow collectors, which store information from one or more devices' NetFlow caches, placing it into a table for NetFlow analyzers to analyze. There are several companies selling different NetFlow analyzers, and which tool you choose is often a matter of desired features and budget.

Performance Monitoring

Performance monitoring tracks the performance of some aspect of a system over time and lets you know when things aren't normal. Performance monitors are usually tied to a particular operating system or application and require a very detailed understanding of the low-level aspects of the system to answer common questions like "How many requests per second occurred on my web server over the last hour?"

The two most common performance monitoring tools are Performance Monitor (perfmon.exe) for Windows and syslog for macOS and Linux. Although they do the same job, they do it very differently and use different terms to describe the same tasks. As we look next at certain aspects that are common to any good performance monitoring tool, I'll point out the differences in terminology.

BASELINE METRICS

The only way to identify when a problem is brewing on your network is to know how it performs when all is well. Part of any proper performance monitoring is the ability to create baseline metrics: a log of performance indicators (such as CPU usage, network utilization, and other values) that gives you a picture of your network and servers when they are working correctly. A major change in these values can point to problems on a server or the network as a whole.

A typical scenario for baselines is for techs and administrators to create and use appropriate documentation and diagrams to demonstrate how the network optimally performs. They then use this information to manage the network over time. *Anomaly alerting/notification* can spring into action in the event that some factor exceeds the baseline, ensuring that the situation can be identified and fixed in a timely fashion.

LOGS

Performance monitors use system logfiles to track performance over time. Logs store information about the performance of particular aspects of a system, which different programs refer to by different terms. Performance Monitor calls them *counters*; syslog calls them *facilities*. A logfile might record a specific Ethernet port's percentage of utilization over time, for example, or the average throughput of a network connection.

Network device logs can provide a lot of information that's useful in troubleshooting. Devices can log traffic, SSH connections, and more (assuming they're set up to do so). Part of device configuration is to set up the device logging—local logging—to capture the data you'll need. The worst time to discover that logging wasn't set up properly is when devices go down and you're troubleshooting.

Any system that generates electronic logfiles has two issues related to log management. The first is security: logfiles are valuable because of the information they provide. Because they often contain private or sensitive data, logs must be protected and access carefully controlled, with read access rights given only to specific users. In many cases, the logging application has only write access to the files, as it's not a good idea to give root access to critical logfiles.

The second issue is maintenance: logfiles will continue to grow until they fill the mass storage where they're located. To prevent this, it's common to make logfiles cyclical, meaning that when a file grows to a certain size, it begins to cycle: as a new record appears in the file, the oldest record is deleted. It's also common for logfiles to be re-created on a set schedule. Depending on the utility, you can set a new logfile to be created daily, weekly, hourly—or whatever interval is most convenient for the administrators—and then back them up.

Many laws today require organizations to retain logfiles for a certain period of time. Check with your legal department to see if you need to keep any files longer than your standard backup timeframes.

LOG AGGREGATION

Log aggregation—consolidating data from many different log sources into a central location—is essential for an effective and accurate reading of what's happening on your network. Log aggregation can range from simple centralized collection to comprehensive SIEM platforms.

Syslog Collector

A syslog collector (also known as a syslog receiver or server) collects messages from many network devices, allowing for review of traffic and audit logs, for example. Syslog listens on UDP port 514, logging incoming messages from clients, and can automatically tag messages according to logging levels or severity levels. Syslog severity levels range from 0 (Emergency: system is totally down) to 7 (Debug: used when debugging a program):

0. Emergency
1. Alert
2. Critical
3. Error
4. Warning
5. Notice
6. Informational
7. Debug

Devices must be configured to send messages to a syslog collector, which aggregates them by timeframe, level, and other criteria. Administrators can then access and manage logs from many sources (routers, switches, servers, etc.) in a single location.

SIEM

Security information and event management (SIEM) is used to monitor and manage an organization's network. SIEM is an industry-standard term, but many products are marketed as SIEM solutions.

SIEM is a mashup of two processes: security event management (SEM) and security information management (SIM). SEM is based on real-time monitoring of security events. The SEM framework calls for monitoring the entire enterprise, often through edge devices at monitor points, then saving the logged events to a location that supports single-viewpoint event review and analysis. In addition to active event monitoring, another task of SEM is to collect and centralize otherwise disparately located security and event logs. Once logs are created and saved, the second SIEM process, security information management, kicks in: here, the logfiles are reviewed and analyzed by automated and human interpreters.

One place SIEM comes into play is with *file integrity monitoring* (FIM), checking for changes in various aspects of files, such as attributes (file size, permissions, etc.), configuration values, content, credentials, and hash values. The verification process compares a baseline or known good copy of the file with the current file, checking for differences. Any changes discovered could indicate that an attack has occurred or is in progress.

SIEM systems are complex solution suites that are found in large, enterprise environments. Organizations may manage them internally or contract with a managed security service provider (MSSP) to administer them.

API Integration

With application programming interface (API) integration, the tools that monitor the network—and even the routers, switches, firewalls, and other devices themselves—can communicate with a centralized device. This communication activates automatic workflows that use the devices' native protocols. For example, in a cyberattack, the APIs could trigger an incident response plan in conjunction with the routers and firewalls to stop or contain the threat.

Network Discovery

Have any rogue or legitimate devices been added to the network? In the case of rogue devices, you'll want to stop them in their tracks. These unauthorized devices can pose serious security risks, including data breaches, lateral movement, or backdoor access for attackers. It's crucial to identify and isolate them immediately using scanning tools.

In the case of legitimate devices, have they been documented properly? Every authorized device should be inventoried with details such as IP and MAC addresses, assigned user or department, physical location, and compliance with security baselines. Ensuring proper documentation helps maintain network visibility, enforce access policies, and support incident response efforts. Regular network scans, asset audits, and real-time monitoring are essential to catch new or unapproved connections early.

AD HOC

An ad hoc network discovery technique is an on-demand scan of your infrastructure. If you suspect an unauthorized device or something isn't working like it should, you should perform this scan immediately. This is a key step of the troubleshooting process.

SCHEDULED

Scheduled network discovery is regular, periodic scanning that provides proactive maintenance and monitoring. In addition to helping you determine what belongs on the network and what doesn't, it supports performance monitoring, availability monitoring, and configuration monitoring.

Availability Monitoring

The CIA triad is a foundational model in cybersecurity, representing confidentiality, integrity, and availability (discussed in detail in Chapter 17). Availability ensures that authorized users can access systems and data when needed.

To maintain availability, organizations implement measures such as fault tolerance, load balancing, and protection against distributed denial-of-service (DDoS) attacks. These controls help ensure systems remain operational even during cyber incidents or other disruptions.

Constantly monitoring the availability, or uptime, of critical infrastructure (routers, switches, firewalls, IDSs, IPSs, servers, and more) is essential to prevent downtime. For some organizations, such as data centers, financial institutions, and healthcare providers—even minimal downtime can be damaging, devastating, or even fatal. These systems strive for the "five nines of uptime" (99.999 percent), meaning that they will be down for only around 5 minutes per year. Table 15-1 shows how different availability levels translate to actual downtime.

TABLE 15-1 Uptime measures

NINES OF AVAILABILITY	UPTIME	MAXIMUM DOWNTIME PER YEAR
1	90.0%	36 days, 12 hours
2	99.0%	3 days, 15 hours, 36 minutes
3	99.9%	8 hours, 46 minutes
4	99.99%	52 minutes, 34 seconds
5	99.999%	5 minutes, 15 seconds

Configuration Monitoring

The configurations for routers, switches, servers, and other devices are constantly being modified. Are these changes in line with company policies and standards, regulatory and compliance standards, and legal requirements? Were these changes approved or implemented by an authorized user? Have the changes been documented? It is important to keep track of all configuration changes and audit them from time to time.

Centralized configuration management and monitoring solutions streamline network administration by providing a unified platform that manages device configurations, monitors performance, and enforces security policies across an organization's infrastructure. This reduces operational complexity, improves consistency, and enhances visibility, making it easier to maintain compliance and troubleshoot issues. A well-known example is Cisco Catalyst Center, which offers a comprehensive dashboard that automates network provisioning, applies configuration templates, monitors real-time health metrics, and leverages AI-driven insights. With the actionable analytics provided by this centralized control, administrators can manage enterprise networks efficiently and proactively.

Chapter Review

Questions

1. Which of the following devices sends and receives traffic between clients and servers and pretends to be the client to the server and vice versa?
   A. Load balancer
   B. Proxy
   C. Firewall
   D. IDS
2. What's the difference between a stateless firewall and a stateful firewall?
   A. A stateless firewall is for private IP addresses, while a stateful firewall uses public IP addresses.
   B. A stateless firewall is for Layer 3 traffic, while a stateful firewall is for Layer 2 traffic.
   C. A stateless firewall treats each packet individually, while a stateful firewall links packets of a certain flow together.
   D. A stateless firewall is for inbound traffic, while a stateful firewall is for outbound traffic.
3. Which of the following are reasons for deploying an IDS and IPS? (Pick two.)
   A. Malicious traffic that originates inside the network is not filtered by network-based firewalls.
   B. Network-based firewalls cannot detect all types of malicious activity on the network.
   C. An IDS or IPS can replace firewalls in high-security environments.
   D. Traffic that evades a firewall can enter a network.
4. Which of the following is not associated with a client-to-site VPN?
   A. Clientless VPN
   B. Split tunnel
   C. Full tunnel
   D. Two router endpoints
5. Which of the following should be used today for console-based access of a remote machine?
   A. Telnet
   B. SSH

C. RDP

D. RDC

6. Which of the following is a device that can access and manage devices in a zone that has greater security needs than the zone it is located in?
   A. DMZ
   B. Active Directory
   C. Jump box/host
   D. Remote Desktop Gateway
7. Which of the following is an example of out-of-band management?
   A. Console port
   B. Router port
   C. Switch port
   D. TCP port
8. What does SNMPv3 use for authentication?
   A. Community strings
   B. Hashing
   C. Encryption
   D. Traps
9. Which of the following lets you know how, under normal conditions, traffic should flow on your network?
   A. Baseline metrics
   B. Performance monitoring
   C. Availability monitoring
   D. Configuration monitoring
10. Which of the following is used for log aggregation? (Pick two.)
    A. Port mirroring
    B. API integration
    C. Syslog collector
    D. SIEM

Answers

1. **B.** A proxy offers security and caching between clients and servers.
2. **C.** A stateless firewall—for example, a stateless packet filter in the form of an ACL—looks at rules and judges each packet individually. A stateful firewall looks at state (for example, established TCP flows).
3. **A** and **D.** Malicious traffic originating from inside a network and packets that evade firewalls are two reasons for deploying an IDS and an IPS.
4. **D.** When each of the two endpoints is a router, the VPN is site-to-site.
5. **B.** Telnet and SSH are the only two console options. Telnet is old and obsolete because it doesn't encrypt the traffic. SSH should always be used over Telnet, because it cryptographically protects the traffic.
6. **C.** A jump box/host can be used to manage a DMZ host from a trusted infrastructure. It can also be a data center system that controls access to Active Directory.
7. **A.** A console port allows you to manage a router or switch without sending traffic over the TCP/IP network.
8. **B.** Hashing is used for SNMPv3 authentication, which replaced community strings from SNMPv1 and SNMPv2c. Encryption is used for confidentiality in SNMPv3.
9. **A.** Baseline metrics allow you to understand how your network behaves when everything is working correctly.
10. **C** and **D.** A syslog collector and SIEM aggregate logs from various devices.

Processes and Procedures

IN THIS CHAPTER, YOU WILL LEARN HOW TO

- Develop documentation for assets and business functions
- Implement life-cycle management
- Implement change management
- Implement configuration management
- Explain disaster recovery concepts

Previous chapters have covered important organizational processes and procedures in the context of broader topics, such as physical versus logical diagrams, rack diagrams, cable maps, wireless surveys/heat maps, and high-availability approaches (active-active, active-passive). This chapter focuses specifically on processes and procedures themselves, covering several that haven't been discussed yet but are equally vital to organizations.

Test Specific

Organizations have *standard operating procedures* (SOPs) that detail how to do most organizational tasks. Any changes made to procedures should be reflected in an updated SOP document. Ideally, these documents should be like process guides to new staff. Employees should not have to rely on institutional knowledge; everything they need to know should be listed in the operating procedures.

Documentation

Documentation is a collection of technical information about infrastructure, hardware, software, policies, and procedures. It helps keep a network running smoothly and securely and can aid the troubleshooting process when problems arise.

Asset Inventories

An *asset* is something of value. From an organizational perspective, an asset could be hardware, software, licensing, and warranty support.

Many organizations use asset tags to simplify managing their *asset inventory*. Asset tags allow them to track all their devices without having to rely on a serial number as a main ID criterion in inventory systems. These tags typically include a number and barcode to make it easier to record inventory information. They should be attached to a fixed part of the device so that the assets don't get mixed up when technicians are working on multiple computers at the same time. For integrity purposes, asset tags should also be tamperproof and difficult to remove. Some companies use labels, while others use small metal plates affixed with super-strong adhesive.

At a minimum, the asset inventory should include when the assets were acquired, who they were acquired from, who acquired them, who deployed them, where they appear in the infrastructure, and when replacements might be needed. Having this inventory allows organizations to stay in compliance with regulatory laws; adhere to their licensing agreements with vendors; and more easily troubleshoot, repair, replace, add, and purchase devices—all processes that help keep systems up and running smoothly as well.

HARDWARE

Hardware assets include client computers, servers, routers, switches, and stand-alone security devices (firewalls, IPSs, etc.). Cables, racks, and other physical tools or components also fit into this category.

SOFTWARE

Software assets include operating systems, applications, and tools, as well as client and server services (DHCP, DNS, etc.).

LICENSING

Licensing assets include agreements with vendors dictating how the organization can use the software. For example, a *seat license* permits one user (in one seat, hence the name) to use the software. A *site license*, in contrast, allows some or all users at a specific site (headquarters, branch office, etc.) to use the software.

Some hardware licenses can unlock certain features of a device to expand its capabilities.

WARRANTY SUPPORT

Warranty support assets include a vendor's guarantee that software or hardware will work as intended for a certain timeframe; otherwise, the vendor must fix or replace any faulty parts. Warranty support is a form of insurance that can save time and money if something goes wrong.

IP Address Management

IP Address Management (IPAM) is a collection of processes and tools for managing DNS and DHCP. It allows for greater integration between the two protocols and provides a single console from which to manage both.

For DNS, resource records (A, AAAA, PTR) are automatically updated whenever DHCP assigns a device an IP address, linking the device's hostname to its assigned address. For DHCP, IPAM tracks IP addresses along with the associated MAC addresses and user accounts, allowing administrators to identify which device or user held a particular IP at a given time.

IPAM also offers insights such as IP address utilization trends, lease history, and name resolution activity to aid in troubleshooting and security analysis.

In addition, it can collect detailed historical data useful for audits, investigations, and overall network documentation.

Service-Level Agreements

A *service-level agreement* (SLA) is a contract between a customer and a service provider that defines the scope, quality, and terms of the service to be provided. SLAs are a core part of business continuity and disaster recovery. They're also widely used in IT, given the large number of services available in the industry. ISPs, for example, typically provide SLAs to customers that define the following:

- **Service provided** Defines the minimum and/or maximum bandwidth and describes any recompense for degraded services or downtime.
- **Equipment** Specifies what (if any) equipment the ISP provides, as well as the type of connections.
- **Technical support** Defines the level, type (phone, web, or in-person), and cost of technical support to be given.

Some companies also use internal SLAs between IT, which acts as the service provider, and other departments. These agreements establish clear expectations for service levels, such as system uptime, reliability, and responsiveness. In turn, these expectations guide IT in determining the appropriate hardware redundancy, high-availability systems, and associated costs needed to meet the agreed-upon standards.

Life-Cycle Management

All corporate resources have a finite lifespan that generally follows predictable phases: planning, procurement, implementation, and, eventually, decommissioning. *Life-cycle management* deals with resources from the first phase to the last.

Software Management

Software management involves planning for future software, then developing, implementing, monitoring, and administering that software. In essence, software management deals with software deployment from the initial idea to full deployment.

PATCHES AND BUG FIXES

Patches and bug fixes aren't just the handy tools provided by Microsoft Windows or Ubuntu Linux. Almost every piece of software and firmware on almost every type of equipment you own is subject to patching and bug fixes: printers, routers, wireless access points, desktops, programmable logic controllers (PLCs), and more. Everything needs a patch or bug fix occasionally.

Think of a *patch* as cutting out part of a program's source code and patching up the hole with a new part. Security is usually the driving factor behind patches. For example, if a vulnerability is found in a program that will allow cybercriminals to exploit it, that part of the code needs to be fixed. Patches are deployed to the public in the form of updates that users need to install.

In a network environment, patching is a routine but crucial process consisting of the following steps:

- **RESEARCH** When a critical patch is announced, it's important to do some research to verify that the patch will do what you need it to do and that users who have already installed it aren't having problems.
- **TEST** When possible, it's a good idea to try out a patch on a test system.
- **BACK UP** Make sure you can revert to a previous configuration (as discussed in the "Backup Configuration" section later in this chapter).

A single system may need many patches over time. Sometimes, you might find that you have to roll back an update, returning to an earlier version. This process is usually pretty easy on PCs because the OS tracks each update. With firmware, the best approach is to track and keep a copy of each upgrade so that you can revert to a safe version if necessary. In fact, some devices may do this automatically.

A bug fix addresses known defects in a program that can cause glitches, annoyances, and errors. Efficiency, stability, and smoothness are usually the driving factors behind bug fixes. Like patches, bug fixes are deployed through updates.

Applying patches and bug fixes for software and firmware is critically important in hardening networks. Bad actors know about system flaws and will attack the network through any unpatched and unfixed gaps.

FIRMWARE UPDATES

Firmware updates enable programming upgrades that make network devices more efficient, more secure, and more robust. Manufacturers release firmware patches to unlock new features and fix or refine current features. Unlike software updates, firmware patching is typically a manual process and occurs less frequently—usually in response to a known issue, to add new features, or for optimization purposes. The patching process varies by device and typically involves downloading a patch from the manufacturer and applying it through the device's browser-based interface or central management system.

Firmware updates, while a crucial network hardening measure, are inherently risky. A bad patch can brick a device, making recovery difficult or impossible. Thus, firmware patching requires careful planning and consideration. Best practices include researching patches thoroughly before applying them, ensuring stable power during the update process, verifying backups and having a recovery plan, and testing in non-production environments when possible.

Some enterprise networking devices, SAN equipment, and even SOHO routers have two firmware slots that alternate during updates, allowing for quick rollback and recovery from the other slot if necessary.

OPERATING SYSTEM UPDATES

OS updates are easily the most common type of update. Users install automatic updates on their OSs routinely, but when you're updating OSs across many systems, especially critical nodes like servers, it's never a good idea to apply all OS updates without first doing some due diligence. Most operating systems provide some method of network server–based patching, giving administrators the opportunity to test before distributing patches.

OS updates typically include device driver updates as well. Device drivers often need patching to fix an incompatibility, incorporate new features or updates, repair a bug, or address a security vulnerability.

All software, regardless of complexity, has flaws. New hardware can expose flaws, newer applications can create unexpected interactions, and security standards can change over time. All these factors mean that responsible companies patch their products after they release them. When a major vulnerability is discovered, vendors tend to respond quickly by creating a fix and distributing an update or patch. Updating devices to protect them against vulnerabilities is a best practice for hardening networks.

Lesser vulnerabilities get patched as part of a regular patch cycle. For example, Microsoft has sent out patches for deployment on the second Tuesday of the month—known as *Patch Tuesday*—since October 2003. These patches are released for a wide variety of Microsoft products, including operating systems, productivity applications, and utilities.

End of Life

Organizations sometimes complain that they had no warning when an OS or device reaches *end-of-life (EOL)* and is no longer supported. However, vendors typically provide advance notice and sometimes even give specific EOL dates when the OS or device is released. Customers should start planning for the decommissioning process the day they install a new OS or device as part of a proactive life-cycle management strategy.

End of Support

End-of-support (EOS) systems are no longer supported or patched by the OS vendor. When facing this scenario, you need to consider the system's function and decide whether to update or replace the OS. If neither is possible, you should isolate the legacy system on a locked-down network segment with robust firewall rules that restrict unnecessary access but still allow the system to perform its required tasks, protecting the rest of the network if it is compromised.

Decommissioning

Every computing device has a system life cycle, from shiny and new, to patched and secure, to "You're still using that old junk?," to safely decommissioning.

Life-cycle management policies approach asset decommissioning with the philosophy of reduce, reuse, and recycle. You shouldn't just throw away your old gear. Your outdated switches and routers might be perfect for a nonprofit's network. Donate them and take a tax write-off. Repurpose older access points as simple bridges for devices that don't need high speed—for example, multifunction printers. Make sure to remove all your data and custom configurations from the devices as part of the decommissioning process.

Change Management

An IT infrastructure is constantly changing: applications are updated, operating systems change, and server configurations adjust. But while change is inevitable, it shouldn't come at the cost of security.

Change management is the process of creating change in your infrastructure in an organized, controlled, and safe way. It usually begins with a change management team. This team, consisting of people from departments across your organization, is tasked with the job of investigating, testing, and authorizing all but the simplest changes to your network.

Changes tend to be initiated at two levels. *Strategic-level* changes are typically initiated by management and major in scope (like replacing Windows servers with Linux servers). *Infrastructure-level* changes are typically initiated by a department making a request to the change management team, as in the following example scenario.

Say you're in charge of IT network support for a massive art department. There are over 150 graphic artists, each using a powerful macOS workstation. The artists have discovered a new graphics program that they claim will dramatically improve their ability to do their job. After a quick read of the program's features on its website, you're also convinced that this a good idea. It's now your job to make the change happen.

Service Requests

To begin, create a *service request*. Depending on the organization, this might be an official form or simply a detailed email message, but regardless, it should document the reason for this change. A good service request will include the following:

- **TYPE OF CHANGE** Software and hardware changes are obviously part of this category, but it could also encompass issues like backup methods, work hours, network access, and workflow changes.

- **CONFIGURATION PROCEDURES** What is required to make this change happen? Who will help? How long will it take?
- **ROLLBACK PROCESS** If this change has such a negative impact that you need to undo it, what will it take to roll back to the previous configuration?
- **POTENTIAL IMPACT** How will this change impact the organization? Will it save time? Save money? Increase efficiency? Will it affect the perception of the organization?
- **NOTIFICATION** How will you notify the organization about this change?

With your service request in hand, it's time to get the change approved. In most organizations, change management teams meet at fixed intervals, so you'll usually have a deadline. Most teams rely heavily on a well-written change request form to get the details. The approval process usually involves both considering the points listed in the change request as well as securing management approval and funding.

Once your change is approved, the real work starts. Equipment, software, and tools must be purchased. Configuration teams must be trained. The change committee must provide an adequate *maintenance window*: the time it will take to implement and thoroughly test the coming changes. As part of that process, the committee must authorize downtime for systems and departments. Your job is to notify people who will be affected by the change and provide alternative workplaces or equipment if possible.

Request Process Tracking

The last step, which is ongoing, is *request process tracking*. All changes must be clearly documented, including but not limited to the following:

- Network configurations, such as server settings and router configurations
- Additions to the network, such as servers, routers, and switches
- Physical location changes, such as relocated workstations, servers, routers, and switches

As noted earlier in the chapter, organizations have SOP documents that detail how to do most organizational tasks. Any procedures affected by the change management process should be reflected in an updated SOP document.

Configuration Management

Originating from the US military, *configuration management* is the process of maintaining hardware and software in a specific state to ensure predictable behavior. Proper configuration management can help you troubleshoot issues, identify needed patches and bug fixes, and uncover configurations that need modification.

Production Configuration

A *production configuration* is what is currently deployed on an infrastructure's hardware and software. The production configuration must allow devices and software to perform their functions in accordance with their intended purposes while also ensuring security (through access control, permissions, and more). As you might expect, production configurations aren't just thrown into a live network; they are tested thoroughly before deployment.

Backup Configuration

The *backup configuration* process varies by platform and device, but almost all PCs can back up their system setups, and switches and routers have well-known backup commands.

A backup configuration is especially critical for firmware. If you know your systems have outdated firmware, back it up prior to upgrading. Since vendors usually allow you to download only the latest version or two of the firmware, if you need to restore your current setup, using your backups will be your only option.

Baseline/Golden Configuration

Once an infrastructure is up and running efficiently, you should document the *baseline configuration* (also known as a *golden configuration*) for each device. Note that this is a *network* baseline rather than a *performance* baseline. The latter examines throughput, bandwidth, and the like, while a baseline configuration describes the definitive standard for all the components, including computers, servers, switches, routers, and every installed software package. The baseline configuration also includes network topology and placement of devices in the organization.

The baseline configuration provides the foundation for future upgrades. When an organization upgrades the network, it should update the baseline configuration documentation to the new standard.

NOTE This definition of baseline/golden configuration reflects the best practices outlined in NIST Special Publication 800-128, *Guide for Security-Focused Configuration Management of Information Systems*.

Disaster Recovery

Disaster recovery (DR) is a critical part of contingency planning that supports full or partial recovery from a disaster—an event that disables or destroys substantial amounts of infrastructure. While natural disasters like hurricanes and floods are often the first thing that comes to mind, a powerful cyberattack also qualifies as a disaster if it impacts critical infrastructure.

Disaster recovery starts before a disaster occurs, with an organization developing a disaster recovery plan. The actual plan will vary by the type of disaster, with different solutions specified for each scenario, but this section will discuss a few common areas the plan addresses.

DR Metrics

Despite the best efforts of competent techs, bad things happen. An organization should identify and prepare for any situation that could hurt or compromise its people, systems, or ability to function. *DR metrics* help organizations determine how to respond when something goes wrong.

RECOVERY POINT OBJECTIVE

The *recovery point objective* (RPO) specifies how much data loss an organization can tolerate if it must restore from a backup after an incident, effectively dictating the backup frequency. RPO is expressed as the maximum amount of time after which the data loss will exceed the organization's threshold. An RPO of four hours, for example, requires an organization to perform a backup every four hours. In that case, a business process recovery could succeed within four hours of a failure. Any duration longer than that would hinder the recovery process.

RECOVERY TIME OBJECTIVE

The *recovery time objective* (RTO) specifies how long an organization can tolerate an outage before full functionality must be restored to avoid negative consequences like financial loss or reputational damage. An RTO of four hours, for example, requires a company to allocate substantial preparation and budget to ensure that systems can be recovered quickly. An RTO of a week, on the other hand, requires less preparation and a smaller budget.

EXAM TIP SQL servers illustrate effective RPO and RTO strategies. Database systems like Microsoft SQL Server store active logs separately from data files, committing transactions to the logs prior to writing them to data. This separation provides great RPO when logs are protected and backed up to remote storage frequently (as often as every five minutes, since each log is small). For example, if only the data drive in a server fails, you can back up the current log with no data loss. Alternatively, if you lose an entire server, you can recover all data from remote backups and lose only minimal data (a maximum of five minutes' worth).

SQL recovery solutions often include a spare SQL server where backups can be restored quickly, keeping the RTO and RPO low. SQL Log Shipping automates this process by sending transaction log backups from primary servers to secondary servers, further reducing RTO while limiting RPO to the last five-minute backup (or less if the active log is recoverable).

MEAN TIME TO REPAIR

The *mean time to repair* (MTTR) is the amount of time it takes to fix a system after it fails, including time to replace components, repair parts, and restore the system to its fully functional state. When devices have a low MTTR, they can be placed back into production quicker, supporting high availability.

MEAN TIME BETWEEN FAILURES

The *mean time between failures* (MTBF), which typically applies to hardware components, represents the manufacturer's best guess (based on historical data) about how much time will pass between major failures of that component. This assumes that more than one failure will occur, which means that the component will be repaired rather than replaced. Organizations take MTBF into account because it may affect the likelihood and impact of the risks associated with critical systems. Components with high MTBF are generally more reliable, requiring less redundancy and maintenance, whereas components with low MTBF may prompt organizations to implement additional failover systems, maintain spare parts, and increase monitoring to reduce downtime and associated risks.

NOTE Although not covered by the CompTIA Network+ objectives, *mean time to failure* (MTTF) and *annualized failure rate* (AFR) are also DR metrics worth discussing. Hard drive manufacturers often list MTBF, but the metric is actually MTTF, as a hard drive must be replaced when it fails. MTBF applies only to repairable components, such as other parts of the computer or parts of an automobile.

Hard drive manufacturers and other industries have also started using AFR, which is the expected percentage of failure per year based on the device's projected lifetime. For example, if a manufacturer rates its drives with a 5-year lifespan and publishes an AFR of 2.5 percent, this means that if you own 100 drives, 2 or 3 are expected to fail in any given year of that 5-year period.

DR Sites

When a disaster prevents its primary infrastructure from operating, an organization should have processes in place and a plan of action—known as *business continuity* (BC)—to maintain operations. Organizations plan for BC with *business continuity planning* (BCP), the output of which is a *business continuity plan* that details risks to critical systems, costs to replace or repair them, and strategies to implement those solutions in a timely fashion.

One aspect of BCP that is especially critical to plan well in advance of a major disaster is the backup site. Every business continuity plan should outline how to set up some form of secondary location that enables an organization to continue operating should its primary site no longer function. One prime example is the *DR site*, which comes in three types:

- **COLD SITE** A cold site consists of a building, facilities, desks, toilets, parking—everything that a business needs, except computers. A cold site generally takes more than a few days to bring online and is used when cost is a primary concern and some downtime is acceptable.
- **WARM SITE** A warm site has everything found in a cold site, but adds computers loaded with software and functioning servers—a complete hardware infrastructure. A warm site lacks current data and may not have functioning internet/network links. Getting this site up and running involves activating your network links and loading data from recent backups. A warm site should only take a day or two to bring online and is used when a balance between cost and recovery time is needed.
- **HOT SITE** A hot site has everything a warm site does but also includes very recent backups. It might need just a small amount of data restored from a backup to be current, but in many cases a hot site is a complete duplicate of the primary site. A hot site typically takes only a few hours to bring online and is used when critical systems must have minimal downtime.

Testing

Having a disaster recovery plan in place is good, but you need to make sure you can put that plan into action effectively during a real incident. Tabletop exercises and validation tests help ensure that implementing the disaster recovery plan will go as smoothly as possible.

TABLETOP EXERCISES

Tabletop exercises are simulations and discussions to help teams understand the steps involved in the disaster recovery plan and determine whether there are opportunities for improvement. Through tabletop exercises, employees get familiar with their roles and responsibilities, and the organization can gauge the effectiveness of its plan before a disaster strikes. This process is similar to a play's cast doing a table read long before the live performance.

VALIDATION TESTS

Validation tests take tabletop exercises to the next level by simulating a real disaster as closely as possible, with actual hardware, software, and employees acting in their designated roles. Continuing the analogy of a play's cast, this is akin to a full dress rehearsal just before opening night. Validation tests will answer questions like: Will there be any hitches in deploying the DR site? Are the backups current and accessible? They can even serve as wake-up calls to improve or change the existing plan.

Chapter Review

Questions

1. Which of the following is not a reason for asset inventory?
   - **A.** Allows organizations to stay in compliance with regulatory laws
   - **B.** Allows organizations to stay within the licensing agreements with vendors
   - **C.** Aids in troubleshooting, repairing, replacing, adding, and purchasing assets
   - **D.** Protects systems from cybercriminals
2. Which protocols does IPAM control?
   - **A.** DNS and SSH
   - **B.** DHCP and SSH
   - **C.** DNS and DHCP
   - **D.** DNS, DHCP, and SSH
3. Which of the following is a document between a customer and a service provider that defines the scope, quality, and terms of service to be provided?
   - **A.** SLA
   - **B.** EOL
   - **C.** EOS
   - **D.** DNS
4. What is a service request most related to?
   - **A.** Decommissioning
   - **B.** Change management
   - **C.** Life-cycle management
   - **D.** Configuration management
5. Which of the following is not a part of configuration management?
   - **A.** OS configuration
   - **B.** Production configuration
   - **C.** Backup configuration
   - **D.** Baseline/golden configuration

6. When is a disaster recovery plan developed?
   A. Before a disaster
   B. During a disaster
   C. After a disaster
   D. Determined by each organization differently
7. Which of the following sets an upper limit for how long an organization can tolerate an outage before full functionality must be restored?
   A. RPO
   B. RTO
   C. MTTR
   D. MTBF
8. Which of the following represents the amount of time it takes to fix a system after it fails?
   A. RPO
   B. RTO
   C. MTTR
   D. MTBF
9. Which of the following DR sites lacks current data and possibly networking links, but has computers and other technology in place that can spring into action?
   A. Cold site
   B. Warm site
   C. Hot site
   D. Recovery site
10. What's the difference between tabletop exercises and validation tests?
    A. Tabletop exercises are used for DR, but validation tests aren't.
    B. Validation tests are used for DR, but tabletop exercises aren't.
    C. Tabletop exercises involve hands-on activities, while validation tests are just discussions.
    D. Validation tests involve hands-on activities, while tabletop exercises are just discussions.

Answers

1. **D.** An asset inventory system doesn't directly protect an infrastructure from cybercriminals.
2. **C.** IPAM controls DNS and DHCP.
3. **A.** SLA is a service-level agreement between customer and service provider.
4. **B.** Change management includes a service request and request process tracking.
5. **A.** Configuration management includes production configuration, backup configuration, and baseline/golden configuration.
6. **A.** A disaster recovery plan needs to be developed before any disaster so that it can be implemented in a time of need.
7. **B.** The recovery time objective (RTO) is the amount of time needed to restore a business process after an incident or disaster.
8. **C.** Mean time to repair (MTTR) is the amount of time it takes to fix a system after it fails.
9. **B.** A warm site is quicker to bring up than a cold site, but not as quick as a hot site.
10. **D.** Tabletop exercises are just talk, but validation tests involve hands-on activities in a DR simulation.

PART IV

Network Security and Troubleshooting

IN THIS PART:

- CHAPTER 17: Network Security
- CHAPTER 18: The Troubleshooting Methodology

Network Security

IN THIS CHAPTER, YOU WILL LEARN HOW TO

- Explain the importance of basic network security concepts
- Summarize various types of attacks and their impact to the network
- Given a scenario, apply network security features, defense techniques, and solutions

TCP/IP wasn't designed with security in mind. It was designed to standardize networking, allowing different systems to communicate regardless of vendor, operating system, software, hardware, ISP, or speed. This was long before cybercriminals engaged in the kinds of network attacks that have unfortunately become all too commonplace today.

This chapter will explore numerous security concepts, but I'll start by clarifying some terminology. You'll often hear three terms used interchangeably—*information security, cybersecurity,* and *network security*—but they have subtle differences. The one most commonly used today, cybersecurity, is defined by the National Institute of Standards and Technology (NIST) as follows:

> *Prevention of damage to, protection of, and restoration of computers, electronic communications systems, electronic communications services, wire communication, and electronic communication, including information contained therein, to ensure its availability, integrity, authentication, confidentiality, and nonrepudiation.*

Cybersecurity applies to digital information and includes processes and policies that affect physical security of those systems (like securing server rooms). Cybersecurity is a subset of information security, a broader domain that also deals with information stored physically (printed).

Network security is a subset of cybersecurity that focuses on securing networks, networking devices, and the network traffic. In Chapter 15, you learned about some devices that provide network security, such as a firewall, an intrusion detection system (IDS), and an intrusion prevention system (IPS).

NOTE You can hear me talk on TV news and talk radio about many of this chapter's topics at *youtube.com/weissman52* in the TV News Cybersecurity Expert and Radio Cybersecurity Expert playlists.

With those nuances settled, it's time to dive into the wonderful world of network security!

Test Specific

Foundational Network Security Concepts

Credit card numbers, passwords, and other sensitive information should never be sent over the internet without encryption, which keeps the bad guys from reading it and then using it to their advantage (and your detriment). Similarly, if you send someone the "secret decoder ring" to unscramble an encrypted item, the recipient needs to have a way to confirm that the decoder ring actually came from you. We'll begin by discussing these and other basic network security concepts before covering attacks and defense techniques.

Vulnerabilities

Vulnerabilities are weaknesses, flaws, or gaps in an operating system, program, device, network, and even a human process that provide a way for cybercriminals to gain entry into a system or network. Examples include weak authentication (proving you are who you say you are) checks, default username/password combinations, incorrectly configured firewalls, susceptibility to buffer overflows, susceptibility to SQL injection attacks, and even a gullible or naive employee. Some vulnerabilities are obvious, such as connecting to the internet without a firewall or forgoing file permissions. Other vulnerabilities are unknown or missed, and that makes them a very important topic for a network tech to study.

The *Common Vulnerabilities and Exposures* (CVE) database hosted by MITRE Corporation at *cve.org* is a public reference of identified vulnerabilities and exposures. Each vulnerability is assigned a CVE ID, which is included in security advisories issued by researchers and vendors and helps cybersecurity specialists synchronize on vulnerabilities that need to be addressed immediately.

How do vulnerabilities come to light? Who discovers them? From the *black hat* (malicious intent) camp, attackers do. From the *white hat* (helpful intent) camp, security researchers do. Both sides poke and prod operating systems, software, and hardware day in and day out. Black hat hackers, if caught, go to prison. White hat hackers—also known as *penetration testers* (*pentesters*) or *ethical hackers*—get paid, have thrilling careers, and are highly regarded in the cybersecurity community. They do the same things that black hat hackers do but with explicit permission from system or network owners. Companies hire white hat hackers to find and exploit vulnerabilities so that those weaknesses can be identified and fixed before they are discovered by black hat hackers.

Gray hat hackers, as the name implies, combine black hat and white hat hacking. While gray hat hackers have no malicious intentions (the white hat component), they access systems and networks without permission, which is illegal (the black hat component), to find and exploit vulnerabilities. Once they identify a vulnerability, they report it to the organization at risk and request a fee to fix it. If a company doesn't want to pay, the gray hat hacker could post the vulnerability online to raise public awareness, which may actually make it easier for black hat hackers to exploit it. Some gray hat hackers operate solely for the excitement of it, relishing the challenge of finding and exploiting vulnerabilities.

Some vulnerabilities are labeled *zero-day*. These are vulnerabilities that are discovered but not publicly announced before they are (or can be) exploited. Therefore, the companies and individuals who would normally patch them now have zero days to fix the problems or recommend mitigation techniques. Zero-day exploits (also known as *zero-day attacks*) aren't used against many targets because increased use raises the likelihood that they will be detected (by anti-malware programs and IDS/IPS devices) and analyzed. Sometimes even a single well-examined attack is enough for vendors (or researchers) to discover the underlying vulnerability and issue patches. A zero-day used too often won't be a zero-day for long! Therefore, attackers stockpile them and use them in certain "emergency" situations.

Governments can stockpile them, too, sometimes weaponizing them instead of notifying vendors of vulnerabilities in devices and software their own citizens use (although many governments use internal review processes like the US Vulnerabilities Equities Process to decide whether to keep or report these vulnerabilities). For example, a zero-day stockpile would be very valuable for reconnaissance and cyberattacks against adversaries. However, serious negative outcomes, such as ransomware attacks or large-scale system compromises, can occur if these stockpiled zero-days are used offensively, leaked, or stolen by malicious actors.

Exploits

Exploit, used as a noun, is a tool or method used to penetrate a system through vulnerabilities. When used as a verb, *exploit* means the actual act of penetrating a system: attackers exploit vulnerabilities. Interestingly enough, exploits are usually named after the vulnerability they exploit. For example, MS08-067 (MS stands for Microsoft Security Bulletin, 08 is the year, and 67 denotes the 67th bulletin released that year) is the identifier for a well-known 2008 Windows vulnerability, and the MS08-067 exploit is the code that targets it, allowing cybercriminals to gain control of Windows XP and Windows Server 2003 systems. More recently, in 2021, the Hafnium cyberespionage group unleashed multiple zero-day exploits attacking Microsoft Exchange Server, prompting the publication of CVE-2021-26855, CVE-2021-26857, CVE-2021-26858, and CVE-2021-27065.

NOTE Although common, exploits aren't always named after the vulnerability they exploit. Sometimes the vulnerability has one name (e.g., Heartbleed, Dirty COW), while the exploit is separate and may have its own name (e.g., Metasploit modules and exploit kits).

Pentesting and cyberattacks follow the same algorithm for their exploits:

1. Find systems.
2. Find programs or services on those systems.
3. Find vulnerabilities in those programs or services.
4. Develop and execute an exploit against the identified vulnerabilities.
5. Use the compromised systems to pivot to other systems on the same network as well as systems on different networks.

Payload is the code delivered by an exploit that performs the attacker's intended action on the compromised system. Payloads can provide remote access (such as reverse shells or bind shells), carry out malicious activities like ransomware encryption or data exfiltration, escalate privileges, establish persistence, or act as "stagers" that download and execute additional malicious components. The exploit delivers the payload, but the payload is what actually executes the attacker's objectives.

Imagine two burglars driving in a van. The driver rams the van into a storefront. The passenger jumps out and starts looting the store. In this scenario, the van is the exploit, and the looter filling his bags is the payload. As another example, think of a missile: the rocket, fuel, and guidance system are the exploit. The warhead—which is what does the actual damage—is the payload. Take out the warhead, and the missile doesn't have a strong impact. Likewise, a warhead can't do much unless it's delivered by a rocket.

Threats

From a cybersecurity perspective, you are looking to protect *assets*—entities that have value to an organization, such as hardware, software, information, data, trade secrets, and employees. *Threats* represent potential events or actions (looming dangers) that can negatively impact assets, operations (including reputation, functions, and mission), and even individuals through violations of confidentiality, integrity, or availability.

INTERNAL

Internal threats originate from individuals within the organization who threaten security by acting maliciously (for example, sabotage or data exfiltration) or carelessly (such as falling for a phishing email). Because these insiders already have some level of access, means, and opportunity, they can do far greater damage than outside actors.

EXTERNAL

External threats come from outside the organization. Deliberate examples include cyberattacks such as malware infections or network intrusions. Environmental and accidental examples include natural disasters (fires, floods, earthquakes) and equipment failures (server crashes or accidental disconnections).

THREAT AGENTS

Threat agents or actors are the ones carrying out the threats. They exploit vulnerabilities or circumstances to cause harm to assets or operations. Cybercriminals, including a person, organization, or even a nation-state, are the first examples that come to mind. However, Mother Nature—through earthquakes, tornadoes, fires, and floods—is also a threat agent.

NOTE Another example of a threat agent is . . . squirrels! See the following articles for evidence:

- *theweek.com/articles/452311/forget-hackers-squirrels-are-bigger-threat-americas-power-grid*
- *arstechnica.com/information-technology/2017/01/whos-winning-the-cyber-war-the-squirrels-of-course/*

Risk

Risk combines the probability of a threat coming to fruition along with the consequences that would result from it. Risk assessment uses the following equation:

Risk = Probability of threat × Impact of threat

Risk considers the potential for loss, damage, or destruction of an asset as a result of a threat exploiting a vulnerability. Risk carries uncertainty about how or whether a threat will impact something you value.

We take risks every day by walking to a car, driving to and from work, crossing the street, eating out, and otherwise living our lives. You might get hit by a truck, have a car accident, get mugged, slip on ice, fall down stairs, cut your finger, get a stomach bug, and more.

Do you actually analyze all these risks? You probably do without even realizing it, as it's become second nature. You look both ways before crossing the street. You drive responsibly and obey traffic laws. You stay aware of your surroundings, use a handrail, handle sharp objects carefully, and wash your hands.

In cybersecurity, the same principles apply. Organizations assess and manage risk by identifying threats, evaluating vulnerabilities, estimating likelihood and impact, and implementing controls to reduce potential harm to assets. A security risk analysis involves the following steps:

1. Identify the assets to be protected (*asset valuation*).
2. Define specific threats (*threat analysis*).
3. Calculate *annualized loss expectancy* (ALE), a fundamental concept in risk analysis, estimating potential monetary loss over a year:

   ALE = Single loss expectancy × Annualized rate of occurrence

4. Select and implement appropriate preventive, detective, and corrective *risk controls*, measures that reduce risk to limit the potential damage from threats.

To identify an asset, ask the following: What's important to you? To your company? What is considered of value? Here are some examples:

- Funds (cash, bank accounts, or financial resources)
- Hardware (servers, computers, networking equipment, or devices)
- Location (physical sites, facilities, or data centers)
- People (employees, contractors, or other stakeholders)
- Data (raw facts, figures, logs, or measurements)
- Information (processed or organized data that provides meaning, insight, or value to the organization)
- Knowledge (expertise, processes, or organizational know-how)
- Technology (software, applications, or technical systems)
- Intellectual property (patents, trademarks, or copyrighted materials)
- Reputation (brand image, public trust, or credibility)

After you've identified your assets and noted the risks, you can adopt any of four strategies:

- **AVOIDANCE** Eliminate the risk or its causes, or change the plan to avoid the risk. For example, take a vulnerable hardware device or software deployment out of production, or relocate servers away from areas prone to water damage.
- **MITIGATION** Apply risk security controls (through hardware, software, or people) to reduce the potential impact. Controls can be preventive, detective, or corrective, but they can never completely eliminate risk.

- **TRANSFERENCE** Contractually engage with a third party who takes on the risk for money (cyber insurance).
- **ACCEPTANCE (risk retention)** Acknowledge the risk and choose to take no action, accepting the potential consequences if the risk materializes.

Risk security controls can be either nature-based or time-based.

NATURE-BASED RISK SECURITY CONTROLS

- **PHYSICAL** Tangible measures to protect people, assets, or information (fences, doors, locks, fire extinguishers)
- **PROCEDURAL** Policies and processes that guide behavior and response (incident response (IR) process, security awareness and training, management oversight)
- **TECHNICAL** Electronic or software-based measures to control access and detect threats (user authentication, logical access, antivirus software, firewalls, other systems)
- **LEGAL** Regulatory or contractual measures that enforce compliance and define responsibilities (privacy laws, policies, clauses)

TIME-BASED RISK SECURITY CONTROLS

- **DIRECTIVE** Guidelines to direct the use or implementation of controls (policies, procedures, or standards)
- **PREVENTATIVE** Measures that prevent bad things from occurring (account lockouts)
- **DETECTIVE** Mechanisms that identify and characterize incidents in progress (intruder alarms, notifications)
- **CORRECTIVE** Safeguards that limit damage caused by the incident (system patches, restoring from backup, applying configuration changes to prevent further damage)
- **FORENSICS OR RECOVERY** Measures that provide after-event data to allow some event that has happened in the past to be uncovered or the organization to get back to work (audit logs, forensic imaging of compromised systems, disaster recovery procedures, backup restoration)

There are several reasons why you might perform a risk analysis:

- To comply with laws or regulations, such as Sarbanes Oxley (SOX) Audit Standard 5 or the Federal Information Security Management Act (FISMA)
- To adhere to standards and best practices, such as ISO/IEC 27001 and 27002, for minimizing business disruption and continuing operations in the event of an incident.
- To protect your organization from lawsuits and cybersecurity risks and to inform your security budget decisions

You can't expect what you don't inspect: if you don't look for potential liabilities, you're not likely to find them, but someone else might!

Risk falls into four zones or impact areas, as shown in Figure 17-1.

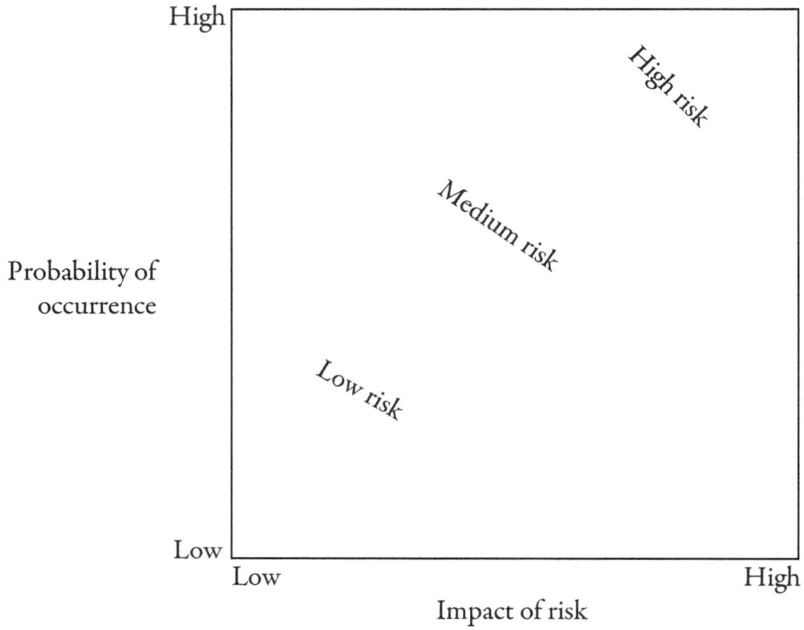

FIGURE 17-1 Risk impact areas

The four quadrants are as follows:

- **LOW IMPACT/LOW PROBABILITY** A risk in the bottom-left corner can usually be ignored.
- **LOW IMPACT/HIGH PROBABILITY** A risk in the top-left corner is moderately important. You can probably deal with it without worry, but mitigation is always a good strategy.
- **HIGH IMPACT/LOW PROBABILITY** A risk in the bottom-right corner is of very high importance but not that likely to happen. Mitigate a risk here and make sure that there are plans in place if it comes to fruition.
- **HIGH IMPACT/HIGH PROBABILITY** A risk in the top-right corner is critically important and should be prioritized accordingly.

Confidentiality, Integrity, and Availability

Just as networking education starts with the OSI model, security education starts with the *CIA triad* (also known as the *CIA model*), shown in Figure 17-2. CIA stands for *confidentiality*, *integrity*, and *availability*, which are the tenets of information security, used to protect systems and data. Every breach, cyberattack, vulnerability, and exploit affects at least one of these components, and every cybersecurity control and mitigation technique is designed to safeguard one or more aspects of the triad.

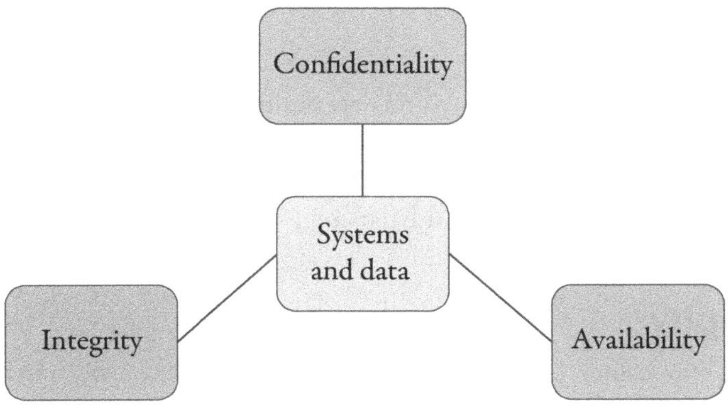

FIGURE 17-2 The CIA triad

NOTE Every security technique, practice, and mechanism put into place to protect systems and data relates in some fashion to ensuring confidentiality, integrity, and availability.

Confidentiality means preventing unauthorized people from accessing data, messages, and files, while ensuring access for authorized people. Systems enforce confidentiality through encryption (converting readable plaintext into ciphertext that only certain parties can read, as discussed in the next section) and access controls like operating system permissions.

Integrity ensures that data isn't changed (either accidentally or maliciously) while being stored, transmitted, processed, or received, unless the alteration is authorized and intentional. Mechanisms such as hashing and digital signatures are commonly used to verify integrity.

EXAM TIP Hashing enforces integrity at the file/message level. Other methods for enforcing integrity take place at various layers of the OSI model. As discussed in earlier chapters, a cyclic redundancy check (CRC) is used for Ethernet and 802.11 frames, while a checksum is used for ICMP packets, TCP segments, and UDP datagrams. A CRC or checksum is meant to detect accidental changes but is not designed to protect against malicious modifications. In contrast, cryptographic hashing is used to detect malicious changes and is designed to reliably detect malicious changes. Hashing will be discussed in more detail shortly.

Availability refers to keeping systems and data online and operational for authorized users to access whenever needed. Any potential downtime for users or the entire network—for example, after a distributed denial-of-service (DDoS) attack—can be devastating. Availability is enforced through fault tolerance, load balancing, system redundancy, data backups, business continuity, and disaster recovery.

Cryptography

Cryptography is the science and practice of securing information by transforming it with mathematical algorithms. Cryptography directly supports the CIA triad by ensuring confidentiality (via encryption) and integrity (via hashing). While cryptography does not directly provide availability, breaches in confidentiality or integrity can indirectly compromise availability. Protecting information from unauthorized access or modification helps ensure that it remains accessible and reliable to authorized users.

Encryption

A file or message in plaintext is human-readable or in another directly usable format. Plaintext also refers to any data, including binary files like images or programs, that you can view or use in its original form without first having to transform it into another representation. When a message is sent as plaintext over an insecure channel, an attacker could intercept a copy and understand it just as the intended recipient would. The insecure channel could be wired or wireless, ranging from a Wi-Fi infrastructure to the full internet.

All data starts as plaintext. To make it difficult for unauthorized parties to read, the data must be encrypted using a *cipher*, a mathematical algorithm that defines specific steps for transforming data. When plaintext is processed by a cipher using a *key*, a string of 1s and 0s, the result is encrypted data called *ciphertext*. See Figure 17-3.

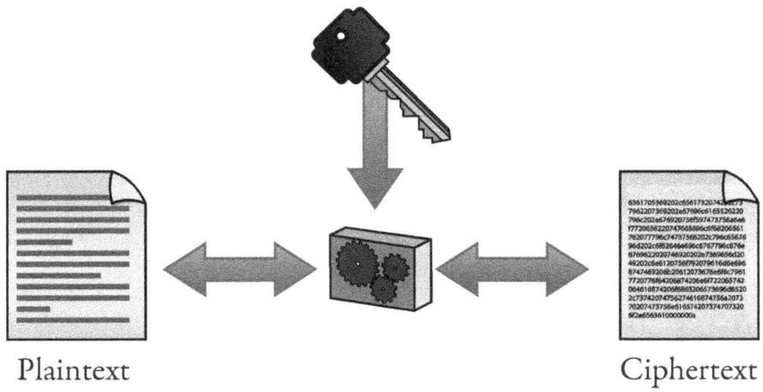

FIGURE 17-3 The encryption process

When a message is sent as ciphertext over an insecure channel, an attacker can still get a copy of it, but it will look like random gibberish with no information that is useful or meaningful to the attacker.

NOTE The term *encrypt* originates from the Greek word *kryptos*, which means hidden or secret. The word combines *en* (to make) and *crypt* (hidden).

Decryption works in reverse. The intended recipient, unlike the attacker, will have the key. By entering the key and the ciphertext into the cipher, the recipient can transform the ciphertext back into the original plaintext in order to read it.

You might think that the algorithm by itself is sufficient, but it's not. Plaintext fed into an algorithm without a key will also output ciphertext, but there's a big problem: encryption algorithms aren't secret. It's common knowledge how they work mathematically, and which ones are used for certain protocols. So, if no key was used, an attacker could simply reverse the publicly known algorithm to recover the original message. The security lies in the key. To avoid compromising the encryption and confidentiality, you must protect the key and avoid letting any unauthorized entity see it.

XOR AND ENCRYPTION

To understand how encryption algorithms use keys to transform plaintext into ciphertext, let's look at a fundamental operation used in many cryptographic systems: XOR (exclusive OR). Say you have a string of 1s and 0s that looks like this:

```
0100101001010011010101111
```

This string may not mean much to you, but if it's part of an HTTP segment, a web browser instantly recognizes it as Unicode—that is, numbers representing letters and other characters—and converts it into text:

```
01001010 01010011 01010111
    J       S        W
```

NOTE The American Standard Code for Information Interchange (ASCII)/Unicode character *J* is 4A in base 16 (hexadecimal), which is 01001010 in base 2 (binary). See *asciitable.com* for a complete ASCII table and *rapidtables.com/convert/number/hex-to-binary.html* for a hexadecimal-to-binary conversion table. Early character encoding systems like ASCII are now largely obsolete, replaced by Unicode, which can represent virtually all characters used in modern computing.

Many cryptographic algorithms include a derivation of the logical OR: the logical XOR (exclusive OR). Single-byte XOR outputs a 1 if the first or second bit, but not both, is a 1, as shown in Table 17-1.

TABLE 17-1 XOR

IF THE PLAINTEXT IS . . .	AND THE KEY VALUE IS . . .	THEN THE RESULT IS . . .
0	0	0
0	1	1
1	0	1
1	1	0

Line up the key (52 in base 10 in this case) against the first eight values in the plaintext and perform the XOR operation:

```
010010100101001101010111
00110100
01111110
```

Then align the next eight bits with the same single-byte key:

```
010010100101001101010111
0011010000110100
0111111000111011
```

Then the final eight bits:

```
010010100101001101010111
001101000011010000110100
------------------------
011111100110011101100011
```

This outputs the following ciphertext:

```
011111100110011101100011
```

If you want to decrypt the ciphertext, you need to know the algorithm and the key. By XORing the ciphertext and the key together, you get the original plaintext:

```
011111100110011101100011
001101000011010000110100
------------------------
010010100101001101010111
```

NOTE As a bitwise operation, XOR operates on each pair of corresponding bits. At this level, letters and numbers are all just binary 1s and 0s—XOR works on any data you can throw at it.

Although XOR by itself is far too weak for modern encryption, it is widely used in practice, especially in malware. Malware authors frequently use single-byte or multibyte XOR to obfuscate strings, configuration data, and payloads because it is fast, trivial to implement, and—since XORing data changes its byte patterns—effective at evading simple signature-based detection.

XOR is also a building block in modern encryption algorithms like AES, where it is used to combine round keys with data. Beyond encryption, XOR appears in hash functions, hash-based message authentication code (HMAC), and error detection codes such as parity calculations. Its versatility makes XOR a foundational operation in both security tools and attacks.

The example in Table 17-1 was simplified for illustration purposes; in practice, single-byte XOR encryption is insecure and easy to break. Real-world encryption relies on:

- Longer keys to make brute-force attacks more difficult
- Complex algorithms to transform data in ways that are computationally hard to reverse without the key

Over the years, cryptographers have developed hundreds of algorithms for encrypting binary data. Only a few are commonly used in TCP/IP networks today. All of these algorithms share two essential components: a complex cipher algorithm and a key (or keys) for encryption and decryption.

DATA IN TRANSIT

Data in transit, moving across a network from a source to a destination, should be encrypted. Using encryption protocols like Transport Layer Security (TLS) for web traffic and Secure Shell (SSH) for remote access, protects against attacks that could compromise confidentiality, integrity, or availability.

DATA AT REST

Data at rest, files stored on a machine, should be encrypted as well. Encryption protects this data not only from prying users but also from anyone who gets hold of a lost or stolen device.

NOTE *Homomorphic encryption* enables you to work with encrypted data without having to decrypt it. You can process, manipulate, and analyze the ciphertext while keeping the data confidential and sharing it with others for computation.

SYMMETRIC ENCRYPTION

Symmetric encryption, also called *secret key cryptography*, is a method of encrypting data in which the same key is used for both encryption and decryption. If you want someone to decrypt what you encrypt, you must make sure that they have the key as well as a tool that can handle the algorithm.

Symmetric algorithms are either block ciphers or stream ciphers. *Block ciphers*, the more common type, encrypt data in single "chunks" of a certain length at a time. Let's say you want to encrypt a Microsoft Word document. An approach that uses a block cipher would take the file, split it into 128-bit chunks, and encrypt each block separately, as shown in Figure 17-4.

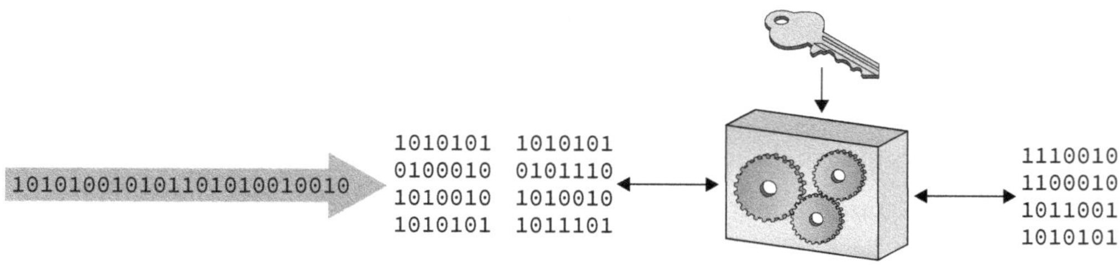

FIGURE 17-4 A block cipher

Advanced Encryption Standard (AES), the most common block cipher, uses a 128-bit block size and 128-, 192-, or 256-bit key size. AES is incredibly secure, practically uncrackable (for now at least), and so fast that even applications that traditionally used stream ciphers (such as TLS) have switched to AES.

Stream ciphers take a single bit at a time and encrypt on the fly, as shown in Figure 17-5. They're very popular for data that comes in long streams, as in cellular networks, but advances in hardware have made block ciphers like AES the preferred choice for most noncellular applications.

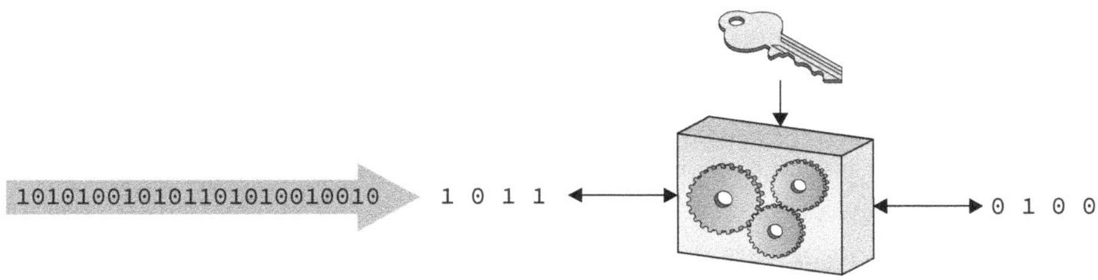

FIGURE 17-5 A stream cipher

ASYMMETRIC CRYPTOGRAPHY

Symmetric encryption has one serious weakness: anyone who gets the key can encrypt or decrypt data with it. The nature of symmetric encryption forces you to send the key to the other person in one way or another, making it a challenge to use symmetric encryption safely by itself (see Figure 17-6).

FIGURE 17-6 How can the sender get the key to the intended recipient safely?

Asymmetric cryptography, also called *public key cryptography*, solves this problem using a *key pair*: a public key and a private key. The public key can be shared openly and is used to encrypt data intended for the key's owner, while the private key is kept secret and is used to decrypt data encrypted with the corresponding public key. Conversely, data encrypted with the private key can be decrypted with the public key, allowing the owner to create digital signatures (discussed shortly) that verify authenticity and integrity. Using this system, users can securely transmit a symmetric key without ever sending it in plaintext, enabling safe communication even over unsecured channels.

NOTE In this chapter, I use the term *symmetric encryption* (note the word *encryption*) to describe methods that use the same key for both encryption and decryption, and I use the term *asymmetric cryptography* (note the word *cryptography*) to describe methods that use a pair of keys, since asymmetric keys are also used for key exchange and digital signatures, not just for encrypting data.

In practice, asymmetric cryptography is not used for the encryption of bulk data because it is computationally expensive. Instead, it is used to securely encrypt small, critical pieces of data, such as symmetric session keys, authentication information, digital signatures, or key exchange material, which then enable the efficient encryption of bulk data with symmetric keys.

Imagine that two people, Bob and Alice, want to exchange email securely. See Figure 17-7.

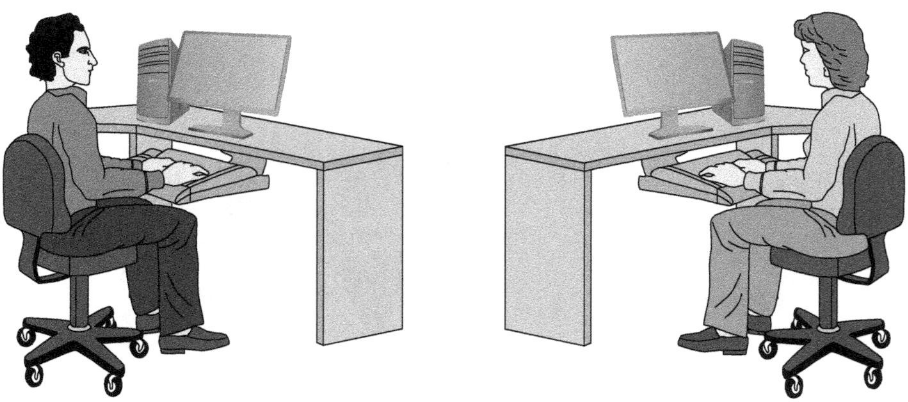

FIGURE 17-7 Bob and Alice using cryptography

In this story, Alice and Bob are using Pretty Good Privacy (PGP), a program or software standard that can be integrated with email clients to secure messages using hybrid encryption.

1. Bob generates a key pair: a private key, which he keeps secret, and a public key, which he shares with Alice (Figure 17-8).
2. Alice encrypts her message using a randomly generated symmetric session key. She then encrypts the symmetric key with Bob's public key and sends the encrypted session key along with the ciphertext in a single message.
3. Bob uses his private key to decrypt the session key, then uses that key to decrypt Alice's message.

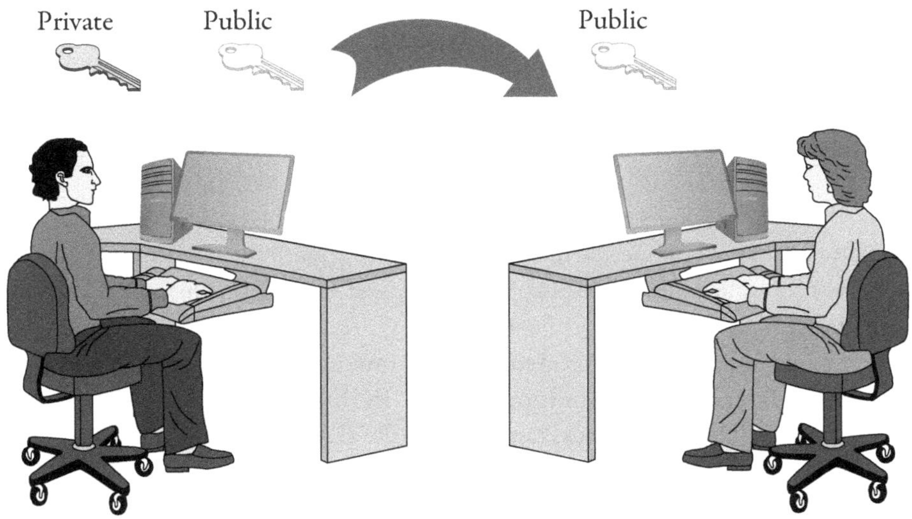

FIGURE 17-8 Bob sends his public key to Alice

This hybrid approach combines the speed of symmetric encryption for large amounts of data with the security of asymmetric cryptography for key distribution. Modern web traffic, such as TLS 1.3, uses elliptic-curve Diffie–Hellman (ECDHE) or other Diffie–Hellman key exchange methods to establish a shared symmetric key and digital certificates, discussed next, to authenticate servers to clients.

NOTE Some asymmetric algorithms you will see these days are Rivest, Shamir, Adleman (RSA; named after its creators), Digital Signature Algorithm (DSA), and Elliptic Curve DSA (ECDSA).

Certificates

Public key cryptography solves the key distribution problem, but how do you know that a public key actually belongs to the person sending it? If an attacker intercepts Bob's public key and substitutes their own, Alice would unknowingly encrypt her message with the attacker's public key instead. *Digital certificates*, electronic documents (data files) that prove the identity of a website, organization, or individual, solve this problem. Digital certificates and asymmetric cryptography are closely linked because digital certificates verify the ownership of public keys.

A *certificate authority* (CA) is an entity that issues digital certificates. Think of it like a digital notary, as both parties must trust the CA for the system to work. For example, online banking relies on certificates to protect both the account holder and the bank. The account holder would surely want to use encryption to avoid having their identity and money stolen. The bank wants to use encryption, too, to avoid getting sued.

When issuing a certificate, the CA creates a *digital signature* by encrypting the organization's certificate data with the CA's private key. This signature proves the certificate is authentic and hasn't been tampered with. Anyone can verify the signature using the CA's public key—if the signature is valid, they know the certificate came from that CA and hasn't been modified.

The CA service runs on a server owned by a corporation that issues digital certificates. CAs are trusted publishers of public certificates, and organizations rely on them for public-facing services. These are called public or third-party CAs, and examples include DigiCert, Sectigo, and Let's Encrypt.

Large organizations may also create their own internal CAs to issue certificates within the company for internal systems and applications. The organization distributes the internal CA's certificate to all internal devices, establishing the CA as a trusted authority within the organization.

PUBLIC KEY INFRASTRUCTURE

When an organization wants to create a secure website, it gets a certificate signed by a root CA such as DigiCert. A *root* certificate is the top-level, self-signed certificate that belongs to the CA itself and comes preinstalled in operating systems and browsers as a trusted certificate. The new website's certificate will contain DigiCert's digital signature, proving DigiCert issued it.

NOTE Becoming a root certificate authority with enough respect to have browsers install your certificate is very difficult!

In most situations, DigiCert doesn't directly sign these certificates with its root certificate—it keeps that under lock and key (we hope). Instead, they'll use an *intermediate* certificate, which they've signed with their root certificate, to sign the organization's certificate. This creates a tree or chain of certificate authorization, with the root certificate authorities at the top and issued certificates at the bottom.

You can also have additional intermediate certificate authorities, although these are not as heavily used. A CA that directly issues certificates to organizations or devices is also sometimes called an *issuing certificate authority*. Together, this hierarchy is called a *public key infrastructure* (PKI). See Figure 17-9.

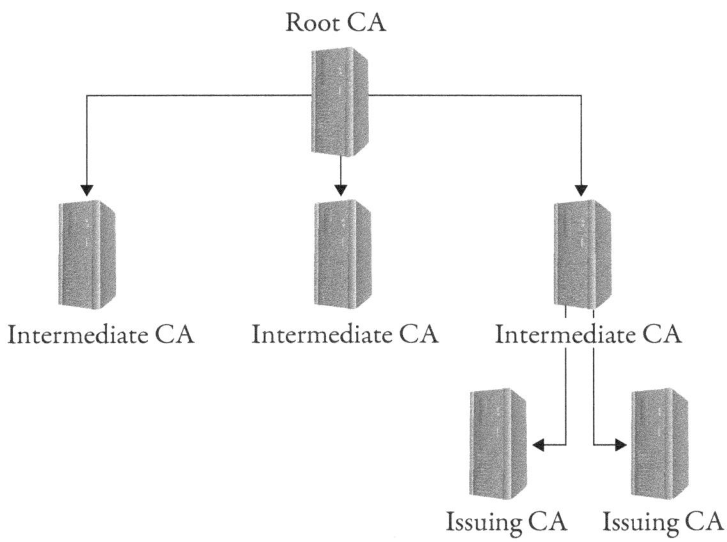

FIGURE 17-9 PKI hierarchy

When a browser goes to a website, the browser transmits a list of algorithms it supports to the web server. The server selects algorithms to use and sends its digital certificate to the browser. The browser then verifies that the digital certificate isn't revoked or expired. If the certificate is valid, the browser extracts the server's public key from the certificate.

SELF-SIGNED CERTIFICATES

You don't have to use PKI to use certificates. You can create and self-sign your certificates. This approach is perfectly fine for lower-security situations (such as internal services), but don't expect anyone to buy products on a website or send highly sensitive email without a certificate signed by a well-known CA like Sectigo, DigiCert, or Let's Encrypt.

THE ISSUANCE PROCESS

To obtain a certificate from a CA, an organization generates a public/private key pair. Then the organization creates a Certificate Signing Request (CSR) that contains the public key (the private key is kept internally and never transmitted) and information about the organization, including its name and domain name. After verifying the organization's domain ownership, the CA signs the CSR with its private key (digital signature), creating a digital certificate. The CA sends this digital certificate to the organization, who installs it on the web server.

When a customer goes to the organization's website, the web server presents this digital certificate to the client's browser. The browser verifies the CA's digital signature with the CA's trusted certificate in the system or application-level trusted root certificate store. Upon successful verification, the browser can now trust the public key and the server's identity.

The browser and server then perform the TLS 1.3 *handshake*:

1. They agree on encryption algorithms and parameters to use.
2. Both client and server participate in a Diffie–Hellman key exchange, which allows them to independently calculate a shared secret (the *premaster secret*) without transmitting it directly.
3. From this shared secret, both sides derive the *session keys*, which are symmetric keys used to encrypt and decrypt all subsequent communication.

This process ensures the connection is secure, private, and tamper-proof before any sensitive data is transmitted.

NOTE Nowadays, companies like Let's Encrypt provide free digital certificates to help encrypt as much of the web as possible. Recent data suggests that a large majority, roughly 90–98 percent, of web traffic (loads/requests) now occur over HTTPS (HTTP over TLS). Even sites that don't deal with personally identifiable information (PII) should use TLS. Any unprotected resources, like ads between websites and users, can be exploited. Cybercriminals aggregate information to identify your users. TLS is required for cutting-edge features and new technologies.

Hashing

Hashing ensures the integrity of files, messages, certificates, and software updates. It's also used to store password verifiers securely so that systems never need to store plaintext passwords.

Hash functions, also known as *hash algorithms*, are given plaintext input, apply some math to it, and then output a message digest, also known simply as a *hash*. Figure 17-10 illustrates this process.

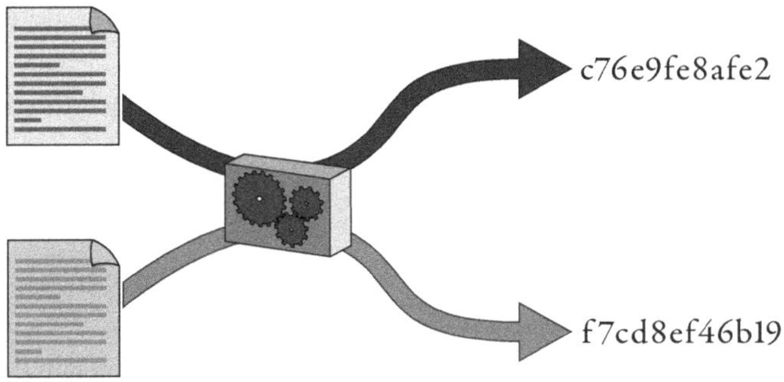

FIGURE 17-10 Hashing in action

Hash functions have five important characteristics:

- The input is of variable length, but the output length is fixed. You could input the Declaration of Independence into a hash function or just your name, and the output message digest will be the same size.
- If just one bit of the input changes, the output hash is completely different. This means an input of `bob` hashes to something completely different than an input of `Bob`.
- Hashing is designed to be a one-way function. It should be computationally infeasible to recover the input from the hash. This is known as *preimage resistance*.
- For a given input, it should be extremely difficult to find a second input that, when fed into the same hash function, produces the same hash. This is known as *second preimage resistance*. For example, if you know someone's password hashes to a specific value, you shouldn't be able to find a different password that produces the same hash.
- It should also be very difficult to find two different inputs that produce the same hash. This is known as *collision resistance*. Unlike second preimage resistance, where you're given a specific input, here you're comparing *any* two inputs. It's like the difference between finding someone who has the same birthday as you and finding any two people that share a birthday.

Hashing serves multiple security purposes, from verifying file integrity to protecting password databases. Let's look at how it is used in practice.

INTEGRITY OF FILES

How do you know that file that you're downloading is the original and not an altered version laced with malware or spyware? When you've downloaded a file in the past, you might have seen its hash next to the link you clicked. If you run your downloaded file through the same hash algorithm and get the same message digest, you know that you got the file intact and that no bits were changed accidentally (due to transmission errors, which are less common now than in the past) or maliciously in transit.

For a file on a hard drive—that is, data at rest—if the stored hash doesn't match a newly computed hash, you know the file has been altered since the last hash.

INTEGRITY OF MESSAGES

Suppose Alice hashes her message and then encrypts that hash with her private key. This encrypted hash is her digital signature. Bob decrypts the signature using Alice's public key, recovering the original hash Alice created. Bob also hashes the decrypted email himself. If Bob's computed hash matches Alice's decrypted hash, he knows the message is exactly what Alice sent and that no bits were changed accidentally or maliciously in transit.

This process also provides *nonrepudiation*, meaning Alice cannot credibly deny having sent the message. Only Alice has her private key, so only she could have created the digital signature that Bob successfully verified with her public key.

INTEGRITY OF CERTIFICATES

When your browser connects to a web server using TLS 1.3, it needs to confirm that it's really talking to the legitimate server. The server proves it owns the private key corresponding to the public key in its digital certificate by signing part of the handshake. The browser verifies this signature using the public key from the certificate. It also checks that the certificate itself was issued by a trusted CA, confirms its validity period, verifies it has not been revoked, and ensures the certificate's hostname matches the URL being accessed. To do this, the browser refers to its *root certificate store*, a list of preinstalled trusted CA certificates. Depending on the platform, this store may be maintained by the browser itself, the operating system, or both. Once all these checks pass, the browser knows the server is legitimate and can safely establish an encrypted session.

INTEGRITY OF SOFTWARE UPDATES

When a software update or patch comes from Microsoft, Apple, or any other vendor, how do you know it's really from them? Each update includes a hash that's encrypted with the vendor's private key. The client computes its own hash of the downloaded update and decrypts the provided hash with the vendor's public key. If the hashes match, the client can be confident the update is authentic and hasn't been tampered with.

SECURE PASSWORD STORAGE

Hashing protects password databases from both system administrators with prying eyes and cybercriminals out to steal those databases. Passwords should always be stored as hashes, not plaintext, so that anyone who views or steals a password database won't be able to read the passwords. When you log in to a local or remote machine, your password is hashed and compared to the stored hash on the authenticating system, which never needs to store or display the plaintext password. The same thing happens at an ATM when you enter your PIN.

Secure password storage combines hashing with *salts*, random values added to each password before hashing, and slow, computationally expensive algorithms such as PBKDF2, bcrypt, scrypt, Argon2, and yescrypt. Salts and slow hashing make brute-force, dictionary, rainbow table, and similar attacks far more difficult, because each hash is unique and costly to compute. (These attacks aren't part of the Network+ objectives, but you can research them.)

NOTE Contrary to what you hear in the media, password databases today are *never* encrypted. Encryption is a two-way function, so if passwords were stored as ciphertext, a key for decryption wouldn't be too far away. If the attackers got the ciphertext, they'd most likely get the key too. As a one-way function, hashing is a stronger form of password storage than encryption. Before hashes were used, passwords were stored in <gulp> plaintext, so once the attackers got the password database, they could use it right away. They could also launch a credential stuffing attack, trying the same username/password combination on other sites to see if the users had reused passwords—a security no-no!

Identity and Access Management

When you think about security, physical devices and controls often come to mind. Unlike physical security mechanisms like padlocks and alarm systems, *logical security* uses software to protect systems, and it can be implemented in many different ways. You've just seen how cryptography accomplishes this, so now let's explore some other methods.

Beyond encryption and hashing, organizations need to control who can access their systems and resources. An organization's applications, files, and more should be accessed only by those authorized to do so, and only to the authorization level indicated by the *principle of least privilege* (accessing only the resources you need and no more). This principle applies to both on-premises and remote users, which include not just employees but also vendors, contractors, business partners, and even customers.

Identity and Access Management (IAM) is a framework consisting of technologies, processes, systems, and policies used to efficiently verify digital identities and then grant the permissions required to access specific resources at specific times. Users can be verified in multiple ways.

Two subsets of IAM are *Privileged Access Management* (PAM) and *Privileged Identity Management* (PIM). PAM ensures legitimate access to privileged accounts by controlling credentials, enforcing the principle of least privilege, and monitoring sessions to detect misuse.

PIM, on the other hand, manages who can be temporarily elevated to privileged roles, usually inside cloud-based IAM systems (such as Microsoft Entra ID—formerly Azure Active Directory—and AWS IAM).

Authentication

Authentication validates the identification of users trying to gain access to a system, network, or some data. Whereas identity is who you are, identification is claiming or stating that identity. Authentication is proving it. The first exposure to authentication for most users is local authentication—entering a username and password to sign in to a computer. However, there are many other ways to authenticate, especially when networking is added into the mix. A network technician should understand how different authentication methods control usernames and passwords, as well as some of the authentication standards used in today's TCP/IP networks.

MULTIFACTOR AUTHENTICATION

What if someone obtains your username and password? To defeat those types of threat actors, some systems require a second form of authentication known as *multifactor authentication* (MFA). MFA means using two or more distinct methods for authentication. When only two authentication methods are used, you might see the term *two-factor authentication* (2FA). These methods fall into one of three categories, and it's a good idea to be able to recognize examples of all of them:

- *Something you know* (a knowledge factor) is a password, a passphrase, or a personal identification number (PIN).
- *Something you have* (a possession factor) is either a hardware token (e.g., YubiKey) that you plug into a USB port, or a temporary code you get from a smartphone app (e.g., Google Authenticator or Microsoft Authenticator).
- *Something you are* (an inherent or inherence factor) is a unique biometric characteristic such as facial features, a fingerprint, an iris or retina, a voice, or hand geometry.

MFA through SMS text messaging is neither safe nor recommended. SMS messages are not encrypted, and cybercriminals can intercept and read codes that banks and other organizations send you. Then, with a SIM Swap attack, they can take over your accounts and clean you out.

Platforms like Microsoft Azure can implement conditional access policies that have different authentication requirements depending on certain factors. For example, they might permit access with just a username and password as long as a user is located in the corporate offices. Access from registered offsite locations (based on IP address) would require MFA. Access from other countries could be denied altogether.

SINGLE SIGN-ON

SSO is a process whereby a client performs a one-time login to an authenticating system. That system, in turn, authenticates the client for any other connected systems the client is authorized to access. *Federated authentication* extends the SSO concept to allow users from one organization to use their credentials to access another organization's resources, which mitigates risk by keeping the credentials stored locally to each user's organization, and sharing only a secure token or assertion with the other organization.

SSO cuts down on overwhelming users with numerous username/password combinations, which ultimately aids security since users won't be practicing bad password hygiene (such as writing down their passwords). SSO also boosts productivity: users spend less time reentering passwords, and administrators and help desk workers don't have to field as many password calls. However, because access to multiple systems depends on a single set of credentials, SSO accounts become high-value targets. Strong authentication methods like MFA are recommended to mitigate this risk.

TERMINAL ACCESS CONTROLLER ACCESS-CONTROL SYSTEM PLUS

The authentication methods discussed so far focus primarily on user access to applications and data. But network infrastructure devices—routers and switches—also need secure authentication and authorization. In a simple network, you can access the administration screen for each router and switch by entering a username and password for each device. When an infrastructure becomes complex, with many routers and switches, logging into each device separately can become administratively messy. Authentication, Authorization, and Accounting (AAA) is a centralized framework for managing access to network devices.

As previously mentioned, authentication is proving you are who you say you are. Once you do that, you are authorized to perform certain (but not all) actions and access specific (but not all) data, following the principle of least privilege. Accounting is keeping track (through logs and alerts) of what users do or attempt to do. *Terminal Access Controller Access Control System Plus* (TACACS+) is a networking administration protocol developed by Cisco through which administrators can authenticate, gain authorization, and have their actions logged. TACACS+ uses TCP port 49 by default; separates authorization, authentication, and accounting into different parts; and encrypts the entire packet.

REMOTE AUTHENTICATION DIAL-IN USER SERVICE

Remote Authentication Dial-in User Service (RADIUS) is an IETF standard/protocol and, as its name implies, was created to support ISPs with hundreds or thousands of modems in hundreds of computers to connect to a single central database. While originally designed for dial-up connections, RADIUS still works hard in a huge variety of networks, both wired and wireless, and is the protocol of choice for implementing AAA for network access (in contrast to TACACS+, which is preferred for remote management of routers and switches).

Unlike TACACS+, RADIUS combines authentication and authorization, and only the password in the access request packet is encrypted (the rest of the packet is sent in cleartext). Modern RADIUS uses UDP ports 1812 (authentication) and 1813 (accounting) as defined by the IETF, although older implementations may use UDP ports 1645 (authentication) and 1646 (accounting). RADIUS works in conjunction with 802.1X, described later in this chapter.

LIGHTWEIGHT DIRECTORY ACCESS PROTOCOL

Programs use Lightweight Directory Access Protocol (LDAP) to store, query, and modify directory information used by the network. These directories track aspects of networks, such as username/password hash combinations, computers connected to a domain, signed-in users, or the location of printers. One of the most complex and commonly used databases is Active Directory, found on Microsoft Windows domain controllers. Active Directory powers services like SSO and central management of network information. Every Windows domain controller stores a copy of the Active Directory database.

In most environments, programs and services use LDAP automatically and transparently; administrators rarely interact with it directly. LDAP uses port 389 (TCP and UDP) by default. The older secure version, LDAP over SSL (LDAPS) on TCP port 636, is now largely obsolete; LDAP version 3 and modern deployments rely on LDAP over TLS (STARTTLS) to secure communications.

LDAP supports multiple authentication methods, known as *binding methods*, including simple bind (username/password in cleartext), Simple Authentication and Security Layer (SASL), and anonymous bind. Simple bind should only be used over a secure channel (TLS) because it transmits credentials in cleartext. SASL provides stronger authentication options, such as Kerberos, which is widely used in Active Directory environments.

SECURITY ASSERTION MARKUP LANGUAGE

Security Assertion Markup Language (SAML) is an open standard by which identity providers pass authorization credentials to service providers. SAML enables SSO, allowing a user to log in to multiple websites (Active Directory, email, customer relationship management software, and more) with one set of credentials.

Identity providers and service providers communicate via Extensible Markup Language (XML) to authenticate the user and grant permissions and authorizations to resources and services.

TIME-BASED AUTHENTICATION

As mentioned earlier, MFA includes other factors besides a password (something you know). These include biometrics (something you are) and a *time-based authentication* code (something you have), which is generated and valid for a limited period of time.

Authenticator apps like Google Authenticator and Microsoft Authenticator generate new codes every 30 seconds using the Time-Based One-Time Password (TOTP) algorithm, and you must enter the code in addition to your password to log into accounts. TOTP codes usually expire every 30–60 seconds, limiting the window during which an attacker could use a stolen code. Authenticator apps and hardware tokens rely on a shared secret initially established between the server and the app/token.

Some apps, like Duo, can also send push notifications to your smartphone for one-tap authentication. All you need is one authenticator app, and it works for all the sites you sign into. Similarly, hardware tokens like Yubico's YubiKey and RSA's SecurID generate keys every 30 seconds.

This way, if you fall for a phishing attack or a company you use gets breached and cybercriminals get your password, they can't get into your account without the code, and they can't get the code without your phone. Even if they had your phone, they'd need to know your phone's passcode to use an authenticator app.

NOTE To read my comments on a crazy story in which criminals actually stole phones to bypass MFA, see *nypost.com/2024/02/12/news/tren-de-aragua-gang-uses-migrants-in-nyc-phone-robberies/*.

KERBEROS

Kerberos, a cross-platform authentication protocol, has been the default authentication protocol for Windows domain controllers for over two decades. A client authenticates once to the authentication server and gets a Ticket-Granting Ticket (TGT). From that point, the client can pass the TGT to the Ticket-Granting Service/Server (TGS) to request a ticket to a specific resource. The authentication server and the TGS are part of the key distribution center (KDC). Symmetric encryption is used to ensure the confidentiality of messages.

When the client proves its identity, the server never sees the actual password. Instead, the client derives a secret key from a password hash, which is the result of hashing the password together with a salt to prevent precomputed attacks such as rainbow tables. The server sends a message encrypted with this key. If the client enters the correct password, it can generate the correct secret key and decrypt the message, proving it knows the password without transmitting it. On Windows domain controllers running Active Directory, password hashes are stored in the *C:\Windows\NTDS\ntds.dit* file.

The tickets issued by the KDC contain two encrypted components: one encrypted with the client session key (a temporary symmetric key generated for that session and known only to the client), and one encrypted with the service's secret key, which only the service can decrypt. This ensures that only the intended parties can access and use the session information.

GEOFENCING

Geofencing is the process of using a device's GPS, Wi-Fi, or cellular data to enforce geographical restrictions on access or device usage. Geofencing works in several ways, including as a wireless network security option. Say an organization uses very high-security mobile devices that must never be taken beyond its campus. The organization can install a geofencing application on each device such that if the device leaves the campus perimeter, an alert is triggered or access is restricted.

Although not technically geofencing, similar location-based restrictions can be enforced through IP address ranges. Corporate or user devices that are not in the designated IP subnet/network segment are considered out of range. Streaming services use IP ranges to determine if you are in a country that should not be receiving specific content.

Authorization

Even when a user has identified themselves and authenticated, they don't have free rein over the system or network. *Authorization* is predefined for users and groups and determines which resources they can access. It can also be dynamically evaluated with conditional access policies.

LEAST PRIVILEGE

On any system, it's important to implement the principle of least privilege. As mentioned previously, this is the concept that users and processes should have only the permissions (rights, privileges, and access levels) they need to perform their jobs, and nothing more. Any additional permissions could result in accidental or even malicious CIA compromise. You are not authorized to do anything you want, only what your role requires.

ROLE-BASED ACCESS CONTROL

Role-based access control is a security best practice that assigns permissions to roles, not individual users. *Roles* are sets of permissions granted based on job function, such as Application Manager, Help Desk, or Security Administrator. Those roles are typically assigned to group objects, and when an administrator's user account is added to the group, they inherit the associated permissions.

Assigning resource permissions to user objects would be an administrative nightmare. If a user were being moved from a department with access to 100 resources to another department with access to 100 other resources, you'd have to make 200 changes!

If resource permissions were tied to group objects in that scenario, however, all you'd have to do is remove the user from the original group and add them to the new group—only 2 changes instead of 200. Furthermore, users serving in multiple roles (as is commonly the case) can easily inherit the cumulative permissions of multiple groups.

Physical Security

Physical security is just as important as the logical controls just discussed. In a college lab, for example, you might find servers, routers, and switches that are physically accessible to students. Even when these systems are locked down or attached to racks, students can often still access cables and components.

In enterprise networks, however, servers, routers, and switches are kept in locked rooms where access is restricted to authorized personnel. These networks must implement and enforce strong physical security to avoid putting confidentiality, integrity, and availability at risk.

Cameras

Video surveillance involves monitoring facilities and assets for nefarious or accidental security breaches from authorized or unauthorized parties. An IP camera setup is a common implementation of video surveillance. IP video streams can be monitored by anyone who is authorized to access the network on which the cameras are installed, and the footage can be saved to a hard drive or network storage device. Multiple workstations can simultaneously and easily monitor video streams from many cameras.

Many small office/home office (SOHO) video surveillance systems rely on motion detection systems that start and stop recording based on movement, which saves storage space by filming the bad guys only as they're breaking into your house or stealing your garden gnomes. Door sensors, window sensors, and glass break sensors provide additional security.

Locks

If a room with devices and equipment cannot be secured, the rack should be. If the room houses many types of equipment, all of that equipment needs to be secured into separate racks so that a company can apply extra security to the rack housing its payroll server or ERP system, for example.

Start with the simplest approach: a lock. Locking the door to the network closet or equipment room that holds servers, switches, routers, and other network gear goes a long way toward protecting the network, but it's equally vital to lock racks and cabinets. Typically, in a colocation data center, a company's rack is locked front and back with keys that only that company—and colocation staff for emergencies—can access. This prevents employees from other companies from handling equipment that doesn't belong to them.

Key control—assigning keys to appropriate staff, tracking key assignments, and collecting the keys from departing personnel—is critical here. Guard access by creating and enforcing key control policies. The administrator should never assign a key to someone without completing the appropriate procedures and documentation.

Deception Technologies

Imagine a server with lots of personally identifiable information, including passwords stored in plaintext, credit card numbers, addresses, and even healthcare-related information. Now imagine the administrators deliberately not applying any strong form of cybersecurity to that server. Is this a bad dream? No, it's by design, and the PII is fake.

Honeypots

A server like the one just described is called a *honeypot*—a decoy system deployed on networks to lure potential attackers away from critical systems. Typically, honeypots encourage attackers to stay on the system long enough for administrators to document the attack, observe attacker behaviors, and collect telemetry for improving defensive controls such as firewall rules, intrusion detection signatures, and threat intelligence. Honeypots also allow security specialists to collect information about attackers' tools, techniques, and procedures (TTPs).

Honeypots should include enough simulated protection to convince a cybercriminal that they are real. The level of protection should be somewhat challenging and take some time to exploit. Without any protection at all, they're easily identifiable as honeypots.

Honeynets

A network of honeypots combined with monitoring and analysis infrastructure is called a *honeynet*.

NOTE *Deception software* represents the new wave of honeypots. These decoys can be centrally managed, integrated with other security tools, and deployed through virtualization. Intruders can be deceived at many layers—network, endpoint, application, and data—by decoy workstations, fake browser credentials, phony files, fabricated datasets, and more. For example, a Linux endpoint might be configured to present itself as a particular version of Windows in order to trick malware into attempting exploits against vulnerabilities the system doesn't have. A company could create a decoy document that appears to contain new product designs or embed it with a tracking capability that will indicate when and where it was opened.

Audits and Regulatory Compliance

A data center should conduct thorough *audits*, annually at a minimum, to assess *regulatory compliance* with every applicable industry law and regulation (the standards covered in this section are just the tip of the iceberg). An outside organization that specializes in auditing should perform this audit to avoid any potential conflicts of interest or bias. Afterward, the auditing firm will produce an audit and assessment report that details all of its findings and recommendations.

Data Locality Laws

Data locality laws require organizations to store and process data close to where it originates. Doing so reduces latency, improves performance, and helps maintain availability. Many countries also mandate that certain types of data must be stored and processed within their borders before it can be transmitted elsewhere.

Cloud service providers must place data centers in specific regions to meet these regulatory requirements and to deliver low-latency services to customers. Auditors verify that an organization meets data locality requirements as part of regulatory compliance checks.

PCI DSS

The Payment Card Industry Data Security Standard (PCI DSS) protects credit cards and other financial information exchanged between the organization and external parties. A data center absolutely needs to be PCI DSS compliant.

GDPR

The General Data Protection Regulation (GDPR) gives individuals greater control over their personal data, which affects any business collecting information on European citizens, especially if that company conducts business in the EU. Many US companies updated their data collection and usage policies, especially with data center concerns, because of the GDPR.

ISO/IEC 27001

ISO/IEC 27001, published jointly by the International Organization for Standardization (ISO) and International Electrotechnical Commission (IEC), provides a framework for managing and securing organizational assets. Organizations implement an information security management system (ISMS) to plan, organize, and maintain their security controls effectively.

ISO/IEC 27002

ISO/IEC 27002 provides guidance for organizations to develop, implement, and maintain security policies across all levels of the enterprise.

HIPAA

The Health Insurance Portability and Accountability Act (HIPAA) is a US federal law that governs how organizations handle health information. It establishes rules to protect patient privacy, secure data, and ensure confidentiality, integrity, and availability of sensitive health records.

Network Segmentation Enforcement

It's safe to say that a network failure isn't a happy occurrence. On the low end of the spectrum, losing your home network is super annoying when you want to watch Netflix. Taking it to the other extreme, many systems—from those that run oil refineries to those that keep our electrical infrastructure up and running—are crucial for everyday living. The potential consequences of a network failure in those systems are far worse than missing a show! *Network segmentation* is designed to helps prevent such failures by isolating different parts of a network to limit the scope of outages and security incidents..

The OSI model, particularly the first three layers, is a great way to explain network segmentation:

- **LAYER 1 (PHYSICAL)** Physically separating one network from another (different cabling, switches, or physical locations)
- **LAYER 2 (DATA LINK)** Separating a physically connected network into multiple broadcast domains (think VLANs)
- **LAYER 3 (NETWORK)** Separating broadcast domains into distinct subnets or filtering traffic between them using routing policies
- **ABOVE LAYER 3** Separating networks using VPNs, unique SSIDs, different Windows domains, or virtualization

Segmentation serves multiple purposes. It improves security by limiting lateral movement for attackers, reduces network congestion, optimizes performance, supports compliance with laws and standards, and simplifies troubleshooting when problems arise.

NOTE Reasons for network segmentation include security, performance optimization, load balancing, and compliance.

Internet of Things

The *Internet of Things* (IoT) refers to nontraditional computing devices, smart home appliances, wearables, industrial sensors, medical devices, and more that connect to networks and the internet. Unlike standard computers, many IoT devices have limited processing power and memory, making them unable to support complex security mechanisms.

IoT devices often use lightweight networking protocols such as Message Queuing Telemetry Transport (MQTT) for publish/subscribe messaging; Constrained Application Protocol (CoAP), a RESTful protocol for constrained devices; and mesh networking protocols like

Zigbee, Z-Wave, and Thread. IoT's rapid growth is also driving IPv6 adoption because of the need for a vast number of unique IP addresses.

Due to convenience, cost, or oversight, many IoT devices have default passwords, weak encryption, or no authentication at all, making them attractive targets for attackers. Compromised IoT devices can be exploited for botnets, DDoS attacks, and unauthorized access to sensitive data. Physical attacks are also a concern for devices without tamper-resistant hardware. Because many of these devices are always online, security is frequently overlooked—hence the joke "the S in IoT stands for security."

NOTE One of my favorite IoT-related stories is about a casino that got hacked through its internet-connected fish tank thermometer. Read about it at *thehackernews.com/2018/04/iot-hacking-thermometer.html*.

Network administrators can reduce IoT risks by:

- Inventorying and monitoring devices for unusual traffic or vulnerabilities
- Segmenting IoT devices from critical network resources using separate VLANs or subnets
- Changing default credentials and enforcing strong passwords
- Keeping firmware and software up to date
- Encrypting communications using TLS/HTTPS when possible
- Integrating logging and alerts
- Using stronger authentication, such as device certificates or token-based methods, when supported

IoT devices often communicate with cloud services, so data locality laws and edge computing are important for both regulatory compliance and performance. Understanding the behavior and vulnerabilities of IoT devices is essential for maintaining network performance and security.

Industrial Internet of Things

The *Industrial Internet of Things* (IIoT) consists of devices, sensors, applications, and associated networking equipment, all working together to collect, monitor, and analyze data from industrial operations (such as energy management, transportation, oil and gas, mining, and manufacturing).

The IIoT increases visibility, makes troubleshooting and maintenance easier, streamlines processes, decreases costs, promotes regulatory compliance, and improves safety and security.

SHODAN

Shodan is a search engine for the internet itself, scanning publicly reachable devices rather than web pages. It collects service banners, which reveal metadata like software version, device type, supported features, and sometimes authentication settings. When combined with geolocation and IP data, banners highlight vulnerable devices, including those with hardcoded credentials or backdoors.

Although widely known, Shodan is primarily used by cybersecurity professionals, penetration testers, researchers, and law enforcement to identify and secure devices. It can also generate statistics about device versions, geographic trends, and vulnerabilities.

IoT devices Shodan has found include the following:

- Traffic light controls without login credentials that displayed warnings like *"DEATH MAY OCCUR!!!"*
- Hospital heart monitors and neurosurgery wing power switches
- Webcams, retail cash registers, school labs, and industrial control systems (discussed in the next section)
- Building management systems, including one at Google, that lacked authentication

Shodan can detect almost any network-facing device, including smart TVs, refrigerators, wind turbines, water treatment systems, and electrical grids.

You can read more about Shodan discoveries at *forbes.com/sites/kashmirhill/2013/09/05/the-crazy-things-a-savvy-shodan-searcher-can-find-exposed-on-the-internet/*.

Operation Technology

Operation technology (OT) refers to programmable systems and devices that manage or interact with the environment. This section looks at the ones covered on the CompTIA Network+ exam.

INDUSTRIAL CONTROL SYSTEMS

Any given industrial plant, power grid, or pipeline is full of elements that must be monitored (e.g., temperature, power levels, fill quantity, illumination, and mass) and controlled (e.g., heaters, voltage, pumps, retractable roofs, and valves). Pretty much any industry that makes things, changes things, or moves things—from mousetraps to ice cream—is filled with equipment to do those jobs. Robots control the factory, machines help automate packing and shipping, and air conditioning cools buildings.

The overall system that monitors and controls machines is called an *industrial control system* (ICS). The ICS isn't a new concept; it's been around for over 100 years in the form of monitoring tools, such as telescopes and horns, and control mechanisms like pneumatics. But ICSs really started to take off when computers were integrated with digital sensors and control interfaces.

Today, ICS is moving from stand-alone networks to interconnect with the internet, which carries serious security implications. Competent network techs know the basic ICS variations and the three basic components that make up an ICS: input/output (I/O) functions on the machine, a controller, and the interface for the operator. See Figure 17-11.

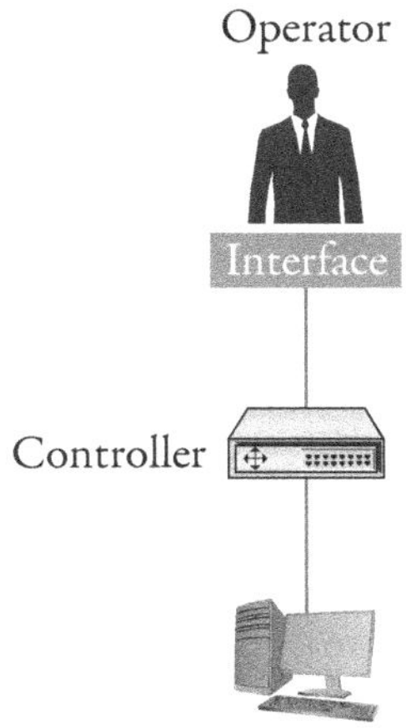

FIGURE 17-11
A simple ICS

Input and output work through sensors and actuators. *Sensors* monitor elements like temperature, for example, and *actuators* modify that temperature. The *controller*, some sort of computer, manages the process, such as "keep the temperature between 50 and 55 degrees Fahrenheit." The *operator* watches some kind of monitor—the interface—and intervenes if necessary.

What if you have multiple machines that accomplish a big task, like in a factory that produces some finished product? For example, imagine a company that manufactures products in stages, with a machine at each stage that needs monitoring and control. Back when computers were really expensive, the controller was a single computer. All the sensors from each of the machines had to provide feedback to that single controller. The controller would compute and then send signals to the various actuators to change things, managing the process. See Figure 17-12.

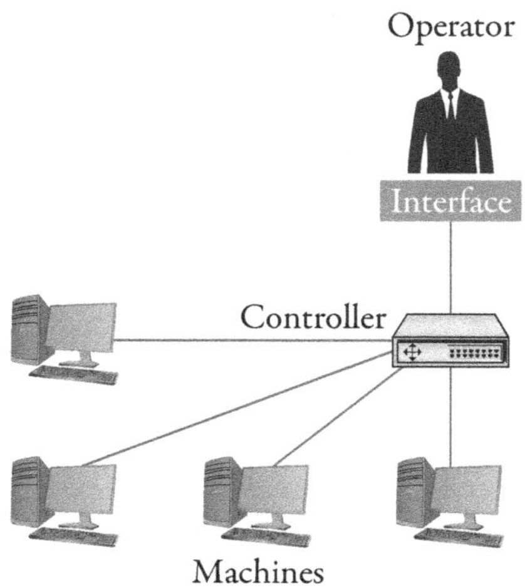

FIGURE 17-12
An early computer-assisted ICS

DISTRIBUTED CONTROL SYSTEMS

As computing power increased and costs decreased, it made much more sense to put smaller controllers directly on each machine to distribute the computing load. This is a *distributed control system* (DCS). In a modern DCS, each local controller connects (eventually) to a centralized controller called the *ICS server*, which manages global changes. See Figure 17-13.

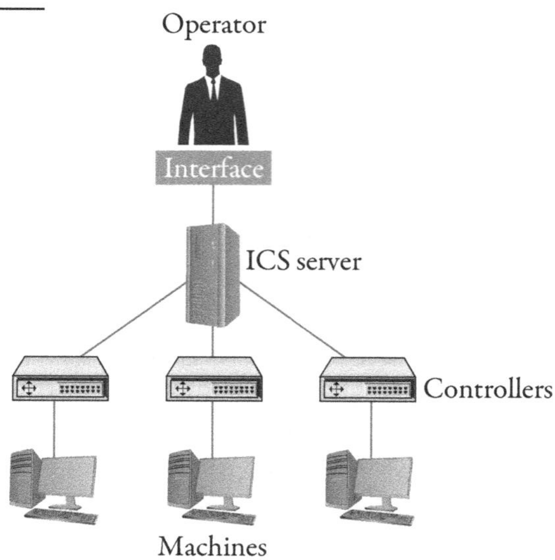

FIGURE 17-13
A simple DCS

SUPERVISORY CONTROL AND DATA ACQUISITION

A *supervisory control and data acquisition* (SCADA) system is a subset of the ICS. Generally, a SCADA system has the same basic components as a DCS but differs in two very important ways. First, a SCADA system is designed for large-scale, distributed processes such as power grids, pipelines, and railroads. Second, due to the distance involved, a SCADA system must function on the premise that remote devices may or may not have ongoing communication with the central control.

Operators interact with controllers through a control or computer called a *human–machine interface* (HMI). Early HMIs were usually custom-made boxes with gauges and switches. Today, an HMI is most likely a PC running a custom, touchscreen interface. See Figure 17-14.

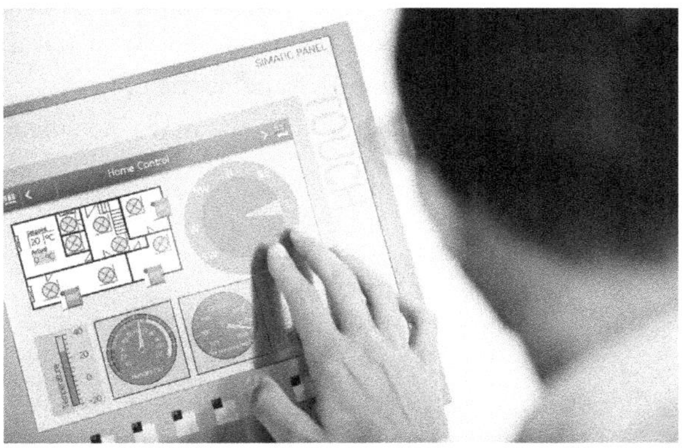

FIGURE 17-14 SIMATIC HMI Basic Panel with a touch screen (© Siemens AG 2014, All rights reserved)

It's important to appreciate that HMIs are not general purpose. You wouldn't run Microsoft Office on an HMI, even if the PC on which it is built is capable of it. It's very common for an HMI to show a single interface that never changes.

In general, a SCADA system is going to be a DCS using servers, an HMI, sensors, and actuators. SCADA systems typically use *remote terminal units* (RTUs) for distributed control. RTUs provide the same function as controllers but have two major differences: they have some autonomy in case they lose the connection with the central control, and they can take advantage of long-distance communication such as telephony, fiber optic, or cellular WANs.

An ICS is by definition a *closed network*—that is, a network that strictly controls who and what may connect to it. However, connectivity is increasing in two main areas. Many SCADA systems use public wireless networks to connect RTUs, and, in some cases, SCADA servers connect to the internet to provide intranet access. The biggest single line of defense for these two scenarios are virtual private networks (VPNs). A VPN is the standard method for securing ICS or SCADA systems that require internet connectivity.

RTUs, PLCs, and SCADA systems often communicate using industrial control protocols such as Modbus, DNP3, or IEC 60870, which are optimized for monitoring and controlling industrial devices.

PROGRAMMABLE LOGIC CONTROLLERS

A DCS makes sense for a process that requires a continuous flow. The sensors provide real-time feedback to the controllers, and the controllers are sophisticated enough to keep the machines functioning properly, making changes via the actuators. In a process that instead follows specific, ordered steps, a different kind of system would make more sense.

A classic *programmable logic controller* (PLC) is a computer that controls a machine according to a set of ordered steps. See Figure 17-15. Take, for example, a machine that produces cakes. Each step in the process of producing a cake follows a certain pattern (add ingredients, mix, bake, etc.) that must proceed in order and at the proper time. The PLC monitors sensors (like timers and oven temperatures) and tells the machine when to take the next step in the process.

FIGURE 17-15 Siemens SIMATIC S7-1500 PLC (© Siemens AG 2014, All rights reserved)

PLCs are often part of a larger control system and can communicate with other controllers or SCADA systems.

NOTE Although ICS predates them, the predominance of Ethernet and TCP/IP has yielded several ICS solutions that use these protocols instead of proprietary cabling systems and communication protocols. If you were building an ICS from scratch today, you would likely use Ethernet as your interconnection of choice.

Guest Network

A *guest network* is a wireless network separate from the primary network used by employees or devices. Any device connected to a guest network will have internet access but won't be able to access anything on the primary network. Isolation is typically enforced through separate SSIDs, VLANs, and firewall rules to prevent unauthorized access to internal systems.

Bring Your Own Device

A *bring your own device* (BYOD) policy and deployment allows employees to use their personal mobile devices and laptops for company work. The company installs its applications on employees' devices, and employees install their corporate email accounts on them. Organizations enforce security through mobile device management (MDM) or enterprise mobility management (EMM). BYOD requires tight controls and separation of personal data from corporate data.

BYOD deployments have benefits and challenges. The benefits are fairly obvious: the organization saves money because employees pay for their own devices, and employees get to use the devices they prefer, which can increase morale and productivity.

On the flip side, BYOD presents challenges with security, end user support, and privacy. A lost or stolen device puts both company information and private information at risk. Can the support staff provide help with every device type and model? Does monitoring software installed on an employee's device remain active during off-hours? What about users who unwittingly bring in devices that are already compromised, jeopardizing the security of other devices (not to mention the organization's data)?

Often, a personal device used to access company data must be enrolled in the company's device management solution to ensure it meets the minimum security standard to store corporate data, including email. Devices should be enrolled in MDM/EMM solutions to enforce minimum security standards. Newer features allow for the separation of business and personal profiles so that when an employee loses their device or leaves the company, only the business data will be deleted, not any of their personal data.

Test Specific

Types of Attacks and Their Network Impact

It's never been a fair fight, and it never will be. As a cybersecurity defender, you have to protect all of your company's vulnerabilities. Cybercriminals, on the other hand, only have to exploit one. Attackers can choose from many effective technology-based attacks, but they also have great success with social engineering attacks that instead prey on gullible and naive humans.

Denial-of-Service and Distributed Denial-of-Service

Denial-of-service (DoS) and *distributed denial-of-service* (DDoS) attacks attempt to compromise system and network availability. Internet-based servers are generally designed to handle a large volume of requests, so a single-source DoS attack often has limited impact on enterprise-grade systems (though it can still disrupt smaller or midsize servers). Far more menacing, and far more common, are DDoS attacks—coordinated attacks that use hundreds, thousands, or even millions of infected computers under a single operator's command and control.

DDoS operators usually don't own these computers but instead use malware (discussed later in this chapter) to take control of them. These devices can include poorly secured computers, IoT devices, or other internet-connected endpoints. The security and robustness of a public-facing server (accessible through the internet) depends on the organization hosting it as well as whoever is responsible for it within that organization. Take a college as an example. Both the college's main website and its course enrollment website would have higher-capacity servers than those of individual departments, but they could still fall victim to a DDoS attack. A specific department might be dealing with faculty funded and acquired servers that are less secure, less robust, and often overlooked, but they really should be protected from DDoS attacks as well. Similarly, in business, some departments with shoestring budgets use discarded devices and equipment for critical business services without considering DDoS defense mechanisms for them.

Mitigation options include DDoS protection services that detect and filter abnormal traffic, rate limiting, upstream traffic scrubbing, and firewalls designed to absorb or block malicious traffic.

VLAN Hopping

An older type of attack that still comes up from time to time is called *VLAN hopping*, which comes in two forms. The first, *switch spoofing*, is when an attacker sends traffic to the switch, convincing the switch to change the attacker's port from an access port to a trunk port. This allows the attacker to read traffic from and inject traffic to other VLANs.

The second form, a VLAN *double tagging attack*, injects traffic from one VLAN into another by sending two 802.1Q tags (which mark frames with VLAN identifiers for VLAN tagging). The attacker sends a frame with an outer 802.1Q tag matching their own access port VLAN and an inner tag matching the target VLAN. For this attack to work, the trunk link from the attacker's switch to another switch must use a native VLAN that matches the attacker's access port VLAN. When the frame reaches the trunk port, the switch strips off the outer tag and forwards the frame, with the inner tag still intact, to the switch at the other end of the trunk link. The receiving switch then sends the traffic to access ports in the VLAN specified by the inner tag (as well as to any trunk ports), allowing the attacker to inject traffic (which could be malicious or part of a DoS) into a VLAN other than their own.

VLAN hopping is rarely seen today because modern switches are all designed to prevent it by dropping all tagged frames received on access ports.

To prevent a switch spoofing attack, hardcode all access ports as such and disable Dynamic Trunking Protocol (DTP).

To prevent a double tagging attack, change the native VLAN on all trunk ports to an unused VLAN and explicitly tag frames from the native VLAN.

MAC Flooding

Ethernet switches learn where hosts are by analyzing the source Media Access Control (MAC) address field in Ethernet frames as the frames enter switch ports. The switches maintain mappings of MAC addresses to ports in a table stored in RAM called the MAC address table, source address table (SAT), or content addressable memory (CAM) table, as discussed in Chapter 6. Each switch can store a specific number of MAC addresses in this table. The size of the table and the number of entries vary by switch.

In a *MAC flooding attack*, also known as a *CAM overflow attack*, an attacker connects a device to a port and runs a tool or script that sends thousands of Ethernet frames into the port with different, randomly generated MAC addresses. The switch happily enters each MAC address into the MAC address table, associating each address with the same physical port as the attacker. Eventually, the MAC address table runs out of space, and the switch simply starts flooding all traffic from all hosts out of all ports except the originating port. This attack essentially turns a switch into a hub—the very device that the switch and its MAC address table put out of business.

With this attack, the attacker is now able to *sniff* (capture and read) every single frame sent into the switch. The attacker could be an insider, physically on the premises, or an outsider who has compromised an internal system and can generate traffic from that system. Confidentiality is at great risk. Tools like macof, part of the dsniff suite of tools, can generate hundreds of thousands of random MAC addresses and flood them through a switch, either for cybersecurity purposes (to test your switch's resistance to such an attack) or malicious ones.

To prevent a MAC flooding attack, use the techniques discussed in the "Port Security" section later in this chapter.

On-Path Attack

In an *on-path attack* (previously known as a *man-in-the-middle attack*), an attacker inserts themselves into the communication path between two systems, covertly intercepting traffic. The attacker may simply read the data or modify it before passing it along to the intended destination.

On wireless networks, an attacker might create a rogue access point that nearby clients mistakenly connect to, allowing the attacker to monitor or manipulate their traffic. Once clients connect, the attacker can silently monitor their traffic and capture sensitive information such as passwords, shared keys, or session data.

On wired or wireless LANs, attackers commonly perform on-path attacks using an *Address Resolution Protocol (ARP) poisoning/spoofing* attack, described next.

ARP Poisoning/Spoofing

An *ARP poisoning/spoofing* attack is a specific type of on-path attack in which the attacker forges ARP messages. The attacker intercepts, relays, and possibly alters the communication, while the two parties believe they are communicating directly and privately with each other.

Consider a network with a router, a DHCP server, and two hosts plugged into a switch, as shown in Figure 17-16.

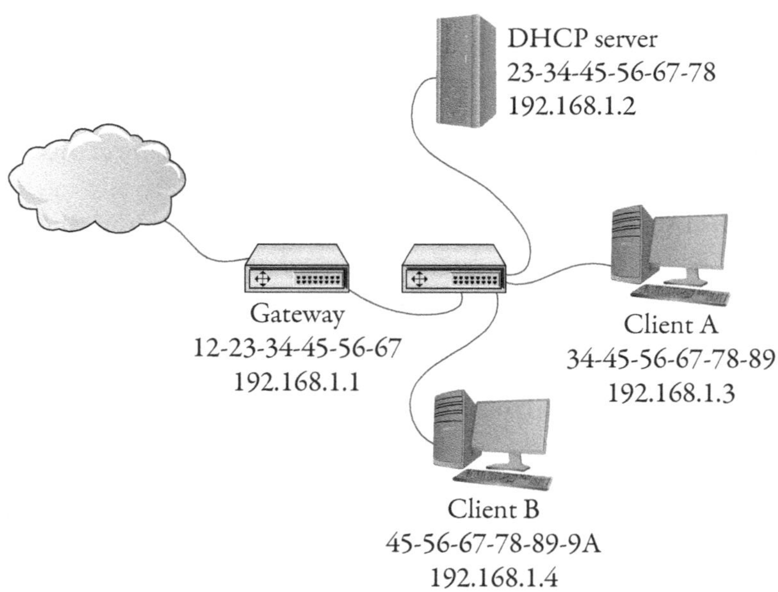

FIGURE 17-16 The network before the attack

When Host A has remote traffic to send, it must first send a broadcast ARP request to find the MAC address of the default gateway (if the entry isn't already cached). The gateway sends its MAC address to Host A in a unicast ARP reply. Host A caches this address and then uses it in subsequent frames as the destination MAC address for remote traffic. Since most (if not all) traffic is destined for devices on different networks, a gateway's MAC address typically remains in a host's ARP cache.

Now suppose that the clients' ARP caches show that the MAC address of the default gateway, 192.168.1.1, is 12-23-34-45-56-67. See Figure 17-17.

ARP Cache

	MAC	IP
Gateway	12-23-34-45-56-67	192.168.1.1
DHCP	23-34-45-56-67-78	192.168.1.2
Client A	34-45-56-67-78-89	192.168.1.3
Client B	45-56-67-78-89-9A	192.168.1.4

FIGURE 17-17 The clients' ARP cache before the attack. Clients won't have entries for themselves in their ARP cache.

Using tools like Cain and Abel, Ettercap, or arpspoof, the on-path attacker (the evil computer shown in Figure 17-18) sends out ARP messages claiming that the MAC address of 192.168.1.1 is actually FE-ED-DC-CB-BA-A9. These messages can be sent as requests or replies, unicast to a specific host or broadcast (like a standard ARP request) to the entire network. The clients look at this ARP and say, "Hmm, it was 12-23-34-45-56-67. I guess they put a new NIC in that device. I'll update my ARP cache accordingly." Each client overwrites the correct gateway MAC address with the evil computer's MAC address.

The evil computer then poisons the gateway's ARP cache by sending another ARP message that changes the MAC address the gateway has on file for Client A (34-45-56-67-78-89) to the evil computer's MAC address (FE-ED-DC-CB-BA-A9). This would need to be done for each client whose traffic will be intercepted.

Now, when the person sitting in front of Client A wants to go to a website, Client A gets the IP address of the web server from its local DNS server and uses it as the destination IP address in the outgoing IP header. After determining that the destination is not on the same network, Client A retrieves the "gateway" MAC address—which now points to the evil computer—from its ARP cache. Thus, instead of sending the traffic to the actual default gateway, the switch sends it to the evil computer (see Figure 17-19).

	MAC	IP
Gateway	~~12-23-34-45-56-67~~ FE-ED-DC-CB-BA-A9	192.168.1.1
DHCP	23-34-45-56-67-78	192.168.1.2
Client A	34-45-56-67-78-89	192.168.1.3
Client B	45-56-67-78-89-9A	192.168.1.4

FIGURE 17-18 The clients' ARP cache after the attack

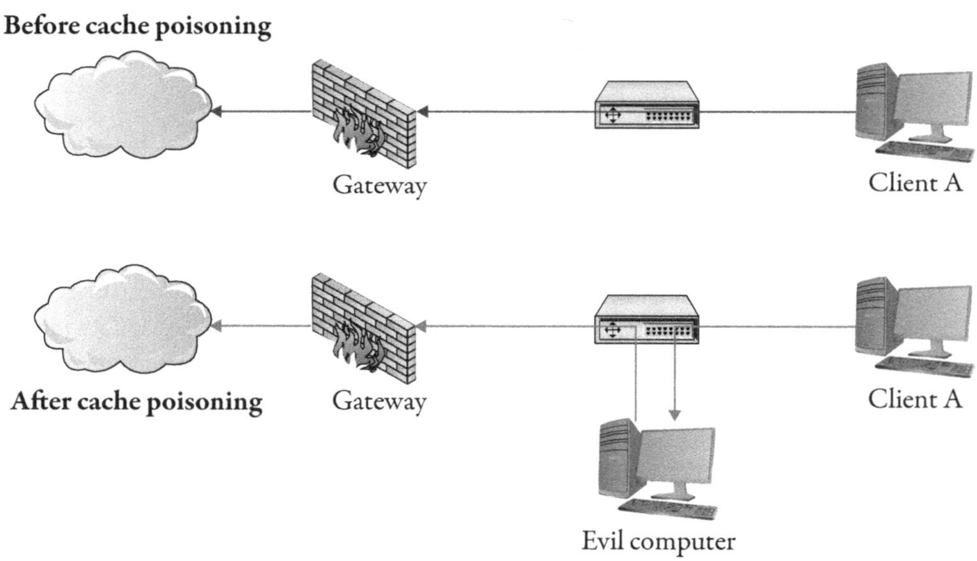

FIGURE 17-19 ARP cache poisoning, before and after

Next, the evil computer reframes the packet. The new source MAC address is that of the evil computer, and the new destination MAC address is that of the real default gateway. The normal IP routing process gets the packet to the web server, which will send return traffic back to the evil computer because of the poisoned gateway ARP entry. The attacker will now be able to read all the data exchanged between the Client A user and the website. The attacker can modify the traffic as desired before sending it back to the victim. Even with HTTPS and HTTP Strict Transport Security (HSTS), attackers can still capture metadata like

IP addresses and DNS queries, execute downgrade attacks on misconfigured servers, or exploit unencrypted traffic from legacy and IoT devices.

To prevent an ARP poisoning/spoofing attack, use dynamic ARP inspection (DAI) or private VLANs, neither of which is covered in the CompTIA Network+ objectives (Google them anyway!).

DNS Poisoning

Another common attack today is *DNS poisoning*, also known as *DNS cache poisoning*, in which an attacker sends unsolicited DNS answers to caching DNS servers. The server then caches the incorrect information, redirecting users to malicious sites even when they enter the correct domain name. For example, if an attacker changed the cache on the RIT DNS server to associate *www.rit.edu* with an IP address for a malicious website (such as a phishing site or one containing a drive-by-download exploit kit, both described shortly), any downstream RIT client making requests would be given that incorrect IP address and led to that site. If this happened to an ISP's DNS server cache, all ISP customers would be affected. If it happened to a root server or an authoritative TLD DNS server, all ISPs and customers downstream would be affected through the poisoned referrals provided by these servers. The false DNS resource records would even make their way to DNS caches on user machines. Furthermore, cybercriminals could change the time-to-live (TTL) values to keep those false entries in cache for a long time.

An incident with China's "Great Firewall," in which Chinese DNS servers intentionally map blocked sites to an incorrect IP address, provides a real-world example of large-scale DNS poisoning effects. In 2010, a non-Chinese ISP accidentally misconfigured its DNS servers to query those Chinese DNS resolvers. As a result, it cached the incorrect, censorship-based DNS records locally. Other ISPs that relied on this provider's DNS data then pulled the same poisoned records, spreading them across parts of the global internet. For a short period, users outside China—including in the United States—were unable to reach sites such as Twitter (now known as X), Facebook, and YouTube because their DNS lookups returned the false IP addresses China had been using for censorship.

DNS Spoofing

A related attack is *DNS spoofing*, in which an attacker impersonates a legitimate DNS server and sends forged DNS responses directly to a client or resolver. In this attack, the goal is not necessarily to poison a cache, but to trick the victim into accepting a false response before the legitimate DNS server replies. If the client accepts the spoofed response, it will use the incorrect IP address supplied by the attacker, redirecting the user to a malicious site even though the correct domain name was requested.

For example, an attacker on the same network as a victim could monitor DNS queries and quickly respond with a fake DNS answer that associates a legitimate domain name, such as *www.flcc.edu*, with the IP address of a phishing website. If the attacker's response arrives first, the client may accept it and connect to the malicious server. The impact of DNS spoofing is often limited to specific clients or sessions, rather than affecting all users of a caching DNS server as with DNS poisoning.

DNS spoofing exploits the fact that traditional DNS does not authenticate responses.

DNS Snooping

Yet another attack on DNS today is *DNS snooping*, which is a form of surveillance. By default, DNS queries and responses are sent in plaintext, which allows ISPs, cybercriminals targeting public Wi-Fi networks, governments, and others to see (breach of confidentiality), change (breach of integrity), or even censor (breach of availability) DNS traffic.

DNS Attack Mitigations

Because DNS is a foundational part of the internet, it is a frequent target for attacks like poisoning, spoofing, and snooping. These attacks exploit the trust that clients and servers place in DNS responses. Several mitigation techniques have been developed to defend against these threats. Domain Name System Security Extensions (DNSSEC) protect against DNS poisoning and spoofing by ensuring that DNS responses are authentic and have not been tampered with. DNS over TLS (DoT) and DNS over HTTPS (DoH) protect against DNS snooping by encrypting DNS queries and responses, preventing eavesdropping and on-path attacks.

NOTE DNSEC, DoH, and DoT are included in the CompTIA Network+ exam objectives under the Network Operations domain. To follow naturally from the three DNS attacks just mentioned, they are being discussed here rather than in the mitigation-focused "Network Security Features, Defense Techniques, and Solutions" section at the end of the chapter.

DOMAIN NAME SYSTEM SECURITY EXTENSIONS

DNSSEC is an addition to DNS that uses public key cryptography to sign DNS responses, providing authentication (verifying that they came from the correct source) and integrity (ensuring that an attacker hasn't changed them). DNSSEC does not encrypt DNS queries. It only validates authenticity. A chain of trust, from the root servers to the authoritative TLD DNS servers to the second-level domain (SLD) DNS servers, establishes the destination domain. Each higher-level entity validates each lower-level one: the root zone verifies the TLDs, which in turn verify the SLDs. The root zone is vetted through a thorough security procedure that includes root-signing ceremonies held alternately at two secure facilities: one in El Segundo, California, and one in Culpeper, Virginia.

DNS OVER TLS AND DNS OVER HTTPS

DoT and DoH are protocols designed to prevent DNS snooping by encrypting DNS queries and responses. Encryption ensures that eavesdroppers cannot read the queries or responses (confidentiality) and prevents attackers from covertly modifying the data (integrity). Both DoT and DoH encrypt DNS traffic between a DNS client and DNS server. This prevents DNS queries and responses from being intercepted, modified, or spoofed by an on-path attacker. However, it doesn't protect against compromised or untrustworthy DNS servers as DNSSEC does.

DoT uses port 853 and TLS, which allows network administrators to easily identify, monitor, or block DNS traffic. DoT is commonly deployed in system-wide configurations—for example, in routers and OS-level settings.

DoH uses port 443 and HTTPS, which makes it harder for network administrators to detect or filter DNS traffic, since it blends in with regular web traffic. As a result, DoH can circumvent network-based filtering, which has implications for enterprise security policies. Thus, DoH is more likely to succeed in bypassing censorship and surveillance, but it can be challenging from an enterprise management perspective. DoH is commonly implemented in individual applications like web browsers.

NOTE DoT uses TLS. DoH uses HTTPS. TLS is the encryption layer. HTTPS is a secure version of HTTP that runs over TLS. Anytime HTTPS is used, that implies TLS is used. However, as with DoT, not all TLS connections use HTTPS.

Rogue Devices and Services

Rogue devices and services running on a network, whether introduced through malicious means or by users just trying to "get something done," are severe vulnerabilities.

ROGUE DHCP SERVER

Most DHCP servers in a company are on a subnet with other servers, such as DNS servers. In other words, clients are not on the same subnet as their servers. As discussed in Chapter 7, relay agents convert DHCP Discover broadcasts into unicasts and forward them to the DHCP servers, which return DHCP Offers through the relay agents back to the clients. If a client gets multiple DHCP Offers (there should be more than one DHCP server for fault tolerance and load balancing), it usually accepts the first offer.

As you can imagine, a DHCP server on a client's own subnet can respond to a DHCP Discover broadcast a lot quicker than legitimate DHCP servers, which have to wait for traffic to be routed through the relay agents across multiple hops. An attacker can exploit this by placing a rogue DHCP server on a client subnet. The rogue DHCP server will answer a DHCP Discover message with a DHCP Offer containing the normal information given out to the clients in that autonomous system, with one small difference: it lists itself as the default gateway!

When clients send traffic off their network and ARP for their default gateway's MAC address, they'll contact the attacker's MAC address instead, inadvertently sending all remote traffic directly to the attacker.

Several programs can detect the presence of a rogue DHCP server, and they all follow the same algorithm: send a DHCP Discover message and check if any DHCP Offers come back from IP addresses that are not on an authorized DHCP servers list.

To prevent a rogue DHCP server attack, enable DHCP snooping (which is not covered in the CompTIA Network+ objectives—Google it anyway!).

ROGUE AP

A *rogue access point* (AP) is simply an unauthorized access point. Rogue access points have tortured every wireless network since the day Linksys came out with the first cheap wireless router back in the early 2000s. Most rogue APs are evil, but some are installed by authorized users seeking to connect to the wired network from a location that doesn't have decent Wi-Fi coverage from existing authorized APs (without authorization). Evil rogue act as a backdoor to a network or an on-path attack, grabbing usernames and passwords, among other sensitive information.

To prevent a rogue AP attack, use wireless intrusion prevention systems (WIPSs) or wireless LAN controllers (like the ones from Cisco) that have rogue AP detection built in.

EVIL TWIN

The most infamous form of a rogue AP is called an *evil twin*, which intentionally mimics an existing service set identifier (SSID; the name of a Wi-Fi network) to get people to connect to it instead of the legitimate AP. Evil twins work best in unsecured networks such as those you see in airports and hotels. It's easy to access the wrong SSID. Some 802.11 devices are notorious for moving their list of discovered SSIDs in such a way that you think you're clicking one SSID when you're accidentally clicking another.

Attackers can easily create an evil twin SSID to mimic common public SSIDs like AT&T's attwifi hotspot service and trick unsuspecting people into connecting to it. Using enterprise authentication (WPA2/WPA3-Enterprise) and carefully verifying SSIDs can reduce risk.

Social Engineering

Human and environmental attacks rely not on technology, but rather on how humans behave in certain situations. Humans are, have been, and will always be the weakest link in any security implementation. Any hardware or software security implementation can be undone extremely quickly by a gullible or naive human.

Social engineering is an art and science cybercriminals use to convince people to grant their requests. Social engineering attacks use psychological tricks to get victims to reveal information they normally wouldn't so the criminals can access systems, networks, and infrastructures. It's much easier to ask someone for a password than it is to break into a system and get it.

The following are some examples of social engineering tactics:

- "Hello, this is tech support. We need your help to fix a problem with your account. Can you help us out today? Okay, great. What's your password?"
- "Hi, I'm from corporate. Today I'm just doing a security assessment, and I need you to check out a few things for me."
- "I'm here to fix the heating in the data center. See the logo on my polo shirt?"
- "Hold the door, please. I forgot my badge."
- *Look what I found in the employee parking lot—a flash drive labeled "Corporate finances, top secret." Let me plug it in and see what's on it.*

These are all scary examples of social engineering, the only threat to cybersecurity that doesn't involve technology. You can patch a computer, but you can't patch people. You can teach them the signs of social engineering, but they forget and make mistakes. As computer vulnerabilities get more difficult for cybercriminals to exploit, people become their most obvious targets. Skilled social engineers fool victims with their body language, facial expressions, voice and tone, word choice, and more:

- "I really need you to help me right now! Time is of the essence!"
- "This is Bob Jones. We met last year at the company picnic. You know me."
- "Alice told me that you're a great worker, willing to help out whenever you can."
- "If you don't give me the information, I'm going to complain to your manager."
- "I'm the one who actually signs your checks. You don't want me on your bad side."
- "Your colleague did this for me last week."

Using social engineering, cybercriminals can commit fraud, network intrusion, industrial espionage, and identity theft, and otherwise disrupt systems and networks. Potential targets include telephone companies, answering services, big name corporations, financial institutions, military and governmental agencies, hospitals, and even you!

The social engineering process starts with information gathering. Attackers do their homework to figure out what the victims like and don't like. They find any potential weaknesses and vulnerabilities of the victims that can be exploited. Online information is a great resource. In many cases, companies don't even realize how much public-facing information could be used against them in a social engineering attack. Employees' names, titles, phone numbers, and more are just sitting there, waiting for an opportunist to take advantage.

Why is social engineering so effective? People want to help others. They don't want to get in the way, especially if someone is carrying a clipboard and glancing at it as if they're completing an assignment. Just look and act like you belong there, and no one will ask questions. People don't like conflict or to question authority. They *do* like free stuff and will sometimes give out usernames, passwords, or other information to participate in some random survey in exchange for a gift. That free chocolate bar could prove to be very expensive in the long run, though.

Mitigation of social engineering involves teaching users right from wrong. Enforce organizational security policies and test employees to make sure they're following them. Incentivizing them with legitimate rewards can help ensure they're not tempted by offers from cybercriminals.

PHISHING

The digital form of social engineering is called *phishing*. It involves sending out "bait" to a large number of people in hopes that some users will reveal usernames, passwords, credit card details, and other sensitive information. It is primarily accomplished through email but can also occur through SMS text messages (*smishing*) or phone calls and voicemail (*vishing*).

When a user clicks a link in a phishing email, a web page opens that looks and feels like a legitimate site (such as PayPal, eBay, Facebook, or LinkedIn). Therefore, the user feels safe and secure in entering sensitive information, which goes directly to the attacker.

Simply visiting phishing sites (without clicking anything on the page) could install malware on a victim's machine. The page could use a *drive-by download exploit kit*, which automatically collects information from a victim's machine; finds vulnerabilities in operating systems, browsers, and other software such as video players; determines appropriate exploits; and executes malware. These exploit kits are usually hosted on a legitimate website that's been hacked or delivered through third-party advertisements.

Phishing attacks can also:

- Ask users to click a link to view content or install a program, which actually installs malware
- Pop up *scareware* windows prompting users to scan for viruses, which install malware when clicked
- Display phone numbers for victims to call, allowing social engineers to obtain their credit card numbers or gain remote access to "fix" nonexistent problems on their machines
- Include attachments such as ZIP files or Microsoft Office documents with macros. While modern malware scanners often detect malicious ZIP contents, enabling macros in Office files can still allow malware to execute on the user's machine. In fact, this is exactly how the 2015 Ukraine power grid cyberattack started.

Phishing often involves sending emails to random addresses that may or may not be valid (such as *bob1@gmail.com*, *bob2@gmail.com*, *bob3@gmail.com*, and so on). *Spear phishing* takes this to another level by targeting users in a specific company (*alice@company.org*, *bob@company.org*, *eve@company.org*, etc.). *Whaling* attacks extend this further still by going after the "big fish" of a company, such as a senior executive (*ceo@company.org*, *daboss@company.org*, *ciso@company.org*, etc.).

There are many ways to spot phishing emails and fake sites:

- **SUSPICIOUS URLS** On desktop machines, hovering over a link before clicking it shows you the real destination address. On mobile devices, pressing and holding a link is the equivalent of previewing it, but you risk accidentally tapping it instead; instead, open a new browser window or tab and type the URL directly. Legitimate domain names in the wrong position (linkedin.attackersite.com) are malicious. HTTP instead of HTTPS can indicate a fake site.
- **GENERIC GREETINGS** Using a greeting like "Dear customer" instead of your actual name is often a sign of something amiss.
- **SPOOFED OR SUSPICIOUS EMAIL ADDRESSES** Email addresses might appear legitimate at first glance but can have subtle differences (like one character being off) or even be noticeably wrong.
- **EXCESSIVE INFORMATION REQUESTS** Be suspicious if you're asked to fill in information that should not be required.
- **URGENT OR THREATENING LANGUAGE** Phishing emails often include a desperate story that asks the user to act urgently or even threaten the user with consequences for not acting.
- **POOR FORMATTING** The appearance of the email or website, including the quality of images, is another giveaway. Images of text, instead of actual text, are suspicious, as they can't be keyword scanned by phishing filters. An email consisting of just a single image or a single web link is highly suspicious.
- **IMPROPER SPELLING AND GRAMMAR** While it's true that many phishing campaigns originate from non-English-speaking countries, these errors may be introduced deliberately to filter out all but the most gullible recipients, evade spam filters, and appear more authentic (that is, having a few typos makes it seem like a human wrote the email).
- **GENERIC SIGNATURES** As with generic greetings, phishing emails often include a generic signature without any contact information.
- **ATTACHMENTS OR SCRIPTS** These are often a dead giveaway.

To avoid being the victim of a phishing attack, never click any links in email; instead, type in URLs directly. Never download and open any attachments without verifying that they are legitimate by contacting the alleged sender via email (compose a new one instead of replying to the message you received) or phone.

NOTE Hovering over a link is becoming less reliable. This article from August 2021 explains why: *microsoft.com/en-us/security/blog/2021/08/26/widespread-credential-phishing-campaign-abuses-open-redirector-links/.*

DUMPSTER DIVING

Dumpster diving is another information-gathering technique used by social engineers. Attackers will dive into corporate dumpsters and sift through trash cans looking for any useful information. They're not really looking for obvious things like passwords; phone directories, calendars, company memos, and more can prove to be even more valuable.

Suppose an attacker finds a discarded invoice from an HVAC company or a computer contractor. All the attacker needs to do is make a knockoff polo shirt with a logo and show up for some "maintenance repairs." The next step is exploitation. Social engineers develop relationships, rapport, trust, and credibility with their victims. Alternatively, they might threaten, intimidate, impersonate, use scare tactics, and convey a sense of urgency. In this step, the attackers get what they want by any means necessary.

SHOULDER SURFING

Shoulder surfing is the process of surreptitiously monitoring people ("looking over their shoulder") as they are accessing a system, trying to ascertain their passwords, PINs, or other personal information. Shoulder surfing is an old but still very common method of social engineering.

TAILGATING AND PIGGYBACKING

Tailgating is when an unauthorized person enters a room or area through a door just unlocked and opened by an authorized person. The authorized person has no idea that an unauthorized person followed them in. *Piggybacking* is very similar except that the authorized person is aware that they are letting someone in but not necessarily that the person is unauthorized. It exploits the human tendency to "hold the door" for someone coming in behind you.

Tailgating and piggybacking are especially easy in large organizations where not all employees know each other. If the unauthorized person dresses like everyone else and has a badge that looks legitimate, they probably won't be challenged. And if they're also holding an armload of gear, who could blame you for holding the door for them?

Guards can help mitigate tailgating and piggybacking attempts because they get to know everyone's faces. They are there to protect assets; secure building, room, and office access; and patrol the facility. The guard station can serve as a command center for security systems such as video surveillance and key control. Like all humans, however, security guards can be subject to attacks such as social engineering, so proper training is essential.

Another option to prevent tailgating is the use of turnstiles, which can be connected to the badge access system to allow only one person through at a time. An alternative is an access control vestibule (also known as a *mantrap*), a small room with two doors that both require scan access but can't be open at the same time.

Malware

Malware, short for *malicious software*, is intended to damage or break systems, steal or manipulate data, conduct espionage, or gain unauthorized control on a computer system or network without the user's knowledge or approval. There are many different types of malware, but the two most often confused ones are viruses and worms.

EXAM TIP Although the CompTIA Network+ exam objectives do not list specific types of malware, you will be expected to know about the ones covered in this section.

Most malware propagates via phishing, unsecured ports, and stolen credentials.

VIRUSES AND WORMS

Let's start with some background definitions. A *computer program*, also known as *software* or an *application*, is a collection of instructions that use algorithms to solve problems or accomplish tasks. These instructions are executed by the central processing unit (CPU), the brain of the computer.

Viruses and worms differ in three primary ways. First, a virus injects malicious code into a program's instructions. When the CPU executes the infected program, it also executes the malicious code. Just like a biological virus, a computer virus needs a host file to infect—a program, a data file, or even the boot sector of a hard drive—and that file must be run for the virus to execute. In contrast, a worm does not infect host files. It stands alone in its own file.

The second difference relates to how viruses and worms spread. Viruses can spread and replicate to other files on the same machine automatically, but spreading and replicating to other machines requires human intervention (such as when someone forwards an email attachment). Worms propagate all by themselves across networks all around the world by exploiting vulnerabilities in protocols, networks, and configurations. Worms can get into your email system, compose messages, attach themselves to emails, and mimic content from trusted sources, but modern email filters often prevent this.

Third, most viruses contain a malicious payload intended to cause harm, but a worm doesn't require one (although some worms do have one). Worms are often used instead to build *botnets*—networks of infected computers, known as *zombies*—for DDoS attacks (described earlier in this chapter). An attacker can use a worm to infect thousands of machines, with each infected machine spreading the worm to thousands more. The attacker can then command all of the zombies to simultaneously flood a target server with traffic, overwhelming it.

MACRO VIRUSES

A *macro virus* is any type of virus that exploits application macros to replicate and activate. Macros exist in applications with built-in macro languages, such as Microsoft Excel, and can be programmed to handle repetitive tasks. Modern Office applications disable macros by default and prompt the user, so exploitation requires social engineering.

LOGIC BOMBS

A *logic bomb* is a type of malware sometimes embedded in malware, scripts, or applications and distinguished by its delayed execution. A certain date, time, or event triggers a logic bomb to run. From the malware author's perspective, the longer the malware remains undetected, the better. This allows the malware to silently spread and then, after a period of time, boom—it executes simultaneously on all infected systems.

One famous story involves a software engineer who suspected he was going to get fired. He programmed the company's software such that if human resources generated payroll and his name was missing, it would trigger actions detrimental to the company. He knew that if he were fired, his computer rights would be revoked first, so this was his way of getting revenge before the fact. If he was wrong, nothing would happen. But as it turns out, he was right. He got fired, and his logic bomb did a lot of damage to the company and its data. He got caught and was handed a stiff fine and prison sentence.

Another programmer wrote a logic bomb into his company's software before resigning. He was hoping to be rehired at a big premium to save the company from the malware that he had launched. Yet another programmer wrote logic bombs into company sites all around the world. The company sent him on trips worldwide to fix these issues, and he gained fame and fortune doing so . . . until he got caught.

TROJAN HORSES

A *Trojan horse* is malware named after the famous story about Greek troops hiding inside a big wooden horse during the Trojan War. Thinking the Greeks were gone, the Trojans took this horse into their city as a trophy. At night, the soldiers hiding in the horse jumped out, opened the gates, and let in the rest of the Greek army. They destroyed Troy and ended the war.

The malware version of a Trojan horse works the same way: what appears to be a legitimate program also contains hidden malicious code. There is a social engineering component as well in that Trojan horses do not replicate on the local machine or across a network. Trojan horses require user action to install and typically rely on social engineering. When users click links for free screensavers, ringtones, or WeatherBugs, they get all those things but also unknowingly install malicious programs. These hidden programs can damage computers, spread malware, spy on user activities, and use the computer as part of a botnet.

RATs

A *remote administration tool* (RAT) is a piece of software used to remotely access or control a computer. This tool can be used legitimately by systems administrators to access client computers or servers, but cybercriminals can also use it maliciously to control a system without the user's knowledge. In that case, it's known as a *remote access Trojan*. Remote access Trojans are often included in pirated software (including patches and cracked games) delivered via email attachments, Trojans, phishing links, or malicious downloads. Most popular RATs can perform keystroke logging, packet capture, screen capture, camera capture, file access, code execution, registry management, password sniffing, and more. After the infection, they perform unauthorized operations while hiding their presence from the user.

ROOTKITS

A *rootkit* is a set of software tools that allow an attacker to maintain persistent and often undetectable access to a computer. Rootkits can hide their presence, conceal installed malware, and even sanitize logs or repair timestamps to cover the attacker's activity. They can operate in user mode (running like normal applications and hiding files, processes, or registry entries at the user level) or in kernel mode (operating at the core of the operating system, which makes them harder to detect and able to conceal nearly anything on the system).

Rootkits often also install *backdoors*, malware that cybercriminals leave behind after initially penetrating a system so they can bypass the normal authentication process the next time. It's like breaking into a physical location and propping open an unmonitored window or door to get back in later.

ADWARE AND SPYWARE

Adware and spyware are two types of programs that are similar to malware in that they try to hide themselves to some extent. *Adware* monitors the types of websites you visit and uses that information to generate and automatically display targeted advertisements, usually pop-up windows. It's often bundled with a product or package and it's common in *shareware*, software offered on a free trial basis with limited functionality until the user pays to continue. Adware isn't inherently malicious, but many adware makers use sneaky methods to trick users into installing it, such as displaying web pages with deceptive messages ("Your computer is infected with a virus—click here to scan NOW!"). Some of these ads actually do install malware if you click them, so avoid doing so.

Spyware covertly monitors and reports on a user's activities for financial gain. This could include selling the data to third parties, redirecting web activity to ad sites, and presenting targeted ads and pop-ups through adware. The type of information spyware collects depends on the program, but may include browsing history, keystrokes, or email contacts. Some spyware makers bundle their products with ads to make them look innocuous. Adware, therefore, can contain spyware.

Some modern potentially unwanted programs (PUPs) combine adware and spyware functionality.

For mitigation of all types of malware, use a good anti-malware program, as well as Windows Security real-time protection.

Test Specific

Network Security Features, Defense Techniques, and Solutions

Defending against the kinds of attacks you've just read about requires a layered approach combining network security features, defense techniques, and monitoring solutions. This section covers the key defenses organizations use to protect their networks.

Device Hardening

Device hardening aims to eliminate attack vectors by patching vulnerabilities and turning off nonessential services. By eliminating needless functionality and deploying secure configurations and settings, hardening reduces the risk of vulnerabilities being exploited and helps ensure that an infrastructure is compliant with regulations. Device hardening is an ongoing process; patching, monitoring, and configuration reviews should all be done periodically.

DISABLE UNUSED PORTS AND SERVICES

A good way to prevent someone from plugging unauthorized cables and devices into switches to inject or capture traffic is to disable unused switch ports by disabling the port or, for Cisco devices, issuing the shutdown command. This defends against attacks like MAC flooding, VLAN hopping, or unauthorized access.

Another hardening best practice is to disable unused services. The logical TCP/UDP ports (not to be confused with the physical ports just mentioned) on which these services listen can provide unauthorized access if the services are vulnerable. Without proper security, these open ports become exploitable attack vectors.

CHANGE DEFAULT PASSWORDS

Every configurable device, like a router or switch, has a default password and settings that present security vulnerabilities if not changed. Curious users can discover these defaults with a simple Google search. For example, a user might note the IP address of a network device, run SSH "just to see" what they can find, and log in using the default credentials. One unauthorized change on that device can cause a whole lot of pain for the network tech or administrator.

Dealing with such authentication issues is straightforward. Before bringing any system online, change the default passwords. This is particularly critical for administrative accounts. Also, disable or delete any "guest" accounts (make sure you have another account created first!).

NOTE Insecam (insecam.org) allows you to view webcams around the world whose passwords haven't been changed. According to the site, the way to remove your camera from their directory is simply to . . . set a password! This is an example of a real-world consequence rather than a routine attack vector. Both 802.1X and MAC filtering were introduced in Chapter 12.

INCREASE PASSWORD LENGTH

Overly complex or frequently changed passwords are hard for users to remember, prompting them to write those passwords down and store them insecurely. Furthermore, keystroke logging, phishing, and social engineering attacks work just as well on complex passwords as they do on simple ones. A longer password using a single character set is generally stronger than a shorter password with multiple character sets. In other words, password length often provides more security than password complexity alone.

Network Access Control

Network access control (NAC) is a standardized approach to verify that a node meets certain criteria before it is allowed to connect to a network. There are several mechanisms for managing and controlling who can access a network.

PORT SECURITY

Port security is a switch feature that mitigates MAC flooding attacks (discussed earlier in this chapter). It works by controlling which MAC addresses can access specific ports and limiting the number of allowed addresses per port.

First, you identify allowed MAC addresses either statically or dynamically as frames enter a port. The next step involves specifying the maximum number of MAC addresses that can access the port. By default, port security allows only one MAC address per port.

In a switched environment, there are legitimate reasons why more than one MAC address might appear on a single port:

- **SWITCH UPLINKS** When a port connects to another switch, all traffic from hosts on the downstream switch will pass through that single uplink port. For example, if Switch A connects to Switch B, all traffic from hosts connected to Switch B will enter Switch A through the port connecting the two switches. Thus, Switch A will see multiple MAC addresses (one for each host on Switch B) on that single port. For this reason, trunk ports should generally be exempt from strict port security.
- **VIRTUAL MACHINES** VMs send frames with the MAC address of their virtual NIC, which differs from the MAC address of the host's physical NIC. A single physical port can therefore see traffic from multiple MAC addresses—one for the host and one for each VM.
- **VOICE OVER IP PHONES WITH PC PASSTHROUGH** A VoIP phone with an internal switch can connect to a PC, with a single cable connecting upstream to another switch. This results in two MAC addresses (the phone's and the PC's) appearing on a single port on the upstream switch.

A violation occurs when a port detects a new MAC address after reaching the maximum number of allowed addresses. On ports that are statically configured for certain MAC addresses, an unknown MAC address would trigger a violation as well. When a violation occurs, the switch will enter one of three modes and take appropriate action:

- **SHUTDOWN MODE** The port is immediately shut down. No frames can enter or exit, and a Simple Network Management Protocol (SNMP) trap notification is sent. The network engineer must re-enable the port manually, although the switch can be configured to bring ports back up automatically after a certain period of time.
- **RESTRICT MODE** The port doesn't shut down, but all frames from violating MAC addresses are discarded. The switch logs the number of violating frames and can send an SNMP trap, as well as a syslog message, if configured to do so.
- **PROTECT MODE** The port doesn't shut down, but all frames from violating MAC addresses are discarded. This mode is the same as restrict except that no violations are logged. (I've never heard of a valid use case—or even a contrived one—that works for this state. No sane administrator would want to stick their head in the sand and ignore violations!)

As if preventing a MAC flooding attack weren't enough motivation, there are other compelling reasons to implement port security. In organizations that deal with sensitive PII, such as healthcare groups or government agencies, every device on the network should be tightly controlled and tracked, while personal devices should be forbidden. After the port learns the MAC address of a company device (which will happen instantly when the device is set up for the first time), users would not be able to unplug that device and plug in their own. If someone tried that, the port would be shut down and an administrator would need to manually bring it up again.

Port security also prevents users from plugging unauthorized switches into ports to connect multiple personal devices to the network. In this case, the switch could use restrict mode instead of completely shutting down to allow the user to keep working while preventing unauthorized devices from sending traffic into the switch. In this case, too, the administrator will get alerts.

Finally, in the case of a VoIP phone or public kiosk computers available to employees or visitors, port security will prevent someone from unplugging that device and connecting one of their own.

NOTE 802.1X and MAC address filtering were discussed in Chapter 12.

Key Management

As mentioned earlier, both TLS and SSH use asymmetric cryptography (to securely establish a shared secret and, in SSH, authenticate the server and optionally the client) and symmetric encryption (to encrypt and decrypt the data).

The life cycle of the asymmetric key pairs (public and private keys) includes generation (using a strong algorithm), distribution (through a secure connection), use (in actual encryption and decryption), storage (for subsequent access), rotation (replacing older or potentially compromised keys with newer ones that are longer/stronger), backup/recovery (in the event that the server storing them gets corrupted), revocation (immediately stopping the key's use), and destruction (deleting the key permanently such that it can never be re-created). Each phase requires security to protect the keys—if they get into the wrong hands, confidentiality, integrity, and availability are all at great risk.

Furthermore, organizations must carefully consider how to transmit secure keys to users (especially remote employees), including how to ensure the key reaches only the intended employee and how to renew private keys.

Security Rules

Security rules are ordered, explicit lists that define whether to permit or deny access. They include access control lists, URL filtering, and content filtering.

ACCESS CONTROL LISTS

Say you have some subnet hosts that should have access to all other subnets in your autonomous system except for one where servers are storing sensitive data. Or maybe one host from a subnet should be allowed to access a specific service on a certain machine, but not others. Or perhaps government privacy regulations require you to prevent or allow packets from reaching certain servers. Enter the *stateless packet filter*, which permits or denies inbound or outbound packets based on certain criteria.

The best example of a stateless packet filter is an IP *access control list*. Standard ACLs filter only by source IP address, while extended ACLs can filter by source IP address, destination IP address, protocol, and port number (the only optional criterion for extended ACLs). An ACL can be applied to a router interface or configured on a dedicated firewall device.

With ACLs, the terms *inbound* and *outbound* are reversed, as they're relative to the router rather than the network. Inbound to the router means traffic entering the router from a connected network (outbound from a network), and outbound means leaving the router toward a network (inbound to a network).

IP ACLs filter at Layers 3 and 4 of the OSI model, so they don't use MAC addresses (found in Layer 2 frames) as criteria. To filter at Layer 2, you'd use a MAC ACL instead. Other types of ACLs include VLAN ACLs and port ACLs.

An ACL contains multiple lines of instructions that are processed sequentially until a match is found. As soon as a packet matches a statement, it's either permitted or denied immediately, regardless of statements that come later in the ACL. In other words, if an early general statement denies a specific packet, it remains denied even if a more specific statement later would permit it; the packet never reaches the later line. There's no branching, looping, or comparison between general and specific statements.

The order of instructions in an ACL is crucial. Ordering the instructions incorrectly could mean the ACL does the opposite of what you intended: packets you mean to deny could be permitted, and those that should be permitted could be denied. This could leave you vulnerable to a cybersecurity breach or a DoS attack.

URL FILTERING

URL filtering permits or denies access to websites based on web address. Blocking malicious websites not only protects devices and infrastructure from cyberattacks but also boosts user productivity by restricting visits to high-bandwidth streaming sites and social media sites. Modern filters often return a block page or redirect to a warning site.

Dan Pollock (*someonewhocares.org*) uses an interesting alternative approach: mapping blocked domains, such as those serving ads, malware, or adult content, to the loopback address (127.0.0.1). When your browser attempts to access one of these sites, it queries your local machine instead of your DNS server. Because the site isn't actually hosted locally, the connection fails and the content is effectively blocked. You can implement this technique by copying the contents of his hosts file into your system's hosts file: *C:\Windows\System32\drivers\etc\hosts* on Windows, or */etc/hosts* on Linux and macOS. This file acts as a manual override for DNS, mapping hostnames to IP addresses to prevent access to unwanted sites.

In fact, both malware and security tools may modify the hosts file as well: malware to redirect or block access, and anti-malware or ad blockers to prevent connections to known malicious or unwanted sites.

URL filtering can be configured by category (social media, news, shopping, job searching, etc.), user or group (admins can be allowed to go to more sites than non-admins), location (headquarters, specific branch offices), time of day (work hours vs. off hours), keywords (words indicating prohibited content), and even reputation (based on various sources of data).

CONTENT FILTERING

Whereas URL filtering looks at the web address to decide whether to allow a browser to access a site, *content filtering* examines the actual content on a web page or within an email to make that determination. This includes images, text, files, and themes.

If a legitimate site is hacked and laced with pornography, malware, or other undesirable items, URL filtering wouldn't protect you (since the URL is legitimate and allowed), but content filtering would.

Modern content filtering often uses deep packet inspection (DPI) or proxy servers to analyze the payload of network traffic, not just headers. DPI allows administrators to block malware, phishing attempts, inappropriate material, or sensitive data leaks even when the URL appears legitimate. By examining text, images, attachments, and file types, DPI provides a more precise and flexible layer of protection than simple URL or domain-based filtering.

Content filtering is used both at home, such as when parents want to block their children from accessing inappropriate content, and at work, where administrators want to block users from accessing malicious or non-work-related content (such as malware, phishing, or sites that reduce productivity).

Zones

Putting traffic and devices into controlled segments, known as *zones*, is an effective way to limit traffic and implement network security.

SCREENED SUBNET

Using a single firewall between the network and the ISP works well in simple networks or when you want strong isolation for all clients inside the firewall. But a screened subnet with internal/external firewalls may be a better option when you have servers that need less restricted access to the internet.

A *screened subnet*—previously known as a *demilitarized zone* (DMZ)—is a network segment carved out by firewalls to provide a zone on the network for servers that need to be publicly accessible from the internet (see Figure 17-20). By definition, a screened subnet uses network segmentation as a mitigation technique against attacks on the network.

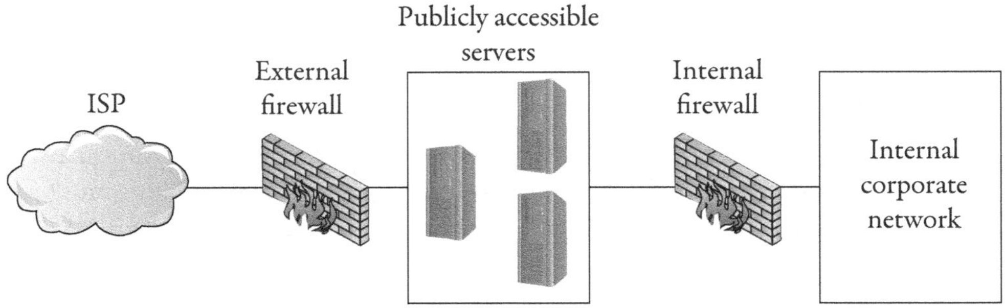

FIGURE 17-20 Screened subnet

A *bastion host* is a system in a screened subnet that is directly exposed or connected to the unfiltered internet. As such, it requires extra hardening and ongoing security monitoring. The name refers to the *bastion* structure—a fortified projection from a castle wall that, being exposed, must be extra strong and well defended.

Bastion hosts are not corporate file servers or corporate application servers; those systems reside on the internal corporate network behind the internal firewall, and the public has no business accessing them. Instead, bastion hosts include a company's web servers, DNS servers, and mail servers—resources the public *should* be able to access. In fact, bastion hosts can also act as proxies for internal servers to handle all communication with external clients, providing another layer of defense for those servers.

TRUSTED VS. UNTRUSTED NETWORKS

The most common screened subnet design uses two routers with firewalls to create a perimeter network. In this design, the two firewalls carve out areas with different levels of trust.

The external firewall sits between the perimeter network and the *untrusted* internet, protecting the public servers from known internet attacks while still allowing traffic through to the public-facing servers. These servers are still publicly accessible, though, and remain more vulnerable to attack and takeover. That's acceptable for the public-facing servers, but the light protection afforded by the external firewall is unacceptable for internal systems. That's where the internal firewall comes in; it sits between the perimeter network and the *trusted* network that houses all the organization's private servers and clients.

The internal firewall provides extremely strict ACLs to protect internal servers that, unlike the bastion hosts, should be accessed only by employees. Having the screened subnet, with the public-facing servers segmented from the internal devices, limits a potential breach to an individual server, thereby protecting the other servers in the screened subnet and any internal devices.

Chapter Review

Questions

1. Which of the following represents a weakness, flaw, or gap in security?
   - **A.** Exploit
   - **B.** Vulnerability
   - **C.** Threat
   - **D.** Risk
2. Which of the following is true regarding risk?
   - **A.** It is just the probability of a threat coming to fruition.
   - **B.** It is just the consequences that would result from an attack.
   - **C.** It combines the probability of a threat coming to fruition along with the consequences that would result from such an attack.
   - **D.** It has nothing to do with the probability of a threat coming to fruition or with the consequences that would result from such an attack.
3. Which element of the CIA triad uses encryption to prevent unauthorized parties from seeing a file or message?
   - **A.** Confidentiality
   - **B.** Integrity
   - **C.** Availability
   - **D.** All of the above
4. What are the two main states of encrypted data?
   - **A.** At rest and processed
   - **B.** In transit and processed
   - **C.** In transit and with integrity
   - **D.** In transit and at rest
5. Which of the following MFA types is the most common and thus should be supplemented with another?
   - **A.** Something you know
   - **B.** Something you have
   - **C.** Something you enjoy
   - **D.** Something you are

6. Which of the following attacks uses malware to take control of computers?
   - A. VLAN hopping
   - B. DDoS
   - C. MAC flooding
   - D. Evil twin
7. Which of the following is not a form of a social engineering attack?
   - A. Dumpster diving
   - B. Shoulder surfing
   - C. Tailgating
   - D. Rogue DHCP
8. Which of the following forms of NAC directly addresses a MAC flooding attack?
   - A. Port security
   - B. 802.1X
   - C. MAC filtering
   - D. All of the above
9. Which of the following is a stateless packet filter?
   - A. URL filter
   - B. Content filter
   - C. ACL
   - D. 802.1X
10. Which of the following involves placing public servers on a different segment than internal servers?
    - A. VLAN
    - B. VPN
    - C. VM
    - D. Screened subnet

Answers

1. **B.** A vulnerability is a weakness, flaw, or gap in an operating system, program, device, network, or even a person.
2. **C.** Risk combines the probability of a threat coming to fruition along with the consequences that would result from such an attack.

3. **A.** Confidentiality means keeping data secret from anyone who isn't allowed to see or interact with it while ensuring access for authorized people.
4. **D.** Aside from homomorphic encryption, data is encrypted when in transit and at rest.
5. **C.** Something you know, in the form of a password, should be supplemented with another form of authentication—either something you have (smartphone app or hardware token) or something you are (biometrics). Something you enjoy is not a form of MFA.
6. **B.** A DDoS (distributed denial-of-service) attack uses hundreds, thousands, or even millions of malware-infected computers under the command and control of a single operator.
7. **D.** Social engineering is the only type of attack that doesn't use technology but rather preys on gullible and naive humans. Dumpster diving, shoulder surfing, tailgating, and phishing are forms of social engineering attacks. A rogue DHCP server is not.
8. **A.** Port security secures a switch against a MAC flooding attack.
9. **C.** The best example of a stateless packet filter is an IP access control list (ACL), which will permit or deny inbound or outbound packets based on criteria such as source IP address, destination IP address, protocol, and port number.
10. **D**. A screened subnet (previously known as demilitarized zone, or DMZ) is a network segment carved out by firewalls to provide a zone on the network for any servers that should be publicly accessible from the internet. By definition, a screened subnet uses network segmentation as a mitigation technique against attacks on the network.

The Troubleshooting Methodology

IN THIS CHAPTER, YOU WILL LEARN HOW TO

- Explain and implement the CompTIA Network+ troubleshooting methodology
- Relate the methodology to any form of troubleshooting

Previous chapters touched on important troubleshooting concepts and protocols in the context of discussing issues with cabling and physical interfaces, network services, or performance. This chapter takes a broader view and walks you through the methodology you should apply to *any* troubleshooting situation, no matter the specific problem or environment you're dealing with.

Test Specific

Have you ever seen a network tech walk up to a broken network and seem to know all the answers? They type in a few commands, and magically the system or network works again. The reason it seems so effortless is that they tend to follow the same steps for similar problems—looking in the same places, typing the same commands, following the same algorithms. When someone performs a task the same way every time, they're probably following a plan. They understand what tools they have to work with, and they know where to start and what to do second and third and fourth until they find the problem.

Primary troubleshooting tools help you formulate a troubleshooting process, guiding you on where to look for different sorts of problems. I will admit, though, that sometimes when I'm helping my students troubleshoot issues in the labs at Rochester Institute of Technology and Finger Lakes Community College, all I have to do is walk over and watch them execute the same commands they've been executing for the past 10 minutes. Somehow, some way, when I'm watching, it suddenly just works. As much as I'd like to think I can use Jedi Mind Tricks on technology, obviously the students must have made a change or two before calling me over. They were following a troubleshooting process, and they'd actually made progress without realizing it.

The CompTIA Network+ exam objectives include troubleshooting methodology steps that can transform seemingly magical problem-solving into a learnable, repeatable skill. Let's dig into them now.

Identify the Problem

First, you need to identify the problem. That means grasping the *true* problem, rather than what someone tells you it is. For example, say a user calls in and complains that she can't access the internet from her system. While that might be the actual problem, it's also possible that the entire wing of her office building just went down, and you've got a much bigger task on your hands. The following steps will help you get to the root of the problem.

Gather Information

Just like Lieutenant Columbo, you can often identify the problem by collecting bits and pieces of information and then putting them together. Gathering information might involve talking to people or using software tools. With tools like the ones discussed in Chapter 15, you can generate information to analyze, but existing resources like logs might already have the details (timestamps, error messages, etc.) you're looking for.

Question Users 1

If you're troubleshooting in person or even over the telephone, you will need to question users. You can ask simple yes or no questions ("Can you see a light on the front of the monitor?") or open-ended questions ("What have you already tried to fix the problem?"). The type of question you ask depends on the information you need and the user's knowledge level. If the user seems technically savvy, you can probably ask more close-ended questions because they'll be able to follow along with you. If, on the other hand, the user seems confused, open-ended questions will allow them to explain what's going on in their own words.

Identify Symptoms

To determine the problem's cause, you first need to understand the extent of the problem by identifying the symptoms. Is it specific to one user or is it network-wide? Sometimes answering this question entails trying the task yourself from both the user's machine and another one. If you're working directly on an affected system and not relying on a caller's version of events, you can identify symptoms yourself by observing what is (or isn't) happening. Are the symptoms indicative of a problem for one user, multiple users, or everyone? There's a difference—both in urgency and in possible sources and solutions—between an internet outage limited to one user versus one spread across multiple users or the entire company. What about a system slowdown? Is one machine possibly infected with malware, or has it spread to multiple machines? Is it just a PC? A switch somewhere? A router? A firewall?

Determine Whether Anything Has Changed

Next, you'll need to determine whether something has changed recently on the affected system or network that might have caused the problem. Sometimes you get a quick answer and sometimes it can take quite a bit of time and effort behind the scenes. Here are some examples of questions to ask:

- "What exactly was happening when the problem occurred?"
- "Has anything been changed on the system recently?"
- "Has the system been moved recently?"

Be careful not to use the word *you*, as in "Have you changed anything on the system recently?" to avoid implicitly blaming the user. Being nice never hurts, and it makes the whole troubleshooting process friendlier. You should also ask yourself some questions, such as "Was that machine involved in the software push last night?" or "Didn't a tech visit that machine this morning?" (Note that you'll only be able to answer these questions if your documentation is up to date!) Sometimes, isolating a problem may require you to check system and hardware logs, such as those stored by routers and other network devices, so make sure you can access them.

EXAM TIP Avoid aggressive or accusatory questions when trying to get information from a user.

Keep in mind that in larger corporate environments, this step includes consulting change management documentation to determine if anything has changed on the network.

Try to Duplicate the Problem

If a user is experiencing problems going to a certain website, go to their machine and try to access the website yourself. In other words, try to duplicate the problem. This enables you to see the symptoms yourself and can often tell you whether the problem is due to user error.

Next, try the same thing from a different machine. If possible, ask other users in the area if they're experiencing the same problem to see if it's affecting more than one user. Determine whether the problem is occurring in only one part of your company or across the entire network.

Essentially, this step tells you how big the problem is and helps you narrow down the source. If nobody in an entire remote office can log in, you might start to suspect that the problem is the network link or the router connecting that office to the server. If nobody in any office can log in, it might mean the server is down or not accepting logins. If it's only one user in one location who can't log in, the problem may be with that user, that machine, or that user's account. Once you've identified the problem and verified it by duplicating it, you can remediate it to ensure it doesn't happen again.

Approach Multiple Problems Individually

If you encounter a complicated scenario—say, various machines that can't access the network as well as potential server room or wiring problems—break it down. Approach multiple problems individually to sort out the root causes, and then methodically tackle them. If you try to identify and solve multiple problems at once, it will be hard to tease out the root cause and solution for each one.

Establish a Theory of Probable Cause

Once you've identified one or more problems, establish a theory of probable cause. In other words, try to figure out what could have happened. Keep in mind that a theory is not a fact, however. You might need to revise your theory later in the process or dismiss it altogether in favor of a new one.

This step comes down to both experience and good use of the support tools at your disposal, such as your knowledge base. Don't spend your time stabbing in the dark. Select the most probable cause from all the possibilities to improve the likelihood that the first solution you choose fixes the problem. Start by questioning what seems obvious and considering multiple angles.

Question the Obvious

When establishing a theory of probable cause, first question or investigate the obvious. If a user can't print to the networked printer, for example, check to see that the printer is plugged in and turned on. It may be hard to believe, but the obvious causes are sometimes the actual causes!

Consider Multiple Approaches

Considering multiple approaches will keep you from locking your imagination into a single train of thought. Two possible approaches are discussed next.

TOP-TO-BOTTOM/BOTTOM-TO-TOP OSI MODEL

You can use the OSI seven-layer model as a troubleshooting tool to help you establish a theory of probable cause. As an example scenario, imagine that a user can't access the database server at the start of the workday. They open the database client from a workstation computer and click on Recent Documents to access the project that management has currently assigned to their team. Nothing happens. Normally, the database client connects to the database that resides on the server on the other side of the network.

Table 18-1 provides some ideas on how starting with a *top-to-bottom OSI model* approach might help.

TABLE 18-1 Top-to-bottom/bottom-to-top OSI model

OSI LAYER	TROUBLESHOOTING
7, Application	Could there be a problem with the API that enables the client database application to connect to the database server service?
6, Presentation	Could there be a problem with encryption between the application and the database server? Maybe, but the user would probably see an error message rather than nothing.
5, Session	Could the fact that a socket can't be established be the cause?
4, Transport	Is an incorrect port specified? Maybe there's something keeping the TCP three-way handshake from completing.
3, Network	Is an IP access control list incorrectly configured? Maybe an incorrect IP address is manually specified or returned by DNS.
2, Data Link	Could an incorrectly (and ill-advised) MAC address filter be configured? As explained in Chapter 17, an attacker can thwart MAC filtering with a blacklist by spoofing their MAC address, while MAC filtering with a whitelist requires a human to collect all of the MAC addresses, which is impossible on a transient network. Furthermore, whitelisting is prone to human error in the MAC address collection/recording process or in the configuration of the whitelist itself.
1, Physical	Could a cable be disconnected? Is a NIC faulty?

You might start with the reverse model (bottom-to-top) in some situations. If the network was newly installed, for example, running through some of the basic connectivity at Layers 1 and 2 might be a good first approach.

DIVIDE AND CONQUER

Another option for tackling multiple options is the divide-and-conquer approach. While it appears to be a compromise between the top-to-bottom/bottom-to-top OSI model approaches, it's actually better. If you arbitrarily always perform top-to-bottom troubleshooting, you'll waste a lot of time at Layers 7 through 3 if the issue is in Layer 1 or 2.

Divide and conquer is a time saver for developing a theory of probable cause. As you gather information for troubleshooting, you'll develop a general sense of where the problem lies. Place this likely cause at the appropriate layer of the OSI model, and begin to test your theory and related theories at that layer. If your theory bears out, follow the appropriate troubleshooting steps. If it doesn't, move up or down the OSI model with new theories of probable causes. For example, executing `ipconfig` (Windows), `ip a` (Linux), or `ifconfig` (Mac) could reveal valuable information. Pinging the default gateway could also be very telling.

Test the Theory to Determine the Cause

After identifying the problem and establishing a theory of probable cause, test your theory in a way that does not permanently alter the system or network and does not compromise confidentiality, integrity, or availability (CIA). Use only non-intrusive, reversible tests that avoid creating new issues.

If Theory Is Confirmed, Determine the Next Steps to Resolve Problem

Regardless of how many times you must go through this process, you'll eventually reach a theory that seems right. When you confirm the theory, determine the next steps to resolve the problem. For example, if you have theorized that the probable cause for a user not being able to print is that the printer is turned off, go look to confirm that theory. If that's the case, plan your next step to resolve the problem. Don't act yet! That step comes next.

If Theory Is Not Confirmed, Establish a New Theory or Escalate

If you can't confirm your theory, you have two options: establish a new one or escalate the problem to someone with more expertise. For the first option, you can go back to the previous step and determine a new probable cause. Once you have another idea, test it. But remember, don't act yet: you might not have permission to make the fix, or the fix might have repercussions you don't yet fully understand.

For example, if you walk over to the print server room to see if the printer is powered up and online and find the door padlocked, that's a whole different problem. In this situation, you need to escalate the problem to management, which is presumably responsible for locking the door. Even if you can access the printer, trying solutions like rebooting the print server could also pose problems. Maybe the machine the print server is running on is also running a database server.

Escalate has two meanings: seeking guidance from relevant parties about the problem or passing off the job to someone who has more control over the device or behavior that's most likely causing the problem. Say you have a server with a bad NIC. This server is used heavily by the accounting department, so taking it down may affect them in ways you can't predict. You need to escalate the problem to the accounting manager.

Alternatively, you'll come across problems over which you have no control or authority. A misbehaving server across the country is the responsibility of another person (hopefully) to whom you need to hand over the job. You could also escalate to someone outside of your organization. For example, you might need to call the vendor support line or open a support case or ticket with the applicable vendor, such as Cisco, Microsoft, or Broadcom.

Establish a Plan of Action

By this point, you should have some ideas as to what the problem might be. It's time to "look before you leap" and establish a plan of action to resolve it and identify its potential effects. An action plan defines how you are going to fix this problem. Most problems are simple, but if yours is complex, you need to write down the steps.

As you do this, think about what else might happen as you undertake the repair. Identify the potential—and especially the unintended—effects of your planned actions. If you take out a switch without having a replacement switch at hand, users might experience excessive downtime before you find a new switch and move them over. If you replace a router, can you restore all the old router's settings to the new one, or will you have to reconfigure them from scratch?

Implement the Solution or Escalate

Once you think you've isolated the cause of the problem, determine the best way to fix it and then implement the solution or escalate as necessary. Solutions could include advising a user over the phone, installing a replacement part, or adding a software patch. Or, if the solution you propose requires more skill than you possess now or falls into someone else's purview, escalate it as necessary to get the fix implemented. If you're the implementer, follow these guidelines, and be sure to try only one likely solution at a time. If you install several patches at once, you won't be able to tell which one fixed the problem!

Similarly, avoid replacing several items of hardware (such as a hard disk and its controller cable) at the same time, because then you can't tell which part (or parts) was faulty. As you try each possibility, always document what you do and what results you get. This isn't just for a future problem either; during a lengthy troubleshooting process, it's easy to forget exactly what you tried two hours before or which attempt produced a particular result. Although being methodical may take longer, it will save time down the road and may help you pinpoint what to do to prevent a recurrence, reducing future call volume to your support team—and, as any support person will tell you, that's definitely worth the effort!

Then you need to test the solution. This is the part everybody hates. Once you think you've fixed a problem, you should try to make it happen again. If you can't, great! But if you can, then you know you haven't finished the job at hand. Many techs want to slip away as soon as everything seems to be fine, but it won't impress your customer when the problem flares up again 30 seconds after you've left the building—and you won't appreciate making another two-hour trip the next day to fix the same problem for an even unhappier client!

EXAM TIP Always test a solution before you walk away from the job!

Verify Full System Functionality and Implement Preventive Measures

Once you've changed something on the system to solve one problem, you must think about the wider repercussions of that change to ensure it doesn't cause another. If you've replaced a faulty NIC in a server, for instance, will the fact that the MAC address has changed (remember, it's built into the NIC) affect the logon security controls or the network management and inventory software? Did installing a patch on a client PC change the default protocol or any other default settings that may affect other functionality? Did changing a user's security settings affect the user's ability to access other network resources? You're not only testing your solution to make sure it works properly, but also considering the impact of your work on the system as a whole.

Make sure you verify full system functionality and implement preventive measures if applicable. If you think you fixed the problem between a workstation and the database server, for example, have the user open the database while you're still there. That way, you don't have to make a second tech call to resolve an outstanding issue. This saves time and money and helps your customer do their job better. Everybody wins.

In a scenario where you're providing support to someone else rather than working directly on the problem, have them try to re-create the problem. This both educates them and confirms that they understand what you've been telling them, reducing the chance that they'll call you back later and ask, "Can we just go through that one more time?"

NOTE For a funny video that illustrates this objective very well (medieval helpdesk with English subtitles), see *youtu.be/pQHX-SjgQvQ*.

After testing the full system functionality, implement any necessary preventive measures—steps taken through software, hardware, or human interaction—to avoid a recurrence of the problem. Such measures might include adding automation through scheduled tasks, installing software to patch a system, or deploying a new router, switch, or PC. You might need to educate users on what to do or not do, but be sure to teach them tactfully.

Document Findings, Actions, Outcomes, and Lessons Learned

Documenting findings, actions, outcomes, and lessons learned from every support call is vital for two reasons. First, you're creating a support and knowledge database so that other support team members can identify and resolve new problems quickly without having to duplicate someone else's research efforts. Second, documentation enables you to track problem trends, anticipate future support needs, or even identify a particular brand or model of device, such as a printer or a NIC, that seems to be less reliable or more labor intensive than others.

Don't skip this step—it really is essential! That said, the unofficial repository for documentation for almost every problem, cause, and solution is, of course, Google. If you're having a problem, it's almost guaranteed that someone else has had the same or a similar problem, posted to a forum, and gotten an answer.

EXAM TIP Expect a Network+ question on soft skills, such as communication, professionalism, documentation, and empathy. In addition to technical troubleshooting, the exam may test your knowledge of how to speak with end users, handle difficult situations professionally, and interact respectfully with coworkers.

Network troubleshooting can be a fun but also often frustrating part of your network career. By applying a consistent troubleshooting methodology and constantly building your network knowledge, you can develop into a great troubleshooter. Mastering this art takes time, naturally, but stick with it. Begin the training. Use the Force. Learn new things, document problems and fixes, and talk to other network techs about the issues they encounter. Every bit of knowledge and experience you gain will make the troubleshooting process that much easier for you when a network disaster occurs—and as any experienced network tech can tell you, one *will* occur, even on the most robust systems.

Chapter Review

Questions

1. Which of the following is not a reason to use a structured approach for troubleshooting?
   A. It allows for finding random solutions.
   B. It allows techs to follow a gameplan.
   C. It allows for following algorithms.
   D. It helps techs understand what they have to work with.
2. When a user complains that they can't access a website, which of the following isn't a step toward identifying the problem?
   A. Gather information.
   B. Question users.
   C. Identify symptoms.
   D. Question the obvious.

3. Which of the following is not an approach to establish a theory of probable cause?
   A. Top-to-bottom OSI model
   B. Bottom-to-top OSI model
   C. Inside-to-outside OSI model
   D. Divide and conquer
4. What layer of the OSI model might help you diagnose issues with MAC addresses?
   A. 1
   B. 2
   C. 3
   D. 4
5. How should multiple problems be solved?
   A. All at once
   B. One at a time
   C. In groups of two
   D. In groups related to each network
6. Which of the following is not true about testing a theory to determine the cause?
   A. If the theory is confirmed, duplicate the problem if necessary.
   B. If the theory is confirmed, determine the next steps to resolve the problem.
   C. If the theory is not confirmed, establish a new theory.
   D. If the theory is not confirmed, escalate.
7. Which of the following are caused by establishing a plan of action to resolve a problem?
   A. Just intended effects
   B. Just unintended effects
   C. Both intended and unintended effects
   D. Neither intended nor unintended effects (just side effects)
8. Which of the following is not part of implementing a solution?
   A. Installing a replacement part
   B. Installing a software update
   C. Trying to make the problem occur again
   D. All of the above

9. Which of the following isn't a reason to ask a remote user to try to re-create a problem after you've solved it?
   A. It allows you to focus on other troubleshooting issues.
   B. It shows they understand what you've been telling them.
   C. It educates them.
   D. It lessens the chance they will call back about the issue.
10. What is the final step of troubleshooting?
    A. Documentation
    B. Testing
    C. Gathering information
    D. Evaluating

Answers

1. **A.** Solutions that are found with a structured approach have more to do with logic and reason than randomness.
2. **D.** You must first identify the problem. Then, you establish a theory of probable cause, which includes questioning the obvious.
3. **C.** There is no inside-to-outside OSI model approach to troubleshooting.
4. **B.** MAC addresses are found at Layer 2, the Data Link layer.
5. **B.** If you try to solve multiple problems at once, it will be hard to tease out each unique problem and its solution.
6. **A.** Duplicating the problem is in the "Identify the problem" step, not the "Test the theory to determine the cause" step.
7. **C.** You must consider both intended and unintended effects when establishing a plan of action to resolve a problem.
8. **D.** Implementing hardware and software as well as trying to make the problem occur again are part of implementing a solution. If you don't try to repeat the problem, you can't be sure that you've fixed it.
9. **A.** A tech can work on multiple issues at a time, but you wouldn't ask a remote user to re-create a problem so that you can focus on other issues.
10. **A.** Documentation, as the last step, creates a support database and enables you to track problem trends.

PART V

Appendixes

IN THIS PART:

- Appendix A: Exam Objective Reference
- Appendix B: About the Online Content

APPENDIX A

Exam Objective Reference

CompTIA Network+ Certification Exam

The CompTIA Network+ exam will certify your knowledge of essential networking tools and concepts. According to CompTIA, you will be assessed "on your abilities in network connectivity, documentation, service configuration, data centers, cloud, virtual networking, monitoring, troubleshooting, and security hardening." Passing the exam validates that the successful candidate has the knowledge and skills required to work successfully in job roles including technical support, network operation, and system administration.

NOTE The lists under each objective cover all the headings in the objectives listing at the time of publication. Refer to the CompTIA website for the most complete and up-to-date objectives list.

DOMAIN	PERCENT OF EXAMINATION
1.0 Networking Concepts	23%
2.0 Network Implementation	20%
3.0 Network Operations	19%
4.0 Network Security	14%
5.0 Network Troubleshooting	24%
Total	100%

OBJECTIVE	CHAPTER
Domain 1.0 Networking Concepts	
1.1 Explain concepts related to the Open Systems Interconnection (OSI) reference model.	
Layer 1 – Physical	1
Layer 2 – Data link	1
Layer 3 – Network	1
Layer 4 – Transport	1
Layer 5 – Session	1
Layer 6 – Presentation	1
Layer 7 – Application	1
1.2 Compare and contrast networking appliances, applications, and functions.	
Physical and virtual appliances	2
Router	2
Switch	2
Firewall	15
Intrusion detection system (IDS)/intrusion prevention system (IPS)	15
Load balancer	15
Proxy	15
Network-attached storage (NAS)	14
Storage area network (SAN)	14
Wireless	12
Access point (AP)	12
Controller	12
Applications	8
Content delivery network (CDN)	8
Functions	8
Virtual private network (VPN)	14
Quality of service (QoS)	3
Time to live (TTL)	3
1.3 Summarize cloud concepts and connectivity options.	
Network functions virtualization (NFV)	13
Virtual private cloud (VPC)	13
Network security groups	13
Network security lists	13
Cloud gateways	13
Internet gateway	13
Network address translation (NAT) gateway	13

OBJECTIVE		CHAPTER
Cloud connectivity options		13
VPN		13
Direct Connect		13
Deployment models		13
Public		13
Private		13
Hybrid		13
Service models		13
Software as a service (SaaS)		13
Infrastructure as a service (IaaS)		13
Platform as a service (PaaS)		13
Scalability		13
Elasticity		13
Multitenancy		13
1.4 Explain common networking ports, protocols, services, and traffic types.		
Protocols	**Ports**	4
File Transfer Protocol (FTP)	20/21	4
Secure File Transfer Protocol (SFTP)	22	4
Secure Shell (SSH)	22	4
Telnet	23	4
Simple Mail Transfer Protocol (SMTP)	25	4
Domain Name System (DNS)	53	4
Dynamic Host Configuration Protocol (DHCP)	67/68	4
Trivial File Transfer Protocol (TFTP)	69	4
Hypertext Transfer Protocol (HTTP)	80	4
Network Time Protocol (NTP)	123	4
Simple Network Management Protocol (SNMP)	161/162	4
Lightweight Directory Access Protocol (LDAP)	389	4
Hypertext Transfer Protocol Secure (HTTPS)	443	4
Server Message Block (SMB)	445	4
Syslog	514	4
Simple Mail Transfer Protocol Secure (SMTPS)	587	4
Lightweight Directory Access Protocol over SSL (LDAPS)	636	4
Structured Query Language (SQL) Server	1433	4
Remote Desktop Protocol (RDP)	3389	4
Session Initiation Protocol (SIP)	5060/5061	4

OBJECTIVE	CHAPTER
Internet Protocol (IP) types	4
Internet Control Message Protocol (ICMP)	3
Transmission Control Protocol (TCP)	3
User Datagram Protocol (UDP)	3
Generic Routing Encapsulation (GRE)	15
Internet Protocol Security (IPSec)	15
Authentication Header (AH)	15
Encapsulating Security Payload (ESP)	15
Internet Key Exchange (IKE)	15
Traffic types	2
Unicast	2
Multicast	2
Anycast	8
Broadcast	2
1.5 Compare and contrast transmission media and transceivers.	
Wireless	12
802.11 standards	12
Cellular	12
Satellite	12
Wired	9
802.3 standards	9, 10
Single-mode vs. multimode fiber	9
Direct attach copper (DAC) cable	9
Twinaxial cable	9
Coaxial cable	9
Cable speeds	9
Plenum vs. non-plenum cable	9
Transceivers	10
Protocol	10
Ethernet	10
Fibre Channel (FC)	14
Form factors	10
Small form-factor pluggable (SFP)	10
Quad small form-factor pluggable (QSFP)	10
Connector types	9
Subscriber connector (SC)	9
Local connector (LC)	9

OBJECTIVE	CHAPTER
Straight tip (ST)	9
Multi-fiber push on (MPO)	9
Registered jack (RJ)11	9
RJ45	9
F-type	9
Bayonet Neill–Concelman (BNC)	9
1.6 Compare and contrast network topologies, architectures, and types.	
Mesh	11
Hybrid	11
Star/hub and spoke	11
Spine and leaf	14
Point to point	14
Three-tier hierarchical model	14
Core	14
Distribution	14
Access	14
Collapsed core	14
Traffic flows	14
North-south	14
East-west	14
1.7 Given a scenario, use appropriate IPv4 network addressing.	
Public vs. private	3
Automatic Private IP Addressing (APIPA)	3, 7
RFC1918	3
Loopback/localhost	3
Subnetting	3
Variable Length Subnet Mask (VLSM)	3
Classless Inter-domain Routing (CIDR)	3
IPv4 address classes	3
Class A	3
Class B	3
Class C	3
Class D	3
Class E	3
1.8 Summarize evolving use cases for modern network environments.	
Software-defined network (SDN) and software-defined wide area network (SD-WAN)	14
Application aware	14

OBJECTIVE	CHAPTER
Zero-touch provisioning	14
Transport agnostic	14
Central policy management	14
Virtual Extensible Local Area Network (VXLAN)	14
Data center interconnect (DCI)	14
Layer 2 encapsulation	14
Zero-trust architecture (ZTA)	14
Policy-based authentication	14
Authorization	14
Least privilege access	14
Secure Access Secure Edge (SASE)/Security Service Edge (SSE)	14
Infrastructure as code (IaC)	13
Automation	13
Playbooks/templates/reusable tasks	13
Configuration drift/compliance	13
Upgrades	13
Dynamic inventories	13
Source control	13
Version control	13
Central repository	13
Conflict identification	13
Branching	13
IPv6 addressing	8
Mitigating address exhaustion	8
Compatibility requirements	8
Tunneling	8
Dual stack	8
NAT64	8
Domain 2.0 Network Implementation	
2.1 Explain characteristics of routing technologies.	
Static routing	5
Dynamic routing	5
Border Gateway Protocol (BGP)	5
Enhanced Interior Gateway Routing Protocol (EIGRP)	5
Open Shortest Path First (OSPF)	5
Route selection	5
Administrative distance	5

OBJECTIVE	CHAPTER
Prefix length	5
Metric	5
Address translation	5
NAT	5
Port address translation (PAT)	5
First Hop Redundancy Protocol (FHRP)	5
Virtual IP (VIP)	5
Subinterfaces	5
2.2 Given a scenario, configure switching technologies and features.	
Virtual Local Area Network (VLAN)	6
VLAN database	6
Switch Virtual Interface (SVI)	6
Interface configuration	6
Native VLAN	6
Voice VLAN	6
802.1Q tagging	6
Link aggregation	6
Speed	6
Duplex	6
Spanning tree	6
Maximum transmission unit (MTU)	6
Jumbo frames	6
2.3 Given a scenario, select and configure wireless devices and technologies.	
Channels	12
Channel width	12
Non-overlapping channels	12
Regulatory impacts	12
802.11	12
Frequency options	12
2.4GHz	12
5GHz	12
6GHz	12
Band steering	12
Service set identifier (SSID)	12
Basic service set identifier (BSSID)	12
Extended service set identifier (ESSID)	12

OBJECTIVE	CHAPTER
Network types	12
Mesh networks	12
Ad hoc	12
Point to point	12
Infrastructure	12
Encryption	12
Wi-Fi Protected Access 2 (WPA2)	12
Wi-Fi Protected Access 3 (WPA3)	12
Guest networks	12
Captive portals	12
Authentication	12
Pre-shared key (PSK) vs. Enterprise	12
Antennas	12
Omnidirectional vs. directional	12
Autonomous vs. lightweight access point	12
2.4 Explain important factors of physical installations.	
Important installation implications	11
Locations	11
Intermediate distribution frame (IDF)	11
Main distribution frame (MDF)	11
Rack size	11
Port-side exhaust/intake	11
Cabling	11
Patch panel	11
Fiber distribution panel	11
Lockable	11
Power	11
Uninterruptible power supply (UPS)	11
Power distribution unit (PDU)	11
Power load	11
Voltage	11
Environmental factors	11
Humidity	11
Fire suppression	11
Temperature	11

OBJECTIVE	CHAPTER
Domain 3.0 Network Operations	
3.1 Explain the purpose of organizational processes and procedures.	
Documentation	11
Physical vs. logical diagrams	14
Rack diagrams	14
Cable maps and diagrams	11, 14
Network diagrams	11, 14
Layer 1	14
Layer 2	14
Layer 3	14
Asset inventory	16
Hardware	16
Software	16
Licensing	16
Warranty support	16
IP address management (IPAM)	16
Service-level agreement (SLA)	16
Wireless survey/heat map	12
Life-cycle management	16
End-of-life (EOL)	16
End-of-support (EOS)	16
Software management	16
Patches and bug fixes	16
Operating system (OS)	16
Firmware	16
Decommissioning	16
Change management	16
Request process tracking/service request	16
Configuration management	16
Production configuration	16
Backup configuration	16
Baseline/golden configuration	16
3.2 Given a scenario, use network monitoring technologies.	
Methods	15
SNMP	15
Traps	15
Management information base (MIB)	15

OBJECTIVE	CHAPTER
Versions	15
v2c	15
v3	15
Community strings	15
Authentication	15
Flow data	15
Packet capture	15
Baseline metrics	15
Anomaly alerting/notification	15
Log aggregation	15
Syslog collector	15
Security information and event management (SIEM)	15
Application programming interface (API) integration	15
Port mirroring	15
Solutions	15
Network discovery	15
Ad hoc	15
Scheduled	15
Traffic analysis	15
Performance monitoring	15
Availability monitoring	15
Configuration monitoring	15
3.3 Explain disaster recovery (DR) concepts.	
DR metrics	16
Recovery point objective (RPO)	16
Recovery time objective (RTO)	16
Mean time to repair (MTTR)	16
Mean time between failures (MTBF)	16
DR sites	16
Cold site	16
Warm site	16
Hot site	16
High-availability approaches	14
Active-active	14
Active-passive	14

OBJECTIVE	CHAPTER
Testing	16
Tabletop exercises	16
Validation tests	16
3.4 Given a scenario, implement IPv4 and IPv6 network services.	
Dynamic addressing	7
DHCP	7
Reservations	7
Scope	7
Lease time	7
Options	7
Relay/IP helper	7
Exclusions	7
Stateless address autoconfiguration (SLAAC)	8
Name resolution	7
DNS	7
Domain Name Security Extensions (DNSSEC)	7
DNS over HTTPS (DoH) and DNS over TLS (DoT)	7
Record types	7
Address (A)	7
AAAA	7
Canonical name (CNAME)	7
Mail exchange (MX)	7
Text (TXT)	7
Nameserver (NS)	7
Pointer (PTR)	7
Zone types	7
Forward	7
Reverse	7
Authoritative vs. non-authoritative	7
Primary vs. secondary	7
Recursive	7
Hosts file	7
Time protocols	15
NTP	15
Precision Time Protocol (PTP)	15
Network Time Security (NTS)	15

OBJECTIVE	CHAPTER
3.5 Compare and contrast network access and management methods.	
Site-to-site VPN	15
Client-to-site VPN	15
Clientless	15
Split tunnel vs. full tunnel	15
Connection methods	4, 15
SSH	4, 15
Graphical user interface (GUI)	15
API	15
Console	15
Jump box/host	15
In-band vs. out-of-band management	15
Domain 4.0 Network Security	
4.1 Explain the importance of basic network security concepts.	
Logical security	17
Encryption	17
Data in transit	17
Data at rest	17
Certificates	17
Public key infrastructure (PKI)	17
Self-signed	17
Identity and access management (IAM)	17
Authentication	17
Multifactor authentication (MFA)	17
Single sign-on (SSO)	17
Remote Authentication Dial-in User Service (RADIUS)	17
LDAP	17
Security Assertion Markup Language (SAML)	17
Terminal Access Controller Access Control System Plus (TACACS+)	17
Time-based authentication	17
Authorization	17
Least privilege	17
Role-based access control	17
Geofencing	17
Physical security	17
Camera	17
Locks	17

OBJECTIVE	CHAPTER
Deception technologies	17
Honeypot	17
Honeynet	17
Common security terminology	17
Risk	17
Vulnerability	17
Exploit	17
Threat	17
Confidentiality, Integrity, and Availability (CIA) triad	17
Audits and regulatory compliance	17
Data locality	17
Payment Card Industry Data Security Standards (PCI DSS)	17
General Data Protection Regulation (GDPR)	17
Network segmentation enforcement	17
Internet of Things (IoT) and Industrial Internet of Things (IIoT)	17
Supervisory control and data acquisition (SCADA), industrial control system (ICS), operational technology (OT)	17
Guest	17
Bring your own device (BYOD)	17
4.2 Summarize various types of attacks and their impact to the network.	
Denial-of-service (DoS)/distributed denial-of-service (DDoS)	17
VLAN hopping	17
Media Access Control (MAC) flooding	17
Address Resolution Protocol (ARP) poisoning	17
ARP spoofing	17
DNS poisoning	17
DNS spoofing	17
Rogue devices and services	12, 17
DHCP	17
AP	12, 17
Evil twin	12, 17
On-path attack	17
Social engineering	17
Phishing	17
Dumpster diving	17
Shoulder surfing	17
Tailgating	17
Malware	17

OBJECTIVE	CHAPTER
4.3 Given a scenario, apply network security features, defense techniques, and solutions.	
Device hardening	17
Disable unused ports and services	17
Change default passwords	17
Network access control (NAC)	17
Port security	17
802.1X	17
MAC filtering	17
Key management	17
Security rules	17
Access control list (ACL)	17
Uniform Resource Locator (URL) filtering	17
Content filtering	17
Zones	17
Trusted vs. untrusted	17
Screened subnet	17
Domain 5.0 Network Troubleshooting	
5.1 Explain the troubleshooting methodology.	
Identify the problem	18
Gather information	18
Question users	18
Identify symptoms	18
Determine if anything has changed	18
Duplicate the problem, if possible	18
Approach multiple problems individually	18
Establish a theory of probable cause	18
Question the obvious	18
Consider multiple approaches	18
Top-to-bottom/bottom-to-top OSI model	18
Divide and conquer	18
Test the theory to determine the cause	18
If theory is confirmed, determine next steps to resolve problem	18
If theory is not confirmed, establish a new theory or escalate	18
Establish a plan of action to resolve the problem and identify potential effects	18
Implement the solution or escalate as necessary	18
Verify full system functionality and implement preventive measures if applicable	18
Document findings, actions, outcomes, and lessons learned throughout the process	18

OBJECTIVE	CHAPTER
5.2 Given a scenario, troubleshoot common cabling and physical interface issues.	
Cable issues	11
Incorrect cable	11
Single mode vs. multimode	9
Category 5/6/7/8	9
Shielded twisted pair (STP) vs. unshielded twisted pair (UTP)	9
Signal degradation	9
Crosstalk	9
Interference	9
Attenuation	11
Improper termination	11
Transmitter (TX)/Receiver (RX) transposed	11
Interface issues	6
Increasing interface counters	6
Cyclic redundancy check (CRC)	6
Runts	6
Giants	6
Drops	6
Port status	6
Error disabled	6
Administratively down	5
Suspended	6
Hardware issues	12
Power over Ethernet (PoE)	12
Power budget exceeded	12
Incorrect standard	12
Transceivers	11
Mismatch	11
Signal strength	12
5.3 Given a scenario, troubleshoot common issues with network services.	
Switching issues	6
STP	6
Network loops	6
Root bridge selection	6
Port roles	6
Port states	6

OBJECTIVE	CHAPTER
Incorrect VLAN assignment	6
ACLs	17
Route selection	5
Routing table	5
Default routes	5
Address pool exhaustion	3, 8
Incorrect default gateway	7
Incorrect IP address	7
Duplicate IP address	8
Incorrect subnet mask	7
5.4 Given a scenario, troubleshoot common performance issues.	
Congestion/contention	12
Bottlenecking	15
Bandwidth	12
Throughput capacity	12
Latency	12
Packet loss	12
Jitter	12
Wireless	12
Interference	12
Channel overlap	12
Signal degradation or loss	12
Insufficient wireless coverage	12
Client disassociation issues	12
Roaming misconfiguration	12
5.5 Given a scenario, use the appropriate tool or protocol to solve networking issues.	
Software tools	15
Protocol analyzer	15
Command line	4, 5
ping	4, 5
traceroute/tracert	4, 5
nslookup	7
tcpdump	15
dig	7
netstat	4
ip/ifconfig/ipconfig	2
arp	2

OBJECTIVE	CHAPTER
Nmap	15
Link Layer Discovery Protocol (LLDP)/CiscDiscovery Protocol (CDP)	5
Speed tester	11
Hardware tools	11, 12
Toner	11
Cable tester	11
Taps	12
Wi-Fi analyzer	12
Visual fault locator	11
Basic networking device commands	5, 6
show mac-address-table	6
show route	5
show interface	5
show config	5
show arp	5
show vlan	6
show power	12

APPENDIX B

About the Online Content

This book comes complete with TotalTester Online customizable practice exam software, which includes:

- TotalTester Online customizable practice exam software with 230 practice exam questions
- A video introduction to the N10-009 CompTIA Network+ certification
- More than an hour of video training episodes from Mike Meyers's CompTIA Network+ Certification video series
- More than 20 sample simulations from Total Seminars' TotalSims for Network+
- Links to a collection of Mike Meyers's favorite tools and utilities for network troubleshooting

System Requirements

The current and previous major versions of the following desktop browsers are recommended and supported: Chrome, Microsoft Edge, Firefox, and Safari. These browsers update frequently, and sometimes an update may cause compatibility issues with the TotalTester Online content or other content hosted on the Training Hub. If you run into a problem using one of these browsers, please try using another browser until the problem is resolved.

Your Total Seminars Training Hub Account

To access the online content, you will need to create an account on the Total Seminars Training Hub. Registration is free, and you will be able to track all your online content using your account. You may also opt in if you wish to receive marketing information from Total Seminars, but this is not required for you to gain access to the online content.

Privacy Notice

Total Seminars values your privacy. Please be sure to read the Privacy Notice available during registration to see how the information you have provided will be used. You may view our Corporate Customer Privacy Policy by visiting *www.totalsem.com*. Click **Privacy** at the bottom of the page.

Single-User License Terms and Conditions

Online access to the digital content included with this book is governed by the Total Seminars License Agreement, outlined next. By using this digital content, you agree to the terms of that license.

ACCESS To register and activate your Total Seminars Training Hub account, simply follow these easy steps.

1. Go to this URL: *https://hub.totalsem.com/aioclaim*.
2. To register and create a new Training Hub account, enter your email address, name, and password on the Register tab. No further personal information (such as credit card number) is required to create an account.
3. If you already have a Total Seminars Training Hub account, enter your email address and password on the Log In tab.
4. Enter your Product Key: **pp6m-c20m-q0z4**.
5. Click to accept the user license terms.
6. For new users, click the **Register and Claim** button to create your account. For existing users, click the **Log in and Claim** button.

You will be taken to the Training Hub and will have access to the content for this book.

DURATION OF LICENSE Access to your, the user's, online content through the Total Seminars Training Hub will expire one year from the date the publisher declares the book out of print.

Your purchase of this Total Seminars product, including its access code, through a retail store is subject to the refund policy of that store.

RESTRICTIONS ON TRANSFER The user is receiving only a limited right to use the Content for the user's own internal and personal use, dependent on purchase and continued ownership of this book. The user may not reproduce, forward, modify, create derivative works based upon, transmit, distribute, disseminate, sell, publish, or sublicense the Content or in any way commingle the Content with other third-party content without Total Seminars' consent.

LIMITED WARRANTY The Total Seminars Content is provided on an "as is" basis. Neither Total Seminars nor its licensors make any guarantees or warranties of any kind, either express or implied, including, but not limited to, implied warranties of merchantability or fitness for a particular purpose or use as to any Total Seminars Content or the information therein or any warranties as to the accuracy, completeness, correctness, or results to be obtained from accessing or using the Total Seminars Content, or any material referenced in such Content or any information entered into the licensee's product by users or other persons and/or any material available on or that can be accessed through the licensee's product (including via any hyperlink or otherwise) or as to noninfringement of third-party rights. Any warranties of any kind, whether express or implied, are disclaimed. Any material or data obtained through use of the Total Seminars Content is at the user's own discretion and risk, and the user understands that they will be solely responsible for any resulting damage to their computer system or loss of data.

Neither Total Seminars nor its licensors shall be liable to any subscriber or to any user or anyone else for any inaccuracy, delay, interruption in service, error, or omission, regardless of cause, or for any damage resulting therefrom.

In no event will Total Seminars or its licensors be liable for any indirect, special, or consequential damages, including, but not limited to, lost time, lost money, lost profits, or lost goodwill, whether in contract, tort, strict liability, or otherwise, and whether or not such damages are foreseen or unforeseen with respect to any use of the Total Seminars Content.

TotalTester Online

TotalTester Online provides you with a simulation of the CompTIA Network+ exam. Exams can be taken in Practice Mode or Exam Mode. Practice Mode provides an assistance window with hints, references to the book, explanations of the correct and incorrect answers, and the option to check your answers as you take the test. Exam Mode provides a simulation of the actual exam. The number of questions, the types of questions, and the time allowed are intended to be an accurate representation of the exam environment. The option to customize your quiz allows you to create custom exams from selected domains or chapters, and you can further customize the number of questions and time allowed.

To take a test, follow the instructions provided in the previous section to register and activate your Total Seminars Training Hub account. When you register, you will be taken to the Total Seminars Training Hub. From the Training Hub home page, select your certification from the Study drop-down menu at the top of the page to drill down to the TotalTester for your book. You can also scroll to it from the list on the Your Topics tab of the home page, and then click on the TotalTester link to launch the TotalTester. Once you've launched your TotalTester, you can select the option to customize your quiz and begin testing yourself in Practice Mode or Exam Mode. All exams provide an overall grade and a grade broken down by domain.

Other Book Resources

The following sections detail the other resources available with your book. You can access these items by selecting the Resources tab, or by selecting CompTIA Network+ All-in-One Exam Guide 9e (N10-009) from the Study drop-down menu at the top of the page or from the list on the Your Topics tab of the home page. The menu on the right side of the screen outlines all of the available resources.

COMPTIA NETWORK+ VIDEO TRAINING SAMPLE

More than an hour of training videos is available for free. Select **CompTIA Network+ All-in-One 9e (N10-009) Resources** from the Your Topics list on the home page. Click the **TotalVideos** tab. The videos are organized by chapter, and more than one hour of free videos is available for study. You can purchase the complete video training series from the Total Seminars website at *www.totalsem.com*.

PLAYING THE COMPTIA NETWORK+ INTRODUCTION VIDEO

You can watch the video introduction to the **CompTIA Network+ exam online. Select CompTIA Network+ All-in-One 9e (N10-009)** Resources from the list of "Your Topics" on the home page. Click the Resources tab, and then select the Network+ Intro button.

TOTALSIMS SAMPLE FOR COMPTIA NETWORK+

From your Total Seminars Training Hub account, select **CompTIA Network+ All-in-One 9e (N10-009) Resources** from the list of "Your Topics" on the home page. Click the TotalSims tab. The simulations are organized by chapter, and there are over 20 free simulations available for reviewing topics referenced in the book, with an option to purchase access to the full TotalSims for Network+ (N10-009) with over 120 simulations.

MIKE'S COOL TOOLS

Mike loves freeware/open source networking tools! Access the utilities mentioned in the text by selecting **CompTIA Network+ All-in-One 9e (N10-009)** Resources from the list of "Your Topics" on the home page. Click the Resources tab, and then select Mike's Cool Tools.

Technical Support

For questions regarding the TotalTester or operation of the Training Hub, visit *www.totalsem.com* or email *support@totalsem.com*.

For questions regarding book content, email *support@totalsem.com*.

INDEX

Numbers

3-1-4 rule, 218
4TO6, 219
5G technology, 409–410
6-byte binary addresses, 249
6IN4, 219
6P4C (6 position 4 conductor/contact) connectors, 234
8P8C (8 position 8 contact) connectors, 234, 253, 327
10BASE-FL fiber-optic cable, 255–257
10BASE-T Ethernet, 245, 250–251, 255, 265
10GBASE-ER, 271
10GBASE-EW, 271
10GBASE-Ey, 271
10GBASE-L4, 271
10GBASE-LR, 270
10GBASE-LRM, 271
10GBASE-LW, 270
10GBASE-Ly, 270
10GBASE-SR, 270
10GBASE-SW, 270
10GBASE-Sy, 270
10GBASE-T, 272
10GBASE-xy, 270
10GBASE-ZR, 271
10 GbE (10 Gigabit Ethernet), 269–274
10 Mbps Ethernet, 257
40 Gigabit Ethernet, 275
48-bit binary addresses, 249
66-punchdown block, 293
100BASE-FX Ethernet, 263
100BASE-SX Ethernet, 264
100BASE-T Ethernet, 261–263
100 Gigabit Ethernet, 275
100 Mbps Ethernet, 245, 261–265
110-punchdown block, 291–293, 296
802 Working Group, 239
802.1AB LLDB, 136
802.1Q VLAN tag, 153
802.1X, 365, 366
802.11a, 356
802.11ac, 359, 398, 399
802.11a-ht/802.11g-ht, 358
802.11ax, 360, 398, 399
802.11b, 356
802.11be, 360
802.11bn, 361
802.11g, 357
802.11n, 357, 398, 399
802.11 standards, 25, 50, 240, 344–354, 381, 382, 395, 396, 400, 401, 403
802.3, 246–247, 250, 257, 263
802.3ab, 265
802.3af, 374
802.3bz, 272
1000BASE-LX Ethernet, 265, 266
1000BASE-SX Ethernet, 265, 266
1000BASE-T Ethernet, 265–266
1000BASE-X Ethernet, 265

A

AAAA host addresses, 181, 218
absorption, signal, 400
abstraction, 421–422
access control, network, 597–599
access/edge layer, 458
access management, 563–568
access points, rogue, 588
access points, Wi-Fi. *See* WAPs (wireless access points)
access ports, 153, 155, 580, 581
ACK (Acknowledge), 92–94
Ack, DHCP, 193, 196
ACLs (access control lists)
- incorrect configuration of, 168
- for large network security, 112
- MAC address filtering for, 369
- overview of, 600
- packet filtering and, 491
- subnetting and, 67
- traffic-checking on routers, 491

active-active/active-passive HA, 470, 471
activity lights, 331, 332
actuators, 575
adapters, wireless network, 346
addressing
- address pool exhaustion, 198
- anycast addressing, 176
- classless, 68, 76, 77, 206, 625
- DNS host types, 180–188

addressing (*continued*)
dynamic vs. static, 77–78, 173
IP (Internet Protocol) address, 205
IPv4 address classes, 62–76
IPv4 notation, 206
IPv6, 204–212
link-local address, 194–195
Local and Foreign, 97
for local/remote communication, 42–54
prefix lengths, 208
solicited-node multicast address, 212–214
special categories of, 78
subnet broadcast address, 73, 74
See also IP (Internet Protocol) address; MAC address
ad hoc network discovery, 520
ad hoc networks, 349, 351, 380–381
administration
at the demarc, 299
of DNS zones, 184
enterprise wireless, 372–374
firewall, 489
for IoT devices, 573
jump box/host for, 508
performance monitoring, 517–520
of primary DNS server, 175
remote, 506
subnetting for ease of, 67
See also management
administrative distance, 124–125
Advanced Research Projects Agency Network (ARPANET), 172
advertisements, router, 215–216
adware, 595–596
AES (Advanced Encryption Standard), 367, 553, 555
aggregating logs, 518–519
AH (Authentication Header), 503
AirMagnet Survey Pro, 376, 377, 378, 401
air quality, 305, 335, 337
ALE (annualized loss expectancy), 546
ALG (application layer gateway), 491
Amazon Web Services (AWS), 433, 434, 443, 444, 447, 448, 450, 451
analyzers, packet, 515
analyzers, wireless, 376, 401
angled physical contact (APC) connectors, 268
annualized failure rate (AFR), 534
anomaly-based IDSs/IPSs, 495
ANSI (American National Standards Institute), 232, 253
Ansible, 440–441
ANSI/TIA-568 standards, 253–254, 282, 285, 293, 298, 303, 323, 326
ANSI/TIA-606-C, 294
ANSI/TIA fiber-optic standards, 237
antennas, 381–386, 397
anycast addressing, 176, 211–212
AP (access point). *See* WAPs (wireless access points)
API integration, 520
APIPA (Automatic Private IP Addressing), 194, 208, 395
APIs (Application Programming Interfaces), 8
Apple, 60, 562
Application layer, 6, 8–9, 492
applications (apps)
API integration, 520
app-specific functions, 8
authenticator apps, 567
CI/CD for, 442
in cloud service model, 432
IaC automation for scaling, 440
PaaS for deploying, 433–436
SaaS for user access to, 436
scaling up/down, 443
in SDNs, 430
SD-WAN awareness of, 467
TCP vs. UDP use by, 11
See also software
AR (augmented reality) systems, 360
architecture. *See* network design; topology
areas, OSPF, 120
ARIN (American Registry for Internet Numbers), 63, 205, 206
ARP (Address Resolution Protocol)
broadcast requests, 45, 46, 150, 212
cache vs. MAC address table, 493
gratuitous, 194–195
for local communication, 45, 46
MAC address gathered via, 42, 50, 128
poisoning/spoofing attack, 582–585
for remote communication, 47, 49
subnetting to shrink domain of, 67, 112
as unicast messages, 46, 47, 50
viewing router ARP cache, 137
ARPA (Advanced Research Projects Agency), 13, 172, 203
`arp -a` command, 46
ASAv (Adaptive Security Virtual Appliance), 422
ASCII (American Standard Code for Information Interchange), 552

ASes (autonomous systems), 112–113, 116–117, 121
ASN (autonomous system number), 116–117
asset inventories, 480, 525–526
asset protection, 544
asset valuation, 546
association time, 404
asterisks (*) in `tracert`, 101
ASUS WAP, 387–388, 390, 392
asymmetric cryptography, 555–557
AT&T, 60
attacks
  BGP in, 124
  client disassociation, 404
  and cloud multitenancy, 445
  CompTIA exam objectives on, 633–634
  DDoS, 190, 580
  defense techniques, 596–602
  DoS, 444, 494
  exploits/attacks defined, 543–544
  hashing vs., 560–563
  information sharing and, 137
  MAC address spoofs, 16, 369
  overview of, 580–596
  on-path attacks, 216, 506, 582
  via physical switch access, 152
  port scanning and, 505–506
  security threats, 544–545
  spoof attacks, 16, 369, 491
  SSH to prevent, 506
  by threat agents, 545
  on unencrypted networks, 402
  VLAN hopping attacks, 154
  WPS, 361
  zero-day attacks/exploits, 543
  See also malware; response plans; security
attenuation, signal, 235, 323, 400
A type host address, 180, 188, 218
audits, security, 571–572
AUP (Acceptable Use Policy), 370
authentication
  changing default passwords, 597
  for cloud accounts, 444–445
  DKIM for email, 186
  EAP for, 363–366
  hardening via, 362
  OSPF for network, 120
  Remote Desktop Gateway, 508
  SNMP, 511
  in SSH session, 506–507
  TLS (Transport Layer Security), 505
  of user identity, 564–568
  of VPN packets, 503–505
authoritative/non-authoritative DNS responses, 188–189
authoritative TLD DNS servers, 174–180, 182
authorization
  and least privilege principle, 563
  predefined access via, 568
  for telecommunications room, 283, 306
  in ZTA, 469
autoconfiguration, IPv6, 216
automatic translations (stateless mapping), 221
automation, IaC, 440
automation, scaling, 444
Auto-MDI/MDI-X, 261, 266
autonomous AP, 373
Autonomous System Path, 123
AUX ports, 509
availability, data, 549–550, 572
availability monitoring, 520–521
A/V connections, 296
Azure, 187, 434, 438, 443, 444, 448, 451, 564
Azure Stack, 438

B

backbone (vertical) cabling, 274–275, 284, 299
backbone, core layer, 460
backbone routers, 66, 78, 112, 121, 128, 269
backbone switches, 275
backdoors, malware, 595
backoff period, 354
backups, 528, 532
backward compatibility, 9
balanced loads, 115, 139, 420, 461–462, 470
band steering, 354
bandwidth
  defined, 233
  in EIGRP networks, 120
  full duplex, 264
  horizontal cabling and, 286
  in OSPF cost calculation, 117–119
  saturation, 399
  traffic shaping for, 496
  of wireless frequencies, 353
  See also throughput
bandwidth-efficient encoding schemes, 233
barrel connectors, 229, 230
BASE (baseband), 251
base 2 system. *See* binary system
base 10 system. *See* decimal system
base 16 system. *See* hexadecimal system

baseline configurations, 480, 532
bastion hosts, 602
battery backups, 472
BC (business continuity), 534
BCP (business continuity planning), 534
beacon frame, 388
beam antenna, 385
beamforming, 358
Belanger, Phil, 344
bend radius limitation, 324
BGP (Border Gateway Protocol), 121–125, 212, 450
BIA (burned-in address), 42
Bidirectional (BiDi) transceivers, 273
binary system
  binary-to-decimal conversion, 28
  decimal-to-binary conversion, 28–32
  hexadecimal numbering in, 15
  hexadecimal-to-binary conversion, 34–35
  in local communication, 43–46
  for MAC vs. IP addresses, 42
  overview of, 26, 27–32
  physical data in, 23–25
  subnetting via, 68, 71–72
BIOS (Basic Input/Output System), 417
bits, defined, 27
BIX blocks, 296
black hat hackers, 542
blacklist, 369
block ciphers, 554
blocked ports, 159, 163, 166
block ID, 16, 42
blocks, 63, 463
BNC connectors, 226
bonding ports, 157
Boolean tools, 100
botnets, 594
bottlenecking, 494
bottom-to-top OSI model, 610–611
BPDUs (bridge protocol data units), 158, 159, 161
branching, DVCS, 441
Branscombe, Mary, 431
bridges
  bridge ID, 161
  bridge priority, 161
  and collision domains, 260
  NIC/VPN concentrator, 428
  root bridge selection, 159, 161–163
  wired, 159
  wireless, 159, 393–394
bridging loops, 158
broadband vs. baseband connection, 251
broadcast address, 210–211
broadcast domains, 67, 150, 151, 153
broadcast forwarding, 48, 197–198
browsing, 90, 559, 639
BSS (basic service set), 351
BSSID (basic service set identifier), 351, 371
buffer, fiber-optic, 235
bug fixes/patches, 528
Building Industry Consulting Service International (BICSI), 282
bursting, cloud, 438
bus topology, 54, 227, 245, 250, 257–259
BYOD (bring your own device), 579
bytes, 27, 93

C

CA (certificate authority), 558
cable drop, 304
cable maps/diagrams, 304, 318, 319
cable modems, 133, 228
cable service, 110
cable trays, 307
cabling
  10BASE-FL, 255–257
  10BASE-T UTP, 251–254
  100 Mbps Ethernet, 261–265
  vs. cables, 225
  cloud Direct Connect, 451
  CompTIA exam objectives on, 626–627
  copper cables/connectors, 226–235
  CSMA/CD, 257–259
  diagnostics/repair, 332–338
  fiber-optic cables, 235–238
  fire ratings for, 238–239
  Gigabit Ethernet, 265–269
  horizontal cabling, 284–286
  installation of structured, 303–327
  for ISP diversity, 472
  labeling/organizing, 294
  making your own, 254
  maps/diagrams of, 479–480
  mechanical connection variations, 268
  media converters for, 255, 256, 268–269
  in network design, 225
  standardization for, 232, 237, 239–240
  structured cabling, 225, 280–303
  telecommunications room to work area, 283
  testing/troubleshooting, 316–327, 334–335
  tracing cables, 337

caches
- ARP cache poisoning attack, 582–585
- ARP caches, 46
- client resolver cache, 173, 176
- DNS, 173, 174, 176, 179–180
- IPv6 destination cache, 215
- neighbor cache, 212, 214
- NetFlow, 517
- proxy caching, 486

cameras, security, 569
canonical name (CNAME) resource record, 181
capacitance, 229
captive portals, 370–371
Carrier-Grade NAT (CGNAT), 143, 144
carrier sense, 257
CASB (Cloud Access Security Broker), 469
Cat (category) ratings, 232, 294
Cat6/6a cables, 234
CCMP, 367
CDMA (code-division multiple access), 408
CDNs (content delivery networks), 211
CDP (Cisco Discovery Protocol), 136–137
cellular service, 110, 134
cellular WAN, 405–410
censoring packets, 491
central policy management, 467
Cerf, Vinton, 13, 203
certificates, digital, 558–560, 562
certifiers, cable, 323
change management, 530–531
channel bonding, 357
channels, Wi-Fi
- ad hoc mode for, 380
- configuring frequency and, 390–392
- overview of, 353–354
- troubleshooting, 395

checkpoints/snapshots, 420
checksum, 550
child domains, 178–179
CIA (confidentiality, integrity, availability) triad, 520, 549–550, 571
CI/CD (continuous integration/continuous deployment), 442
CIDR (Classless Inter-Domain Routing), 68, 76–77, 206, 625
ciphertext, 550, 554–555
Cisco
- AD chart, 124–125
- EAP-FAST, 364
- EIGRP, 117, 120
- EtherChannel, 157
- IOS, 135–138, 197
- NetFlow, 516–517
- port states, 161
- routers, 133, 134
- switches, 150, 156, 275
- three-tiered architecture, 458, 460
- WAPs, 348

cladding, fiber-optic, 235
Class A networks, 63–64, 78
Class B networks, 64–65, 68, 76, 78
Class C networks, 65–66, 68, 76, 78
Class D networks, 66
Class E networks, 66
classes, IPv4 address, 62–76
classful addressing, 63–76, 77, 204
classic data center architecture, 456–466
classless addressing, 68, 76, 77, 206
CLI (command-line interface), 54
clientless VPNs, 501
clients
- configuring wireless, 392–393
- in DHCP DORA process, 190–193
- DNS, 174
- installing Wi-Fi network, 379–380
- ports and requests from, 11
- resource sharing via, 3
- in SSH session, 506–507
- VLAN pooling for enterprise, 373
- VPN client software, 498

client-to-site VPNs, 497–498
clock synchronization, 505
closed ports, 86
cloud bursting, 438
cloud computing
- cloud providers, 415
- cloud resource management, 443–446
- CompTIA exam objectives on, 622–623
- container technology for, 422
- costs, 443
- defined, 431
- deployment models, 437–439
- desktop virtualization, 446–448
- DNS provider for, 190
- IaC for, 440–442
- integrating local and, 448–450
- security for, 444–446
- TXT to validate ownership in, 187
- virtualization and, 415, 431, 433, 439
- VMs in the cloud, 428

cloud computing (*continued*)
  VPNs for, 448–450
cloud gateways, 439
clustering, 471
`cmd` prompt, 97
coaxial cables, 226–230, 334
collapsed core architecture, 460–461
collisions
  avoiding wireless, 354–355
  in bus topology, 258–259
  collision domain, 259, 260
  collision resistance, 561
colocation, 466
colons, in IPv6 notation, 207
command line interface (CLI), 348
commands, 137, 193
common polarization, 386
communication
  API integration, 520
  local, 42, 43, 44–46
  MAC and IP addresses for, 42–43, 52–54
  via ports/services, 83
  remote, 42, 43, 47–52
  re-routing, 114
  sockets as endpoints of, 97
  soft skills in, 615
  TCP for secure, 91–94
  three-way handshakes for data, 92–94
  timing to prevent collisions, 258–259
  UDP for real-time, 95
  VLANs for boundaries in, 152
community strings, 511
CompTIA, vii, xxxiii–xxxiv, xxxiv
CompTIA Network+ certification
  education for, xxxv–xxxvi
  exam for, xxxvi–xxxvii, 3, 621–637
  overview of, xxxiv–xxxv
  practice exams, 639, 641–642
  understanding networks via, xxxiii
CompTIA Network+ Certification All-in-One Exam Guide, xxxv–xxxvi
concentrators, 428–429, 501
conceptual network models, 4–6
confidentiality, 549–550
configuration
  automated, 440, 442
  of backups, 532
  baseline/golden, 532
  change management, 531
  configuration drift, 441
  configuration management, 531–532
  DHCP, 190–197
  documenting baseline data center, 480
  encryption, 390
  enterprise wireless, 371–376
  incorrect ACL, 168
  IP address, 77–78
  IP helper/relay agent, 197
  IPv6 autoconfiguration, 216
  monitoring, 521
  NAT-compatible routers, 140–144
  of network security devices, 495
  PoE (Power over Ethernet), 375
  production configuration, 532
  RA (Router Advertisement), 216
  router, 109, 110, 113, 127, 134, 135
  switch port, 160
  VLAN, 153, 156
  WAP, 347–348
  Wi-Fi, 376–394
  WPS for IoT, 361
configuration utility, 347, 348
congestion/contention, 378
connections/connectors
  10GbE, 272
  CompTIA exam objectives on, 624–625
  connector mismatches, 324
  connector standards, 239–240
  copper cables and, 226–235
  at the demarc, 299, 302–303
  fiber-optic cables/connections, 235–238, 255–258, 268
  IPv4 and IPv6, 205, 221
  link lights for, 330–332
  in physical network setup, 310–316
  physical NIC, 328–330
  PoE, 37
  punchdown blocks for, 291–294
  router, 134–139
  routing table for info on, 127
  SAN (storage area network), 464
  securing. *See* security
  SFF connectors, 266–268
  slow wireless, 398–401
  TCP, via three-way handshakes, 91
  troubleshooting cable runs, 316–327
  troubleshooting Wi-Fi, 394–404
  VPNs for secure, 496–503
  WAP connection types, 358
console cables, 134

console ports, 509
consoles, 135
consumer access points, 386–392
containerization, 422, 442
content addressable memory (CAM) table, 148
content filtering, 601
continuity, electrical, 317, 318
controllers, ICS, 575
control plane, 430
convergence, 117, 120, 133, 161
converters, 472
copper cables/connectors
  for 10GbE, 269, 272
  overview of, 226–235
  testing/troubleshooting, 316–320
core, fiber-optic, 235
core layer, 460–462
cost(s)
  asymmetric cryptography, 556
  cable, 255
  cloud computing, 443
  network installation, 304
  of router pathways, 118
counters/facilities, 518
couplers, 334
CPE (customer-premises equipment), 302
CPU, 151, 417–418, 424, 445, 470, 494, 512, 517, 593
CRC (cyclic redundancy check), 18, 19, 20, 166, 550
crimping cables, 252–253, 311–313, 317
crossover cables, 138, 152, 254, 260, 266, 293
cross-polarization/misalignment, 386
crosstalk, 231, 293, 321–322
cryptography, 550–563
  See also encryption
CSMA/CA (carrier-sense multiple access with collision avoidance), 354–356
CSMA/CD (carrier-sense multiple access with collision detection), 257–259, 354–355
CSPs (cloud service providers), 432
CST (Common Spanning Tree), 161
CVE (Common Vulnerabilities and Exposures), 542
cybersecurity. *See* security

D

DAD (duplicate address detection), 217
daemons. *See* services (daemons)
DARPA (US Defense Advanced Research Projects Agency), 13
DAS (direct-attached storage), 465
data
  in data centers, 455
  Ethernet transmission of, 247
  facility/infrastructure support, 472–473
  fragmentation, 11
  frames for, 17, 22
  IP addressing for packets of, 60–61
  methods for moving, 225
  NIC reading of, 52, 59
  passed between layers, 9
  regulatory security compliance, 571–572
  SaaS and control of, 437
  voice data streams, 155
databases, VLAN, 156
data centers
  assessments of, 481
  classic architecture/design of, 456–466
  the cloud as, 431
  cloud connections for, 451
  configuration drift at, 441
  defined, 455–456
  documentation at, 474–481
  high availability in, 289, 456, 464, 470–473, 525, 527, 534, 630
  location of, 464–466
  modern architecture/design of, 466–469
  NFV technology for, 429
  PDUs for, 289
  physical scalability for, 306
  site surveys, 481
  storage at, 463–464
  traffic flows at, 462
  virtual scalability for, 444
Data field, 18, 249
datagrams, 60
Data Link layer (Layer 2)
  ACL configuration in, 168
  ARP at, 212
  as belonging to VLANs, 152
  frames at, 247
  LLDP and CDP at, 136–137
  network segmentation in, 572
  NIC at, 83
  overview of, 6, 14–23
  physical connectivity at, 60
  routers and data from, 133
  switching at, 147
  in three-tiered architecture, 458
  virtual switching at, 426
  VXLANs and, 468

data locality laws, 572
Data Over Cable Service Interface Specification (DOCSIS), 133
data plane, 430
DCF (Distributed Coordination Function), 355
DCI (Data Center Interconnect), 468
DCI (deep content inspection), 491–492
DCS (distributed control system), 576, 577
DDoS (distributed denial of service) attack, 190, 580
dead ports, 261
dead spots, signal, 358, 379, 398
debugging, 446, 528
decapsulation, 23
deception technologies, 570
decibels, 316–317
decimal system
  binary-to-decimal conversion, 28
  decimal-to-binary conversion, 28–32
  decimal-to-hexadecimal conversion, 37–38
  hexadecimal-to-decimal conversion, 35–37
  IPv4, 206
  in local communication, 43–46
  for MAC vs. IP addresses, 42
  overview of, 26–27
decommissioning devices, 530
decoy software, 570
decryption, 551
dedicated switches, 458
default gateway, 47, 193
defaults
  changing default passwords, 597
  default DHCP gateway, 193, 199
  default DHCPv6 gateway, 217
  default route cost, 120
  default route errors, 133
  default subnet mask, 71
  default switch port setting, 157
  route on routing tables, 128
  TTL, in SOA records, 185
defense-in-depth architecture, 492
degradation, signal, 316, 323–324, 396, 397
demarc (demarcation point), 299–302, 477
demarc extension, 302
demilitarized zone (DMZ), 601
deployment, app, 442
deployment models, cloud, 437–439
designated ports, 163, 164–166
desktop computers
  cloud virtualization of, 446–448
  as VMs, 416
  wireless clients in, 379
Destination Address, 215, 248–249
destination cache, 215
development environment, 440, 442
device drivers, 347
device ID, 16, 42
devices
  EUI-64 to track, 209
  hardening, 596
  life-cycle management, 527–530
  management of employee, 579
  mean time to failure (MTTF), 534
  network device logs, 518
  OT (operation technology) for, 574–579
  rogue, 520, 587–588
  saturation of, 399
  See also hardware; IoT (Internet of Things) devices; *specific device by name*
DFS (Dynamic Frequency Selection), 353
DHCP (Dynamic Host Configuration Protocol)
  as an application, 8
  as client-server protocol, 3
  commands, 193
  DHCPv6 vs., 217
  DORA process, 190–193
  dynamic addressing by, 173
  dynamic vs. static IP assignment by, 195–196
  IPAM to oversee, 526–527
  leases, 194–195
  message types, 196–197
  overview of, 173–174
  ports associated with, 85, 88
  relay agent/IP helper, 197–198
  rogue servers, 138, 587–588
  troubleshooting, 198–199
  UDP use by, 95
DHCPv6, 205, 217
diagnostics
  by ISPs, 300
  via OSI model, 25
  physical cabling, 332–338
  ping utility for, 61, 98, 99–100
  See also troubleshooting
dial-up internet, 9, 405, 496, 509, 565
Diffie–Hellman Key Exchange (DHKE) algorithm, 506, 557
DigiCert, 558, 559
`dig` utility, 180
dipole antennas, 383–384

direct attached copper (DAC) cable, 230
direct communication, 41, 47
Direct Connect, 451
directed broadcast, 131
directional antennas, 384–385
disassociation, client, 404
disaster recovery, 532–535
Discover, DHCP, 190, 194, 196, 197, 198, 215
disks, virtual, 463
distributed switches for virtual networks, 426–427
distributed systems, DNS, 178
distribution layer, 459
diverse paths, 472
DKIM (DomainKeys Identified Mail), 186
DMARC (Domain-based Message Authentication, Reporting and Conformance), 187
DNS (Domain Name System)
  as an application, 8
  as client-server protocol, 3
  dots in DNS names, 184
  global hierarchy in, 176
  hosts file vs., 172–173
  IP address gathering via, 42
  IPAM to oversee, 526–527
  for IPv6, 205
  ports associated with, 88
  resource record types, 180–188
  structure and query resolution, 174–180
  website lookup via, 171–173
DNS over HTTPS (DoH), 175
DNS over TLS (DoT), 175
DNSSEC (DNS Security System Extensions), 586
DNS servers
  attacks on, 585, 586–587
  authoritative/non-authoritative responses from, 188–189
  authoritative TLD DNS servers, 177–180
  DHCP and incorrect, 199
  internal vs. external, 189–190
  IPv6 and, 218
  primary, 175
  query response by, 174
  root name servers, 176–177, 178
  UDP use by, 11, 95
documentation
  asset inventories, 525–526
  of changes, 531
  CompTIA exam objectives on, 629
  of configuration changes, 521
  data center, 474–481
  on optimal performance, 518
  of troubleshooting outcomes, 614–615
DoH, 587
Domain Name Security Extensions (DNSSEC), 177
domains
  global hierarchy of, 176, 179
  and subdomains, 175, 178–179
  validating ownership of cloud, 187
  www as needed for certain, 183
DORA (Discover, Offer, Request, and Ack) process, 190–193, 194
DoS (denial of service) attacks, 444, 494, 580
DoT, 587
DPI (deep packet inspection), 491
DR (disaster recovery), 532–535, 630–631
drive-by download exploit kit, 590
drivers, NIC, 330
drops, cable, 167, 304, 307
DSA (Digital Signature Algorithm), 557
DSL modems, 110, 133
DSSS (direct-sequence spread-spectrum), 353
DUAL (diffusing update algorithm), 120
dual stacks, 219
dumb terminals, 135
dumpster diving, 592
Duo, 567
duplex fiber-optic cables/connectors, 235–236, 238, 272
duplex settings, 157
duplicates
  DAD (duplicate address detection), 217
  DHCP and duplicate IP addresses, 199
DVCS (distributed version control system), 441
Dyn, 190
dynamic addressing, 78, 173, 208, 215, 631
dynamic inventories, 441
dynamic IP assignment, 195–196
dynamic key generation, 367
dynamic load balancing, 420
dynamic ports, 86, 190
dynamic routing
  EGP for, 121–125
  IGP for, 117–121
  overview of, 113–117
  troubleshooting, 132–133

E

EAP (Extensible Authentication Protocol), 363–364
EAP-FAST (Flexible Authentication via Secure Tunneling), 364

EAP-MD5, 364
EAP-MSCHAPv2, 363–364
EAPOL (EAP over LAN), 365
EAPOW (EAP over Wireless), 365
EAP-PSK, 363
EAP-TTLS (Tunneled TLS), 363
east-west traffic, 462
eavesdropping, 506
eBGP (External BGP), 122
EBSS (extended basic service set), 351
ECDSA (Elliptic Curve DSA), 557
Echo requests/replies, 98, 99, 101, 142, 195
ECMP (Equal-Cost Multipath), 461
EDGE (Enhanced Data rates for GSM Evolution), 406, 407
edge layer, 458
edge routers, 113, 121
EGP (Exterior Gateway Protocol), 121–125
EHT (Extremely High Throughput), 360
EIGRP (Enhanced Interior Gateway Routing Protocol), 120–121, 125
EIRP (effective isotropic radiated power), 398
elasticity, 444
electing root bridges/ports, 162
electricity/power
    binary data transmission via, 23–25
    for data centers, 472–473
    for enterprise networks, 374–376
    increasing, 397
    multimeters for testing, 319
    PDU for managing, 289
    signal loss and insufficient, 396
    to telecommunications room, 305
    testing copper cables for, 317–320
    troubleshooting issues with, 335–337
    UPSs, 335
email
    DKIM to authenticate, 186
    message integrity, 562
    phishing, 590–592
    TCP for, 90
emergency procedures, 473
EMI (electromagnetic interference), 226
enable mode, 136
encapsulation, in networks, 11, 23, 51, 61, 498, 500, 503
encryption
    configuring Wi-Fi, 390
    encryption protocol mismatch, 395
    Kerberos, 567
    overview of, 550–557
    SNMP, 511
    in SSH session, 506
    TKIP, 367
    TLS (Transport Layer Security), 505
    VPN, 496–503
    wireless data encryption, 362
    XOR (exclusive OR), 551–553
enterprise SaaS, 437
enterprise wireless setup, 371–376
environmental monitors, 337, 455–456, 473, 575
EOL (end-of-life) management, 529
ephemeral ports, 86
equipment racks
    in classic data center design, 458, 459, 461, 466
    diagrams of, 474–479
    installation of, 287–291
    power supply to, 472
ERP (effective radiated power), 398
errdisable port state, 161
errors
    ICMP to report, 61, 86, 98, 112, 142
    IPv4 packet header to check, 62
    power budget exceeded, 375
    from switching loops, 158
ESP (Encapsulating Security Payload), 503
ESS (extended service set), 351, 352
ESSID (extended service set identifier), 352, 371
ESX hypervisor, 418, 419
ESXi hypervisor, 419
EtherChannel, 157
Ethernet
    10GbE, 269–274
    40 GbE, 100 GbE, and Terabit, 275–276
    100 Mbps, 261–265
    802.3 standards, 246–247
    address for IPv6 multicasts, 210
    connectors, 14
    EAP for, 365
    early standards, 250–259
    enhanced/extended, 259–261
    frames, 18, 19, 247–249
    Gigabit Ethernet, 265–269
    for ICSs, 579
    interfaces, 120, 132
    origins of, 246
    PoE (Power over Ethernet), 374–376
    switches, 260–261
    switch/node length, 298
    wireless connectors, 50

ethical hacking, 542
EUI-64 (Extended Unique Identifier, 64-bit), 209
Europe Norm (EN), 280
evil twins, 403, 588
expansion slots/cards, 328
explicit tagging, 153
exploits/attacks. *See* attacks
Extension Mechanisms for DNS (EDNS), 177
external DNS servers, 189–190
external security threats, 545
extranet-based VPNs, 502

F

facilities and infrastructure support, 289, 335, 472–473
facilities/counters, 518
failures
- mean time to failure (MTTF), 534
- from mishandling VTPs, 156
- OSPF repair of, 120
- ping utility, 100
- segmentation enforcement for, 572

false positives/negatives, 495
far-end crosstalk (FEXT), 321–323
Fast Ethernet
- 100BASE-T as, 262
- interfaces, 120
- for LANs, 264

fault tolerance, 114
FC (Fibre Channel), 464, 465
FCoE (Fibre Channel over Ethernet), 464
F connectors, 228
FCS (frame check sequence), 18, 19, 166, 249
feasible successor routes, 121
federated authentication, 565
FHRP (first hop redundancy protocol), 139
FHSS (frequency-hopping spread-spectrum), 353
fiber distribution panel, 302
fiber-optic cables/connections
- 10BASE-FL, 255–257
- 10GbE, 269–274
- mechanical connection types, 268
- overview of, 235–238
- for SAN connections, 464
- tools for working with, 325–327
- troubleshooting, 323–327, 334–335

fiber-optic NICs, 327
file integrity, 561–562
file transfers, 90
filtration
- content filtering, 601
- firewalls for, 489–490
- of ICMP, 101
- incorrect ACL configuration and, 168
- MAC address, 362, 369, 389
- port, 86, 505
- SSE and URL, 469
- stateful/stateless packet filtering, 490–491
- URL filtering, 600–601

FIM (file integrity monitoring), 520
FIN flag, 94
fire ratings, cable, 238–239
fire suppression, 305, 473
firewalls
- filtered ports and, 86
- IDS/IPS to support, 492
- next-generation firewall (NGFW), 492
- overview of, 489–490
- virtual, 426, 427

firmware, 528–529
first hop redundancy protocols (FHRPs), 471
fish tape, 307
flags
- IPv4 packet header, 62
- RA (Router Advertisement), 216
- in routing tables, 126
- TCP, 91–94

flat-surface connector, 268
FLCC DNS, 188
flexibility, virtual software, 423
floor plans, 303, 473, 475
flow monitoring, 516–517
Fluke MicroScanner, 334
forced tunnel with exceptions, 502
Foreign Address, 97
forward lookup zones, 189
forward proxy, 488
four-pair UTP, 285
four-post (server rail) rack, 289
Fox and Hound toner, 337, 338
FQDN (fully qualified domain name), 171, 172, 176, 180, 181, 183, 185, 187, 199
fragmentation, 11, 19, 158, 177
frames
- Ethernet, 247–249
- flooded by switches, 148–151, 159
- incorrect ACL configuration and, 168
- jumbo frames, 158
- latency for, 323
- MAC addresses in, 61
- monitoring switch interfaces, 167

frames (*continued*)
movement of, 20–23, 52
overview of, 17–19
packets vs., 514
PDUs and, 24
frequency configuration, Wi-Fi, 390–392
FTP (File Transfer Protocol), 3, 84, 87, 90, 143
full duplex, 157, 252, 259, 264–265
full tunnel VPNs, 501
fusion splicer, 326
FWaaS (Firewall as a Service), 469

G

Gartner, 469
gateway, default, 193, 199, 217
gateways, cloud, 439
GBIC (gigabit interface converter), 268
GDPR (General Data Protection Regulation), 571
generators, power, 473
geofencing, 371, 568
giants, 167
Gigabit Ethernet, 265–269
Git, 441
GLBP (Gateway Load Balancing Protocol), 139, 471
global hierarchy, 176
golden configuration, 532
Google, 8, 95, 172, 174, 574, 615
Google Authenticator, 564, 567
Google Cloud, 415, 451
Google Drive, 437
gray hat hackers, 543
GRE (Generic Routing Encapsulation), 504
greenfield mode, 358
GSM (Global System for Mobile Communications), 406–407
GUA (global unicast address), 209–210, 215, 217
guest networks, 370, 579
GUI (graphical user interface), 54, 507
Guide for Security-Focused Configuration Management of Information Systems, 480, 532

H

hacking. *See* attacks
half duplex, 157, 252
handshakes, 560
hard drives, 28, 463, 534, 593
hardening devices/network, 362, 596, 634
hardware
airflow for, 289, 473
asset inventories, 526
cable management, 314
change management, 530
copper cables/connectors for, 226–235
data center, 472–473
diagrams of, 478–479
EMI from, 226
enterprise wireless, 371–372
equipment racks, 287–291
EUI-64 to track, 209
firewall, 489
hardening, 596
installation vs. servicing 100BASE-, 263
load balancing, 486
MAC addresses for, 15–17
network, 4
NFVs to replace, 429–431
physical environment for, 305–307, 337
protocols, 6
redundancy of, 471
routing table use by, 128
switches, 19, 426
in three-tiered architecture, 457–459
troubleshooting issues with, 335–337, 420
underutilization of, 416
VMs (virtual machines), 417–421
Wi-Fi network client, 379–380
wireless networks, 345–347
See also cabling; connections/connectors
hashing, 550, 560–563
HBA (Host Bus Adapter) storage cards, 465
HDLC (High-level Data Link Control), 50
headers
ICMP, 99
IP, 13, 98
IPv4 packet header, 61–62
TCP, 92–94
in Transport layer, 12
heat map, 378
Hello messages, 117
Heroku, 435, 436
hexadecimal system
decimal-to-hexadecimal conversion, 37–38
hexadecimal-to-binary conversion, 34–35, 209
hexadecimal-to-decimal conversion, 35–37
for IPv6, 207
for MAC vs. IP addresses, 42
overview of, 15, 26, 32–33
hierarchy
DNS and global, 176, 179
in network design, 112, 113

Hi-Fi (high fidelity), 344
high availability, 289, 456, 464, 470–473, 525, 527, 534, 630
HIPAA (Health Insurance Portability and Accountability Act), 571
HMI (human-machine interface), 577
homomorphic encryption, 554
honeypots/honeynets, 570
hopping/shifting frequencies, 353
hops, 101, 102, 118, 179, 215
horizontal cabling, 282, 283, 284–286, 294, 297, 309
hosts
- address creation by IPv6, 217
- bastion hosts, 602
- calculating number of subnet, 70
- in the cloud, 431
- configuring IP addresses for, 77–78
- host-based firewalls, 489, 490
- host-based IDS/IPS, 495
- host ID, 42
- host-only virtual networks, 426
- vs. IPv6 interface, 207
- lessening traffic to, 151
- local, 78
- MAC and IP address known by, 42
- resource sharing via, 3
- in subnet mask, 71, 73
- subnetting for, 67
- virtual network, 425
- VM as website, 420

hosts file, 172–173, 174
HSPA+ (Evolved High-Speed Packet Access), 408
HSRP (Hot Standby Router Protocol), 139, 154, 471
HSTS (HTTP Strict Transport Security), 584
HTTP (Hypertext Transfer Protocol), 3, 9, 85, 88, 90, 486, 584, 587
HTTPS (HTTP over TLS), 85, 89, 90
hub and spoke topology, 281
hubs, 250, 259–260
HughesNet, 405
humidity, 305, 337
Hurricane Electric, 220
HVAC systems, 473
hybrid public/private cloud, 438
hybrid topology, 281, 282
hypervisors, 417–421, 425, 428

I

IaaS (Infrastructure as a Service), 433, 434, 443
IaC (infrastructure as code), 440–442, 626
IAM (Identity and Access Management), 563
IANA (Internet Assigned Numbers Authority), 62, 85, 86, 116, 205
iBGP (Internal BGP), 122
IBSS (independent basic service set), 349, 351
ICANN (Internet Corporation for Assigned Names and Numbers), 63, 205
ICMP (Internet Control Message Protocol)
- ARP and, 42
- Echo request/reply, 98, 99, 101, 142, 195
- error messages, 61, 97, 98, 142
- filtration of, 101
- inside IP, 98–99
- for IPv6, 212
- Verizon Fios and, 102

ICMP QueryID, 142
ICS (industrial control system), 574–576
ICS (Internet Connection Sharing), 350
IDF (intermediate distribution frame), 286, 302, 475, 477–478
IDS (intrusion detection system), 490, 492–495
IEEE (Institute of Electrical and Electronics Engineers)
- 10 GbE standards, 270
- cable/connector standards, 239–240
- LACP, 157
- LAN standards, 25
- MAC addresses from, 15
- *See also* individual standards by number

IEEE 802.1Q VLAN tag, 153
IETF (Internet Engineering Task Force), 78, 116, 204, 467
IFG (interframe gap), 354
IGP (Interior Gateway Protocol), 117–121
IIOT (Industrial Internet of Things), 573
IKE (Internet Key Exchange), 503–504
IKEv2, 504
IMAP (Internet Message Access Protocol), 8, 90
impedance, 229
implicit tagging, 152
in-band management, 509–511
incompatible updates, 403
incorrect pinout, 318
indirect communication, 41
information security, 541
infrastructure layer, 430
infrastructure-level changes, 530
infrastructure networks, 350–351, 381–392
infrastructure support, data center, 472–473
inputs for virtualization, 423

insufficient wireless coverage, 396
insulating jacket, fiber-optic, 235
integrity, data, 549–550, 561–562
interbuilding connections, 299
interfaces
  HMI (human-machine interface), 577
  IPv6, 207
  monitoring switch/router, 166–167
  vs. ports, 149
  router, 138
interference, 316, 318, 321–322, 338, 378–379, 397, 400–401
intermediate certificates, 559
internal DNS servers, 189–190
internal networks, 117
internal security threats, 544–545
internet
  and the cloud, 431–432, 439
  connection at data centers, 471
  connections for ICS, 574–576
  decentralized governance of, 116
  dynamic routing on, 116
  inexpensive connections via, 496
  overlay tunnels for, 220
  satellite, 405
intranet-based VPNs, 502
intrusion in cloud computing, 446
inventories, asset, 525–526
inventories, dynamic, 441, 480
IoT (Internet of Things) devices
  IPv6 for, 204
  RFI from, 401
  security for, 572–573
  wireless configuration for, 361
IP (Internet Protocol) address
  address pool exhaustion, 198
  ad hoc mode for, 380
  for authoritative TLD DNS, 178
  for CGNAT, 143
  configuration for, 77–78
  configuring router ports, 136, 138
  DHCP and conflicting, 194–195
  DHCP to obtain, 190
  vs. DNS, 171–173
  and DNS resource record types, 180–188
  for DNS root name servers, 176–177
  duplicate, 199
  dynamic vs. static assignment of, 195–196
  exclusion ranges for, 196
  geofencing for, 568
  how to find, 54–55
  incorrect, 199
  iterative/recursive lookup of, 179–180
  for local communication, 42
  vs. MAC address, 15, 42–43
  NAT and, 140–144
  need for both MAC and, 52–54
  at Network layer, 97–98
  in remote communication, 42, 47–52
  routing based on, 110, 115, 125
  as socket component, 10
  special categories of, 78
  subnet broadcast address, 74
  subnetting for, 66–68
  TCP/IP protocol, 12–13
  in traceroute, 101
  TTL field in, 48
  VPNs for, 498
  website lookup via name vs., 171–172
  See also IPv4 (Internet Protocol version 4) address; IPv6
IP ACLs, 168
IPAM (IP Address Management), 526–527
`ipconfig`, GUA and, 210
`ipconfig /all`, 16, 54, 193
`ipconfig` command, 16, 54, 179
ipconfig /release, 193
ipconfig /renew, 193
IP helper/relay agent, 197–198
`iproute`, 129, 132
iproute2, 97
IPS (intrusion prevention system), 490, 492–495
IPsec tunneling protocols, 503–505
IPSes (intrusion prevention systems), 469
IPv4 (Internet Protocol version 4) address
  address classes, 62–76
  addressing process, 60–61
  CompTIA exam objectives on, 625, 631
  for DNS root name servers, 176–177
  IPv4/IPv6 compatibility, 219–221
  IPv4 packet header, 61–62
  multicasting in, 211
  NAT for depletion of, 140, 143
  OSPF version 2 for, 120
  space limitations for, 204
  type A host address, 180, 188
IPv6
  addressing system, 205–212
  address space in, 204
  CompTIA exam objectives on, 626, 631

deployment of, 216–218
DNS extensions for, 177
IPv4/IPv6 compatibility, 219–221
NDP (Neighbor Discovery Protocol), 212–216
at Network layer, 61
origins of, 204
type AAAA host address, 181
iSCSI (Internet Small Computer System Interface), 464, 465
ISO (International Organization for Standardization), 6, 232, 571
ISOC (Internet Society), 116
ISO/IEC 27001, 571
ISO/IEC 27002, 571
isolation, network, 370
ISPs (Internet Service Providers)
and BGP policy, 124
and CGNAT, 143
data center access to, 457, 471
demarc between network and, 300
DNS of, 172, 178
IP addresses from, 43, 63
multiple networks and, 112–113
NFV technology for, 429
SLAs from, 527
VLSMs for, 77
iterative IP lookup, 179–180

J

jitter, 399
jumbo frames, 158, 464
jump box/host, 508

K

Kahn, Robert E., 13
KDC (key distribution center), 567
KDF (Key Derivation Function), 506
Kerberos, 567
kernels, 417
Kevlar fibers, 251
keys
in asymmetric cryptography, 555–557
digital certificates for, 558–560
managing, 599
processing ciphers via, 550
PSK (pre-shared key), 363, 367–368, 390, 392
SSH (Secure Shell), 506
symmetric encryption, 554–555
TKIP, 367
in XOR, 551–553
Krone blocks, 296
Kubernetes, 442

L

LAN (local area network), 25, 109, 119, 141, 206, 264, 373, 446, 448–450, 467–468
LAN NICs, 327
Large-Scale NAT (LSNAT), 143
latency, 323, 356, 360, 399, 572
layers
in OSI networks, 3–4, 6–25
vs. planes, 430
in three-tiered architecture, 457–460
layout, network, 68–69
LC fiber-optic connectors, 237–238, 267
LDAP (Lightweight Directory Access Protocol), 8, 89, 187, 566
LDAPS, 89
leaf switches, 461
lease, DHCP, 194–195, 198
least privilege access, 445, 468, 469, 563, 565, 568, 626, 632
LEDs (light-emitting diodes)
as activity lights, 332
for fiber-optic signals, 236
as NIC link lights, 330
RFI from, 401
legacy mode, 358
Let's Encrypt, 558, 559, 560
licensing, 526, 640
life-cycle management, 527–530, 629
light leakage, 324
lightweight AP, 373
Lightweight EAP (LEAP), 364
limited broadcast, 131
linear networks, 113
link lights, 330, 332
link-local addresses, 194–195, 208–209
links
IPv6, 206
link aggregation, 157
OSPF repair of, 120
recovering from downed, 113–114
wireless link states, 347
Linux
daemons in, 83
`ip a`, 16, 55
iproute2 in, 97
MAC addresses for, 16
`netstat` utility, 10

Linux (*continued*)
  NIC drivers, 330
  routing table info in, 129
  traceroute, 102
LLC (Logical Link Control), 22
LLDP (Link Layer Discovery Protocol), 136–137
load balancing, 115, 139, 420, 461–462, 470
Local Address, 97
local communication, 42, 44–46
local hosts, 78
Local Preference, 122
locks, for physical security, 569
logging cloud use, 446
logical address protocol, 12–13, 15, 52
logical AND operation, 45, 47
logical network diagrams, 478
logic bombs, 594
logs, 518–519
loopback adapters, 333, 334
loopback addresses, 78
loops, 130, 158, 164
loss of signal, 316–317, 323–324, 396, 397
Lotus Notes, 259
LSA (link-state advertisement), 117, 118, 120
LSDB (link-state database), 117
LTE (Long Term Evolution), 408–409
LTE networks, 110, 134
LWAPP (Lightweight Access Point Protocol), 374

M

MAC address
  BSSID as wireless equivalent, 352
  in DHCP message, 191
  in Ethernet networks, 247, 248–249
  filtering, 362, 369, 389
  flooding attacks, 581
  in frame movement, 20–23
  how to find, 54–55
  vs. IP address, 12, 42–43
  and IPv6, 209
  for local and remote communication, 42–54
  MAC address table, 493–494
  need for both IP and, 52–54
  overview of, 15–17
  port security for, 597–599
  in switch decision-making, 148–151
  for virtual networks, 426
  in wireless NICs, 25
macOS
  daemons in, 83
  DNS caches, 180
  `ifconfig`, 16, 55
  `netstat` utility, 10
  NIC drivers, 330
  routing table info in, 129
  traceroute, 102
macro viruses, 594
maintenance window, 531
malware
  DPI checks for, 491
  honeypots/honeynets for, 570
  overview of, 593–596
  via phishing emails, 590
  and slow connections, 398
  VM to prevent, 421
  XOR in, 553
  See also attacks; security
managed devices, 134
management
  asset inventories, 526–527
  in-band vs. out-of-band, 509–511
  of changes, 530–531
  CompTIA exam objectives on, 629–630, 632
  documentation for, 525–527
  of employee devices, 579
  jump box/host for, 508
  key management, 599
  life-cycle, 527–530
  monitoring data flows, 516–517
  of network device access, 565
  of network security devices, 495
  NTP (Network Time Protocol), 505
  packet sniffing for, 514–516
  via performance monitoring, 517–520
  port scanning, 505–506
  RDP (Remote Desktop Protocol) for, 507–508
  remote, 506
  resource management, cloud, 443–446
  SD-WAN and central policy management, 467
  SIEM for security, 519–520
  SNMP (Simple Network Management Protocol), 511–514
  SSH (Secure Shell) for, 506–507
  See also administration
management plane, 430
man-in-the-middle attack, 506, 582
MANO (management, automation, and network orchestration), 429
mantraps, 593
manual translations (stateful mapping), 221

mass storage devices, 463
Maximum Transmission Unit (MTU), 158, 167
MDF (main distribution frame), 286, 302, 476–478
MDM (mobile device management), 579
mean time between failures (MTBF), 534
mean time to failure (MTTF), 534
mean time to repair (MTTR), 534
media converters, 255, 256, 268
memory, 28, 421
mesh networks, 349, 394, 461
message integrity, 562
metadata, 12, 574
metrics, DR, 533–534
metrics, routing, 114–116, 127
Meyers, Mike, 639
MHz (megahertz), 232
MIB (management information base), 512
micrometers/microns, 236
microservices, 422
Microsoft, 60, 529
Microsoft 365 apps, 437
Microsoft Exchange, 259
Microsoft SQL Server, 533
MIMO (multiple input, multiple output), 358, 398
misalignment, antenna, 386
MITRE Corporation, 542
mixed mode, 357, 358
MLDv2 (Multicast Listener Discovery version 2), 211
MLS (multilayer switch), 148, 154–155
MMS (multimedia messaging system), 408
mobile devices
    cellular WAN for, 405–410
    wireless clients in, 379
modal dispersion, 324
modal distortion, 236
mode, wireless networking, 348
models, network, 4–6
modern data center architecture, 466–469
module interfaces, 133
monitoring. *See* management
mounting brackets, 309
MPLS (Multiprotocol Label Switching), 456
MS08-067 exploit, 543
MSAs (multisource agreements), 272
MT-RJ connectors, 238, 267
multicasting
    Class D addresses for, 66
    IPv4, 211
    IPv6 multicast addresses, 210–211, 213
    solicited-node multicast address, 212–214
    switches to flood multicasts, 150
Multi-Exit Discriminator (MED), 123–124
multifactor authentication (MFA), 508, 564, 566
multimeter, 319, 320
multimode fiber (MMF), 236, 255
multipathing, 464
Multiple-fiber Push-On (MPO) connectors, 238, 267
multiple networks, 112
multitenancy, 445
MU-MIMO, 398
multispeed networks, 274
multiple access, 258
MX (mail exchanger) resource record, 183

N

NA (Neighbor Advertisement), 214, 217
NAC (network access control), 597–599
name resolution, website, 171–173, 180
nanometers, 237
nano-SIM cards, 408–409
NAS (network attached storage), 465
NAT (Network Address Translation), 79, 109, 140–144, 425, 499
NAT64, 220–221
NAT gateways, 439
native mode, 357
NAT traversal, 219
nature-based risk security controls, 547
Nazareth University, 182
NDP (Neighbor Discovery Protocol), 205, 212–216
near-end crosstalk (NEXT), 321–323
NEC (National Electrical Code), 307
neighborships, 117
`netstat -a` command, 97
`netstat` utility, 10, 96–97
Network+. *See* CompTIA Network+ certification
network-based firewalls, 489
network blocks, 63
network controllers, 430
network design
    cabling in, 225
    components of, 282–284
    CompTIA exam objectives on, 281, 625
    defense-in-depth architecture, 492
    demarc (demarcation point), 299–302
    Ethernet, 247, 250–259
    hierarchical, 112
    horizontal cabling, 284–286
    and installation, 303–327

network design (*continued*)
MDF in, 302
for NFVs, 429
and NIC installation, 327–332
patch panel as mirroring, 316
SNMP architecture, 512
SPF (Shortest Path First) algorithm, 117
structured cabling installation, 303–327
telecommunications room in, 282–284, 286–297, 305–307
testing cable runs, 316–327
VLANs for flexible, 151
work area, 297–298
See also topology
network device logs, 518
network ID
in local communication, 44
in routing table, 77, 126
via subnet masks, 42, 71, 76
network ID extension, 71, 72, 74
Network layer (Layer 3)
Layer 3 switches, 148, 154–155
NAT and, 142
network segmentation in, 572
overview of, 6, 12–13
packets at, 247
protocols and utilities, 97–102
routing at, 110
TCP/IP at, 60–61
in three-tiered architecture, 458
VLANS and, 152
VXLANs and, 468
network loops, 158
network name/SSID, 352
networks
ACL and multiple, 112
API calls in, 8
baseline configurations, 532
basic knowledge of, xxxv
bug fixes/patches, 528
classes of network blocks, 63
communication between, 47–52
complexity of, xxxiii
CompTIA exam objectives on, 621–637
conceptual models, 4–6
diagrams of physical, 474–478
discovery of rogue, 520
dynamic routing for, 113–117
early Ethernet, 250–259
EMI effects on, 226
frame movement in, 20–23
guest networks, 579
hardening, 362
of honeypots, 570
host-only virtual, 426
layers in OSI model, 3–4, 6–25
NAC (network access control), 597–599
network-based firewalls, 489
network-based IDS/IPS, 495
network equality, 6
network metrics, 399
physical. *See* physical networks
resource sharing via, 3, 9
routers and switches for, 13, 109, 110, 111
segmentation enforcement, 572–578
service-related entry point, 299
stub/linear, 113
subnetting for layout of, 68–69
trusted/untrusted, 602
virtual, 421, 425–431
vulnerabilities in, 542–543
wireless/wired hybrids, 351
See also wired networks; wireless networks
next-generation firewall (NGFW)/Layer 7 firewall, 492
NextGenHacker101, 102
Next Hop Address, 215
NFV (network function virtualization), 429–431
NFVI (network function virtualization infrastructure), 429
nibbles, 33
NICs (network interface cards)
100BASE-T vs. 10BASE-T, 262
ad hoc mode for, 380
collision detection by, 258
data reading by, 52, 59
diagnostics/repair, 332–334
in frame movement, 20–23, 52
installing/troubleshooting, 327–332
loopback interface and, 130
MAC addresses for, 43, 53
malfunctioning, 167
NIC bonding, 157
overview of, 14–15, 19
physical communication via, 83
replacing onboard, 333
virtual, 425–426
wireless, 345–347, 379
NIM (network interface module), 134
NIST (National Institute of Standards and Technology), 79, 541

NIU (network interface unit), 300, 303
Nmap, 505
NMS (network management system), 512, 514
NOC (network operations center), 475
non-authoritative DNS responses, 188–189
non-linear networks, 113–117
nonrepudiation, 562
north-south traffic, 462
no shutdown, 137
notation systems, 206–208
Novell, 60
NS (name server) resource record, 187–188
NS (Neighbor Solicitation), 212, 214, 215, 217
`nslookup` utility, 180–188
NTP (Network Time Protocol), 88, 197, 505
NTS (Network Time Security), 505
numeral systems, 26–38

O

octets, 44, 63, 206
OCx, 456
OFDM (orthogonal frequency-division multiplexing), 353
OFDMA (orthogonal frequency-division multiple access), 360
Offer, DHCP, 191–192, 193, 196
Ohm rating, 229
OID (unique object identifier), 512
OM (optical multimode) fiber-optic cable, 255
omnidirectional antennas, 382–384
online UPSs, 336
on-path attacks, 216, 506, 582
ONT (optical network terminal), 110
open/damaged cable connections, 317, 323
open networks, 402
open ports, 86
operating systems (OSes)
- Cisco IOS, 135–138
- console ports to access, 509
- for containerization, 422
- DNS caches by, 180
- DNS resource record lookup, 180
- EUI-64 used by, 209
- finding IP addresses on, 54–55
- finding MAC addresses on, 16, 54–55
- IPv6 support by, 219
- `netstat` utility in, 10
- NIC drivers in, 330
- NIC troubleshooting via, 333
- routing table info in, 129
- updates, 529
- virtualization for, 417–421, 423, 447

operators, ICS, 575
Optical Carrier (OC) rates, 270
orchestration, 442
orchestrators, NFV, 429
OSI (Open Systems Interconnection)
- CompTIA exam objectives on, 622
- DNS resolution and, 173
- encapsulation/decapsulation in, 23
- hosts files, 172–173
- integrity checks in, 550
- layers in OSI model, 6–25
- network segmentation in, 572
- ports in, 84
- tools provided via, 3
- troubleshooting via, 3, 25, 610–611

OSPF (Open Shortest Path First), 117–120, 125
OT (operation technology), 574–579
OTDR (optical time-domain reflectometer), 326
OUI (organizationally unique identifier), 16, 42, 53
out-of-band management, 509–511
outputs for virtualization, 423
overcapacity issues, 399
overflow attacks, 581
overlay tunnels, 220
overutilization, hardware, 416

P

PaaS (Platform as a Service), 433–436, 443
packets
- capturing/sniffing, 514–516
- defined, 24
- flow monitoring, 516–517
- vs. frames, 247
- frames and, 17, 212, 514
- IPv4, 60–62
- load balancing of, 115
- monitoring discarded, 167
- in Network layer, 12
- router pathways for, 118
- routing, 125, 127–128
- stateful/stateless filtering of, 490–491
- stateless packet filters, 67
- troubleshooting lost, 399
- VPN, 498–503

Pad field, 248, 249
PAgP (Port Aggregation Protocol), 157
PAM (Privileged Access Management), 563
parabolic antenna, 385

PARC (Palo Alto Research Center), 210
parent domains, 178–179
passwords
  changing default, 597
  incorrect, 395
  increasing length of, 597
  key-based authentication vs., 507
  secure storage of, 562–563
PAT (Port Address Translation), 141–143, 220
patch antennas, 385
patch bay, 296
patch cables, 268, 295, 298, 311–314
patches
  life-cycle management, 528
  VMs to test, 420
patch panels, 291–294, 302, 314–316, 477
path diversity, 472
Path Maximum Transmission Unit (PMTU), 215
payload, data, 9, 18, 60, 503
payload, exploit, 544
PBAC (policy-based access control), 468
PCF (Point Coordination Function), 355
PCI (Peripheral Component Interconnect), 328
PCI DSS (Payment Card Industry Data Security Standard), 572
PCIe NIC, 379
PC-over-IP (PCoIP), 448
PDU (power distribution unit), 289, 472, 513
PDU (protocol data unit), 24, 513
peer-to-peer networks, 349
penetration testers (pentesters), 542
performance
  assessing baseline, 480, 517
  data locality laws for, 572
  logs, 518–519
  monitoring, 517–520
Performance Monitor, 518
peripherals, network segmentation for, 572
permissions, 444–445, 568
Peterson, Frank Thomas, 84
pfSense, 428
phishing, 590–592
physical contact (PC) connector, 268
Physical layer, 6, 22, 23–25, 60, 83, 316, 572
physical networks
  cable diagnostics/repair, 332–338
  CompTIA exam objectives on, 628
  data center facilities, 472–473
  documentation of, 474–481
  horizontal cabling, 284–286
  installation of, 303–327
  ISP redundancy at, 471–472
  NIC installation, 327–332
  physical security for, 290–291
  physical security threats, 290–291, 305
  physical signal obstructions, 400
  structured cabling for, 225, 280–303
  telecommunications room, 286–297
  testing/troubleshooting cables, 316–327
  work area in, 282, 297–298
piggybacking, 592–593
PIM (Privileged Identity Management), 563
ping utility, 61, 98, 99–100
pipelines/workflows, 442
PKI (public key infrastructure), 558
PLC (programmable logic controller), 578–579
plenum, 239
pods, 459
PoE (Power over Ethernet), 374–376
point-to-multipoint bridges, 159, 394
point-to-point bridges, 159, 394
point-to-point networks, 350
polarization, 386
Pollock, Dan, 600–601
PON (passive optical network), 133
port 68, 191
port 80, 11
port 443, 11
port bonding, 157
PortFast ports, 160–161
ports
  aggregating, 157
  blocked, 159
  broadcast flooding of, 494
  cable type detection by, 266
  CompTIA exam objectives on, 623
  console ports, 509
  dead Ethernet, 261
  disabling unused, 596
  dynamic, 86, 190
  Ethernet, 14, 261
  filtering, 86, 505
  fixed UDP, 191
  logical vs. physical, 87, 149
  mismatched connections, 324–325
  NAT changes to, 142
  overview of, 84
  patch panel, 294
  physical root port, 163–166
  physical switch ports, 153

port forwarding, 143–144
port mirroring, 493–494
port numbers, 84, 85, 86, 142, 174, 190
port scanning, 144, 505–506
port security, 597–599
port states, 86–90
protocols associated with, 87–90
root port selection, 163–164
router, 110, 127
as socket component, 10
source and destination, 84, 91
STP port states, 159–161
TCP and UDP, 11
types of, 85–86
UDP, 94–95

Postel, Jon, 62
power. *See* electricity/power
power budget exceeded, 375
power redundancy, 472
PPP (Point-to-Point Protocol), 50, 363–364, 365
PPPoE (Point-to-Point Protocol over Ethernet), 133
Preamble field, 248
prefixes
DHCPv6 Prefix Delegation, 217
length of IPv6, 206

preimage resistance, 561
premaster secret, 560
Presentation layer, 6, 9
preventing future bugs, 614
privacy
of cloud data, 445
private IP addresses, 78–79
at TotalTester Online, 639

private addresses, 78, 79, 140, 143
private clouds, 438
private DNS servers, 189
private ports, 86
privileged EXEC mode, 136, 137
probable cause theories/testing, 610–612
problem identification, 608–610
problem solving. *See* troubleshooting
procedures, operational, 525
production configuration, 532
programmable SDN controllers, 430
Protected EAP (PEAP), 363
protocols
CompTIA exam objectives on, 623
defined, 6
dynamic routing, 113–114, 115
history of network, 60
IPv4 packet header, 62
Network layer, 60–61, 97–102
in OSI layers, 7–25
PDU (protocol data unit), 24
for physical connectivity, 60
port forwarding, 144
ports associated with, 87–90
protocol suite, 13, 60
redundancy, 154
TCP/IP protocol, 12–13, 60
Transport layer (Layer 4), 90–97
VPN, 504
wired vs. wireless, 344
See also individual protocol by name

proxies, 486–488
pruning, 153
PSH flag, 93
PSK (pre-shared key), 363, 367–368, 390, 392
PTI (Public Technical Identifiers), 63, 205
PTP (Precision Time Protocol), 505
PTR (pointer) resource records, 185–186
public cloud, 437–438
public DNS servers, 189
public key cryptography, 556
pulling cable, 307–310
punchdown blocks, 291–293
PuTTY, 135, 510
PVC (polyvinyl chloride), 239

Q

QAM (quadruple-amplitude modulated), 359
QoS (Quality of Service), 62, 496
QSFP (quad small form-factor pluggable), 274
QSFP+ (enhanced quad small form-factor pluggable), 276
quad A record type, 181, 218
quartets/hextets, 207
queries
DNS process for resolving, 174–180
and DNS resource record types, 180–188
SNMP, 512–513

QUIC (Quick UDP Internet Connections), 95

R

RA (Router Advertisement), 215–216, 217
raceways, 305
rack diagrams, 478–479
Radio Guide (RG) rating, 229
RADIUS (Remote Authentication Dial-In User Service), 363, 365, 391, 565–566

RAM (random access memory), 28, 398, 417–418
range, wireless, 351, 393
RAT (remote administration tool), 595
RC4, 367
RDC (Remote Desktop Connection), 507
RDP (Remote Desktop Protocol), 89, 448, 507–508
Reachable state, 214
receiver (RX), 318
recovery. *See* response plans
recursive IP lookup, 179–180
recursive loops, 130
redirect packets, 216
redundancy
  in core switches, 460
  CRC for switches, 166
  high availability and, 471
  loops for switching, 158
  protocols for switches, 154
  router, 139
re-encapsulation, 51
reflection/refraction, signal, 400
registered (user) ports, 85
regulation, Wi-Fi channel, 353
regulatory security compliance, 571–572
remote access Trojans, 595
remote communication, 42, 47–52
Remote Desktop Gateway, 508
remote loopback, 300
Request, DHCP, 192, 194, 196
request process tracking, 531
reservations, DHCP, 194, 195, 196
resource management, cloud, 443–446
resource record types, DNS, 180–188
resource sharing via, 568
response plans
  API integration for, 520
  attack types and, 580–596
  defense techniques, 596–602
  disaster recovery, 532–535
  SLAs in, 527
  SQL solutions, 533
  testing, 535
  See also attacks; security; troubleshooting
reverse lookup zones, 189
reverse proxy, 488
Reynolds, Joyce K., 62
RF (radio frequency), 343
RFC 1338, 77
RFC 1519, 77
RFC 1918, 78
RFC 4291, 209
RFC 5952, 207, 208
RFI (radio frequency interference), 400
RIRs (Regional Internet Registries), 62–63, 77, 205, 218
riser-rated cables, 239
risk assessment, security, 545–547
RIT (Rochester Institute of Technology), 15, 112, 142, 171
RJ (registered jack) connectors, 234
RJ11 connectors, 234
RJ45 ports/connectors, 234, 251, 252, 298, 310, 327
roaming, 352, 404
rogue access points, 403–404, 588
rogue devices, 520, 587–588
role-based access control, 568
rollover cable, 134
ROM (Read-Only Memory), 15
roootkits, 595
root bridge, 159, 161–163
root certificates, 558, 562
root guard, 161
root name servers, 176–177
route aggregation, 121
routers/routing
  access controls for, 565
  administrative distance in, 124–125
  assigning IPv6 prefixes to, 217
  backbone routers, 66, 78, 112, 121, 128, 269, 274–275
  CompTIA exam objectives on, 626–627
  connections for, 134–139
  defined, 13
  edge routers, 113, 121
  frame movement and, 21
  function of, 132
  IGP and EGP for, 117–125
  indirect communication via, 41, 47
  interfaces as relay agents, 197
  metrics, 211–212
  module interfaces for, 133
  monitoring router interfaces, 166–167
  NAT-compatible, 141
  non-Ethernet, 133–134
  OSPF on, 117
  overview of, 110–112
  port-forwarding routers, 143
  router interfaces, 48, 52
  router redundancy, 139
  routing costs, 118

routing tables, 49, 77, 112, 115, 125–133, 216
RS (Router Solicitation), 215
SOHO, 110, 111
static vs. dynamic routing, 113–117
and switches, 109, 112, 126
in three-tiered architecture, 457
`traceroute` for, 100–102
troubleshooting, 132–133
virtual, 426, 427
virtual SD-WAN, 467
VPN packets, 498, 500, 502
See also cabling
RPO (recovery point objective), 533
RS (Router Solicitation), 215
RSA (Rivest, Shamir, Adleman), 557
RSSI (received signal strength indication), 396
RST flag, 94
RTO (recovery time objective), 533
RTSP (Real-Time Streaming Protocol), 95, 159, 161
RTUs (remote terminal units), 577
runs, cable, 283, 304, 316–327
runts, 166

S

SaaS (Software as a Service), 436–437
salts, hashing and, 563
SAML (Security Assertion Markup Language), 566
SAN (storage area network), 157, 463–464, 465
SAP business management, 259
SASE (Secure Access Secure Edge), 456, 469
SAS/SCSI, 465
satellite internet, 405
saturation, device, 399
SCADA (supervisory control and data acquisition), 577–578
scalability
of anycast addressing, 176
cloud-based DNS for, 190
and cloud resource management, 443
hosts file limitations on, 172
IaC for app, 440
of OSPF networks, 120
subnet, 75
for telecommunications room, 306
of VMs, 424
scanning ports, 144, 505–506
scareware, 590
SC fiber-optic connectors, 237–238, 255
scheduled network discovery, 520
scope, multicast message, 210
SDN (software-defined networking), 430, 466, 625
SD-WAN (software-defined wide area network), 449, 456, 466–467, 469
second preimage resistance, 561
secret key cryptography, 554
Sectigo, 558, 559
security
ACLs (access control lists), 600
ALG (application layer gateway) for, 491
attack types/impacts, 580–596
authoritative TLD DNS servers and, 179
and BYOD, 579
and CIA triad, 549–550
in cloud computing, 190, 444–446
CompTIA exam objectives on, 632–634
cryptography for, 550–563
at data centers, 455–456
decoy honeypots/honeynets, 570
defense techniques, 596–602
defined, 541–542
exploits/attacks defined, 543–544
firewalls for, 489–490
geofencing for, 371
hashing for, 560–563
identity/access management, 563–568
IDS/IPS to support, 492–495
information sharing and, 137
jump box/host to manage, 508
and lessening host traffic, 151
MAC address filtering for, 362, 369, 389
mesh network, 394
via multiple networks, 112
NAT and, 142
via network isolation, 370
network segmentation for, 572–578
via obscurity, 79, 144, 369
packet sniffing for, 515
performance logs and, 518
physical, 290–291, 569
port security, 597–599
private addresses for, 79
proxies for, 486–488
risk assessment, 545–547
role of IDS/IPS in, 492–495
SASE and SSE for, 469
SIEM for managing, 519–520
telecommunications room, 290
threats, 544–545
in three-tiered architecture access layer, 460
via traffic zones, 601–602

security (*continued*)
  URL and content filtering, 600–601
  and use of SaaS, 437
  for VMs, 421
  VPNs for, 496–503
  vulnerabilities to, 542–544
  Wi-Fi, 361–371
  ZTA (zero trust architecture), 468–469
  See also attacks; malware
security type mismatches, 395
segmentation, data, 11, 60, 572–578
self-signed certificates, 559
sensors, ICS, 575
Serial interfaces, 120
servers
  authentication/RADIUS, 365
  cloud VM servers, 428–429
  at data centers, 455–456
  data center server farms, 475
  defined, 83
  DHCP, 190–193, 197
  DHCPv6, 217
  DNS. *See* DNS servers
  equipment racks for, 289
  ICS, 576
  ports and responding to requests, 11
  proxy servers, 486
  resource sharing via, 3
  in SSH session, 506–507
  in three-tiered architecture, 457
  virtual, 433
service models, cloud, 432–437
service-related entry point, 299
service requests, 530
services (daemons)
  in the cloud, 432–437
  CompTIA exam objectives on, 623
  defined, 83
  disabling unused, 596
  DNS and DHCP as, 171
  rogue, 587–588
  SLAs (service-level agreements), 527
session hijacking, 506
Session layer, 6, 9–11
SFD (start frame delimiter), 248
SFF (small form factor) connectors, 267
SFP (small form-factor pluggable) connectors, 268, 323
SFP+ (enhanced small form-factor pluggable), 272
SFTP, 87
shaping traffic, 496
Shodan, 574
shorts, electrical, 317
shoulder surfing, 592
`show interfaces`, 137, 166
`show ip arp`, 137
`show ip route`, 137
`show power inline`, 375
`show running-config/show startup-config`, 137
`show vlan` command, 156
SIEM (security information and event management), 519–520
signal analysis, 338
signal attenuation, 235, 400
signal degradation, 316, 323–324, 396
signal loss, 316–317, 323–324, 396
signal mismatch, 324–325
signal strength, 316, 347, 398
signature-based IDSs/IPSs, 495
SIM (subscriber identity module) cards, 407
single-mode fiber (SMF), 236
SIP (Session Initiation Protocol), 90
site surveys, 376, 481
site-to-site VPNs, 502–503
SLAAC (stateless address autoconfiguration), 205, 208, 216–217
SLAs (service-level agreements), 527
SLD (second-level domain), 176, 178, 179, 184
smartjacks, 300
smartphones, 155, 405–410
SMB (Server Message Block), 9, 83, 89
smishing, 590
SMTP (Simple Mail Transfer Protocol), 8, 11, 88, 90
sniffing attacks, 514, 581
SNMP (Simple Network Management Protocol), 8, 89, 511–514
SNMP PDU, 513
snooping attacks, 491, 586
Snort, 495
SNR (signal-to-noise ratio), 401
SNTP (Simple Network Time Protocol), 505
SOA (start of authority) resource record, 175, 184–185
social engineering attacks, 588–590, 592
sockets, 10, 97
soft skills, 615
software
  asset inventories, 526
  bug fixes/patches, 528
  change management, 530
  defined, 593

firewall, 489
history of network protocol, 60
honeypots/honeynets, 570
hypervisor, 417
life-cycle management, 527–529
load balancing, 486
malicious. *See* malware
network, 4, 8
for NFV functions, 429
NFV vs. software-defined networking, 430–431
protocols, 6
session software, 10
update integrity, 562
virtual, 421–422, 425
VPN, 498
Wi-Fi, 347–348, 379–380
See also applications (apps)
SOHO (small office/home office) routers, 110, 138, 197, 371
solicitation, router, 215
solicited-node multicast address, 212–214
solid core, 285
SONET (Synchronous Optical Network), 270
SONET/WAN-based signaling, 270
SOPs (standard operating procedures), 525
Source Address, 248–249
source address table (SAT), 148, 150
source control, 441
southbound traffic, 462
SPAN (Switched Port Analyzer), 493–494
speed(s)
100 Mbps Ethernet, 261–265
802.11 standards for, 356–361
for backbone routers, 269
crosstalk and testing cable, 321
horizontal cabling and, 286
switch, 157–158
in three-tiered architecture core, 460
UDP vs. TCP for, 94
wireless standards and, 356–361
See also Ethernet
SPF (Sender Policy Framework), 186
SPF (Shortest Path First) algorithm, 117
spine-and-leaf architecture, 456, 461–462
splitter, coaxial, 229
split-horizon DNS, 189
split tunnel VPNs, 501
SPOG (single pane of glass), 467
spoof attacks, 16, 369, 491, 582–585
spread-spectrum radio waves, 352–353
SPS (standby power supply), 336
spyware, 595–596
SQL (Structured Query Language) server, 89, 533
SRV (service) resource records, 187
SSDs (solid-state drives), 463
SSE (Security Service Edge), 456, 469
SSH (Secure Shell), 3, 86, 87, 132, 139, 506–507, 553
SSID (service set identifier), 352, 361, 368, 369, 380, 387, 392, 402
SSID broadcast, 352
SSL VPN, 504
SSO (single sign-on), 565
`ss` tool, 97
stacks, 20, 219
standby UPSs, 336
star topology, 251, 282, 284, 286, 299, 350
stateful DHCPv6 server, 217
stateful mapping (manual translations), 221
stateful packet filtering, 490–491
stateless DHCPv6 server, 217
stateless mapping (automatic translations), 221
stateless packet filters, 67, 490–491, 600
State University of New York (SUNY), 188
static IP address, 78, 173, 195–196
static routing, 113, 125, 132–133
ST fiber-optic connectors, 237–238, 255
storage
bytes for measuring, 28
at data centers, 456, 463–464
IaaS for cloud, 433
jumbo frames for reading/writing to, 158
link aggregation for moving data to, 157
SAN, 463–464, 465
SAN vs. NAS, 465
secure password storage, 562–563
STP (shielded twisted-pair) cable, 231–232
STP (Spanning Tree Protocol), 158–166, 461
stranded core, 285
strategic-level changes, 530
stream ciphers, 555
streaming, 95, 211, 360, 404, 568, 600
streams, MIMO, 358
structured cabling
installation of, 303–327
overview of, 225, 280–303
stub networks, 113
subdomains, 175, 178–179
subnet masks
binary code for, 71
calculating number of, 72–76

subnet masks (*continued*)
  CIDR notation for, 68
  for classful addressing, 63–66, 68–69
  DHCP and, 193, 199
  in IP addresses, 42
  for IPv6, 206
  in local communication, 44–46
  network ID via, 43
  in remote communication, 47–52
  in routing table, 126, 127
  VLSM (variable-length subnet mask), 77
subnetting
  calculating number of subnets, 72–76
  CIDR for, 77
  creating subnets, 71–72
  host calculation for, 70
  for IPv6, 205, 218
  network layout via, 68–69
  overview of, 59, 66–68
  scaling subnets, 75
  screened subnets, 601
  for small networks, 197
  VLAN, 152–153
successor routes, 121
supernetting, 77
supplicant, 365
surge/spike protection, 335
surveys, wireless, 377, 378
SWG (Secure Web Gateway), 469
switched virtual interfaces (SVIs), 154
switches
  access controls for, 565
  backbone switch, 275
  bridges as, 159
  broadcasts sent by, 494
  CompTIA exam objectives on, 627
  configuring, 134
  data center, 458, 477
  defined, 19
  designated port selection, 164–166
  direct communication via, 41
  duplex settings, 157
  Ethernet, 260–261
  implicit tagging on, 152
  information gathering/decision-making by, 148–151
  at Layer 2, 147
  link aggregation of, 157
  mismatched connections, 324–325
  MLS (multilayer switch), 148
  monitoring switch interfaces, 166–167
  physical, 426
  ports on, 153
  root bridge selection, 161–163
  routers and, 109, 112, 126, 147
  speed of, 157–158
  spine-and-leaf architecture, 461
  spoof attacks, 580
  STP (Spanning Tree Protocol), 158–166
  switch interfaces, 48
  in three-tiered architecture, 457, 459
  virtual, 426
  VLANs and, 151–153
  wireless LAN, 373
switching loops, 158
symmetric encryption, 554, 557, 567
symptom identification, 608
SYN (Synchronize), 92–94
SYN/ACK, 92–94
Syracuse University, 182
syslog, 89, 518, 519
system (well-known) ports, 85

T

T1/E1, 456
tables
  made by switches, 148
  routing, 49, 77, 112, 115, 125–133, 216
tabletop DR exercises, 535
TAG (Technical Advisory Group), 240
tagging
  attacks, 580
  explicit VLAN, 153
  implicit VLAN, 152
tailgating, 592–593
taps, network, 338, 494
TCN (topology change notification), 159
TCP (Transmission Control Protocol)
  accuracy via, 90
  data segments and, 60
  DNS use of, 175, 177
  PDUs and, 24
  ports associated with, 87–88
  in Session layer, 10
  in Transport layer, 11–12, 90–94
TCP/IP
  CIDR for, 77
  for ICSs, 579
  IP for logical addressing in, 12
  IPv4 in history of, 204

IPv6 as future of, 204
iSCSI as built on, 464
origins of, 13, 60
security for, 541
subnets for, 59
testing local, 78
TDMA (time-division multiple access), 407
TDR (time-domain reflectometer), 319, 334
teaming NICs, 157
telecommunications room, 282–284, 286–297, 305–307, 335–337, 475
telephone connectors, 234
Telnet protocol, 139
temperature monitors, 337
Terabit Ethernet, 276
Terminal Access Controller Access Control System Plus (TACACS+), 565
terminal emulators, 135
terminals, remote, 507
terminal servers, 507, 511
termination standard, 253
test environment, 440
TFTP (Trivial File Transfer Protocol), 88
theories of probable cause, 610–612
threads, 84
threats, cybersecurity, 544–545, 546
three-tiered architecture, 457–458
three-way handshakes, 91
throughput
DSSS, 353
goodput and, 356
high-throughput, 358
jumbo frame, 158
link aggregation and, 157
UTP cable, 233
Wi-Fi 6, 360
of wireless frequencies, 353
See also speed(s)
TIA (Telecommunications Industry Association), 280
TIA/EIA (Telecommunications Industry Association/Electronics Industries Alliance), 253
TIC (Tunnel Information and Control), 220
Ticket-Granting Service/Server (TGS), 567
Ticket-Granting Ticket (TGT), 567
Tier One backbone, 128
tiers, 456
time-based authentication, 566–567
time-based risk security controls, 547
timers, 175
time synchronization, 505
TKIP (Temporal Key Integrity Protocol), 367
TKIP-RC4, 367
TLD (top-level domain), 176, 185
TLD DNS servers, 177–180, 187
TLS (Transport Layer Security), 85, 363, 402, 499, 504, 506, 553, 560, 587
tone generators, 337
tone probes, 337
top-of-rack switching, 458
topology
baseline configuration and, 480, 494
bus, 227, 246, 250, 257–259, 354
classic data center, 456–466
CompTIA exam objectives on, 625
EIGRP and, 120
Ethernet, 250–259
iBGP (Internal BGP) and, 122
mesh, 461, 462
modern data center, 466–469
for NFVs, 429
patch panel as mirroring, 316
routing protocols to assess, 49, 113, 117
star, 251, 282, 284, 286, 299, 350
switches and, 151, 159, 161, 166
wireless network types, 349–351
See also network design
top-to-bottom OSI model, 610–611
Tor (The Onion Router), 402
ToS (Terms of Service), 370
Total Seminars Training Hub, 639
TotalTester Online, 639–642
TOTP (Time-Based One-Time Password), 567
TPC (Transmit Power Control), 353
traceroute, 100–102
`tracert`, 98, 100–102
traffic flows, 456, 462
traffic shaping, 496
trailers, 18
transceivers, 268, 273–274, 324, 624
transition mechanisms, IPv4-to-IPv6, 219, 221
transmission frequency, 352
transmit beamforming, 358
transmitter (TX), 318
transport agnosticism, 467
Transport layer (Layer 4)
overview of, 6, 11–12
protocols and utilities, 88–97
VXLANs and, 468
transposition, TX/RX, 318
`Trap` messages, 513

Trojan horses, 594–595
troubleshooting
  cable runs, 316–327
  CompTIA exam objectives on, 634–637
  DHCP, 198–199
  documentation to support, 316, 614–615
  DR plans, 535
  dynamic routing for, 113
  Ethernet switches, 261
  information sharing for, 137
  logs for, 518
  methodology for, 607–615
  network design and, 282
  NICs, 327–332
  `nslookup` utility for DNS, 180
  OSI model for, 3, 25
  plan of action for, 613
  pre-deployment, 532
  probable cause theories/testing, 610–612
  problem identification, 608–610
  and problem prevention, 614
  remote loopback for, 300
  routing tables, 132–133
  solution implementation, 613
  switch interfaces, 166–167
  verifying functionality, 614
  of VLAN assignments, 152
  Wi-Fi, 394–404
  work area, 298
  See also diagnostics
trunking, 153, 155
trunk ports, 153
trust, administrative distance and, 124–125
trusted/untrusted networks, 602
TSP (Tunnel Setup Protocol), 220
TTL (time to live), 48, 101, 158, 179–180, 185
tunnel brokers, 219, 220
twinaxial cables, 230
twisted-pair cabling, 231, 251–254
two-factor authentication (2FA), 564
two-post racks, 289
TXT (text) resource record, 186–187
Type field, 18, 249
typos, 133

U

Ubiquiti EdgeMax router, 132
Ubiquiti EdgeRouter Pro, 110
UDP (User Datagram Protocol)
  datagrams, 17, 21, 24, 60, 102
  for DNS queries, 175, 179
  forwarding, 197–198
  IPv4 packet protocol and, 62
  PDUs and, 24
  ports associated with, 88–90
  in Transport layer, 10, 11–12, 94–95
  as used by DHCP, 190
UHR (Ultra High Reliability), 361
ultra-physical contact (UPC) connectors, 268
unbounded media, 344
unencrypted networks, 402
unicast addressing
  ARP requests/replies with, 46, 50
  and DHCP forwarding, 198
  and frame movement, 20
  IPv6, 209–210, 213
unicast frame, 20, 150
Unicode, 552
unidirectional antennas, 384–385
unified threat management (UTM) appliance, 492
UNIX, 60, 102, 516
untrusted networks, 602
updates
  automating, 441
  firmware, 528–529
  integrity of software, 562
  operating system, 529
  untested/incompatible, 403
UPSs (uninterruptible power supplies), 289, 335, 472
uptime, infrastructure, 521
URG flag, 93
URL filtering, 469, 600–601
USB (Universal Serial Bus)
  console ports, 509
  NICs into USB ports, 329, 380
  wireless network adapters, 346
user (registered) ports, 85
users
  access to data centers, 458
  SaaS for access by, 436
  soft skills with, 615
  troubleshooting with, 608
USM (User-based Security Model), 511
US Vulnerabilities Equities Process, 543
UTP (unshielded twisted pair) cable, 24, 232–235, 251–254, 263, 284, 294, 311

V

validation tests, DR, 535
VCSEL (vertical-cavity surface-emitting laser), 236

VDI (virtual desktop infrastructure), 446
Verizon Fios, 102
version control, 441
vertical cabling (backbone cabling), 284
vertical cross-connect, 302
VIP (virtual IP), 471
virtual disks, 463
virtualization
- abstraction and, 421–422
- and the cloud, 415, 431, 433, 439
- component relocation and, 423–424
- flexibility via, 423
- hypervisors, 417–421
- of modern data centers, 466
- overview of, 416–417
- rerouting inputs/outputs, 423
- resource sharing via, 424
- SDN (software-defined networking) as, 430–431
- virtual networks, 425–431

viruses, 593–594
vishing, 590
visual fault locator, 324
VLAN ACL (VACL), 168
VLAN pooling, 373, 374
VLANs (virtual local area networks)
- hopping attack, 580–581
- overview of, 151–153
- switches and, 425
- trunking, 153
- VLAN ACL (VACL), 168
- VLAN database, 156
- voice VLANs, 155
- VXLANs and, 468

VLSM (variable-length subnet mask), 77
VMs (virtual machines)
- abstraction and, 421–422
- component relocation in, 423–424
- hypervisors, 417–421
- isolation of/security for, 445
- overview of, 416–417
- and port security, 598
- rerouting inputs/outputs in, 423
- resource sharing via, 424
- scalability of, 424

VMware, 426, 465
VMware Horizon, 446
VMware Workstation Pro, 417, 418, 425
VNFs (virtualized network functions), 429
vNICs (virtual network interface cards), 425–426
VoIP (Voice over IP), 155, 598, 599
voltage event recorders, 336
VPC (virtual private cloud), 439
VPNs (virtual private networks)
- vs. eavesdropping, 402
- encrypted tunnels via, 496–503
- heavy data traffic over, 507
- IaaS to support, 433
- IPsec tunneling protocols, 503–505
- overview of, 449–450
- public Wi-Fi and, 499
- VPN concentrator, 428–429

VR (virtual reality) systems, 360
VRRP (Virtual Router Redundancy Protocol), 139, 154, 471
vSphere Client, 419
VTEPs (VXLAN tunnel endpoints), 468
VTP (VLAN Trunking Protocol), 156
vulnerabilities, network, 542–544, 574
VXLANs (Virtual Extensible Local Area Networks), 456, 467–468, 626

W

WANs (wide area networks)
- cellular, 405–410
- routing to connect with, 109
- SD-WAN and, 466–467
- SONET for, 270
- VPNS to connect with, 449

WAPs (wireless access points)
- adding additional, 393
- antennas, 381–386
- channels, 353
- configuring, 347–348
- connection types, 358
- consumer access points, 386–392
- enterprise, 371–374
- infrastructure networks, 381
- in network topologies, 349–351
- overworked, 399
- PoE for enterprise, 374
- rogue, 403–404
- on routers, 110
- signal interference from, 401

warranties, 526
wavelength, 266
wavelength mismatch, 325
WDM (wavelength division multiplexing), 273
websites
- building, 415
- digital certificates for, 559

websites (*continued*)
DR/backup, 534–535
name resolution, 171–173
PaaS for deploying, 433–434
VMs for hosting, 420
well-known (system) ports, 85
WEP (Wired Equivalent Privacy), 362
white hat hackers, 542
whitelist, 369
WIC (WAN interface card), 134
Wi-Fi
802.11 standards, 356–361
BSSID, SSID, and ESSID, 351–352
channels, 353–354
CSMA/CA, 354–356
extending, 392
hardware, 344–346
installing/configuring, 376–394
network types, 349–351
physical data movement in, 25
public, 499
range, 351
security, 361–371
software, 347–348
standards, 355–361, 395
testing networks, 394
transmission frequency, 352
transmission methods, 352–353
troubleshooting, 394–404
See also wireless networks
Wi-Fi 4, 358
Wi-Fi 6, 358, 360
Wi-Fi 8, 361
Windows OS
destination cache in, 215
DNS cache clearing, 179
DNS client resolver cache, 173
ipconfig /all, 16, 54
MAC addresses for, 16
neighbor cache in, 214
`netstat` utility, 10, 97
NIC drivers, 330
remote access to, 86
routing table info in, 129
services in, 83
`tracert`, 100–102
virtual networks in, 425
wired bridges, 159
wired networks
CompTIA exam objectives on, 624
protocols for, 60
wired/wireless hybrids, 281
wireless vs., 344
wireless bridges, 159
wireless channel utilization, 390
wireless LAN controller, 373
wireless networks
802.11 frames for, 50
cellular WAN, 405–410
channels, 353–354
CompTIA exam objectives on, 624, 627–628
CSMA/CA, 354–356
enterprise wireless setup, 371–376
extending, 392
hardware for, 345–347
installing/configuring, 376–394
overview of, 344–361
physical data movement in, 25, 60
protocols for, 60
range for, 351
security for, 361–371
standards, 355–361, 395
survey tools for, 376
technologies used in, 343–344
topology types, 349–351
transmission frequency, 352
upgrading existing, 376–377
wired/wireless hybrids, 281
See also Wi-Fi
wire maps, 304, 318, 319
Wireshark, 515, 516
Wireshark OUI Lookup, 53
wiring. *See* cabling
WLAN (wireless local area network), 240, 348, 350, 370, 374, 396
work area, 282, 297–298, 310–311, 446–448
workflows/pipelines, 442, 530
WorkSpaces, 447, 448, 449, 450
Workstation Pro, 417
worms, 593–594
WPA (Wi-Fi Protected Access), 362–363
WPA2 (Wi-Fi Protected Access 2), 367, 394
WPA2-Enterprise, 368
WPA2-PSK (Pre-Shared Key), 367–368
WPA3 (Wi-Fi Protected Access 3), 368
WPA-Enterprise, 365
WPS (Wi-Fi Protected Setup), 361
WWNN (World Wide Node Name), 465

X

XOR (exclusive OR), 551–553

Y

Yagi antenna, 385
Y Combinator, 102
Yost cable, 134

Z

zero-configuration networking, 194, 208
zero-day attacks/exploits, 543
zero-touch provisioning, 467
zombies, 594
zone files, 174–175, 184, 188, 189
zones, traffic, 601–602
zone transfers, 11, 175
ZTA (zero trust architecture), 456, 468–469, 626

www.ingramcontent.com/pod-product-compliance
Lightning Source LLC
LaVergne TN
LVHW082003200926
848481LV00010B/2797
* 9 7 8 0 9 8 1 6 2 1 7 3 9 *